Midwest Library
$475.00
P.O. 87929
12-03-03

S0-BSP-791

Brooks-Cork Library
Shelton State Community College
DISCARDED

DISCARDED
Brooks-Cork Library
Shelton State Community College

ENCYCLOPEDIA
OF THE
STATELESS NATIONS

ENCYCLOPEDIA OF THE STATELESS NATIONS

Ethnic and National Groups Around the World

VOLUME III
L–R

James Minahan

GREENWOOD PRESS
Westport, Connecticut • London

Library of Congress Cataloging-in-Publication Data

Minahan, James.
　　Encyclopedia of the stateless nations : ethnic and national groups around the world /
James Minahan.
　　　p. cm.
　　Includes index.
　　ISBN 0–313–31617–1 (set : alk. paper)—ISBN 0–313–32109–4 (v. 1 :
　alk. paper)—ISBN 0–313–32110–8 (v. 2 : alk. paper)—ISBN 0–313–32111–6 (v. 3 :
　alk. paper)—ISBN 0–313–32384–4 (v. 4 : alk. paper)
　　　1. World politics—1989—Dictionaries. 2. Nationalism—History—20th century—
Dictionaries. 3. Ethnic conflict—History—20th century—Dictionaries. 4. Stateless-
ness—Dictionaries. I. Minahan, James. Nations without states. II. Title.
D860.M56 2002
909.82'9'03—dc21　　　　2001033691

British Library Cataloguing in Publication Data is available.

Copyright © 2002 by James Minahan

All rights reserved. No portion of this book may be
reproduced, by any process or technique, without the
express written consent of the publisher.

Library of Congress Catalog Card Number: 2001033691
ISBN: 0–313–31617–1 (set)
　　　　0–313–32109–4 (Vol. I)
　　　　0–313–32110–8 (Vol. II)
　　　　0–313–32111–6 (Vol. III)
　　　　0–313–32384–4 (Vol. IV)

First published in 2002

Greenwood Press, 88 Post Road West, Westport, CT 06881
An imprint of Greenwood Publishing Group, Inc.
www.greenwood.com

Printed in the United States of America

The paper used in this book complies with the
Permanent Paper Standard issued by the National
Information Standards Organization (Z39.48–1984).

10 9 8 7 6 5 4 3 2 1

CONTENTS

Contents

Contents

Contents

PREFACE

This volume is an updated and greatly expanded sequel to the award-winning *Nations without States: A Historical Dictionary of Contemporary National Movements*, which was published in 1996 and contained information on over 200 national groups and their homelands. Since that time, many new national groups have emerged as part of the nationalist revival that began with the end of the Cold War a decade ago. The purpose of this encyclopedia is to provide readers with an easy-to-use, accurate, up-to-date guide to the many national groups in the contemporary world. It is being published at a time when national identity, ethnic relations, regional conflicts, and immigration are increasingly important factors in national, regional, and international affairs.

Encyclopedia of the Stateless Nations: Ethnic and National Groups Around the World follows the development of over 300 national groups from the earliest periods of their histories to the present. That collection of national surveys is an essential guide to the many emerging groups and the national groups that the world ignored or suppressed during the decades of the Cold War, the longest and most stable peace in the history of the modern world. The Cold War did give the world relative peace and stability, but it was a fragile peace and a stability imposed by force. When reading the descriptions of national groups and the analyses of their histories, it is important to keep in mind the broader context—the growing role of national identity worldwide. This encyclopedia, like its 1996 predecessor, addresses the post–Cold War nationalist resurgence, by focusing on the most basic element of any nationalism, the nation itself.

This encyclopedia contains 350 national surveys, short articles highlighting the historical, political, social, religious, and economic evolution of the many national groups that are now emerging to claim roles in the post–Cold War world order. The worth of this encyclopedia in part derives from its up-to-date information on the often virtually unknown national groups that are currently making news and on those that will produce future headlines, controversies, and conflicts.

In this book I have followed the same general approach taken in the previous book for choosing which national groups to cover. Selecting the national surveys to be included in the encyclopedia again presented numerous problems, not the least of which was the difficulty of applying a uniform criteria that could accommodate language, religion, common history, occupational specialization, regional localization, common culture, self-identification, and identification by others. In general, strict adherence to official government lists of ethnic groups has been avoided, as the compilation of such lists is often driven by political considerations. If government criteria were followed, national groups in such states as Turkey or Japan would not be included, because of government claims that there are no national minorities within their borders.

The national groups chosen for inclusion represent a perplexing diversity that share just one characteristic—they identify themselves as separate nations. The arduous task of researching this diversity has been made more complicated by the lack of a consensus on what constitutes a "nation" or "nation-state." There is no universally accepted definition of "nation," "country," or "state." The subject continues to generate endless debate and numerous conflicts.

An attempt to apply the criteria used to distinguish independent states foundered on the numerous anomalies encountered. Size is definitely not a criterion. Over 40 states recognize a building in Rome, covering just 108.7 acres, as an independent state. Nor is United Nations membership the measure of independence; Ukraine and Belarus (Byelorussia) were founding members of the United Nations in 1945 yet became independent only in 1991. Membership in such international organizations as the International Olympic Committee (IOC) or the Organization of African Unity (OAU) does not necessarily signify political independence. Antarctica issues postage stamps but has no citizens; Palestine has citizens and embassies in dozens of countries but is not in practice an independent state; and so on.

Webster's Unabridged Dictionary defines the word *nation* as "a body of people, associated with a particular territory, that is sufficiently conscious of its unity to seek or possess a government particularly its own." On the basis of this definition, the criteria for selecting nations for inclusion was narrowed to just three important factors, modified by the diversity of the nations themselves. The three factors are self-identity as a distinctive group, the display of the outward trappings of national consciousness (particularly the adoption of a flag, a very important and very emotional part of any nationalism), and the formation of a specifically nationalist organization or political grouping that reflects its claim to self-determination. Many stateless nations were eliminated from the encyclopedia when one of these three factors could not be found during the exhaustive research process. National identity is often difficult to define and is very tricky to measure. For that reason this definitive volume of twenty-first-century nationalism contains a number of national groups whose identity is disputed but that met the criteria.

In any compilation, the selection process for choosing which material to include is a complex evolution of subtractions and additions. Estimates of the number of national groups in the world run as high as 9,000, making the selection process truly a process of elimination. The nations included in these volumes therefore represent only a fraction of the world's stateless nations.

Each national survey is divided into several parts or headings: the name and alternative names of the group; population statistics, incorporating the total national population and its geographical distribution; the homeland, including location, size, population, capital cities, and major cultural centers; the people and culture; the language and religion; a brief sketch of the national group's history and present situation; the national flag or other pertinent flags; and a map that places the national homeland in a local geographic setting.

Most of the nations included in this encyclopedia played little or no role in international politics before the end of the Cold War. Some of the national groups will be familiar, historically or more recently as news items, but the majority are virtually unknown and do not have standardized names or spellings in English. Familiar names often were, or are, the colonial or imposed names that in themselves represented a particularly harsh form of cultural suppression. That situation is now being reversed, with scholars, cartographers, and geographers attempting to settle on the definitive forms of the names of national groups, territories, and languages. Until that process is completed, many of the names used in these volumes will not only be unfamiliar but will not appear in even the most comprehensive reference sources.

The population figures are the author's estimates for the year 2002. The figures are designated by the abbreviation "(2002e)" before the appropriate statistics. The figures were gleaned from a vast number of sources, both official and unofficial, representing the latest censuses, official estimates, and—where no other sources were available—nationalist claims. Where important disparities over group size exist, both the official and the claimed population figures are included. Official rates of population growth, urban expansion, and other variables were applied to the figures to arrive at the statistics included in the encyclopedia. Since very few of the world's national groups are confined to one territory, the population statistics also includes information on geographic distribution.

Information on the homeland of each national group includes the geographic location and general features of the territory. Most of the national groups are concentrated in defined national territories—a state, province, region or historical region, department, etc. The corresponding features are included in this section, even though most territorial claims are based on historical association, not modern ethnic demographic patterns, provincial boundaries, or international borders. The geographic information incorporates the size of the territory, in both square miles (sq. mi.) and square kilometers (sq. km). The population figures for the larger cities cover the populations within city limits, and where appropriate, populations of surrounding urban or metropolitan areas. The two figures are included in an effort to reconcile the vastly different methods of enumerating urban populations used by the various governments and international agencies. A list of the principal statistical sources is provided at the end of this section.

Current political events have graphically demonstrated that the overall numbers are much less important than the level of national sentiment and political mobilization. A brief sketch of the people and their culture accompanies each entry, highlighting the cultural and national influences that have shaped the primary national group. A related section covers the linguistic and religious affiliations of each national group.

Each of the stateless nations has its own particular history, the events and conflicts that have shaped its national characteristics and level of mobilization. The largest part of each national survey is therefore devoted to the national history, the historical development of the national group. The national history survey follows the evolution and consolidation of the nation from its earliest history to the present. Although meticulous attention has been paid to the content and objectivity of each national survey, the polemic nature of the subject and, in many cases, the lack of official information have made it impossible to eliminate all unsubstantiated material. The author apologizes for the unintentional inclusion of controversial, dubious, or distorted information gathered from myriad and often unsatisfactory sources.

The national flags and other flags intimately associated with national groups are images of the actual flags; however, due to the informal use of these flags and a lack of information on actual size, all are presented in the same format. In many cases more than one flag is presented, particularly when a national flag has not been adopted or when other flags are equally important. The maps are the author's own, provided to complement the text. They are simple line drawings provided to aid the reader and as supplements to a comprehensive atlas.

The two appendices will allow the reader to develop a better understanding of the historical evolution of national sentiment over the past century and of the rapid proliferation of national organizations that has attended the post–Cold War wave of nationalism. Appendix A sets the numerous declarations of independence in a historical and chronological context, explicitly illustrating the waves of nationalism that have paralleled or accompanied the momentous trends and events of contemporary history. Appendix B provides a geographic listing, by region and nation, of the ever-expanding number of national organizations that herald the mobilization of national sentiment. The number of groups that exist within each national movement graphically illustrates the range of nationalist opinion, although little is known or published about the ideologies, aims, or methods of the majority of these national organizations.

Very few of the stateless nations developed in isolation; they were shaped by their relations with various governments and neighboring peoples. Accordingly, nations mentioned in the various entries that are themselves the subjects of separate entries appear with an asterisk (*). An extensive subject index is provided at the end of the last volume. Each encyclopedia entry also includes a short bibliographic list of sources.

This historical encyclopedia was compiled to provide a guide to the nations in the forefront of the post–Cold War nationalist resurgence, a political process all too often considered synonymous with the more extreme and violent aspects of nationalism. This work is not presented as an assertion that a multitude of new states are about to appear, even though political self-rule is the ultimate goal of many the national groups included in the survey. This encyclopedia is presented as a unique reference source to the nonstate nations that are spearheading one of the most powerful and enduring political movements in modern history, the pursuit of democracy's basic tenet—self-determination.

PRINCIPAL STATISTICAL SOURCES

1. National Censuses 1998–2001
2. *World Population Chart*, 2000 (United Nations)
3. *Populations and Vital Statistics*, 2000 (United Nations)
4. *World Tables*, 2000 (World Bank)
5. *World Demographic Estimates and Projections*, 1950–2025, 1988 (United Nations)
6. *UNESCO Statistical Annual*, 2000
7. *World Bank Atlas*, 1998
8. The Economist Intelligence Unit (Country Report series 2000)
9. *World Population Prospects* (United Nations)
10. *Europa Yearbook*, 2000
11. U.S. Department of State publications
12. *CIA World Factbook*
13. *United Nations Statistical Yearbook*, 2000
14. *United Nations Demographic Yearbook*, 2000
15. *The Statesman's Yearbook*, 2000
16. *Encyclopedia Britannica*
17. *Encyclopedia Americana*
18. Bureau of the Census, U.S. Department of Commerce 2001
19. National Geographic Society

20. Royal Geographical Society
21. *Webster's New Geographical Dictionary*, 1988
22. *Political Handbook of the World*
23. The Urban Foundation
24. *The Blue Plan*
25. Eurostat, the European Union Statistical Office
26. Indigenous Minorities Research Council
27. The Minority Rights Group
28. Cultural Survival
29. World Council of Indigenous Peoples
30. Survival International
31. *China Statistical Yearbook* (State Statistical Bureau of the People's Republic of China)
32. Arab Information Center
33. CIEMEN, Escarré's International Centre for Ethnical Minorities and Nations, Barcelona
34. International Monetary Fund
35. American Geographic Society

INTRODUCTION

The human race has never been a uniform whole, composed of rigorously identical individuals. There are a certain number of characteristics common to all human beings, and other attributes belonging to each individual. Besides the division of the human race by sex, age groups, and class divisions of economic origin, there is another very important separation, which is of a linguistic, ethnic, religious, or territorial type: the division into discernible national groups. Just as social classes are defined by economic criteria, even though they include global human realities and not just economic parameters, national groups are characterized not simply by linguistic or ethnic realities but also by global human realities, such as oppression or other forces of history.

The emphasis on the rights of states rather than the rights of the individuals and nations within them has long dictated international attitudes toward nationalism, attitudes buttressed by ignorance and failure to understand the "nation" versus the "nation-state." The use of condemnatory labels—separatist, secessionist, rebel, splittist, etc.—has been a powerful state weapon against those who seek different state structures on behalf of their nations. The rapid spread of national sentiment, affecting even nations long considered assimilated or quiescent, is attracting considerable attention, but the focus of this attention is invariably on its impact on established governments and its effect on international relations. As the Cold War withered away, it was replaced by a bewildering number and variety of nationalisms that in turn spawned a global movement toward the breakdown of the existing system of nation-states.

Current trends toward decentralization of government and empowerment of local groups inadvertently fragment society into often contending and mutually unintelligible cultures and subcultures. Even within a single society, people are segmenting into many self-contained communities and contending interest groups, entities that often take on the tone and aims of national groups.

The human race was divided into national groups long before the division of labor and, consequently, well before the existence of a class system. A class is defined by its situation in relation to production or consumption, and it is a universal social category. Each individual belongs to a horizontally limited human group (the economic class) and to a vertically limited group (the nation or national group). People have had identities deriving from religion, birthplace, language, or local authority for as long as humans have had cultures. They began to see themselves as members of national groups, opposed to other such groups, however, only during the modern period of colonization and state building.

An offshoot of the eighteenth-century doctrine of popular sovereignty, nationalism became a driving force in the nineteenth century, shaped and invigorated by the principles of the American and French revolutions. It was the Europeans, with their vast colonial possessions, who first declared that each and every person has a national identity that determined his or her place within the state structure. Around the world colonial and postcolonial states created new social groups and identified them by ethnic, religious, economic, or regional categories. Far from reflecting ancient ethnic or tribal loyalties, national cohesion and action are products of the modern state's demand that people make themselves heard as groups or risk severe disadvantages. Around the world, various movements and insurgencies, each with its own history and motivations, have typically—and erroneously—been lumped together as examples of the evils of nationalism.

Over the last century, perhaps no other subject has inspired the passions that surround nationalism and national sentiment. We can distinguish two primary kinds of nationalism, often opposed: unifying or assimilative nationalism; and separatist nationalism, which seeks to separate to some degree from the nationalism of the nation-state. Unifying nationalism shades off gradually into assimilation and imperialism, which reached its apex in the nineteenth century and continues to the present. Nationalism, in its most virulent forms, has provoked wars, massacres, terrorism, and genocide, but the roots of nationalist violence lie not in primordial ethnic and religious differences but in modern attempts to rally populations around nationalist ideas. Nationalism is often a learned and frequently manipulated set of ideas rather than a primordial sentiment. Violent nationalism in political life is a product of modern conflicts over power and resources, not an ancient impediment to political modernity.

The question of what a nation is has gained new significance with the recent increase in the number of claims to self-determination. The legitimacy of these claims rests upon the acceptance of a group in question as a nation, something more than just a random collection of people. The international community primarily regards nations as territorially based, and the consolidation of nations within specific territories has lent legitimacy to self-determination struggles in many areas. Yet this limited definition can give both undue influence to territorially consolidated groups seeking full sovereignty and independence, as well as undermine equally legitimate claims for self-determination among nonterritorial groups that do not aim for statehood but aim, rather, at greater control over their own lives.

National identity becomes nationalism when it includes aspirations to some variety of self-government. The majority of the world's stateless nations have embraced nationalism, but even though nationalists often include militant factions seeking full independence, most nationalists would probably settle for the right to practice their own languages and religions and to control their own territories and resources. Although the nationalist resurgence has spawned numerous conflicts, nationalism is not automatically a divisive force; it provides citizens with an identity and a sense of responsibility and involvement.

The first wave of modern nationalism culminated in the disintegration of Europe's multinational empires after World War I. The second wave began during World War II and continued as the very politicized decolonization process that engulfed the remaining colonial empires, as a theater of the Cold War after 1945. The removal of Cold War factionalism has now released a third wave of nationalism, of a scale and diffusion unprecedented in modern history. In the decade since the end of the Cold War, regionalist movements across the globe have taken on the tone and ideology of nationalist movements. The new national awakening, at the beginning of the twenty-first century, in many respects resembles the phenomenon of the turn of the twentieth century. Ethnicity, language, culture, religion, geography, and even economic condition—but not nationality—are becoming the touchstones of national identity.

Nationalism is often associated with separatism, which can be an offshoot of nationalism, but the majority of the world's national movements normally mobilize in favor of greater autonomy; separatism and separatist factions usually evolve from a frustrated desire for the basic tenet of democracy, self-determination. The conflicts resulting from this latest nationalist upsurge have reinforced the erroneous beliefs that nationalism is synonymous with extremism and that separatism is confined to the historical "hot spots" in Europe and Asia. One of the basic premises of this encyclopedia is that the nationalist resurgence at the end of the twentieth century is spreading to all corners of the world and is likely to mold the world's political agenda for decades to come. Academics too often define nationalism in terms of its excesses, so that its very definition condemns it.

The post–Cold War revival of nationalism is not limited to any one continent, nor is it a product of any particular ideology, geographic area, religion, or combination of political or historical factors. The latest wave of nationalism affects rich and poor, large and small, developed and developing, indigenous and nonindigenous peoples. National diversity is often associated with political instability and the likelihood of violence, but some of the world's most diverse states, though not without internal nationalisms, have suffered relatively little violence between national groups, while countries with relatively little cultural or linguistic diversity, including Yugoslavia, Somalia, and Rwanda, have had the bloodiest of such conflicts.

Nationalism has become an ascendant ideology, one that is increasingly challenging the nineteenth-century definition of the unitary nation-state. The worldwide nationalist revival is an amplified global echo of the nationalism that swept Europe's stateless nations in the late nineteenth and early twentieth centuries, now including the indigenous-rights movements that are major moral, political, and legal issues in many states, and a growing number of groups based on religious distinction that have taken on the characteristics of national groups.

The United Nations estimates that only 3% of the world's 6,000 national groups have achieved statehood. Although the last decade has seen the emergence of an unprecedented number of new states, the existing world order remains conservative in the recognition of new states. There is no perfect justice in dealing with nationalist aspirations; each case should be viewed as separate and distinct. Joining the club of independent states remains a privilege of few of the world's national groups.

The failure to understand national identity and nationalism is often reinforced by the view that nationalism represents a tribal, waning stage of history. The world's insistence that national structures conform to existing international borders for the sake of world peace was one of the first casualties of the revolution brought on by the world's new enthusiasm for democracy and self-determination. Between the end of World War II and the end of the Cold War, nationalism spawned only three new states—Iceland, Singapore, and Bangladesh—while the decolonization process created many more. However, between 1991 and 2001 nationalism accounted for the splintering of the Soviet Union and Yugoslavia, and the partitions of Czechoslovakia and Ethiopia, leading to the emergence of twenty-two new states. The belief that political and economic security could be guaranteed only by the existing political order faded as quickly as the ideological and political divisions set in place after World War II.

The world is in the midst of an extended post–Cold War transition that will last well into the present century. The community of democratic states is expanding, but this era of transition remains complex and dangerous. In much of the world there remains a potentially explosive mix of social, demographic, economic, and political conditions that run counter to the global trends toward democracy and economic reforms. The transition has taken the lid off long-simmering ethnic, religious, territorial, and economic disputes and has stimulated the growth of national identities on a scale unimaginable just a decade ago.

The definition of a "nation" remains controversial and undecided. The nineteenth-century French scholar Ernest Renan stated that a nation is a community of people who have endured common suffering as a people. National identity and nationalism are highly complicated and variable phenomena that resist simple diagnoses of any kind. The most basic premise remains that nations are self-defining. In a broad sense, a nation may be defined as any group of people that perceives itself to be a nation.

The growth of national sentiment can be based on a common origin, language, history, culture, territorial claims, geographical location, religion, economics, ethnicity, racial background, opposition to another group, or opposition to bad or oppressive government. The mobilization of national sentiment is most often a complicated mixture of some or all of these components. No one of these factors is essential; however, some must be present if group cohesion is to be strong enough to evolve a self-identifying nationalism. None of the world's national groups is a hermetically sealed entity. All are influenced by, and in turn influence, other national groups. Nor is any national group changeless, invariant, or static. All national groups are in states of constant flux, driven by both internal and external forces. These forces may be accommodating, harmonious, benign, and based on voluntary actions, or they may be involuntary, resulting from violent conflict, force, or domination.

Democracy, although widely accepted as the only system that is able to provide the basis of humane political and economic activity, can be a subversive force. Multiparty democracy often generates chaos and instability as centrifugal forces, inherent parts of a free political system, are set loose. The post–Cold War restoration of political pluralism and democratic process has given rise to a rebirth of ethnicity and politicized national identity, while the collapse of communism in much of the world has shattered the political equilibrium that had prevailed for over four decades. The Cold War blocs had mostly succeeded in suppressing or controlling the regional nationalisms in their respective spheres, nationalisms that now have begun to reignite old national desires and ethnic rivalries. Around the globe, numerous national groups, their identities and aspirations long buried under decades of Cold War tensions, are emerging to claim for themselves the basic principle of democracy, self-determination. The centrifugal forces held in check by the Cold War have emerged to challenge accepted definitions of a nation and its rights. The doctrine of statism is slowly being superseded by a post–Cold War internationalism that is reshaping the world's view of the unitary nation-state and, what is more important, the world's view of who or what constitutes a nation.

Two main trends are vying to shape the post–Cold War world. One is the movement to form continental or regional economic-political groupings that would allow smaller political units as members. The other is the emergence of smaller and smaller national units as older states are broken up. The two trends are not mutually exclusive. The nation-state, with its absolute sovereignty, is fading and giving way to historical trends—the nation rather than the nation-state in one direction, and supranational bodies, such as the United Nations, the European Union, and even

NAFTA, in the other. The rapidly changing political and economic realities have swept aside the old arguments that population size, geographic location, and economic viability are deterrents to national self-determination. The revival of nationalism is converging with the emergence of continental political and economic units theoretically able to accommodate ever smaller national units within overarching political, economic, and security frameworks.

The third wave of modern nationalism, with its emphasis on human rights and democratic self-determination, is set to top the international agenda for decades to come. The nationalist revival, global in scope, has strengthened submerged national, ethnic, and regional identities and has shattered the conviction that assimilation would eventually homogenize the existing nation-states. The nationalist revival is now feeding on itself, as the freedom won by many historically stateless nations has emboldened other national groups to demand greater control of their own destinies.

A unique feature of this current wave of nationalism is the growing mutual cooperation and support among and between the stateless nations, both nationally and internationally. A number of national groups in countries such as Russia, China, and Myanmar have joined together to work for common goals. Many of the nations selected for inclusion in the encyclopedia are members, or aspiring members, of two organizations that for the first time provide legitimate forums in which to gain strength through numbers and to publicize causes without recourse to violence. The larger of the organizations, the Unrepresented Nations and Peoples Organization (UNPO), was formed in 1991 by six stateless nations, four of which have since been recognized as independent states. The organization, its membership now swollen by the representatives of dozens of stateless nations, is already referred to as an alternative United Nations, representing over 100 million people. The second group, the Free Europe Alliance, is less global in scale but, like the UNPO, is inundated by membership applications.

The political and cultural renaissance spreading through the world's national groups is inexorably moving global politics away from the present system of sovereign states, each jealously defending its authority, to a new world order more closely resembling the world's true national and historical geography. A world community dominated by democracy must inevitably recognize the rights of the world's stateless nations, including the right of each to choose its own future. The twin issues of national identity and self-determination will remain at the forefront of international relations. The diffusion and force of contemporary national movements make it imperative that the nationalist phenomenon be studied and understood. One of the most urgent concerns of our time is to fashion a principled and effective policy toward all national groups.

ENCYCLOPEDIA
OF THE
STATELESS NATIONS

Ladakhis

Ladakis; Ladaphis; Ladhakhis; Ladaks; Ladwags; Bhotias

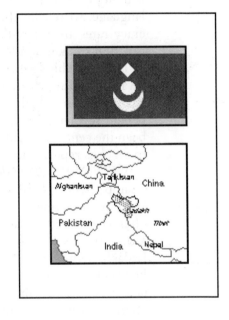

POPULATION: Approximately (2002e) 144,000 Ladakhis in the Kashmir region of northwestern India and northern Pakistan. Outside the region there are Ladakhi communities in other parts of Kashmir, in Himalayan India, and in Nepal and Tibet.

THE LADAKHI HOMELAND: The Ladakhi homeland occupies an extremely mountainous region in the Karakoram Range of the Himalayas at the conjunction of the Indian, Pakistani, and Chinese borders. Ladakh is one of the most elevated inhabited regions of the world. The thinly populated region, sometimes called "Little Tibet," was divided between India and Pakistan in 1949 and now forms the Ladakh and Kargil Districts of the Indian state of Jammu and Kashmir, the Ladakh District of the Northern Areas of Pakistani-controlled Kashmir, and the Aksai Chin region, under Chinese control since 1962. *Region of Ladakh*: 45,762 sq. mi.—118,524 sq. km, (2002e) 264,000—Ladakhis 51%, Balts and Balawaris* 35%, Kashmiris* 10%, other Indians and Pakistanis 4%. The Ladakhi capital and major cultural center is Leh, (2002e) 33,000.

FLAG: The Ladakhi national flag, the flag of the national movement, is a green field bordered by narrow yellow stripes at the top, bottom, and hoist, bearing a centered white disc, a white crescent moon, and a white diamond.

PEOPLE AND CULTURE: The Ladakhis are a people of Tibetan origin. Culturally, ethnically, and linguistically the Ladakhis retain many ties to the Tibetans.* Traditionally the Ladakhis are Buddhists; the Muslim Ladakhis are called Balts or Balawaris. The region has a basically Tibetan culture with an admixture of customs and traditions adopted from the neighboring Muslim peoples. The Buddhist religion, as in Tibet, is an integral part of Ladakhi culture, and at any given time one in six Ladakhis is doing religious duties in one of the numerous lamasaries that dot the landscape. The majority of the Ladakhis remain rural, although the number living in the region's small urban areas is increasing.

LANGUAGE AND RELIGION: The Ladakhis speak western dialects of Tibetan, which is part of the Tibetan-Burmese branch of the Sino-Tibetan language group. The Ladakhi language in India is spoken in five major dialects: Leh or Central Ladakhi, Zangskari, Changtang, Shamma or Lower Ladakhi, and Nubra. Each of the dialects is further divided into subdialects, particularly Changtang, with seven subdialects. The language is thought to be 30 to 40% mutually intelligible with Tibetan. The literary language, written in the Tibetan script, is based on the Leh dialect. Literacy rates are lower than the Indian national average, partly due to the isolation of many Ladakhi communities.

The Ladakhis are primarily Buddhists, practicing the Tibetan form, Vajrayana Lamaism; there is a Muslim minority in the Kargil region. The Ladakhi religion is a mixture of Lamaism, Hinduism, Islam, and pre-Buddhist beliefs, involving spirits, faith healing, and exorcisms. The lamasaries have been the centers of Ladakhi culture and religion for centuries and continue to serve as repositories of the Ladakh national identity.

NATIONAL HISTORY: The Ladakhis trace their history to Nya tri Tsampo, who ruled Ladakh in the third century B.C. Traditionally populated by immigrants from western Tibet in prehistoric times, Ladakh was often considered an outer province of Tibet until the tenth century. About A.D. 900, the Tibetan state collapsed, and the border regions, including Ladakh, became independent under a member of the Tibetan royal family. For centuries Ladakh remained isolated from the outside world with tenuous ties only to Tibet. The inhabitants lived a traditional Tibetan way of life under their own kings.

The first Ladakhi king extended the territory under his control, but his descendants were defeated by the Muslim Balts, who laid waste all of the important lamasaries in Ladakh. A generation later the Balts were conquered by the Ladakhis, but the Ladakh kingdom was divided among heirs and soon lost power. In 1523 the Ladakhis concluded the "Treaty of Perfect Friendship" with Tibet after years of cross-border raids.

In 1531 the weakened Ladakhi kingdom lost its western districts in Baltistan to invading Kashmiri Muslims. A descendant of the Tibetan kings, Chovang Namgyal, conquered eastern Ladakh in 1533 and established the Namgyal dynasty. Under the Namgyal dynasty the Ladakhis reconquered Baltistan and defeated the Kashmiris.

Raiding by caravans crossing the mountains and a slave trade that resulted from continual warfare resulted in the wide dispersal of the Ladakhis in the high mountain valleys. Passes suitable for foot traffic across the mountains led northward from Skardu and Leh into China and the Silk Road. Buddhist monasteries exercised great control over subjects and land in the eastern districts.

The Tibetans again invaded the kingdom in the early 1640s. In 1644, the Ladakhi king appealed for assistance against the invaders to the Mogul emperor in Delhi. The Moguls, exacting the price of making Ladakh a tributary kingdom, cleared the kingdom of Tibetan invaders in 1650. The Ladakhis formed treaty relations with the Mogul Empire, which again sent troops to assist the Ladakhis against the Tibetans in 1681–83. Invading Mongols defeated the Mogul troops in 1685 and overran the Ladakhi kingdom. In desperation the Ladakhis turned to their old enemies, the Kashmiris, for military aid. In the next decades, under a series of weak rulers, the Ladakhi kingdom gradually became a vassal state of Kashmir.

The kingdom, rich from the caravan trade between India, China, Tibet, and Central Asia, gradually threw off Kashmiri rule in the eighteenth century. In 1809, threatened by the expanding Sikhs,* Tsepal Namgyal sought an alliance with the British, but his remote kingdom had little to offer the Europeans, and they rebuffed his appeal. The Dogras of Jammu, allies of the Sikhs, invaded Ladakh in 1834. Appeals to the Tibetans and British were ignored, and the kingdom finally surrendered in 1842. The Dogras deposed the Ladakh monarchy but allowed the Namgyal family to retain Stok Palace, where it remains to the present. As part of the Dogra state of Kashmir, the former kingdom eventually came under British rule in the nineteenth century.

The Simla Conference between the British and Chinese authorities finally delimited Ladakh's formerly indefinite boundaries and for the first time established a firm frontier between Ladakh and Tibet. Despite the official boundaries, Ladakhis and Tibetans continued to move freely back and forth, and caravans continued to connect the high mountain valleys. Cut off from November through June when the high mountain passes were closed, the Ladakhis retained their traditional culture, and the Buddhists and Shi'a and Sunni Muslims continued living in harmony as they had for centuries.

The Ladakhis after World War II communicated to the British their unwillingness to become part of either Hindu-dominated India or Muslim Pakistan. The Indian government laid claim to the region based on tribute sent to the Mogul emperors in the seventeenth century. The British ignored the Ladakhi protests and demands for separation from both India and Pakistan. Ladakh remained part of the disputed state of Jammu and Kashmir when India and Pakistan gained independence in 1947. The first Indo-Pakistani war, ended by a United Nations cease-fire in January 1949, marked the first partition of Ladakh. India retained southern Ladakh, but the northwestern districts, including Baltistan, came under Pakistani control. The Indian authorities opened the first airstrip in Ladakh in 1948, allowing year-round communications for the first time.

In 1957 the Chinese government built a military road across Aksai Chin, the largely high-desert region of Ladakh lying between Chinese-held Tibet and Sinkiang. China, following its conquest of Tibet in 1959, laid claim to all of Ladakh as a historical appendage of Tibet. In 1962 Chinese troops invaded Indian Ladakh from Tibet. The invasion formed part of an advance all along the frontier that provoked war with India. The Indian government rushed troops to the formerly ignored district, but the Chinese troops continued to advance. A cease-fire in the region left China in control of the strategically important but mostly uninhabited Aksai Chin. The Chinese take over of Aksai Chin marked the second partition of Ladakh.

In the mid-1960s, the first stirrings of Ladakhi nationalism focused on a proposal for a neutral Ladakhi state on the sensitive Kashmir-Sinkiang-Tibet border. Never reconciled to foreign rule, the Ladakhis began to agitate for the reunification of their homeland. In Indian Ladakh, nationalists argued that if India was unable to defend them, the Ladakhis would be better off making their own international agreements.

The Indian military, often seen by Ladakhis as an occupation army, supported an Indian government's decision to introduce the Kashmiri and Punjabi languages to the region's schools. In 1974 the Ladakhi king died and was succeeded by Queen Diskit Wangmo, who assumed the role of Ladakh's political leader.

In the late 1980s, influenced by the Chinese repression in Tibet and the dramatic rise of Kashmiri nationalism, the Ladakhis began to organize in both India and Pakistan. The Ladakhis and Balts, having lived in harmony for over a thousand years, began to demand reunification. The violence that broke out in Kashmir in 1988 accelerated the growth of Ladakhi nationalism, which focused in India on separation from Kashmir and the creation of a separate Ladakhi territory within India. In Pakistan the religious issue fueled Ladakhi nationalism, as tension increased between the mostly Sunni Muslims in the Northern Areas and Pakistani Kashmir and the Shi'a Muslim Ladakhi Balts. In August 1989 severe ethnic violence between the Ladakhis and the Muslim Kashmiris erupted in Indian Ladakh.

The Ladakhi national movement in the wake of the Cold War evolved into a separatist faction claiming that the partition of Ladakh was the result of big-power politics and pressed for reunification as a first step to restoring Ladakh's sovereignty. Ladakhi militants pointed to the region's thousand years of independence as a basis for claims to sovereignty. The increasingly violent Kashmiri separatist movement in the 1990s frightened many Ladakhis, who feared the spread of violence to their homeland. The ideal behind Ladakhi separatism in both India and Pakistan was the creation of a neutral, multi-ethnic, multireligious Ladakh, a zone of peace in one of the world's least peaceful regions.

Following several years of discontent and agitation in Ladakh, the Indian government passed the Ladakh Autonomous Hill Development Councils

Act in May 1995. The act established autonomous councils in the Leh and Kargil Districts and allowed limited powers in the areas of economic development, land use, and taxation. Militants denounced the move as a sop, but even limited autonomous powers were seen as progress. The Ladakhis ignored a Kashmiri Muslim-called boycott of elections in the region in December 1995. In 1997 the Jammu and Kashmir legislature passed a new autonomy bill for Ladakh, but the majority of the Ladakhis rejected the bill as too limited.

In June 1999, Pakistani and Indian troops fought several skirmishes in the Kargil region on the demarcation line that divides Ladakh. The spring thaw always brings violence across the provisional border that separates Pakistani and Indian-controlled zones. Militants sponsored by the Pakistani government have crossed the border in an effort to wrest additional territory in Ladakh from India. The dispute nearly brought the two nuclear-armed countries to the brink of war, but the Ladakhis once again saw their protests ignored.

Increasing rivalry between the Ladakhi Buddhists and Shi'a Muslims in Ladakh has decreased the effectiveness of the movement for separation from Kashmir. In September 1999, a high number of Ladakhi voters participated in the general election in spite of threats and a boycott called by militant Kashmiris.

In June 2000 the Ladakh Autonomous Hill Development Council rejected yet another autonomy plan and unanimously passed a resolution at its general council meeting demanding "separation" from Jammu and Kashmir and the status of a Union territory. On 1 July the Jammu and Kashmir government described as 'illegal' the resolution adopted by the Ladakh Autonomous Hill Development Council against the autonomy motion passed by the state legislature.

The Ladakhis have resisted assimilation and continue to look to their former royal family for guidance. An Indian military force of over 40,000 remains in Ladakh to guard the sensitive Pakistani and Chinese frontiers, but to many Ladakhis they remain an occupation force. In February 2001 members of the former royal family called for a reduction of the military presence in Ladakh and supported a proposal for the separation of Ladkah, Jammu, and Kashmir as separate states as the only way to address the region's instability.

SELECTED BIBLIOGRAPHY:

Kaul, H.N. *Rediscovery of Ladakh*. 1998.
Kaul, Shridhar, and H.N. Kaul. *Ladakh through the Ages: Towards a New Identity*. 1993.
Rizvi, Janet. *Ladakh: Crossroads of High Asia*. 1998.
Srinivas, Smriti. *The Mouth of People, the Voice of God: Buddhists and Muslims in a Frontier Community of Ladakh*. 1998.

Ladins

Ladinos; Dolomitos; Nones; Ladini

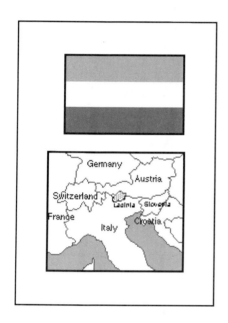

POPULATION: Approximately (2002e) 36,000 Ladins in northern Italy, concentrated in the Dolomite Alps region of the Trentino-Alto Adige and Veneto regions. Outside Europe there are Ladin communities in several areas of the United States.

THE LADIN HOMELAND: The Ladin homeland lies in the Dolomite Alps in northern Italy, occupying high alpine valleys between the Piave and Isarco Rivers just south of the Austrian border. The region is famous for the striking outline of the Dolomites, named for the stone of which it is formed. The majority of the Ladin population lives in the Val di Badia and Val di Gardena of Bolzano Province, with other groups in the provinces of Trento, the Val di Fiemme, and Belluno, the parishes of Val Moena, Cortina d'Ampezzo, Pieve-di-Livinallongo, Colle-Santa-Lucia, Cles, and Val di Non. The Ladin homeland, called Ladinia, has no official status. The region claimed by Ladins as the heartland of their small nation forms the Cadore district of Belluno Province of Veneto, and Val Gardena district of Bolzano Province of Trentino-Alto Adige region. *Ladinia (Patrje Ladine)*: 920 sq. mi.—2,382 sq. km, (2002e) 57,000—Ladins 55%, Tyroleans* 35%, other Italians 10%. The Ladin capital and major cultural center is Cortina d'Ampezzo, called Ampëz in Ladin, (2002e) 8,000. Another important cultural center is San Martino in Badia, called San Martin de Tor Val Badia in the Ladin language, the largest town of the Badia Valley.

FLAG: The Ladin national flag, the flag of the national movement, is a horizontal tricolor of pale blue, white, and green.

PEOPLE AND CULTURE: The Ladins are a Rhaeto-Romantic nation living in the high valleys of the Dolomite Alps. They traditionally trace their ancestry to the ancient Celtic tribes conquered and Latinized by the Romans. The Ladin culture developed in the isolation of the high mountain valleys, which were often cut off during the winter months. Mostly ignored by the conquerors that swept through northern Italy over the centuries, they clung to their distinct identity. The Ladins are the smallest of the three Rhaeto-Romantic nations that inhabit the eastern Alps. The related nations are the Romansch* of southeastern Switzerland and the Friulis,* who inhabit the region just southeast of Ladinia.

LANGUAGE AND RELIGION: The language spoken by the Ladins is derived from ancient Latin. The language belongs to the Rhaeto-Romance branch of the Gallo-Romance group of languages spoken in Western Europe. Due to the relative isolation of their high alpine valleys, a number of dialects of the language are spoken, the most important being Atesino, Cadorino, Fassano, Gardena, Nones (Parlata Trentina), Badiotto, Marebbano, Livinallese, and Ampezzo. A Venetian-influenced dialect, called Zoldino, is spoken in the southern valleys. The oldest known document in the language is a fourteenth-century paper from the Venosta Valley. The literary language, written since 1700, which is taught in area schools, is based on Fassano, spoken in the Fassa Valley. The language has a degree of official recognition in the Trentino and South Tyrol but none in the Fodom and Ampezzo Valleys of the Veneto region. Many Italian scholars until World War II claimed that Ladin was really a Veneto-Lombard dialect of Italian. Although many consider the language threatened with extinction, it appears to retain its vitality among the mostly rural Ladins. Newspapers are published in the language, and radio broadcasts began in the 1970s. Ladin has been taught in primary schools in the Gardena and Badia valleys since the 1940s. Most Ladins are bilingual in Italian, but they retain a fierce pride in their own language.

The Ladins are mostly Roman Catholics, with a small but important Protestant minority. The Catholic religion, an integral part of the Ladin culture, with its many feast days and ceremonies, traditionally has been the center of Ladin life, providing a focus for both the secular and religious aspects of the Ladin communities.

NATIONAL HISTORY: In 44 B.C., after the campaigns of Julius Caesar, the Roman Empire in Europe remained divided by a vast mountain chain inhabited by a diverse collection of indigenous Celtic tribes. The Rhetic and Noric tribes in the eastern Alps independently resisted integration into the Roman Empire, while their mountain homeland effectively divided Italy from Caesar's conquests in Germania. Emperor Augustus between 25 and 15 B.C. directed several military campaigns against the tribes. Some tribes were decimated, while others were sold as slaves and deported to far-flung corners of the Roman Empire. Finally subjected, the various peoples were forcibly united into the new Roman province called Rhaetia by Drusus and Tiberius, stepsons of Augustus.

The colonization of the region by the Romans and the influx of soldiers, merchants, officials, and colonists that it brought spread the Latin language into the new province. The structure of the Latin was modified by the local inhabitants, who wove it into their existing language structures. The arrival of the new Christian faith and its Latin language strengthened the Latin character of the dialects spoken in the Dolomites. The Ladin language evolved over several centuries to become a separate language by about A.D. 450. Most scholars are certain that at one stage the whole of the Tyrol was culturally and linguistically Ladin.

After three centuries of relative peace and stability in the region, the Roman Empire began to disintegrate. The alpine peoples once again were under attack after A.D. 400, this time from successive invasions of Goths, Franks, Bavarians,* and Lombards.* Many of the small tribes disappeared completely. The Lombards and other invaders settled in the lowlands south of the Alps and spread into the mountains, displacing or absorbing all but a few of the Rhaetian peoples. Most of the Ladin homeland formed part of a Lombard county until the eighth century, when the expanding empire of the Germanic Franks took control.

The Germanization of the Alps was assisted by a period of glacial retreat between the tenth and twelfth centuries, which raised the vegetation limits by as much as 6,561 feet (2,000 meters), allowing more extensive colonization of the valleys and easier passage through the high alpine passes. Under Germanic rule the Ladins formed a small minority, overlooked in their isolated alpine valleys, where they were able to maintain their own cultures and dialects.

In the eleventh century the western Ladin valleys came under the rule of the bishops of Brixen and Trent. In 1420 the Cadore and Zoldo regions in the east came under Venetian rule. The Austrian Habsburgs extended their influence into the area in the fourteenth century. In 1797 the Austrians took control of Venice, and the eastern Ladin valleys came under Austrian rule. Habsburg rule was extended to the western Ladin valleys following the secularization of the bishoprics of Brixen and Trent in 1802.

The Ladins lived under the cultural and linguistic domination of the neighboring Tyroleans and Venetians* for centuries. In the multi-ethnic Habsburg empire the Ladins formed one of many different ethnic groups, and pressure to assimilate eased. Their basically alpine culture took on many borrowed traits and customs, and their dialects absorbed many foreign words and usages. Each valley evolved its own particular customs and dialect, with little collective feeling of kinship or ethnic identity. Each group identified with the valley in which it lived. In 1866 the Austrians ceded the Veneto to Italy, again partitioning the small Ladin nation. Its culture and language remained mostly rural, and Italian quickly became the language of the towns and of local administration.

The European national revival in the latter half of the nineteenth century was felt throughout the vast, multi-ethnic Austro-Hungarian Empire. The movement, as interpreted by the Ladins, provoked a renewed interest in their unique history, culture, and dialects with demands for the unification of their valleys in one administrative unit. The cultural revival in the 1880s and 1890s began to reverse centuries of assimilation. The standardization of the language on the basis of the Fassano dialect strengthened the ties between the Ladin inhabitants of the isolated alpine valleys. The Ladin national movement focused on the reunification of the divided Ladin territories in Italy and Austria, but it also promoted the survival of the culture and the various Ladin dialects.

The first openly nationalist organization, the Ladin Union (Union de Ladins), was founded in Innsbruck in 1905. The nationalists proposed the political and administrative unification of the Ladin valleys as a third nationality in the Tyrolean region, along with the Italians and Tyroleans. The Ladin Union had by the outbreak of World War I chapters in most villages in both Italian and Austrian Ladinia.

The large Italian and the small Ladin populations of South Tyrol were objects of Italian irredentist claims in the first decade of the twentieth century. Promised the South Tyrol and other Austrian territories with large Italian populations by the allies after the outbreak of war in Europe in 1914, the Italians finally entered the war on the allied side in 1915. The heavy fighting between the Italians and Austrians in the Dolomites swept through the Ladin's alpine valleys, leaving devastation. The front line finally settled down to a war of attrition along the Piave River in 1917–18.

Nationalist Tyrolean opposition to the Italian claims fueled a movement for Tyrolean independence at the end of the war. The Tyroleans promised autonomy and gained some support among the Ladins, though unification under Italian rule became the theme of Italian propaganda directed at the Ladin population in Austrian territory. In October 1918 the Tyroleans convened an assembly of all of the region's peoples; it approved a plan for a federation of autonomous cantons, based on the Swiss model. On 24 April 1919, the Tyroleans declared the independence of their homeland, which included western Ladinia, but the movement was blocked by the allies. The Italian kingdom annexed the South Tyrol, but the Ladin valleys remained separated by provincial Italian boundaries.

In a conciliatory gesture soon after annexation, the Italian government made Italian, German, and Ladin official languages of the annexed Austrian territory. Italian guarantees of cultural and linguistic freedom lasted only until the Fascists took power in Rome in 1922.

The Fascist authorities closed all Ladin cultural institutions, schools, and publications and forbade the use of the Ladin language. Standard Italian was the only language allowed in education, the courts, and in local administration. In 1926 the authorities decreed that all family and place names must conform to Italian guidelines. In 1939 the Italian government arrested most nationalist leaders. The Ladin leaders charged that the policies of the fascist Italian government amounted to the suppression of the Ladin past, culture, and language.

During World War II, following Italy's surrender in 1943, German troops occupied the alpine regions and united them under one administration. The Ladins' brief administrative reunification under German rule between 1943 and the end of World War II initiated the growth of modern Ladin nationalism. After the war, the Ladins, led by the Committee for National Liberation (Comitati de Liberazione Nazionale), attempted to win Allied support for the creation of an independent state, modeled on Liechtenstein and under the protection of the new United Nations. The Allies, preoccupied with the reconstruction of Europe, refused to accept their petitions.

Influenced by the larger Tyrolean nationalist movement, the Ladins pressed for linguistic, economic, and cultural autonomy in a united Ladin district within Italy. The Ladins, overwhelmed by the Italianization of their homeland, organized numerous marches and demonstrations demanding the unification of and special status for the five major Ladin valleys in the Dolomites.

The Ladin valleys remained remote and very sparsely populated until the 1960s tourism boom. Expensive ski resorts and second homes for Italians from the lowlands proliferated. Resentment of the exploitation of their homeland without their consent or participation gave new impetus to demands for self-government and a say in the development of the resources of the Ladin homeland.

Ladin nationalism experienced a resurgence in the 1980s as Europe began to unite in a proposed federation of independent states. The European ideal, theoretically able to accommodate an independent Ladinia that was economically integrated with the rest of the union, spurred the growth of nationalism since 1988. The Ladin nationalists claimed that their movement was not separatist but worked for the equality of their small nation with the other nations of a united Europe.

After centuries of resisting assimilation, the Ladins are still fighting for the survival of their small nation. They are no longer threatened by armed invasion but by rural depopulation and the cultural transformation associated with mass tourism. Organizations such as Inant Adum and the Uniun Generela di Ladins organized in the 1980s and 1990s to safeguard the culture and language of the Ladin nation. Demands for the unification of Ladinia in one administrative unit, the primary aim of the nationalists since the late nineteenth century, continue to fuel nationalist sentiment in the high valleys of the Dolomites.

In mid-2000, the Italian government rejected a petition for the creation of a separate Ladin autonomous region in the Dolomites. As an alternative, the Ladins were allowed to create a partially elected government, including a president of the Ladin nation.

SELECTED BIBLIOGRAPHY:

Facaros, Dana. *Northeast Italy.* 1990.
Goldsmith, Annie. *Dolomites of Italy.* 1989.
Hofmann, Paul. *South Tyrol and the Dolomites.* 1995.
Toscano, Mario. *Alto Adige, South Tyrol: Italy's Frontier with the German World.*
    1991.

Lahu

Lohei; Lahuna; Launa; Mussuh; Muhso; Musso; Massur; Masur

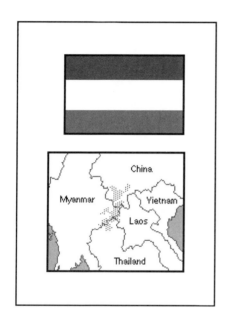

POPULATION: Approximately (2002e) 680,000 Lahu in southeastern Asia, concentrated in the jungle region at the conjunction of the borders of Myanmar (with 290,000), China (with 275,000), Thailand (with 75,000), and Laos (with 30,000). There are smaller groups in Vietnam and in other parts of Myanmar and Thailand.

THE LAHU HOMELAND: The Lahu homeland occupies part of the Shan Plateau in northeastern Myanmar and adjacent areas of China, Thailand, and Laos, a mountainous region east of the Salween River. The Lahu population is concentrated in the foothills and middle levels of the mountains. Popularly called Lahuland, the region has indefinite boundaries and no official status, forming several districts of Shan State of Myanmar. The Lahu capital and major cultural center is Mong Thon, (2002e) 15,000.

FLAG: The Lahu national flag, the flag of the national movement, is a horizontal tricolor of red, white, and green, the white half again as wide as the red and green stripes.

PEOPLE AND CULTURE: The Lahu, called Masur by the Thais and Shans,* are a small nation distantly related to the Tibetans.* There are four major divisions among the Lahu, historically based on geography and the color of their clothing. The four—the Black Lahu (Lahu Na'), Red Lahu (Lahu Nyi), Yellow Lahu (Lahu Shi), and She-Leh Lahu—mostly live in villages at high altitudes. There are no clans among the Lahu, thus no surnames. This creates administrative difficulties, so many families have adopted family names from surrounding peoples. Traditionally the Lahu were slash-and-burn agriculturists, but since the 1950s they have increasingly settled in permanent villages and towns. The Lahu are not self-sufficient and must maintain contact and trade with the peoples of the valleys and plains for survival. Lahu society is patrilineal, with inheritance through the male line, although relationships have great importance on both the paternal and maternal side. Extended families live together in large houses built on stilts, although now there are signs that many of the traditional ways are breaking down. The small, often-warring Lahu tribes were transformed into a nation in the twentieth century.

LANGUAGE AND RELIGION: The Lahu language is a language belonging to the Yi or Lolo subgroup of the Lolo-Burmese branch of the Tibeto-Burman group of languages. The language, like Chinese, is tonal, with seven distinct tones. Because the Lahu tribes have been heavily influenced by both the Shans and Burmans, many are bilingual; Shan is the favored language of trade. Missionaries developed a Latin script for the language. The language is spoken in three major dialects—Na (Black), Nyi (Red), and Shehleh—and several subdialects exist, based on geographic and clan affiliations. Lahu Shi or Yellow Lahu, spoken by about 10,000, including a small immigrant group in California, is considered a distinct language. Not all the dialects and subdialects are mutually intelligible.

The majority of the Lahu retain their traditional spiritual beliefs, which involve a supreme being, Geusha, who has overall control of all other deities, and worship of their ancestors. There are Buddhist communities, mostly in Thailand and Laos, and one Christian, mainly Baptist; Christians make up about 30% of the Lahu population. Even many Christian and Buddhist Lahu have retained their beliefs in evil spirits, *nats*. They believe that while all *nats* are evil, some are worse than others and that all must be appeased. If the *nats* are pleased, the harvest will be bountiful and the Lahu will enjoy good health. Belief in these spirits is strongest among the most isolated groups. The most important festival, the five-day new year's ceremony, the Kho Cha Lor, is held to thank Geusha for the blessings of the year. The new year's festival is also the courting period for young Lahu couples; a go-between for the man asks the girl to ask permission of his friend to marry her. During the betrothal ceremony, the village elders pray for Guesha's blessings on the couple.

NATIONAL HISTORY: The Lahu are thought to have originated in the upper Salween River area of Yunnan in China. They migrated south along the river in prehistoric times, settling a wider area than their present homeland. They lived in tribal groups, often warring among themselves. Gradually stronger peoples pushed them into the less accessible mountains, into which they retreated whenever threatened. The tribes maintained a precarious independence but never evolved a unified political system.

Invading Shans, a Tai* people, took control of the lowlands in the seventh century A.D. They established small monarchies in the region but only nominally controlled the Lahu highlands. Ethnic Burmans, now called Myen, originally from Tibet, began to penetrate the region in the ninth century as conquerors. They received tribute both from the settled Shans and the Lahu tribes of the mountains in exchange for being left to live their traditional ways of life. The tribute paid to the Burman kings established the basis of later Burmese claims to the region.

The highland region was often crossed by invading armies, forcing the Lahu to form an alliance with the Shans, who held the lowlands, and the Wa,* who held the passes. The three peoples established a feudal system dominated by the more numerous Shans. The frequent invasions established a Lahu military tradition of fierce resistance to threats to their independence. The Lahu tribes continually fought the imposition of direct Burman rule in the sixteenth and seventeenth centuries.

In the nineteenth century, the lowlands Shans formed a series of small kingdoms that nominally controlled the tribal lands of the Lahu. In the 1870s the Shan princes ceased paying tribute to the Burman king, opening the way for increased British influence in the region. The British took effective control of the region and continued the Burman practice of retaining traditional state and tribal hierarchies.

Christian missionaries arrived in the Lahu homeland in the 1880s. They introduced various Christian sects, but more importantly, they also brought Western-style education and new ideas. Chiefs' sons educated in mission schools, and often Christian, emerged as the leaders of the Lahu nation in the early twentieth century, ruling their traditional tribal structures under the guidance of British agents. Under the leadership of the Christian-educated minority, the Lahu began to identify with a larger national unit rather than with their immediate tribal identities.

The Lahu leadership, relieved of Shan and Burman oppression by the presence of the British authorities, remained fiercely loyal during World War II. They served as guides to the Allied forces and following the Japanese conquest of the British territories in the region formed guerrilla groups that terrorized Japanese troops behind the front lines.

At the end of the war, without being consulted, their homeland was included in the new Burmese state, which was granted independence in 1948. The Burmans of the Irrawaddy Delta to the south, with little experience of the tribal peoples, moved into the Lahu tribal lands as the new administrators. Their harsh and arbitrary rule soon alienated the majority of the tribes. The Lahu formed a loose alliance with other non-Burman minorities, particularly the Shans in the early 1950s, with the aim of winning autonomy within the Burmese state. In 1958 the Lahu joined the Shans in open rebellion against the increasingly oppressive Burmese government.

A Burmese military government that took power in the country following a coup in 1962 imposed such an oppressive regime that the Lahu again openly rebelled. Nationalists, many drawn from the Christian minority, formed the Lahu National Organization (LNO). The LNO formed a military alliance with the neighboring Shans to fight the government troops sent to pacify the region. By the mid-1960s some Lahu leaders had abandoned the idea of autonomy within a Burmese federation and had embraced independence of Greater Lahuland, including the Lahu territories in neighboring states.

Many of the Lahu tribes turned to opium and other drug production to finance the growing nationalist insurgency in the 1970s. Attacks by the Burmese military, using helicopters and weapons supplied by the United States to fight the drug trafficking, were directed at unarmed civilians indiscriminately, while many Burmese officers grew rich from drugs being produced in the region known as the Golden Triangle.

After the communist Pathet Lao takeover of Laos in 1975, thousands of Lahu fled across the border to refugee camps in Thailand. Some were returned to Laos, but others, after years in the camps, finally settled in Thailand or emigrated to the United States. There are now Lahu groups in California, Minnesota, and North Carolina.

Most of the Lahu remained hunters until a lack of game and a shortage of primary forest forced many to settle on agricultural land. They had little experience in farming, so they were not efficient at producing food. For this reason, Lahu hired out to other peoples as laborers, and the Lahu language thus became a lingua franca spoken throughout a wide area.

In the 1980s, the vestiges of the old feudal system dominated by the Shan nobility increasingly made efforts at a cooperative defense difficult. The Lahu nationalists opposed the Shan claims to their territory and resented Shan domination of the joint military operations. The Burmese military, in order to isolate further the rebellious Lahu, stationed troops along the main trade routes, preventing the traditional trade between the two peoples.

A democracy movement that drew in most of the national groups in Burma was brutally suppressed in 1988, although elections were allowed two years later. In 1990 the ruling military government refused to accept the victory of the democracy movement and relinquish power. The Lahu rebels, in a show of support for the democratic movement, had promised to end decades of resistance once a democratic federal state had been established in Burma. The Lahu, along with many other minority groups, refused to accept the terms offered by the military government, and fighting continued.

The Burmese military government, in an effort to divide and rule, offered development funds in exchange for cease-fires by the military forces of the minorities. The leadership of the Lahu National Organization (LNO) in 1994, nearly without arms and the people suffering hunger and disease, finally accepted the government offer. Thousands of acres of poppy plantations were destroyed by government troops, against Lahu resistance. Fighting again flared in several areas, and thousands of Lahu fled to refugee camps in Thailand.

In the late 1990s, forced labor, particularly as porters for military units, decimated many of the more accessible Lahu villages. Lahu men and women were forced to clear land and to provide food and housing for government troops. Lahu refugees in Thailand told of laborers being forced to march along roads that had been mined by rebel groups. Illegal logging, smuggling of minerals, and the production of drugs were often controlled by the nationalist organizations to finance their war, but increasingly these activities involved army officers in areas under government control. For the Lahu, the oppressive military government of Myanmar is one of five traditional enemies, along with fire, flood, famine, and plague.

SELECTED BIBLIOGRAPHY:

Bhruksasri, Wanat. *Hill Tribes of Thailand and Relevant Matters.* 1987.
Fisher, Frederick. *Myanmar.* 2000.
Gall, Timothy L. *Worldmark Encyclopedia of Culture and Daily Life.* 1998.
Wongsprasert, Sanit. *Semi-Nomadic Highlanders of Northern Thailand: A Historic Perspective.* 1993.

Leonese

Lleónesas; Lleonese; Leonese-Sanbrese

POPULATION: Approximately (2002e) 1,300,000 Leonese in Spain and Portugal, concentrated in the historical region of León in northwestern Spain, and the Mirandese region of northeastern Portugal.

THE LEONESE HOMELAND: The Leonese homeland lies in the north-central region of the Iberian Peninsula in southwestern Europe. The region, traversed by the Duero (Douro) River, is mostly rolling plain, rising to the Cantabrian Mountains in the north. Pastures and woodlands continue to be communal in the mountainous eastern region. The heartland of León, locally spelled Lleón, comprises the provinces of León, Salamanca, and Zamora. The adjacent provinces of Valladolid and Palencia are disputed with Castile but historically formed part of León. Nationalists also claim the area of Portugal in Beira Alta between the Coa River and the international border with Spain. *Region of León (Lleón):* 21,078 sq. mi.—54,591 sq. km, (2002e) 1,726,000—Leonese 68%, Castilians 18%, Asturians* 6%, Galicians* 5%, other Spanish 3%. The Leonese capital and major cultural center is León, called Lleón by the Leonese, (2002e) 137,000. The other major cultural centers are Zamora, called Sanabria in Leonese, (2002e) 68,000, and Valladolid, (2002e) 319,000. The major cultural center of the Mirandese in Portugal is Miranda do Douro, called Miranda'l Douru in Mirandese and Miranda del Douro by the Leonese, (2002e) 5,000.

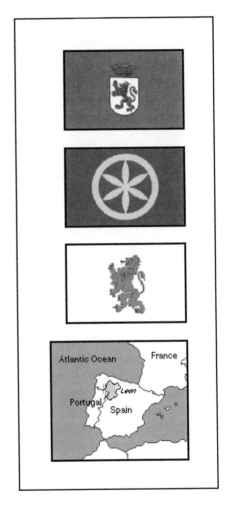

FLAG: The Leonese national flag, the flag of the national movement, is a dark pink field bearing the historical coat of arms, a pink lion rampant under a gold crown, centered. The flag of the Conceyu Xoven, the major nationalist organization, is a red field bearing a gold Celtic sun centered within a gold circle. The traditional flag of León is a white field bearing a pink rampant lion.

PEOPLE AND CULTURE: The Leonese population has declined since 1900, due to emigration to Madrid and other parts of Spain. Rural depopulation is particularly acute in some districts, and the population is now concentrated in the towns, especially the provincial capitals. *Minifundios*, or small landholdings, predominate in the rural areas and have led to fragmentation of the available farmland. The rural quality of Leonese society until the mid-twentieth century helped to maintain the distinct culture of the region in spite of gradual assimilation into Castilian culture and the prohibition of regional cultures and languages during the Francisco Franco dictatorship from the late 1930s to 1975.

LANGUAGE AND RELIGION: The Leonese language derives from the vernacular of the Visigothic period and is still spoken in León, Zamora, Salamanca, and Valladolid Provinces. Leonese forms part of a group of dialects in the northwestern Iberian Peninsula called Asturian-Leonese or Astur-Lleonés, which are transitional dialects between Castilian Spanish and Galician and Portuguese. The dialects, spoken by over 300,000 people in the region, form a historical bridge from Galician and Portuguese on the west and Castilian Spanish on the east. Leonese is spoken in three major dialects—Lleón, the most widely spoken; Sanbrese, mostly spoken in the province of Zamora; and Mirandese, spoken in adjacent areas of Portugal. Mirandese (Mirandés) is spoken by about 20,000 in the region of the towns of Miranda do Douro and Vimioso in the Portuguese district of Bragança. Some steps toward standardization are under way, and the literary language is being revived. The language has no official status; the majority who are able to speak it are unable to read or write in the dialect. Teaching Leonese in area schools is prohibited by the regional governments of Castile and León in Spain, while Mirandese has been introduced to schools in the two municipal areas of Miranda do Douro and Vimioso in northeastern Portugal.

The Leonese in both Spain and Portugal are overwhelmingly Roman Catholic, with religious beliefs traditionally intertwined with the yearly cycle. In recent years evangelical Protestant sects have been making headway in the region, partly due to the Catholic Church's long and close association with Franco. Although the influence of the church has declined in recent years, saints' days and traditional Catholic festivals and celebrations remain an integral part of the Leonese culture.

NATIONAL HISTORY: The region south of the Cantabrian Mountains was settled by Celtic tribes in the eighth to sixth centuries B.C. The Celts were gradually brought under Roman rule by the first century B.C.; the conquest was completed by the emperor Augustus in 19 B.C. Forming part of Farther Spain, Baetica, the area remained sparsely populated, with few towns and only one Roman garrison. The decline of Roman authority led to invasions by barbarian tribes, particularly the Vandals, in the fifth century A.D. Conquered by the Visigoths in the sixth to eighth centuries, the region formed part of the Visigothic kingdom, with its capital at Toledo.

The invasion of southern Spain by Muslim Moors from North Africa in 711 began the rise of the Asturian kingdom, as Visigothic nobles fled north to the mountainous region. León received a large number of Mozarabic immigrants following the Moorish conquest. These immigrants introduced a strong Arabic linguistic and cultural influence in the region. The small Leonese kingdom bore the brunt of the Moorish attacks but seems to have been the first Peninsular kingdom to evolve popular parliamentary institutions. The reconquest of Leonese territory from the Moors was completed in the eleventh century.

The rise of the medieval Leonese kingdom began with García I (909–914), the son of Alfonso III of Asturias, who set up his court on the site of the former Roman camp of Legnio Gemina after abandoning the former capital of the kingdom at Oviedo, in Asturias. The kings of León ruled León, Galicia, Asturias, and much of the country of Portugal before the Portuguese won their independence in 1139.

The Muslim caliphate of Cordoba during the tenth century extended its authority into the southern districts of the kingdom. The Leonese kings often had to accept de facto submission to the Moorish caliphs. The Leonese kings had inherited from the Asturians a strong attachment to Visigothic tradition, and they sometimes took the title of emperor or "king of all Spain," and they furthered the reconquest of Muslim Spain whenever possible.

The period of Leonese hegemony in Christian Spain nominally lasted until the death of Alfonso VII in 1157. His kingdom was divided between his sons; Sancho III received Castile, and Fernando II was given León. Conflicts between the various Christian kingdoms created great difficulties in the effort to expel the Muslims from the northern Spanish territories.

The Leonese kingdom's decline began in the early eleventh century when the conquests of Sancho III of Navarre elevated Castile from a county to a kingdom at his death in 1035. Fernando I of Castile conquered León in 1037, but at his death in 1065 the Leonese kingdom regained its independence. León and Castile were again united in 1072 under Alfonso VI and again separated in the twelfth century. The second period of Leonese power, from 1157 to 1230, occurred when the kingdom was ruled separately from Castile by its own kings. Relations with Castile were rarely amicable, but the kingdom was remarkably stable during this period, and the Leonese won several notable victories over the Moors in Leonese Extremadura, the region just south of the Leonese heartland.

After political union with Castile in 1230, Leonese political and administrative institutions were maintained and a sense of separate identity survived, but they slowly gave way to Castilian. The Leonese language by the fourteenth century had been relegated to the status of a rural, peasant dialect, while the towns became mostly Castilian speaking. Castilian became the language of the administration, and officials were dispatched from Castile to fill political and ecclesiastical positions throughout the Leonese lands.

León rapidly lost political power as the Castilian administration was transferred south to territories reconquered from the Moors in the thirteenth and fourteenth centuries. In 1561 Madrid, in central Spain, was made the center of the kingdom, and all remnants of Leonese autonomy were abolished.

In the nineteenth century, León was occupied by French troops following Napoleon's invasion of the Iberian Peninsula in 1808. The French, with their revolutionary ideas of nation and equality, had a profound effect on the formerly isolated region. The ideas disseminated during the French occupation of 1808–12 saw the modest beginnings of a Leonese national movement in the mid-nineteenth century.

The unstable Spanish kingdom was finally overthrown in the early 1930s, but subsequent elections seriously divided the Spanish state. The Leonese initially supported the more conservative elements, but as civil war spread in 1936, many joined the anti-Fascist groups fighting in the northern mountains. The victory of the Fascists under Franco in 1939 ended a Leonese drive to win autonomy within a democratic Spanish state.

The development of industry began only after the civil war and remains modest to the present. The majority of the Leonese remained rural and lived in villages or small towns, where their culture and language had been preserved. Only in the 1970s did the relative prosperity of the coastal zones begin to be felt in the region. Dams in the provinces of Salamanca and Zamora generate a quarter of Spain's hydroelectricity.

With Franco's death in 1975, Spain rapidly democratized, and regionalist and nationalist organizations proliferated. Groups such as Conceyu Xoven formed in León, with the aim of autonomy for the Leonese. The Spanish government, wishing to diffuse rising regionalist demands, offered autonomy to the kingdom's historical region. Regionalists put forward a proposal for a regional government to cover the Leonese heartland, the provinces of León and Zamora, plus plans for referendums on joining the new region in areas also claimed by the Castilians—the province of Salamanca, and the districts of La Liebana, Valdeorras, the left bank of the Valderaduei River, and the Carrion Strip of the provinces of Valladolid and Palencia. Nonetheless, the Leonese provinces, over the protests of many inhabitants, were incorporated into the autonomous community of Castile-León in 1979. Separation from Castile became the focus of the nationalists, and a movement formed to revive the Leonese culture and language.

Spain joined the European Economic Community, later called the European Union (EU), in 1986, bringing new demands from the Leonese nationalists. The majority supported autonomy within democratic Spain, but small militant groups called for independence and the reunification of the Leonese territories in Spain and Portugal as part of an Iberian federation within the EU.

The linguistic issue continued to fuel the nationalist movement in the 1990s. The Leonese language has no official status, but nationalists hope that separation from Castile would allow the language to become an official language of the proposed new region. The lack of self-government is felt to be the major reason for the decline of the Leonese culture and language. The three major demands of the national movement are for the unification of all the Leonese territories, self-government for the Leonese nation, and official status for the Leonese language. Activists demand the same autonomy granted to the neighboring region of Galicia.

SELECTED BIBLIOGRAPHY:

Griffiths, Helen. *León*. 1994.
Kern, Robert W. *The Regions of Spain: A Reference Guide to History and Culture.* 1995.
Llamas, David Diez. *The Leonese Identity*. 1978.
Reilly, Bernard F. *The Kingdom of León-Castilla under King Alfonse VII, 1126–1157.* 1998.

Lezgins

Lezgians; Lezghi; Lezgi; Lesghians; Kuris; Kurins; Akhtas; Akhtins

POPULATION: Approximately (2002e) 485,000 Lezgins in the North Caucasus, 287,000 in the Dagestan Republic of southern European Russia, 195,000 in the adjacent districts of northern Azerbaijan, and smaller communities in neighboring regions and countries. Outside the former Soviet Union the largest Lezgin community is in Turkey. Lezgin nationalists claim a national population of 1.2 million in Russia and Azerbaijan. Other Lezgin populations live in Central Asia, Turkey, and Georgia. Lezgin national organizations estimate the actual Lezgin population in Azerbaijan at between 600,000 and 900,000, much higher than the official estimates. The disparity arises from the number of ethnic Lezgins who registered as ethnic Azeris during the Soviet period and continue to claim Azeri nationality to escape job and education discrimination in Azerbaijan.

THE LEZGIN HOMELAND: The Lezgin homeland lies along the Samur River in southeastern Dagestan and northeastern Azerbaijan. The river forms part of the international boundary between the Dagestan Republic of the Russian Federation and the Republic of Azerbaijan. Most of the region lies in the eastern Caucasus and is very mountainous, but a small portion is included in the Caspian Sea lowlands around the mouth of the Samur River. Never united as a single political entity, Lezginistan remains divided and, according to nationalists, forms the Kurakh, Kasumkent, Magaramkent, Akhty, Derbent, and Dokuzpara Rayons of Dagestan in the Russian Federation, and the Kuba, Khachmaz, and Qusar (Gusar) Rayons of the Republic of Azerbaijan. *Lezginistan (Lezghistan):* 2,984 sq. mi.—7,729 sq. km, (2002e) 625,000—Lezgins 75%, Dagestanis* 12%, Azeris 10%, Russians 2%, others 1%. The Lezgin capital and major cultural center is Derbent, called Derbend by the Lezgins, (2002e) 97,000. The Lezgin traditional capital is the town of Magaramkent, called Maharamdxür by the Lezgins, (2002e) 10,000. Other important Lezgin cultural centers are Quba, called Kuba by the Lezgins, (2002e) 24,000, and Säki, called Sheki (2002e) 63,000, in Azerbaijan.

FLAG: The Lezgin national flag, the flag of the national movement, is a horizontal bicolor of green over blue bearing a black and white eagle against a yellow and pale blue background within a centered white-outlined disk.

PEOPLE AND CULTURE: The Lezgins are a Caucasian people of unknown origin, one of the indigenous nations of the Caucasus Mountain region of southeastern Europe. The Lezgins traditionally lived in free societies, consisting of patriarchal groups or clans led by male elders responsible for all major decisions. The clans, the *turkum*, remain to the present, but with modernization and emigration the clans have become less important, although the Lezgins still generally marry within their own clans. The elder women are very influential. Because of their geographic isolation and their resistance to state authority, Lezgin educational levels remain among the lowest in the region. Unemployment is very high, mostly due to the concentration of Soviet-era arms industries that have closed since 1991; the mostly rural Lezgins have not been as hard hit as those in urban areas. The most important folk tradition is the *Lezginka*, a traditional dance both for couples and for males, who dance imitating the eagle, the Lezgin national symbol.

LANGUAGE AND RELIGION: The language spoken by the Lezgins belongs to the Samurian group of northeastern Caucasian languages. The relative isolation of the Lezgin communities fostered the development of seven dialects: Kiuri, Akhty, Kuba, Gjunej, Garkin, Anyx, Stal. The most important of the dialects are Kiuri or Kurin, which are spoken by the majority of Lezgins and are the basis of the literary language; Akhty, spoken on both sides of the international border in the high Caucasus region; and Kuba, which differs considerably from standard Lezgi and is spoken mostly in Azerbaijan. The three dialects reflect the division of the Lezgins into three subgroups, the Kurin, the Kuba, and the Akhty or Sumar. Some of the dialects are not mutually intelligible with others. The language shows considerable borrowings from neighboring Turkish languages, particularly Azeri. The written language was created in the mid-nineteenth century. In the 1920s, the Soviet authorities changed the alphabet from the Arabic script to Latin, then in 1938 from Latin to the Russian Cyrillic. The Russian authorities also attempted to replace Arabic and Persian words with Russian words. Before the Russian Revolution, the Lezgins were undergoing assimilation by the Azeris to the south; presently most Lezgins speak Azeri as a second language.

The Lezgins are primarily Sunni Muslims, although there is a substantial Shi'a Muslim minority in the Dokuzpara area in Azerbaijan. Many of their former animist beliefs have been mingled with their Islamic practices. During the spring, as well as during planting and harvesting seasons, several ancient rituals are still practiced. The bones of animals are believed to have magical and healing powers. The names of many pagan deities have become synonymous with the name of Allah, and pre-Islamic harvest and spring festivals remain important. Younger, urban Lezgins are more secular and tend to observe those parts of the Islamic religion that function as part of modern urban life.

NATIONAL HISTORY: For thousands of years invaders from Europe and Asia crossed or conquered Lezgistan, driving the early clans into mountain strongholds in the high Caucasus. The clans formed loose federations for defensive purposes. The Lezgins are believed by historians to have their origins in the amalgamation of three ancient tribal federations that spoke similar dialects and shared many cultural traits—the Akhty, Alty, and Dokuz Para.

Muslim Arabs conquered the lowlands in A.D. 728, introducing their new Islamic religion, with its unifying religious and social system. A flourishing Muslim civilization developed in the coastal plains, centered on Derbent, on the edge of Lezgin territory. The city became a major political and cultural center of the Muslim empire known as the Caliphate. The influence of Muslim society converted most of the lowland clans, but the highland clans continued to resist all invaders and to cling to their own folk religions until the eighteenth century. Politically, the Lezgins were divided; those in the north were included in the Derbent khanate, while the southern clans formed part of the Kuba khanate.

Invading Mongols devastated the Lezgin lowlands in the early thirteenth century, forcing most of the clans to withdraw to traditional mountain strongholds. The Persians extended their rule to the coastal lowlands in the fourteenth century, beginning a long rivalry between the Persian and Turkish empires that eventually facilitated the Russian conquest of the Caucasus.

Until the fifteenth century the majority of the Lezgin clans remained animists, but other religions were making inroads. Persian traders introduced Islam to the highland clans in the south in the fifteenth century, and the Golden Horde brought Islam to the northern clans in the sixteenth and seventeenth centuries. The Ottoman Turks occupied the region in the sixteenth century, and under their rule Islam became the major religion.

The Lezgins, unlike other Dagestani peoples, offered their loyalty to tribal and clan federations and never formed their own principality or state, though a khan of the Kuris exercised loose cultural authority in the region. The Laks took control of the Lezgin territories for a time in the eighteenth century, but real authority mostly remained with the local Lezgin leaders.

In 1723 the Russians took control of the plains of northern Dagestan, and a weakened Persia ceded the rugged, mountainous south in 1813. The Russians created a new political entity in the Lezgin territories, the Kiurin Khanate, which was later dissolved and made the Kiurin District. The

Lezgins fiercely resisted Christian Russian rule. Stirred to religious and nationalist fervor, they followed the religious leader of the Avars,* Imam Shamil, in a long holy war against the Russians. Effective guerrilla tactics in the high mountains halted the Russian advance for over two decades. Thousands died in the final Russian conquest of Lezginistan in 1859–60. The last of the fierce Lezgin warriors did not submit to Russian rule until 1877. A profound hatred of the Russians continues to permeate Lezgin culture. The term "Lezgin" was also applied to other Dagestani groups, the Aguls, Rutuls, and Tabasarans, until the early twentieth century.

The Lezgin clans were progressively assimilated into the larger Azeri culture until the First World War and the turmoil that followed. The Lezgin clans openly supported Muslim Turks when war began in 1914, and they celebrated the news that revolution had broken out in Russia in February 1917. Effectively independent as civil administration collapsed, in May 1917 the Dagestani peoples called a Muslim conference that elected Mullah Gotinsky as their political and religious leader.

The Bolshevik takeover of the Russian government in October 1917 created chaos in the region as local Bolsheviks attempted to take power. The Muslim peoples joined with the Terek Cossacks* to declare an independent Terek-Dagestan republic on 20 October 1917, but the new state, undermined by ethnic, religious, and territorial disputes, collapsed in December 1917. The Muslim peoples formed a separate state in March 1918 and attempted a cooperative defense as the Russian Civil War spread south. The anti-Bolshevik forces, the Whites, took control of the region in January 1919, but forced conscription of Muslims generated strong resistance. Promised autonomy, the Muslims mostly went over to the Reds. The last of the White forces withdrew in January 1920.

The Soviet authorities created the Mountain Autonomous Republic, with Arabic as the official language. The Lezgins, along with many other Muslim highlanders, opposed the Soviet antireligious policy and rebelled. The government then created a separate Dagestan for the highland peoples of the eastern Caucasus. In 1925 the Soviets began an anti-Islamic campaign; this involved closing mosques and religious schools, eliminating the use of Arabic, and executing or deporting local Lezgin religious leaders. Azeri was declared the official language of the region, but in 1928 Lezgin was made an official language in Dagestan, and a Latin alphabet was devised. Over the next decades, the Russian language was imposed on administration, education, and intergroup communications.

The political and social manipulations of the Soviet authorities increased Lezgin resentment of Russian and Soviet domination. The Lezgin clans resisted attempts to move them from their mountain villages to lowland towns and collective farms, and as a result they remained largely rural until the 1970s. The later move to the nearby towns and cities, particularly Derbent, forced on them by the need to find work, increased the popular resentment of the Soviet authorities. Government attempts to suppress their religion, relocate them away from their homelands, and manipulate their language created a powerful unity among the Lezgin clans.

The political reforms begun by Mikhail Gorbachev allowed the Lezgins finally to give voice to their grievances, accumulated over decades. The Lezgin national movement, Sadval (Unity), was founded in July 1990 in Derbent. In April 1991, the autonomous Soviet republic of Dagestan passed a resolution making itself a sovereign republic. The Lezgin regional *soviets* (councils) opposed the transformation, as it made no provision for the creation of a separate Lezgin republic.

Lezgin nationalism exploded with the collapse of the Soviet Union and the independence of Azerbaijan, which effectively partitioned the Lezgins between two new states. In December 1991, the All–National Congress of Lezgins called for the immediate creation of a Lezgin national state.

The border between Dagestan and Azerbaijan was only nominal when the two formed part of first the Russian Empire and later the Soviet Union, but following the disintegration of the Soviet Union it became a frontier separating two independent states. In 1992, when the Russian Federation and Azerbaijan agreed to a formal boundary at the Samur River, thousands of Lezgins demonstrated. Lezgins on both sides of the new border today maintain family and trade ties across the frontier. The new border controls greatly interfere with the Lezgins' traditional way of life. The Lezgins have never complained about cultural or political repression in Dagestan, but they continue to accuse the Azeri government of suppressing the Lezgin language and culture. They claim they are forced to lie about their ethnic origins for fear of discrimination. Some observers believe that the Russian government is encouraging Lezgin nationalism in order to increase pressure on the Azeris with regard to oil quotas and pipelines.

The mobilization of the Lezgins in Dagestan started with the collapse of the Soviet Union, but those in Azerbaijan joined the movement later, a result of forced military conscription for duty in Nagorno-Karabakh, and the settlement of Meskhetians* on land claimed as Lezgin territory. Initially Lezgin nationalism remained stronger in Russia than in Azerbaijan, where large numbers of Lezgins had settled in the Azeri capital, Baku. In March 1993 the Azeri police fired on a Lezgin demonstration of over 70,000 people, killing at least six demonstrators. The "Lezgin massacre" fueled the dramatic rise of nationalism in Azerbaijan. Further demonstrations led to violence in 1994–95 in Derbent between local Azeris, Lezgins, and the police, leaving several dead and many wounded. A considerable degree of ethnic cohesion was formed during the mass demonstrations in Azerbaijan.

In 1995 the new Azeri government banned the Sadval movement in Azerbaijan and appealed to the Russian government to ban the group's activities in Russia. Seven activists arrested in Azerbaijan were put on trial for treason, terrorism, and banditry, including one of the leaders of Sadval, a citizen of Russian Dagestan. Other activists escaped to Russia, where they supported demands for the liberation of the seven, also demanding dual Azeri-Russian citizenship for all Lezgins and that a share of the proceeds from oil extracted from their region be set aside for Lezgin development. The Azeri court sentenced the seven activists to terms in prison, mostly between 13 and 15 years. In July 1996 some 300 militants took four Azeri policemen hostage and blocked the Baku-Rostov highway to protest the arrest of Lezgin nationalist leader Nariman Ramazanov, the head of Sadval. Ramazanov was released after two days in custody.

The Lezgin nationalist leadership sent a statement to the Russian and Azerbaijani governments in late 1996 calling for the unification of the Lezgin nation. They warned that they might resort to arms very soon in defense of their rights. The statement emphasized the treatment of the Lezgins in Azerbaijan. A later statement appealed to the two governments to consider dual citizenship for Lezgins in Azerbaijan, which would allow the resumption of family and business contacts between the two halves of the Lezgin nation.

The seventh convention of the Lezgin nationalists in Derbent in November 1998 led to a serious split in the movement. The more radical faction demanded a sovereign Lezgin state within the Russian Federation, to which the Lezgin-populated *rayons* of northern Azerbaijan would also be annexed. Militants called for the creation of a military wing of the Sadval organization. Moderate nationalists supported autonomy within Dagestan as a first step in the sovereignty process. The Lezgin homeland in Dagestan is the least developed in the republic.

The Russian attack on the separatist Chechens* in 1999 frightened the more moderate Lezgins, but controversy over the drafting of young Azeri Lezgins for the Nagorno-Karabakh fighting has renewed the more militant organizations. The Lezgins view that conflict as an ethnic war between Azeris and Armenians, one that that has nothing to do with them, but universal conscription continues to be pursued in Azerbaijan.

The Lezgin demands for unification continue to be one of the major problems in the North Caucasus. The border, closed except for temporary openings since the war in neighboring Chechnya began in 1999, has become the focus of Lezgin nationalism. Nationalist activities by members of Sadval declined in the late 1990s since support by the Russian government ended. The Russians, satisfied with deals made with Azerbaijan over oil and natural gas, ended overt support, but tension between Lezgins and other groups continue to be tense. The Lezgins are the least advantaged of the Dagestani groups, and there appears to be little effort on the part of the government of Dagestan to rectify the situation. The radical wing of Sadval and other more radical groups have stepped up their activities. In April 1999, the chairman of Dagestan's State Council accused the Armenian intelligence service of training and arming Lezgin militants.

The Lezgin congress in Derbent in early 2000 discussed economic and social problems, but did not, as it had in the past, reiterate demands for the creation of a separate Lezginistan republic. Instead, it called for national-cultural autonomy while remaining part of Dagestan. It also did not repeat its previous claim to territory in Azerbaijan. The congress, boycotted by more militant organizations, indicated a willingness to compromise, but the issue of the divided Lezgin nation remains a major problem in a volatile area.

SELECTED BIBLIOGRAPHY:

Bremmer, Ian, and Ray Taras, eds. *Nations and Politics in the Soviet Successor States.* 1993.

Goldenberg, Suzanne. *Pride of Small Nations.* 1995.

Krag, Helen, and Lars Funch. *The North Caucasus: Minorities at a Crossroads.* 1994.

Tutuncu, Mehmet. *Caucasus: War and Peace.* 1998.

Ligurians

Ligures; Liguris; Ligurianos; Ligurs

POPULATION: Approximately (2002e) 1,859,000 Ligurians in Italy, concentrated in the Liguria Region, with other populations in the neighboring Italian regions of Piedmont, Emilia-Romagna, and Tuscany, and in France and Monaco. Outside Europe the largest Ligurian communities are in the United States, Canada, Australia, and South America.

THE LIGURIAN HOMELAND: The Ligurian homeland lies in the southwestern part of northern Italy on the Ligurian Sea. The region forms an arc from the mouth of the Roia River to the Magra River, embracing the southern slopes of the Ligurian Alps and the Apennines around the Gulf of Genoa. Protected by their mountains, the Ligurians live in a zone of mild, Mediterranean climate that is often called the Italian Riviera. The Region of Liguria, comprising the provinces of Genoa, Imperia, La Spezia, and Savona, was reestablished in 1948 and was granted limited autonomy in 1970. *Region of Liguria*: 2,089 sq. mi.—5,410 sq. km, (2002e) 1,611,000—Ligurians 82%, French 8%, other Italians 10%. The Ligurian capital and major cultural center is Genoa, (2002e) 632,000, metropolitan area 891,000.

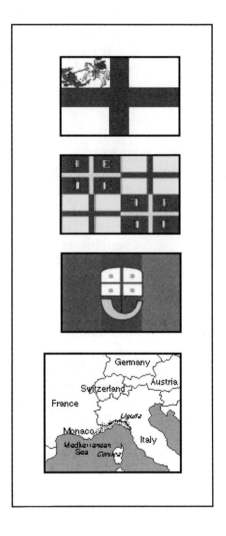

FLAG: The Ligurian national flag, the flag of the national movement, is a white field with a centered red cross with St. George killing a dragon on the upper hoist. The flag of the Ligurian League is quartered, with the red cross on white of Genoa on the upper hoist and lower fly, and red fields with gold crosses and Byzantine designs on the lower hoist and upper fly. The official flag of the Liguria region, adopted in 1997, is a vertical tricolor of green, red, and blue bearing a silver ship with a white sail charged with a red cross and four silver mullets.

PEOPLE AND CULTURE: The Ligurians are an ancient people, the descendants of the region's pre-Roman population and later migrants. The culture and traditions of the Ligurians were formed during the centuries of the Republic of Genoa, one of the most powerful maritime states of medieval Europe. Heavily influenced by the nearby French, their culture and dialect differ greatly from those of the Italian heartland in Rome and the central regions of Italy. The culture, influenced by many other Mediterranean cultures because of their long maritime tradition, is unique in Italy in its borrowings from non-Italian cultures. In Liguria, more than any other region in Italy, the distribution of the population is determined by topography. An estimated 90% of the Ligurian population live in the coastal towns, with a consequent depopulation of the hilly or mountainous inland areas.

LANGUAGE AND RELIGION: The language spoken by the Ligurians, called Ligurian or Ligure, is a Gallo-Romance language, often referred to as a Celto-Romance or Italo-Celtic dialect. The language has two major dialects, Ligurian and Genoese or Genovese; the latter is spoken around the capital, Genoa, and with variations in other areas of the region. It is spoken in the towns of Caloforte and Calasetta and several small islands in Sardinia and in Corsica. The Monégasque dialect, also called Ventimigliese, of Ligurian is spoken along the coast west of San Remo and across the border in France and Monaco. The language is not intelligible to speakers of standard Italian, although all Ligurians are bilingual in that language. In most areas Ligurian remains the language of daily life.

The Ligurians are mostly Roman Catholic, with a small Protestant minority. Their Catholic religion has long been associated with the sea, around which Ligurian life revolves. Religious ceremonies marked the seasons and maritime activities, but not fishing, which is not important in the region. Saints associated with the sea are particularly venerated.

NATIONAL HISTORY: The ancient Ligurii, who gave their name to the modern region, occupied the Mediterranean coast from the Rhone to the Arno. A people of pre–Indo-European stock, the Ligurians controlled the inland Po Valley to the foothills of the Alps. In the fourth century B.C., the Ligurian tribes were driven from the highland regions by the Celtic migrations, and Greeks, Phoenicians, and Carthaginians colonized the Ligurian coast. The region early developed a maritime tradition, establishing trade ties with the civilizations of the Mediterranean.

The tribes west of the Rhone River were gradually subdued by the Romans during the second century B.C. The Ligurian town of Genua was first mentioned in Roman records in 218 B.C. and later flourished under Roman rule. Genua, later called Genoa, developed as the major trading center of Roman Liguria, which stretched west to present-day Nice and north to where Turin now stands.

Roman authority declined in the fourth and fifth centuries A.D., gradually reducing the area protected by Roman troops. Barbarian tribes from beyond the Roman borders overran and devastated the region. Visigoths passed through the Roman province, and in 539 the Germanic Burgundians* conquered Liguria. In 679, the Germanic Lombards* extended the boundaries of their kingdom to encompass Liguria. The region was later included in the kingdom of the Franks.

In the tenth century, the city of Genoa developed as a free commune governed by consuls. Its maritime power increased with the growth of trade around the Mediterranean Sea. The city-state increased its territory at the expense of weaker neighboring communes. Allied to Pisa, the Genoans drove the Arabs from Corsica and Sardinia, but rivalry over Sardinia ruptured the alliance. A long series of wars ensued, which finally ended with Pisa's defeat at the naval battle of Meloria in 1284. In return for assistance against Venice, the Byzantines awarded the Genoans special privileges at Constantinople, as well as colonies at Chios, Lesbos, and Samos in Greece, and at Kaffa and Azov on the Black Sea.

Genoa developed into a major financial center, the center of a far-flung mercantile empire, and one of the principal maritime powers in Europe. A series of wars with the Venetians* ended with the Peace of Turin, signed in 1381, which slightly favored Venice. The Crusades furthered the prosperity of the region, due to the new trade routes to the eastern Mediterranean. Prosperity facilitated the great cultural flowering of the Renaissance in northern Italy, which permanently changed the civilization of Western Europe.

In the fourteenth century, the Genoese Republic was weakened by factional strife between the Guelphs and Ghibellines, representing respectively the nobility and the growing middle class. In 1339 the first *doge* was elected, to serve for life. Although Genoa, from the late thirteenth through the sixteenth century, gained control of the various territories of the Ligurian coast, it gradually lost its overseas colonies. The republic, which included the Ligurian coast, became the object of a French and Milanese rivalry; it eventually came under nominal French rule. The power of the republic was revived under the military leader Andrea Doria, who expelled the French and wrote a new republican constitution in 1528. The decline of republic accelerated, however, as the French, Spaniards, and Austrians vied for influence in Liguria.

A popular uprising in the region drove the Austrians from the area in 1746, but in 1768 the Genoese, unable to control the Corsicans,* were forced to sell the island, their last overseas possession, to France. In 1797 French military pressure forced the end of aristocratic rule in the republic and the formation of the Ligurian Republic, which was annexed to Napoleonic France in 1805. The annexation of the republic ended over a thousand years of Ligurian independence. The Ligurian Republic had existed from June 1797 to May 1800 and from June 1800 to June 1805, and would again from April to December 1814. The periods of semidemocratic rule under the French sparked the first stirrings of Ligurian regionalist sentiment. The republic used the same flag as had the former Genoese republic, a white field with the red cross of St. George, which was later adopted as the flag of the newly emerged nationalist movement.

The Congress of Vienna was convened in 1815 to remap the continent of Europe after the upheavals of the Napoleonic wars. Liguria, over the protests of the region's leaders, was given to the kingdom of Sardinia. During the Risorgimento, the Sardinian kingdom, centered on nearby Turin, expanded to include almost all of Italy. In 1861, Victor Emmanuel II of Sardinia was proclaimed king of united Italy. The Ligurians played a leading role in the Risorgimento and contributed significantly to the union of Italy. Genoa became the major port of the unified kingdom, rivaling Marseilles in the Mediterranean.

The consolidation of the Italian kingdom, with the inclusion of the Papal States in 1870, was followed by a period of national consolidation. To overcome the problem of dozens of different dialects, a Tuscan dialect was selected as the new national language. The dialect, in 1871, was spoken by only 10% of the Italian population and was written by just 1%. The adoption of a standard language failed to impose national unity; loyalty to regional dialects and cultures endured. The Ligurian language began to give way to the standardized Italian dialect only with the arrival of radio in the 1930s.

The Ligurians enjoyed the fruits of the liberal constitution adopted by the Sardinian kingdom in 1848 until the rise of the Fascist dictatorship in the 1920s. The Fascist industrialization of the northern regions of Italy in the early 1900s caused unrest related to an economic depression and the change from an agrarian to an industrialized society. After World War I, political and social dissatisfaction increased, furthering the growth of Fascism. In 1922, the Fascist leader, Benito Mussolini, promising the restoration of order, was made premier by the king. Under his government the regional dialect was suppressed, and all regionalist and nationalist sentiment was severely punished.

The Fascist regime, although unpopular with the Ligurian middle class, gained support among the workers and the rural population. In the 1930s there were frequent clashes between Fascists and communists, especially in industrial Genoa. Migrants from the poor, backward south were resettled in the region by the government, further raising tension in the region.

When World War II broke out, the Ligurians, although initially supportive, soon lost enthusiasm as fighting broke out on their border with France. In 1943 the Italian government surrendered to the Allies, but the northern Italian region, including Liguria, was occupied by German troops; the Ligurians were treated as a conquered nation until they were liberated by American troops. Partisan groups fighting the German occupation formed the nucleus of the postwar regionalist movement.

The Ligurians, in 1946, began to agitate for regional autonomy, including the teaching and official use of their distinct dialect. In 1947 the Italian government promised broad autonomy, but a year later only very limited self-government had been granted. In the postwar period, in spite of political agitation, the northern Italian industrial triangle—Turin, Genoa, and Milan—experienced an economic boom and led the so-called Italian Economic Miracle. In the 1950s and 1960s these cities attracted an influx of workers from rural areas and from the poorer regions of southern Italy. The conflict between the Ligurians and the culturally and dialectically different southerners erupted in the 1970s into often violent confrontations. The Ligurians resented the southerners, whom they saw as living off the prosperous Ligurian economy while contributing very little.

The Ligurians' standard of living reached the level of the more prosperous European nations, but at a cost to the environment. The depopulation of the upland areas, as well as the excessive concentration of industrial plants in certain districts, became serious problems. Badly planned urban growth, and the construction of the tourist industry in the region, which is often called the Italian Riviera, caused further damage; all this had been frequently motivated by speculation.

In the 1960s the Ligurians, like the other nations of northern Italy, pressed for greater economic and political autonomy. The movement was triggered by resentment that much of their wealth was used in Italy's poor and corrupt southern regions. Regional self-government was finally granted in 1970 and became effective in 1972, but it fell far short of the self-government demanded by Ligurian activists. An new appreciation of their glorious history as a maritime republic and of their unique culture and dialect fueled the regional movement in the 1970s and 1980s.

Traditionally oriented to the Mediterranean trade routes, the Ligurians enthusiastically supported Italy's integration in the European Union (EU). A Europe without borders would allow the Ligurians to reestablish their historical ties to Europe's inland regions by serving as the natural outlet for much of southern Europe. By 1998 an estimated two-thirds of the active population was employed in the service industries related to the port cities.

Resentment of the corruption and political instability in Rome continues to generate calls for autonomy or even independence from Italy. Many Ligurians support the Northern League, which advocates the secession of the northern Italian regions into a confederation to be called Padania. The Northern League's alliance in 1999–2000 with the four-party right-wing coalition (including the "postfascist" National Alliance) led by the controversial tycoon, Silvio Berlusconi, later the prime minister of Italy, alienated many Ligurians. They object to the northern nationalist forces allying themselves with the neofascists and with Berlusconi, who had been convicted of several crimes, including bribery. However, in regional elections in April 2000, the Right, including the nationalist forces, easily won power in Liguria, partly by its stand on illegal immigration, a growing concern for the Ligurians.

The Ligurians are among the most affluent groups in Italy, partly due to their long association with regions outside the country. Nationalists would like to refine those ties and establish a relationship with the European Union as an autonomous European state loosely associated with a federal Italy, not under the political control of Rome. The chronic political chaos in Italy continues to stimulate support for Ligurian autonomy and for direct ties to the European Union, without the need to consult Rome on every decision.

Much of the nationalism in Liguria is based on economic grievances. Taxes are higher than in most parts of Europe, red tape still hampers local businesses, and too many grandiose projects seem to go nowhere. Patronage and cronyism, particularly at the federal level, too often have a negative impact on Liguria.

The meeting of the G8 group of most industrialized states in Genoa in late July 2001 led to massive violence between anti-globilization and local police, horrifying many Ligurians, particularly the brutality of Italian police against unarmed protestors. The violence was blamed on the Italian government's lack of preparation and the overreaction of police.

SELECTED BIBLIOGRAPHY:

Facaros, Dana. *Northwest Italy*. 1991.
Hearder, Harry. *Italy in the Age of the Risorgimento, 1790–1870*. 1983.
Monteverde, Franco. *The Ligurians: An Italian and Mediterranean People*. 1994.
Toso, Fiorenzo. *The Linguistic History of Liguria*. 1991.

Livonians

Livs; Liivs; Livians; Livods; Livlis; Liivlist; Liivnikad; Liibõd

POPULATION: Approximately (2002e) 100,000 Livonians in Europe, concentrated in northwestern and northern Latvia and southwestern Estonia. Many Livonians live elsewhere in Latvia, mostly in Riga, in other parts of Estonia, and in Finland and Sweden. Outside Europe the largest Livonian communities are in the United States, Canada, and Australia.

THE LIVONIAN HOMELAND: The Livonian homeland, Liivimaa, lies on the eastern shore of the Baltic Sea around the Gulf of Riga in Latvia and Estonia. In Latvia the region is included in the historical regions of Kurzeme, on the western shore of the Gulf of Riga, and western Vidzeme, on the eastern shore of the gulf. In Estonia the Livonian homeland includes the coastal region south of the city of Parnu. Much of the region is lowland swamps and forests, which helped to protect the isolated Livonian communities. Livonia has no official status, although a small part of the Livonian homeland, approximately a 50-mile-long (80 km) strip of land in extreme northwestern Latvia, was officially designated the Livonian Coast (Livõd Randa) in 1992. The Livonian capital and major cultural center is Mazirbe, called Îre by the Livonians, in northern Latvia. The city of Ventpils, called Vänta by the Livonians, (2002e) 42,000, at the southern edge of the Livonian homeland, is also a major cultural center, as is Riga, the Latvian capital. In Estonia the most important Livonian cultural center is the town of Massiaru.

FLAG: The Livonian national flag, recognized by Livonians in both Latvia and Estonia, is a horizontal tricolor of green, white, and pale blue. The white stripe is half the width of the green and blue stripes.

PEOPLE AND CULTURE: The Livonians are a Finno-Ugric people related to the Estonians and Finns, although culturally they are close to the Baltic Latvians. The Livonian population is concentrated in Latvia, both east and west of the Gulf of Riga, with smaller numbers in southeastern Estonia and on the Estonian island of Saaremaa. The total number of Livonians in the region is uncertain, as most Livonians have traditionally registered as ethnic Latvians or Estonians. Officially, only those who speak the Livonian language are counted as ethnic Livonians. Traditionally the Livonians are divided into two groups—the Raandali, the "people of the seashore," west of the Gulf of Riga; and the Kalamied, "fishermen," on the eastern shore of the Gulf of Riga, straddling the border between Latvia and Estonia. Culturally, the Livonians were strongly influenced by the Germans and were severely affected by the domination of the Soviet era. The Livonians have been declared the second indigenous nation, alongside the Latvians, in Latvia, and they now have their own representative in the Latvian parliament.

LANGUAGE AND RELIGION: The Livonian language belongs to the southern group of the Balto-Finnic languages. It is related to Estonian and Finnish, and more distantly to Hungarian; it was formerly spoken in two distinct dialects—Western Livonian in Kurzeme, and Eastern Livonian in Vidzeme. Western Livonian, also called Raandalist or Kurzeme, is spoken on a daily basis by less than 50 people and is used by between 400 and 1,000 frequently, although an estimated 1,700 in eight villages west of Kolka (Kolkasrags) in Kurzeme have some knowledge of it. The spoken language includes three subdialects based on geographic area. Most of the dispersed Livonian population in Latvia and Estonia have some knowledge of the language. A concerted effort to revive the language has gained support since the early 1990s. Eastern Livonian or Vidzeme became extinct in the late nineteenth century. The first book written in Livonian was published in 1863, although a written form of the language was standardized only in 1935. The modern written language has been heavily influenced by Latvian in its grammar, pronunciation, and vocabulary. Livonian linguists are attempting to unify the spelling and standardize the vocabulary, deliberately avoiding Latvian elements.

The Livonians are nearly all Lutherans, the predominant religion of the Baltic region. The major concentration of Livonians, in the cities of Riga and Ventpils, has recently been exposed to evangelical Protestant sects.

NATIONAL HISTORY: The Livonians claim to have inhabited their present homeland for over 5,000 years. The descendants of Finno-Ugric tribes migrated to the northern Baltic Sea region from central Russia in pre-Christian times. The Finnic tribes were pushed into the coastal regions by the Slav migrations of the sixth and seventh centuries A.D. The ancient Livonians were farmers, herders, and fishermen. Settled in an area of important trade routes, they evolved a remarkably well-developed material culture. The established trading relations with Gotland, Kievan Rus', and the Finns.

Historical Livonia traditionally consisted of the region east of the Gulf of Riga from the Daugava River into present Estonia, and in the northern districts of Kurzeme west of the Gulf of Riga. The Livonians developed from the fusion of the Finnic tribes and the earlier Baltic and Germanic peoples who inhabited the region. They settled a wide area around the Gulf of Riga, with their major centers around the mouths of the Dvina and Gauja Rivers.

German merchants landed at the mouth of the Daugava River in the twelfth century, establishing trading posts and Roman Catholic missions. In 1201 Bishop Albert founded the town of Riga on Livonian territory, and a year later the Livonian Knights, also called the Livonian Order, were formed to serve the bishop by Christianizing the pagan Livonians. The knights, a strict military religious order, defeated the Livonian tribes in 1206 and took control of the territory known as Livonia. The Livonians were forced to take part in subsequent military campaigns against the related Estonians to the north.

The German victory over the Livonian tribes began 700 years of foreign domination. Latvian tribes began to settle in the depopulated Livonian territories. According to chronicles of Henric the Lett, at the beginning of the thirteenth century Livonians lived on the shores of the Gulf of Riga, the lower reaches of the Daugava River, and on the Gauja and Salaca Rivers.

The Livonian state of the Germanic knights was a militarily strong one that threatened Lithuania and Novgorod in the thirteenth and fourteenth centuries. The knights divided the territory into numerous feudal manors and reduced the Livonians to serfs. Peasant uprisings were frequent; the subsequent reprisals produced an enduring hatred of the German masters. In 1554, the Master of Order, the head of the Livonian Order, Walter von Plettenberg, fearing a wider uprising, declared Protestantism the official religion of the region. The decision weakened the feudal state and allowed the expanding Russians to gain influence. The Livonian Wars from 1558 to 1583 were fought partly due to Moscow's desire for a warm-water port on the Baltic Sea.

To prevent a Russian conquest of the region, the German aristocrats dissolved the Livonian Order, except in Kurzeme and Riga, and placed their vast estates under the protection of the powerful Roman Catholic Lithuanian-Polish state in 1561. The remains of the Protestant order were secularized, and Catholicism was again proclaimed the state religion. Following the dissolution of the Livonian Order, the Livonian homeland was contested by the Poles, Russians, and Swedes. Kurzeme, called Courland, became a separate duchy under Polish suzerainty, with the last grand master of the Livonian Order as its duke.

The Swedish kingdom, which had controlled northern Estonia from 1521, wrested most of Livonia from Poland between 1621 and 1626. Swedish rule reinforced Lutheranism as the predominant religion of the Livonians. The Swedes retained the Livonian territories for almost a century.

The Livonian territories were devastated by the Polish-Swedish War of 1654–60 and the Russo-Swedish War of 1654–61. The rivalry between Sweden and Russia for domination in the Baltic region culminated in the Northern War, which again devastated the region between 1700 and 1721. By the terms of the 1721 Treaty of Nystad, most of the region passed to Russian rule. In 1783, Livonia was constituted as Russian province. Courland, under Russian influence since 1737, became a Russian province in 1795, following the third partition of Poland. Under Russian rule, the German "Baltic Barons" retained their power, and German was the official language. The Livonians were relegated to a rural, peasant existence, and their language was gradually replaced by the more extensive Estonian or Latvian.

In the eighteenth and nineteenth centuries, the Livonians began to assimilate into the larger neighboring cultures of the Estonians and Latvians. The language gave way to Latvian in the south and Estonian in the north, although Livonian culture, much influenced by that of the Latvians, remained dominant throughout the region. In the nineteenth century the Livonians east of the Gulf of Riga adopted Latvian as their mother tongue, and the eastern dialect of Livonian virtually disappeared. In 1817–19, the Livonian serfs were emancipated, but by that time the Livonian language was nearly entirely extinct. In 1835 only 2,074 considered Livonian their first language, although the ethnic population was estimated at over 200,000.

During World War I, the Russian authorities ordered thousands of Livonians living along the Baltic Sea to leave their villages and move inland. Their deserted coastal villages were patrolled by troops from the coastal defense installations. After the war many of the dispersed Livonians remained where they had resettled, mostly in the nearby cities of Ventspils and Riga.

The independence of Latvia and Estonia following the Russian Revolution further endangered the Livonian nation. In 1918 it was divided between the two new states, which sparked a national awakening. Inspired by the independence of the Estonians and Finns, the Livonians began to resuscitate their disappearing language and culture. The Latvian government supported the revival, and after 1923 the Livonian language was taught in area schools, textbooks were compiled, a newspaper was issued, and books in the Livonian language were again published.

A nationalist organization, the Livonian Association, was formed to promote the culture and to intercede with local and national governments on behalf of the Livonian people. The Livonian flag was approved at the first meeting of the Livonian Association, on 2 April 1923. A plebiscite among the Livonians approved the creation of an autonomous enclave but was opposed by the Latvian government. A renewed national awakening and movement to develop the Livonian culture was spurred by the establishment of closer ties to the related Estonians and Finns in the 1920s and 1930s. In 1939, with support from the Estonian and Finnish governments, the Livonian Community Center was built at Mazirbe. Such progress was effectively annulled by the beginning of World War II.

Soviet troops occupied Latvia and Estonia in 1940 and quickly eliminated all resistance. The Livonian coast became the western border of the Soviet Union. The beaches were closed, barbed wire blocked access to the sea, and the sands were mined. Many Livonians were deported to Siberia or Central Asia along with their Latvian neighbors; many others, unable to continue fishing, were forced to search for work in the nearby cities.

The Germans attacked their Soviet ally in June 1941 and quickly overran the region. Many young Livonians were conscripted or volunteered to fight the communists. Livonians were once again forced to abandon their homes as war swept over them. Many Livonians fled, mostly to neutral Sweden. In 1944, the Soviet authorities again took control of the area, and new deportations eliminated the Livonian cultural and political leadership. The economic and cultural life of the coastal Livonians was extinguished. In 1949 thousands were deported, along with other Baltic peoples. According to the regulations covering the coastal zones, the Livonians were not allowed to go to sea, even to fish. In 1955 Soviet military bases were built between the coastal villages. Many were forced to move inland, and many villages were almost completely emptied. All elements of the Livonians' national culture was banned, and the nationalist Livonian Union was dissolved. Organizations among the emigrant population, particularly in the United States and Sweden, became the centers of Livonian culture.

In succeeding Soviet censuses the Livonians, fearing official attention, registered as ethnic Latvians or Estonians. In the Soviet census of 1959 only 200 claimed Livonian nationality. In the 1970 census no Livonians were counted in the region. In the 1979 census, several hundred people of Livonian descent in Latvia wished to identify themselves as Livonians but were ignored. In the late 1980s there were only about 35 people who could still speak Livonian, and only 15 of them fluently. A modest movement to save the vanishing language and culture began in the late 1980s among the large number of ethnic Livonians living in the Latvian capital, Riga.

The Livonian nation, considered assimilated by the Soviet authorities after the 1960s, reemerged with the disintegration of the Soviet Union and the independence of Latvia and Estonia. Overseas Livonians supported the revival with monetary and cultural aid. The Livonian Cultural Society, later renamed the Livonian Union, was founded in Latvia, where the Livonian language was again taught in area schools. Choirs developed in Riga and Ventpils and became famous as the spiritual centers of the reviving Livonian nation.

Young Livonians, in order to safeguard the future of their nation, began to learn the language and to sing in the Livonian choirs. On 4 February

1991, the Latvian government approved the creation of a special cultural region, the Livonian Coast, in a territory of about 50 miles (80 km) long, on the extreme northwestern shore of Latvia, which is inhabited by last speakers of the Livonian language. In 1996 the University of Latvia's Foreign Languages Faculty began offering Livonian-language courses. Great interest in Livonian culture was shown by Finnish and Estonian researchers keen to learn more about a related culture, and the Livonian language is now taught in Finnish and Estonian universities.

On 3 August 1996, the Livonian nation held its seventh annual festival in the Livonian capital at Mazirbe. Tens of thousands of young people of Livonian ancestry attended the festival. The Livonians claim to have inhabited the region for over 5,000 years, and in the first years of the twenty-first century they seem determined that their small nation will survive.

SELECTED BIBLIOGRAPHY:

Beitina, Ligita. *Livs of the River Gauja.* 1995.
Boiko, Kersti, ed. *The Livonians.* 1994.
Plakans, Andrejs. *Historical Dictionary of Latvia.* 1997.
Raun, Toivo U. *Estonia and the Estonians.* 1991.

Logonese

Southern Chadians

POPULATION: Approximately (2002e) 2,920,000 Logonese in Chad, concentrated in the far south Logon region of the country.

THE LOGONESE HOMELAND: The Logonese homeland occupies the flat wooded savanna lands of southern Chad, the only agricultural zone in the country. The fertile region includes the basins of the Chari and Logone Rivers, which drain into Lake Chad to the north. The region forms Mayo-Kebbi, Tandjilé, Logone-Occidental, Logone-Oriental, and Moyen-Chari Departments of Chad. *Logone*: 49,213 sq. mi.—127,461 sq. km, (2002e) 3,296,000—Logonese 86%, Northern Chadians* 4%, other Chadians 10%. The Logonese capital and major cultural center is Moundou, (2002e) 113,000. The capital and major cultural center of the largest of the Logonese groups, the Sara, is Sarh, (2002e) 85,000. The other important Logonese cultural center is the Chadian capital, N'Djamena, on the dividing line between the black Logonese and the Arabized north, (2002e) 601,000.

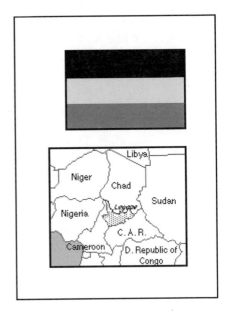

FLAG: The Logonese national flag, the proposed flag of the separatist Logone Republic, is a horizontal tricolor of black, yellow, and red.

PEOPLE AND CULTURE: The Logonese represent a compact group of related agricultural peoples. The Logonese, unlike the Arabized peoples of northern and eastern Chad, were integrated into European culture under French colonial rule. The major Logone group is the Saras, also known as Ngambaye or Mbaye. Other large Logone groups are the Massa, Moussei, and Moundang, in the eastern departments. Smaller groups include the Laka and Mbum west of the Saras, the culturally distinct Gula and Tumaks, and Tangale peoples along the banks of the Chari and Logone Rivers and in the region between the two rivers. The Kotoko, who are thought to be descended from the ancient Sao, live along the lower reaches of the Logone and Chari Rivers. The population of the region is growing at a comparatively low rate for an African country. Emigration, especially to Nigeria and northern Cameroon, resulting from drought, conflict, and famine probably accounts for this.

LANGUAGE AND RELIGION: The Logonese speak various languages, though French and Arabic are the only official languages of the country. Many Logonese speak French as a second language, and fewer speak Arabic dialects. French is used in intergroup communications and in education. Radio broadcasts in the region are in French, but also in Arabic, Sara, Tubari, and Mundang. A regional patois, showing local linguistic peculiarities, is widely spoken in the urban areas; few in the rural areas understand it.

The majority of the Logonese are Roman Catholic, a legacy of French colonial rule. In recent years Protestant evangelical groups have made converts. Religious discrimination has been a serious problem since the late 1970s, with Christians often segregated or suffering from discrimination by Chad's Muslim majority in employment and education. A minority practice traditional religion, which involves nature spirits and ancestor worship. The conflicts between government supporters from the politically dominant north and the Logonese rebels from the politically subordinate south have religious overtones.

NATIONAL HISTORY: The region around the Logone River has been inhabited for thousands of years. In ancient times the Sahara area was not totally arid, and it had a more even distribution of population than at present. Animist Bantu tribes populated the areas of the southern Sahara, but they were slowly pushed south by nomadic peoples influenced by the cultures of ancient Egypt and Sudan. The Sao people lived along the Chari and Logone Rivers, but their weak chiefdoms were overcome by more powerful neighboring kingdoms.

An area at the southern edge of the Sahara, mentioned by Arab historians as settled by nomadic pagan Arabs in the early seventh century A.D., received an influx of Berber refugees fleeing the Arab invasion of north Africa in the seventh and eighth centuries. The Arab and Berber migrants conquered or weakened the tribal states in the region, and an Arab-Berber culture spread across the northern regions. In the eighth century newcomers from the upper Nile Valley moved into the area and established walled city-states in the fertile lands at the southern edge of the Sahara. Invading Muslim Arabs conquered the area and introduced Islam, traditionally in the year 1090. Controlled by a sophisticated Muslim Berber-Arab pastoral elite, the states of the region grew wealthy on the trans-Saharan caravan trade.

The Muslims raided the black Logone tribes to the south for captives to send north to the slave markets of North Africa. Many of the northern tribes adopted Islam, as Muslims were not permitted to enslave other Muslims. These tribes gradually Arabized, adopting much of the culture and the language of the desert peoples. Other tribes fled south to escape the raiders and settled among the related peoples in the forested areas around the Chari and Logone Rivers. The raids led to isolation of and antagonism among the southern tribes.

In 1891, French colonial power was extended to the southern river valleys. Various territories were united in the French protectorate of Chad in 1900. The Muslim peoples from the beginning rejected inclusion in a territory with tribes they had formerly raided for slaves and booty. The Muslims of the north fought French rule and remained in a state of nearly constant rebellion. During the colonial period, French development programs, particularly schools and health care, largely favored the south. The southern tribes were offered better educational and political opportunities and economically advanced more rapidly than the Muslim north. However, French administrators established cotton farms, taking a head tax and imposing quotas; they therefore soon lost their popularity in the south as well.

After World War II, in 1946, Chad became a province of French Equatorial Africa, and in 1958 it was made an autonomous republic of the French Union. Chad became an independent republic in 1960, with the Logonese in control. Francois Tombalbaye, a southerner, was sworn in as Chad's first president. The first postcolonial government was rejected in the Muslim north. Tombalbaye proclaimed a one-party state in 1962 and openly adopted policies that favored the Logonese. In 1963 rioting broke out between Muslim Northern Chadians and Logonese in N'Djamena, leaving over 100 dead.

The French maintained a strong military presence, which created a precarious calm, but in 1965 the Chadian government requested their withdrawal. In 1965 a tax revolt by Muslims escalated rapidly, setting the Muslim north, center, and east against the southern-led government. The Muslim's demands for autonomy, a larger share of power, and a fairer distribution of development funds were rejected by the French-backed Chadian government in N'Djamena. By the late 1960s most of the estimated 200 ethnic groups in Chad had affiliated with one of two regional cultural traditions—Arab and Saharan/Sahelian Muslim in the north, center, and east; and the Christian and animist groups in the south.

In 1969 French troops intervened on behalf of the Tombalbaye government, which became increasingly repressive and irrational. Most Logonese continued to support the government in spite of the dictatorial and erratic behavior of the president, due to fear of the northern Muslims. Fierce fighting between various Muslim factions, however, reduced rebel pressure on the government. The Tombalbaye government continued to decline despite French-assisted administrative reform and mediation efforts, while the Muslim rebel groups, supported by Libya and Sudan, gained strength. Tombalbaye often claimed that he had survived more coups and plots on his life than any other African leader, but his luck ran out in 1975—he was killed in an army coup.

French pressure led to the formation of a government of national reconciliation, including northern Muslim leaders. The new government collapsed after three turbulent years, and the Muslim rebellion resumed in 1978. In March 1979 Muslim forces took control of N'Djamena and drove the Logone tribes from power. Hundreds of Logonese were massacred. In retribution, Logonese militants killed between 5,000 and 10,000 Muslims. As a result, civil war spread to all regions of Chad; 11 major factions were engaged in the fighting.

In 1980 Libyan and French troops intervened in the region, deepening the crisis; conflicts between various Muslim groups erupted in violence. International attempts to bring about the formation of a government with both northern and southern representation were unsuccessful throughout the 1980s. The southern tribes supported the creation of Codos Rouge, the first organization actively opposing the Muslim-dominated government. Talks between the Codos and the government collapsed in 1984, resulting in violent clashes in four of the five southern prefectures. Northern troops rampaged through the south, killing civilians and destroying villages, and by 1985 the government had regained control over most of the south.

Several Logonese groups in the south joined a reconciliation government in 1986, but this government was driven from power in December 1990 by Muslim forces led by Idriss Déby. In the 1990s, crises and coups continued to sour relations between the southern Logonese and the Muslims, particularly Déby's Zagawa ethnic group. In 1992 Logone leaders alleged that Muslim troops had carried out massacres in the south. The League of Human Rights accused the Republican Guard, an elite division loyal to Déby, of genocide in the southern prefectures. Logonese leaders claimed the government was engaged in religious and ethnic cleansing. Thousands of Logonese villagers fled to safety in neighboring areas of the Central African Republic.

The continuing violence increased the tension and antagonism between the peoples of northern and southern Chad. Rebel groups threatened to sabotage government-supported oil exploration in the region. Several Logonese leaders in late 1993 demanded reparations for the alleged massacres by the Republican Guard, the introduction of a federal system, and the withdrawal of the Republican Guard from the five southern prefectures. Other rebel leaders, having experienced only violence and repression within Chad, proposed the secession of the five prefectures and the creation of a separate Logone Republic.

In July 1994, government troops launched a new initiative against the Logonese rebels. Peace in the region became more urgent when several Western oil companies investigated the growing oil reserves at Doba. The oil finds, in the most fertile part of the Logone region, threatened to open the region to rapid and unfettered exploitation. An oil pipeline through the southern prefectures into Cameroon soon disrupted a wide area, with many people being driven from their homes near its right of way.

In August 1994, the Chadian government and southern Christian rebels signed a peace agreement. The government agreed to withdraw the hated Republican Guard, grant a full amnesty to rebels, and recognize the major rebel movement, the CSNPD, Committee of National Revival for Peace and Democracy (Comité de Sursaut pour la Paix et la Démocratie), as a legal political party. Other rebel groups refused to participate.

The government announced in May 1995 that Arabic would become the only language of instruction in schools and that the Islamic Shari'a was the source of civil law in the country. Clashes broke out between southern farmers and northern traders, and quickly spread across the region. Renewed efforts to form a government with representatives of both north and south resumed in 1996. Most southern rebel groups, cut off from rear bases and resources in Cameroon and in the Central African Republic, had to agree to peace talks and eventually signed deals. In August 1997, members of FARF/VA, Armed Forces for the Federal Republic/Victims of Aggression (Forces Armés pour la République Fédréale), signed a peace agreement with the government, following the disappearance and presumed death of the group's leader, Laokein Barde Frisson.

Human-rights abuses continued in spite of government denials. Within months of the August 1997 agreement, fighting had resumed. In early 1998 many people suspected of belonging to or supporting rebel groups were summarily executed. Entire villages were destroyed for suspected rebel ties. Many Logonese fled into the countryside or to urban areas, such as Moundou and Sarh. Extrajudicial executions, torture, disappearances, and other abuses were routinely used by the government to control the civilian population of Logone and other regions. The leaders of the Logone organizations denounced in early 2000 the presence of French troops in Chad. They claimed that the foreign troops represented an outmoded colonialism and that they were there to bolster the personal rule of Déby.

The government of Idriss Déby is dominated by his own ethnic group, the Arabized Zaghawas. Most other Muslim groups support the government; the north-south split in Chad remains in politics, culture, and religion. Christian-led Logonese continue to advance the idea of a federal state in Chad, or failing that, the division of the country into two. The Logonese rebels, regrouped and rearmed, have begun to attack the oil installations being built in their homeland. How the revenue from the oil and how the Logonese are affected by the building of wells and other structures will partly determine the future of the region.

The increasing flow of oil from Doba in the Logone region has added economic grievances to the already long list of conflicts. The Logonese perception is that southern wealth is being spirited away by the Muslim elite in N'Djamena. Critics claim that the oil project has effectively become an asset of Déby's extended family, with profits being siphoned off by Déby and his clan. International donors have criticized the Déby regime for spending a large portion of the oil revenue on arms to fight rebel groups throughout the country instead of to improve the region's abysmal health and educational systems.

The spread of Islamic fundamentalism throughout northern Chad has encouraged many Muslim groups to pursue a more active policy in Chad. The increasingly fundamentalist influence in the Chadian government has further antagonized the Logonese and renewed the bitter competition between north and south Chad. The north-south, Muslim-Christian fault line, rather than disappearing as planned by the French colonial administration and various successive governments, is growing ever wider.

The Logonese groups also have opposed the application of Shari'a law and the use of Arabic as the official language as a form of genocide. The increasingly radical Islamic strictures of the Chadian government have alienated even moderate Logonese leaders.

SELECTED BIBLIOGRAPHY:

Azevedo, Mario J. *Chad: A Nation in Search of Its Future*. 1998.
Collins, Robert O. *Africa's Thirty Years War: Libya, Chad, and the Sudan 1963–1993*. 1999.
Manning, Patrick. *Francofone Sub-Sahara Africa 1880–1985*. 1988.
Safran, William, and Ramon Maiz, eds. *Identity and Territorial Autonomy in Plural Societies*. 2000.

Lombards

Lombardi; Lombardos; Lombardians

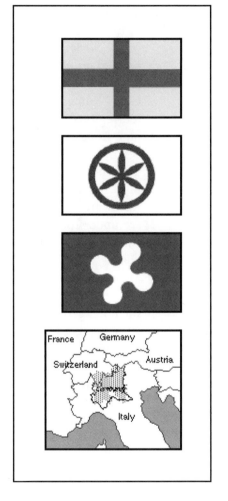

POPULATION: Approximately (2002e) 8,221,000 Lombards in Italy, concentrated in the Lombardy region. Outside Italy there are sizable Lombard groups in Ticino and Graübunden Cantons of Switzerland, and in France and Germany. Lombard immigrants have established communities in the United States, Canada, Australia, Brazil, Argentina, and Uruguay.

THE LOMBARD HOMELAND: The Lombard homeland lies between the Lepontine and Rhaetian Alps in Ticino and Graübunden and the Po River in northern Italy. Three distinct natural zones are easily distinguishable in Lombardy—mountain, foothill, and plain. Most of the region occupies the broad Lombard Plain, which extends north to the foothills of the Alps. The rich Po Valley, the Val Padana, in which irrigated agriculture has been practiced since Roman times, is one of the most fertile regions in Europe. It is also the primary industrial region of Italy, producing textiles, iron and steel, automobiles, and chemicals. Lombardy forms a semi-autonomous region of the Italian Republic, comprising the provinces of Bergamo, Brescia, Como, Cremona, Lecco, Lodi, Mantua, Milan, Pavia, Sondrio, and Varese. *Region of Lombardy (Lombardia)*: 9,202 sq. mi.—23,833 sq. km, (2002e) 9,052,000—Lombards 77%, other Italians and non-Italians 23%. The Lombard capital and major cultural center is Milan (Milano), (2002e) 1,301,000, metropolitan area 4,811,000.

FLAG: The Lombard national flag, the flag of the national movement, is a white field charged with a centered red cross. The Padania flag, the flag of the proposed federation of states in northern Italy, is a white field with a green "Sun of the Alps" centered. The official flag of the region of

Lombardy is a pale green field bearing a centered white device called the Rosa Camuna, an ancient cross.

PEOPLE AND CULTURE: The Lombards are a distinct Italian nation descended from the early Celtic and Latin populations and the later Germanic Langobard or Lombard tribes. Innovative, energetic, and pro-European, the Lombards are the most advanced of the Italian peoples. Although the separatist movement began over economic grievances, it has reinforced a formerly weak sense of national identity. Prior to the 1980s, the majority of the population identified with towns, cities, or districts. The Lombards' history and culture, distinct from central and southern Italy, as well as the creation of the European Union (EU) and the collapse of the Soviet Union, strengthened the Lombards' sense of identity, with a parallel growth of nationalism, in the late twentieth century.

LANGUAGE AND RELIGION: The Lombard language belongs to the Gallo-Romance group of the Romance language group and is spoken in ten regional dialects. Milanese, Eastern Lombard, Western Lombard, Alpine Lombard, Latin Fiamazzo, Latin Anaunico, and Bergamasco are spoken in Lombardy; Novarese Lombard is spoken in eastern Piedmont; Trentino Western is spoken in Trentino-Alto Adige Region; and Ticinese in Switzerland. The group of dialects that make up the Lombard language varies greatly from region to region, but all have much in common and are understood by the majority of the population. Lombard, called Lombardo, is very different from standard Italian, however, and the two languages are not mutually intelligible. Nationalists are standardizing the Milanese dialect as the literary language of all the Lombard dialects.

The majority of the Lombards are nominally Roman Catholic, with a small but growing Protestant minority in northern Lombardy, where Swiss influence is the greatest. The influence of the Catholic Church has been declining rapidly in recent decades; precepts on abortion, birth control, and other issues pressed by church officials are mostly ignored. The Lombards have one of the lowest birthrates in Europe, producing a crisis as the population ages. Traditionally the Roman Catholic Church was a central institution in the region, often allied to the ruling cliques, but with the urbanization and modernization of the region since the early 1950s, its influence declined considerably.

NATIONAL HISTORY: An ancient region populated by Celtic tribes came under the rule of the Etruscans as early as 500 B.C. The Romans, extending their authority to the north, absorbed the Etruscan cities one by one after the Second Punic War (218–201 B.C.). Added to the Roman province of Cisalpine Gaul, the northern cities developed as centers of Roman culture and art, and they continued to flourish for a time after the division of the empire in A.D. 395. The rapid decline of Roman power left the wealthy region nearly defenseless as the Roman garrisons withdrew.

The region suffered heavily in the barbarian invasions that ended the western Roman Empire.

The Lombards, also called Langobards, originated in the lower Elbe Valley in present-day Germany. They were mentioned by Tacitus in the first century A.D. as one of many tribes collectively known as the Suebi or Swabians.* Tacitus noted that they were small in number and hemmed in by more powerful Germanic tribes but that they found safety not in submission but in war. They played little role in the Germanic invasions of the collapsing Roman Empire, moving into northern Austria only in the wake of other tribes about 486, long after the Romans had departed.

The Lombards moved into Pannonia early in the sixth century; there they established themselves as a powerful presence. In 547 Emperor Justinian of the eastern Roman Empire allowed them to settle permanently in Pannonia and Noricum, in what are now eastern Austria and Hungary. The Lombards, under their kings Wacho and Audoin, became allies of the empire and assisted imperial forces against the Ostrogoths and Franks. During the wars they helped Byzantine emperor Justinian to reconquer the fertile Po Valley from the Goths. When they came under pressure from the advancing Avars,* they migrated southwest to settle on the plains of the Po River in 568.

The Lombards erected a small kingdom centered on Pavia and extended their rule to much of northern Italy while adopting the culture and language of the surviving Latin population. The kingdom soon divided into 36 duchies in a loose federation; the region fell into chaos from 575 to 584. Finally the Lombard nobility gathered to elect a new king to wear the Lombard "iron crown" and to unite the Lombard lands against the threats by the expanding Franks and the growing power of the papacy. In the early seventh century the Lombard kingdom replaced the autonomous duchies. The Lombards gradually converted to Christianity, although the Lombard kings initially resisted conversion.

Lombard power reached its peak during the reign of King Liutprand in the early eighth century, but after his death the pope enlisted the Franks to defeat them. In 755, Pepin the Short, king of the Franks, invaded Lombardy at the direct invitation of the pope. Lombard rule was finally destroyed by Pepin's son, Charlemagne, in 773. The next year he was crowned, and the Lombard kingdom disappeared. The region was divided into a number of feudal fiefs, most based on a nuclear city under the control of a powerful vassal of the Frankish kingdom.

The breakup of Charlemagne's empire in 843 shifted secular power in the region to a number of independent states, mostly cities ruled by local counts or bishops after 887. Feudal rule proved unpopular, and a number of Lombard cities were able to throw off the rule of their overlords and evolve into self-governing communes that became the commercial centers of Europe. The Lombard cities formed a defensive alliance in 1167, the

Lombard League. In 1176 the Lombards defeated the forces of the Holy Roman Empire and forced the emperor to recognize their status as free cities in 1183.

Conflicts within the Lombard communes between the Guelphs and Ghibellines continued into the fourteenth century, allowing the rise of local despots, particularly the Visconti and Sforza families of Milan and the Bonacolsi and Gonzaga families of Mantua. Milan became the strongest of the Lombard city-states and gradually extended its rule over many neighboring cities.

The cultural revival of the northern Italian cities initiated the Renaissance, the great medieval flowering of European culture. The region flourished but soon became involved in warfare as France and Spain fought for dominance in divided Italy. Wars between the city-states and vicious family rivalries accelerated the rise of Milan and the loss of territories to Venice and other powers in the fifteenth and sixteenth centuries. The Swiss intervened and conquered Milan; they were eventually defeated but retained control of the eight northern districts of Milan on the Ticino River.

The dominant Lombard power, the duchy of Milan, came under Spanish Hapsburg rule in 1535 and passed to the Austrian branch of the Hapsburgs in 1713. Mantua retained its independence until it too came under Austrian rule, along with Milan. The region became a battleground following the French Revolution and Napoleon's invasion of northern Italy. Taken from Austria by Napoleon in 1796, the Lombards were mostly under French rule during the Napoleonic Wars. Austrian authority was reestablished in 1815 in the guise of the Lombardo-Venetian Kingdom, set up under Austrian rule and garrisoned by Austrian troops.

The territorial exchanges and the imposition of differing laws, languages, and political systems sparked a Lombard national movement that culminated in widespread disturbances in 1848. Nationalists demanding the independence of Lombardy skirmished with Austrian troops. Lombardy remained part of the Lombardo–Venetian Kingdom until its liberation by French and Piedmontese* troops following a Lombard uprising in 1859. In 1861 the Lombards joined the Risorgimento, the union of the numerous Italian states in a united Italian state, the kingdom of Italy.

The numerous Italian peoples, united between 1861 and 1870, spoke dozens of regional dialects, many mutually unintelligible. The new Italian government chose a Tuscan dialect as a national language, a dialect spoken by only 10% of the population, and written by just 1%. The adoption of a standard language failed to impose national unity on the diverse Italian peoples, who remained loyal to their regions, dialects, and cultures. The Lombard language, like many others, began to give way to standard Italian only with the beginning of radio broadcasts in the 1930s.

Lombard industrialization, accelerated after unification, evolved an urbanized, middle-class culture, unlike most of agrarian Italy. The Fascist government in the 1920s and 1930s began to settle poor, culturally and linguistically distinct southern Italians in Lombardy to work in the booming factories.

The Lombard industries, vitally important to Italy during World War II, suffered massive destruction from bombing. Following Italy's withdrawal from the war in 1943, Lombardy was occupied by German troops. Many Lombards joined the anti-Nazi resistance, and the region suffered harsh reprisals before it was liberated.

The Lombards recovered quickly in the postwar era. Their region became the center of the "Italian Miracle," the rapid industrial expansion of the 1950s based on the triangle of Milan, Turin, and Genoa. Millions of poor southerners from Italy's underdeveloped Mezzogiorno migrated north to the expanding Lombard industrial cities. The influx further strengthened standard Italian as a lingua franca used by southern workers and Lombard supervisors, but it set off severe conflicts between the culturally and linguistically distinct groups. Lombardy's postwar growth raised Lombard living standards to the equal of any region in Europe, but increased prosperity exacerbated tension between the Lombards and the poorer southern Italian immigrants.

The unification of Europe, widely supported in Lombardy, began to raise questions and resentment in the 1970s. In 1978 Umberto Bossi published a tract advocating Lombard secession from Italy. The tract was widely denounced as the work of a lunatic. Undeterred, Bossi organized the Northern League in 1981. Anti-Rome and anti-immigrant (meaning both foreigners and the southern Italians), the league's nationalist message struck a cord in Lombardy, which pays more taxes to the Italian state than the entire area south of Rome. Growing dissatisfaction with Rome's huge, and hugely inefficient, bureaucracy—which lavished Lombard taxes on tax-evading southern Italy, where it lined the pockets of corrupt officials and organized-crime bosses—fueled Lombard nationalism in the 1980s. The movement raised the Lombard League's portion of the vote from only 8% in 1988 to 20% in 1989, and to between 37% and 46% in local elections after 1992.

In the 1990s, the idea of a federation of independent northern Italian states within a united Europe, to be called Padania, gained support across northern Italy. The proposed federation, to include the Lombards, Piedmontese, Venetians,* Ligurians,* and other nations in northern Italy, remains the goal of many of the pro-European Lombards. On 15 September 1996 Umberto Bossi symbolically declared the independence of the Federation of Padania at a rally in Lombardy attended by an estimated two million people. Opponents of federalism and of Lombard nationalism, many of them southern Italians living in the region, attended two progovernment unity rallies held in Milan.

Severe and violent clashes between Lombards and immigrant gangs in

1999–2000 led to calls for greater security and to harsh criticism of Rome's policy on immigrants and violent crime. Although the birthrate is very low in Lombardy, many of the inhabitants are increasingly fearful of the massive influx of legal and illegal immigrants to the region.

Italy's chronic corruption scandals, affecting hundreds of politicians and officials of the traditional political parties, have outraged many Lombards, who see themselves as Europeans first and Italians second. The pull of Europe, the idea of an independent Lombardy that participates as an equal in a united Europe, continues to fuel nationalism and support for a reversal of the Risorgimento—which would make Italy once more a mere geographical expression.

In 1999 Umberto Bossi, as head of the Northern League, joined a coalition government in Rome led by Silvio Berlusconi. The move, denounced by the more radical militants among the Lombard nationalists, seemed to work in Lombardy's favor when a new plan for devolution of powers to the region was debated in late 2000. The devolution process requires a referendum in Lombardy, probably in 2002. The devolution plan was denounced as playing a "dangerous game" by pandering to the separatist sentiments of the Northern League.

SELECTED BIBLIOGRAPHY:

Carello, Adrian N. *The Northern Question: Italy's participation in the European Economic Community and the Mezzogiorno's Underdevelopment.* 1989.

Greenfield, Kent R. *Economics and Liberalism in the Risorgimento: A Study of Nationalism in Lombardy 1814–1848.* 1978.

Hine, David. *Governing Italy: The Politics of Bargained Pluralism.* 1992.

Williams, William K. *The Communes of Lombardy from the Sixth to the Tenth Centuries.* 1995.

Lozis

Barotse; Rotse; Rutse; Barotsis; Malozis; Luyanas; Aluyis; Silozis; Rozis; Tozvis

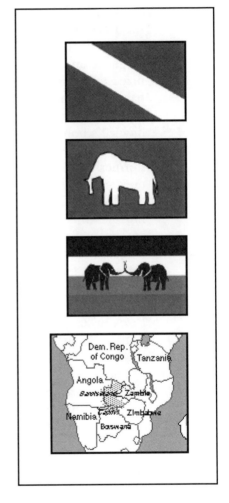

POPULATION: Approximately (2002e) 1,950,000 Lozis in south-central Africa, 1,505,000 Lozis in Zambia, 100,000 in Namibia, and other communities in Angola, Botswana, Democratic Republic of Congo, and Zimbabwe. Outside the traditional Lozi territory there are sizable Lozi populations in the large urban centers just to the east, in the Copperbelt and Lusaka regions of Zambia.

THE LOZI HOMELAND: The Lozi homeland occupies the fertile flood plains of the upper Zambezi River and its tributaries in south-central Africa, comprising territory in Zambia, Namibia, Angola, Botswana, and Zimbabwe. The Lozi heartland, called Barotseland, lies in western Zambia west of the Kafue River. Historical Barotseland comprises the Western, Northwestern, and Southern provinces of Zambia. Some nationalists claim six of Zambia's ten provinces as traditional Lozi territory. The Lozi territory in Namibia comprises Liambezi Province, formerly called the Caprivi Strip. *Barotseland*: 130,307 sq. mi.—337,493 sq. km, (2002e) 2,624,000—Lozis 49%, Tsongas 18%, Lundas 11%, Luvale 10%, Mbunda 7%, Nkoyas 4%, other Zambians 1%. *Liambezi (Caprivi/Itenge)*: 4,453 sq. mi.—11,533 sq. km 102,000—Lozis 78%, Tsongas 8%, other Namibians 14%. The Lozi capital and major cultural center is Lealui, the royal capital, (2002e) 11,000. Other important Lozi cultural centers are Livingstone, (2002e) 108,000, and Mongu, (2002e) 36,000, in Zambia. The capital and major cultural center of the Caprivian Lozis in Namibia is Katima Mulilo, (2002e) 15,000.

FLAG: The Lozi national flag, the flag of the Barotseland national movement, is a red field bearing a broad white diagonal stripe from the upper hoist to the lower fly. The traditional flag of the Lozi kingdom is a red field charged with a centered white elephant. The flag of the Caprivi Lozis is the flag of the former autonomous state, consisting of four horizontal stripes of black, white, green, and pale blue with two black elephants, trunks entwined.

PEOPLE AND CULTURE: The Lozis, called Barotse or Marotse by their neighbors, are a Bantu people thought to be the descendants of Lunda tribesmen from present eastern Zaire. The Lozi nation comprises 32 tribes of six interrelated cultural groups spread over a large area of south-central Africa. The Mafwe, Subiya, and Mayeye, all subgroups of the Lozis, constitute the majority of the population of the Caprivi Strip. Further divided into numerous clan groups, the Lozi are united by their language and their unique history. Traditionally Lozi society was organized into a social hierarchy of aristocrats, commoners, and serfs, but urbanization has weakened the traditional system. The *litunga* (king) is revered throughout the Lozi territories, even though the Lozi nation is divided among Zambia, Angola, Namibia, Botswana, and Zimbabwe. The desire for Lozi unity grew throughout the 1990s and into the new century. Formerly one of the wealthiest peoples in southern Africa, the Lozi are now among the poorest.

LANGUAGE AND RELIGION: The Lozi language, a legacy of the nineteenth-century Kalolo conquerors, is related to the Sotho language spoken in South Africa and Lesotho far to the southeast. Although the language exhibits some modifications, especially in phonetics and vocabulary, it is considered a Sotho-Tswana dialect of the Benue-Congo languages of the Niger-Congo language group. The literary language is based on the dialect spoken around the royal capital at Lealui, in Zambia. Most Lozis in Zambia, Namibia, Zimbabwe, and Botswana have some knowledge of English, while the Lozi population of Angola generally speak either English or Portuguese as a second language.

The majority of the Lozis are nominally Christian, mostly Roman Catholic. They were converted by nineteenth-century missionaries, who introduced the first educational facilities in the region. Christian beliefs are mixed with traditional survivals, including belief in not only a supreme being but in spirits and other supernatural beings. Elaborate rituals and offerings are carried out at the tombs of former Lozi kings.

NATIONAL HISTORY: Bantu peoples, thought to belong to the large Lunda tribe, conquered the Zambezi lowlands around A.D. 1600. Several of the small kingdoms established by the conquerors eventually united under a paramount king at Lealui. A highly advanced bureaucratic state, the Lozi kingdom expanded by absorbing neighboring peoples and eventually controlled over 25 subject states. The Lozis gradually developed the three major organs of a modern political community—a centralized authority, a well-defined administrative machinery, and established judicial institutions. The subject peoples did not enjoy the same privileges as the Lozi.

In the early eighteenth century, Portuguese traders entered the Lozi homeland in search of ivory, copper, and gold. By the early nineteenth century slavery had surpassed ivory and gold as the main export of the lower Zambezi region. In the mid-nineteenth century the Bembas to the east traded slaves for guns from Arab traders. The Bembas began an era of territorial expansion that greatly weakened the Lozi hold on the vast Zambezi lowland.

The Kalolo, a Sotho tribe from the southeast displaced during the massive Zulu migrations, conquered the declining Lozi kingdom in the 1840s. The highland Kalolo, unused to the wet lowlands, were soon decimated by malaria, endemic along the Zambezi River. In 1864 the resurgent Lozis overthrew the weakened Kalolo administration and reestablished their kingdom. In spite of the brevity of the Kalolo domination, their Sotho language replaced the earlier Lozi dialects.

British explorer and missionary David Livingstone, visiting the kingdom in 1851, found a highly sophisticated and cultured state in control of a vast multi-ethnic empire. In 1871 a British trader, George Westbuch, reached the kingdom and so impressed the Lozi king with his guns that he was allowed to establish a trading post and later became a close advisor. King Lewanika, realizing that with the arrival of the Europeans his kingdom would need powerful new allies, sent an appeal to the British authorities in Cape Town asking for Queen Victoria's protection. The British South Africa Company established in 1889 a protectorate in Barotseland, although the wily King Lewanika signed away the lands and mineral rights of only the subject peoples.

The Germans of South-West Africa demanded that the British authorities grant them access to the Zambezi River and a land link to German East Africa in 1890. The result was the partition of the Lozi kingdom, with a strip of territory ceded to the Germans and named for the German chancellor, Count Leo von Caprivi. German rule proved harsh and arbitrary. In 1891 the British and Portuguese agreed to delineate Barotseland's western border but were unable to agree on the territorial extent of Lozi influence. The king of Italy, asked to arbitrate the dispute, finally drew a straight line north to south. In 1903, despite protests of the Lozis that the transfer deprived them of over half their traditional lands, a vast area of Lozi territory became part of Portuguese Angola.

The Victoria Falls Treaty of 1900 gave the British the right to open the lands of the subject peoples to European settlement. Under British pressure Lewanika abolished slavery in the kingdom in 1906, devastating the agricultural base until the king devised schemes to grow and sell fruits and vegetables in the growing European city of Livingstone, founded in Lozi territory in 1905. In 1911 Barotseland was incorporated into the British colony of Northern Rhodesia as a self-governing protectorate, with Livingstone as its administrative capital. Five years later Lewanika died, having retained at least the outward trappings of the monarchy.

In 1920, following Germany's defeat in the First World War, South-West Africa, including the Caprivi Strip, was given to South Africa as a League of Nations mandate. English-speaking administrators were posted to the region, even after the electoral victory of the Afrikaners,* who established an apartheid system. The ability to speak English was more widespread in the Caprivi region than in the rest of present Namibia.

Barotseland was neglected by the colonial government, which concentrated its attention on the lucrative copper mines in the east. The Lozi homeland formed a vast labor pool; the proud tribesmen were forced to seek work in other areas. In the 1920s Lozi resentment sparked the first stirrings of nationalism and a campaign for Lozi self-government. Once the richest nation in the region, the Lozi became progressively poorer as development schemes favored the commercially important Copperbelt mining region, where many Lozi migrated in search of work.

Lozi separatist agitation peaked in the early 1960s as the British prepared Northern Rhodesia for independence. Fearing domination by the more numerous and sophisticated Bembas, the dominant tribe in the colony's heartland to the east, Lozi nationalists demanded separate independence, citing their kingdom's long and separate ties to Great Britain. In 1961, Lozi representatives traveled to London to petition for separate independence for Barotseland but failed to win British support.

The Lozi king, Sir Mwanawina Lewanika III, the litunga of Barotseland, finally signed under British pressure the Barotseland Agreement on 18 May 1964, on the eve of Northern Rhodesian independence. The agreement awarded Barotseland special autonomous status and renounced the kingdom's special relationship with the British crown, thus removing the last barrier to Zambian independence in October 1964.

The government of the new nation, having abolished all opposition, ignored the Barotseland autonomy agreement and appointed a resident minister as the political head of the regional government in place of the litunga. The Constitutional Amendment Act of 1969, which overrode the provisions of the Barotseland Agreement 1964, was passed following a national referendum; it made Barotseland no more than equal to the other provinces. The majority of Zambians voted for the amendment, but 69% in Barotseland voted against it. The abrogation of the Barotseland agreement, viewed by Lozi nationalists as the unilateral termination of the union between Zambia and Barotseland, gave legal force to the self-determination of Barotseland. Lozi nationalists nonetheless sought a dialogue with the socialist Zambian government, but they were rebuffed.

The push by the Caprivi Lozis for regional autonomy in South-West Africa was recognized in 1972 under the South African "bantustan" system.

The Caprivians were granted a separate legislative assembly and considerable self-government, which disappeared when Namibia became independent in 1990. Since that time the Lozis of the Caprivi Strip have been neglected, as priority has been given the more populous regions of the country, particularly the homeland of the dominant Ovambos.

In Zambia, political parties were banned and a one-party state established in 1972. Corruption and nepotism, particularly along tribal lines, became the rule. The country, one of the richest in sub-Saharan Africa at independence, gradually became one of the poorest. Heavily subsidizing the Copperbelt and the urbanized east of the country, the government ignored Barotseland and its rich agricultural potential. The government's failure to develop an efficient road system to connect the regions effectively cut off the Barotse provinces from the Zambian heartland.

Lozi nationalism in Zambia reemerged in the late 1980s as the country moved toward multiparty democracy. The Bemba-dominated government of Zambia portrayed Lozi nationalism and the 1964 Barotseland agreement as a tribal conflict, and the Lozis as unbending secessionists. The Lozi nationalists countered that Barotseland had voluntarily joined Zambia under the Barotseland Agreement, and that agreement having been terminated, the Lozi territory should be allowed to revert to its former status as a self-governing kingdom.

One-party rule in Zambia ended in November 1991. President Kenneth Kuanda stated that he would reexamine Lozi demands for autonomy if he was reelected, but he was defeated; the opposition candidate, Frederick Chiluba, became Zambia's first president elected under a multiparty system. The end of the copper boom fanned smoldering ethnic tension. In December 1992 Lozi nationalists, led by the Barotse Patriotic Front, demanded the restoration of the monarchy, reversion to the name Barotseland, and a return to Barotseland's autonomous political status of 1964. The rapid growth of Lozi national sentiment added to Zambia's increasing instability. In March 1993 the government declared a state of emergency as economic and political difficulties multiplied.

On 20 July 1993, leaders of the Lozi national movement gave the Zambian government 28 days to respond to their demands for autonomy or they would opt for secession. The government of Frederick Chiluba countered with arrests and threats that secession would not be tolerated. When Chiluba went to Barotseland in February 1994, his motorcade was stoned. About 3,000 Lozis took up arms after rumors that the litunga was being sought by government forces in March 1994. Over the next year Zambian police seized caches of weapons in the region, reportedly bought from Angolan rebel groups.

Lozi leaders ordered their lawyers in late 1994 to seek legal arbitration for the settlement of the secession issue, possibly through the International Court of Justice. In November 1995, a mass meeting, called a "Pizo," was summoned to consider the continuing impasse over the termination of the 1964 Barotseland Agreement. The participants agreed that if the government of Zambia continued to ignore the agreement, the people of Barotseland had the right to revert to their self-governing state that had existed prior to the agreement. Adoption of a land-reform law in 1995 further angered the Lozis; it took away traditional land tenure and distribution rights from the Lozi chiefs and put these powers in the hands of the national government.

In early 1997, the Barotseland prime minister, the *ngambela*, sent a written petition to the United Nations Security Council, the Commonwealth Secretariat, and the Organization of African Unity outlining the Lozi position on separation from Zambia. In 1998 several nationalist leaders demanded a referendum to allow the people to decide whether Barotseland should continue living as a captive nation, as they called it, or reclaim independence as a free state, an independent, democratic, and self-governing monarchy. Many Lozis agree with the nationalists that real political freedom, power sharing, and equal justice are impossible in Zambia. More moderate Lozi leaders press for a federal system in Zambia, which would allow the Lozi provinces to create autonomous governments. All agree that centralized government in Zambia has been a political and economic disaster.

The Caprivi region is one of the least developed and poorest in Namibia. The high levels of unemployment and poverty and its neglect by the Namibian government enabled Lozi nationalists to win support. In October 1998 the Namibian army discovered a training camp for nationalists in the region.

The leader of Agenda for Zambia and of the Lozi nationalists, Akashambatwa Lewanika, held meetings in late 1998 with Lozi leaders from Namibia on a possible common agenda. Boniface Manili, the Lozi chief in Namibia, fled to Botswana in November 1998, claiming persecution. He is linked to the growing Lozi separatist movement in the Caprivi Strip, where lack of development in the region fuels antigovernment sentiment. He later traveled to Zambia to meet with nationalist leaders. On 2 August 1999 members of the Caprivi Liberation Army fought a fierce battle with Namibian security forces in the Caprivi capital, attempting to take control of the local television station and the airport. The separatists were routed, and over 2,000 Lozis fled the region. At least 75 people were prosecuted for treason and other crimes. The Caprivi region was placed under a strict curfew, and the number of troops in the region was increased, although the majority of the population does not support the secessionist movement. They believe that the Caprivi region is too small and isolated to survive as an independent state; they refused to consider union with Barotseland in Zambia. The brutal military response to the uprising did little to reconcile the Lozis of Namibia to the Ovambo-dominated national government.

The Lozis have long complained of neglect by the Zambian government, and this neglect continued under the Chiluba government. In February 1998 Lozi members of parliament pointed out that while budgets for other regions had grown, the budget for Barotseland remained static and that nothing had been allocated for the region's dilapidated and unpaved road system. Widespread discontent stimulated rumors that the Lozis of Zambia were arming themselves with heavy weapons.

Guerrillas of the Caprivi Liberation Army launched attacks in Caprivi in August 1999. The rebels were reportedly backed by the UNITA group of Angola; the Caprivi Strip was a vital supply route for UNITA fighters in northern Angola. Widespread human-rights abuses were reported in the region, including the beating of women and children during searches for separatists. Up to 500 people were arrested in the region, and several thousand fled into Botswana.

In July 2000 the litunga of Barotseland died, and the peaceful succession was seen as a sign of the continuing stability of the Lozi monarchy. Nationalists of all stripes support the monarchy, with even separatists seeking an independent Barotseland under the rule of the traditional kings.

Lozi nationalists in Zambia presented their case for separation from Zambia to the Organization of African Unity in July 2001. They presented the representatives of the various member states with copies of the 1964 Barotseland Agreement. They stated that the agreement has not been honored and warn they will break away unless the Zambian government lives up to its pledges. Under the provisions of the agreement, Barotseland was to retain autonomy in all matters of governance except for security, monetary policy, and international affairs.

The trial of 125 men accused of participating in the attack on Katimo Mulilo in August 1999 again raised tensions across the Lozi territories. The trial, which began in August 2001, raised many questions as to its legality as only one Namibian lawyer had agreed to defend the men.

SELECTED BIBLIOGRAPHY:

Brown, Ernest Douglas, and A.M. Ibeanu. *Lozi.* 1997.
Burdette, M.M. *Zambia: Between Two Worlds.* 1988.
Caplan, Gerald L. *The Elites of Barotseland: A Political History of Zambia's Western Province.* 1973.
Charles, Douglas Elliott, and Romaine Stirke. *Barotseland: Eight Years among the Barotse.* 1978.

Maasai

Maasai; Arusa; Lumbwas

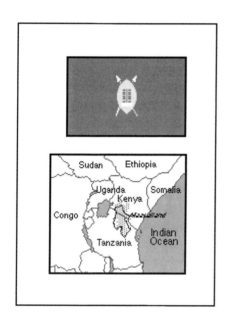

POPULATION: Approximately (2002e) 1,100,000 Maasai in East Africa, concentrated in the Rift Valley of Kenya and the Serengeti Plains and Maasai Steppe regions of Tanzania. The national population is almost evenly divided between the two African states, with 450,000 Maasai in Kenya and about 650,000 in Tanzania. Outside the traditional territories the most important Maasai community lives in Nairobi.

THE MAASAI HOMELAND: The Maasai homeland lies in East Africa, straddling the international border between Kenya and Tanzania. Most of the region is rolling arid and semiarid grassland in the Great Rift Valley, the Serengeti Plain, and the Maasai Steppe, rising to the mountains. A prolonged dry season and unsuitable soils make the region inhospitable to agriculture, although dry-land crops now threaten the pastoral nature of the region, which has a greater diversity and density of large mammals than anywhere else on earth. Maasailand is a nonpolitical region forming the Kajiado and Narok Districts of the Kenyan province of Rift Valley and the Tanzanian province of Arusha. *Maasailand*: 40,391 sq. mi.—104,612 sq. km, (2002e) 1,860,000—Maasai 54%, Kikuyu 11%, Chagga 10%, Kisii 3%, Kamba 3%, Gogo 1%, other Kenyans and Tanzanians 18%. The Maasai capital and major cultural center is Magadi, (2002e) 40,000. The other important cultural center in Kenya is Nakuru, (2002e) 145,000. The major cultural center of the southern Maasai is Arusha, called Arusa by the Maasai, (2002e) 255,000.

FLAG: The Maasai national flag, the flag of the national movement, is a red field bearing a centered white and black Maasai shield over crossed white spears.

PEOPLE AND CULTURE: The Maasai are a tall Nilotic people, the most southerly of the Nilotes. A pastoral people, the Maasai consider things taken from the earth as impure; however, a Maasai minority has settled on permanent farms in recent decades. "Maasai" was formerly a linguistic term, referring to the groups speaking dialects of the Maasai language, which include the Maasai of the Great Rift Valley of Kenya and Tanzania, the Samburu of Kenya, and the semipastoral Arusha and Baraguyu of Tanzania. Most Maasai still live in *manyattas*, villages fortified by walls of thorn bushes, and sustain themselves on a diet of milk and blood taken from their herds of longhorn cattle. The traditional Maasai culture and value system revolves particularly around cattle. The Maasai have only recently begun to urbanize, mostly in small towns but also in the cities of Arusha, Nakuru, and Nairobi, just northeast of the Maasai homeland in Kenya. The urbanized Maasai live in the cities during the week, but on weekends most return to their villages in the countryside. In spite of increasing education and urbanization, the Maasai have maintained a semi-nomadic lifestyle closer to their traditional culture than any other national group in East Africa. The Maasai suffered discrimination under the colonial and postcolonial governments, and they continue to be looked down on by the rest of the regional population.

LANGUAGE AND RELIGION: The Maasai speak a Paranilotic, formerly called Nilo-Hamitic, language of the Eastern Sudanic language group of the Chari-Nile branch of the Nilo-Saharan language family. The language, probably originally of Hamitic origin, is called Ongama Maa or Maa and is spoken in 14 major dialects based on geographic areas. The Maasai are the southernmost Nilotic speakers and are linguistically most closely related to the Turkana and Kalenjin of Kenya.

The traditional Maasai religion is based on the belief on an all-powerful god, Enkai, and many lesser gods and spirits. The center of the religion lies in the "Cathedral of Seven Trees," in the Loita Forest. Many religious ceremonies are performed within and around the sacred forest. Herbs, trees, and plants found in the forest are used by local healers, who combine religious beliefs with ancient medicine. The cow is slaughtered as an offering during important ceremonies marking completed passage through age-grade groups.

NATIONAL HISTORY: The creation of the world, according to Maasai legend, began when God, Enkai, allocated the earth's resources to his sons. The Maasai claim descent from the son who was given cattle; therefore all of the earth's cattle belong to the Maasai. For centuries the Maasai warriors raided neighboring peoples to appropriate their cattle, held illegally and against God's will. According to their tradition, the Maasai originated near Lake Turkana. They probably arrived with their herds in the area west of Mount Kilimanjaro in the mid-eighteenth century. The Maasai continued to push south until checked by hostile tribes in the 1830s. Expanding across the grasslands, the Maasai reached the coast south of Mombasa in 1859.

Considered invincible by neighboring tribes, the Maasai established their dominance over much of East Africa. At the height of their power, in the 1870s, the Maasai controlled some 80,000 square miles of territory and raided as far west as Lake Victoria and east to the Indian Ocean. Prior to the colonial period, land was divided ecologically; the Maasai remained in the dry savanna, where the soil was too poor for agriculture, while Kikuyu, Kalenjin, and other agricultural tribes farmed in the wetter areas, where the tsetse fly made herding impossible.

First visited by German missionaries in 1848–49, few Maasai showed an interest in the new religion, which would deny their right to the world's cattle. An epidemic of rinderpest swept the Maasai herds in the 1880s, setting off wars with the neighboring tribes the Maasai raided to replenish their livestock wealth. In the 1890s smallpox, inadvertently introduced by European visitors, decimated the Maasai tribes; up to 75% of the Maasai population died in the epidemic. Even during this time of troubles the Maasai maintained their domination.

The British, seeking to open trade routes to the kingdoms of the highland region around Lake Victoria, needed first to pacify the Maasai, whose territory straddled the trade routes. Weakened by their tribulations, the Maasai could not sustain a long war. Treating them with caution and respect, the British authorities pacified the Maasai with diplomacy; the fierce Maasai accepted nominal British rule. The southern groups came under German authority. The boundaries between the British territories and German East Africa, fixed by negotiations between 1886 and 1890, included provisions for supposedly inalienable Maasai land reserves in the Rift Valley, the highlands northwest of Nairobi, and the southern Maasai Steppe in Tanganyika. Much of this Maasai land was arable but had never been farmed. Only just recovering from the severe epidemic and from drought in the 1890s, the Maasai were manipulated with relative ease into a treaty that allowed the colonial authorities to take the most fertile lands in the Rift Valley in 1904.

The British authorities, determined to construct an agricultural economy in Kenya, viewed the Maasai as a barrier to progress and their way of life as worthless and destructive. Many officials believed that their lands must be divided into private farms and their migrations stopped. The authorities, ignoring the earlier agreements, moved the Maasai into restricted grazing lands in southern Kenya in 1911. The colonial government again reduced the Maasai reserves in 1913. The reserve lands taken for European settlement became the so-called White Highlands, the heartland of the European settler community of colonial Kenya. Many Maasai were expelled from the region as unsuitable for farm labor; workers were recruited from among the agricultural tribes.

During World War I, British troops from Kenya moved south to capture German East Africa. In spite of Maasai demands for the reunification of their homeland, the British maintained the former international boundaries as colonial boundaries. The Maasai remained divided, under two colonial administrations.

Their lands reduced to small, inadequate reserves, the disillusioned Maasai began to reject modernization. In the 1920s Kikuyu tribesmen began to move into the Maasai grazing lands to set up farms. Unable to interest the British officials in their problems, in the 1930s the Maasai retreated into egocentric tribalism. The colonial authorities discriminated against the pastoral Maasai in favor of the agricultural peoples. In 1939, the colonial regime settled over 4,000 Kikuyu squatters in areas that had traditionally belonged to the Maasai.

Rival tribes, particularly the numerous Kikuyu in Kenya, advanced more rapidly than the Maasai and often filled administrative positions in the Maasai districts. Disputes over land and water rights sparked the beginning of Maasai nationalism in the 1950s during the Mau Mau uprising, led by the Kikuyus. Nationalists formed the Maasai United Front (MUF), a coalition of Maasai organizations in Kenya and Tanganyika. The nationalists demanded separate Maasai independence as the British began decolonizing the region in the late 1950s.

Poorly educated and unfamiliar with politics, the Maasai failed to make their case for separation. Many supported an opposition political group centered among the related Kalenjins, the Kenya African Democratic Union (KADU), which represented the smaller and less advantaged ethnic groups. The KADU leaders advocated the creation of ethnic-based semi-autonomous regions in a federal Kenya. In December 1963, KADU was defeated by the Kikuyu-dominated Kenya African National Union (KANU), and federalism was abandoned.

In both Kenya and Tanzania, one-party states were created after independence. Although some Maasai were brought into the government in Kenya, they were mostly ignored and marginalized. Land disputes, especially in Kenya, escalated in the 1960s and 1970s. Rapid population growth among the settled farming tribes put enormous pressure on the open Maasai grazing lands. The Kenyan government of Jomo Kenyatta, dominated by the Kikuyus and other agricultural tribes, determined to divide the Maasai lands for food production. In Tanzania, the new socialist government appropriated and nationalized the Maasai grazing lands, exacerbating the growing Maasai alienation. In both countries the Maasai suffered great poverty and social disorganization. Land claims by Maasai evicted from their best lands during the colonial period were dismissed by both governments.

Younger, educated Maasai moved into the leadership of the tribe in the 1980s as land pressure increased dramatically. Unsuccessful appeals to national governments to stop the encroachments of farming peoples and Somali herdsmen led to demands for the return of nationalized lands in

Tanzania and the reunification of the Maasai nation. Moves to introduce multiparty democracy greatly increased ethnic and tribal rivalries.

The status of the Maasai in Kenya changed when Daniel arap Moi, a Kalenjin, came to power in 1978 at Jomo Kenyatta's death. Moi's government, dominated by the Kalenjins, was unable to sustain its control alone and was forced to make political alliances with other, smaller tribal groups. This gave the Maasai a voice in government, and several Maasai gained high government posts. Many Maasai were employed as armed units against Moi's political opponents. Many outsiders in the 1980s saw the Maasai as the lackeys of an increasingly authoritarian Moi regime.

In 1991 serious ethnic violence broke out in Kenya's Rift Valley and quickly involved the Maasai. Disputes over land and water rights in the region spread across the Maasai districts in 1992–93. The Maasai, trying to drive Kikuyu and others from disputed lands, were repeatedly used as agents of political repression in ethnic violence in 1991–94 that displaced over 300,000 and left over 1,500 dead. In 1992 moderate Maasai, including the small nationalist organizations, held their first conference on culture and development of Maasailand. The event, bringing together Maasai from both Kenya and Tanzania, rejected the growing violence in Kenya; the delegates reiterated the Maasai land claims but refused to pursue them at the cost of war.

A group of Maasai businessmen, the Maasai Development Trust, attempted in the 1990s to gain control of the forested Loita Hills, the heartland of Maasai culture. The region, adjacent to the overexploited and degraded Maasai Mara wildlife reserve, had been under the sustainable management of the Loita Maasai and had been preserved in its natural state. Maasai mobilization in the 1990s to save their threatened culture focused on the Loita region, which had spiritual, cultural, and economic significance. Development of the region as a mass tourist region would wipe out the traditionally strong influence of the Maasai elders. The situation in Loita was an example of the growing conflict between the Maasai and conservation interests that funnel the economic benefits of tourism away from those who bear the cost in lost land rights.

In January 1994, a meeting of reconciliation between the Maasai and Kikuyus was held, but it failed to curb the growing conflict. The violence extended into the highlands above Nairobi; violent confrontations occurred in the Nakuru and Naivasha regions. Maasai youths often attacked "foreigners," mostly Kikuyus and Kisiis, the largest groups among the agriculturalists who had settled on traditional Maasai lands. Retaliatory attacks on Maasai often targeted communities not involved in the conflict.

The Moi government in Kenya banned tribal organizations within the ruling KANU political party in 1995, but ethnic violence, often instigated by government agents, continued. In May 1996 a Maasai leader and local government minister, William ole Ntimama, claimed that in spite of government restrictions, other groups were again encroaching on Maasailand. In the past, the Maasai and their herds had been forbidden to enter the huge areas set aside as wildlife parks. Under the Moi government, the Maasai were again allowed into the reserves, but they were in competition with the wildlife.

The ethnic violence abated in the run-up to the December 1997 elections, which were again won by President Moi, who then dismissed his Maasai vice president. In March 1998, Maasai leaders joined other tribal leaders in calling for an end to the ethnic violence in Kenya. The Maasai, having benefited from their alliance with the ruling Kalenjins, were by then suffering the consequences of twenty years of misrule and corruption in Kenya.

In August 1998, the Kenyan and Tanzanian governments agreed to carry out a major operation to flush out Maasai bandits and cattle rustlers along their common border. The operation was particularly aimed at groups responsible for the growing insecurity in Kenya's Maasai Mara and Amboseli, and Tanzania's Serengeti wildlife reserves.

The Maasai increasingly turned to nationalism as tribal and ethnic conflicts proliferated, seeking a united, independent Maasailand free of Kenya's tribal violence and Tanzania's economic woes. As an interim step, Maasai nationalists have demanded the introduction of "majimboism" in Kenya, a federal system based on ethnicity. The system would mandate that only members of indigenous groups would have political and economic rights in the Rift Valley areas. Maasai leaders demand that ethnic groups who settled on Maasai lands since the 1920s and those who illegally bought land since the independence of Kenya be expelled. Majimbo rallies have continued throughout the Maasai territories in Kenya in spite of government efforts to curtail them. In late 1998, several Maasai leaders accused the government of denying the Maasai the right to development, as had the colonial and postindependence governments.

The Maasai alliance with the ruling Kalenjins in the Kenyan government of Daniel arap Moi has improved their historically disadvantaged situation but leaves them vulnerable should the increasingly authoritarian government fall. The Kikuyus, largest tribe in Kenya, suffered the most from Maasai expulsions and attacks in the 1990s, and they are now attempting to regain power in the country. The Maasai, should the ethnic violence of the early 1990s resume, could become the targets of the more numerous Kikuyus, Luos, Luhyas, and Kisiis, the tribal groups they claim have illegally stolen their ancestral lands.

A severe drought in mid-2000 forced tens of thousands of Maasai off the land and into the cities, particularly Nairobi. The Maasai refuse to give up their cattle and have taken to grazing them on golf courses and in city parks. The decimation of the Maasai herds could take years to reverse, seriously threatening the traditional Maasai culture.

SELECTED BIBLIOGRAPHY:

Hetfield, Jamie. *The Maasai of East Africa*. 1997.
Nechkbrouck, V. *Resistant Peoples: The Case of the Pastoral Maasai of East Africa*. 1993.
Spear, Thomas. *Being Maasai: Ethnicity and Identity in East Africa*. 1993.
Spense, Glenys. *Caught in the Crossfire: The Maasai and Majimboism in Kenya*. 1996.

Mabas

Wadaians; Waddayens; Ouadaï; Ouaddaiens; Mabangis; Mabans; Mabaa; Mabaks; Borgu

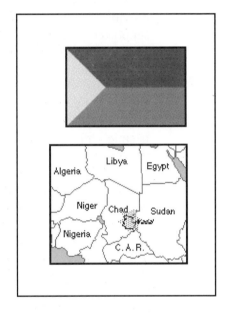

POPULATION: Approximately (2002e) 695,000 Mabas in north-central Africa, concentrated in the Ouaddaï, Biltine, Batha, Guera, and Salamat prefectures of Chad, and the western districts of Darfur province of Sudan.

THE MABA HOMELAND: The Maba homeland lies in north-central Africa, a region of savanna grasslands crossed by the Saharan caravan routes. Most of the region is semi-desert with some tropical forests and grazing lands on the fertile Maba Plateau that rise to the Wadai Mountains in the east. The Maba heartland, Ouaddaï, locally called Wadai, formerly an independent sultanate, now forms a prefecture of the Republic of Chad. *Prefecture of Ouaddaï (Wadai):* 29,436 sq. mi.—76,238 sq. km, (2002e) 615,000—Mabas, Zagawa Arabs, Tamas, Dajus, Fulanis. The Maba capital and major cultural center is Abéché, (2002e) 63,000. The center of Maba culture in Sudan is al-Junaynah, called Ajjinena, (2002e) 118,000.

FLAG: The Maba national flag, the flag of the national movement, is a horizontal bicolor of blue over red with a yellow triangle at the hoist.

PEOPLE AND CULTURE: The Mabas are an Arabized Negroid Sudanic people of mixed Hamitic and Arab descent. The largest of Chad's non-Arab Muslim groups, they form a nucleus surrounded by a number of groups who, while possessing their own languages, form a distinct culturally Maba unit. The name Maba is actually used to describe all the mountain tribes in Wadai into which other ethnic groups have been assimilated. There are various Maba subgroups, the Marfas, the Djene, and the Mandabas being the most important. The Mabas are mostly herders and farmers and are fiercely independence. Their society is clan-oriented, with each clan controlling specific grazing lands, wells, and oases. Chiefs and members of royal clans still possess a high degree of power and prestige. Urbanization, accelerating since the 1970s, has somewhat diluted the traditional way of life, but even in the towns and cities the Mabas tend to cluster tightly together.

LANGUAGE AND RELIGION: The Maba group of languages form an interrelated cluster in eastern Chad and western Sudan. Masalit is the most extensive of the dialects spoken in Sudan. The language, often including the related dialects and called the Ouaddaïan Languages, is a Nilo-Saharan language called Maba or Mabang, which is closely related to the Masalit and Runga languages. Many of the Mabas also speak Arabic as a second or trade language. The origins of the language are obscure although the distribution of the 13 Maba dialects implies origins farther east, a theory supported by Maba oral tradition. Although some scholars separate Tama, Dadju, and Mimi, others consider them part of the larger Ouaddaïan group, which stretches from central Chad to western Sudan.

The majority of the Mabas are Sunni Muslims of the Malakite sect, although their belief system retains many pre-Islamic traditions. Mysticism plays a big role in the Islamic life of the Mabas, whose ceremonies mix Islamic and pre-Islamic traditions. The chastity of women, as written in the Koran, is considered to be of prime importance among the Mabas.

NATIONAL HISTORY: The history of Wadai before the seventeenth century is uncertain, although scholars believe that the kingdom emerged in the sixteenth century as an offshoot of the state of Darfur under the non-Muslim Tungur people. In about 1640, a Maba chieftain, Abd-el-Kerim, conquered the country and overthrew the Tungur dynasty, which had originated among the Fur* to the east. Adb-el-Kerim installed a Muslim dynasty and over the next two centuries the Mabas, led by Abd-el-Kerim's descendants, fought intermittent wars with the Bagirmis and Kanuris,* mostly to maintain Wadai's supply of slaves for shipment north on the caravan routes.

Initially, the Mabas of Wadai were forced to pay tribute to the more powerful kingdoms of Kanem-Bornu and Darfur, but by the early eighteenth century the Mabas had gained enough strength to assert their sovereignty. They carried on raids on Kanem-Bornu for plunder and on black African tribes for slaves. The Mabas adhered to the Islamic ban on enslaving other Muslims and raided the peoples to the south, who lacked states and complex social hierarchies and who maintained traditional religious practices. Often the black slaves embraced Islam to escape slavery and many were absorbed into the Maba tribal structure.

The Kado, the ruling clan, once formed an aristocracy among the Mabas, and ruled an empire that dominated much of central Saharan Africa in the seventeenth and eighteenth centuries. During much of the eighteenth century, the Mabas resisted attempts by the Furs to incorporate Wadai into Darfur. By the 1790s, the Mabas had thrown off Fur influence and began a period of rapid expansion.

In about 1800, during the reign of Sabun, the sultanate of Wadai began to expand its borders and powers. A new trade route across the Sahara was discovered and Sabun sponsored royal caravans to travel north. He began minting his own coinage and used it to import chain mail, firearms, and military advisors from the Muslim states of North Africa. Salt, horses, and glass were brought south by the caravans, while Maba traders carried ivory and especially slaves to the markets of North Africa. Sabun's descendants were less able, and the Fur again gained influence in the region.

Muhammad al-Sharif, the sultan from 1835 to 1858, reasserted his authority and rejected the Fur meddling in his kingdom. He was influenced by the teachings of the Sanussis,* the Islamic brotherhood that spread from Cyrenaica. It remained the dominant political and religious force until the French conquest. Sharif conducted military campaigns as far west as Lake Chad and the Chari River.

Though Arab geographers had described the area, Wadai was not generally known to Europeans until after 1873, when it was explored by the German geographer Gustav Nachtigal. Wadai was recognized as within the French "sphere of influence" according to a Franco-British agreement of 1899, the Mabas retained effective independence until after 1904, when they attacked French outposts in the Chari region. Fighting between the Mabas and French colonial forces continued sporadically until 1908, when the sultan, Doud Murra, proclaimed a *jihad*, a holy war, against the French. Doud Murra divided his army into units under his subordinates, but he was no match for the well-armed French troops and was quickly defeated. By 1912, the French had taken control of the vast territory and abolished the Maba sultanate, which was joined to the French Chari-Ubangi colony. The French occupation put an end to the Mabas' lucrative trans-Saharan trade.

A famine swept the region in 1913–14 and devastated Wadai. European diseases decimated the remaining population as major epidemics swept the defenseless population. From an estimated population of two million in the sultanate in the 1870s, the inhabitants, mostly Mabas and related groups, were reduced to less than 300,000 by 1917.

As soon as the French had established their authority, they began leaving the stricken region, making Wadai the most neglected of colonial outposts. The French authorities reversed the traditional dominance of the Islamic northerners and concentrated their efforts in the fertile southern districts of the Chad colony inhabited by the black African tribes formerly taken as slaves by the Muslims. The northern Muslims lacked the educational opportunities offered in the south, allowing the Christian and animist southerners to dominate the colonial administration. The Black southern tribes were viewed by the Mabas as either subjects or slaves, certainly not leaders.

Banditry, long prevalent in Wadai under French rule, evolved into guerrilla warfare following Chadian independence in 1960. Independence came at a time of political instability and economic weakness. In November 1965, rebellion broke out and quickly spread from the Mabas of Guéra prefecture to the Maba heartland in Wadai. Civil unrest among the northern Muslims turned into civil war. The Muslim Mabas fought the southern Christians and animists who formed Chad's first independent government. The Black African Chadian government banned opposition political parties and carried out massacres of Muslim peoples. Thousands fled to refugee camps in neighboring Sudan.

The Mabas' territory was particularly hard hit by the severe drought that began in the late 1960s and continued unabated into the 1970s. The economic hardships that accompanied the loss of their valued herds added to Maba discontent.

Several liberation groups formed, including the most prominent, the National Liberation Front of Chad (FROLINAT) in June 1966. Personality, ideological, and ethnic differences soon led to the fragmentation of the front. Most Mabas abandoned the united Muslim philosophy and formed their own Maba-Wadai Liberation Front (FLMO). By 1970, the FLMO had also splintered along tribal and clan lines. Some groups claimed a wide region of central and eastern Chad formerly under the rule of Wadai as traditional Maba territory.

In 1968, French troops were dispatched in an effort to end the fighting between the northern Muslims and the southern-dominated government forces. The French intervention was useless, and in 1971 the Libyan government began supplying arms to the Mabas and other rebel groups. The Chadian government, led by Ngarta Tombalbaye, was further destabilized when Tombalbaye virtually lost control. In a frenzy of voodoo and nationalist fervor, he forced the entire population of Chad to change their names to traditional African ones. Anyone who refused was summarily executed. The Mabas, whose names reflect their Muslim culture, joined other northern Muslim groups in a widespread rebellion, but they soon broke with the other groups and recreated the separate Maba national movement that sometimes cooperated with the North Chadians,* but just as often fought against domination by other northern peoples, particularly the dominant Toubou and Zaghawa Arab peoples after they took control of the Chadian government in 1990.

Fighting continued sporadically into the 1980s because of the state's ongoing civil war. The cyclical droughts coupled with the continuing war led to widespread hunger and destruction. Herds were lost and many of the region's semi-nomadic peoples were forced to settle in permanent villages or to live in the shantytowns that grew up around the towns and cities. Chad continued in a cycle of military crackdowns and attempted coups.

French and Libyan interference in the continuing ethnic and religious violence led to a splintering of both government and rebel forces. In 1992 and 1993, there were five coups and numerous crackdowns, but the Zaghawas of northern Chad continued to control the government.

In 1991, clashes broke out on the indefinite Chad-Sudan border. The closing of the border most affected the Mabas, who have populations in both countries and had always crossed and recrossed the border. The Chadian government, supporting Maba claims to territory in Sudan, pressed for revision of the border. In 1994, the two countries demarcated the border, officially dividing the Maba nation. Activities by anti-government groups continued in the region although serious clashes declined following a peace accord that was signed by the Maba rebels and the Chadian government in October 1994.

The Chadian army, gendarmes, police, national guard, and intelligence services are dominated by the Zaghawa ethnic group of Chad's President Déby. In the late 1990s, the security forces were accused of committing serious abuses in the Wadai area, where opposition Maba forces continued to harass the troops and garrison towns following government forced conscription of young Mabas without informing their families. There remain some limits on assembly and association and on freedom of movement.

In 1993, there were serious clashes between demonstrators and government forces by Mabas protesting alleged massacres in the Chokoyan district, near Abéché. Maba leaders claim that the massacres were carried out by special units of the army, but a government investigation failed to uncover any of those guilty of the violence. In early 1994, following renewed fighting in the region, a curfew was declared throughout the Wadai region. In a leaflet distributed in Abéché, Islamic fundamentalists ordered Christians to leave the region or face reprisals.

The traditional hierarchy of Wadai remains in spite of decades of strife. The palace of the sultan of Wadai is situated in Abéché and is considered the center of the nation. The sultan serves as the head of the Mabas and as the secular and religious leader of the region. Nationalists revere the sultan and any proposals for greater autonomy, independence, or federalism focus on the leadership of the Maba sultan.

The Mabas, from safe havens on the Chad-Sudan border, continue to skirmish with government troops, but the violence has abated in 2000–2001. Government appeals to Muslim solidarity and the planned introduction of Islamic law in all of Chad has convinced some rebels to disarm, but many Mabas remain suspicious of the Chadian government, which was first dominated by Christian tribes from the south, then by their historic enemies the Zaghawas and Toubous of northern Chad.

SELECTED BIBLIOGRAPHY:

Azevedo, Mario J. *Chad: A Nation in Search of Its Future*. 1998.
Carter, Gwendolen Margaret, ed. *National Unity and Regionalism in Eight African*

States: *Nigeria, Niger, the Congo, Gabon, Central African Republic, Chad, Uganda, and Ethiopia.* 1996.

Collins, Robert O., ed. *Africa's Thirty Years War: Libya, Chad, and Sudan 1963–1993.* 1999.

Kelly, Robert C., ed. *Chad Country Review 2000.* 1999.

Madeirans

Madeira Islanders; Madeiranos

POPULATION: Approximately (2002e) 355,000 Madeirans in Europe, the majority in the autonomous Portuguese region of Madeira, but with substantial Madeiran populations in mainland Portugal, France, Germany, and Luxembourg. Outside of Europe there are Madeiran communities in Brazil, the United States, and in South Africa. The Madeiran diaspora is estimated to number 1.5 million.

THE MADEIRAN HOMELAND: The Madeiran homeland is an island group in the Atlantic Ocean 440 miles (708 km) west of Morocco and 530 miles (852 km) southwest of the Portuguese mainland. The archipelago comprises the large island of Madeira, the smaller island of Porto Santo, and two groups of barren, uninhabited islets, the Desertas and Selvagens. The islands, of volcanic origin, are mountainous, with deep, green valleys and high basalt cliffs along parts of the shore. The equitable climate, marred only by the occasional *leste*, a dry, hot Saharan wind, makes the islands a major tourist destination. Madeira has formed an autonomous region of the Republic of Portugal since 1976. *Autonomous Region of Madeira (Arquipélago da Madeira)*: 314 sq. mi.—813 sq. km, (2002e) 242,000—Madeirans 92%, other Portuguese 8%. The Madeiran capital and major cultural center is Funchal, (2002e) 103,000.

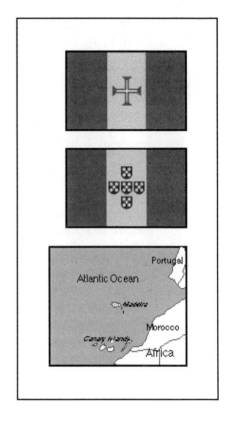

FLAG: The Madeiran national flag, the official flag of the autonomous region, has three vertical stripes of blue, yellow, blue with a centered cross of the Order of Christ, a square white cross outlined in red, in the center. The same blue, yellow, blue flag, but with five blue shields, each with five white *guinas* (roundels), in the form of a centered cross, is the flag of the largest nationalist organization, the Madeira Archipelago Liberation Front (FLAMA).

PEOPLE AND CULTURE: The Madeirans are an island people, descendants of early Portuguese settlers, with later admixtures of African slaves brought in to work the sugar plantations, and of Berbers and Arabs from the Moroccan mainland. Emigration, particularly in the twentieth century, resulted in a large overseas population, estimated at over 1.5 million, primarily in South America and South Africa. The emigrants contribute to the Madeiran economy and are the most nationalistic and ardent supporters of the Madeiran national movement. An insular, conservative nation, the Madeirans are culturally distant from mainland Portugal. Many traditions and customs that form part of the Madeiran culture were brought to the islands by the early colonists but have since disappeared from mainland Portuguese culture.

LANGUAGE AND RELIGION: The dialect of Portuguese spoken in the archipelago is the Madeira-Azores dialect, quite different from the Portuguese of mainland Portugal, which is based on the Extremenho dialect spoken around Lisbon and Coimbra. The dialect is further divided into two subdialects, Madeiran and Azorean. The Madeiran dialect has incorporated many words from Arabic, Berber, African, and other European languages brought to the islands by traders, slaves, and tourists.

The conservative Madeirans are overwhelmingly Roman Catholic. The religion, an integral part of island culture, remains an important pillar of Madeiran society. The annual observances and festivals associated with the religion mark the rhythm of island life.

NATIONAL HISTORY: The islands, lying in the eastern Atlantic Ocean, are believed to have been visited by the Phoenicians. They were known to the Romans as the Purple Islands, due to their frequent haze. They were lost to all but legend following the coming of the Dark Ages to Europe, although they are depicted on an Italian map of 1351. A Portuguese navigator, João Gonçalves Zarco, sighted Porto Santo in 1418, having been blown off course by a storm while exploring the African coast. Zarco, sailing under orders from Prince Henry the Navigator, claimed the uninhabited islands for Portugal in 1420. The name of the largest island, Madeira, the Portuguese word for wood (in reference to the island's extensive forest cover), became the name of the entire archipelago.

Colonists from mainland Portugal established in 1421 a settlement at Funchal, Portugal's first overseas colony. The dense forests were felled and burned, the fires reportedly burning for seven years. The cleared lands were brought under cultivation by a growing number of colonists. By 1425 several Portuguese settlements had been established in the islands. The introduction of sugar cane cultivation in 1452 transformed Madeira, as sugar requires a large workforce to cultivate. Madeira is thought to have been the location of the world's first sugarcane plantation; the sugar trade quickly became important.

The Madeirans bought black African and Moorish slaves in the slave markets of nearby Morocco to work on the sugar and tropical fruit plantations. The Portuguese, free from the strong racial prejudices common in other parts of Europe, freely mixed with the large slave population, and many colonial families included members of mixed race. The sugar and wine industries suffered temporarily when slavery was abolished in 1755.

The islands, lying on the sea routes between Europe, Africa, and the Americas, prospered in the sixteenth and seventeenth centuries. However, during the colonial period, the Madeirans, drawn by tales of riches, emigrated to the new Portuguese colonies, particularly Brazil. The tradition of leaving the islands in search of work or fortune continued for centuries.

Madeira was occupied by the British during the Napoleonic Wars. While the British controlled the islands, a number of British families settled in the islands, most to engage in the lucrative wine trade. The production of the famous Madeira wine began when a shipment of red wine to the East Indies was returned unsold. On opening the cask, the owner discovered that the heat of the ship's hold had considerably enhanced the flavor. The production of the unique Madeira wine, which involves heat, after that time became one of the Madeirans' major industries.

In 1850 an Englishwoman, Mrs. Phelps, introduced embroidery to the women of Funchal. At first a way for women to earn extra money, embroidery grew into a major cottage industry. By the mid-twentieth century embroidery and lace making employed thousands of Madeiran women.

In the nineteenth century thousands of Madeirans continued to leave the neglected, overpopulated, and underdeveloped islands, some to settle as far from their homeland as Hawaii, where they introduced the musical instrument called the ukulele. Between 1900 and 1920 more thousands of Madeirans emigrated in search of jobs, most to the United States, Brazil, and Argentina.

Tourism, particularly from Britain, brought much-needed income in the early twentieth century. The island of Madeira was a favorite holiday destination of Winston Churchill. In the twentieth century, the economic mainstays of tourism, sugar, wine, and lace making provided for only a fraction of the burgeoning population. In the 1950s, banana production replaced sugar as the major export crop. By the early 1960s, emigration reduced Madeira's population by an average of 2.5 to 3% a year.

The Madeirans experienced a cultural and linguistic revival beginning in the 1960s, partly in response to the need to leave their beloved islands to find work. The cultural movement quickly evolved into a strong nationalist faction following the leftist revolution in Portugal in 1974. Portugal's revolutionary government moved quickly to dismantle the costly remnants of the Portuguese Empire, granting independence to remaining overseas possessions. Nationalists, led by the Madeira Archipelago Liberation Front (FLAMA), created a provisional government in anticipation of the granting of independence to Portugal's oldest overseas possession.

The Madeirans, considering themselves a separate nation and not part of metropolitan Portugal, were disappointed by the government's refusal to grant independence to Madeira as it had its other overseas territories. Thousands of Madeirans joined demonstrations in Funchal and other towns demanding immediate independence for the archipelago. The leftist rhetoric of the revolutionary government prompted a majority of the population to support the independence movement.

In 1975 political conditions in Lisbon stabilized under a new centrist government, and mass support for Madeiran separation waned, due to fear that the islands would suffer economically and lack trained administrators. Many nationalists agreed that premature independence might prove a disaster; national organizations pressed for association status or other forms of independence. In 1976, the Madeirans accepted a government offer of broad economic and political autonomy, an arrangement seen by the more militant nationalists as an interim step to eventual independence. Militant nationalists, citing long neglect and a string of broken promises, continued to demonstrate for full independence. In the late 1970s and early 1980s, however, increasing prosperity and ample autonomy satisfied many of the demands of the islanders.

The island's rising prosperity, accelerating with Portugal's entry into the European Economic Community, later the European Union (EU), in 1986, gave the Madeirans new confidence. Madeiran membership in the community again raised the question of independence within a united Europe. Emigration, once a necessity, had reversed, and the population again began to grow slowly. Many Madeirans found work in the expanding financial and banking industries spawned by the islands' emergence as a major offshore European financial center, tax haven, and free port.

The nationalists again became active in the late 1980s, renewing demands for independence within an integrated European federation. A plan was drawn up for a federation of the Madeiran, Azorean, and Canary Islands. The Madeiran national movement, with the support of the large emigrant Madeiran population, particularly those in Brazil, focused on ending the state's semicolonial status and sought full national sovereignty within the EU.

In October 1990, the president of the regional government met with nationalist leaders to discuss the independence issue and to forestall threatened separatist activities. After that meeting the autonomous government moved closer to the nationalists; this cooperation benefited the autonomous island state. In September 1993, during a heated dispute with the Lisbon government, the governor, Social Democrat Alberto Joan Jardim, threatened to throw his government's support behind the separatists. In 1994 Portuguese intelligence officers were exposed spying on Madeiran leaders, further harming relations between the Madeiran and Portuguese governments.

Portuguese law makes advocating secession a grave offense, and nationalist organizations are banned under the terms of the Portuguese constitution, forcing the Madeiran nationalists to seek broad support as legal political parties. The nationalists have begun to integrate themselves into local politics, making the Portuguese prohibitions on secession and nationalism irrelevant, in light of the increasingly close relationship between the nationalists and the autonomous Madeiran government.

Emigration again became necessary during the 1990s, particularly for many young Madeirans unable to find jobs in the islands. The population, which reached a high of 253,000 in 1991, had fallen to 242,000 in 2001.

SELECTED BIBLIOGRAPHY:

Bragança-Cunha, Vicente. *Revolutionary Portugal.* 1976.
Duncan, Thomas Bently. *Atlantic Islands: Madeira, the Azores, and the Cape Verdes in Seventeenth-Century Commerce and Navigation.* 1972.
Ludtke, Jen. *Atlantic Peeks: An Ethnographic Guide to the Portuguese-Speaking Islands.* 1989.
Rogers, Francis M. *Atlantic Islanders of the Azores and Madeiras.* 1979.

Mahoris

Mahorais; Mahorians; Mayottis; Mauris; Maore

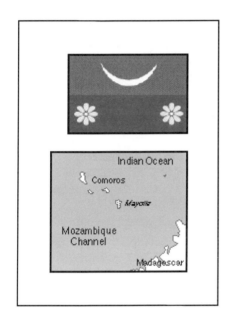

POPULATION: Approximately (2002e) 112,000 Mahoris in the French territories of the Indian Ocean. The Mahoris mostly live on Mahore, the southernmost of the Comoro Islands, with a smaller community living in French Réunion. Other Mahori communities live in mainland France.

THE MAHORIAN HOMELAND: The Mahorian homeland, Mahore, is the southernmost island of the Comoro Archipelago, lying in the Indian Ocean about halfway from northern Madagascar to northern Mozambique, on the African mainland. Due to a shortage of farmland, much of the food consumed on the island must be imported. Mahore forms a territorial collective under French rule. *Territorial Collectivity of Mayotte (Mahoré/Mahore)*: 144 sq. mi.—373 sq. km, (2002e) 166,000—Mahoris 63%, Malagasy 26%, French 5%, Anjouanis* 5%, others 1%. The Mahori capital and major cultural center is Mamoutzou, called Mamutsu, (2002e) 43,000.

FLAG: The Mahori national flag, the unofficial flag of the island, is a horizontal bicolor of blue over red, bearing a white crescent moon on the upper half and two yellow flowers on the lower half.

PEOPLE AND CULTURE: The Mahoris are of mixed ancestry, combining Malay, African, Persian, and Arab strains. Although ethnically related to the peoples of the neighboring Comoran Islands, the Mahoris consider themselves culturally, religiously, and linguistically distinct. Their long association with France has given their island and culture a distinct Creole character. Most of the Mahoris are fishermen; others herd cattle, sheep, goats, and donkeys in the interior of the island. A growing number work in industry or in jobs related to tourism. Polygamy is widely practiced, particularly among the Muslim population.

LANGUAGE AND RELIGION: The Mahoris speak a dialect of Comoran Swahili called Mahorian or Mahoran. The language, an Arabized dialect of Swahili, has absorbed many borrowings from French, which is widely spoken as a second language and is the official language of the island. The Mahorian dialect, called Shimaore, was used in the publication of parts of the Bible in the 1980s. French is spoken by about 35% of the population as a second language.

Although for political reasons French officials often claim that there is a Roman Catholic majority on the island, most Mahoris are Sunni Muslims. The Muslims adhere to the Shafi branch of Sunni Islam and are markedly less fundamentalist than many other Islamic groups in the region. Both Christianity and Islam on the island have been mixed with earlier traditional beliefs. There remain strong elements of occultism and spirit possession.

NATIONAL HISTORY: The island was originally inhabited by settlers from the African mainland. Over 2,000 years ago Malays from southeast Asia came; the majority settled on nearby Madagascar, but small groups settled the Comoro Islands. Their Asian culture soon dominated that of the African peoples.

The island became a center for dhows that traded as far east as India. In the eighth century A.D., Arabs settled on the islands, bringing their Islamic religion. The mixture of the original black Africans, the Malays, and the later Arabs produced a distinct people and culture in the Comoro Islands.

In the early ninth century, the island of Mahore was acquired by the Sultanate of Oman as part of its East African empire, which also included Zanzibar and part of the African mainland. The island remained under Omani rule until the sixteenth century, when a Shirazi dynasty created a separate sultanate on the island. The Shirazis, claiming descent from Shiraz in Persia, originally came to the Comoros as traders and adventurers.

Sultan Andriantsuli granted the French the right to use the island as a military base in 1840. Under increasing French pressure, he ceded his sultanate to French control in 1841. Sultan Andriantsuli continued to rule the island under French authority until 1843, when the island was made a colony, the first European colony in the Comoros. Mahore remained the center of French activity in the region, including that of Christian missionaries. Many Mahoris were converted to Catholicism, and mission education was introduced. The Catholic minority became the most prosperous group in the Comoros, attracting even more Mahoris to the church. The other Comoran islands remained overwhelmingly Muslim.

The other islands of the archipelago were proclaimed a French protectorate in 1886; only Mahore, called Mayotte by the French, continued as a separate French colony. The powerful Roman Catholic minority on Mahore firmly opposed French moves to integrate Mahore into the Comoro Islands protectorate. In 1912, the other Comoran islands were made dependencies of Mahore, but in 1914 the entire chain of islands was made a dependency of the French colony of Madagascar.

Mahore, dominated by French planters and the Christian Mahoris, prospered under colonial rule, further widening the rift between it and the other islands of the group. During World War II, a basic naval-military facility was built on Mahore by the British, augmenting an important base of the French Foreign Legion. Wartime activity brought even more prosperity to the Mahoris, who found work on the bases and in related activities.

The French government in 1947 joined Mahore to the other islands to form the French Overseas Territory of the Comoro Islands. The colonial authorities began to allow a degree of local rule in the islands in 1958, but the Christian Mahoris, aided by the important Creole planters, opposed Muslim domination of the local Comoran government and demanded separation. The islands were granted self-government in 1960 under an autonomous government. Mahore was relegated to a dependent role when the capital of the archipelago was transferred to the largest of the islands, Grand Comoro.

The loss of power was greatly resented by the more prosperous Mahoris. Their island, fertile and underpopulated, was chosen to receive excess population from the other, more densely populated islands. In 1966 the Mahoris formed the Mahorais People's Party (PPM) to fight inclusion in the proposed independent Comoran state. The Mahoris' refusal to be ruled by Grand Comoro delayed their independence for a number of years.

In 1974, in an effort to end the dispute, the French government decided to allow each of the four islands of the group to decide its own fate. On 8 February 1974 99% of the Mahoris voted to retain their ties to France. The French legislature voted in June 1975 to postpone Comoran independence for six months to allow for a second referendum. The Comoran government responded by unilaterally declaring independence on 6 July 1975, claiming all of the Comoros, including Mahore. The French government reacted by ending all financial aid, which represented over 40% of the Comoran national budget.

After independence, the politically unstable Comoros underwent a brutal reign of terror, which French-protected Mahore escaped. The new Comoran government, in an attempt to unite the Comoran population, reiterated its claim to the island, with the support of the United Nations and the Organization of African Unity (OAU). When the French reiterated their determination to respect the results of the 1974 vote, Comoran military forces attempted to invade Mahore, only to be repulsed by French Legionnaires.

The Mahorais People's Party, led by Marcel Henry, became the dominant political organization. The islanders, solidly pro-French, repeatedly rejected overtures from the Comoran government. The new Comoran government accused Henry of fabricating Mahoran "uniqueness" to perpetuate Mahore's Creole, non-Muslim elite.

The United Nations admitted the Comoro Islands on 12 November 1975. At the same time, the world body recognized the Comoran claim to Mahore. The French government held a second plebiscite on 11 April 1976. The Mahoris again voted, by an 80% majority, to remain a French territory. In December 1976 the island was made a "territorial collectivity," construed as something between an overseas territory and an overseas department. The island's name was officially changed from Mayotte to the local name, Mahore. Some 2,000 settlers from the other Comoran islands were expelled following violent pro-Comoran agitation.

The United Nations reaffirmed the Comoran claim to Mahore in 1979 amid widespread demands by African and other governments for the decolonization of the island. The French authorities refused to relinquish the island unless the majority of the Mahoris approved. In unofficial polls during the 1980s, the majority of the Mahoris remained stubbornly pro-French; most favored full departmental status for the island, which would give the Mahoris the same rights as the continental French departments. In late 1984, the Mahoris again voted overwhelmingly to remain associated with France. Departmental status, scheduled for 1985, had to be postponed indefinitely due to continuing Comoran and UN objections.

The French government heavily subsidized the Mahorian economy, and through its association with France, the island became much more prosperous than the Comoros under an unstable independent government. The dispute created a modest Mahorian national movement, pro-French and anti-Comoran. The nationalists stated in 1992 that the Mahoris would prefer separate independence rather than inclusion in the Comoros, should the French leave the region. In 1992–93, Mahori paramilitary groups attacked Comoran immigrants to the island.

The French presence in Mahore has caused friction between France and many African states, as the OAU condemns the continuing French authority as colonialist and illegal. Many Africans believe that the preference of Mahoris for French association is a fabrication by France as a pretext to hold the only deep-water port in the Comoros.

In 1997, the Anjouanis of the neighboring Comoran islands attempted to separate from Grand Comoro, adding to the instability in the islands. The islanders of Anjouan and Moheli, where unemployment is over 90% and gross domestic product hovers around $30 per head, were drawn by the Mahoris' free education and health care, guaranteed monthly wage of $400, and French citizenship. The separatist leaders requested a return of French rule, which was rejected by the French government.

In a bid to rekindle Comoran nationalism, the Comoran government again demanded the return of Mahore. The French government would be pleased to leave the costly relic of its former empire, but its promise to the Mahoris remains in force. Attempts by destitute Anjouanis and Mohelians to cross the shark-infested waters to Mahore have been steadily rising since the early 1990s, although their presence has become a nationalist issue on the island.

The French have upgraded education, built roads, and improved food production, while the Comoros have sunk deeper in crisis and chaos. The Comoros have been in nearly constant political upheaval since independence in 1975 and hold little attraction for the Mahoris. Every year the UN passes with near unanimity a resolution calling on France to relinquish Mahore to the Comoros, and the OAU issues annual condemnations.

SELECTED BIBLIOGRAPHY:

Fasquel, Jean. *Mayotte: The Comoros and France.* 1991.

Fontaine, Guy. *Mayotte.* 1995.

Lambeck, Michael. *Knowledge and Practice in Mayotte: Local Discourses of Islam, Sorcery, and Spirit Possession.* 1993.

Mahamoud, Ahmed Wadaane. *Mayotte: The Conflict between France and the Comoros.* 1999.

Majerteens

Majeerteens; Puntlanders

POPULATION: Approximately (2002e) 1,394,000 Majerteens in Somalia, concentrated in the self-proclaimed state of Puntland in the northeast on the Atlantic Ocean and the Gulf of Aden. Outside the region, there are Majerteen communities in Yemen, Saudi Arabia, and in western Europe.

THE MAJERTEEN HOMELAND: The Majerteen homeland lies in northeastern Somalia, a hilly, semi-desert region with some fertile lands in the coastal lowlands on the Atlantic Ocean and the Gulf of Aden to the north. The homeland comprises the Somali provinces of Bari, Nugaal, and Mudug. The region was declared the autonomous state of Puntland in 1998. *Puntland*: 41,568 sq. mi.—107,660 sq. km, (2002e) 1,593,000—Majerteens 86%, Warsangeli 8%, Dulbahante 6%, other Somalis. The Majerteen capital and major cultural center is Garowe (2002e) 19,000. The other important centers are Galkayo, (2002e) 42,000, which is being rebuilt after being fought over, and is the only town in Somalia to have streetlights. The other important center is Bosaso, called Boosaaso locally, (2002e) 53,000.

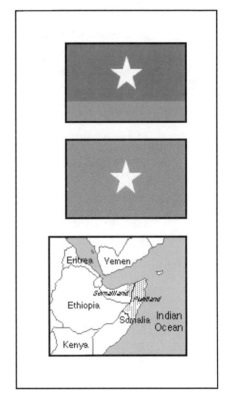

FLAG: The Majerteen national flag, the flag of the clan movement, is a pale blue field bearing a green stripe at the bottom and a small white five-pointed star centered. The official flag of Puntland is temporarily the flag of Somalia, a pale blue field bearing a centered five-pointed white star.

PEOPLE AND CULTURE: The Majerteens are a distinct division of the Harti group of the Darood clan that stretches south to the Kenyan border and is one of the six major clans of Somalia. The Majerteens, the dominant clan in the northeast of Somalia, is further subdivided into subclans, the Osman Mahmood, Issa Mahmood, Omar Mahmood, Ali Suleiman, and the smaller Sikwakroon and Ali Jibril. The Warsangali and Dulbahante clans are distinct, although related, Darood clans. The Majerteens, unlike the southern Somali clans, retain their traditional structures, which have been used to set up the Puntland government based on the consent of the leaders of the clan and its subclans. The Majerteens are known as self-reliant and tough, with a strong sense of clan identity.

LANGUAGE AND RELIGION: The Majerteens speak the northeastern dialects of Somali, an East Cushitic language of the Afro-Asiatic groups of languages. The dialects, commonly referred to as Northern Common Somali, show considerable Arabic influence, particularly the dialects spoken in the port cities. Arabic, the lingua franca of the region, is widely spoken as a second language and is the language of trade and religion.

The Majerteens are overwhelmingly Sunni Muslims, belonging to the orthodox branch of Islam that is predominant in the nearby Arabian Peninsula and around the Gulf of Aden. The religion, which has incorporated many pre-Islamic traditions, particularly having to do with the seasons and livestock, is less restrictive than in many Muslim cultures. The veneration of local saints is widespread, with many of the saints associated with the pre-Islamic culture of the region.

NATIONAL HISTORY: The region probably formed part of the land of Punt mentioned in the chronicles of ancient Egypt. To the ancients, Punt was a place of legend and fable, known through Herodotus' historical account of the exploits of Egyptian pharaoh Sesostris, who took a fleet of ships and made conquests along the shores of the Erythraean Sea (the Red Sea). Voyages to Punt eventually became routine and many expeditions were undertaken by Egyptian rulers between 2200 to 1450 B.C. The trade routes to Punt were opened to the Greeks after Alexander the Great conquered Egypt in the fourth century B.C.

Between the seventh and twelfth centuries A.D., Muslim traders from the nearby Arabian Peninsula and Iran settled on the coast founding cities along the gulf of Aden. They carried on a lucrative trade in slaves, precious gums, and ostrich feathers. The Muslims organized themselves in small sultanates and often warred with the Christian kingdoms of the Ethiopian highlands.

The nomadic Somali clans occupied the region between the tenth and fifteenth centuries. The clans adopted Islam and served in the armies of the Muslim sultanates. Gradually, the sultanates came under Somali control, increasing ties to the states of the Arabian Peninsula across the narrow Red Sea.

British explorers were the first Europeans to visit the region in the 1820s. In the nineteenth century, several European colonial powers gained influence among the various Somali clans. In the 1880s, the Italians declared a protectorate over Somalia with the objective of safeguarding trade links and to exclude other Europeans interested in the region. In 1897, Ethiopia, France, Italy, and Britain signed a series of treaties dividing the

Somali clans into four separate colonial territories. Italian rule was finally extended to the northeast during the 1920s.

During World War II, the British defeated the Italians and took control of Italian Somaliland. The Italians renounced their claim to Somalia in 1947, but in 1950 returned as the administrating country of a United Nations Trust Territory, which was to lead to independence in 10 years.

In 1960, British and Italian Somaliland were united to form the independent Republic of Somalia. The Somalis are racially, religiously, linguistically, and culturally homogeneous, but clan loyalty overrides all other national sentiments and Somali society remained divided along clan lines. The clans in the country lived in relative peace for nine years after independence.

In 1969, the Somali president, a member of a southern Darood clan, was assassinated by a disgruntled Majerteen soldier. Amid the confusion following the assassination, General Mohamed Siad Barre staged a bloodless coup on 21 October 1969 and gained control of the country. Barre ruled Somalia by playing one clan against another, and was able to hold off any real threat to his administration until the late 1970s when he waged war on neighboring Ethiopia over control of the Ogaden region of the Western Somalis.* Barre's troops invaded in 1977 and quickly overran 90% of the Ogaden. The Ethiopian government appealed to the Soviet Union for help, which was quickly granted. The Somalis were driven back by Ethiopian, Cuban, and Soviet military units and were finally defeated in 1978. The defeat greatly weakened the Barre dictatorship.

The Majerteens were the first to revolt against Siad Barre's dictatorship in 1978, led by the Somali Salvation Democratic Front (SSDF). The Majerteens, along with the Hawiye and Isaaks,* were among the most effective opposition to the Siad Barre dictatorship. They were also the principal targets of repression. Barre's troops retaliated by killing large numbers of civilians in the region. In 1986, the town of Bosaso had only 10,000 inhabitants, but as violence spread across Somalia Majerteens living in Mogadishu and other areas fled back to their homeland in the northeast. Most settled around the port of Bosaso, which provided contact with the outside world and a market for their herds. Bosaso became the only large city in Somalia that did not experience widespread violence in the 1990s.

Somalia ceased to exist as a country, with some areas and clans reverting to local rule while others, particularly in the south, were sinking into seemingly unending violence. The differences between the region reinforced the clan divisions and stimulated local regionalist and nationalist movements. The Majerteens joined with several clan-based groups in the north and south to finally drive Barre from power in January 1991. The northeastern provinces, mostly populated by Majerteens, began to distance themselves from central and southern Somalia, where clan militias fought a vicious civil war.

In the spring of 1991, clan militias of the Hawiye clan of central Somalia invaded the region. Since the local militia, the SSDF, was weak, it abdicated power to the Committee of Elders, which was temporarily put in charge of defending the region. A particular division of power developed, the administrative network paralleled by a *maamul guddi* or traditional administration of clan elders. The joint administration allowed the clan leaders to control the younger, better educated but less prudent members of the clan and prevented conflicts between the Majerteen subclans. In the absence of a centralized administration, taxes were collected by the clan authorities, which the leaders used for maintenance, rehabilitation, or development purposes.

Many Majerteen clan leaders clamored to follow the neighboring Isaaks in secession from the disintegrated Somali state, but clan elders, fearing violence among the subclans, refused to support separatism, but gave their consent to the creation of regional administrative bodies. The decision to cut ties to the south saved the region from the anarchy and clan fighting in that area during the 1990s. Neighboring Ethiopia sent special envoys to the region and a close relationship was established between the two governments.

The last United Nations peacekeeping troops finally pulled out of Somalia in 1995, having failed to end the violence between the many clan militias. Somalia remained divided into numerous fiefs ruled by local warlords. Any attempt to rebuild Somalia was seen internationally as a waste of time and money so long as the warlords retained their power over the clans. The withdrawal of the UN left behind a patchwork of warlords who cared little for the welfare of their respective clans. Later UN efforts to bring together clan leaders in a power-sharing arrangement also failed.

The leader of the Majerteens, Abdullahi Yusuf Ahmad, was chosen head of the new state called Punt or Puntland after the ancient state that controlled the region. In 1993, the Puntland government issued a statement supporting the agreement of various Somali factions to make peace in the country, but reiterated that Puntland will only rejoin Somalia when a democratic, federal state is established. The Puntland administration was accepted as the legitimate authority in the region at conferences in Egypt in 1996–97. In July 1998, Ahmad declared the autonomy of Puntland, pending an overall peace agreement in Somalia.

The Majerteens, rather than to follow the Isaaks into secession and unrecognized independence, have refrained from any of the symbolic trappings of independence while quietly separating their homeland from the remains of Somalia. In early 2000, a serious confrontation broke out between the Majerteens and the Isaaks of neighboring Somaliland over territory in the Sool and Sanaag regions, which is claimed by both states. Majerteen forces moved into the disputed area. Abdullahi Yusuf Ahmad claimed that Sool and Sanaag are required to be part of Puntland on the grounds of clan affiliation, but the Somaliland government threatened to fight to protect the borders of their breakaway state. In late 1999, troops from the two states clashed in Sool, bringing fears that the chaos and violence of the rest of Somalia could extend to Somaliland and Puntland.

The Majerteen leaders of Puntland have repeatedly stated that they are not advocating secession, which has prompted poor relations with the neighboring Isaaks of the secessionist Somaliland to the west. With the widespread support of the Majerteens, the Puntland government has tried to establish its credentials as an autonomous, responsible administration within Somalia. The clan leaders have proposed a plan for a federal Somali state, with broad regional autonomy for each of the clan territories. In ten years with little outside assistance, the Majerteens have become self-reliant and tough, living as do the average Tanzanians and Zambians.

A severe drought in mid-1999 wiped out half the cattle herds, the major economic asset of the Majerteens. No rain fell in the region since October 1998 and the authorities were forced to declare a state of emergency. The serious threat of famine was met by clan resources and reinforced militants who are pushing for complete separation from Somalia.

In August 2000, after complicated negotiations in Djibouti, the leaders of the southern Somali clans put together a peace plan, but the Majerteens, like the neighboring Isaaks, refused to participate. On 27 August 2000, a new Somali president was inaugurated in Mogadishu. The Majerteen leaders, relishing the relative stability of their homeland, rejected the peace process due to the fact that not all Somali clans and factions were represented.

In a bitter conflict that involved rivalries between Majerteen subclans, Abdullahi Yousuf Ahmed was ousted as head of state and was replaced by Yousuf Haji Nur in late 2000. The clan rivalry threatened to repeat the disintegration that has overtaken most of the rest of Somalia.

In August 2001, 500 clan elders met to elect a parliament as the region sees little hope of a reunited Somalia. The parliament will then elect a new leader for the republic. The creation of the functions of an independent state are seen by many Majerteens as a confirmation that Somalia may never be reunited. Despite reiterating their position that they are not secessionist, the Majerteen leadership increasingly ignore the rest of Somalia.

The majority of the Majerteens support the reunification of Somalia, but with a central government responsible for such institutions as a central bank, roads, defense, and international affairs, leaving the six or seven regions that currently exist to govern themselves. A loose confederation of independent states would suit the Somali social structure and mirror traditional Somali administrative structures.

Following the terrorist attacks on the United States in September 2001, the relationship between the Puntland government and organizations named as having ties to terrorist groups were questioned. In October the "acting president," Yusuf Haji Nur, denied reports that there are camps run by suspect organizations in Puntland.

SELECTED BIBLIOGRAPHY:

Farah, Nuruddin. *Yesterday, Tomorrow: Voices from the Somali Diaspora.* 2000.
Kelly, Robert C., ed. *Somalia Country Report 1998/1999.* 2000.
Lewis, Ioan M. *Blood and Bone: The Call of Kinship in Somali Society.* 1994.
Ricciuti, Edward. *Somalia: A Crisis of Famine and War.* 1999.

Malaitans
Malans; Malaita Islanders; Kwaio

POPULATION: Approximately (2002e) 180,000 Malaitans in the Solomon Islands, concentrated in Malaita province, the islands of Malaita and Maramasike. Immigrant Malaitans have settled on the more fertile islands of the Solomon Islands, particularly nearby Guadalcanal.

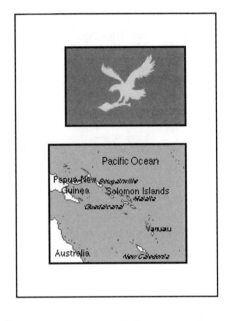

THE MALAITAN HOMELAND: The Malaitan homeland lies in the southwestern Pacific Ocean in the Coral Sea east of the large island of New Guinea. Malaita is a volcanic, tropical island lying 30 miles (50 km) northeast of the central island of the Solomons, Guadalcanal, across Indispensable Strait. The island is about 115 miles (185 km) long and 22 miles (35 km) at its widest point. The island is mountainous and covered in dense forests. It is separated from Maramasike Island at its southeastern end by a narrow channel. Malaita and Maramasike form a province of the Republic of the Solomon Islands. *Province of Malaita*: 1,870 sq. mi.—4,843 sq. km, (2002e) 118,000—Malaitans 92%, Polynesians 2%, other Solomon Islanders 6%. The Malaitan capital and major cultural center is Auki, (2002e) 5,000.

FLAG: The Malaitan national flag, the official flag of the island, is an orange field bearing a centered yellow eagle holding a curved Malaitan sword.

PEOPLE AND CULTURE: The Malaitans are a Melanesian people, part of the large Melanesian group in the southwestern Pacific. Traditionally the Malaitans were divided into numerous small clans headed by local chiefs later called "Big Men." The Malaitans are often identified with the Kwaio, the major group in the central part of the island. Their leadership is based on status achieved through material success or prowess in warfare. Warfare and feuding were endemic in precolonial Malaita, although the importance of warriors has waned or been eclipsed by leaders in competitive feasting and other exchanges. In many areas local groups are not concentrated in villages, but are dispersed through territories in scattered homesteads. Some villages are large and are packed together on coral platforms in the lagoons of northern Malaita. Residential separation of the sexes was traditional, but this practice has begun to break down. Men's clubhouses, a focus of ritual and military solidarity, were formerly common throughout the area.

LANGUAGE AND RELIGION: The Malaitans speak several closely related dialects of the Malaita–San Cristobal group of Solomonic languages of the Austronesian language group spoken throughout the Melanesia region of the South Pacific. There are 11 Malaitan dialects and a number of subdialects. Other dialects, such as Longgu, are spoken by Malaitan early immigrants on the east coast of Guadalcanal and are no longer intelligible to speakers of the modern Malaitan dialects. The largest are Kwaio, Are'are, Kwara'ae, Lau, and To'abaita. Pijin, an English-based pidgin, is widely used as a second language. The basic vocabulary is closer to standard English, but the grammar shows Melanesian features. Pronunciation varies according to local languages. There have been recent efforts to standardize the language. English is spoken by a small elite, mostly educated in church-operated schools.

Officially 95% of the Malaitans are Christian, mostly Protestant, although many pre-Christian traditions and customs have survived. Deaths were often attributed to sorcery, and accusations of sorcery commonly triggered vengeance murders.

NATIONAL HISTORY: The Solomon Islands were initially settled by at least 2000 B.C. The first settlers were probably peoples of the Austronesian language group. The settlers colonized the fertile coastal strip and established small, territorial clan groups.

Leaders of local clans characteristically emerged on the basis of success in prestige economy and warfare. Many became hereditary chiefs, who ruled the islanders at the time for the first European visits. The chiefly succession to leadership was based on a complex relationship between hereditary rights and demonstrated ability. Large-scale armed confrontations between rival groups of warriors were marked by pageantry and ritual posturing and few lives were lost. Traditionally territory was neither gained nor lost. Large-scale combat was rare, but blood feuds were endemic. Raiders from Malaita often raided neighboring islands, most often nearby Guadalcanal.

The first European to reach the island was the Spanish explorer Alvaro de Mendaña in 1568. Unjustified rumors led to the belief that he had not only found gold but had found where biblical King Solomon had obtained gold for his famed temple in Jerusalem. The islands were named the Islas de Solomón. Later Spanish expeditions, in 1595 and 1606, were unable to confirm the discoveries reported by Mendaña. Initial attempts to colonize the islands failed and the islands were not visited again for nearly 200 years.

French, German, Dutch, and British explorers later visited the islands. They charted and explored the islands but made little effort to colonize. After the British settlement was established at Sydney in 1788, British naval and commercial shipping increasingly passed though the waters around the islands.

In the mid-nineteenth century, Christian missionaries from Australia, the United States, and the United Kingdom established mission stations on the island. Anglican missionaries began working with the Malaitans in the 1850s. A number of mission stations had been established by the 1870s. A Roman Catholic mission failed in the 1840s, but a Catholic mission was established in 1898. Church-funded and -operated schools began to provide basic formal education to small groups of islanders, mostly the sons of local chiefs. The educated elite, in the late nineteenth century, became the leaders of the island.

The development of sugar plantations in northern Australia and Fiji in the mid-nineteenth century led to a sometimes brutal recruitment of Melanesians taken from the islands. The raiders, called Black Birders, raided the narrow coastal strip where the majority of the islanders lived. Thousands were rounded up and put aboard ships to be sold to colonial planters. The raids provoked reprisals by the islanders, who often attacked European visitors.

To protect their colonial interests, Germany and Britain divided the Solomons between them in 1886, with Malaita included in the British zone. In 1893, the British established a protectorate in the eastern Solomon Islands. German claims to the northern Solomons, except Bougainville and Buka, were transferred to the United Kingdom in 1898–99 in return for British recognition of German claims in Western Samoa. The British colonial authorities mostly left the islands to live in their traditional manner under local chiefs but attempted to provide protection against Black Birder raids.

British rule in Malaita was generally humane, but the colonial authorities were more concerned with promoting the interests of European traders and planters than those of the indigenous Malaitans. The islanders were harshly punished for offensives against colonial law and order.

Anti-colonial feeling began to grow in the early 1920s. The murder of government tax collectors on Malaita in 1927 prompted a savage punitive expedition, which was supported by an Australian warship. The leader of the attackers, Basiana, was later hanged and his young children were forced to witness the execution. The event, still recalled by the Malaitans, has become part of their national myth and Basiana is now revered as a national hero.

The British evacuated the islands shortly before the Japanese invaded during World War II. The Japanese troops took control of Malaita and the other islands in 1942, but were opposed by an invasion of Allied troops.

1153

The Allies, mostly American troops, fought the Japanese for control of the islands over the next three years. Fighting was particularly severe on nearby Guadalcanal. The Allied troops were strongly supported by the islanders.

British rule was restored at the end of the war, but already nationalist stirrings were evident. Ethnic identity tended to be local, with the people of each island forming a distinct national group. The ethnic dispute between the peoples of the two major islands of the archipelago began at the end of the war and remained a simmering crisis.

A strongly anti-colonial movement known as Marching Rule united the Malaitans and aimed to dominate local government. An agreement in the 1950s between the colonial government and the leaders led to the creation of an organized local Malaitan council for the first time.

A united nationalist movement obtained support throughout the archipelago in the 1950s. The British authorities granted a new Solomon Islands constitution that provided a council with some local representation. The protectorate was granted internal self-government in 1975, and full independence in 1978.

The ethnic rivalry between the inhabitants of the two largest ethnic groups in the islands erupted in violence in the early 1990s, often over the question of land. The Malaitans, lacking agricultural land on their island, have been settling on the major island of the group, Guadalcanal, since the 1970s. The land issue prompted the growth of nationalism among the Malaitans, who saw their group as disadvantaged. Conflicts on Guadalcanal, where many Malaitans had settled over many decades, became a serious problem in the 1980s.

In the mid-1990s, militant Isatabus, the indigenous peoples of Guadalcanal, began attacking Malaitan settlements on the north coast of the island. The Isatabus claim that the immigrant Malaitans take their jobs and land. By 1998, violent attacks eventually drove over 20,000 Malaitans to flee their homes and return to their homeland on Malaita. Over 60 Malaitans died in the violence. The influx of refugees from Guadalcanal stretched the limited resources of the Malaitans and raised ethnic tensions across the archipelago. Malaitans in other parts of the country, particularly in Western province, also came under attack.

Bartholomew Ulufa'alu, an ethnic Malaitan, after the 1997 general elections, was chosen prime minister by the legislature. Ulufa'alu attempted to mediate in the growing ethnic confrontation between the Malaitans and the inhabitants of Guadalcanal. The prospects of increased prosperity from a new gold mine on Guadalcanal fueled the dispute. The Malaitans, whose island has less agricultural land available than is needed by the fast growing population, claimed that neglect and poverty were due to development on Guadalcanal.

In early 1999, the islanders of Guadalcanal, the Isatabus, particularly the militants of the Isatabu Freedom Movement, began trying to drive the remaining ethnic Malaitan settlers out of Guadalcanal, the Solomons' main island. They were opposed by the Malaitan national organization, the Malaita Eagle Force led by Andrew Nori. Foreign diplomats attempted to intercede in the escalating violence, but without success. The Malaitans raided police stations and an armory. The stolen arms gave them an advantage over the lightly armed Isatabus.

On 5 June 2000, the Malaitans of Guadalcanal, after eighteen months of ethnic fighting, took control of the Solomons capital, Honiara. The rebels seized Prime Minister Bartholomew Ulufa'alu, placed him under house arrest and demanded his resignation. The people of Guadalcanal, led by the IFM, continued to fight the Malaitans on the island, often forcing settlers from Malaita to flee back to their home island. The Malaitans declared "all-out" war against the Isatabus, but after several days they released the prime minister. The prime minister is an ethnic Malaitan, but nationalists accuse him of being a turncoat.

The fighting around the Solomons' capital left at least 50 dead, hundreds injured, and more than hundreds of refugees forced from their homes. Hundreds of foreign residents were evacuated by the Australian and New Zealander warships. On 15 June 2000, Prime Minister Ulufa'alu resigned in an effort to end the crisis as the system of law and order in the islands collapsed.

Diplomats from Australia and New Zealand flew to Honiara in an attempt to end the violence and to help end the crisis. Peace talks began between the warring Malaitans and Isatabus. The diplomats met with the Solomons' new prime minister and rebel leader, Andrew Nori, but a temporary cease-fire was all the Malaitans would allow. The premier of Malaita, David Oeta, urged the Malaitans not to embrace secession, but to negotiate an end to the crisis.

The ongoing conflict has seriously divided the Solomon Islands. The Solomon Islands government reported having ties to the nationalist Bougainvillans* in neighboring Papua New Guinea territory. Armed groups, reportedly with ties to the Bougainville secessionist movement, became active in the western islands of Gizo and Choiseul, where fighting spread between Malaitans and migrants from Bougainville. Mercenaries from Bougainville were brought in to intimidate settlers from Malaita. They announced that their mission was to expel Malaitans from the western province.

In late June, the Solomon Islands legislature elected a new prime minister to replace Bartholomew Ulufa'alu in an effort to end the ethnic fighting. The new prime minister, the opposition leader Manasseh Sogavare, pledged to promote national unity and reconciliation. The Malaitans accepted the new government's offer of negotiations as the former prime minister was considered a traitor to the Malaitan cause. The Malaitan rebels threatened to declare war if the crisis was not resolved to their satisfaction.

The Malaitans and Isatabus signed a cease-fire agreement in Honiara on 2 August 2000. Both sides agreed to lay down their arms and begin formal peace talks. They agreed to allow an unarmed police force to begin re-establishing law and order. International monitors were invited to oversee the cease-fire. The government promised to appoint a new police commissioner to help restore Malaitan faith in the police, most of whom had sided with the Isatabus.

On 8 August 2000, a Malaitan of the MEF was shot by a sniper in a contested area near Honiara. The outraged Malaitans threatened to terminate the cease-fire agreement. The cease-fire was further threatened by ongoing territorial disputes. The Malaitans hold territory on Guadalcanal around Honiara, mostly areas populated over many decades by immigrants from their home island. The ethnic fighting is the most serious unrest the Solomon Islands have experienced in over twenty years of independence.

The Malaitans remain divided among those who seek to remain in the Solomon Islands, but in a position equal to the Isatabus, and nationalist groups seeking to separate Malaita and other dissatisfied islands, particularly the ethnically and linguistically related island of San Cristobal, from the republic. In October 2000, a meeting of the two warring groups was held in Townsville, Australia. Malaitan nationalists threatened secession and civil war if the talks failed.

A peace settlement, signed in October 2001, allowing the election of a new national government of the Solomon Islands. The elections, held in December 2001, were peaceful, although Malaitans warned that should their interests again be contravened, the integrity of the island state would be in serious jeopardy.

SELECTED BIBLIOGRAPHY:

Alasia, Sam, and Hugh Laracy. *Ples Blong Iumi: Solomon Islands, the Past Four Thousand Years.* 1989.

Ewing, Debra, ed. *Solomon Islands Country Review 1999/2000.* 1999.

Hogbin, Herbert Ian. *Experiments in Civilization: The Effects of European Culture on a Native Community of the Solomon Islands.* 1991.

Keesing, Roger M. *Custom and Confrontation: The Kwaio Struggle for Cultural Autonomy.* 1992.

Malayalis

Keralans; Cherans; Alealums; Malayalees; Malayalanis; Maleans; Maliyads; Mallealle

POPULATION: Approximately (2002e) 34,620,000 Malayalis in India, concentrated in the southwestern state of Kerala, with smaller communities in neighboring states, the United Arab Emirates, Malaysia, Singapore, the United Kingdom, and Fiji.

THE MALAYALI HOMELAND: The Malayali homeland lies in southwestern India, occupying a tropical coastal plain on the Arabian Sea rising to the rocky highlands of the Cardamon Hills and the Western Ghats in the interior. A chain of lagoons, lakes, and backwaters along the coast form the so-called Venice of India. Kerala is the most densely populated state in India, although only about 20% of the population is urban. *State of Kerala*: 15,003 sq. mi.—38,857 sq. km, (2002e) 32,112,000—Malayalis 84%, Tamils 12%, Hindis 3%, other Indians 1%. The Malayali capital and major cultural center is Trivandrum, called Thiruvananthapuram in Malayalam, (2002e) 645,000, metropolitan area 1,045,000. The other important cultural centers are Cochin, called Kochi by the Malayalis, (2002e) 659,000, metropolitan area 1,434,000, and Kozhikode, formerly Calicut, (2002e) 490,000, metropolitan area 991,000, and the urban area of Tellicherry (Thalassery in Malayalam), (2002e) 139,000, and Cannanore (Kannur), (2002e) 88,000, metropolitan area 1,010,000.

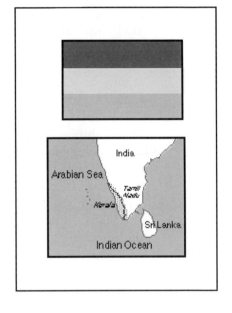

FLAG: The Malayali national flag, the traditional flag of the state of Travancore, is a horizontal tricolor of red, yellow, and turquoise.

PEOPLE AND CULTURE: The Malayalis are a Dravidian people, the descendants of peoples driven into southern India by the ancient Aryan invasions of northern India, with some Aryan admixture. Malayali society embraces four major divisions, high-caste Hindu Nairs and low-caste Hindu Ezhavas, the Christians (further divided among several sects), and the Moplahs, Muslim Malayalis of mixed Dravidian and Arab background. There is also a small, ancient Jewish community. All Malayali groups encompass castes and subcastes, including the Christian and Jewish communities. The culture heritage contains elements of ancient Hindu culture that have been enriched by long contact with maritime peoples from both Europe and Asia. Women enjoy high social status and participate in all facets of life. The Ezhava caste, constituting about a quarter of the total population, were up to the turn of the century a despised people, not to be touched or even seen by upper-caste Hindus. Ezhava men and women were forced to go bare chested so that upper-caste passers-by could recognize them quickly, avoid looking at them, and avoid being spiritually polluted. The Ezhavas have climbed the caste ladder to merely officially "backward" and have prospered economically. Many Ezhavas have also embraced Islam or Christianity to escape the harsh caste system.

LANGUAGE AND RELIGION: The Malayalis speak Malayalam, belonging to the Tamil-Malayalam branch of the Dravidian language of southern India. The Malayali language, with its own script, is based on Old Tamil, from which it separated in the tenth century to develop as a separate literary language in the eleventh century. The language is spoken in three regional subgroups, North, Central, and South, divided into eleven dialects and many subdialects, based on caste and communal group. The rate of literacy is substantially higher than the national average; about 80% of the population are able to read and write the Malayalam language. The Malayalis have one of the most advanced educational systems in India. English is widely used as a second language. In 1889 Chandu Menon wrote *Indulekha*, the first notable novel in Malayalam, setting the tone for broad modern use of the language.

Kerala, only about half Hindu, has the largest Christian population, about 30% of the society, and one of the largest Muslim populations in India, about 20%, with small Jewish and Jain populations. The plurality of the Malayali population are Hindus, belonging to the Vaisnava or Vishnuite (Saivite) branch, with traditions and ceremonies very different from the Brahmanism of northern India. The region contains many Vaisnava shrines and pilgrimage centers. The Malayalis have a unique record in India of harmonious coexistence of diverse religions. Kerala's impressive display of Hindu temples with typical copper roofs, later Muslim mosques with "Malabar gables" (triangular projections at the rooftops), Jain temples, and colonial and modern churches attest to religious tolerance and interweaving. The Christian denominations include Roman Catholics, 1.8 million; Syrio-Malabar Catholics, 3.3 million; Syrian Orthodox (Methran Kakshi), 550,000; Jacobite Syrian Orthodox (Bava Kakshi), 1.2 million; Independent Jacobites (Thozhiyur), 10,000; Marthomites, 500,000; St. Thomas Evangelicals (Mar Thoma), 500,000; Nestorians and Surais, 110,000; and various Protestant sects, including Church of South India, 750,000.

NATIONAL HISTORY: Dravidian peoples, pushed south by the Aryan invasions of northern India between 1500 and 1200 B.C., established a number of small, independent states in the coastal plain along the Indian Ocean. Hindu culture, replacing the earlier Buddhism by 200 B.C., helped to unite the region's peoples. Kerala was first mentioned as the region of Keralaputra in a rock inscription of the third century B.C. Indo-European immigrants from northern India introduced Hinduism during this period. A powerful maritime kingdom, called Kerala and later Chera, emerged in the early Christian era as the region's dominant power.

Greeks and Romans knew of the region and its spices, especially pepper. Kerala's trade ties, extending as far west as the Roman provinces of Arabia, brought new cultural and religious traditions. By the first century A.D., Malayali development had begun to diverge from the uniform Hindu Dravidian culture of south India. By tradition, St. Thomas brought Christianity to the kingdom, in the first century A.D. The first Jewish refugees established themselves in the kingdom in 69 A.D., and a Syrian Orthodox Christian community had settled in Kerala by 325.

Literature and learning, in both Tamil and Sanskrit, flourished in the region from the second century A.D. Conquered by the Tamils in the fourth century, the Malayalis developed an intense hatred, which remains to the present, of the Tamil conquerors, who are related to them. The Malayalam language, a dialect of ancient Tamil, began to diverge in the tenth century. The language, like the culture, absorbed influences from the many maritime peoples to visit the Malayali ports, particularly the Arabs, who settled the Malabar Coast, bringing with them their Islamic religion. Under the Kulashekhara dynasty, between the ninth and twelfth centuries Malayalam emerged as a distinct language, and the Hindu religion became the predominant belief system of the region.

The region divided into a number of petty states before the first European, the Portuguese explorer Vasco de Gama, rounded the Cape of Good Hope and reached the Malabar Coast in 1498. The Europeans recorded their amazement to find native Christians whose existence was unknown in Europe. Jewish refugees, expelled from Portugal in 1496, used the new sea routes to join the region's ancient Jewish community, where they were tolerated and generally flourished. Pedro Álvares Cabral founded the first European settlement on Indian soil at Cochin in 1500. Vasco de Gama established a "factory" (a trading station), at Cochin two years later, and in 1503 the Portuguese viceroy Alfonso de Albuquerque built the first European fort in India in the town. In 1510 the Portuguese built the first European church in India, to serve the growing number of traders, although the native Christians already had an organized hierarchy. The Syriac Christians, "lost" to Rome for centuries, established new ties to the Vatican in 1599.

English, Dutch, French, and Danish expeditions followed the Portuguese, and an intense European rivalry developed for control of the lucrative Indian trade. The Europeans introduced diseases to which the local population had no immunity. In 1616 the Black Plague ravaged the population.

In 1635, the English established a trading post at Cochin and later another at Calicut. The Dutch took control of the important Portuguese port at Cochin in 1663, expelling both the English and the Portuguese. The Dutch made alliances with the Muslim Moplahs, who controlled most of the spice trade, and converted Cochin into a major center of the important spice trade, shipping pepper, cardamom, and other spices to Europe. The Dutch expansion was ended by their defeat by Maharaja Marthanda Varma of Travancore in 1741.

The descendants of the ancient Chera kings united the southern Malayali states in the early 1700s. Two other Malayali states, Travancore and Cochin, with close dynastic ties, established a military and political alliance in 1757. The northern part of the Malayali homeland, called the Carnatic, remained outside their political control. The British defeated the remaining Dutch in 1759, and after an intense rivalry, defeated the French in 1763. Cochin and Travancore established separate treaty relations with Great Britain in 1795. By 1806 Cochin and Travancore, as well as Malabar to the north, had become subject territories under the authority of the British Madras presidency. In 1814, the Dutch formally ceded their interests in the region to the United Kingdom.

In the mid-nineteenth century, Christian missionaries became active in the region, gaining many converts, often among the already Christian population. The number of Christian sects proliferated, bringing rivalries and at times violence. By the 1880s Christian missionaries had established a network of educational and medical institutions, giving the Malayalis a tradition of literacy and good health care that still exists in Kerala State.

Staunch British allies, the two Malayali states provided troops to Britain's colonial army. In return British troops supported the states' Hindu rulers by suppressing a Moplah Muslim uprising in 1921, and by limiting the ethnic and religious disturbances and the communist agitation that plagued the states in the 1930s. Sporadic clashes between Hindus and Muslims continued up to World War II. Indian nationalism, gaining widespread support in northern India, won few adherents in the region.

Local nationalism increased after the war, partly as a backlash against Tamil claims to the region, and grew dramatically as India prepared for independence in the early months of 1947. The rulers of the Malayali states expressed their preference for association with, but not incorporation into, the new Indian state. Sir C.P. Ramaswani Aiyer, the prime minister of Travancore, announced the adoption of a new constitution and withdrew the state from all Indian political bodies. Malayali nationalists claimed that Travancore, with its considerable coastline and near monopoly on several important commodities, was better fitted for independence than any other state in British India. The governments of Travancore and

Cochin rejected Indian overtures and threats and refused to join to India. On 15 August 1947, the day India became independent, Aiyer proclaimed Travancore a sovereign state, and neighboring Cochin prepared to follow suit.

The Indian government threatened reprisals, and Malayali appeals to the British brought only pressure to negotiate. Following protracted talks, the two Malayali states finally accepted guaranteed autonomy, under their traditional rulers, with the Indian government responsible only for defense and foreign relations. Disturbances, led by nationalists and communists, broke out at the news of the compromise, but also among the Muslim Moplahs, who vehemently opposed inclusion in predominantly Hindu India.

In 1948, in spite of the earlier guarantees, the Indian government ended the states' autonomy and combined the two into a new state called Travancore-Cochin. In 1949 the two maharajas, under pressure, renounced their political rights, retaining only their personal privileges and properties. As part of the government's 1956 reorganization, most of the Malayalam-speaking regions—Travancore, Cochin, and the Malabar district of southwest India—were united in a new state called Kerala.

Opposition to Indian rule coalesced around the Kerala Socialist Party (KSP), a communist-dominated party that openly advocated secession from India. In 1957 the KSP won state elections and on 5 April 1957 formed the world's first freely elected communist government. The Kerala government quickly developed separatist leanings, alarming the Indian federal government. In 1959, claiming a breakdown of law and order, the federal authorities dissolved the government of "Red Kerala" and in 1962 passed a law making advocacy of secession a serious crime.

The communists again gained control of the state government in 1967 and 1970, gaining Moplah support by shifting district boundaries to the benefit of the Muslim areas. After years of rule by parties affiliated with India's ruling Congress Party, the communists returned to power in Kerala in 1987, further straining relations between the Malayalis and the federal government.

Malayali nationalism, based on anti-Aryan and anti-Tamil traditions, remains a strong force in the state, particularly among the non-Hindus. The state, with India's highest literacy rate, best health care, and most extensive road system, has little in common with the rest of the country. The neat and clean Malayali cities are remarkably free of the squalid slums and communal tension that dominate most of India. In August 1999, a high court in Kerala banned smoking in public places, the first time in India that such a ruling had been handed down, again highlighting the differences between the Malayalis and the rest of India.

In part because of a long flirtation with communism, the collapse of the Soviet Union brought changes to Kerala. Economics, not ideology, had become the prime national issue in the state at the turn of the twenty-first century. The underdevelopment and backwardness of the regional economy has forced thousands to seek work abroad, many in the oil rich states of the Persian Gulf. Money sent by the overseas Malayalis is a major source of income for the state and the basis of the region's relative prosperity in the late 1990s.

A controversy over the distribution of the waters of the Cauvery River reignited nationalist fervor in 2001–02. The neighboring states of Karnataka and Tamil Nadu attempted to divide the resource bilaterally, effectively excluding the Malayalis from the bargain. Demonstrations in several large cities turned into anti-Tamil marches.

SELECTED BIBLIOGRAPHY:

Mathew, George. *Communal Road to Secular Kerala*. 1990.

Menon, Dilip M. *Caste, Nationalism and Communism in South India: Malabar 1900–1948*. 1993.

Osella, Filippo, and Caroline Osella, eds. *Social Mobility in Kerala: Modernity and Identity in Conflict*. 2000.

Padmanabha, K.P, and T.K. Menon, eds. *History of Kerala*. 1982.

Manchus

Niuchi; Man; Manchurians; Mandzhu; Mandju; Mandjuris; Mandjury; Mandzhuris; Mandzhury; Mandzhurians

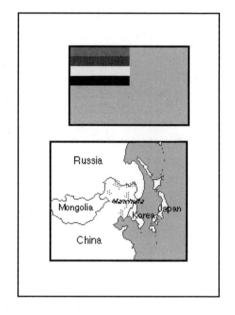

POPULATION: Approximately (2002e) 11,475,000 Manchus in north-central Asia, concentrated in Heilongjiang, Jilin, and Liaoning Provinces in the northeast; in Hubei Province, around Beijing; and in Inner Mongolia. Outside northeastern China, there is a Manchu group, the Xibe or Western Manchu, numbering abut 200,000, in Xinjiang in western China. Outside China there are Manchu communities in the Russian Far East and in North Korea.

THE MANCHU HOMELAND: The Manchu homeland lies in northeastern China, in the Tung-pei-sheng, the Northeast Provinces. The region, mostly fertile lands west of the Great Kingan Mountains, occupies the vast Manchurian Plain. Industrialized in the late nineteenth and early twentieth century, the region is now overwhelmingly Han Chinese. The small regions that still have Manchu majorities enjoy no official status, due to traditional Chinese hostility to the Manchus dating from the centuries of Manchu domination prior to the 1911 Chinese Revolution. The Manchu capital and major cultural center is Bei'an, called Pehanchen by the Manchus, (2002e) 153,000.

FLAG: The Manchu flag, the flag of the former Manchurian state, is a dark gold field bearing a canton of four equal horizontal stripes of red, blue, white, and black.

PEOPLE AND CULTURE: The Manchu, calling themselves Niuchi, thought to mean simply "people," are a robust Tungus people, on average five inches taller than the majority Han Chinese. In spite of decades of communist egalitarianism, the Manchu tend to be more prosperous and better educated than the Han Chinese. The government of the People's Republic of China asserts that the Manchu do not now, and never did, exist as a separate people. The Xibe or Western Manchu are descendents of an eighteenth-century military garrison and are now an official nationality in China. Since 1911, when the Manchu dynasty was overthrown, the

1163

Manchus have grown considerably in number, but they have not been allowed their own autonomous territory, as have most other minority groups in China. Traditionally the Manchus were farmers, but by 1990 over half lived in cities, where the Manchu revival movement was strongest. The extended family remains strong; three or four generations often live together. Until the 1980s, the Manchu were considered assimilated, but since that time a movement has arisen to reclaim their ancient culture and heritage.

LANGUAGE AND RELIGION: The Manchu languages belong to the geographically widespread Manchu-Tungus subfamily of the Altaic language family. The Manchu speak a Southwest Tungistic language of the Tungistic group of the East Altaic languages. The language, called Kuoyu, has been written in its own script since the seventeenth century and was an official language in China until 1911. A majority of the Manchu, estimated at 99%, are now bilingual, also speaking the northeastern Chinese dialects or the official Mandarin language. The Manchu language is a literary language, written in a modified variation of the Mongol script. The Xibe language is also a literary language, using a modified Manchu-Mongol script. The language, officially discouraged by successive Chinese governments since 1911, is now mostly spoken by older people and their grandchildren, who have taken a new interest in reviving Kuoyu.

The majority of the Manchus are Buddhists, although religious practices have been severely curtailed under the rule of the Communist Party. Many Manchus also adhere to many traditional shamanistic beliefs alongside their Buddhist rites. The Xibe in western China retain a shamanist belief system. The ancient festivals of spring planting, autumn harvest, and the new year are still observed. Traditionally the Manchus depended on shamans or healers to cure the sick by magic, communicate with the gods, and control events. Ancestor worship remains strong, particularly in rural areas.

NATIONAL HISTORY: The Manchu, according to tradition, are descended from the Jurchen, a tribe known since the seventh century A.D., although the Manchu claim to have inhabited the region since at least the third century B.C. Originally a nomadic people, the Manchu settled in permanent communities near the grazing lands. In early Chinese records they are known as the Tung-ihu, the Eastern Barbarians. The Jurchen founded the Chen kingdom in A.D. 698; it became the P'o-hai kingdom in 712. At its height the kingdom covered nearly all of Manchuria and northern Korea. The kingdom was overthrown by a Mongol group called the Khitan in 926.

Renowned warriors, the Manchu resisted sporadic Chinese attempts to conquer the region and in the twelfth century defeated the Mongols, then a rising power. They settled in the Sungari Valley, where they developed an agrarian civilization and gradually increased their territory. By 1115 their dynasty had secured control over northeastern China. The kingdom was annihilated by the Mongols in 1234, and the surviving Jurchen were driven into northeastern Manchuria.

Three centuries later the descendants of the Jurchen were again a powerful people. Calling themselves Manchu, they regained control of Manchuria. The Manchu created a powerful state about 1616 under Nurhatsi, known as Nurachu to the Chinese. Manchu soldiers launched raids into northern China and captured Han laborers, whom they forced to settle in Manchuria. In 1644 the Manchu invaded the weakened Chinese Empire and installed a Manchu dynasty in Beijing, the Ch'ing dynasty. By 1680 the Manchus had confirmed their authority over all parts of China. Han Chinese immigration to the Manchu homeland was forbidden by imperial decree in 1668, but the ban was never effectively enforced.

The Manchu adopted many Chinese customs and cultural traits while retaining their own language and culture. Some Chinese customs, such as the Golden Lilies—the deliberately deformed feet so prized by the Chinese upper classes—never found favor with the Manchu. Their own custom of braiding their hair into queues, or pigtails, was forced on their Chinese subjects as a sign of loyalty to the new dynasty. Apart from this they made little effort to impose their culture on the vastly more numerous Chinese.

The Manchu authorities in the spring of 1764 dispatched a large Manchu force from Manchuria to help garrison the newly acquired territory of Xingjiang, mostly populated by Muslim Uighurs.* After a long journey across Mongolia, the Manchu troops settled and took wives from the local ethnic groups. Their descendants, called Western Manchus or Xibe, have only reestablished ties to the Manchus of northeastern China in the last few decades.

Some four million Manchu formed an elite nobility, ruling an empire of more than 400 million Chinese. The Manchu emperors, in spite of their patronage of Chinese art, scholarship, and culture over the centuries, made strenuous efforts to prevent the Manchu from being absorbed by the Chinese. The Manchus were urged to retain their own language and to educate their children in Manchu. Intermarriage between the Manchu nobility and their Chinese subjects was strictly forbidden, so as to keep the Manchu ethnically pure. Even social intercourse between the Manchus and Chinese was frowned upon. All these efforts proved fruitless. During the nineteenth century, as the dynasty decayed, efforts to preserve the Manchu culture and ethnic separateness gradually broke down. The Manchus began to adopt Chinese customs and language, and to intermarry.

The Manchus managed to maintain a brilliant and powerful government until about 1800, after which they seemed to lose energy and ability rapidly. Manchu territory was threatened by the advance of the Russians, while British, French, and other Europeans encroached on other parts of the empire.

Manchuria, the ancestral homeland, remained closed to non-Manchu settlement until severe population pressure forced the Manchu government to allow limited Chinese immigration in 1878. Even restrictive immigration soon reduced the Manchu to minority status in their homeland. Russian influence, growing with construction of the Chinese–Eastern Railway, prompted the Manchu rulers to open Manchuria to unlimited immigration in 1896. In 1900 the immigrant Han Chinese formed 80% of Manchuria's population, and further Han settlement was encouraged.

Russia established a virtual protectorate over Manchuria as Manchu power waned in China. The Japanese, after defeating China in a brief war in 1895, sought to assert their influence as well in the mineral-rich area, resulting in a war with Russia in 1904–1905. The victorious Japanese quickly consolidated their economic and political influence. As Manchuria developed into an important industrial region, large urban centers evolved, and immigration increased, particularly from rural areas.

The long decline of Manchu power finally ended in revolution in 1911. The last Manchu emperor, the child Pu-Yi, was deposed and a Chinese republic proclaimed. The weak republican government soon lost control of many areas to local factions and warlords. Chang Tso-lin, named governor of Manchuria in 1918, created a virtually independent state supported by a strong military force drawn from the numerous White Russian refugees fleeing Russia. The influx of Han immigrants was especially heavy after 1923. The immigrants brought a vast area of virgin prairie under cultivation. On 9 February 1926 Chang declared Manchuria independent of China, and in the ensuing war his forces drove republican troops back on Beijing.

The Japanese, taking advantage of the turmoil, persuaded Chang to give them responsibility for the important South Manchurian Railway. They used Chang's assent as a pretext to occupy key positions in the state and to grab power when Chang Tso-lin died in a mysterious bomb explosion in 1931. The League of Nations recommended an autonomous Manchurian state under nominal Chinese rule. Both the Japanese and the Manchurian nationalists rejected the recommendation.

Encouraged by the Japanese, the nationalists declared the independence of Manchukuo, the Manchu State, on 9 March 1932. The nationalists and their Japanese allies installed Pu-yi as the state's chief executive. In 1934 Pu-yi assumed the Manchu throne as Emperor Kang Teh. In spite of the trappings of sovereignty, ultimate power rested with the Japanese advisors assigned to all high Manchu officials. In 1937 the Manchu state served as base for the Japanese invasion of China, and in 1941 the Japanese-dominated government declared war on the United States and its allies.

At the Yalta Conference of February 1945, the Soviet premier Joseph Stalin demanded the restoration of all the former Russian rights and privileges in Manchuria as the price for Soviet entry into the war in the Pacific, an offer readily accepted by his American and British allies. In May, Soviet troops began to be transferred from Europe to Asia. On 8 August 1945, the Soviet Union declared war on Japan and invaded Manchuria. By 15 August the war was over, and Manchuria was under Soviet occupation. The Soviet troops quickly removed as much as possible of the huge industrial capacity established by the Japanese. Other troops arrested Pu-yi, who was later turned over to the Soviets' allies, the Chinese communists.

The Soviets supported the Chinese communists in the Chinese Civil War of 1945–49 and retained considerable influence in Manchuria. The Manchurian leader Kao Kang was made, for his support of the communists, the head of an autonomous Manchurian state in 1949. Accused of attempting to resurrect Manchurian independence in 1954, Kao Kang was dismissed, and in 1955 he disappeared. Divided into three provinces, Manchuria as such disappeared from Chinese official maps. Ignoring the fact that the Manchus had ruled China from 1644 to 1911, the communist authorities decreed that no separate Manchu people had ever existed and forbade the use of the names "Manchu" and "Manchuria" and all references to over two centuries of Manchu domination in China.

Manchurian regionalism, supported by the majority Chinese and the minority peoples, again became a strong force in the 1980s, sparked by government policies that neglected the Northeast Provinces, with their aging heavy industries and traditionally independent-minded people, in favor of economic development in the provinces near Hong Kong and opposite Taiwan. By the late 1980s the average incomes in the favored coastal provinces were more than double those of the Northeast.

The relatively relaxed atmosphere of the period allowed the Manchu to emerge from decades of enforced obscurity. In 1990, for the first time since the communist victory of 1949, the Manchu were counted as a minority people in the official census. The Manchu population of China officially numbered 9,821,000, considerably higher than expected, even without adjustment for the unknown number of ethnic Manchu who had listed themselves as ethnic Han Chinese for decades to escape persecution.

The memories of the grimmer aspects of the Japanese military occupation having faded, a wave of nostalgia swept the region in the late 1980s. The Manchu flag of the 1930s appeared in demonstrations in the large cities in 1988–89. This nostalgia and the emerging Manchu cultural movement were crushed along with the prodemocracy movement in China in a vicious military campaign in June 1989.

The region in the 1990s experienced the highest level of unrest since the Cultural Revolution of the 1960s. The unrest was propelled by falling incomes—lower than the dismal Chinese average and only a quarter of those in the privileged southeast. The overthrow of communism in, and the disintegration of, the Soviet Union also reverberated in Manchuria. In 1994 the three Northeast Provinces put forward a plan for economic independence, including direct access to the Sea of Japan through the delta of the Tumen River, on the narrow frontier between Russia and Korea. The loosening of communist control in China allowed Manchuria to turn away from ideology and to emphasize economic and political ties with the countries that have shaped so much of its modern history, Japan and Russia.

The Manchus, who ruled China for over 250 years, are hated by the vast majority of the Chinese population. In 1998, Manchu cultural leaders organized a plan for the creation of autonomous counties for the Manchu population in northeastern China. The majority of the Manchus, living in the industrial heartland of China, support the cultural revival, but politics, after decades of oppression, remains a painful subject to the Manchus, one to be publicly avoided.

SELECTED BIBLIOGRAPHY:

DuRuofu, Vincent F. *Ethnic Groups in China*. 1995.

Harrell, Steven, ed. *Cultural Encounters on China's Ethnic Frontiers*. 1996.

Lee, Chong-Sik. *Revolutionary Struggle in Manchuria: Chinese Communism and Soviet Interest, 1922–1945*. 1983.

Rhoads, Edward J.M., ed. *Manchus and Han: Ethnic Relations and Political Power in Late Qing and Early Republican China, 1861–1928*. 2000.

Manx

Mannins; Manxmen; Manxians

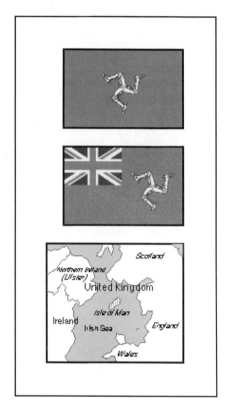

POPULATION: Approximately (2002e) 89,000 Manx in the United Kingdom, concentrated in the Isle of Man, in the Irish Sea between England and Ireland. There are important Manx communities in England and Scotland, and in Canada, Australia, New Zealand, and the United States.

THE MANX HOMELAND: The Manx homeland is a small island lying in the Irish Sea, nearly equidistant from Ireland, Scotland, England, and Wales. The island, 33 miles (53 km) long and from 6 to 12 miles (10 to 19 km) wide, is ringed by high cliffs indented by numerous bays. The Calf of Man is a detached rocky islet off the southwest coast. In the north of the island there is a flat plain with lazy rivers and streams that cross fertile farmlands behind long, sandy beaches. Some of the river valleys have rich pastures, and livestock is raised extensively. The island has a mild climate; subtropical plants and crops are grown without protection. About 40% of the island is uninhabited. The population is concentrated in several urban areas, particularly the Douglas-Onchan area, which accounts for about half the total population. The Island of Man is not part of the United Kingdom but rather a crown possession, with its own parliament, laws, currency, and taxation. *Isle of Man (Ellan Vannin/Mannin)*: 221 sq. mi.—572 sq. km, (2002e) 79,000—Manx 89%, other British 8%, Irish 1%, others 2%. The Manx capital and major cultural center is Douglas, called Doolish in Manx, (2002e) 24,000. The other important cultural center is Onchan, Kione Droghad in the Manx language, (2002e) 10,000.

FLAG: The Manx national flag, the official flag of the autonomous state, is a red field bearing three white legs called the Trinacria, armored and spurred, detailed in gray and yellow. The official flag of the state is a red field bearing the Trinacria on the fly and the Union Jack as a canton on the upper hoist.

PEOPLE AND CULTURE: The Manx are a distinct European nation of Norse-Celtic descent. They are the descendents of the island's early Celtic inhabitants, Celts driven from the mainland by invasions of Anglo-Saxons, and admixtures of Scandinavians, Scots, and Welsh. The Manx culture and language developed over many centuries in the relative isolation of the island. The culture, including many features and traditions that have disappeared from the other Celtic cultures, has revived in recent decades and is once again flourishing. Throughout the centuries the Isle of Man developed a way of life and a culture all its own. Many of the events that shaped the nearby islands, such as the Roman and Norman invasions of Britain, passed it by, leaving its Celtic culture intact. The arrival of the Vikings, however, did leave a lasting mark on the small Celtic nation. After a period of turbulence, the Celts and the Vikings merged as one nation under a unique system of government, the Tynwald, brought to the island by the Scandinavians.

LANGUAGE AND RELIGION: The Celtic language of the Manx, called Manx or Manx Gaelic, belongs to the Goedelic branch of the Celtic languages. The language was nearly extinct by the 1950s, but it has been revived as part of the Manx cultural resurgence. English remains the first language of the island, but it has become a matter of pride for the Manx to learn and use their ancient language. The last native speaker died in 1974.

The Manx are mostly Protestant, the majority Methodists, although other Protestant denominations, including the Society of Friends, as well as the Roman Catholics are represented.

NATIONAL HISTORY: Traces of Neolithic peoples abound on the island—ancient crosses and other stone monuments, a round tower, an ancient fort, and several castles. Celtic clans are thought to have migrated from mainland Britain around 500 B.C. The island was ruled by a Welsh line of kings from the sixth to the ninth centuries A.D. and remained a Celtic kingdom while most of Celtic Britain was falling to, successively, the Germanic Angles, Saxons, and Jutes. The Celtic stronghold on the Isle of Man was reinforced by refugees fleeing the Germanic invasions of the nearby mainland territories.

In A.D. 798, the Celtic inhabitants of the islands experienced the first of many terrifying Viking raids. Norse raiders eventually overthrew the Celtic monarchy in 800. Norse settlers from Scandinavia settled the island and mixed with the earlier Celtic inhabitants, adding many Norse words to the Celtic language. The island became a dependency of the kingdom of Norway. The system of government evolved under Norwegian rule has remained practically unchanged since that time. In 1266 the Norwegian king sold the island to Alexander III of Scotland. The Manx, unhappy under

Scottish rule, placed their island under the protection of the English king Edward I in 1290. The island came under English control in 1341. From that time on the island's feudal lords, calling themselves "kings of Mann," were all English.

The island's mixture of Celtic and Scandinavian influences evolved a distinct culture by the fifteenth century, with traditions and customs quite unlike those of the neighboring islands. The Scandinavian heritage remained, but the culture, although influenced by contact with the neighboring peoples, developed in the isolation of their island homeland.

In 1405 King Henry IV gave the island to the Stanley family, who refused to be called kings. They took the title "lord of Mann." The Stanleys, later the earls of Derby and Salisbury, ruled the Isle of Man for over three centuries. In 1651 the Manx, led by Illiam Dhone, rebelled and attempted to drive the foreigners from their island. The rebels were defeated, and Dhone was executed in 1663.

The island passed to the duke of Athol in 1736. In the decades that followed, the island's economy revolved around smuggling between Ireland, Scotland, Wales, and England. Many Manx fortunes stemmed from this illegal trade. In an effort to stop the Manx smuggling of goods into England, which deprived the British government of lucrative customs, the British crown purchased the island in 1765, for £70,000. The purchase was designed to save the British treasury approximately £100,000 per annum, but it deprived the Manx of their main sources of income.

The British parliament acquired the Athol family's remaining feudal prerogatives in 1828. The island then became a self-governing crown dependency and possession. A statute confirming local autonomy was passed in 1866. The Manx were given the right to choose representatives to the House of Keys, the lower house of their thousand-year-old parliament, the Tynwald, the upper house of which is the Legislative Council. The Manx would remain subject to the British monarch, but not to Parliament.

English in the eighteenth and nineteenth centuries gradually took over as the language of Manx daily life. By 1871 only a quarter of the population could still speak Manx. The island's mild climate, beautiful scenery, and unique culture attracted many visitors; the island became one of the premier resorts of Victorian Britain, a fact that reinforced the use of English. By 1900 only 5,000 could still speak their Celtic language. Opposition to presence of thousands of English tourists sparked periodic demands for independence, but no serious negotiations were undertaken, as the authorities considered the island too small for viable nationhood.

During World War I, the Manx supplied many volunteers to the allied cause, but after the war, nationalism, influenced by the example of the Irish, began to gather support, and the Manx began to take measures to save their ancient culture from extinction. In World War II many Manx again fought, but there was more sentiment for neutrality, as in nearby Ireland.

After World War II the island again prospered as a major British resort. Younger Manx, fearing that tourism meant the extinction of their ancient culture and language, began a campaign to save them. In 1961 only 165 people spoke the Manx language, but the numbers began to grow as younger Manx took pride in learning and using it. The Manx renewed ties and contacts with the other Celtic peoples of Europe; annual Celtic festivals and congresses sustained a growing cultural and national revival. In 1968 the Executive Council, part of the local autonomous government, decreed that the Union Jack would no longer fly from public buildings on official holidays—only the Manx flag, even on royal birthdays.

In 1973, when the United Kingdom joined the European Economic Community (EEC), the Manx signed a separate associate agreement, which initiated a dramatic economic surge. Offshore banking and financial services flourished under favorable tax laws and less restrictive banking rules than those of the neighboring islands. The financial-services industry brought much income to the island, but tourism, with over 500,000 visitors a year, remained the island's major support until the 1980s. The prosperity of the island attracted many new residents from the British mainland.

From 1980 the population grew rapidly, raising housing prices to a level higher than in London, far beyond the reach of the average Manx. The situation sparked renewed Manx nationalism, accompanied by a campaign of arson against holiday homes owned by foreigners in 1989–90. Pressed by the nationalist agitation, the island's government passed laws restricting immigration from the mainland and giving special protection to the Manx culture and language. In 1992 the government introduced the Manx language in the school curriculum, and the nearly extinct Manx language began to revive dramatically.

The Manx retain, and are proud of, their thousand years of political stability and parliamentary government. The laws passed by the Tynwald must receive royal assent, after which, every July 5—known as Midsummer Day, or Tynwald Day—they are read aloud from Tynwald Hill, first in Manx, then in English. The British monarch, as Lord of Man, appoints the lieutenant governor of the island. The Manx are not bound by acts of Parliament unless they are specifically mentioned. There are no political parties; members of the local parliament all sit as independents.

In 1996 moderate nationalists formed the Alternative Policy Group (APG), which argued that the chief minister of the island had too much power. The group, which broke with the tradition of nonparty politics, presented an independence manifesto. They claimed it was time to scrap the veto that the British government wielded, though rarely used, over Manx legislation. The nationalists also claimed that independence would allow the Manx to develop their financial industry further.

A new bill passed in early 2000 highlighted the peculiar nature of the Manx relationship with the United Kingdom—a new residency law that would give the island government power to stop people moving to the island. The law is to be a contingency measure, as the Manx government already requires people moving to the island to have work permits. The new power allows the Manx to control the flow of rich immigrants attracted to the island's income tax of only 20%, the absence of a capital-gains tax, and low crime rates. Wealthy immigrants willing to pay high prices continue to drive the Manx out of the property market. The Manx government currently backs subsidies to enable Manx first-time home buyers to compete in the housing market.

The increasing unification of western Europe in the European Union (EU) has given Manx nationalism a new focus. The Manx nationalists now look to the EU, which is theoretically able to accommodate smaller nations, and not to Great Britain, as their future. A nationalist campaign favors transforming the island's relationship from the British crown to a similar connection with the government of an integrated European federation, by which the Manx would maintain control of their island homeland.

SELECTED BIBLIOGRAPHY:

Killip, Christopher. *Isle of Man: A Book about the Manx*. 1980.
Kinvig, R.H. *The Isle of Man: A Social, Cultural, and Political History*. 1976.
Moore, A. *A History of the Isle of Man*. 1991.
Robinson, V., and D. McCarroll, eds. *The Isle of Man: Celebrating a Sense of Place*. 1990.

Maoris

Southern Polynesians; Maaoris

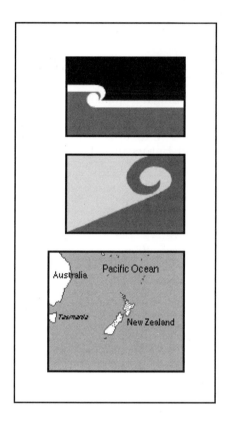

POPULATION: Approximately (2002e) 468,000 Maoris in New Zealand, concentrated in the urban areas of North Island. Some scholars and Maori activists claim a national population of up to 600,000, including the numerous part-Maoris.

THE MAORI HOMELAND: The Maori homeland lies in northern New Zealand; 90% of the Maori population lives on North Island. The islands of New Zealand comprise two large islands, North Island and South Island, and several smaller islands. North Island is mostly rolling hills and grazing land. South Island is more rugged, with the Southern Alps running the length of the island. New Zealand is called Aotearoa by the Maoris. *New Zealand (Aotearoa)*: 103,736 sq. mi.—268,676 sq. km, (2002e) 3,899,000—New Zealand white (Pakeha) 74%, Maoris and part-Maoris 12%, Pacific Island Polynesians 3%, Cook Islanders* 1%, other New Zealanders 10%. The unofficial Maori capital is Rotorua, (2002e) 55,000. The major cultural centers are Auckland, called Tamaki-Makaurau by the Maoris, (2002e) 388,000, metropolitan area 1,132,000, and Hamilton, called Kirikiriroa, (2002e), 114,000, and Rotorua (2002e) 55,000.

FLAG: The flag of the Maori Independence Movement (Tino Rangatiratanga) is black over red, with a thin white stripe broken by a spiral pattern toward the hoist. The flag was the winning design in a 1990 contest to select a Maori national flag. The flag of the North Island Maoris is a pale yellow field bearing a green *koru*, a traditional Maori symbol, on the fly.

PEOPLE AND CULTURE: The Maoris are an East Polynesian ethnic group, the indigenous population of New Zealand. The Maori population is divided into tribal groups, each with a distinct ancestry and a common allegiance to a chief or chiefs. The most important social group is the subtribe, the primary landholding group and the one within which marriage is preferred. The extended family is also important, although less so among the increasingly urban population. In 2000 an estimated four-fifths of the Maoris were urban dwellers, mainly living in Auckland and other cities on North Island. Urbanization has meant adoption of urban New Zealand culture and increased contact with the white New Zealanders. The rate of intermarriage has steadily increased since the 1970s. A disproportionate number of urban Maoris remain in occupations of low status and low pay, although there is a sprinkling of Maoris at all levels, and job discrimination is minimal. Social discrimination is minor; Maoris worry more about social domination and the loss of their culture. The Maoris call the New Zealand descendants of European settlers "Pakehas," but the majority of Maoris have some European ancestry, and many who identify themselves as Maoris are actually of predominantly European ancestry. Only those with 50% or more Maori ancestry are considered indigenous in government statistics. Identification has become a question of culture rather than genetics.

LANGUAGE AND RELIGION: The Maori language is Tahitic language of the Polynesian branch of the Malayo-Polynesian group of Austronesian languages. The language, spoken by about a third of the adult Maori population, is divided into seven geographical dialects: North Auckland, South Island, Wanganui, Bay of Plenty, Rotorua-Taupo, Taranaki, Moriori. The Moriori dialect, formerly spoken in the Chatham Islands, is now extinct. The language is about 70% intelligible to the Hawaiians,* who speak a related language. Most Maori speakers are bilingual in English. Since the 1980s there has been a tendency to politicize Maori language issues. There is a strong movement to revive the language, and teaching in the language is widespread. In 1987 Maori was made an official language of New Zealand. In the late 1990s, there were over 300 government-funded language schools in New Zealand. In 1993, the Maoris launched a campaign to promote the use of the language.

The Maoris are mostly Christian, belonging to a number of Protestant denominations. Mormons* have had particular influence on Maori religious beliefs since the Second World War. Traditional Maori beliefs included ancestor worship and belief in spirits that inhabit nature. They believed in a pantheon of numerous gods under a supreme being known as Io. Christianity mostly destroyed traditional Maori beliefs, though not quickly.

NATIONAL HISTORY: New Zealand was the last large land mass to be settled by humanity. Archeological evidence suggests that the first Polynesians arrived a mere 800 years ago and that they came from the Society or Marquesas Islands in eastern Polynesia. Maori oral history describes their origins in terms of waves of Polynesian migration beginning about

A.D. 1150. The migrations culminated in the fourteenth century in the arrival by a "great fleet" of eight to ten large canoes in a land they called Aotearoa from islands they called Hawaiki, usually identified as Tahiti.

The Polynesian settlers spread across the land and organized themselves into geographical tribal groups. Land was held in common at the subtribal level. Intertribal wars were endemic, although the rituals and ceremonies of war were often more important that the actual fighting, and few warriors were killed before tribal honor was satisfied.

Abel Tasman was the first European to visit the lands he called New Zealand. He arrived off the coast in December 1642. He was driven off by a Maori tribe on the South Island and left the region largely unexplored. The Maoris living on the two large islands were left to their traditional way of life for over a century. In 1769–70, when Capt. James Cook sailed around the two major islands, there were an estimated 100,000 to 200,000 Maori inhabitants. His reports told of the intelligence of the Maoris and the suitability of New Zealand for European colonization.

Whalers, sealers, and other European adventurers seeking profit were initially welcomed to the islands by the Maoris. With the European introduction of firearms, disease, and Christian missionaries, however, traditional Maori culture and social structure began to disintegrate. The acquisition of European muskets resulted in the so-called Musket Wars, a devastating series of tribal conflicts in the early nineteenth century. By the late 1830s, New Zealand was claimed as part of the British Empire, and settlers from Britain began to settle the islands.

The British government officially assumed control of New Zealand in 1840, under the terms of the Treaty of Waitangi, signed by representatives of some Maori tribes and Queen Victoria. By the treaty the Maoris ceded sovereignty in exchange for protection and guaranteed possession of their ancestral lands. Soon, however, European settlement and increasingly intrusive British authority alarmed the Maori tribes, especially on North Island. In 1845 Maori bands attacked the European settlements around the Bay of Islands and other areas of the far north. The attacks, sometimes collectively called the First Maori War, were not fully suppressed by colonial troops until 1847. The defeated Maoris remained at peace from 1847 to 1860.

In 1857 several tribal groups of the Waikato areas of North Island elected a new king and established a council of state, a judicial system, and a police organization. The creation of state symbols was intended to further the Maori resolve to retain ancestral lands and stop intertribal warfare over the land issue. Not all Maori tribes accepted the authority of the king, but the majority shared with the *kingitanga*, the King Movement, the intention not to sell additional land to the Europeans.

The Maoris of North Island retained most of the island territory until 1860, but a large increase in the number of European immigrants in the

1850s led to demands for greatly increased land purchases by the colonial government. In 1859, Te Teira, of the Taranaki region, sold his riverside land without the consent of his tribe. The unapproved sale precipitated the First Taranaki War of 1860–61, although only the extremist wing of the King Movement joined in the fighting. The war was generally fought as a number of successful sieges of Maori fortified villages by British troops and colonial militias. The fighting ended in a stalemate and resumed in April 1863. While fighting raged in the Taranaki area, violence broke out in the Waikato region in July 1863, the center of the King Movement tribes.

During the Maori Wars of the 1860s a religious-military cult was formed. The members of the Pai Marire, the Good and Peaceful Religion, were called Hauhau. A mixture of Maori, Jewish, and Christian tenets, the cult held that the Maoris were the new chosen people. Their immediate work was to drive the European settlers from New Zealand and to recover their traditional lands. The Hauhau went into battle believing they would be protected from bullets; large-scale European confiscation of Maori lands drove many Maoris to embrace the movement. The Maoris, unable to stand up in pitched battles to the well-armed troops, began to employ guerrilla tactics. The British troops, aided by gunboats and colonial volunteers, won notable victories in October and November 1863. The fall of the Maori stronghold at Orakau pa in early 1864 brought the fighting in the Waikato region essentially to an end.

The last of the Maori Wars was fought from 1864 to 1872. Hostilities spread to virtually the whole of North Island. The main warrior groups in the mid-1860s were the fanatic Hauhaus. The British government indicated that it wanted to conclude a peace in 1864, but the colonial authorities, wishing to acquire additional lands, continued the war and assumed a larger share of the fighting. From 1968 to 1872 the Hauhau were supplemented by a new warrior cult, the Ringatu. All fighting finally ended in 1872, with the defeat of the last warrior bands. Large tracts of Maori land were confiscated, and Maori society was permanently disrupted. Supporters of the King Movement retreated to "King Country," in the west-central part of North Island. This area was closed to European colonization and remained under Maori control until 1881, when it was released to the government.

The Maori Representation Act of 1867 created four Maori seats in New Zealand's parliament. The act was originally intended to be temporary; when Maori landholdings were converted from communal to individual ownership, the Maoris were to join the general electoral rolls. Because of the difficulty of dividing the Maori land holdings, however, the act was made permanent in 1876. By 1896, as a result of war and disease, the Maori population had fallen to just 42,000.

Maori relations were exceptionally tranquil for over a century, from the end of the Maori wars until the 1970s. Many people proclaimed New Zealand a model of ethnic relations, but the truth was closer to the Maori view—that they were recovering from their status as a "dying nation" and were in any case largely out of sight and neglected in their rural communities.

The difficult living conditions in the tribal areas and the whites' insistence on cultural assimilation spurred a migration to the cities beginning in the 1950s. By the 1970s the migration had transformed tribal demographics. Closer contact with white New Zealand society stimulated politicization of Maori grievances over economic neglect, quality of life, and particularly land rights. Renewed interest in developing Maori culture, society, and economic well-being was reflected in the establishment of numerous Maori organizations, mostly in the urban areas. In 1971, annual Maori demonstrations at celebrations of Treaty of Waitangi Day, a New Zealand national holiday, began.

The general global trend toward group and civil rights contributed to an increased awareness and political activism among the Maoris. Questions of land and culture remained the major issues, but demands grew for greater access and opportunities in New Zealand society. Activists demanded formal biculturalism in place of the former assimilation, as well as sovereignty over Maori affairs.

In 1975, tens of thousands participated in a protest march over the length of North Island. The march began a period of strikes, sit-ins, and occupations of public buildings. An increase in their traditional forms of political association and a marked decrease in electoral participation prompted promises of concessions and accommodations by the New Zealand government. In a symbolic gesture, a Maori was appointed as governor general of New Zealand in 1985, the same year that the government changed the law to allow Maoris to put forward claims for lands they believed had been illegally taken since 1840.

By 1990 an estimated 70% of New Zealand was subject to land claims. In December 1994, the government proposed a "take it or leave it" settlement of a billion New Zealand dollars, both in land and cash, to settle all outstanding claims. The proposal, rejected by the majority, set off a series of often violent confrontations. In 1995, radical nationalists threatened to carry out acts of terrorism in New Zealand unless the Maoris were consulted on all land claim proposals and foreign investment schemes.

In 1992, the New Zealand government established a new Ministry of Maori Development to give advice on Maori health, training, education, resources, and economic development. A Maori leader in February 1993 called on New Zealanders to rename the country Aotearoa, the "Land of the Long White Cloud," the Maori name for it. An uproar resulted when New Zealand's prime minister agreed to consider the change. In 1997 the New Zealand government expressed profound regret and apologized unreservedly for suffering it had inflicted in the past, and for and grave injustices that had significantly impaired the development of a major South Island tribe. Maori activists demanded that the government apologize to the entire Maori nation and reiterated demands for compensation for lost lands.

In mid-2000 several militant leaders expressed support for the overthrow of the Fijian government by indigenous activists, contradicting the New Zealand government's condemnation of the hostage taking that accompanied the coup. One radical leader threatened a Maori-led coup in New Zealand if the government did not recognize the Maoris' indigenous rights.

Racial or social discrimination is minimal in New Zealand, and many Maoris are assimilated into New Zealand culture. For many Maoris the most significant issues in New Zealand remain land claims and failure to consult them on issues regarding their nation. Since the end of the Maori Wars, land entitlements have been systematically abrogated and the Maoris are now in possession of only about 5% of their original territory. Conscious of the injustices of the European land purchases and confiscations of the nineteenth century, they are suspicious of government changes in the land laws. Laws that make it easier to sell individual Maori holdings are strongly opposed by activists, who argue that land is held in trust by one generation for the next.

The Maoris remain well behind white New Zealanders in income and education, while leading in most crime statistics. Maori unemployment is three times higher than among European New Zealanders, and the educational disparity is the widest. Although nationalist activism has increased dramatically since 1980, often stimulated by development and educational questions, most Maoris would be satisfied if the New Zealand government simply honored the terms of the partnership agreement between Maoris and Pakehas embodied in the 1840 Treaty of Waitangi.

SELECTED BIBLIOGRAPHY:

Alves, Dora. *The Maori and the Crown: An Indigenous People's Struggle for Self-Determination.* 1999.

Brookfield, F.M. *Waitangi and Indigenous Rights: Revolution, Law, and Legitimation.* 1999.

Rosenfield, Jean Elizabeth. *The Island Broken in Two: Land and Renewal Movements among the Maori of New Zealand.* 1999.

Sharp, Andrew. *Justice and the Maori: The Philosophy and Practice of Maori Claims in New Zealand since the 1970s.* 1997.

Mapuches

Mapuch; Araucanians; Araucanos; Maputongos

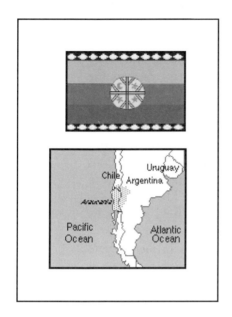

POPULATION: Approximately (2002e) 1,755,000 Mapuches in southwestern South America, concentrated in the Araucania region of Chile and Neuquén Province of Argentina, where some 200,000 Mapuches live. Outside Araucania there are sizable Mapuche populations in Santiago and other Chilean cities, and in the United States.

THE MAPUCHE HOMELAND: The Mapuche homeland occupies a fertile plain in south-central Chile between the Bío-Bío River and the Gulf of Ancud. In the east the region rises to the Andes Mountains, which form the international border with Argentina and physically divide the Mapuche nation. The Mapuche homeland, called Mapu by the Mapuches, has no official status, although to the Mapuches it is divided into four regions, Puelmapu, the "Land of the East"; Pikunmapu, the "Land of the North"; Lafquenmapu, the "Land on the Ocean"; and Huillimapu, the "Land of the South." In Chile the region, popularly called Araucania, is included in the regions of Bío-bío, Araucanía, and Los Lagos. *Araucania (Mapu)*: 21,209 sq. mi.—54,946 sq. km, (2002e) 1,965,000—Mapuches 76%, other Chileans 24%. The Mapuche capital and major cultural center is Temuco, called Temuko by the Mapuches, (2002e) 284,000. The major cultural centers of the Argentine Mapuches are Zapala, (2002e) 27,000, and Cutral-Có, (2002e) 63,000.

FLAG: The Mapuche flag, the flag of the national movement, is a horizontal tricolor of light blue, green, and red bearing narrow black stripes, with white geometric designs, at the top and bottom and charged with a centered yellow disc bearing the national symbols in brown.

PEOPLE AND CULTURE: The Mapuches, often called Araucanians, are a native American people traditionally divided into fourteen distinct castes or tribes. The most important of the Mapuche groups are the Mapuche, the "People of the Land," traditionally farmers; the Moluche, the "People of O," traditionally warriors; the Pipuche, the "People of the

Pines," mountain dwellers; the Huilliche, the "People of the South"; the Pehuenche, the "People of the North"; and the Laiquenche, the "People of the Coast." Although most Chileans have at least some indigenous blood, they continue to discriminate against the indigenous peoples. By 2000 an estimated third of the total Mapuche population lived in urban areas. Alcohol, disease, and illiteracy continue to be the major problems of both urban and rural Mapuches. The Mapuches are the poorest sector of regional society and continue to lose land to privatization and settlers.

LANGUAGE AND RELIGION: The Mapuches speak a number of related dialects, collectively called Mapudungun or Mapudhnquen, which means "language of the land." They make up a separate language family of the Andean branch of the Andean-Equatorial languages. Most Mapuches speak Spanish as their second language, as it is the sole official language in both Chile and Argentina. The language until recently was oral; Spanish was used as the literary language. There are a number of organizations working toward the creation of a Mapuche alphabet in order to preserve and sustain the oral tradition. Huilliche, spoken south of the Mapuche heartland by about 175,000, is barely intelligible to speaker of the central dialects.

The Mapuches, although nominally Roman Catholic, have retained their traditional religious beliefs and traditions—including holding their lands in common, an important part of Mapuche culture and religious beliefs. The traditional belief system is based on the idea that the world was created by a celestial family, headed by the forces of creation, embodied in Ngenechen, and the destroyer, Wakufu; the celestial family were the creators of all beings as well as holders of the power of nature. Traditional shamanism is centered on medical and spiritual ceremonies performed through a shaman or *machi*, who is the spiritual leader of village groups. Other pre-Christian customs, such as consulting spirits or ancestors, are also still frequently practiced.

NATIONAL HISTORY: The Mapuche tribes, under constant Inca pressure from the twelfth century, evolved a warrior tradition. They later halted the southern expansion of the Inca Empire, defeating invasions launched by Tupai Yupanqui between 1448 and 1482. The Incas, unable to penetrate the area, finally withdrew in the face of fierce Mapuche resistance, leaving the Mapuches the most powerful nation in the southern part of the South American continent prior to the arrival of the Europeans. Mapuche territory stretched from the Pacific Ocean eastward to the Atlantic. Although they dominated a vast territory, the Pre-Columbian Mapuches did not recognize any political or cultural entity above the village level.

Spanish forces under Pedro de Valdivia moved south into present Chile from Peru in 1540, founding Santiago in 1541. The Spanish eventually crossed the Bío-Bío River, which marked the northern border of Mapuche territory, meeting only minimal resistance. The Spaniards founded Concepcíon in 1550, and Valdivia, farther south, in 1552. The Spanish authorities, having established permanent settlements, considered the conquest of Chile complete and the people they called the Araucans pacified.

The Mapuches, led by their warrior chief Lautaro, organized a massive attack on the Spanish settlements in Mapuche territory in 1553, beginning the long series of conflicts known collectively as the Araucanian Wars. The Mapuches learned to use horses and reorganized their widely separated villages into military, political, and economic alliances. The warriors surged north and destroyed the settlements south of the Bío-Bío and in December 1553 defeated Valdivia's colonial army. In a later battle the Mapuches captured and killed Valdivia himself. The victorious Mapuches, intent on driving the Spanish back to Peru, marched on the major Spanish base at Santiago. Only the death of Lautaro and a smallpox epidemic among the Mapuches saved the colony. Betrayed to the Spanish by a Mapuche renegade, Lautaro died fighting his attackers.

The demoralized Mapuche warriors soon withdrew and returned to their homeland south of the Bío-Bío River. Continuing to repulse Spanish incursions from the north, the Mapuches eradicated all signs of the Spanish presence in their homeland by 1598. The Mapuches had defeated what was at that time the world's most powerful state, the Spanish Empire.

The Spanish authorities, unable to defeat the Mapuches, negotiated the Treaty of Quillin in 1641, a hundred years after their first incursion into Mapuche territory. The treaty recognized the independence of the Mapuches and guaranteed Mapuche control of the territory between the Bío-Bío and the Chonos Archipelago. The treaty prohibited further Spanish attempts to conquer the region.

In spite of the guarantees, the Mapuches were forced to repulse renewed Spanish incursions in 1725, 1740, and 1766, as well as numerous slave raids. Pressure on the Mapuches decreased, however, as the Spanish turned their attention to the wars in Europe and to the increasingly restive colonial populations in the Americas.

Argentina and Chile gained independence from Spain in 1810. The new governments revived the struggle to conquer Araucania, which they claimed. Unlike their kin in neighboring Argentina, conquered and nearly exterminated during the "Campaign of the Desert," the Mapuches west of the Andes Mountains repeatedly defeated Chilean military offensives. By 1845, the Chilean government had decided to colonize the land south of the Bío-Bío. The government began selling European settlers land grants in Mapuche lands. In the 1850s the Mapuches began to raid settlements established by German immigrants, thus preventing further expansion of colonial settlements in Araucania. In 1866, nonetheless, the Chilean government passed a law allowing the sale of public lands. The Mapuche land was considered "public," and large portions were sold to European immigrants.

The Chilean government, determined to take control of all of Araucania, sent a large military force south in 1873, but once again the Mapuches defeated the invaders. In 1880 the Chileans returned, this time with their entire national army. Unable to hold out against such a large force, the Mapuches were finally defeated in 1881, ending over three centuries of resistance to the Spanish expansion. The Mapuches were the last indigenous nation of South America to be conquered. The Mapuches signed treaties with the Chilean government, and most were settled on reservations farther to the south in 1884, thereby losing even more land to Chilean colonization. The last Mapuches were defeated in Patagonia by a combined force of Chileans and Argentineans.

The defeated Mapuches, many of their most productive lands confiscated and colonized by Chileans, Argentineans, and immigrants newly arrived from Europe, settled on small farms on their remaining communal lands. Over the next decades the Mapuches lost control of all of their land except for a compact region in the foothills of the Andes; they were ultimately restricted to reservations, under direct Chilean or Argentine government control.

In 1927 the Indian Law was passed, allowing indigenous peoples to purchase individual land titles in Chile. This law was never fully implemented, and much of the remaining Mapuche land was sold to large estates, often those of absentee owners. The decrease in available land and a tripling of the Mapuche population between 1927 and 1961 caused severe poverty, disease, and hunger. Rapid population growth and limited opportunities during the 1950s and 1960s forced many young Mapuches to migrate to the cities in search of work.

Increasingly politicized, urban activists formed cultural and national organizations, many decidedly procommunist—an ideology that appealed to the Mapuches' ancient communal tradition. In 1970, Salvador Allende, a leftist, was elected president of Chile, with overwhelming support from the indigenous peoples. Allende's government passed laws that allowed the Mapuches to reclaim traditional lands. A Directorate of Indigenous Affairs was created to formulate policies in such areas as health care, education, and literacy.

The liberal policies of the Allende government ended with the military coup in 1973. The dictatorship established by Augusto Pinochet murdered Mapuche leaders of organizations that had supported the Allende government. Dozens of Mapuches were killed and their bodies dumped in mass graves. Most of the lands recovered by the Mapuche under Allende were taken away.

The Mapuche situation worsened in the 1970s, during which only 40% of Mapuche babies survived their first year. Forestry companies, helped by large subsidies from General Pinochet's regime, began operations in Araucania. They planted vast tracts of land with pine and eucalyptus. The firms employed few locals, but the worst was that the forests dried up water supplies, making life in the region even more precarious.

In 1978 young nationalists abandoned the Mapuches' long and unsuccessful struggle for acceptance in Chile and formed the Mapuche People's Liberation Organization (AD MAPU). In 1984, following the murder of three AD MAPU leaders, the nationalists adopted a program aimed at eventual independence for Araucania. Several radical organizations turned to violence, while others began a process of occupying lands they claimed as traditional Mapuche national territory.

The Mapuche reservations were abolished in the 1980s over protests that the communal holding of land was part of the Mapuche culture. Violence against the Mapuches continued throughout the 1980s, in spite of protests by international organizations and foreign governments. The Mapuches were not permitted to practice their religion or customs, their language was prohibited in public, and educating their children about their culture and language was forbidden.

A democratic Chilean government elected in 1989 attempted to redress some of the past injustices, but with little success. In 1991 nationalists threatened a secessionist uprising unless preparations were initiated to return 600,000 thousand acres taken from the Mapuches since 1881. The new Chilean government's drive to modernize the economy via road building, hydroelectric dams, and industrialization was often detrimental to the interests of the Mapuches. Many development projects were carried out in contravention of Chile's law concerning the indigenous peoples. According to this law, projects must have the permission of the indigenous landowners, but usually work was pushed through without the consent of the Mapuche communities. Activists organized occupations of lands they claimed had been illegally taken.

Disappointed by their failure to win justice in the Chilean courts, many young Mapuches embraced a more radicalized form of nationalism. The 1992 Chilean census indicated that there were 928,500 Mapuches in Chile, but nationalists disputed the results as failing to count the majority of the growing urban Mapuche population. In late 1992 most of the nationalist organizations supported a demand that the Spanish, Chilean, and Argentine governments recognize and honor past treaties with the Mapuches, which would in effect give legal sanction to Mapuche independence.

The Mapuche tribes, formerly autonomous and disunited, by the early 1990s had formed a viable nation. Mapuche leaders from Chile and Argentina met in Neuquén for the first time to discuss approaches to the creation of an autonomous territory. In September 1992 they adopted a national flag to represent all their groups. They vowed to continue land occupations until the Chilean and Argentinian governments responded to their demands for autonomous status and settled outstanding claims. In January 1993, several thousand acres were awarded to Mapuche communities.

In the late 1990s smoldering tension produced occasional violence, particularly against the forestry companies. The government in 1998 unveiled a plan to construct roads, supply technical help for Mapuche farmers, grant scholarships for their children, write off debt to the state agricultural agency, and allow bilingual schools. The plan, though denounced as too little, was at least the result of consultation with the Mapuches, a first step in the right direction.

The small reservations in Chile and Argentina are inadequate for the number of people in them, and it is increasingly difficult to maintain their traditional life and culture. Mapuche infant mortality is the highest in the region, and the average Mapuche life span is ten years less that of other Chileans and Argentineans. Educational opportunities are limited, and there is a high rate of adult illiteracy. In 1995, a bilingual program sponsored by the United Nations Children's Fund (UNICEF) was implemented to teach young Mapuches from two to five years old their native language, customs, and history, as well as the Spanish language.

In October 1999, Mapuche leaders claimed that repression under the current democratic government of Chile was as bad as it had been under Pinochet. In 1999 alone, 450 Mapuches were detained, including women, old people, and children. The detentions were authorized under the Internal State Security Act, citing the conflicts between Mapuche communities and the forestry companies. Other Mapuches were arrested for participating in outlawed religious ceremonies and in occupation of farms on traditional Mapuche lands.

The Chilean government announced in August 1999 a new development plan for the Mapuches. Like the UNICEF plan of 1995, the plan included new all-weather roads, technical help for farmers, scholarships for Mapuche children, debt write-offs, and bilingual schools. The package of aid, while welcomed by the Mapuches, was denounced by militants as too little because it failed to address the Mapuche land claims.

Members of the Mapuche Inter-regional Council traveled in November 1999 to Madrid to remind members of the Spanish parliament that the Spanish crown had recognized, in 28 international treaties, the independence of the Mapuche nation and its sovereignty over territories to the south of the Bío-Bío River in Chile and the Colorado River in Argentina. In June 2000, while on a speaking tour in Spain, Mapuche leader Aucan Huilcaman declared that the Mapuche nation had no option but to start an armed rebellion to defend its rights.

SELECTED BIBLIOGRAPHY:

Berglund, Staffan. *The National Integration of Mapuche, Ethnic Minority in Chile.* 1991.

Faron, Louis C. *The Mapuche Indians of Chile.* 1986.

Lam, Maivan. *At the Edge of the State: Indigenous Peoples and Self-Determination.* 2000.

Psacharopoulos, George, and Harry Anthony Patrinos, eds. *Indigenous People and Poverty in Latin America.* 1994.

Maris

Mariys; Mariis; Marijs; Maryans; Chermiss; Chermis

POPULATION: Approximately (2002e) 785,000 Maris in Russia, concentrated in the Republic of Mari El, a member state of the Russian Federation. There are sizable Mari populations in the neighboring republics of Bashkortostan, Udmurtia, Tatarstan, as well as the regions of Kirov, Perm, Sverdlovsk, Yekaterinburg, and Nizhni-Novgorod. There are smaller communities in Central Asia, particularly in Kazakhstan.

THE MARI HOMELAND: The Mari homeland, known as Marintasavalta or Land of the Maris, lies in the middle Volga River valley, a region of rolling heavily forested steppe lands extending north from the left bank of the Volga. With only a few good roads and only one railroad, a branch line from Kazan to Ioshkar-Ola, the region is mostly rural and agricultural. The Mari heartland, organized as an autonomous *oblast* in 1920, was raised to the status of an autonomous republic within the Soviet Russian Federation in 1936 and became a member state of the new Russian Federation in 1991. About 48% of the total Mari population of Russia lives outside the boundaries of the ethnic republic, mostly in neighboring provinces and republics. *Republic of Mari-El (Respublika Mariy-El/Marintasavalta)*: 8,958 sq. mi.—23,201 sq. km, (2002e) 751,000—Maris 48%, Russians 42%, Tatars* 6%, Chavash* 1%, Udmurts* 1%, others 2%. The Mari capital and major cultural center is Ioshkar-Ola, called Joschkar-Ola or Charla by the Maris, (2002e) 248,000.

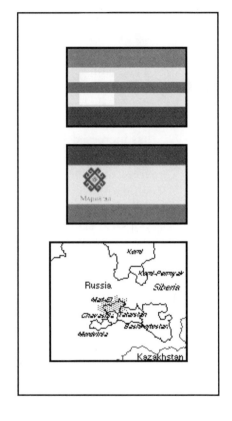

FLAG: The Mari national flag, the flag of the national movement, is a horizontal tricolor of pale blue, white, and red, the white stripe twice the width of the other stripes, and bearing a narrow horizontal stripe across the center. The official flag of Mari republic is horizontal tricolor of pale blue, white, and red, the white twice the width of the other stripes and bearing the Mari national symbol, a stylized brown sun, over the name of the republic on the white stripe.

PEOPLE AND CULTURE: The Maris are a Finnic people, belonging to the Volga branch of the Finno-Ugric nations. They are believed by many historians to be descendents of the Volga region's earliest inhabitants. Closely related to the Udmurts and Mordvins,* they are divided into three basic divisions, distinguished by dialect and cultural traits. The Kuryk Mari—known also as Mountain Mari, Forest Mari, or Highland Mari—inhabit the right bank of the Volga River and are the largest of the three groups. The second group is the Olyk Mari, also called Meadow Mari or Lowland Mari, who live on the left bank of the Volga. The smallest of the three groups, the Upo Mari or Eastern Mari, dwell in Bashkortostan, Tatarstan, and the Sverdlovsk Oblast. In spite of decades of suppression and the use of Russian as the medium of education and administration, the Maris have retained a surprisingly cohesive sense of national identity. The Maris are the only Finno-Ugric nation in Russia whose population has increased steadily, in spite of a slight decrease in the use of their native language. Urbanization has also increased, with about 31% living in urban areas in 2000, but to the Maris, urbanization means Russification and assimilation.

LANGUAGE AND RELIGION: The Finnic language of the Maris, Maryan, also called Finno-Cheremisic, belongs to the Volga-Finnic branch of the Finno-Ugric language group. The language is divided into two major dialects, Highland Mari, also known as Hill Mari, and Lowland Mari, called Woods or Lugovo Mari. Highland Mari is spoken by less than 100,000 people, and its speakers have difficulty reading Lowland Mari, the majority dialect, because of lexical differences. A subdialect of Lowland Mari, called Eastern Mari, is spoken by the Upo Mari. Lowland Mari has one major dialect, Grassland Mari, also called Sernur-Morkin, Volga Mari, or Ioshkar Olin. Highland Mari is spoken in two dialects, Kozymodemyan and Yaran. The two major dialects, although quite similar, have each produced literary languages, one based on the Lowland and Eastern dialects, and another based on the Highland dialect. An estimated 90% of the Maris speak their own dialects, while only 65% are able to speak Russian, even though over half the ethnic Maris live outside the boundaries of their republic. The history of the Maris' language has been closely tied to those of its closest Uralic neighbors, the Mordvin and Permic languages spoken by the Udmurts, Komis,* and Permyaks.* The Maris have retained their language more effectively than any other Finno-Ugric nation in Russia. The language is used in schools, books, newspapers, and in radio and television programming.

For centuries the spiritual life of the Maris was closely connected to their forested homeland. The traditional beliefs developed into a nationalistic animist sect called Kugu Sorta, which remains very influential among the Mari population. Even the Orthodox Mari, about two-thirds of the total, retain pagan and shamanistic beliefs and traditions. Of all the nations of the Middle Volga region, the Maris have been the most successful at retaining their native religion while at the same time resisting Islamization by neighboring peoples. The adherence to their native religion has deeply influenced Mari folklore and cultural life in general, and it remains an important factor in the Mari revival and in Mari politics.

NATIONAL HISTORY: The Mari, believed to be the first inhabitants of the vast Volga River basin, traditionally roamed the steppe lands between the Volga Basin and the Ural Mountains to the east. First mentioned in sixth-century records as seminomadic tribes in the Volga region, the Maris never developed a state system but lived under the political control of stronger neighboring nations, as a group of related, but disunited, tribes or clans. From about A.D. 700, they formed a close relationship with the neighboring Volga Bulgars.

In the eighth century, the Turkic Khazars established a nominal authority in the Volga Basin. The Maris, under Khazar rule, practiced slash-and-burn agriculture, hunting and fishing, and limited trade with neighboring peoples. By the mid-ninth century, the Volga Bulgars, the ancestors of the Chavash, took control of the region. The Bulgars ruled until the mid-twelfth century, leaving a marked cultural and political impression on the scattered Mari tribes. The Bulgar state fell to invading Mongols and Tatars of the Golden Horde in 1236; the Maris came under the rule of the Tatars, who settled the Volga Basin. The Tatar Khanate of Kazan became the primary power in the region following the disintegration of the Mongol Empire in the fourteenth century.

Significant Russian cultural and economic contact with the Maris began as early as the twelfth century, but Russian influence remained nominal until Cossacks and Orthodox missionaries began to penetrate the khanate in the fifteenth century. Under the influence of the Slavs most of the Kuryk Maris converted to Orthodox Christianity, but the Olyk and Upo Maris, living on the other side of the Volga, retained their animist beliefs.

In 1552 the Russians, led by Tsar Ivan the Terrible, conquered Kazan and initiated the Slav colonization of the Volga River basin. The Maris resisted Russian domination and fought a series of defensive wars, called the Cheremiss Wars, in 1552–57, 1572–74, and 1581–84. The wars ended in defeat and massacre. Thousands fled east, and Russian colonization of their homeland accelerated.

The Mari, although more blond and Nordic than the Russians, were subjected to a harsh colonial regime and relegated to virtual slavery on the vast estates of absentee Russian landlords. The Upo Maris began to migrate eastward in the sixteenth century, with more leaving the region in the seventeenth and eighteenth centuries, by which time they had evolved a distinct identity. Some converted to Islam under the influence of the

Bashkorts* and Tatars to the east, while others incorporated elements of Islam into their traditional beliefs.

The process of Mari assimilation to Russian civilization accelerated during the seventeenth century. Social and economic change was countered in many ways, including strong nativistic movements. Pressure to adopt Orthodox Christianity became especially intense in the early 1800s, when Russians began to worry about the number of distinct nationalities living in the empire. The Maris' resistance to Russian-style Christianity resulted in severe persecution and intense assimilation pressures from Orthodox missionaries.

Official efforts to eradicate their languages and culture provoked several serious revolts in the seventeenth and eighteenth centuries. To divide Mari resistance, the tsarist authorities partitioned their lands among several Russian provinces and banned the Mari language and culture. Believing that Christianity and education were closely related, the missionaries worked to develop a literary language for the Maris; it was produced in 1803, and the same year a catechism was published in Kuryk Mari.

Living in conditions of cruelty, ignorance, and poverty, a majority of the Maris clung to traditional shamanistic beliefs, which played a large part in their separate identity. Even the Christian Mari minority incorporated portions of their former animistic beliefs into their religious ceremonies. The Mari effort to preserve animist beliefs stimulated a strong religious and nationalist resurgence, a mass anti-Russian movement, in the latter half of the nineteenth century.

In the 1870s, when a number of Mari leaders began openly to resist Russification and conversion to Christianity, the various Mari religious beliefs were formalized as part of a nationalistic religious sect called Kugu Sorta (Great Candle), intensely anti-Russian and anti-Orthodox. Kugu Sorta was especially influential among the Olyk and Upo Maris. A rebellion broke out, led by members of the Kugu Sorta, protesting against the mission work of the Russian Orthodox church in their homeland.

The Maris, then 90% illiterate, again rose during the 1905 Russian Revolution to attack and burn Russian estates and settlements on their traditional lands. Following a number of skirmishes with government troops, the Mari rebels moved into the thick forests and formed guerrilla bands called the Forest Brethren. The army finally overcame the last rebel bands in 1906. The national awakening of the Maris dates from 1905–1907, when the first efforts to organize on a national basis were realized.

Young Mari conscripts sent to the front during World War I deserted and returned home following news of the revolution in St. Petersburg in February 1917. The Mari soldiers formed the nucleus of a national army that formed to protect the Mari people as civil government collapsed and armed bands roamed the Volga region. Freed from Russian domination, the Maris established the organs of self-rule that oversaw the setting up of hospitals and the organization of literacy classes and Mari language schools, *Likeezes*.

In the summer of 1917 the Maris convened a national congress and voted in favor of a federation of non-Russian states in the Volga–Ural region and the expulsion of the region's Slav settlers. On 24 January 1918 the federation, the Idel-Ural Federation, made up of several Finnic and Turkic nations in the Volga basin, declared independence from Russia. In February 1918, however, before the Volga nations could organize, Bolshevik troops invaded and rapidly overran Mari El, Mari Territory. In July 1918 the Maris rebelled against the excesses of the Red Army and the bureaucratic Soviets. The Red soldiers crushed the Maris and arrested their small, educated elite. Branded "class enemies," all of the Mari's potential leaders were deported or liquidated.

The Soviet government created a nominally autonomous region for the surviving Maris on 4 November 1920. In 1920–21, tens of thousands of Maris perished in the famine that followed the civil war and the inept introduction of communism. Over a third of the 1914 Mari population had died by the end of 1921. The collectivization of Mari agriculture began in the late 1920s and was completed, over Mari protests and resistance, in the early 1930s. Most of the Mari intellectual and professional classes were eliminated in the process.

Under Soviet rule the Mari language was again allowed; it became one of the official languages of the autonomous republic created in 1936. The Soviet government later launched a drive to industrialize the region, and Russian was made the only official language in education and government in the late 1930s. In spite of official Soviet suppression, the Maris made great strides in education and culture.

The small Mari republic was increasingly industrialized and urbanized during World War II, as whole factories and Slav populations were transferred to the region from western Russia. By 1945 the Maris formed a minority in their homeland, which had a mixed population of Maris, Slavs, and other Soviet nationalities. During the 1950s, a new wave of Russian colonization was sponsored by the Soviet government. Resentment of their minority status and the rapid decline in the use of the Mari language sparked a cultural reawakening in the 1960s. Younger Maris took a new interest in their history, their language, and their unique religion as Russian pressure to adopt the ideal of Soviet culture intensified.

The Mari revival, taking on nationalistic overtones in the 1970s, grew into a mass movement following the Gorbachev reforms that liberalized Soviet life after 1987. Unofficial nationalist organizations, organized in 1989, pressured the republican government to change the republic's name and to declare Mari El a sovereign state on 22 October 1990, with three official languages—Lowland Mari, Highland Mari, and Russian. The republic's government unilaterally declared Mari El a full republic within the reorganized Russian Federation following the disintegration of the Soviet Union in August 1991. At the end of 1991 a presidential system was introduced in the republic, and free elections for the local legislature were inaugurated.

In spite of hundreds of years of Russian efforts to assimilate the Maris, they have maintained a cohesive sense of their distinct identity. In the late 1990s, over 80% used Mari as their first language, and less than two-thirds understood the Russian language. Their animistic religion, which venerates the Mari's past, remains a strong influence among all the Maris, but particularly among the Olyk and Upo Maris. Mari schools have been restored in many areas since 1990, and congregations of their indigenous nature religion have been founded in Mari communities, within the republic and in neighboring republics and regions. That the Russian government officially supports a nature religion is unique in all of Europe.

The indigenous Mari religion, which is revered by both Christians and non-Christians, has become a strong political force through the creation of a political organization for the adherents of the *chi marla vera*, the teachings of Kugu Sorta. This organization, called Osh Mari Chi Mari, seeks to legitimize the Maris' traditional religion and, over the protests of the Russian Orthodox Church, to revitalize the Mari religion and culture.

In 1997, the leadership of Mari-El Republic announced that in an effort to attract outside investment, the republic would become an "offshore" zone. There had been little serious investment in the republic's economy in recent years, but investors now enjoyed two years' exemption from all local taxes. The move was partly in response to increased nationalist activity. The Maris complained that ethnic Russians had been encouraged in Soviet times to move into their homeland and that the population transfer had been used to prevent Mari self-determination. Although separatism is not as yet a significant force among the Maris, a lack of raw materials and industrial base that makes them dependent on the federal government for financial support has become a serious national issue.

In January 1997 presidential elections were held in the Mari republic. In the final round of voting, both candidates were ethnic Russians who did not speak the Mari language. The election was won by Vyacheslav Kislitsyn, who removed a number of Mari officials from the government. By 1999, Kislitsyn had come under increasing pressure from the opposition, including Mari nationalists. Local Mari leaders sent two letters to Russian president Vladimir Putin, complaining about the state of the republic's economy under Kislitsyn's rule. Several Mari leaders requested that the republic be placed under the direct rule of the federal government until new elections could be organized.

Economic problems in the region in 2001 led to demonstrations and strikes. The demonstrators, often carrying nationalist flags and chanting nationalist slogans, blame the problems on the Maris' lack of control in their officially "autonomous" republic.

SELECTED BIBLIOGRAPHY:

Fine, Robert. *People, Nation, and State.* 1999.
Hilderley, Jeri. *Mari.* 1990.
Taagepera, Rein. *The Finno-Ugric Republics and the Russian State.* 1999.
Warhola, James W. *Politicized Ethnicity in the Russian Federation: Dilemmas of State Formation.* 1996.

Maronites

Levantines; Maronite Christians; Phoenicians

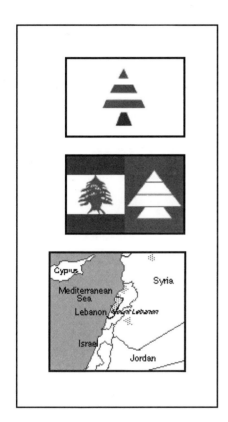

POPULATION: Approximately (2002e) 1,135,000 Maronites in the Middle East, concentrated in the Mount Lebanon region of Lebanon with about 950,000, with smaller communities in Syria, Israel, Cyprus, and Egypt, as well as in Europe, North America, Africa, and South America. The Maronite diaspora is believed to number between three and five million.

THE MARONITE HOMELAND: The Maronite homeland lies in the Middle East, on the Mediterranean coast. The region, largely a coastal plain, rises to the Lebanon Mountains in the east. Mount Lebanon, the Maronite heartland, forms a region of the Lebanese republic. *Lebanon (Republic of Lebanon)* (2002e) 3,964,000—Lebanese 80% (Shi'a Muslims 31%, Maronites 22%, Sunni Muslims 16%, Druze* 6%, Greek Orthodox 3%, Greek Catholic 2%), Palestinians* 12%, Armenians 5%, Syrians, Kurds 3%. *Mount Lebanon (Jabal Lubnän)*: 753 sq. mi.—1,950 sq. km, (2002e) 1,876,000—Maronites 77%, Sunni Muslims 8%, Druze 6%, Greek Orthodox 5%, Greek Catholics 3%, other Lebanese 1%. The Maronite capital and major cultural center is Beirut, (2002e) 1,146,000, metropolitan area 1,867,000. The other major cultural center is Juniyah, called Jounieh by the Maronites, (2002e) 79,000.

FLAG: The Maronite national flag, the flag of the national movement, is a white field with a stylized, centered green and brown cedar tree. The flag of the Phalange (Kataeb), the largest Maronite political party, is divided vertically; the hoist has three horizontal stripes of red, white, and red, bearing a centered green cedar tree; the fly is a green field bearing a stylized white cedar tree.

PEOPLE AND CULTURE: The Maronites are an ethnoreligious people of mixed background, mostly Arabic and European. They are hardy, martial mountaineers of the Lebanon Mountains; they evolved a distinct culture and way of life in the isolation of their strongholds. In the twentieth century their national identity has been reinforced by sectarian warfare and the loss of the power they held in Lebanon before 1975. Their origins are uncertain, although they claim ultimate descent from the ancient Phoenicians of the region. The Maronite culture is basically European, although their music, cuisine, and other cultural traits are Middle Eastern. Until the civil war of 1975–90, the Maronites had considered themselves the foundation of the Lebanese nation, but their national identity was shattered by subsequent events. Emigration has been the Maronite answer to discrimination and their minority status in the Middle East since the early nineteenth century. Activists increasingly refer to the Maronites and the smaller Christian groups as the Phoenician nation.

LANGUAGE AND RELIGION: The Christians speak a dialect of Arabic along with French, the former colonial language. The language of daily life is Levantine Arabic, also called Lebanese-Syrian Arabic. The language is spoken in four major dialects—North, North-Central, South-Central, and South. The Maronite dialect has been heavily influenced by French. In religious services, the Maronites use the Karshuni script with old Syriac letters. Portions of the Bible were published in the Maronite Arabic dialect in 1973.

The origins of the Maronites is uncertain. One version traces them to John Maron of Antioch in the seventh century A.D.; another points to another John Maron, a monk of Homs in the late fourth or early fifth century. The word *maron* or *marun* in Aramaic (Syriac) means "small lord." The Maronites are the largest Uniate or Eastern Church in Lebanon and represent an indigenous church under the authority of the patriarch of Antioch, resident in Lebanon. They reestablished relations with the Roman Catholic Church in the twelfth century but have retained their own rites and canon law and use Arabic and Aramaic in their liturgy.

NATIONAL HISTORY: The Maronites claim descent from the ancient Canaanite peoples, who established a string of coastal city-states and by 1250 B.C. had become the premier navigators and traders of the Mediterranean Sea. First called Phoenician by the Greeks in the ninth century B.C., the wealthy city-states planted colonies around the Mediterranean and as far west as Spain. The region gained fame in the ancient world for the magnificent cedar trees of the Lebanon Mountains. Successively under the rule of Babylon, Assyria, the Greeks, Selucids, Romans, and Byzantines, the region became a patchwork of cultures and languages. Considered part of ancient Syria, the region early came under Christian influence, and by the third century A.D. the majority of the population had become Christians.

The Maronites trace their origins to St. Maron, Marun in Arabic, a

Syrian hermit of the late fourth and early fifth centuries, and also St. John Maron, or Joannes Maron, in Arabic Yuhanna Marun, the patriarch of Antioch in 685–707, under whose leadership the invading Byzantine armies of Justinian II were routed in 684, making the Maronites an independent nation. Although their traditions assert that the Maronites were always Orthodox Christians in union with the Roman church, there is evidence that for centuries they were Monothelites, followers of the heretical doctrine of Sergius, patriarch of Constantinople, who affirmed that there was a divine will, but no human will, in Christ.

In the early seventh century the Christians split over Monotheletism. Many of the Christians of Syria broke with the established Byzantine church and created the Maronite sect, with its own hierarchy. Persecuted by the Byzantine authorities, the Maronites fled en masse from northern Syria to the relative safety of the Lebanon Mountains. There the Maronites formed a distinct community under their own spiritual leader, the patriarch of Antioch.

Muslim Arab invaders conquered the region in 635, rapidly converting a majority of the lowland population to Islam. The isolated Maronites of the Lebanon Mountains rejected Islam and clung to their Christian sect. Tolerated but considered infidels and subjected to special taxes and other indemnities, the Maronites were excluded from government and the professions, and they suffered periodic persecutions.

Shi'a Muslims moved into the region in the ninth century, followed by the Druze in the eleventh century. As they arrived, the groups jostled for geographic position, some of which they still hold. The Maronites took control of the Mount Lebanon region, the Druze settled the Chouf Mountains to their south, the Shi'as settled in the south and in the Beqaa Valley, the Sunnis settled on the coast, dominating the regions both north and south of the Maronites.

The Maronites welcomed the Christian crusaders from Europe in the eleventh and twelfth centuries. In 1110 the Maronite homeland became part of the Christian Kingdom of Jerusalem. The crusaders employed local Christians to administer the region. Under crusader influence the Maronites again accepted the authority of Rome in 1182, although the union was not formally established until the sixteenth century. In 1291 the resurgent Muslims defeated the crusaders. Though the region was a part of the Ottoman Empire after 1516, the Druze became its real rulers, under the nominal rule of the Mamaluks of Egypt. The Maronites and the smaller Christian sects prospered in trade and agriculture, in spite of official discrimination.

The Maronite religious ties to Europe ensured a steady exchange of religious leaders, commercial traders, and explorers. By the seventeenth century, the Maronites had developed a cultural affinity for Europe, particularly France. European culture had a profound influence on the Maronites, who adopted European dress and much of the French culture. The French language became the language of the Maronite upper classes. In 1857–58 Maronite peasants revolted against the large, Europeanized land-owning families.

Rivalry between the Druze and the Christians under Ottoman rule culminated in massacres of the Maronites by the Druze between 1841 and 1860. The massacres of Christians prompted European intervention in the region, led by the French. In 1861 the Maronite homeland, Mount Lebanon, became an autonomous region under a Christian governor. French and British pressure prompted the Turks to establish a semi-autonomous province, a refuge for the besieged Maronite population.

At the end of the First World War, the French established a League of Nations mandate in the former Turkish province of Syria. Under pressure from the Maronites, the mandate authorities added the Beqaa, the coastal cities, and areas of the north and south to Mount Lebanon. The five districts were named Greater Lebanon, a region with a mixed population but a Maronite majority. In 1926 the French split Lebanon from Syria as a protectorate. The French authorities proclaimed Lebanon, dominated by the Maronites, an independent state in 1941. The "Switzerland of the Middle East" flourished as the banking and recreation center of the Arab world.

The idea of power sharing was broached in a 1943 national pact between the Maronites and the Sunnis. Lebanon would be an independent, neutral state. The Maronites would not seek Western protection, and the Muslims would not try to assimilate Lebanon into a larger Arab or Muslim state. Lebanon was to have an Arab facade but a distinct identity. The president was to be a Maronite, the prime minister a Sunni Muslim, and the speaker of the parliament a Shi'a Muslim. In 1944, a sectarian Lebanese government was formed on the basis of a census taken in 1932.

The establishment of Israel on Lebanon's southern border provoked strong Arab resentment and quickly undermined Lebanon's national peace. Under Muslim pressure, Lebanon joined the Arab League and participated in the war against Israel in 1948. The Arab defeat divided the Lebanese population. The Maronites favored an independent course for Lebanon and stressed the state's strong ties to Europe. The fast-growing Muslim population demanded close ties to the more radical Arab states. Thousands of Palestinians settled in refugee camps across Lebanon, adding a new dimension to the patchwork of religious and ethnic groups. A Palestinian revolt in Jordan was violently crushed in 1970–71, adding tens of thousands to the refugee camps in Lebanon.

The growing divisions within Lebanon continued to destabilize the state even as it became wealthy as a Middle Eastern tourist, trade, and financial center. The growing enmity between the Christians and Muslims finally erupted in a Syrian-backed Muslim revolt in 1958, leading to U.S. military intervention, but not to Maronite concessions. In 1967, a group of Maronite leaders of the Phalange, the principal Maronite political organization, attempted to detach Lebanon from the Arab world and affirm its status as a distinct society, on the basis of its Phoenician roots.

The Muslim population, growing more rapidly than the Christian, formed a majority in Lebanon by the early 1970s, although a national census had not been taken since 1932. Demands for greater Muslim political and economic participation in the Maronite-dominated state were given force by the large, radicalized Palestinian refugee population. The tension finally erupted in civil war in 1975. The conflict was initially between the Maronites, representing the established order, and various Muslim militias, particularly the large Palestinian population. The fighting left central Beirut in ruins, divided between the Maronites in the east and Muslims in the west. The war gave the world a new word, "Lebanonization," the breakup of a state into warring enclaves. In 1976, the Maronite leadership invited the Syrian army into Lebanon assist in fighting the Palestinians.

The division of Lebanon into militarized ministates virtually destroyed the country, and it stimulated Maronite nationalist sentiment for secession of the Christian enclave of Mount Lebanon, an undeclared ministate at war with its neighbors. Palestinian militancy and Israeli and Syrian military intervention worsened the situation. The Israelis often answered Palestinian terrorist acts in Israel or by striking at Lebanese targets. American, French, and Italian troops were landed in 1982 but withdrew after heavy casualties.

The Israeli army invaded Lebanon in 1978 and again in 1982, with the assistance of the Maronites. In 1982, the Palestinian Liberation Organization (PLO) was formally expelled from the country by the Israelis. During the fighting around Beirut, Maronite militiamen massacred hundreds of Palestinians in the Chatila and Sabra camps south of Beirut. The event set off another round of intense fighting, which overwhelmed most of the Maronite territories. Thousands of Maronites fled abroad, mostly to Europe, as feudal warlords with private militias fought for control of land, resources, and power. The Maronite defeat ended the long Maronite domination of Lebanon.

A peace plan, approved in 1989, provided for power sharing and the end of the former Christian domination. The plan, overseen by Syrian troops, divided the Christian heartland. Some Christian groups were in favor of it, while others pushed for secession. A Maronite general, Michel Aoun, launched a war to expel the Syrians. General Aoun's attempt to maintain Lebanon's independence made him a hero to some but a terrorist or war criminal to others. In February 1990, fighting broke out between Aoun's forces and the Maronite Lebanese Forces (LF), led by Samir Geagas. By mid-February, when a cease-fire was reached, over 600 Maronites had died and 2,000 had been injured. The conflict provoked a two-year civil war within the Christian enclave that ended only with the intervention of Syrian troops against General Aoun's forces in 1991. Aoun finally took refuge in the French embassy, eventually settling near Paris.

The ingrained sense of superiority that had long influenced Maronite conduct in Lebanon was now shattered. Well aware of the fate of other Christian minorities in the Muslim world, the Christians of Lebanon, however, did not discard the nationalism that had aided the survival of the small nation under centuries of Muslim rule.

In the late 1990s, some 35,000 Syrian soldiers and an unknown number of *mukhabarat*, intelligence officers, continued to oversee Lebanon's internal affairs. For the Maronites, it was a humiliating reminder of the constraints on Lebanon's sovereignty. Although the Maronites still constituted about 25% of Lebanon's population, their influence had been diminished through war, emigration, and the demographic growth of the heavily politicized Shi'a Muslim population, which had surpassed 40% of the total.

On 22 May 1991, Lebanon and Syria signed a treaty in which they agreed to cooperate on military, economic, and political issues. This agreement was a major blow to many Maronites, who viewed Syria's influence in Lebanon as a violation of its sovereignty. Many Maronites boycotted the parliamentary elections in August 1992 to protest Syria's continuing domination of the country. Several high-ranking Maronites in government resigned to protest the elections.

The Israeli troops that had occupied southern Lebanon since 1978 finally withdrew in early 2000, leaving an uncertain situation in Lebanon. The Lebanese state continued to be the pawn of outside interests and the 17 domestic religious-national groups. The Israeli withdrawal prompted calls among Maronites for Syria's troops to pull out as well. In 1994, the Maronite patriarch accused the Syrian-backed Lebanese government of bias against the once-dominant Christians.

In 1995 the Maronite bishops held their first synod since the beginning of the civil war. They urged their brethren to stop fleeing Lebanon and invited back the estimated 900,000 Maronites who had fled the country between 1975 and 1990. By 1999, an estimated half of that number had returned to their homes, but the Maronite diaspora remains large and influential. Tens of thousands return every year, although most maintain ties overseas that would give them refuges in case of renewed war in Lebanon.

In 1996, in a move to appease the Druze, the Lebanese parliament voted to divide Mount Lebanon into six new districts. The only Maronite-dominated region, Mount Lebanon also has a large Druze population in the south. The division was strongly opposed by the Maronites. In August and September 1996, the Maronites, having boycotted the 1992 vote, participated in elections and posed a serious challenge to the Syrian-controlled government.

In May 1997 Pope John Paul II visited Lebanon, intending to help the Maronites become fully integrated in the post–civil war Lebanese society. He called for Lebanon's complete independence and implored the Christian communities, particularly the Maronites, to remain in Lebanon in spite of hardship and discrimination.

In 1998, in another blow to the Maronite position in Lebanon, several non-Maronite politicians called for a new constitution that would end the practice by which parliament appointed the president, who had to be a Maronite. In October 1998, the Maronites welcomed the selection of a Maronite, Emile Lahoud, as the president of Lebanon, but the sense of separate identity continued to grow. In February 1999, several Maronite leaders, including a diaspora leader, Raymon Edde, condemned the Syrian government's decision to place voting booths for a Syrian election on Lebanese territory, arguing that the move indicated that Lebanon had become nothing more than another Syrian province.

The death of President Hafiz Assad of Syria began a new era of uncertainty in Lebanon. The question arose as to whether Bashar Assad, the heir, would maintain Syria's iron grip on Lebanon. Syrian control had meant balancing Lebanon's competing sectarian communities, while binding the two countries ever closer. In early 2000 several Maronite leaders called for the withdrawal of Syrian troops from Lebanese territory. Even moderate Maronites hoped for a diminished role for Syria in Lebanon.

In September 2000 the normally reticent Maronite partiarch, Nasrallah Sfeir, launched a broadside against the Syrian presence. Following months of increasing tensions between the Maronite population and the Syrian occupation troops, the Syrian government in May 2001 began to withdraw troops from Christian areas, particularly around Beirut, and by June had withdrawn all troops from Beirut and the other major cities in the Maronite heartland in Mount Lebanon. The Maronites, unabashedly westernized and relatively rich, had long chafed under the occupation of troops seen as representatives of a grubby, grasping neighboring state.

The spiritual leader of Lebanon's Maronite Catholics, Cardinal Nasrallah Sfeir, made a historic visit to Druze-controlled territory in the Chouf region of Mount Lebanon. Earlier, Cardinal Sfeir said that the two communities had turned the black page of the past, and opened a new era of cooperation and solidarity for the sake of Lebanon. The increasing rapprochement between the Maronites and the Druze was seen a threatening by the Muslim groups. Over 250 Maronite leaders and activists were arrested and put on trial for threatening the integration of the Lebanese state. Although the majority were later released, the arrests raised tensions and sectarian hatreds in the region. Several Maronite activists were accused of planning the secession of Mount Lebanon, East Beirut, Zahlah, Hasbaya, and Rashaya from the Lebanese state.

In early September the Council of Maronite Bishops strongly attacked the influence Syria exerts in Lebanon. The Christian bishops said the presence of thousands of Syrian troops imposed Syrian domination over Lebanese affairs, prevented democratic reforms, and stifled freedoms. The President of Lebanon, Emile Lahoud—himself a Maronite—said the Syrian presence had brought stability. The implication of several Lebanese Muslim in the terrorist attacks on the United States in September 2001 further strained relations between the pro-Western Maronites and the more radical pro-Syrian elements among the Shi'a and Sunni Muslims.

The fragile peace in Lebanon could be merely a pause in the long history of conflict. The Maronite minority that advocates returning to the boundaries of pre–World War I Mount Lebanon, an enclave dominated by the Maronite majority, has been dismissed as a fringe movement, but another round of violence in the region could make separation the last redoubt of the besieged Maronite nation.

SELECTED BIBLIOGRAPHY:

El Khazen, Farid. *The Breakdown of the State in Lebanon, 1967–1976*. 2000.
Moosa, Matti. *The Maronites in History*. 1986.
Salhab, Nasri. *France and the Maronites*. 1995.
Winslow, Charles. *Lebanon: War and Politics in a Fragmented Society*. 1996.

Martinicans

Martiniqueans; Martiniquans; Martiniquais; Madianans; Martinecos; Martinique Creoles

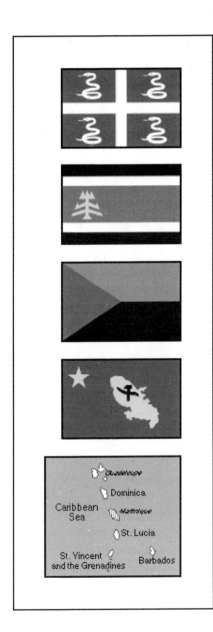

POPULATION: Approximately (2002e) 380,000 Martinicans in the French Caribbean islands, concentrated in Martinique. There are small Martinican communities in the other French islands and in continental France.

THE MARTINICAN HOMELAND: The Martinican homeland, the island of Martinique, lies in the southern Caribbean Sea, one of the Windward Islands. Martinique is located between the island republics of Dominica on the north and St. Lucia on the south. The island, one of the most fertile in the Caribbean, is of volcanic origin and mountainous, with several active volcanoes surrounded by narrow, deeply indented coastal plains. Martinique forms an overseas department of the French Republic. *Department of Martinique (Madiana)*: 436 sq. mi.—1,128 sq. km, (2002e) 388,000—Martinicans (African descent or African, white, Indian mixtures) 94%, French (Béké and Metro) 1.5%, East Indians 2%, Chinese, Lebanese, and others 2.5%. The Martinican capital and major cultural center is Fort-de-France, (2002e) 95,000, urban area 169,000.

FLAG: The Martinican national flag, the flag of the national movement, is a medium-blue field divided by a narrow white cross, each quarter bearing a coiled white snake. The flag of Martinique Independence Movement (Mouvement Indépendantiste Martiniquais) (MIM) is a red field bearing a stylized yellow tree, the Madyoumbe, near the hoist, narrow horizontal black stripes at the top and bottom divided from the red by thin white stripes. The flag of the National Front for the Liberation of Martinique (Front National de Libération de la Martinique) (FNLM) is a horizontal bicolor of green over black bearing a red triangle at the hoist. The flag of the Workers Party of Martinique (Parti des Travailleurs de Martinique) (PTM) is a red field bearing a yellow, five-pointed star on the upper hoist and a map of the island with the local communist symbol imposed.

PEOPLE AND CULTURE: The Martinicans or Martiniquans, called Martiniquais in French, are mostly the descendents of African slaves with some European and Indian admixture. The racial composition of the Martinicans is extremely mixed, but the mulatto element predominates. Locally called Creoles, the Martinicans evolved a distinct culture and language in the isolation of centuries of island life. The Martinican language and culture also reflect mingled African and French influences. Traditions brought to the island by black African slaves, East Indian indentured workers, Lebanese, Chinese, and continental French have all mingled to form the Martinican Creole culture. Since the 1980s, the average annual population-growth rate has been the lowest in the Caribbean, primarily due to extensive emigration of young people. Most emigration is to France or to other Caribbean islands. The French minority includes island-born Europeans called Békés, and metropolitan French, mostly administrators, military, and merchants, called Metros.

LANGUAGE AND RELIGION: The Martinicans speak a French patois called Creole or Lesser Antillean Creole French. Locally called Patwa, the language is related to the Creole languages of the other French-speaking Caribbean islands, particularly that spoken by the Guadeloupeans.* The literacy rate, high for the Caribbean region, is between 89% and 94%; the majority are able to speak standard French to some degree. Increasingly the Martinicans are learning English, the language of tourism, the new growth industry on the island.

The majority, an estimated 95%, of the Martinicans are nominally Roman Catholic. The Catholic traditions of the island are generously mixed with traditions and customs brought from Africa, in a unique Creole belief system. Evangelical Protestant sects, including the Seventh-Day Adventists and Jehovah's Witnesses, have made inroads on the island since the 1970s.

NATIONAL HISTORY: The island was once inhabited by a native tribal people, the Arawaks, and was called Madiana, the "Island of Flowers." Fierce Carib tribes from the South American mainland moved north, conquering the islands and expelling the peaceful Arawaks. Christopher Columbus is credited with the European discovery of the island in 1502, and the establishment of Spain's territorial claim. Fierce Carib resistance to European incursions precluded settlement on Martinique; the Spanish government ignored the island for over a century.

The island remained under Carib control until 1635, when a group of colonists led by Pierre Bélain d'Esnambuc established a colony. Sugarcane cultivation, introduced from Portuguese Brazil in 1654, required a large workforce. The French imported thousands of black African slaves to work the sugar and tropical fruit plantations. By 1658 French settlers on the island numbered about 5,000. The Caribs gradually disappeared as a result of European diseases, conflicts, and assimilation. In 1674, the island became a domain of the French crown.

A French planter aristocracy dominated the island; its most famous representative, Josephine Rose Tascher de La Pagerie, gained fame as Napoleon's empress. Josephine was born in 1763 under British military occupation during one of the intermittent Anglo-French wars for domination in the Caribbean Sea region.

Martinique's large slave population enjoyed a brief period of freedom following the French Revolution of 1789. A guillotine erected in the center of Saint-Pierre, the island's capital city, abruptly ended the domination of the planter aristocracy. During the wars that followed the revolution, the island changed hands several times before returning to permanent French rule in 1814.

The French authorities abolished slavery in 1848, and over 48,000 slaves suddenly became free men. The French planters then imported low-paid East Indians and Chinese plantation workers to take their places. The former slaves settled on small plots as subsistence farmers and fishermen.

Saint-Pierre became the center of French culture in the Caribbean, a sophisticated city nicknamed the "Paris of the West Indies." On 8 May 1902 the volcano above the city, Mount Pelée, erupted and buried the city. Over 40,000 people in the city and its surroundings perished. Fort-de-France, a town in the south away from the active volcanoes, was designated the new administrative center.

The colony, dominated by the Békés, the descendants of colonial families, and the Metros, continental French officials and business people, flourished in the early twentieth century on the trade in sugar and tropical fruit. The European elite ignored the majority Creoles, who were relegated to menial jobs or subsistence farming until after World War II. At that point, Martinique was upgraded to an overseas department of the French Republic. The Martinicans' new status brought all the rights of the inhabitants of metropolitan departments, but no more say in their local affairs. The Martinicans continued to suffer from high unemployment, underdevelopment, and overpopulation. Emigration, mostly to France and encouraged by the French government, became the only outlet for Martinicans seeking jobs or opportunity.

Postwar Martinican politics were greatly influenced by Aimé Césaire, a Martinican writer and one of the founders of the black Martinican emancipation organization known as the Negritude movement. Césaire was elected as a deputy to the French legislature in 1945, but in 1956 he resigned and formed his own political party, the Progressive Party of Martinique. In 1957 Césaire's pro-independence party won the island elections by an enormous margin, and many called for immediate independence, but economic constraints and underdevelopment were major impediments, in spite of continuing unrest. Even visits of Charles de Gaulle in 1956, 1960, and 1964 could not stem the independence movement or the political unrest.

In spite of the continuing overcentralization of government in faraway Paris, the Martinicans benefited materially in comparison to neighboring Caribbean islands. Rising prosperity brought demands for greater Martinican participation in economic and political decisions that pertained to them. In the 1950s and 1960s leftist political parties gained support among the majority Creoles, mostly with demands for the redistribution of wealth and greater participation in the economy by the Creole population. In 1965 antigovernment, pro-autonomy demonstrations turned to rioting, the beginning of the Martinican national movement. In the 1970s, local leftists and communists began to advocate self-determination and independence, setting off numerous strikes and demonstrations.

In the late 1970s, in an apparent about-face, the French government decided to help the island become economically self-sufficient, in preparation for full independence. The Martinicans' economic problems were exacerbated, however, by widespread destruction from severe hurricanes in 1979 and 1980; independence was postponed.

A number of separatist, nationalist, and autonomist groups emerged in the 1970s and 1980s, some demanding immediate independence, others a gradual transition to eventual independence, and others autonomy with continued economic and political ties to France. Pro-independence disturbances rocked the island, particularly in 1974 and 1980–81, and forced the French government to send police reinforcements from France as a series of bomb attacks disrupted the island. Nationalists claimed responsibility for several bombings in Paris. The disturbances continued until 1988, when an uneasy calm settled on the island.

The French welfare state, extended to Martinique after World War II, has given the population one of the highest standards of living in the Caribbean. Pro-French groups point out that Martinique is part of France, not a colony, and vehemently oppose the loss of the generous French benefits and economic subsidies. The local Béké population, the white Creoles, control an important part of the island's economy.

The Creole population, with a birthrate twice that of continental France, remains the power base of the numerous nationalist organizations. With 50% of the population under 20 years of age, the Creoles suffer endemic unemployment and have few economic opportunities; many are forced to emigrate to find work. Nationalists assert that the Creoles' problems, such as domination by the European minority, are those of colonialism.

The nationalists have made substantial gains in local elections since 1990 and hold nearly half the seats in the local assembly. The nationalist upsurge has not generated violence on the scale seen before 1988. Periodic calls for referendums on independence are mostly ignored by the French administration and rejected by the nationalists, who would likely lose a plebiscite on economic issues. The majority of the islanders would probably vote against complete independence and the consequent loss of French subsidies. The island, with virtually no natural resources and 80% of its economy devoted to sugar production, depends on the export of the sugar and the growing number of tourists, but mostly on French subsidies.

SELECTED BIBLIOGRAPHY:

Crane, Janet. *Martinique*. 1995.

Laguerre, Michel S. *Urban Poverty in the Caribbean: French Martinique as a Social Labratory*. 1990.

Miles, William F.S. *Elections and Ethnicity in French Martinique: A Paradox in Paradise*. 1985.

Reno, Fred., ed. *French and West Indian: Martinique, Guadeloupe, and French Guiana Today*. 1995.

Masas

Dimasas; Kacharis; Masa-Cachari

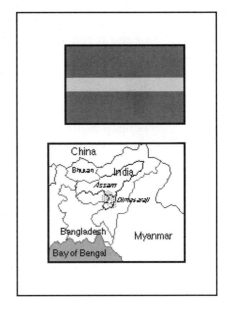

POPULATION: Approximately (2002e) 228,000 Masas, including 148,000 Dimasas and 80,000 Kacharis, concentrated in the Cachar Hills region of southern Assam in northeastern India. Outside the region there are important Masa communities in other parts of Assam, in the neighboring states of Meghalaya and Manipur, and in adjacent areas of Bangladesh.

THE MASA HOMELAND: The Masa homeland, called Dimasaraji, lies in northeastern India in the southern panhandle region of the state of Assam, with smaller areas in the neighboring states of Meghalaya and Manipur. The Masas inhabit the highland region from eastern Meghalaya and Bangladesh to western Manipur, including sizable populations in the Assamese districts of North Cachar Hills, Karbi Anglong, Nagoan, and Cachar. The Masa heartland in the Cachar Hills forms the district of North Cachar Hills in Assam. *North Cachar Hills (Dimasaraji):* 1,887 sq. mi.—4,888 sq. km, (2002e) 391,000—Masas (Dimasas and Kacharis) 48%, Nagas* 27%, Mikirs* 20%, Hmars 3%, other tribal peoples and other Indians 2%. The Masa capital and major cultural center is Haflong (2002e) 34,000.

FLAG: The Masa national flag, the flag of the national movement, is a red field bearing a narrow horizontal yellow stripe across the center.

PEOPLE AND CULTURE: The Masas include two distinct groups, the Dimasas (Sons of the Great River) and the Kacharis (Sons of the Hills), historically and linguistically one nation. They are a patriarchal people, with descent and inheritance through the male line. Some Dimasas have adopted a patriarchal system of family structure, but also have parallel male and female clans according exclusive rights to women. Masa dancing is well known and developed from ritualistic dances performed during traditional ceremonies. Traditionally Masa youth earned a bride by serving her family. Such a form of marriage is presumed to originate the practice of living with the bride's family. The Masas generally follow exogamy. Clan affiliation unites the various tribal groups and are based on animals and plants. The Masas are said to be the earliest inhabitants of the Brahmaputra Valley. Each Masa village is self-contained with merchants, goldsmiths, blacksmiths, coppersmiths, and carpenters and every woman is a weaver.

LANGUAGE AND RELIGION: The Masas speak two closely related dialects of the Bodo group of the Tibeto-Burman branch of the Sino-Tibetan language family. The dialects, Dimasa and Kachari, are divided into a number of regional dialects. The Masas, at the turn of the twenty-first century, were embroiled in a fierce controversy over what should be the script of the Masa languages. Currently the dialects are written in any of the regional scripts used in the state, Roman, Bengali, Devnagari, or Assamese. Older Masas favor the Devnagari script, but younger Masas, particularly from the Dimasa group, demand the official adoption of the Roman script. Many of the Masas of the Nagaon District speak Assamese as their first language, others in the North Cachar Hills speak Mikir or Bengali as their first language. Census figures, based on language, often underestimate the total Masa population.

A majority of the Masas practice what has been dubbed tribal Christianity, which includes many aspects of their former animism and ingredients borrowed from Hinduism. The Masa animism revolves around worship of natural objects such as trees, mountains, and rocks. Cleromancy, the art of divination, is commonly practiced and village oracles, *ojha*, are a respected feature of every Masa village. The Masas believe in the existence of a supreme being, Madai, under whom there are several lesser beings including family deities and evil spirits. The religious practices are reflected in the Masa Daikho system. The system has a presiding deity with a definite territorial jurisdiction and a distinct group of followers, the *khel*.

NATIONAL HISTORY: Evidence of human habitation in the area around the Brahmaputra River basin has been traced back to the early Stone Age. The inhabitants of the valley were Australoid groups who were later absorbed by the Tibeto-Burmans. The ancestors of the Masas and the other Tibeto-Burmans are thought to have settled the valley of the Brahmaputra River from the Tibetan Plateau in the twelfth century. They settled the highlands north and south of the Aryan-dominated flood plains. Their territories were gradually divided into regions controlled by individual tribes. Much of the jungle-clad highlands came under the nominal rule of Hindu states in the Brahmaputra lowlands. Isolated from the mainstream of Indian civilization, the area lay outside most of the great states that arose on the subcontinent. In the early Christian era, the Hindus of the valley formed a state tributary to the Gupta Empire of northern India, but were unable to bring the tribal regions under their rule.

The tribes that settled the area south of the Brahmaputra were driven into the less accessible highlands by more powerful nations. In 1229, the region was overrun by invading Ahoms, a Thai people from the present north Burma-China border region. The Ahoms arrived at a time of turmoil in the region, with only the Kacharis and the Chutias able to offer some resistance.

The Ahoms erected an independent kingdom and mixed with the conquered Aryans to form the Assamese people, but like the former kingdoms they were unable to effectively extend their rule much beyond the Brahmaputra River valley. The Tibeto-Burman tribes withdrew to their jungle strongholds and maintained their control of much of present Assam. The Ahom victory pushed the Masas and other smaller Kachari tribal groups south into the highlands. Separated from their kin north of the Brahmaputra River, the Masas developed a distinct culture based on shifting agriculture and influenced by the cultures of other highland groups.

In the highlands the Masas erected a separate kingdom with its capital at Maibong. The flourishing kingdom traded with China, Southeast Asia, and India. Maibong became known for its architecture and temples favored by the Masa kings. Hot springs, thought to possess spiritual and medical properties, drew visitors from many nations. In the fifteenth century the Ahoms overwhelmed the kingdom, which became tributary to the Ahom kings of Sibsagar in Upper Assam.

The Brahmaputra Valley, after much fighting, finally fell to the Muslim Moguls in 1661–62, but their hold was tenuous and they were quickly expelled by the Ahom, now called Assamese. However, repeated invasions by the Burmans from the east had a more lasting impact on the Tibeto-Burman tribes. The Assamese requested aid from the British in Bengal against the Burmans in the early 1700s. In 1792, the Masas joined a widespread rebellion against Assamese rule and the Assamese again requested British help to put down the rebellion, setting a pattern for later confrontations.

The Burmans again invaded the Brahmaputra Valley in 1822, one of the reasons for the first Anglo-Burmese War in 1824–26. The Burmans were forced to cede all of Assam, including the Masa tribal areas in the Cachar Hills, to British rule in 1826, when Assam became a British protectorate. The Tibeto-Burman tribes were dominant in Assam until about 1825, when they too came under British domination. The Masa territories, administered by British commissioners that accompanied military garrisons, formed part of British Bengal until 1874, when they were included in the new Assam province.

The British conceived the idea of keeping Assam and the northeastern tribal areas separate from the rest of India. Based on the Coupland Plan, they created different authority structures, including the policy of listing some tribal areas as "excluded areas" or "partially excluded areas." These areas were set up as tribal reserves and migration from the lowlands was prohibited. The British policy set in motion the later separatist movements that continue throughout northeastern India. The mutual distrust that grew between the tribal and the plains peoples under British colonial rule continues to the present.

Many Masas were converted to Christianity by British and American missionaries in the nineteenth century. Western-style education began a process of change among the tribal groups. New leaders, educated at mission schools, soon challenged the traditional hold on power of the chiefs and village headmen. Several Masa leaders, educated by Christian missionaries, asked the British authorities for help in preserving their language and culture and for other small cultural concessions in 1929. British colonial authorities encouraged immigration from other parts of India, particularly Bengalis and Biharis to work on British plantations.

During World War II, when Assam was the object of a Japanese thrust into India, the Tibeto-Burman tribes were at first courted as Japanese allies, but their refusal to join the anti-British forces led most to join the British forces fighting the Japanese. After World War II, the British prepared to grant independence to the subcontinent, but rejected numerous demands for separate statehood and finally agreed to the partition of British India into two large states, India, a secular state dominated by Hindus, and Pakistan for the Muslims.

The state of Assam, which included many non-Assamese tribal groups, remained a center of nationalist tensions. Regional cultures and variations were too distinct to remain within a single political administration. New tribal states were carved out of Assamese territory, Nagaland in 1963, followed by Meghalaya and Mizoram in 1971, and Arunchal Pradesh in 1972. The creation of these states spurred numerous separatist movements among the remaining tribal groups in Assam.

Demands for autonomous status by the Masas led to the separation of the Masa heartland in the North Cachar Hills as a separate district in 1951, but the new district left a large part of the Masa population divided among several districts. Years of neglect, economic underdevelopment, and inept local governments created a sharp awareness among the Masas of their ethnic and cultural differences with the dominate Assamese. In 1976, the Masas were granted some autonomy within the district with the creation of the North Cachar Hills Autonomous Council.

The adoption of a money economy left the tribal groups even more isolated. Economic hardships due to poor agricultural practices, mass unemployment, rampant corruption, and a lack of educational and medical facilities further alienated the Masas. Exorbitant prices and the shortage of essential commodities led many young Masas to adopt extremist political views. Political activism became widespread in the late 1960s and early 1970s.

In the 1970s, the Masas mobilized to demand the creation of a separate

Masa state to be called Dimasaraji. Autonomy and self-determination rather than religious, cultural, or economic factors were the major factors in the Masa mobilization. The unequal power relationships between the tribal Masas and the dominant non-tribal groups fueled the growing conflict.

Uncontrolled immigration by Muslim Bengalis from newly independent Bangladesh after 1971 threatened the land remaining under Masa control in the highlands. The arrival of large numbers of Muslims made Assam the fastest-growing area in the subcontinent. Encroachment by lowland Assamese and Bengalis led to conflicts. Activists, in the late 1970s, formed several openly nationalist organizations calling for separation from Assam, an end to Bengali settlements, and greater protection of the Masas' traditional territory. A small militant faction favored separation from India and the establishment of a small, neutral state between India and Bangladesh.

In 1991, the Masas launched a peaceful campaign for separation of the Masa homeland from Assam. Smaller militant groups, allied to Naga separatist organizations, particularly the Dima Halong Daogah (DHD), began a violent campaign to drive non-Masas from traditional territory in 1995. Ethnic conflicts and attacks by DHD militants led to reprisal attacks by non-tribals. By the late 1990s, the Cachar highlands had become one of the most violent areas of Assam. Indian security forces, given broad powers, were accused of the violation of human rights and the brutalizing of the civilian population of the highlands.

Masa activists stepped up their campaign for a separate state in February 2000. They demanded the unification of the contiguous Masa-inhabited territories in one administrative unit. Memoranda sent to the Assamese state government and the federal government in New Delhi were consistently ignored. In November 2000, several Masa groups called a 72-hour general strike that paralyzed southern Assam. The state administration ordered the tightening of security in the districts. Activists of the DHD and other groups used extortion, called revolutionary taxes, to fund their separatist campaign and to buy arms.

Moderate nationalists traveled to New Delhi to present their case for separate statehood. Led by the Dimasa Student's Union (DSU), the nationalists marched to the Indian Parliament, but were refused entry. They accused the Indian government of failing to take into account the demand for separate statehood as per the constitutional provision of Article 244 of the Indian Constitution. Delhi police, to prevent them from marching to the Parliament, charged the demonstrators, leaving over 20 people injured.

The Assamese government gave high priority to the development of the hill districts of North Cachar Hills and Karbi Anglong in November 2000. It also accorded greater autonomy to their autonomous councils, including limited powers to finance development schemes.

The DHD joined thirteen other militant groups in Assam in January 2001 in a general strike against Indian national celebrations such as independence from the United Kingdom. They blamed the Indians for imposing an occupation in the region through the brutal force of the Indian security forces.

In June 2001, the DHD became the first Masa nationalist organization to issue an open threat to the immigrant Bengalis to vacate the hill districts. It started a massive campaign through handbills and posters. The Assamese government, in September 2001, agreed to request additional police and army units in an effort to control the violent situation.

SELECTED BIBLIOGRAPHY:

Bhattacharjee, Chandana. *Ethnicity and Autonomy Movement: Case of the Bodo-Kacharis of Assam*. 1996.

Deaner, Janice. *Assam*. 2000.

Hazarika, Sanjoy. *Strangers of the Mist*. 1994.

Mittal, A.C., and J.B. Sharma. *Tribal Movement, Politics, and Religion in India*. 1998.

Mayans
Maya; Quiche; Tzeltal; Tzotzil

POPULATION: Approximately (2002e) 10,500,000 Mayans in Mexico and Central America, 4,600,000 concentrated in the Mexican states of Campeche, Chiapas, Tabasco, Quintana Roo, and Yucatan and 4,750,000 in northern Guatemala, primarily in the Petén and El Quiche departments. There are smaller communities in Belize, western Honduras, and western El Salvador.

THE MAYAN HOMELAND: The Mayan homeland occupies a nearly continuous territory of Central America from the Chiapas highlands in southern Mexico to the Ulúa River in Honduras, including the Yucatan Peninsula, a limestone plateau shared by Mexico and Belize. The Mayan territory has no official status but is included in several Mexican states, the northern departments of Guatemala, northern Belize, and western Honduras. The Mayan capital and major cultural center is Merida, the capital of Yucatan State in Mexico, called Tihoo or Ho' by the Mayans, (2002e) 699,000, metropolitan area 877,000. Other important cultural centers in Mexico are Campeche, called Kimpech in Mayan, (2002e) 205,000, and San Cristobal de Las Casas, in Chiapas State, called Jobel by the Mayans, (2002e) 106,000. The major cultural center of the Mayans in Guatemala is Quetzaltenango, called Xeelaju' by the Mayans, (2002e) 118,000.

FLAG: The Mayan national flag, recognized across the region, has four triangles—white (hoist), blue (top), yellow (fly), and red (bottom). The flag of the Guatemalan Mayans is a white field with two yellow and two red rectangles and a centered disc bearing the image of a pyramid. The flag of the Zapatista National Liberation (FZLN) is a white field bearing a shooting red star and rainbow on the hoist. The flag of the former republic of Yucatan is has horizontal stripes of red, white, and red, with a broad vertical green stripe on the hoist bearing five white stars.

PEOPLE AND CULTURE: The Mayan peoples, the descendants of the great Mayan Empire, inhabit a large area of southern Mexico and Central America. The Yucatecs of Yucatan call themselves Maya, which was eventually applied to the linguistically and culturally related groups of southern Mexico and Central America. Numerous subgroups remain, including the Tzeltal and Tzotzil of Chiapas; the Yucatecs of the Yucatan Peninsula, northern Belize, and northeastern Guatemala; the Lacandones in southern Mexico; the Quichéan peoples of the eastern and central highlands of Guatamala; the Mamean peoples of western Guatemala; the Kanjobalan peoples of Huehuetenango in northwestern Guatemala and parts of Mexico; the Cholan peoples of northern Chiapas and Tabasco; and the Chortí of eastern Guatemala. The chief division in Mayan culture is between highland and lowland dwellers. Yucatec, Lacandón, and Chontal-Chol are lowland groups. Land is the key element of Mayan culture and traditions; about 80% live in rural areas. The indigenous Mayans are the poorest of a generally poor regional population. In Guatemala, over 87% of all indigenous households are below the official poverty line. Socially, indigenous peoples are considered inferior to those of European descent, and discrimination is rife. For over 500 years, the Mayans have suffered marginalization, poverty, discrimination, exclusion, and contempt for their cultural forms.

LANGUAGE AND RELIGION: The Mayans speak dozens of related languages. The Mayans of the Yucatan Peninsula primarily speak Yucatec, with minorities speaking Itzá and Quiché, languages of the Penutian language group. Yucatec is the most important of the 15 major Mayan dialects. The Mayans are mostly poor farmers, the majority speaking little or no Spanish. The Mestizo middle class and the small upper class, mostly of pure Spanish descent, are concentrated in Merida and the resort cities. Yucatec is spoken on the Yucatan Peninsula and in Belize by over 700,000. The Quiche or K'iche' language is the largest spoken in Guatemala, with some 925,000 speakers in 1995. Other languages spoken in Guatemala are Cakchiquel, Mam (Maya), Tzutujil, Achi, and Pokoman. The most famous work of indigenous American literature, the *Popul Vuh* of the Mayans, was written in Quiche shortly after the Spanish conquest. Many of the largely rural Mayan population speak little Spanish.

The Mayan majority are Roman Catholic, mixing Christian beliefs with many pre-Christian religious traditions and customs to create a unique blend known as "folk Catholicism." Traditional Mayan beliefs revolve around a pantheon of nature gods, including those of the sun, moon, rain, and corn, which have become associated with Christian saints. An elaborate cycle of yearly festivals and rituals marks the Mayan calendar. Since the 1960s, evangelical Christian sects, mostly from the southern United States, have made many converts.

NATIONAL HISTORY: The early history of the Maya peoples is obscure, although scholars agree on three major epochs in Mayan history—the Pre-Classic Era from about 1500 B.C. to A.D. 300, the Classic Era from about 300 to 900, and the Post-Classic, 900 to 1697.

Pre-Classic Mayan civilization developed mostly after 500 B.C., centered in the highlands of Guatemala and El Salvador. There the Mayans developed a sedentary agricultural society, well advanced in the arts and sciences. During this period the Mayans invented an extremely accurate calendar and hieroglyphic writing, and produced major works of art. In the early Classic period Mayan culture spread over a much wider area. Large new cities were characterized by great stone temples, pyramids, and large central markets. During the Post-Classic Era the center of Maya civilization shifted to the city-states of the Yucatan Peninsula.

The Mayans developed the highest culture of pre-Columbian America, reaching their apex between 600 and 900 A.D. Priests made discoveries in astronomy and mathematics comparable to similar achievements in ancient Egypt and Mesopotamia. They developed an advanced writing system and recorded their history. Mayan achievements in ceramics, sculpture, weaving, and painting were often more advanced than those of their European contemporaries. They developed an extremely accurate calendar and complex systems of agriculture, irrigation, and water management. In spite of brilliant advances, however, the Mayans were unable to develop machines such as the wheel, which was used on children's toys but not adapted to any practical application. Animals, other than dogs and turkeys, were not domesticated; all labor was done by human manual labor, directed by a religious and military elite.

Scientists estimate that the Maya numbered some 14,000,000 in the eighth century, mostly south of the Yucatan Peninsula. Their civilization began to decay in the ninth century. The causes are unknown, but scholars surmise that stresses in the social structure, overpopulation, and deforestation all contributed. The collapse of Mayan civilization in the late Classic Era led to the abandonment of the southern cities. Two large migrations from Guatemala and Honduras moved north to the Yucatan Peninsula and the Chiapas highlands, traditionally in 899 A.D. On the peninsula the settlers constructed new cities that became centers of the flourishing Post-Classic period. In the ninth and tenth centuries, Toltec invaders from central Mexico overran the peninsula. Toltec influence disappeared by about 1200, but Maya culture had been drastically changed by such Toltec practices as human sacrifice.

A federation of the three major city-states of the peninsula in the late thirteenth century began a long period of stability and prosperity. The stability crumbled around 1440 when a fierce civil war ended the federation. Whole populations fled, abandoning cities and towns. A series of natural disasters further weakened the Maya. The Itzá, the probable founders of Chichén Itzá, migrated from Yucatan to the region of Lake Petén in present-day Guatemala, known as Watimala, around 1450. The Mayans' civilization was thoroughly in decline, yet they were able to resist subjugation longer than either the Aztec of Mexico or the Inca of Peru.

A shipwrecked Spanish sailor in 1511 taught a Maya girl to speak Spanish. The girl, Malinche, christened Marina, served as the interpreter for Cortez after 1519. Using Campeche as their base, the Spanish launched an expedition against the Mayans in 1531–35. The last Mayan strongholds fell to the Spanish in 1546. The Itzá, the last free Mayan nation, were driven from their capital at Tayasal in 1697, ending the last important independent Mayan state. Not far from Tayasal, the Lacandón Mayans defied the Spanish authorities throughout the Hispanic period in remote jungle and mountain strongholds along the Usumachinta River.

The Spanish systematically destroyed the Mayan culture and religion. Zealous Catholic missionaries gathered and burned all Mayan books and records; only a few scattered examples survived. The inventors of advanced mathematics, astronomy, arts, and sciences were reduced to a subject people, many of them enslaved or bound by debts and forced to work on Spanish plantations. European diseases and social disruption caused by the Spanish conquest wiped out a large part of the native population during the sixteenth century. By 1700 fewer than 250,000 Mayans survived.

In 1821 the newly independent Mexican state claimed most of Central America. One of the wealthiest areas of Spanish America, with plantations worked by Mayan debt slaves following the abolition of slavery, Central America's landowners rejected the Mexican claims. By 1839 the Central American states had broken away, including the Yucatan. Mexican troops sent from the capital ended the Yucatan secession in 1843 but failed to recover the other regions. The Yucatan secession aroused the downtrodden Mayans. A rebellion against the cruel European and Mestizo (mixed race) landlords erupted in 1847. The revolt quickly escalated to civil war, called the War of the Castes, which lasted until 1848. A part of the peninsula remained under Mayan control until 1902. In 1910 there was another revolt; after some initial successes, the Mayans withdrew to the inaccessible areas of Quintana Roo.

Revolution and civil war from 1914 to 1919 left Mexico virtually without a central government. A revolt in Yucatan in 1916, led by Felipe Carillo but with active Mayan involvement, effectively separated the region from the weak Mexican state. On 3 April 1916 Carillo declared the independence of the Socialist Republic of Yucatan, a year before Lenin proclaimed a socialist state in Russia. The Mayans again rebelled in 1923, when renewed political chaos preoccupied the Mexican government. An alliance of Mayan and Mestizo leaders declared Yucatan independent of Mexico on 3 July 1924. The new government, for the first time since the Spanish conquest, made the Mayan language an official language. Quickly defeated and returned to Mexican government control, the peninsula was administratively divided.

The legacy of large estates, effectively excluding the Mayans from participation in the region's economy, remained a well-established mechanism of dominance and subordination into the 1960s. Beginning in 1962, the military took control of Guatemala. The military considered the indigenous people a threat to national security and a major part of an imagined counterinsurgency. The military expanded its role in indigenous areas in the early 1970s. Newly discovered petroleum reserves and the growing importance of tourism also began to change the Mayans' situation in the 1970s. A renewed interest in their rich heritage raised demands for equal rights and for attention to their many cultural and economic grievances. A Mayan rebellion begun in 1975 in Guatemala sparked more militant Mayan nationalism in Mexico. Brutal repression forced between 200,000 and 500,000 to flee and caused the deaths of nearly 50,000. Massive human-rights abuses decimated many Mayan regions of Guatemala.

By 1980, the traditionally pacific Mayans had become more militant. One group took hostages in the Spanish embassy in Guatemala City, which was later stormed; 39 people, including hostages, were killed. The Guatemalan government, in a large press campaign, characterized the Mayans as "conspirators against the government." Death squads systematically eliminated the Mayan leadership, killing over 3,000. The violence declined only after a change of government and a new constitution in Guatemala in 1985.

The mobilization of the Mayans continued into the 1990s. In 1991, the Guatemalan government opened peace talks with the Guatemala National Revolutionary Unit (URNG), an umbrella group. By December 1992, over 45,000 refugees had returned to Guatemala from Mexico. In March 1995, the government and URNG representatives signed a peace accord, which included revising the Guatemalan constitution to recognize the ethnic identity of the indigenous peoples.

The Mayans' habits, culture, and outlook differ drastically from the largely Mestizo Mexicans and Guatemalans. A refusal to assimilate has obliged non-Mayans to learn their language in order to live or work in the region. Merida, alone of the large Mexican cities, is effectively bilingual. As part of the Mayan cultural revival of the 1970s and 1980s, a language academy was established in Merida to standardize and modernize contemporary usage.

The Mayans began casting aside their legendary patience in the 1990s. Nationalist groups began to call for Mayan autonomy and to press for land

and cultural rights in Mexico and Guatemala. In October 1992, the Nobel Peace Prize was awarded to Rigoberta Menchu, a Guatemalan Mayan activist. On 12 October 1992, the anniversary of Columbus's voyage to America, thousands marched in cities across the region to protest what is seen as a disaster by the Mayans.

The Mayans of the Chiapas highlands of Mexico were expelled in the 1980s and 1990s from their farmlands and forest tracts by armed gangs working for wealthy cattle ranchers and logging companies. On New Year's Day of 1994, members the Zapatista National Liberation Army (FZLN) seized the city of San Cristobal de Las Casas to publicize their demands for greater rights for the indigenous Mayans of Chiapas. The Zapatista leader, known as Subcommandante Marcos, demanded local autonomy and economic development for a region long ignored by both federal and state governments. The uprising marked a new radicalism among the Mayans. An initial peace deal was reached in 1996, but talks broke down in early 1997, leaving a tense stalemate between the Mexican army and supporters of the Zapatista rebel movement.

Semi-official paramilitary groups, the Guardias Blancas, often in the pay of the large landowners and under the command of local army officers, have terrorized Mayan communities in Chiapas since 1982. In December 1997, 45 Mayan refugees were massacred by a paramilitary gang, part of an increasingly violent conflict between the Mayans and progovernment groups.

The election in 2000 of an opposition politician as Mexico's first democratically elected president raised hope that the Mayan grievances might at long last be addressed. Although the Mayans of Chiapas have made agreements with the Mexican government to gain more control of local government and on election reform, the majority of the Mayans still face serious discrimination and poverty.

Led by the Zapatistas of Chiapas, thousands of Mayans marched for sixteen days from Chiapas and Yucatan to Mexico City in March 2001. The leaders of the Mayans were received by Mexico's President Vicente Fox, who acknowledged past injustices and promised a place for the indigenous peoples in Mexico's future.

SELECTED BIBLIOGRAPHY:

Carey, James C. *The Mexican Revolution in Yucatan, Nineteen Fifteen to Nineteen Twenty-Four.* 1984.

Cook, Garrett W. *Renewing the Maya World: Expressive Culture in a Highland Town.* 2000.

Feldman, Lawrence H. *Lost Shores and Forgotten Peoples: The Maya of the South East Lowlands of Guatemala.* 2000.

Van Cott, Donna Lee. *Indigenous Peoples and Democracy in Latin America.* 1994.

Meitheis

Manipuris; Monipuris; Kuneis; Kathes; Kathis; Poonas; Miethes; Miteis; Meithais; Meeteis

POPULATION: Approximately (2002e) 1,810,000 Meitheis in South Asia, concentrated in the Indian state of Manipur and adjacent areas of neighboring Indian states and Myanmar, where some 150,000 Meitheis live. Another 135,000 inhabit the Sylhet region of northwestern Bangladesh.

THE MEITHEI HOMELAND: The Meithei homeland occupies a huge valley surrounded by high mountains in northeastern India and western Myanmar. The temperate Manipur Valley, some 690 square miles (1,787 sq. km), lies at an elevation of 2,600 feet (0.8 km). The central feature of the valley is Logtak Lake, the source of the Manipur River. Manipur is somewhat isolated from the most of India and lacks a rail link to the rest of the country. Manipur was made a state of the Indian federation in 1972. *State of Manipur (Kangleipak/Meithei Laipak)*: 8,621 sq. mi.—22,327 sq. km, (2002e) 2,443,000—Meitheis 62%, Bengalis 6%, Kukis 13%, Nagas* 12%, Zomis* 5%, Bodos* 2%. The Meithei capital and major cultural center is Imphal, (2002e) 287,000. The major cultural center of the Meitheis in Myanmar is Tamu, (2002e) 7,000.

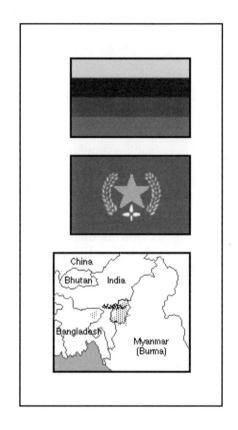

FLAG: The Meithei national flag, the flag of the national movement, has four equal, horizontal stripes of yellow, blue, red, and green. The flag of the Revolutionary People's Party (RPF) is a red field bearing a centered gold star and gold sheaves above a small green cross.

PEOPLE AND CULTURE: The Meitheis are of mixed background, descended from the valley's early tribal Mongoloid inhabitants and the later Khassey, a Thai people. Their name Meithei means "different people." Meithei women enjoy high status and conduct most of the trade in the Manipur Valley. The Meithei culture, which flourished in the great valley, includes an indigenous form of classical dance dissimilar to other Indian dance forms. More than two-fifths of the population is literate, a very high average for India. Traditionally the Meitheis are divided into seven clans or extended families, each claiming descent from one of the seven tribes that merged to form the Meithei nation. Marriage within the clan is forbidden, so Meitheis of marriageable age must find a spouse from another clan. The Manipuris have only one social class, which they believe gives them high-caste status.

LANGUAGE AND RELIGION: The Meithei speak a language related to the Kuki-Chin languages of the state's tribal peoples. The language, Meitheilon, forming part of the Mikir-Meithei group of the Kuki-Naga languages, is not intelligible to neighboring, related languages due to extensive borrowings, particularly from the Aryan languages associated with their Hindu religion. The major dialects correspond to former tribal divisions and include Meithei, Loi, Pangal, and Bishnupuriya. Nearly a third of the state's population, mostly in the hills and mountains around the valley, is made up of 29 non-Meithei Christian and animist tribal groups, some assimilating into the Meithei culture. Manipuri and English are both official languages in the state.

The dominant religion in the region is a form of Hinduism called Vishnavism, incorporating many pre-Hindu beliefs and practices. Traditionally the Meitheis were converted to Hinduism in the sixteenth century, but elements of their pre-Hindu religion, Sana Mahi, remain. In addition to the officially recognized Hindu gods, the Meitheis continue to worship many nature gods, particularly Mani, who supposedly came from the earth in the form of a snake. About 17% of the Meitheis, called Pangans, are Muslims, although they remain culturally part of the Meithei community. The Meithei minority in Bangladesh are mostly Hindu, although there is a sizable Muslim minority that converted following their settlement among the Muslim peoples in the early nineteenth century.

NATIONAL HISTORY: The area of present Manipur was once inhabited entirely by tribal peoples such as the Nagas and Mizos.* Intermarriage and political dominance of the stronger tribes led to a gradual merging of ethnic groups and the formation of the Meithei nations. This league of seven tribal groups consolidated a kingdom that withstood invaders for almost 2,000 years, defeating or absorbing Aryans, Mongolians, and Dravidians.

An enormous valley in the hills, the remains of a prehistoric lake, developed as the center of an early Hindu state with a highly sophisticated civilization. The valley culture incorporated influences from the original tribal peoples and from the Aryans who reached the region during the Aryan invasions of northern India between 1500 and 1200 B.C. Named for the Mani of Ananta, the ancient serpent god of the valley, Manipur evolved into a powerful regional state, often controlling areas beyond the central valley.

According to Meithei tradition, the first recorded historical ruler of Manipur, historically called Kangleipak, was Nongda Lairen Pakhangba, who took the throne in A.D. 33. His ascension established the Ningthouja dynasty. The dynasty expanded its control by integrating neighboring principalities and by assimilating other ethnic groups. The first written recorded history of the region goes back only to about A.D. 900. A written constitution, in the form of a royal decree issued by king Loyumba in A.D. 1110, became the basis of the dynastic rule that continued, with interruptions, until the British conquest.

The state, under the nominal rule of the Tibetans* from the eighth to the twelfth centuries, fell to a Thai people, the Khassey or Moy, in the thirteenth century A.D. The Thai conquerors gradually adopted the language and culture of the valley. By the sixteenth century the Kassey had ceased to be culturally Thai; eventually they were fully absorbed by the older Meithei culture of the great valley.

Manipur's power increased during a series of wars with neighboring Muslim Bengalis and Buddhist peoples in the sixteenth century. The state expanded to control a large area in the surrounding hill districts. A Meithei army, led by Raja Gharib Newaz, the greatest of the Meithei national heroes, devastated Upper Burma, the homeland of their ancient Burman enemies, between 1715 and 1749. The resurgent Burmans in turn invaded Manipur in 1758, forcing the raja to seek British protection. In 1762 the Raja Jai Singh signed a protectorate agreement and with British aid repulsed renewed Burman attacks in 1764 and 1822. Thousands of Meitheis, fleeing the Burman incursions, moved west to British territory in Bengal, later Bangladesh.

Disputed successions were a continual source of political crises until Chura Chand, a five-year-old member of the ruling dynasty, was nominated raja in 1891. For the next eight years Manipur was administered under British supervision. Slavery and forced labor were abolished, and roads were constructed. In 1907 the young raja assumed control of the government, although a British adviser remained at court.

The British authorities added Manipur to British India and began to settle Christian Kubai Nagas in the valley to work in the lucrative citrus groves. The privileged position of the Christian minority incited Meithei resentment and mistreatment. The Meitheis, considering themselves high-caste Hindus, openly discriminated against the tribal peoples, who are traditionally relegated to the lowest rungs of the Hindu hierarchy. The Meithei persecution provoked sporadic rebellions among the Naga and Kuki tribes of the hills that surrounded the central valley.

A serious uprising of the Kuki hill tribes threatened the British hold on the region in 1917. The rebels drove the British from the state. The British flight prompted the Meithei to join the rebellion. Reinforced British forces returned to execute the rebel leaders and to install a new raja, who ruled under strict British supervision. The authorities placed the state under the administration of the British colonial government of Assam.

European missionaries introduced Christianity and Western education in the early twentieth century. The mission campaign, most successful among the pagan hill tribes, allowed all of the population to gain from mission education. A Meithei leadership, educated in the Christian schools, were to lead a strong campaign for separate status as India moved toward independence after World War II.

Indian nationalists, including some Meitheis, allied themselves to the invading Japanese forces during World War II. Promised independence when the British were driven from India, the anti-British forces, led by Subhash Chandra Bose, commanding a combined force of Indians and Japanese, hoisted the Indian tricolor for the first time on Indian soil in Manipur. Fighting devastated much of the Manipur Valley.

Just before India and Pakistan's independence, the British, concerned that India, already partitioned into two states, might splinter, pressured the Meithei leaders to reach an accommodation with the new Indian government. On 15 August 1947, the day India gained its independence, the Manipuri government signed an interim agreement acknowledging Indian responsibility for the state's defense and foreign relations. Faced with large anti-Indian demonstrations and demands for full independence, the Indian government dispatched troops to dissolve the Manipur state administration. Within days the Maharaja of Manipur found himself virtually imprisoned in his residence. The house was surrounded by soldiers and under the pressure of considerable misinformation and intimidation, the Maharaja, isolated from his advisers, council of ministers, and Manipuri public opinion, was made to sign an agreement fully merging his state with India. When the ceremony to mark the transfer of power and the end of this ancient kingdom took place in Imphal on 15 October 1949, a battalion of the Indian army was in place to guard against possible trouble.

The circumstances attending Manipur's merger with India haunts the politics of the state to this day. A number of insurgent groups regard the merger as illegal and unconstitutional, and many among the Manipuri intelligentsia are bitter about the way it was effected. The government imposed direct rule from New Delhi and downgraded the state's status to that of a union territory.

Tanghul and Kubai Nagas, who had begun to assimilate into Meithei culture, launched a campaign to separate their hill tracts from Manipur and to join northern Manipur to the newly created Nagaland state in 1963. The Naga revolt provoked a Meithei nationalist backlash. The campaign became openly nationalist, with Meithei leaders demanding independence for a new country to be called Meithei Laipak or Kangleipak. A violent secessionist war spread across Manipur in 1965. In a futile effort to undermine the nationalist movement, the Indian government granted statehood on 21 July 1972.

In the 1970s the growing numbers of Bengali and Nepalese immigrants entering the state became an explosive issue; nationalists demanded their expulsion. Anti–immigrant violence in the state increased when several of the Kuki and Naga groups joined the Meithei separatists in attacks on the illegal migrants. In 1981 the Indian government suspended the state government and imposed direct rule from New Delhi. Government troops arrested newsmen and closed newspapers for advocating independence. Four years later the authorities declared Manipur a "disturbed area," allowing the Indian military broad powers to combat the separatist bands. In 1990 government troops launched a military campaign called Operation Bluebird in an effort to end the Meithei rebellion.

The Indian anti-insurgency methods, including mass arrests, torture, rape, and executions, alienated many moderates in the state, some joining the renewed rebellion in 1991. The violence in the once peaceful valley in the 1990s involved all of the population groups, fighting either the Indian military or among themselves, raising fears that the separatist war could end with the partition of the ancient state among its various national groups. Attacks on police, soldiers, and Muslim Bengali immigrants increased in spite of widespread repression by the security forces.

Increasing violence between the northern Naga tribes, who sought to unite with a projected independent Nagaland, and the Kuki tribes who disputed their control of the districts, overshadowed the Meithei nationalist activities. Naga attacks on Kuki villages, in an effort to drive the Kukis from the disputed districts, escalated after early 1994 and forced the Kukis to reinforce their ties to the Meithei nationalist organizations. The violence polarized the opposing nationalist forces and converted Manipur into one of the least stable areas in India's turbulent northeastern region.

In 1997, several international organizations published denunciations against the Indian security forces, particularly for the rape and other sexual abuse of women and children in disturbed areas of Manipur. Assaults on suspected members of Meithei nationalist groups often turned into looting and abuse of the civilian population. The Special Forces, under an act passed in 1958, were allowed wide powers to shoot to kill and were protected from prosecution for any acts carried out under its provisions. In June 1999 Manipur was again declared a disturbed area under the 1958 Special Powers Act. A cease-fire was negotiated, which brought relative peace until Indian troops were again accused of abusing the local population. The Special Forces have now been in Manipur for over four decades, which nationalists cite as among the reasons for continuing nationalism among the Meitheis.

The desire for greater autonomy is widespread in the state and is based on the long separate history of the Meithei nation. Although most Meitheis agree on the need for autonomy and self-determination, the fractured nature of the national movement has hindered the formation of a united front. The unification of three of the largest groups in the Manipur People's Liberation Front (MPLF) marked the first concerted effort to overcome the factionalism. In mid-2000, several other smaller groups joined the organization, which reiterated its ultimate goal of a sovereign Meithei state to be called by its ancient name, Kangleipak.

The Indian government's plan to extend the cease-fire in Manipur led to violent demonstrations against the cease-fire plan, which many Meitheis see as giving the military unlimited and unchecked powers over them. In June 2001, over a dozen demonstrators were killed in confrontations with security forces. The state government was suspended and presidential rule, direct rule by the Indian government, was imposed. There are an estimated 35 nationalist, tribal, and religious organizations active in the state in late 2001–2, eighteen of which are considered as armed insurgent groups.

SELECTED BIBLIOGRAPHY:

Hodson, T.C. *The Meitheis.* 1975.
Horam, H., and S.H.M. Rizvi, eds. *Manipur.* 1998.
Singh, N. Lokendra. *The Unquiet Valley: Society, Economy and Politics in Manipur.* 1998.
Zehol, Lucy. *Ethnicity in Manipur: Experiences, Issues and Perspectives.* 1998.

Melayus
Riaus; Rhios; Riau Malays

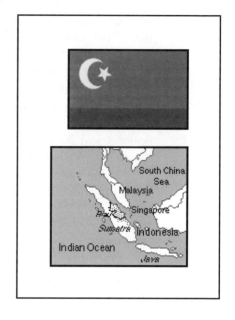

POPULATION: Approximately (2002e) 3,945,000 Melayus in Indonesia, concentrated in Riau Province of Sumatra and neighboring provinces. Outside the region there are Melayu communities living in other areas of Sumatra, on Java, and in Malaysia and Singapore.

THE MELAYU HOMELAND: The Malayu homeland, Riau, lies in southeast Asia south of Singapore on the east coast of Sumatra at the southern entrance to the Strait of Malacca. The region includes the Riau Archipelago, separated from Singapore by the Singapore Strait; it consists of thousands of islands, including Bintan, Bantam, and Karimun. Most of the region is flat lowland; the only uplands are the Batak Plateau and the Padang Highlands of the Barisan Mountains, on the western border. A series of swamps cover part of the coastal region and the greater part of several of the islands. Riau forms a province of the Republic of Indonesia. *Province of Riau (Provinsi Riau/Bangsa Melayu)*: 36,510 sq. mi.—94,561 sq. km, (2002e) 4,474,000—Melayus 72%, Mingankabus 21%, Javanese 5%, other Indonesians 2%. The Melayu capital and major cultural center is Pekanbaru, called Pakan Baru locally, (2002e) 430,000. The other major cultural centers are Tanjungpinang, called Tanjung Pinang locally, the former capital on the island of Bintan, (2002e) 118,000, and Batam, (2002e), just across a narrow strait from Singapore.

FLAG: The Melayu national flag, the flag of the national movement, is a red field bearing a white crescent moon and five-pointed star on the upper hoist and a broad horizontal blue stripe on the bottom.

PEOPLE AND CULTURE: The Melayus are a Sumatran Malay nation closely related to the Malays of the nearby Malay Peninsula of Malaysia. Their culture, based on a long seafaring tradition, is quite different from the other tribal cultures of eastern Sumatra. The Melayus consider themselves the heart of the Malay region of Southeast Asia. The Melayus belong to the Oceanic branch of the Malays, and most live on the eastern coast and the wide southern plains. The Melayu culture has been influenced by centuries of contact between Muslims and Hindus and contains elements of the civilizations that controlled the region in the past. Often called the Coastal Malays or Riau Malays, the Melayus and their culture continue to center on the sea; fishing and trading are traditional pursuits.

LANGUAGE AND RELIGION: The language spoken by the Melayus is the Riau-Jambi dialect of Malay, which belongs to the Austronesian language family. The dialect is the basis of the national language of Indonesia, called Bahasa Indonesian. The infusion of many Javanese words and forms has changed the national language since it was first created in the 1940s and 1950s. The dialect has long served as a lingua franca in much of eastern Sumatra. The first grammar, called *Bustanul Katibin*, was written in the dialect in the early fifteenth century. Since it is relatively simple and widely used and was not associated with any of the dominant ethnic groups in Indonesia, it was accepted as the basis of the national language. In 1972 a uniform revised spelling was agreed to between Indonesia and Malaysia, and communications improved between Riau and the nearby Malaysian states on the Asian mainland.

The Melayus are predominantly Muslim, although many pre-Islamic Buddhist and Hindu customs and traditions survive. Many Muslim ceremonies have incorporated elements from other religions, particularly in the rural areas. The focus of Melayu Islam is the Grand Mosque of Shaykh Burhanuddin in the capital, Pekanbaru.

NATIONAL HISTORY: The region early was the site of the Buddhist Srivijaya empire, and it served as a base for the conquest of the Hindu kingdoms of the Malay Peninsula in the seventh century. Southern Sumatra was the second most important Hindu center, after India, until the twelfth century. The Hindu Majaphahit Empire of eastern Java conquered most of Sumatra; the Srivijaya Empire fell in 1377. Muslim states were established in Sumatra in the sixteenth century, after the disintegration of the Majaphahit Empire. For centuries the islands and the port towns provided safe havens to traders and sailors from India, China, and Southeast Asia who traded in the Straits of Malacca, one of the oldest trading routes in Asia.

The Portuguese seized the state of Malacca on the Malay Peninsula in 1511; its last sultan retained Johore on the peninsula and the Riau Archipelago at its southern tip. The Dutch arrived in the region in 1596 and the English shortly afterward. Colonial rivalries and attacks by sea pirates affected the prosperity of the region. A period of wars for control of the Malay states continued until the middle nineteenth century. The Treaty of London, signed in 1824, gave the Dutch control of all territories south of Singapore.

The last sultan of Riau (called Riouw by the Dutch), Mahmud Muzaffar Shah, was crowned in 1841, resolving to restore the power wielded by his ancestors. He had the tacit support of the Malay states on the east coast of the Malay Peninsula to the north. Mahmud's claim to the throne of the Malay state of Pahang threatened colonial interests, and he was deposed by the Dutch in 1857. His claims to Pahang and his prestige among east-coast Malays and Melayus provided an excuse for further Dutch and British involvement in the affairs of the Malay states.

The Dutch introduced plantation agriculture, producing rubber, palm oil, sisal, and cinchona (quinine). Forced labor and population displacement led to serious unrest and attempts to restore the sultanate in the late nineteenth century. Riau became one of the centers of anticolonial activity in the early years of the twentieth century. A serious rebellion against Dutch rule erupted in 1911, threatening the colonial hold on all of eastern Sumatra.

Riau was occupied by the Japanese military forces during World War II but returned to Dutch control in 1946 following a period of anarchy and nationalist activity following the Japanese surrender in 1945. The province, set up as a separate state by the Dutch administration, was incorporated into the new Republic of Indonesia in 1950. Achmed Sukarno became the first president of Indonesia, limiting the autonomy of the outlying provinces and concentrating power in the capital, Jakarta, on Java. The Javanese dominated the economy and political life of the republic.

A revolt in Riau spread across Sumatra and to other outer islands in 1958. In 1959, in response to the disorders, Sukarno assumed dictatorial powers and increased Indonesia's ties to China and other communist states. The Melayu leadership, conservative and anticommunist, was persecuted and suppressed. Many perished in prisons or disappeared.

An attempted communist coup d'état in late 1965 led to a military take-over in Indonesia, bringing Gen. T.N.J. Suharto to power. Thousands of alleged communists were executed, and a widespread massacre ensued. Several thousand people died in Riau in fighting between autonomists, communists, and conservative Muslim groups.

In the late 1960s and 1970s Riau was designated a transmigration area, to which the government resettled excess population from Java and other overpopulated islands. The settlement of the culturally and linguistically different Javanese, particularly in the Batuampar region, sparked ethnic violence and prompted the organization of the first autonomist organizations among the Melayus. Petroleum production from fields at Dumai worked by the American company Caltex gave the autonomy movement an economic base from the 1970s. The use of Melayu oil wealth for development projects in other parts of the Indonesian Archipelago while Riau remained poor, agricultural, and rural prompted demands for control of their economic resources. Roads are mostly confined to the Pekanbaru region and the oil fields on the coast.

Even moderate Melayu leaders are determined to renegotiate the revenue-sharing system under which the Indonesian government has essentially looted the natural resources of the region. Riau produces more than 70% of Indonesia's oil and gas, worth about seven billion dollars a year, yet government annual expenditure on the province averages less than $150 million. The growing ethnic conflict between the Melayus and the Javanese in the province is based on economic imbalance.

President Suharto, after over three decades in power, was overthrown in a mostly peaceful revolution in 1998. The end of the heavy-handed dictatorship resumed a process of national development among the Melayus that had been interrupted then suppressed since the 1960s. Reculturation and ties to the Malay states of Malaysia stimulated demands for greater cultural and political control of the Melayu homeland. The referendum that led to the virtual separation of the East Timorese* in 1999 led to demands among the Melayus for unspecified self-determination; several groups advocated economic autonomy, federalism, or even outright independence. The discredited Indonesian military virtually withdrew from most of the province, except the oil fields.

In May 1999, new laws decentralizing some powers and increased funding to outlying provinces were passed, but they will take time to implement. Militant groups allied to the Acehnese* demanded Melayu independence and possible federation, or confederation, with an independent Acehnese state. Many nationalists seek a united Sumatra, but the number of ethnic groups that inhabit the huge island makes unity very difficult. As a first step to the restoration of the historical Riau state, militants are pressing for a federal state in Indonesia, with the central government responsible only for defense, foreign affairs, and monetary policy.

Over 1,500 Melayus gathered near Pekanbaru in April 1999 to demand that the Indonesian government honor a promise to return 10% of all Riau's oil revenues to the province. Leaders speaking before the crowd threatened that unless the Melayus began to receive some benefit from the exploitation of their natural resources, they would fight for independence. Asia's largest oil field, operated by Caltex, is situated in Riau. Together with the nearby Duri field, also operated by Caltex, Riau's oil represents 15% of Indonesia's foreign currency revenues. Melayu activists claim that Riau receives a mere 0.02% of its contributions to the national budget. Some locals estimate that Riau contributes as much as 50% of the national budget.

Riau has benefited from its situation in the so-called Sijori Growth Triangle, made up of Singapore, Johore in Malaysia, and Riau. The boom islands of Batam and Bintan have attracted considerable investment from nearby Singapore, which has one of Asia's highest standards of living. The Melayus, whose homeland is potentially much richer than Singapore, are in fact considerably poorer than the Singaporeans, a situation that is increasingly blamed on the corrupt and bloated Indonesian government.

Nationalist sentiment among the Melayus is a recent phenomenon. Although militants are calling for complete separation from the tottering Indonesian state, more moderate groups would probably be satisfied with regional autonomy and a fairer share of Riau's oil profits. The governor of Riau, Saleh Djasit, in 2000 stated that the Melayus simply want a better balance of wealth, but the militants are gaining support for their demands for a renegotiation of Riau's relations with Indonesia, including the possibility of complete separation.

Indonesian nationalism has been a negative factor, and it is now beginning to shatter. It was founded on anti-Dutch resistance and stoked by tirades against the West and the *konfrontasi* with Malaysia in the 1950s and early 1960s. Economic development was the focus of Indonesian unity, but the economic collapse of 1997 removed the positive aspects of Indonesian nationalism. To the Melayus, Indonesian nationalism is now mostly associated with Java, and resentment of Javanese domination of the archipelago is spreading rapidly. The politics of the province, the third poorest in Indonesia, have become identity politics, pitting autonomists and nationalists against the pro-Indonesian groups.

Land disputes are also a growing concern for Caltex as they are for virtually every other company dealing in natural resources in Indonesia. Villagers blockade roads and hijack vehicles, saying Caltex has stolen their land, or demand that Caltex provide solutions the government is unable or unwilling to tackle. But under Indonesian oil and gas regulations, Caltex does not own a square meter of land, a centimeter of pipeline, or a single drop of oil. Like every other oil company in Indonesia, the company operates its fields on behalf of Pertamina, the government-owned monopoly based in Jakarta. After expenses are paid, Caltex gets about 15% of the take; the rest goes to Pertamina and the central government, but very little filters down to the Melayus.

Melayu nationalists claim that unless a more equitable system of distributing wealth is devised, tension between the outlying regions and Java will intensify. The concept of being Indonesian, already tenuous in several parts of the archipelago, is rapidly losing popularity among the Melayus. After three decades of suppression, the political and national identity struggles of the late 1950s and 1960s are resurfacing in Riau. With the center loosening its firm hold on the provinces, the old fault lines are reemerging. Regional, ethnic, tribal, and economic grievances are fueling unrest, and resentment of Javanese domination continues to stimulate Melayu nationalism. The nationalist leader, Tabrani Rab, claims that thousands of Melayus are prepared to fight for independence. The Melayus, already being drawn into the sphere of mainland Asia through their close economic and historical ties to Singapore and Malaysia, are tallying the pros and cons of autonomy, federalism, and continued Indonesian citizenship.

SELECTED BIBLIOGRAPHY:

Andaya, Barbara Watson. *To Live as Brothers: Southeast Sumatra in the Seventeenth and Eighteenth Centuries*. 1993.
Drakard, Jane. *A Kingdom of Words: Language and Power in Sumatra*. 1999.
Omar, Ariffin. *Bangsa Melayu: Malay Concepts of Democracy and Community, 1945–1950*. 1993.
Schwarz, Adam. *A Nation in Waiting: Indonesia's Search for Stability*. 1999.

Merina

Hova; Malache; Antimerina; Imerina

POPULATION: Approximately (2002e) 4,275,000 Merina and 1,885,000 closely related Betsileo in Madagascar. They are called the Highland People, as they are concentrated in the highland provinces of Antananarivo and Fianarantsoa.

THE MERINA HOMELAND: The Merina homeland, called Imerina, lies in the mountainous central highlands of Madagascar, the world's fourth-largest island. The highlands are given over to terraced rice farming, the major occupation of the Merina-Betsileo people. The Merina are concentrated around the city of Antananarivo, while the Betsileo live farther south around the city of Fianarantsoa. The Merina heartland around the Malasy capital forms the division of Antanarivo. *Division of Antanarivo (Faritany Antanarivo/Imerina)*:

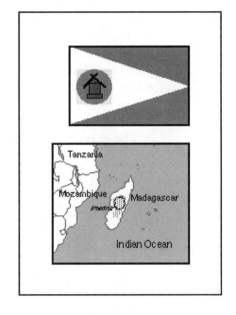

22,503 sq. mi.—58,283 sq. km, (2002e) 4,284,000—Merina 92%, Betsileo 5%, Chinese and other Malagasy 3%. The Merina capital and major cultural center is Antananarivo, (2002e) 1,122,000. The major cultural center of the Betsileo is Fianarantsoa, (2002e) 124,000.

FLAG: The Merina national flag, the flag of the national movement, is red with a large white triangle point to the fly bearing an orange disk charged with a traditional Merina house in red.

PEOPLE AND CULTURE: The island of Madagascar, which was settled from Asia, forms a distinct cultural area. The Merina and the closely related Betsileo, collectively called the Malayo-Indonesian peoples, are mainly of Indonesian origin and live in the central highlands. Unlike the coastal peoples of the island, who are of African, Malayo-Indonesian, and Arab descent, the Merina have retained their Asian physical features and much of their original culture. The practice of endogamy—rejecting intermarriage with other groups—has resulted in the preservation of their Asian heritage. They continue to distinguish between *fotsy* (or white), referring to themselves, and *mainty* (or black), referring to the coastal peoples or former slaves in the highlands. Traditionally they were divided into three castes—the Andriana or nobles; the Hova or free men; and the Andevo, the slaves or serfs. The Merina are the most urbanized of the Malagasy peoples, the urban Merina population rising from about 23% of the total in 1975 to over 40% in 1995.

LANGUAGE AND RELIGION: The Merina speak a Malagasy dialect belonging to the East Borneo group of the Austronesian language family, spoken in southeast Asia and the Pacific. Linguists believe the language shares a common origin with and is closely related to Ma'anyan, a language spoken in southeastern Borneo. The Malagasy dialect contains words from Bantu, Swahili, Arabic, English, and French. The Merina dialect, written in the Latin alphabet, has been an official language of the island. Although there are many local subdialects of Malagasy they are all mutually intelligible. The Merina dialect is the standard and forms the basis of the literary language. French is also widely spoken and is recognized as an official language.

The majority of the Merina are Christians, mostly belonging to Protestant denominations introduced by British missionaries. Protestantism has historically been perceived as the affiliation of the upper classes. Traditionally religious belief revolved around Zanahary, "the Creator," and Andriamanitra, "the Fragrant One." There is a belief in local spirits, and a complex system of taboos marks everyday Merina life. A firm belief in the existence of close ties between the living and the dead is the basis of traditional religious beliefs. Links between the living and the dead include ancestor veneration and the construction of elaborate tombs. Among the Merina-Betsileo the custom of *famadihana*, the placing or turning of the dead—wrapping remains in new shrouds to move them from one tomb to another—is an important family obligation. Many of the traditions of the culture of the dead have been incorporated into Christian services.

NATIONAL HISTORY: Recent research suggests that Madagascar was uninhabited until Malay peoples, probably from the Barito region of Borneo (Kalimantan), migrated across the Indian Ocean, probably in the first century A.D. There is no evidence of how, why, or by what route the first settlers came to the island. It is assumed that the peopling of the island was accomplished by a single cultural group, probably as the result of a single voyage. Eventually eighteen separate tribal groups emerged.

Outside knowledge of the island began in the seventh century, when Arabs established trading posts along the northwest coast. Although they converted some of the local inhabitants to Islam, their primary mission was the purchase of slaves. Slavery became the principal source of revenue and the basis of the island's economy.

The Merina entered the sparsely inhabited central plateau in the fifteenth century. There they established a number of small kingdoms. They organized vast irrigation projects to drain the local marshes and make possible the practice of wet-rice agriculture. In the sixteenth century the Merina spread gradually through the plateau region.

European contact with the island began in the 1500s with the Portuguese explorer Diego Dias, who sighted the island after his ship became separated from a fleet bound for India. The Europeans made contact with the coastal peoples, but few ventured inland to the highland plateau controlled by the Merina kingdom. In the late seventeenth century, the French established trading stations along the east coast. From about 1774 to 1824, the island's coasts were a favorite haunt for pirates, including Europeans and Americans.

The Merina of the highlands alternated between periods of political unity and intervals in which the kingdom was divided into smaller political units. Their plateau homeland afforded some protection from the ravages of warfare among the coastal kingdoms. The political and ethnic distinctions, recognized both locally and among the Europeans, between the central highlanders (the Merina and Betsileo) and the so-called *côtiers* (the coastal peoples) soon exerted a major influence on the island's political system. The Merina developed a unique political institution called the *fokonolona*, the village council. Through the councils, the Merina were able to extend their administrative control across the vast highland plateau.

Two outstanding monarchs established Merina political dominance over the island. The first, Andrianampoinimerina, seized control of one of the Merina kingdoms in 1787. In the late 1790s, he succeeded in establishing hegemony over a large area of the island. By 1806 he had conquered the remaining three Merina kingdoms and established a new capital at the fortified city of Antananarivo. His son, Radama I, succeeded on the death of his father in 1810. A progressive monarch, he adroitly played off competing British and French interests while extending Merina authority over nearly the entire island of Madagascar, including the Betsileo principalities in 1830. The development of a Merina nationalist elite, which exercised considerable influence during the colonial period, laid the foundation of the later anti-French Merina national movement.

The British governor of Mauritius and the Merina ruler concluded a treaty that abolished the slave trade, which was an important element in the Merina economy, in return for British military and financial assistance. British influence remained strong for several decades, during which the Merina elite adopted the Protestant Christianity brought to the island by British missionaries.

King Radama encouraged the London Missionary Society to establish schools and churches and to introduce the printing press. The society devised a written form of the local language using the Latin alphabet, and by 1828 several thousand Merina had become literate. Later the Merina dialect of Malagasy became the official language. In 1896 some 164,000 Merina and Betsileo children attended the mission's primary schools. The

Merina kingdom was governed by a literate bureaucracy, which left abundant archives—diplomatic and administrative correspondence, memoirs, tax and judicial records—one of the few precolonial states in Africa to do so.

Radama II, in the mid-nineteenth century, signed a treaty of perpetual friendship with France; His brief rule ended when he was assassinated by a group of Merina nobles alarmed by his pro-French stance. After 1868, Rainilaiarivony ruled the kingdom. To avoid giving the British or French reason for intervention, he emphasized modernization of the society. He signed a commercial treaty with France in 1868, and with the British in 1877.

The French, based on treaties signed with the coastal Sakalava people, established a protectorate in the northwest of Madagascar in 1882. The British accepted the imposition of a French protectorate over the whole island in 1885, in return for eventual British control of Zanzibar. Queen Ranavalona III refused to recognize French domination of her kingdom and fighting broke out. French troops moved into the highlands from coastal bases in 1895–96 and eventually defeated the forces of the Merina kingdom, which was abolished in 1904. The queen and many of her ministers were deported to Réunion, then to French Algeria.

Nationalist sentiment emerged among a small group of Merina intellectuals in the early twentieth century. A secret society dedicated to the reestablishment of the Merina kingdom was formed in 1913, but the movement was brutally suppressed with the aid of colonial troops drawn from the pro-French coastal peoples. A rivalry developed between the predominantly Roman Catholic coastal peoples, the côtiers, and the predominantly Protestant Merina, who prevailed in the civil service, business, and the professions.

Merina veterans of World War I military service bolstered the embryonic nationalist movement throughout the 1920s. In 1924 a degree of representative government was introduced, although the administration and the economy remained under firm French colonial control. During World War II, Merina troops again fought with the French forces in Europe and the Middle East; following the fall of France in 1940, Madagascar was administered by the pro-German Vichy government. British troops took control of the island from the Vichy forces and turned it over to the Free French in 1943.

Two major political parties formed—the Democratic Movement for Malagasy Restoration (MDRM), dominated by the Protestant highland peoples, and the Party of the Malagasy Disinherited, whose members were mainly côtiers or descendants of slaves from the central highlands. The postwar French assimilationist policy, supported by the côtiers, was rejected by the Merina, who pressed for independence. The rival policies led to a renewal of ethnic tension and the growth of Merina nationalism.

A Merina uprising on 29 March 1947 turned into a nationalist attempt to expel the colonial power from the island. The insurgency was suppressed only after several months of bitter fighting and thousands of deaths, possibly as many as 50,000 to 80,000. The MDRM was outlawed, and 20 of the rebel leaders were executed. Another 5,000 to 6,000 party activists were imprisoned.

From that time the French favored the côtiers over the highland Merina. In 1956 colonial institutions were reformed, bringing many non-Merina into the colonial government. Universal suffrage failed to end the ethnopolitical split between the Merina and the côtiers and reinforced divisions between Protestants and Roman Catholics. Educational and cultural advantages gave the Merina a dominant influence until the 1950s. Then the côtiers, who outnumbered the highlanders, became the dominant group.

The Malagasy Republic was established on 14 October 1958, as an autonomous state within the French community. A period of provisional government ended with the adoption of a constitution in 1959 and full independence from France on 26 June 1960, under a conservative côtier-based government led by Philibert Tsiranana, from the northern Tsimihety tribe. A spirit of unity and reconciliation prevailed in the early 1960s. Tsiranana released those imprisoned since the 1947 revolt, but the highland-coastal rivalry soon reappeared. Tsiranana was reelected in 1972, but two months later he resigned in response to massive antigovernment demonstrations by the Merina in the capital, Antananarivo. The unrest continued, fueled by government attempts to decrease Merina influence.

After several attempts to form a government, Adm. Didier Ratsiraka, from the coast, established a highly centralized government in June 1975, dedicated to Marxist-oriented revolutionary socialism. Only limited and restricted political opposition was tolerated. Opposition to the revolutionary government, mostly underground, formed around the nascent Merina national movement.

Rising political dissent and socioeconomic decline paralleled the collapse of communism in eastern Europe. The end of press censorship and the legalization of political parties in 1989–90 were insufficient to placate the growing opposition in the Merina heartland. Opposition forces known as the Active Forces, the Hery Velona, centered in Antananarivo and the high plateau, led peaceful demonstrations and eventually crippling general strikes. In August 1991, government troops fired on 400,000 peaceful Merina demonstrators, killing more than 30. The killings began a crisis that finally ended Ratsiraka's Marxist government.

In October 1991, a transitional government was formed that set a timetable for a transition to democracy. In August 1992, in spite of attempts to disrupt balloting in several coastal areas, the island's voters approved a new democratic constitution to replace the socialist charter adopted in 1975. After 17 years of Marxist ideology, the economy was in ruins, and relations between the highland peoples and the larger coastal groups had deteriorated. A new government policy of decentralizing resources and authority was intended to enhance the development of the coastal provinces, seen by the Merina as favoring the coasts to the detriment of the more densely populated highlands.

In October 1992, the Merina community in the northern city of Antsirana fled back to the central highlands, claiming that local officials were inciting the côtiers against them. Ethnic violence spread to many areas where Merina had settled outside their highlands. In 1995, the Queen's Building, built in 1839 and considered a symbol of the Merina monarchy, was burned during anti-Merina unrest.

Albert Zafy, a côtier, was inaugurated in March 1993 as the new president of Madagascar, showing the growing strength of the côtier vote in the post-Marxist period. Zafy was impeached for abusing his powers and lost the 1996 presidential elections to Didier Ratsiraka, the leader of the Marxist government that had devastated the country's political life and economy from 1975 to 1991. Ratsiraka became president in 1997 amid widespread Merina opposition and a voter boycott.

The domination of the Malagasy government by the côtiers since the 1970s led to the development of the Merina national movement, which seeks to protect the culture and history by creating a self-governing Merina-Betsileo state in the highlands. Loss of power and influence is the main reason for the rapid growth of Merina nationalism. In July 2001, a group of Merina activists in France published a plan for the partition of Madagascar, which would give the Highland People a separate republic.

SELECTED BIBLIOGRAPHY:

Black, Eugene Robert. *The Madagascar Corundum*. 1998.
Heale, Jay. *Madagascar*. 1998.
Larson, Pier M. *History and Memory in the Age of Enslavement: Becoming Merina in Highland Madagascar, 1770–1822*. 2000.
Middleton, Karen, ed. *Ancestors, Power and History in Madagascar*. 1999.

Meskhetians

Meskhtekis; Meskets; Meskhetinets; Meskhis; Yerlis; Ahiska Turkleri; Ahiska Turks

POPULATION: Approximately (2002e) 350,000 Meskhetians in the former Soviet Union. The majority of the Meskhetians are in Azerbaijan (where 60,000 Meskhetians live), Ukraine, and the North Caucasus region of southern European Russia; a smaller number are in Georgia. Other large Meskhetian populations remain in southern Kazakhstan and Central Asia, in Uzbekistan, Kyrgyzstan, and Tajikistan, where they were deported in 1944.

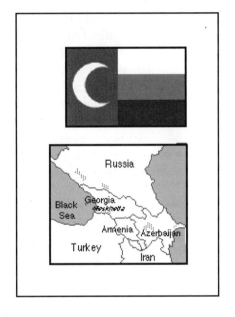

THE MESKHETIAN HOMELAND: The Meskhetian homeland lies in southeastern Georgia and northern Armenia. Traditionally known as Meskheti, the region is a highland in the Meskhetian Range on the Georgian-Armenian border, including a part of the autonomous republic of Ajaristan in Georgia, just north of the Turkish border. The region is very mountainous and lies mostly in the Meskhetian Range of the Lesser Caucasus. Because of the harsh climate, the region is often called "Georgia's Siberia." The homeland of the Meskhetians has no official status; the region claimed by Meskhetian nationalists lies in the Akhaltsikhe, Adigeni, Aspindza, and Borjomi Districts of southwestern Georgia. *Region of Meskhetia (Meskhetistan)*: 1,476 sq. mi.—3,824 sq. km, (2002e) 131,000—Georgians 50%, Armenians 32%, Ajars* 8%, Meskhetians 1%, others 9%. Traditionally the capital and major cultural center of the region is Akhaltsikhe, (2002e) 26,000.

FLAG: The Meskhetian national flag, the flag of the national movement, is a horizontal tricolor of white, green, and black bearing a vertical red stripe at the hoist charged with a white crescent moon.

PEOPLE AND CULTURE: The Meskhetians are one of the world's newest nations, a contemporary example of ethnogenesis. There was no Meskhetian ethnic group in the Soviet Union until the 1950s and 1960s. The small nation, which formed following its deportation from its homeland in the Caucasus Mountains, overcame differences in religion, dialect,

1237

and culture to form a distinct national group. Its members are the remnants and descendents of various Muslim Turkic, Georgian, and Armenian groups deported from the Turkish border region by Joseph Stalin. United by hardships, common experiences, and their Muslim Shi'a religion, the diverse peoples formed a separate nation in exile. The distinct Meskhetian culture incorporates elements of Muslim, Turkish, and Georgian culture. Many Meskhetians claim descent from the ancient Meskhet tribe, which was mentioned in the ancient chronicles of Herodotus and Strabo. Scholars differ on the issue of the Meskhetian origins; some consider them to be Turkicized Georgians; others, including most Meskhetians, consider them an ethnic Turkic group; a small number consider them ethnic Azeris.

LANGUAGE AND RELIGION: The Meskhetians developed a national language in exile, a hybrid dialect combining the Laz dialect of Georgia and admixtures from several East Anatolian Turkish dialects. A lingua franca used for intergroup communication developed as a viable national language. The new dialect, which is close to that of the Ajars, became the national language of the Meskhetian diaspora. In Azerbaijan the Meskhetians have begun primary education in the language, but most speak the languages of the surrounding communities, using their own Meskhetian dialects within the group and in the home.

The majority of the Meskhetians are Shi'a Muslims; a Sunni Muslim minority belongs to the Hanafite school. Although their religious ties are to Iran, their culture is secular and without any tendency toward Islamic fundamentalism. No religious fanaticism has been noted in Meskhetian religious life or in their national movement. Many pre-Islamic traditions and customs have been retained, including unique death rites and belief in magic and sorcery. The practice of inducing rain by magic is common, along with healing by the use of "moon water," water set out overnight under a clear sky.

NATIONAL HISTORY: In the first millennium B.C., the mountainous region was populated by the ancient Meskhet tribes. In the third century B.C., the area formed part of the Iberian Kingdom, with its center in Mtsketa, near present-day Tbilisi. In the second century B.C., the region became part of the Armenian kingdom. In the first century A.D., the Meskheti region had a mixed population of Turks, Georgians, and Armenians. The mountains east of the Black Sea have traditionally been a haven for refugees fleeing wars and invasions. In the high, isolated valleys, the inhabitants developed numerous dialects and cultures. In the early Christian Era, the mountains came under nominal Roman rule.

The Christian population suffered in the Arab invasion in the seventh century. In the eighth and ninth centuries, monks and feudal lords from eastern Georgia settled in Meskhetia. The region later formed part of the early Georgian kingdom in the ninth century, and was under the authority of the Kingdom of Armenia from A.D. 846 to 1046. The region was included in the Georgian principality of Ssanzche-Ssaatabago, which fell to the Mongol conquerors of the Caucasus in the thirteenth century. Tamerlane again devastated the area in the fourteenth century.

The disintegration of the Georgian kingdom coincided with the emergence of the Turkish Ottoman Empire. The Turks took control of the Meskhetia region in 1469, during the intense Turkish-Persian rivalry for control of the Transcaucasian region. The chief town of the area, Akhaltsikhe, was made the capital of a Turkish *pashalik* in the sixteenth century and the center of the Caucasian slave trade. By the seventeenth century the inhabitants of the mountainous region, mostly ethnic Georgian and Armenian Christians, had converted to Islam and had adopted many Turkish cultural traits.

Meskhetia was annexed by the expanding Russian Empire under the terms of the Treaty of Adrianople in 1828–29, beginning decades of Russian efforts to force the small Muslim groups of the Meskhetian Range to revert to the Christian religion. The Meskhetia region was divided between the Batumi and Kars areas of Tiflis (Tbilisi) Province. In spite of the common Christian oppressor, the small groups remained separate, uniting only when threatened by Christian violence, or by attacks on the Shi'a Muslim groups by the majority Sunni Muslim population of the region.

In 1905 serious unrest broke out among the Muslim peoples of the region. The Russians' brutal methods of crushing the disturbances reinforced the pro-Turkish sentiment shared by the diverse groups. Their homeland was on the front line when war began in 1914. As the war dragged on the Muslims suffered increasing persecution for being pro–Turkish. Briefly occupied by Turkish troops after the Russian Revolution in 1917, the Muslims again became the focus of anti-Turkish Georgian and Armenian nationalism when new Transcaucasian republics were set up in 1918. Soviet rule, established in 1921 following the conquest of Georgia and Armenia, was especially harsh for the Muslim peoples, whose loyalty to the new Soviet state was suspect. In the 1920s, the Meskhetians were registered as ethnic Azeris.

During World War II the German forces fought their way into the Caucasus to seize the region's oil reserves, often finding allies among the oppressed Muslim nationalities. Stalin, in 1943–44, accused many of the small Muslim nations of the Caucasus of treason, refusing to differentiate among those who had remained loyal and those who had joined the Nazis to fight the communists. He ordered entire nations deported to the wastes of Kazakhstan and Central Asia. Although neighboring Turkey remained carefully neutral during the war, Stalin regarded Russia's ancient adversary as an enemy and feared that Turkey would conclude a military alliance with Germany.

The small Muslim groups of the Meskhetian highlands, far south of the

German advance, were also charged with treason and suffered deportation, probably for their strong anti-Soviet and pro-Turkish sentiments. The Muslim peoples of southern Georgia, collectively called the Meskheti, were charged with treason and deported. The plan of deportation was prepared by the head of the People's Committee of Internal Affairs, Laventry Beria, and was signed by Joseph Stalin—both men ethnic Georgians.

In 1944 around 130,000 Muslims from the Meskhetia region were secretly driven from their homes and herded onto rail cars. The deportees were a diverse group, in terms of both culture and religion. The largest in number were the Meskhi Turks, Sunni Muslims who lived in the Kura River valley of Georgia. There were also Karapapakh Turks, Shi'a Muslims from northern Armenia; Armenian Sunni Muslims called Kemsils; two groups of Kurds (one Sunni Muslim and the other Shi'a Muslim) from southern Georgia and Ajaristan; and smaller numbers of Azeri-speaking Turkmens, Abkhaz,* and Ajars. The vacated districts were settled by "more reliable" Christian Georgians and Armenians.

Many of the deportees died of hunger, thirst, and cold on the long journey east. Their Soviet guards dumped them at rail sidings across a vast region, often without food, water, or shelter. Surviving Meskhetian soldiers fighting with the Red Army, numbering over 26,000 of the 40,000 conscripts of 1941, began to return to their homes in the Meskhetian hills in 1945, only to face arrest and deportation. The Meskhetians claim that 50,000 of their people died as a direct result of the deportations and the deprivations suffered in exile. In exile they were required to report every two weeks, like prisoners on parole.

At the end of World War II the disparate groups were living in abject poverty in widely scattered communities in Kazakhstan and the Central Asian republics. Their suffering and losses only made them more anti-Soviet, anticommunist, and religious. Putting aside their religious and dialectical differences, they began to solidify as a separate people. They took the name "Meskhetian" as a collective name for the many small groups that were merging into the new national group. They were not included in the rehabilitation of the deported peoples in 1956, when restrictions on free movement were partially lifted. Forbidden to return to their homeland, they were forgotten in the Soviet Union, and their existence was unknown in the West.

The scattered groups strengthened their ties in the 1960s, coordinating petitions, appeals, and agitation for the right to return to their Caucasian homeland. Delegates from the dispersed Meskhetian groups attended a national congress in Tashkent, Uzbekistan, in 1964. The congress voted to form the Meskhetian National Movement (MNM) and to send representatives to Moscow and Tbilisi to plead their case for the right to return to their homes. Finally rehabilitated and restored to full rights as Soviet citizens, the Meskhetians were released from KGB control in 1968, and they stepped up their campaign to win the right to return to their homeland. Details of the secret Meskhetian deportation began to leak out to the West in 1969, bringing international support, particularly among Western human-rights groups. Free from police control for the first time in over two decades, many Meskhetians moved from their scattered settlements to the Fergana Valley in Uzbekistan, the site of the largest Meskhetian exile community.

In the 1970s, the Meskhetian national movement was suppressed, its leaders jailed or exiled to remote regions. They were accused by agents of the Leonid Brezhnev government of spreading lies against the USSR. The growing prosperity of the energetic exiles, who advanced more rapidly than their Uzbek neighbors, raised ethnic and religious tension that worsened with the Soviet liberalization of the late 1980s.

During the 1980s, the national movement split between those favoring returning to their forbidden homeland in Georgia and others who favored migrating en masse to Azerbaijan, which is ethnically, linguistically, and religiously similar to the Meskhetian tradition. Officials in Soviet Georgia demanded that the Meskhetians adopt Georgian family names and renounce their culture. Although some 18,000 Meskhetians adopted Georgian names, very few were allowed to return to Soviet Georgia. The rift between the so-called Turkish Meskhetians and the Georgian Meskhetians remained serious until the violence in Uzbekistan in the late 1980s.

In an incident arising out of the cost of a basket of strawberries, a new tragedy struck the small nation. An Uzbek nationalist demonstration in June 1989 turned into a pogrom when Sunni Muslim demonstrators turned on the Shi'a Muslim Meskhetians, led by a man who claimed he had been cheated while buying strawberries. Enraged Uzbeks hunted the terrified exiles through a week of violence, rape, and murder. Over 100 Meskhetians died, and over 500 were injured before the Soviet military evacuated them to guarded camps outside the Uzbek cities. Told they would be returned to their Georgian homeland within two weeks, the majority of the refugees still languish in the camps. Considered foreigners in newly independent Uzbekistan, as unwanted aliens they can obtain neither work nor housing. Political action groups, including the Meskhetian National Movement and the Temporary Organizing Committee on Returning Home, continue to press for their right to return to their homeland.

After the collapse of the Soviet Union in 1991 allowed Georgia to reemerge as an independent state, the bid of the Meskhetians to return to their homeland was obstructed by the conservative Christian government of newly independent Georgia. The Georgian government of Zviad Gamsakhurdia, ethnocentric and anti-Muslim, offered the Meskhetians an opportunity to register as ethnic Georgians or to accept residence in Georgia outside Meskhetia. A more moderate Georgian government installed in

January 1992 received Meskhetian delegations, but beset by problems on every side, has not allowed the Meskhetians to return home from their long exile. Georgian officials claim that there is a shortage of land in Meskhetia; the Meskhetian homeland is now inhabited by peoples, mostly Christian Armenians and Georgians, settled in the depopulated region during the Stalin era. By 2000 only a handful of Meskhetians had been allowed to resettle in the region. Some Meskhetians have settled in other parts of Georgia, or in Azerbaijan, where the ethnically related Azeris have given them land in districts with large non-Turkic populations.

In November 1992, the nationalist Vatan organization held its first congress in Moscow. The body, representing the majority within the Meskhetian who reject the adoption of Georgian names and culture in order to be repatriated to their homeland, adopted a resolution that expressed their concerns over growing discrimination in many areas. In Krasnodar Krai, in the northern Caucasus region of southern Russia, over 12,000 Meskhetians who had settled after fleeing Uzbekistan in 1989–90 were deprived of their resident permits by local authorities between 1993 and 1998. The Muslim Meskhetians, often at odds with the Kuban Cossacks* in the region, faced increasing discrimination.

In September 1998, a meeting in the Netherlands between representatives of Georgia, Russia, Azerbaijan, and the Meskhetians under the sponsorship of the Organization for Security and Cooperation in Europe (OSCE) set a framework for the return of the first 5,000 Meskhetians to Georgia, although not to their Meskhetian homeland on the Turkish border. The meeting also attempted to address growing tensions before they become confrontations.

The aim of the Meskhetians is to form an autonomous state in their ancient homeland in the region known as Meskhetia, also called Dshavachetia or Achalzychetia, but most realize that as a first step they must gain Georgian citizenship, while maintaining their ethnic identity and preserving their traditional culture. The Meskhetian diaspora has stated its willingness to accept homes in any area of Georgia, but eventually they wish to return to their mountainous homeland on the Turkish border. They see themselves as the indigenous people of Meskhetia with a right to return, but the Georgian government has refused to consider repatriation until they replace their Turkish-sounding surnames and acknowledge themselves as ethnic Georgians. The majority of the Meskhetians still live as stateless persons or refugees over a half-century after their brutal deportation from their mountain homeland.

SELECTED BIBLIOGRAPHY:

Aslan, Kiyas. *The Ahiska Turks.* 1996.
Baratashvili, Marat. *The Legal State of Meskh Repatriates in Georgia.* 1998.
Pohl, J.O. *Ethnic Cleansing in the USSR, 1937–1949.* 1999.
Sheehy, Ann. *The Crimean Tatars, Volga Germans and Meskhetians: Soviet Treatment of Some National Minorities.* 1980.

Métis

Metis; Métiss; Metiff; Mistchiff; Michif

POPULATION: Approximately (2002e) 310,000 Métis in North America, concentrated in the prairie provinces of Canada. The largest communities live Manitoba, Alberta, and Saskatchewan. Other communities live in Ontario, Quebec, and other provinces, and in North Dakota and Minnesota in the United States. Estimates of the number of Métis in Canada vary widely, from 300,000 to 600,000. A proposed federal enumeration of the Métis could provide a more accurate count of Canada's Métis population.

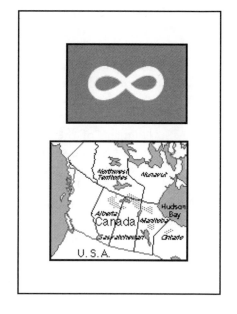

THE MÉTIS HOMELAND: The Métis homeland lies in northwestern Canada, in the vast basin of the Mackenzie Delta, encompassing parts of present-day Ontario, British Colombia, the Northwest Territories, Saskatchewan, Alberta, and Manitoba. Most of the region is included in the Great Plains of North America, the vast grasslands and forests traversed by numerous rivers, formerly the only means of transport across the region. The Métis homeland has no official status, with the exception of the Turtle Mountain Reservation in North Dakota. The Métis capital and major cultural center is St. Boniface, the birthplace of Louis Riel, now part of the Winnipeg metropolitan area in Manitoba. St. Boniface, a largely French and Michif (Mitchif) speaking city, has a population (2002e) of about 35,000.

FLAG: The Métis national flag, the flag of the national movement, is a blue field bearing two white circles forming the infinity symbol, representing the joining of two cultures in one.

PEOPLE AND CULTURE: The Métis are a nation of mixed background, counting French, Irish, Scots, and other Europeans, and Cree,* Blackfoot, Ojibwe,* and Salteaux Indians among their ancestors. Often rejected by both indigenous peoples and whites, the Métis, whose name comes from the Latin "miscere," meaning "to mix," evolved a strong sense of separate identity on the vast plains of North America. Their culture, a unique blend of customs, evolved a strong democratic tradition. The definition of a Métis, according the Métis National Council, is anyone who self-identifies as Métis; is distinct from Indian or Inuit; has at least one grandparent who is aboriginal; and whose application for admission is accepted by the Métis Nation. The dispute over the origins of the Métis, who consider themselves an indigenous people, is often heated. As a distinct nation that developed on the prairies in the eighteenth and nineteenth centuries, the Métis demand the same rights and privileges accorded the indigenous nations in Canada, but their claim to indigenous status is disputed by many scholars who claim they are simply of mixed race and therefore do not constitute a separate aboriginal nation.

LANGUAGE AND RELIGION: The Métis speak a dialect of French, a local patois that incorporates borrowings from English, Cree, and Blackfoot called Michif (Mitchif) or French Cree. The syntax, simplified from the French, has adopted many English forms. The majority of the Métis now speak standard French, taught in many area schools, and English, the language of the Canadian majority. In the 1980s, language organizations from Quebec set up schools and classes in Métis regions where education was mostly in English. Nationalists demand that their dialect be recognized as an official language in areas with large Métis populations.

The majority of the Métis are Roman Catholic, their religion often tempered by customs and beliefs acquired during the development of the Métis culture. In recent decades Protestant denominations have had some success among the scattered groups, but the majority remain devoutly Roman Catholic.

NATIONAL HISTORY: French trappers and traders began moving west from the colony of New France in the sixteenth century. The Métis were born from the marriages of Cree, Ojibwe, and Salteaux women with the trappers, beginning in the mid-1600s. Scots, Scandinavians, Irish, and English were added to the mix as western Canada was explored and developed. Early terms for the mixed population of the frontier were Half Breeds, Black Scots, and Country-born. The Métis quickly became the intermediaries between the Europeans and the various Indian cultures, working as guides, interpreters, and provisioners to the new forts and the companies active in the fur trade.

The redivision of the North American continent begun by the rebellion of the American colonies was intensified in Canada by rivalry in the fur trade. The French fur trade, centered on Montreal, had been taken over by British fur traders in 1763, when the French lost New France. The British conducted the trade with the aid and experience of the Québecois,* the French who remained in the British colonies. The British supplied the capital, while the French-speaking *voyageurs* supplied their skill as canoeists and their knowledge of the country and the indigenous populations.

In 1783, the Quebecker fur traders, called "Montrealers," established the North West Company to challenge the Hudson's Bay Company for dominance in the northwest wilderness. They organized a regular system of canoe convoys between Montreal and the richest trapping areas. They built a chain of fur-trading posts across the west. Explorers working for the company reached the Pacific coast, claiming vast territories for the North West Company.

The rivalry between the North West Company and Hudson's Bay Company at times degenerated into violence and even murder. The fur trade was lucrative for both companies and had a profound impact on the indigenous peoples of the vast region. As the companies pushed inland, contacts between the explorers, mostly French-speaking, and the indigenous peoples expanded.

Many young French-speaking men, called *coureurs des bois*, settled in the prairies to escape organized society. Living under no king or ruler, they produced what they needed and harvested the products of the plains and woods, which they exchanged for salt, cloths, and guns. The number of children of mixed race grew rapidly. They were called "mixed"—Métis, in the French dialect spoken by the trappers. The Métis began to develop a distinct culture and a national ambition of their own, which began to clash with the aims of the fur companies. Their unique plains culture incorporated customs and traditions from the indigenous peoples, the French trappers, and later Irish and other European settlers who joined the Métis communities. As the buffalo herds dwindled, the Métis spread across a vast area of the upper Great Plains.

Sir Thomas Douglas, the fifth earl of Selkirk, the head of Hudson's Bay Company, established the Red River Settlement, also called Assiniboia, on a grant of 116,000 square miles (300,440 sq. km) from the company in southern Manitoba in 1811. The settlement, lying along the main canoe routes of the North West Company, was seen as a threat by the Métis, who formed a majority of the population of the region. Poor European settlers, mostly from Scotland and Ireland, were recruited to colonize the land. Tension between the two groups erupted in violence; the Métis increasingly saw the colonists as a threat to their livelihood, particularly to the buffalo herds. The Métis attacked the settlers at Seven Oaks on 19 June 1816, killing 20 people, including the governor of the Red River colony. In the following days, the Métis forced the remaining settlers to leave to avoid massacre.

The Seven Oaks incident and a number of other violent clashes finally led to a truce between the two fur companies and a merger in 1821. The British government regarded the acquisition of the territories of the North West Company as a transaction in real estate with the Hudson's Bay Company. But Hudson's Bay was not the only authority in the territory. There were many European settlers at the Red River colony, as well as the Métis, who made up more than half the colony but were forgotten in the transfer.

The government's policy was opposed by Louis Riel, a Métis educated in Montreal. He organized resistance in Red River to the land transfer to Canada without the consent of the peoples living in the northwest. Riel, with the support of many armed Métis, seized control of the Red River colony and forced the Canadian government to postpone the transfer in 1869. Armed Métis seized Fort Garry, now Winnipeg, the headquarters of Hudson's Bay Company. The rebellion, known as the Northwest Rebellion, was the first serious threat to Canadian expansion. The rebels, called Nor'Westers, established a provisional government and elected Riel as their first president. He demanded negotiations on acceptable terms for union with Canada. He asserted Métis nationhood and demanded recognition of Métis rights and control over lands and natural resources they had traditionally held.

The government began negotiations, which resulted in the creation of the small province of Manitoba in 1870, with equal status for both French and English as official languages and a bilingual educational system. During the negotiations of Manitoba's entry into the Canadian Confederation, a grant of 1.4 million acres (2,187 sq. mi.—5,665 sq. km) was reserved for the exclusive use of the Métis. The Métis believed that adding this territory to the lands they occupied before the land transfer would provide a viable homeland and ensure the survival of their language and culture against the onslaught of European settlers.

The creation of the Métis territory was undermined by government delay and neglect that facilitated the work of land speculators who profited from the growing demand for land by settlers and the railroads. The Manitoba agreement finally collapsed over the smallness of the province—little more than the original Red River settlement—and the Canadian dominion's control of all natural resources and of the still-vast North West Territory.

In order to extend its authority to the Pacific Ocean, the government negotiated a series of treaties from 1871 to 1877 with Indian groups from northern Ontario to the eastern Rocky Mountains. In return for moving to reserves, the indigenous groups were to receive various subsidies, educational facilities, rations, and health care. These obligations were also mostly ignored, raising tension across a vast area. Because the Métis were outside traditional Indian society, they were excluded from the original treaties that gave rights and privileges to the "status Indians." Denied the recognition of their collective rights by political edict alone, the Métis became Canada's "forgotten people."

The Canadian parliament passed the Manitoba Act in May 1870, establishing the expanded province of Manitoba, including the Red River region. It promised an amnesty to the Métis insurgents, but Riel's court-martial and execution of an English-speaking Canadian soldier aroused all English-speaking Canada against the Métis. The promised amnesty was refused, and Canadian military forces were dispatched to confront Riel and his rebel forces. When Fort Garry was recaptured in August 1879, the rebellion collapsed, and Riel fled. He later became a U.S. citizen and endeavored to organize the American Métis on behalf of the Republican Party.

In 1884, the Métis of Saskatchewan asked Riel to represent their land claims to the Canadian government. At first Riel proceeded legally, but he later rebelled and established a provisional Métis government in March 1885. The uprising was crushed at the Battle of Batoche in Saskatchewan, and Riel surrendered. He was found guilty of treason and was hanged. His death led to violent outbreaks among Métis across Canada and marked the beginning of the modern Métis national movement.

The government began issuing land and money scrip to the Métis outside Manitoba in the late 1880s. Land that had been part of the original 1870 claim was excluded and remained unavailable to the Métis. By issuing scrip on an individual basis instead of collectively to all the Métis, the government forced the Métis to accept it or give up their identity and accept the status of Indians. The government scrip destroyed the base of land and resources that the Métis depended on for their way of life. The Métis were increasingly pushed to the margins of Canadian society. The Métis, unlike the Indians and Inuits, were not officially recognized or afforded any protection under the constitution.

In 1887, the first cultural-national organization was organized in St. Vital, in Manitoba, to preserved the unique heritage of the Métis—L'Union National Métisse St.-Joseph du Manitoba. By the 1930s, nationalist associations had been formed in Saskatchewan and Alberta to press for a territorial base for the Métis nation. In 1936, the Alberta government granted 2,000 square miles (5,180 sq. km) of for Métis settlement, a precedent that allowed the Métis of Alberta to obtain limited control of health care, housing, child welfare, and legal institutions.

Land claims and rights to hunting, fishing, gathering, and trapping began to be taken to the courts rather than to government agencies. Young, educated Métis took over the leadership of the nation from the traditional leaders in the 1960s. The new leaders were more radical and less willing to compromise than their elders. In 1982, the Métis, Indians, and Inuits were officially incorporated into the Canadian constitution as aboriginal groups. In 1983, the Métis of the Native Council of Canada (NCC) left the organization to form the Métis National Council (MNC).

The failure of the 1992 Charlottetown Accord referendum, which would have accommodated the Quebeckers and other French-speaking groups within Canada, alarmed the Métis, who saw the failure as a new threat to their culture and language. Métis leaders in the eastern provinces began a new initiative to keep the Métis issue in the forefront of the national agenda and to create a fresh focus for Métis activism. The national movement, centered on the Métis of the central provinces, favored a prairie-oriented, national definition of Métis. Other groups attempted to avoid further splintering of the national Métis constituency. Also in 1992, the Canadian government recognized Louis Riel as one of the founders of the Canadian Confederation. In March 1993, Yvon Dumont became the first Métis lieutenant governor of Canada.

The majority of the Métis groups favor a mandate for a confederacy of Métis peoples across Canada, while a minority demand an autonomous territory to be carved out of the historical Métis lands in the former North West Territory. A Canadian royal commission report released in 1996 recommended measures to avoid violence, including granting the Métis more land. In early 1998, a national meeting if Métis organizations produced a consensus statement on the idea of a confederacy as a vehicle for encouraging pan-Canadian cooperation of the Métis peoples. A court granted hunting and fishing rights to a group of Métis in December 1998, recognizing for the first time their distinct cultural rights as an aboriginal people.

Militant groups assert that the Métis formed a nation prior to the establishment of the Canadian Confederation, and that the aboriginal peoples of Canada who formed viable nations before union with Canada have a prior claim to traditional territory. Many Métis cite the autonomy agreement applied to the Inuits* of Nunavut in 1999.

The national movement works to restore Métis lands and resources for future generations; achieve the full recognition of the Métis nation and its sovereignty within the Canadian federal system; and promote the cultural, social, economic, and political aims of the nation. Most importantly, it aims to maintain the independence and integrity of the Métis Nation, safeguard its stability, and resist aggression. The Métis were instrumental in the development of western Canada, but unlike the Indians and Inuits, the historical role played by the Métis has not been officially acknowledged, nor have their rights to land and autonomy. At the turn of the twenty-first century none of the promises of lands, rights, or annuities had been fulfilled.

SELECTED BIBLIOGRAPHY:

Bakker, Peter. *A Language of Our Own: The Genesis of Michif, the Mixed Cree-French Language of the Canadian Métis.* 1997.
Giraud, Marcel. *Métis of the Canadian West.* 1999.
Jackson, John C. *Children of the Fur Trade: Forgotten Métis of the Pacific Northwest.* 1995.
Peterson, Jacquelyn, ed. *New People: Being and Becoming Métis.* 1996.

Micmacs

Mi'kmaq; Mi'gmaq; Míqmaq; Míkmaq; Mi'mkaq; Souriquois; Inu; Tarrateen

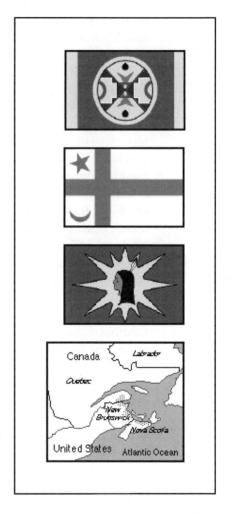

POPULATION: Approximately (2002e) 31,000 Micmac in eastern Canada—14,000 in Nova Scotia, as well as in New Brunswick, Prince Edward Island, Quebec, and Newfoundland. Other communities live in the U.S. states of Maine, Massachusetts, and New York.

THE MICMAC HOMELAND: The Micmac homeland lies in eastern Canada and the northeastern United States. Most Micmac live around the Gulf of St. Lawrence, in the Gaspé region of Quebec, and the coastal regions of New Brunswick, Nova Scotia, and Prince Edward Island. The region is mostly devoted to farming, fishing, and logging. The Micmac homeland, called Mi'kma'ki, or "Land of the Mi'kmaq," has no official status in Canada or the United States. The Micmac capital and major cultural center is Restigouche in Quebec, called Listuguj by the Micmac, (2002e) 3,000. The other important cultural center is Pictou, called Pigtogeoag, in Nova Scotia, (2002e) 5,000.

FLAG: The Micmac national flag is a red field bearing narrow vertical stripes on the hoist and fly and charged with the national shield in yellow, blue, green, and red, centered. The flag of the Micmac Grand Council (Mi'Kmaq Sante' Mawio'mi), is a white field bearing an off-center red cross with a five-pointed red star on the upper hoist and a red crescent moon on the lower hoist. The flag of the Micmac Warriors Society (Mi'kmaq Sma'knis) is a red field bearing a warrior's profile within a 12-pointed yellow sun.

PEOPLE AND CULTURE: The Micmac are the easternmost of the Algonquin peoples of eastern North America. Only a minority live on the officially designated reservations in Nova Scotia, New Brunswick, and

Quebec. Most Micmac live on individual farms or, increasingly, in urban areas but maintain close ties to their culture and nation. The correct name of the nation is Mi'kmaq, which is the plural form of Mi'kmaw. "Micmac," the common name, is a French misspelling of the original name. The Micmac often call themselves Inu, meaning "men" or "human beings." The Micmac are the largest of the indigenous tribes occupying Canada's eastern Maritime Provinces. Due to the traditionally close ties to the French-speaking population of the region, many Micmac are of mixed background and, although they identify with the Micmac nation, are not registered as indigenous. Canada recognizes 28 Micmac bands, but only one Micmac tribe is recognized in the United States—the Aroostook Band of Micmac in northern Maine.

LANGUAGE AND RELIGION: The Micmac language is an Algonquian language belonging to the Eastern Algonquian branch of the language group. Speakers of the Restigouche dialect have difficulty understanding other dialects. The language is distinct from neighboring Algonquian languages, with some features associated with the language of the Innu* of northern Canada. They are the only indigenous tribe in Canada that ever used hieroglyphs, or ideograms, as a means of communication. These were invented in 1677 by Father Leclerq, who took the idea from the drawings of children. A number of manuscripts were written up to the late nineteenth century, when the Latin script was adopted. The Micmac are mostly bilingual in English or French.

The Micmac are staunchly Roman Catholic, the result of missionary activity by French orders in the seventeenth and eighteenth centuries. Since the mid-nineteenth Protestant denominations have been active in the region, but the Micmac have remained steadfast in their fidelity to the Catholic Church. Their traditional ceremonies were reported to be elaborate, but little is known of their rituals or religious beliefs.

NATIONAL HISTORY: There is little known of the history of the Micmac before the arrival of the Europeans. Because their Algonkian dialect differs greatly from that of their neighbors, many scholars believe they were latecomers to the region in prehistoric times. It is thought that they occupied their homeland for a considerable period before A.D. 1500. They were traditionally led by a *saqamaw* or chief, who served for life, and were formed as a confederacy of several clans. The traditional succession of the chiefs followed the male line and was restricted to a few families.

According to Micmac traditions, they held third rank in the original distribution of territory among the confederation of eastern Algonquins. The first place belonged to the most powerful, the Ottawa, who received the "land of origins." The second territory, Wapanakiag, was controlled by the Abenaki, while the third territory, known as Migmagig, was allotted to the Micmac. Until the arrival of the Europeans, an annual ceremony recalled this territorial division. The seminomadic Micmac groups ranged over the present-day Maritime Provinces and the Gaspé Peninsula. They later spread to Newfoundland and New England.

The Micmac were seasonally nomadic. In winter they hunted moose, caribou, and small game, while in summer they fished, gathered shellfish, and hunted seal along the coasts. About 1630 a Micmac band occupied southwestern Newfoundland. The Micmac homeland was traditionally divided into seven hunting districts, each under a separate chief. In 1860 they added another district, for a total of eight.

When Europeans ships visited their shores in the sixteenth and seventeenth centuries, the Micmac welcomed them. They were the first indigenous peoples of the region to be visited by the Europeans. The Micmac were probably visited by Sebastian Cabot in 1497 and by the French explorer Philipe Cortereal in 1501. Jacques Cartier encountered Micmac in the St. Lawrence Gulf region in 1534. Allied to the French, the Micmac delayed the English settlement of Nova Scotia and New Brunswick. The first permanent European settlement in the region was established at the mouth of the St. Croix River in 1604 by Samuel de Champlain and Pierre de Monts but was later moved to Micmac territory in the Annapolis Basin in 1605.

The Micmac population is estimated to have been between 20,000 and 30,000 at the time of European contact. By 1620 epidemics had reduced their numbers to less than 4,000. In 1760 they are estimated to have numbered around 3,000, reaching a low point of 1,800 in 1823. Precise numbers were difficult to establish due to extensive intermarriage with the neighboring French-speaking populations.

The Micmac welcomed the French and their religion, brought to the region by secular priests and Jesuits, and later by the Recollects and Capuchins. Early missionary accounts characterize the Micmac as peaceful and even-tempered. In 1633, several Micmac chiefs visited Rome and were received by the pope. They promised to allow the Catholic missions access to all parts of the nation.

The relationship between the Acadians* and Micmac was, for the most part amiable. The Micmac taught the French settlers how to hunt in the woods and shared with them many facets of herbal medicine. In return the French gave Christianity, but also diseases and alcohol, which the Micmac were not equipped to resist. Dependence on European manufactured goods deprived many Micmac of the traditional ways that had been central to their material civilization.

Though the war practices of the Micmac were less cruel than those of the Iroquois* and other eastern tribes, they proved loyal and brave allies for the French during the French and English wars of the eighteenth century. They developed a lasting hostility to the colonization schemes of the English. Due to extensive intermarriage and long ties, the Micmac at first refused to accept British rule following the cession of the Maritimes by

France in 1713. The British defeat of the French at Quebec brought all of the Micmac territories under British rule. They formally submitted to the British conquerors in 1761. Although more in sympathy with the French, the Micmac honored their trust thereafter and remained loyal to the British crown.

In 1778 the rebel colonists of the United States endeavored to incite the Micmac to revolt against the British, but under the influence of several French priests they remained neutral in the conflict. The Jay Treaty of 1794 between the United Kingdom and the United States gave the Micmac the right to move freely back and forth across the new international border.

In 1849 Protestant missionaries formed the Micmac Missionary Society and began work among the Micmac of Prince Edward Island. In spite of the activities of the Protestants, the Micmac clung to their Catholic religion. The major interest in the Protestant missions was in the educational facilities constructed as part of each mission station.

During the nineteenth century the Micmac slowly recovered from the devastation of European conquest and the diseases that had decimated their small nation. Mostly ignored by provincial and federal governments, most settled as fishermen or farmers. In the late nineteenth century the Canadian government established a number of reserves, mostly in New Brunswick and Nova Scotia, but Micmac living outside the reserves were not obliged to move into them.

A number of bands of Micmac in the 1920s and early 1930s, due to their privileges under the Jay Treaty, were involved in the alcohol trade, which was legal in Canada but illegal in the Prohibition-era United States. Alcoholism, already a serious social problem, increased in the 1940s and 1950s.

In the 1980s, "Red Power" began to influence the formerly acquiescent Micmac. Demands were pressed for full rights, including the rights to hunt, fish, and gather on traditional lands that had been guaranteed in "peace and friendship" treaties signed by the Micmac nation and the British government in 1760 and 1761. (In return the Micmac had agreed to serve the British as lookouts for foreign ships and coastal marauders.)

Micmac activists in the 1990s defied local laws and continued to fish and hunt whenever and wherever they wished on traditional tribal territories and waters. Neighboring fishermen and hunters objected to the Micmac being given more favorable treatment than other Canadian citizens. Sixty activists blocked a road to the Big Hole Tract River in a conflict over fishing rights in July 1995. A dozen Micmac had been arrested for using nets to catch salmon in the shallow river, which activists claimed was a right guaranteed by a British agreement of 1772. In 1997, reacting to indigenous claims, the Canadian Supreme Court ruled that indigenous nations continued to have aboriginal title to their traditional territory. It added that provincial governments had a moral duty to negotiate and settle native claims, including hunting and fishing rights.

In August 1997, the Supreme Court set aside three days to deal with the legal issues surrounding Quebec separation. The Micmac presented their views and reiterated their opposition to Quebec separatism that would divide their small nation between two sovereign states. The Micmac Grand Council opposed Quebec independence and indicated that should Quebec leave the confederation, the Micmac would have to make some hard decisions on sovereignty.

In August 1998, activists from Nova Scotia and New Brunswick blocked a highway in Quebec and refused to disband when presented with an injunction written in French, a language they do not speak. The blockade was initially set up to press for unlimited logging rights in Quebec, instead of being bound by the 350,000 cubic feet (158,574 cubic meters) limit agreed upon by Micmac leaders and the Quebec government. The three-week standoff ended when Micmac and Quebecker officials signed an agreement giving the Quebec Micmac the right to log and creating a number of seasonal jobs in the industry.

The Canadian Supreme Court in September 1999 agreed with the Micmac lawyers that past treaties remained in effect and that the Micmac had the right to fish and hunt while other Canadians were restricted to certain seasons. The Court decided that the Micmac still had the right to earn a "moderate livelihood" from hunting, fishing, and gathering, unconstrained by other restrictions. The decision was applied to all peoples who identified with the Micmac nation, whether they lived on or off the official reservations. Since the treaties had been signed before the establishment of reserves, objections by competing fishermen and businesses were overthrown.

Micmac fishermen in New Brunswick rushed to take advantage of the court ruling. Their nonindigenous competitors, already suffering depleted stocks, promptly destroyed over 3,500 Micmac lobster pots. Boats were rammed, trucks burned, and property and Micmac sacred sites were vandalized. Tension rose until both sides, fearing an outbreak of violence, brought the situation under control and pressed for negotiations.

In August 2000, federal fisheries department boats began to confiscate lobster traps set in defiance of a ban on indigenous fishing. The Micmac have refused to sign an agreement on fishing rights as they believe that they should have control on resources in their traditional territory. To the Micmac, the right to gather applies the gas, oil, mines, minerals, and timber that comes from their traditional lands. The Canadian and provincial governments continue to press negotiations over land claims and aboriginal rights, negotiations that the Micmac hope will lead to the creation of a sovereign Micmac nation, but the question of land and resources rights is a major impediment.

SELECTED BIBLIOGRAPHY:

Paul, Daniel N. *We Were Not the Savages: A Micmac Perspective on the Collision of European and Aboriginal Civilizations.* 1995.

Prins, Harald E.L. *The Mi'Kmaq: Resistance, Accommodation, and Cultural Survival.* 1997.

Raulet, Philippe. *Micmac.* 1982.

Whitehead, Ruth Holmes. *Elitekey: Micmac Material Culture from 1600 A.D. to the Present.* 1991.

Mikirs

Karbis; Mikiris; Manchatis; Arleng

POPULATION: Approximately (2002e) 548,000 Mikirs in India, concentrated in the northeastern state of Assam. Smaller numbers live in other northeastern Indian states, Arunchal Pradesh, Nagaland, and Meghalaya, and in adjacent parts of Bangladesh.

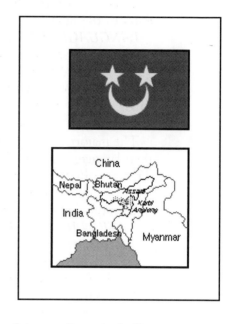

THE MIKIR HOMELAND: The Mikir homeland, Karbi Anglong, lies in northeastern India in the Mikir and Rengma hills mostly in the state of Assam in the Karbi Anglong, North Cachar Hills, and Nagoan districts, the Lower Subansiri District of Arunchal Pradesh, and the Jaintia and East Kashi Hills districts of Meghalaya, and in the hill areas around Dimapur in Nagaland. Most of the region is wet rice lands, although in the highlands more traditional agriculture prevails. The Mikir heartland, called Karbi Anglong by nationalists, forms the districts of Karbi Anglong and North Cachar Hills of Assam State in India. *Karbi Anglong (Karbi Anglong-North Cachar Hills):* 5,916 sq. mi.—15,324 sq. km, (2002e) 1,108,000—Mikirs 43%, Bihars 16%, Masas* (Dimasas) 15%, Assamese* 13%, Nepalis 6%, Bengalis 5%, Bodos,* Kukis, Hmars, and other Indians 2%. The Mikir capital and major cultural center is Diphu (2002e) 48,000.

FLAG: The Mikir national flag, the flag of the nationalist organizations, is a blue field bearing a white crescent moon and two white, five-pointed stars at the points.

PEOPLE AND CULTURE: The Mikirs call themselves Karbis and their language Karbi Barak. They belong to the Mongoloid group. Traditionally the Mikirs are divided into three regional groups, the Chinthong, Ronghang, and Amri. The Mikirs living in the lowlands plains are known as Dumrali. They are further divided into five clans, *kur*, the Terang, Teron, Enghee, Ingti, and Timung. Each of the clans is divided into a number of subclans. Marriage between members of the same clan is forbidden. The Mikirs are a patriarchal people, with descent and inheritance through the male line. Until the 1950s, many Mikirs practiced shifting cultivation, but now almost all are engaged in wet rice agriculture. The traditional Mikir king, the Lingdokpo, still exercises his traditional authority in respect to socio-religious matters. Each Mikir village is headed by a headman called a *rong sarthe* and a village council, the *me*. Traditionally the Mikirs maintained a bachelor's dormitory, the *farla*, which combined some of the functions of a club and a school. Dance and music play an important role in the life of Mikir society. A rich oral history includes their own version of the Ramayana called Sabin Alun which is handed down from one generation to the next.

LANGUAGE AND RELIGION: The Mikirs speak a language of the Mikir group of the Tibeto-Burman languages of the Sino-Tibetan language family. Mikir is spoken in three major dialects, Mikir, Amri, and Bhoi Mynri. Bhoi Mynri is intelligible only with difficulty. Speakers of all Mikir dialects speak Assamese as a second language. The language is written in a Roman script introduced by Western missionaries.

The majority of the Mikirs are Christians. The Bible was translated into their language in 1952. Belief in ghosts and evil spirits remains widespread. Traditionally the highest of the Mikir gods, Barithe, was the god of heaven. Christian beliefs have been mixed with ancient worship of natural objects in a unique belief system.

NATIONAL HISTORY: The original home of the Tibeto-Burman peoples was in western China near the Yang-Tee-Kiang and Howang-ho rivers. From there some followed the courses of the Brahmaputra River and entered present northeastern India from Central Asia in one of many Tibeto-Burman migrations. The ancient history of the Mikirs is difficult to trace in the absence of any written records and other evidence such as archeological remains. Their folk-tales and folklore are the only sources regarding their early history.

According to Mikir tradition, they once lived on the banks of the Kalang and Kapili rivers and are one of the historic nations of the region. They were slowly driven northward by the Jaintias and other peoples. Most lived in autonomous village units in the less accessible mountain areas. Others were under the control of local states controlled by rival tribal groups. At some time in the ancient past, they formed a loose confederation ruled by a king. According to Mikir traditions, their first king, Sat Recho, promised to return at a certain stage of civilization to rule the earth once again.

In the early thirteenth century, a Tai* people, the Ahom, migrated to the Brahmaputra Valley. They established their control of the lowlands and established tribute and trade ties to many of the tribal peoples of the highlands around the huge valley. They remained the dominant political force in the region for nearly 600 years.

At the beginning of the seventeenth century, some Mikirs migrated into the Ahom kingdom in present Assam. There they begged Ahom protection from attacks by other tribal groups. In 1661–62 Mogul troops from Bengal to the south invaded the region, driving many Mikirs from the lowlands.

The Mikirs established a capital at Ronhang Rongbong, in the present Assamese district of Karbi Anglong. There they created a national assembly, the Pinpomar, which then selected a king, the Lingdokpo. In the highlands they maintained their autonomy, often paying tribute to the Ahom kings but mostly left to govern themselves. From the fifteenth to the eighteenth centuries, the region was contested by Burmans, Assamese, and Bengalis.

Burman invasions from the east disrupted the region in the early 1700s. When a Burman supported rebellion broke out against the Ahoms in 1792, the Ahom king enlisted British aid in suppressing the tribal rebels. When the British withdrew, the Burmans again invaded and conquered the Ahom kingdom, driving the Mikirs to take refuge in the deep jungles and the less accessible mountains. In order to save themselves from rape by the invaders, young Mikir girls began to draw a black line from their foreheads to their chins. The line, the *duk*, was designed to make them unattractive to the Burman soldiers. Some Mikir groups migrated to lower Assam, others crossed the Brahmaputra River and settled in the highlands in the north bank.

The British, having driven the Burmans from the region, annexed Assam to the British Empire in 1826. British authority was slowly extended to the highlands, with contact made with the Mikir king and the various Mikir chiefs. Sporadic tribal uprisings occurred when the British authorities attempted to exert more control over the Mikir tribes.

The Mikirs, although inhabiting several distinct regions, maintained their traditional ties to the Mikir kings and the tribal hierarchies. British and American missionary activity facilitated the expansion of Mikir identity in the nineteenth century. Their conversion to Christianity was an offshoot of their efforts to protect their national identity. The missionaries did little to protect their culture, but provided the organizational structure they required to maintain their unity.

British colonial economic control depended on the traditional chief and on a policy of divide and rule. The missionaries concentrated on education, from which new leaders emerged in the early twentieth century. The modern, mission-educated leaders were a threat to the traditional chiefs. By the 1920s, even the traditional tribal leaders had converted to Christianity although the differences between the modern and traditional hierarchies remained.

The British colonial policy set up excluded and partially excluded areas in the tribal highlands. These exclusion orders prohibited settlement by lowland Assamese and Bengalis, but also restricted the social and political mobility of the Mikirs and other tribal groups. Mutual mistrust between the hill tribes and the inhabitants of the lowlands developed. The Mikirs were considered by the lowlanders as nomadic and uncivilized. The Mikirs looked on the lowlanders with distrust and regarded them as outsiders in their traditional lands.

In the 1930s, the traditional chiefs mostly supported the British authorities while the new mission-educated leaders joined the Indian independence movement, which they viewed as a modern institution. The two groups remained united in their efforts to protect Mikir identity and culture. In the late 1930s, as agitation for the end of British rule swept the subcontinent, the Mikirs united to form the Mikir National Council (MNC).

The MNC remained loyal to the British during World War II when the region was invaded by the Japanese from Burma. Although the Japanese promised autonomy and an alliance, the Mikirs mostly rejected Japanese overtures. At the end of the war, the MNC began negotiations with the British for the establishment of an autonomous Mikir district, but their demands were ignored in the rush to Indian independence in August 1947.

The Indian government, in an effort to offset growing Mikir militancy, established the United Mikir and North Cachar Hills District in November 1951. Mikir leaders demanded the creation of a more extensive territory to include the Mikir inhabited territories in the districts of Golaghat, Nagaon, Cachar, and the United Khasi and Jaintia Hills districts. In 1970, the United Mikir and North Cachar Hills District was divided into two separate districts. The Mikir Hill District was given the traditional name of the Mikir homeland in 1976. Karbi Anlong District, although it covered only a portion of the traditional Mikir homeland, became the focus of Mikir nationalism. A 26-member Karbi Anglong Autonomous Council (KAAC) gave the Mikirs of the northern district some limited control, but the council was denounced by the more militant groups as inadequate and too limited to be effective.

In the 1970s, led by Korsing Terang, the Mikirs began to mobilize culturally and politically. Terang became the first chief executive of the Karbi Anglong Autonomous Council and the first Mikir to be elected to the Assam Legislative Assembly. Emigration by lowland Assamese and Biharis and the growing number of Muslim Bengalis forced many Mikirs to embrace nationalism in an effort to maintain their traditional culture and territories.

Long years of neglect, indifference, and ignorance of tribal culture on the part of the Assamese administration created among the Mikirs a sharp awareness of their ethnic and cultural differences from the lowland Assamese. The rapid rise of a money economy forced many Mikirs to adopt new ways of living. Economic hardships due to poor and underdeveloped agriculture, mass unemployment, rampant corruption, a lack of educational and medical facilities, exorbitant prices, and a shortage essential commodities led many young Mikirs to embrace extremist activities. The economic neglect and unimaginative government policies, along with gross ignorance of the tribal ethos, created among the Mikirs and other Tibeto-Burman nations in Assam a sharp awareness of their ethnic and cultural differences from the Indian population. Although the Mikir districts have abundant raw materials, few industries other than tea, sugarcane, and rubber plantations have been established.

In the 1980s, several rebel organizations formed the Karbi National Volunteers (KNV) and the Karbi Peoples Front (KPF). The majority of the Mikirs, calling themselves by the traditional name, Karbi, demanded autonomy in a new Mikir state. Others, including a more militant and violent minority, demanded the independence of a tribal state to be carved out of territory in Assam and Meghalaya along the border with Bangladesh. In 1998, the KNV and KPF united to form the United People's Democratic Solidarity (UPDS) in 1999 and launched a military campaign for an autonomous Mikir state to be called Karbi Anglong. The UPDS united the dissident Mikir groups although the KNV and KPF continued to maintain separate military commands. In July 2000, the UPDS launched a campaign to drive non-Mikirs from the entire region. Retaliatory attacks by Biharis and Nepalis left many Mikirs dead and injured. By December 2000 over 60 people had been killed in the fighting.

Growing violence led to a number of deaths in retaliatory attacks by Mikirs and Biharis in 1999–2000. The Biharis, who opened the forest areas of the Mikir homeland to modern cultivation in the 1950s, now form a majority in some subdivisions of the Mikir districts. The Mikirs resent the Biharis' economic success and political clout. Violent clashes over land and water rights increased tension in the region in 2000–2001.

Dozens of Mikirs and non-tribal peoples died in the fighting that periodically swept the Mikir districts. Mikir villagers joined village defense committees and sent young men for training by the People's Guard, an organization formed to protect the Mikirs from the violent attacks by non-tribal peoples looking for new lands to develop as tea plantations.

Moderate Mikirs, led by Holiram Terang, supported the idea of a separate tribal state within India, particularly following the Indian government's decision, in 2000, to create a number of new states in eastern and central India. The government's lack of response to the creation of a new tribal state fed the growing militancy among the Mikirs.

In May 2000, the UPDS leadership asserted that it would continue its "resistance campaign" against the environmental, ecological degradation and the demographic aggression against the Mikir nation. The UPDS leaders blamed moderate Mikirs and the Indian security forces for "countless extra-judicial killings" in the Mikir districts.

In August 2000, a new executive committee of the KAAC passed a resolution for the creation of an autonomous state of Karbi Anglong along the lines of the new Indian states of Jharkhand, Uttaranchal, and Chattishgarh. The resolution, which has no legislative authority, had widespread public support. Public opinion in the region is increasingly against the continued inclusion of the Mikir homeland within Assam. The demand for a separate Mikir state within India is led by the Autonomous State Demand Committee (ASDC). The ASDC is opposed by the more militant groups who seek to separate the Mikir homeland from India. A factional split among the Mikir leadership in mid-2000 allowed the militants to gain support among the increasingly dissatisfied Mikir majority.

Strikes, including several general strikes, paralyzed the region in 2000–2002. The KNV and KPF, with growing ties to several militant groups of Nagas,* have used the strikes and extortion to press their cause of secession from Assam. More moderate leaders of the two groups demand the immediate introduction of an autonomous state bill for Karbi Anglong and North Cachar Hills in the Indian Parliament in New Delhi.

On 5 June 2001, on World Environmental Day, Mikirs marched through their capital, Diphu, to protest the uncontrolled exploitation of their homeland. The biodiversity of the region includes a number of unique bamboo species and exotic wildlife. A number of militants, carrying the separatist flag, were detained by police for disturbing the peace of the environmental march.

Many Mikir activists have encouraged ties among the various tribal groups in Assam to support the creation of a separate tribal state as the first step to a federation of tribal states that would replace Assamese authority in the region. More militant groups support the idea, but only as the first step toward an independent state. The Mikirs fear that their culture and identity are at stake in future due to the large-scale infiltration of their homeland from the Assamese lowlands, Bangladesh, and Nepal.

SELECTED BIBLIOGRAPHY:

Bower, Ursula Graham. *The Hidden Land.* 1953.
Datta, P.S. *Ethnic Movements in Poly-Cultural Assam.* 1990.
Deaner, Janice. *Assam.* 2000.
Sen, Sipra. *Tribes and Castes of Assam.* 1999.

Miskitos

Mískitos; Mosquitos; Moskitos; Miskitu; Mostiques; Marquitos

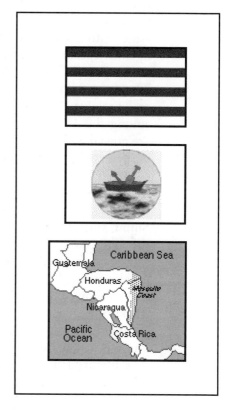

POPULATION: Approximately (2002e) 325,000 Miskitos in Central America, concentrated on the Atlantic coast of Nicaragua with 320,000, and the eastern districts of Honduras, where about 25,000 Miskitos live. The population in Nicaragua includes smaller related groups—10,000 Sumu and 6,000 Rama.

THE MISKITO HOMELAND: The Miskito homeland, called Miskitia or Mosquitia, also the Mosquito Coast, lies on the eastern coast of Central America, a region of river lowlands and swamps some 40 miles wide and about 225 miles long, from the San Juan River in southeastern Nicaragua to the Brus Lagoon on the north coast of Honduras. The Miskito population is concentrated in northeastern Nicaragua and eastern Honduras around the interior mining areas, and along the banks of several rivers that flow east out of the highlands to the Caribbean. The Caribbean lowlands are difficult to reach overland or by river; a paved road to connect the region to central Nicaragua is still in the planning stage. The Miskito region of Honduras forms the department of Gracias a Dios. *Department of Gracias a Dios*: 6,420 sq. mi.—16,628 sq. km, (2002e) 50,000—Miskitos 43%, Mestizo Hondurans 24%, Garifunas* 17%, Creoles 12%, Sumu 2%, others 2%. The homeland in Nicaragua forms two autonomous regions, North Atlantic Autonomous Region (NAAS) and South Atlantic Autonomous Region (RAAS). *Mosquito Coast (Yapti Tasba)*: 22,816 sq. mi.—59,059 sq. km, (2002e) 597,000—Miskitos 52%, Mestizo Nicaraguans 27%, Creoles 15%, Sumu 2%, Rama 1%, Garifunas* 1%, others 2%. The Miskito capital and major cultural center is Waspám, (2002e) 13,000. Other important cultural centers are Puerto Cabezas, often called Bragman's Bluff, but called Bilwi by the Miskitos, (2002e) 29,000, and Puerto Limpera in Honduras, called Tansin by the Miskitos, (2002e) 3,000.

FLAG: The Miskito national flag, the flag of the national movement, has eight horizontal stripes of blue and white. The flag of Almuk Nani (the Elders Council) is considered the traditional flag of the Miskitos, a white field bearing a centered disc bearing a blue sea, a spear and a shovel in a classic brown Miskito canoe, and a yellow sky.

PEOPLE AND CULTURE: The Miskito are a native American people with some admixtures of Jamaicans, Europeans, and escaped slaves. A minority, called Sambos, are of mixed Caribbean black and native American background. The Miskito culture reflects adaptations to contacts with Europeans stretching back to the seventeenth century, as well as intermarriage with Africans brought to the region as slaves. In contemporary Spanish-speaking Central America, a clear ethnic hierarchy assigns indigenous groups like the Miskitos, Sumu, and Rama to the bottom ranks. They remain the most impoverished and least educated, and they are generally relegated to the least desirable occupations. There are five subgroups among the Miskitos; the smaller Sumu and Rama are closely related but are considered non-Miskito. An estimated 80% rate of unemployment has perpetuated poverty and underdevelopment in the region.

LANGUAGE AND RELIGION: The Miskito speak a language of the Macro-Chibchan language group, which includes numerous borrowings from English and Spanish. Miskito is widely spoken by the Rama and Sumu, who speak their own related languages. The language is related to the Chibcha languages of mainland South America. English is the lingua franca of the multi-ethnic region and is spoken by the majority of the inhabitants. The first bilingual education program began in Miskito in 1984, followed by similar programs in the Rama and Sumu languages. The Miskito language is spoken in four major dialects—Cabo (Kabo), Wanki (Wangki), Baymuna (Baldam), and Mam or Honduran Miskito. The language is widely used in primary schools, but secondary schools use Spanish. The literary language is based on Wanki, spoken around Puerto Cabezas. The Sumu or Sumo language, spoken in both Nicaragua and Honduras, is closely related but lacks the European admixtures. Many of the indigenous peoples speak West Caribbean Creole, English, or Spanish as second languages.

The majority of the Miskitos, about 80% of the population, are Protestants, generally Moravians.* The Baptists make up about 10% of the Miskito population. The Roman Catholic minority do not identify with the Spanish-speaking Catholics of the interior; they were mostly converted to Catholicism by priests from the United States rather than from Nicaragua. Christian beliefs are often mingled with folk practices. Moravian ministers remain important figures in Miskito communities. Recently fundamentalist Protestant churches have gained converts.

NATIONAL HISTORY: Chibchan migrants from present-day Colombia are believed to have settled the Caribbean lowlands, where they developed a culture based on fishing and agriculture. The coast was sighted by Christopher Columbus on his fourth voyage in 1502, but fierce Miskito resistance precluded Spanish colonization. Some 500,000 people, members of related tribes west of the mountains in Nicaragua and Honduras, suffered enslavement and effectively disappeared as a separate people by the 1520s. Only the Miskito and the related tribes successfully prevented the colonization of their homeland.

Dutch pirates established bases on the coast in the early seventeenth century, preying on Spanish shipping from their settlement at Bleuwvelt, later called Bluefields. In 1630, English Puritans established a colony on Providence Island. The European immigrants and the native people enjoyed good relations. A chief's son was sent to England for education and returned to convert the Miskito into unabashed Anglophiles. The Spanish destroyed the Providence Island colony in 1641, but many English, including numerous buccaneers, remained on the coast. A slave ship from Africa foundered on the coast in the mid-seventeenth century. The Miskitos adopted the surviving slaves—the origin of the tribe's characteristic Afro-Indian appearance.

The Miskitos were recruited to serve as proxies for English forces in the area; their status as an English ally was institutionalized in 1687 with the establishment of a Miskito kingdom and the crowning of their first monarch. Miskito warriors armed by the English plundered Spanish settlements and raided neighboring tribes for slaves to sell in Jamaica. In the eighteenth century the English imported Jamaican blacks to work the plantations and logging operations. The Jamaicans, later freed, became the basis of the region's Creole population.

Great Britain formally claimed what was by then known as the Mosquito Coast as a protectorate in 1740, but only in 1844 did a British agent arrive to formalize the arrangement. There followed a series of clashes with the Spanish, associated with the constant British-Spanish warfare of the eighteenth century.

German Moravian missionaries arrived in the kingdom in 1849, soon followed by Baptists and other representatives of other denominations. The Miskitos' conversion to Protestantism and the introduction of education in the English language solidified the kingdom's separate character and culture. The Moravian church became an integral part of the distinct indigenous culture of the Caribbean lowlands.

Nicaragua and Honduras, which became independent of Spain in 1835, claimed the Caribbean coasts, with the support of the United States. In 1848 the Mosquito Coast, occupied by British troops, became a point of contention between the United States and the United Kingdom. The Bulwer-Clayton Treaty of 1850 eventually led to the cession of the northern part of the Mosquito Coast to Honduras in 1859 and of the larger, southern district to Nicaragua in 1860. The Catholic, Spanish-speaking

Central American states agreed to grant their respective parts of the region political and religious autonomy, not to interfere in their internal affairs, and not to impose the Spanish language.

Nonetheless, Nicaragua's president, José Santos Zelaya, in 1894 sent Nicaraguan troops to occupy the Mosquito Coast. The British in Jamaica in response moved warships to the coast, but later withdrew rather than confront the United States. The United States invoked the Monroe Doctrine, but it was its interest in a possible canal route from the Caribbean to the Pacific that dictated American support of Zelaya. The Mosquito Convention, adopted by Nicaragua in 1895, deposed the king, ended Miskito autonomy, and renamed the region after the Nicaraguan president, Zelaya.

The United States, indirectly in control of Nicaragua after the turn of the century, landed troops on the Atlantic coast in 1910, provoking fierce Miskito resistance. With the aid of a Nicaraguan peasant army led by Augusto Cesar Sandino, the Miskito expelled the Americans between 1928 and 1930. The Miskito warriors were later defeated by the troops of dictator Anastasio Somoza, installed in the capital, Managua, by the Americans in 1934.

Generally ignored thereafter by the Somoza regime, the region remained isolated and largely English-speaking. The Nicaraguans, called "the Spanish" by the Miskito, maintained only a few National Guard outposts in the main towns. The Miskito continued to live their traditional way of life in numerous scattered villages. The government allowed village leaders to serve as official community liaisons.

Despite some development programs that threatened Miskito interests, the Somoza regime was never despised on the Caribbean coast, as it was in the Nicaraguan heartland. The Miskito took little part in the revolution that finally overthrew the Somoza regime and installed a leftist government in 1979. The revolutionaries, called Sandinistas after the peasant leader of the 1920s and 1930s, desperately needed the revenue of the Miskito region's natural resources. The new government implemented a plan for the total integration of Miskitia into the Sandinista state. The government organized its inhabitants in a self-help organization, Miskito Sumo Rama Asla Tanaka, which means "working together." The organization, known by its initials, MISURATA, was under the leadership of Steadman Fagoth and Brooklyn Rivera.

The Sandinista administration, which enjoyed broad popular support in the Pacific region and the central highlands during the early 1980s, was a political failure in the Caribbean lowlands. The Miskitos and their allies, the Sumu and Rama, barely reconciled to their incorporation into Nicaragua, were unenthusiastic about the new initiatives brought to their homeland from the Pacific coast. Cadres sent to the region were patronizing in their attitude to the indigenous population. First the indigenous peoples resisted literacy programs in Spanish; later they resisted forced resettlement to artificially created villages designed to be more easily controlled by the Sandinista regime.

Sandinista ideology appealed to class interests and anti-American nationalism, sentiments that had little appeal to the Miskitos. Sandinista "anti-imperialism" made little sense to people who had historically depended on the United States and Great Britain to protect them from the Spanish and later the Nicaraguans and Hondurans. The Miskitos identified with Anglo-American culture and appreciated foreign investment, which they associated with the region's former prosperity. These attitudes were reinforced by the anticommunist, pro-American orientation of the Moravian Church.

Accused of fomenting separatism in 1981, the leaders of MISURATA and 3,000 followers fled to Honduras, where they formed an alliance with the anti-Sandinista forces, the Contras, supported by the United States. The Miskito leadership soon split over the question of autonomy or independence, the independence faction favoring the creation of Central America's second English-speaking state. Sandinista forces moved into the rebellious province, burning towns and villages and eventually driving 85,000 refugees from their homes. The Miskito fought back; it was the first time in the twentieth century that a native people had taken up arms against a Latin American government.

The Sandinista government, acknowledging past errors, altered its policies in the region. By 1985 a tense peace had settled over the region, and the majority of the Miskito refugees had returned from Honduras. Broadly based discussions with the leaders of the various ethnic groups led to an accord dividing the area into two autonomous regions. The accord also granted the peoples of the Caribbean coast limited autonomy, cultural guarantees, and a say in the use of the region's natural resources.

The government of Violeta Chamorro, which replaced the Sandinistas following an election in April 1990, attempted to obstruct the development and implementation of the autonomy agreement, claiming that it was a Sandinista plan and was no longer needed. After the demobilization of the Contras, around 35,000 Miskitos returned to Nicaragua from refugee camps in Honduras. In 1990 rioting broke out due to food shortages; troops were sent in to restore order. The government ended funding for bilingual education and attempted to limit Miskito participation in mining, forestry, and fishing development.

In December 1991, activists seized control of the government offices in the coastal town of Puerto Cabezas. They ousted the mayor and leaders of the region's semi-autonomous government. The protesters claimed that Miskito autonomy was not being fulfilled and that massive corruption in the regional council was wasting the limited funds set aside for development. The crisis ended quickly, but the underlying causes of unrest remained. Protesters again took control of government offices and police stations in February 1992, claiming that the Chamorro government was ignoring indigenous rights and had not implemented autonomy measures for the region.

Paseo Pantera, a plan backed by international environmental groups, was fully funded by international governments and organizations and began operation in the Miskito homeland in November 1992. The plan called for the enlargement and creation of parks and biospheres, the implementation of educational programs, and for sustainable development of the Mosquito Coast.

A Miskito group known as Descendants of Mother Earth (Yapti Masrika Nani) or YATAMA was organized and mobilized in early 1993, with the assistance Moravian clergymen, in response to growing discontent with government economic policies, which left most funding to international organizations, and the lack of development in the autonomous regions. In April 1995, a cholera epidemic swept the region, drawing attention to its poverty and poor health and sanitation facilities.

The Nicaraguan government again attempted to extend direct influence over the region's rich natural resources in 1998, following a Miskito demand for a sovereign state federated with Nicaragua. Parliamentary elections in 1996–97 showed that the Mosquito Coast was still a different world from the Nicaraguan heartland, but the Miskitos were outvoted in the region by the rising number of migrants from the western provinces. Ignoring the election results, in March 1998 delegates from 336 indigenous communities convened a conference in Puerto Cabezas, where they decided to form a government of their own. As a first step, they elected four committees to examine respectively the urgent questions of natural resources, jurisprudence, land ownership, and social affairs. Miskito spokesmen talked not of secession but rather of a federal system that would go far beyond the autonomy statute.

Miskito leaders in 2000 accused the Nicaraguan government of viewing the special status of the Mosquito Coast as a product of the hated Sandinistas, something to be eliminated. In mid-2000 several Miskito leaders threatened to declare independence, then negotiate a federation with Nicaragua as an equal member.

A week of violent confrontations in November 2000 left one person dead and 12 badly injured. The conflict had erupted in Puerto Cabezas following a decision by Nicaragua's Supreme Electoral Council that the Miskitos could not participate in upcoming local elections because they had missed the deadline for registering candidates. Many activists were arrested, further escalating the violence. In 2001 activists focused on the reunification of the Miskito homeland in Nicaragua and Honduras, possibly in a transnational autonomy.

In October 2001 presidential elections in Nicaragua pitted the Sandinistas, who controlled the country during the Miskito uprising in the 1980s, against a conservative candidate backed by the Miskitos. The Sandinistas were defeated in a close election, making the defiant statement of a militant minority to declare independence should the Sandinistas return to power unnecessary.

SELECTED BIBLIOGRAPHY:

Garcia, Claudia. *The Making of the Miskitu People of Nicaragua: The Social Construction of Ethnic Identity.* 1996.

Hale, Charles R. *Resistance and Contradiction: Miskitu Indians and the Nicaraguan State, 1894–1987.* 1994.

Kinzer, Stephen. *Blood of Brothers.* 1991.

Nietschmann, Bernard. *Unknown War: The Miskito Nation, Nicaragua, and the United States.* 1989.

Mizos

Lushais; Lusais; Lusheis; Lukhais; Lusagos; Slilaus; Duliens; Hualngos; Whelngos; Le

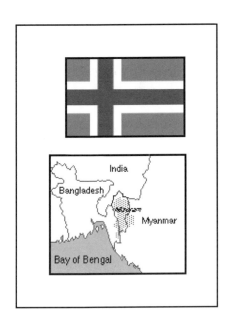

POPULATION: Approximately (2002e) 1,020,000 Mizos in south Asia, concentrated in India's Mizoram state and neighboring states in northeastern India. Other Mizo communities live in adjacent areas of Myanmar and Bangladesh.

THE MIZO HOMELAND: The Mizo homeland, called Mizoram, or "Land of the Mizos," occupies a rugged, mountainous territory formerly called the Lushai Hills, now the Mizo Hills, in northeastern India. Located in northeastern India, Mizoram forms a wedge of Indian territory between Bangladesh and Myanmar. About three-quarters of the region is tropical jungle with fertile regions in the highlands. Mizoram, India's least accessible region, was made a full state of the Indian Union in 1986. *State of Mizoram*: 8,140 sq. mi.—21,081 sq. km, (2002e) 911,000—Mizos 75%, Bengalis 14%, Reangs (Brus) 6%, Chakmas 3%, Ralte, Paite, Baite, Pawi, Lakher, Hmar, Piang and other Indians 2%. The Mizo capital and major cultural center is Aizawl, called Aijal by the Mizos, (2002e) 274,000. The other important cultural center is Lunglei, (2002e) 44,000.

FLAG: The Mizo national flag, the flag of the national movement, is a blue field charged with a red cross, offset toward the hoist and outlined in white.

PEOPLE AND CULTURE: The Mizo, called Lushai by the Indians, are a group of Tibeto-Burman tribal peoples closely related by language and culture. The term Mizo, which is loosely applied to the many tribal groups of the region, means "highlander." The descendents of early tribes pushed into the less accessible hills by successive invasions of the lowlands, the Mizo are closely related to the neighboring tribal peoples, the Zomis* of Myanmar and the Kuki people of Manipur. The Mizos, divided into 49 subtribes, are mostly Christian and have a literacy rate of 46%, one of the highest in India, a result of early Christian missionary activity. Traditionally Mizo society was highly stratified, with chiefs, commoners, serfs, and slaves. One ancient tradition has prevailed in spite of modernization, the use of a single name by all Mizo men. The encouragement and preservation of Mizo culture, based on Christian principles, has been the focus of nationalists since the early 1990s. The Mizo value system, called Tlawmangaina, includes a tradition of public service, a strong sense of clan kinship, courage and generosity, an irrepressible sense of humor, inborn courtesy, and a tremendous love of children.

LANGUAGE AND RELIGION: The Mizo language, often called Lushai, is a Kuki-Chin language of the Tibeto-Burman language group. The language is spoken in six major dialects, Fannai, Mizo, Ngente, Dulien, Ralte, and Pang or Paang, related to the geographic regions of the Mizo homeland. Dulien is spoken mainly in Bangladesh and Ralte is spoken only in Myanmar. The dialects are not all mutually intelligible, as borrowings from neighboring language have influenced the vocabularies and syntax. The Mizos have a high literacy rate for India; an estimated three-fifths are able to read and write. Many are bilingual in English. In 1999 Mizos, who recorded high percentages of growth in literacy in the 1990s, overtook the Malayalis* of Kerala as India's most literate people.

The majority of the Mizo are Christian, mostly Baptist. According to some statistics, the Mizos are over 90% Christian, which explains the cross on their national flag. Many pre-Christian traditions have been retained, however—belief in spirits, witchcraft, and spiritual healing. Missionaries were formerly active in the region. Mission education gave the Mizos their high literacy rate. Drums, symbolizing freedom, are an integral part of Mizo religious and social life, predating the arrival of Christianity in the late nineteenth century. There is a sizable Jewish Mizo community, numbering several thousand, spread over several districts in Mizoram, Manipur, and Nagaland. They are traditionally believed to be the descendents of one of Israel's lost tribes, Manasseh. Several hundred emigrated to Israel in 1994–97.

NATIONAL HISTORY: The origins of the Mizos can be traced to the territory of the Shans* in present-day eastern Myanmar, although they are thought to have originated in eastern Tibet. Following the rivers south, the migrating Lushai and Himar tribes arrived in their present area in the eighth century A.D. Driven into the jungle-covered hills by invasions of the lowlands, the Mizos divided into a number of small tribal states. The states, nominally under the rule of successive empires, absorbed cultural traits from the lowland Indian peoples and the region's many conquerors.

Little is known of Mizoram's early history. Between 1750 and 1850, the Mizo tribes migrated from the nearby Chin Hills and subjugated the indigenous peoples of the region. These similar tribes were assimilated into their own society. The Mizo developed an autocratic political system with some 300 hereditary chieftains.

The Hindu Assamese of the Brahmaputra River valley to the north extended their influence into the hill tracts in the early nineteenth century. The Assamese left the tribal peoples to their traditional way of life and ruled through the local chiefs. The Mizo retained their language, religion, and traditions, including headhunting, an integral part of Mizo culture. The Mizo tribes remained unaffected by foreign influences until the British arrived in the region.

Burman invaders from the east conquered Assam in 1822, provoking war with the British. The defeated Burmans ceded Assam and the hill tracts, including the Lushai Hills, to British India in 1826. The new authorities attempted to stamp out headhunting but, like the former Assamese rulers, generally left the Mizos to govern themselves. British troops entered the hills only to put down occasional revolts and to settle disputes. They suppressed feuding and headhunting but generally administered the region through the indigenous rulers.

The traditional Mizo tribal structure was markedly changed by the British occupation. European administration undermined the traditional tribal hierarchies. The traditionally elective chieftain system was abolished by the British authorities. In its place influential families were granted the hereditary privilege to rule under British advice.

Missionaries, aided by the monotheistic religious beliefs of the Mizos, were quite successful in undermining the traditional animism. The missionaries established stations in the Lushai Hills in the 1840s, converting a majority of the pagan Mizos and introducing modern education through their mission schools. Though the leaders became nominally Christian, the Mizo warriors continued to raid neighboring peoples; sporadic revolts plagued the British administration.

The Christian Mizo leadership led a widespread revolt in 1891 following the formal annexation of the Lushai Hills to the British Empire. The rebels drove the British soldiers from the hills but left the mission stations in peace. A British expedition reconquered the Lushai Hills in 1895. The soldiers were surprised to find the European missionaries safe and protected by Mizo warriors. The conversion of the Mizo majority to Christianity raised yet another barrier between the Mizo and India's Hindu majority. In 1935, the Lushai Hills were declared an "excluded area," with restrictions on migration to the region.

Shortly after World War II, the British government began preparing to leave the subcontinent. The Mizo Union, the first political organization, was formed to press for Mizo independence and to express the opposition of younger Mizo leaders to the domination of the chiefs in Mizo society. The Mizo acknowledged a tacit agreement that they formed a part of the British Empire but denied their inclusion in British India. Loyal British allies during the war, they petitioned the authorities for separate independence and adamantly rejected inclusion in Hindu-dominated India or Muslim Pakistan.

Ignored in the rush to independence, the Lushai Hills legally remained a district of Assam at Indian independence in 1947. The Mizos rebelled as the British prepared to withdraw, determined to resist the imposition of Indian rule. With British military assistance, the Indians subdued the Mizos, and a large Indian contingent of troops and police remained in the region. Access to the Lushai Hills, formerly through the Chittagong Hills, was made more difficult by the division of the region between Pakistan and India.

Large numbers of Hindu refugees from neighboring East Pakistan settled in the region between 1947, at the partition of British India, and 1950. Religious conflicts between the Christian Mizo and the refugee Hindus solidified the Mizos' refusal to acknowledge Indian authority. Nationalists formed the Mizo National Front (MNF) in 1954 to work for autonomy and restrictions on immigration to their territory. The name of their homeland was changed from Lushai Hills to Mizo Hills the same year.

A severe famine, largely ignored by the Indian government, killed several hundred Mizos in 1959. A group of Mizo chiefs warned the administration of Mizoram, which was then a hill district of Assam, that a severe famine was coming. The administrators demanded to know what the basis for their prediction was. It simply had to happen, the Mizo chiefs said. They had a famine every 36 years and it was now almost 36 years since the last one occurred. Nonsense, said the administrators, and turned the tribal chiefs out. They then travelled all the way to Delhi to plead with the prime minister, but returned disappointed; Indira Gandhi had no time for a "bunch of primitive tribals." Then came famine, and a trail of misery. Mau lam, the local term for famine, had kept its date with Mizoram, and it was one of the worst it had experienced. The poor response of both local and federal governments fueled the growth of the Mizos' anti-Indian sentiment. The Mizo National Famine Front was formed in response to official indifference to the famine.

The Mizo National Front won two of three assembly seats in the Mizo Hills of Assam in 1963, showing its growing support in the region. The leader of the MNF, Laldenga (Mizos normally use just one name), used the electoral success to press for separation from Assam. The Mizo leadership, tiring of futile efforts to win autonomy, called for secession and the creation of an independent Mizo state in 1965. Open rebellion broke out in February, 1966; nationalist guerrillas skirmished with Indian troops stationed on the sensitive Pakistani and Burmese borders. Rebel leaders, after capturing Aizawal, declared the independence of Mizoram on 6 July 1966. Indian troops occupied key points in the district and drove the rebels into the jungle-covered hills. Armed by Pakistan and China, the rebels launched a secessionist war from their mountain hideouts. The conflict was the first in which the Indian government bombed and strafed rebel positions.

The Presbyterian and Baptist churches, the dominant religious denominations in the region, attempted to resolve the conflict. The religious leaders deplored the continuing violence, which was taking a heavy toll on the civilian population. Laldenga rejected their pleas to open negotiations with the Indian government.

The Indian government belatedly made concessions in an effort to end the rebellion. In 1972 the authorities separated the Mizo Hills from Assam and created a separate union territory of Mizoram. The change failed to end the Mizo insurgency, which continued throughout the 1970s. In 1976 the Mizos accepted an offer of autonomy but resumed the rebellion when a cease-fire broke down in 1979. The Mizos of the MNF launched another campaign against non-Mizos, largely Bengali migrants (whose presence is viewed as a major threat to the cultural survival of the Mizos), and government military targets. Following futile negotiations begun in 1980, the MNF was banned by the Indian government, and many supporters were arrested.

Mizoram was declared a "disturbed area" in the early 1980s, allowing the Indian security forces broad powers to combat the insurgents. Abuses by Indian soldiers, who could not be prosecuted for their acts, increased rapidly; their offenses included looting, rape, and murder.

In 1986, after two decades of insurgency, Laldenga opened negotiations with the Indian government. Under a new agreement Mizoram became a full state of the Indian union, with Laldenga as its first chief minister. Laldenga called on all members of the Mizo rebel forces to disarm once the statehood agreement was signed. The Indian government began constructing roads throughout the region, not only for development but to provide easier access for the armed forces in case of insurgency. Military patrols were attacked from jungle strongholds in the Mizo Hills as they moved into the less accessible areas.

The 1986 accommodation with the Indian government split the nationalist movement. Moderates accepted the status of statehood within the Indian union on 20 February 1987. More militant nationalists continued to demand independence for a "Greater Mizoram," including the Mizo-populated districts of the neighboring Indian states. Factional disputes and violence provoked a strong government response. In September 1988 the government dissolved the Mizoram state administration and imposed direct rule from New Delhi.

The dramatic growth of Hindu militancy, accompanied by militants' demands that the Indian government end its policy of "coddling" ethnic and religious minorities, alarmed even the most moderate Mizo leaders in the 1980s and 1990s. The new threat forced the Mizos to put aside their factional disputes and cooperate more closely in their fight for an autonomous future for their small nation. Laldenga, the former rebel leader and the chief minister of Mizoram from 1986 to 1988, died in 1990; he was mourned as a national hero.

The rapid growth of the non-Mizo population of the state, particularly immigrant Muslim Bengalis and refugee Jummas* from Bangladesh, led to violence and demands for the expulsion of all non-Mizos. Continuing abuses by the security forces sent in to crush the Mizo national movement include numerous instances of mass killings, torture, rape, and harassment of the civilian population. The unrestricted counterinsurgency rekindled the separatist movement in the 1990s.

In January 1994, the world's largest drum, weighing over half a ton, was used in week-long celebrations marking the advent of Christianity in the Mizo homeland. The drum set the rhythm for hymns sung daily by thousands of Mizos as they recalled the establishment of Welsh* Presbyterian and English Baptist missions in January 1894.

In 1996, following the ending of the five-year uprising of a Mizo splinter group, the government announced that it planned to issue photo identity cards to all citizens in the region. The impact of illegal immigration and drugs on the Mizo homeland grew serious by the turn of the twenty-first century. The high rate of drug use was attributed to the transformation from an agrarian to an industrial society and the subsequent changes in social and ethnic values. According to Mizo leaders it was the product of frustration and discontent among the Mizo population.

In the early 1990s relations between the Mizos and the Reangs (or Brus) deteriorated over Reang demands for an autonomous council in their area in the northeast of the state. Such autonomous district councils have already been constituted for the Chakmas, Lakhers, and Maars of the state. The Bru National Liberation Front (BNLF) began in 1992 a violent campaign to win autonomy, much as the Mizos had in the 1960s. Violent confrontations between Mizos and Reangs in 1997 drove over 35,000 Reangs into Tripura, where they were housed in refugee camps. The Mizo government refused to divide the state further along ethnic lines and denied the refugees the right to return to their villages. In June 1998, the Indian government met with Mizo officials and leaders of the Reang refugees in an effort to reach a solution. The Mizos refused to allow the refugees to be repatriated, claiming that they would be repatriating an insurgency. It is a problem that could reactivate Mizo nationalism.

Setting in motion the process of formation of a new government in Mizoram in 2000, Mizo National Front president Zoramthanga was unanimously elected as leader of the United Legislature Party, a coalition of the MNF and the Mizoram People's Conference (MPC). The president of MPC, Lalhmingthanga, was elected as his deputy. The MNF-MPC combine had unseated the Congress government in the assembly elections, returning the state government to control by Mizo nationalists in 2001.

SELECTED BIBLIOGRAPHY:

Kyndiah, P.R. *Mizo Freedom Fighters*. 1986.
Nag, Chitta Ranjan. *Mizo Polity and Modernization*. 1998.
———. *Post-Colonial Mizo Politics, 1947–1998*. 1999.
Nunthara, C. *Mizoram: Society and Polity*. 1996.

Mohajirs

Mujahirs; Islamis; Undris; Urudus

POPULATION: Approximately (2002e) 11,200,000 Mohajirs in Pakistan, concentrated in Karachi and the other large cities in southern Sind Province. Some nationalists claim a Mohajir population of over 20 million in Pakistan. There is a related Muslim population of some 50 million in India.

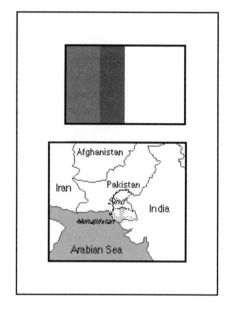

THE MOHAJIR HOMELAND: The Mohajir homeland lies in the fertile delta of the Indus River in southeastern Pakistan. The region, occupying part of the coastline on the Arabian Sea, is heavily urban, particularly in the western districts around Karachi and Hyderabad. The Mohajir homeland has no official status in Pakistan, although nationalists have outlined plans for a separate Mohajiristan, to include all of Sind Province south of the 26th parallel, with its capital at Karachi, which has a population about 75% Mohajir. *Mohajiristan*: 21,490 sq. mi.—55,659 sq. km, (2002e) 23,242,000—Mohajirs 48%, Sindhis* 24%, Pushtuns* 14%, Baluch* 8%, Punjabi 6%. The Mohajir capital and major cultural center is Karachi, (2002e) 10,261,000. The other major cultural center is Hyderabad, (2002e) 1,273,000, metropolitan area 1,359,000.

FLAG: The Mohajir national flag, the flag of the national movement, is a vertical tricolor of green, red, and white, the white twice the width of the green, and the green twice the width of the red.

PEOPLE AND CULTURE: The Mohajirs are the descendents of the Muslim refugees who fled Indian territory during the partition of the subcontinent in 1947. The term "mohajir" refers to refugees who arrived in Pakistan from the areas that fell within the newly constituted India, in the aftermath of partition. It derives its origin from the term Hijr, the flight of the prophet from Mecca to Medina, a journey that was undertaken to escape persecution due to religious beliefs. Although the Mohajirs came to Sind from five different regions of northern India, they had enough in common culturally and ideologically to develop a sense of common identity. The Urdu word "Mohajir" literally means "refugee," but since the 1940s has represented a national entity arising out a historical process. The Mohajir national identity evolved among the refugee population living in the urban areas of the Sind Province in southern Pakistan. The Mohajirs are an urban, largely literate national group that dominates some of Pakistan's largest cities. Originally the Mohajir refugees were mostly bureaucrats, businessmen, and rich landlords. The Mohajirs are still better educated than other communities in Pakistan, giving them an advantage in government bureaucracies and business. Many of the Mohajirs are members of the urban middle class, prominent in business and local government.

LANGUAGE AND RELIGION: The Mohajirs, like the large Muslim population of India, speak Urdu, a language closely related to Hindi, the official language of India, but it has borrowings from Arabic and Persian and is written in a modified Arabic script in the Nastaliq style, with several extra characters. Urdu is a Hindustani language of the West Hindi group of Indo-Iranian languages. The language is spoken as a second or third language by many non-Mohajir Pakistanis.

The Mohajirs are overwhelmingly Sunni Muslims, belonging to several sects or schools. The descendants of sixteenth and seventeenth-century converts to Islam, the Mohajirs mostly lived as religious minorities in Hindu-majority regions of northern India prior to the mass migration to Muslim Pakistan in 1947–48. The more moderate religious views of the Mohajirs has precluded the growth of radical Islamic beliefs prevalent in other parts of Pakistan. A common religion has been too weak to build bonds with other population groups.

NATIONAL HISTORY: In 711–12, Muslim Arabs invaded western India, converting many of the inhabitants to Islam. Much of the territory was added to the Muslim caliphate and was ruled from the Middle East until Turkic peoples overran the region in the eleventh century. In the sixteenth century, the Mogul Empire controlled most of north India, with the Muslim minority forming a ruling elite. In the late 1700s, the Moguls declined, and northern India was divided into numerous small Muslim and Hindu states.

The partition of the subcontinent in 1947 was accompanied by unprecedented levels of violence. Huge caravans of Muslims fleeing India and Hindus leaving Pakistan often clashed or were attacked. Up to two million people died in the partition violence. Many of the Muslim refugees were driven from their homes by militant Hindus, particularly in the Bombay and Uttar Pradesh areas of northwestern India.

The refugees settled mainly in Karachi, the largest urban center and the newly designated capital of Pakistan. Karachi had had a population of 309,000 in 1939, but by 1951 it has swelled to 1.2 million. The influx of Mohajirs relegated the indigenous Sindhis to a rural, backward status in the province. Urdu was made the official language of all Pakistan, even though it was spoken only by the refugee population from India. In 1948 Karachi was separated from Sind as the federal capital, giving the Mohajirs a territorial identity parallel to their political identity.

In 1955, the Pakistani government dissolved the provinces and merged Sind into the single province of West Pakistan. The federal capital was formally transferred to Islamabad, in Punjab, in 1961. Sind was again made a separate province in 1970, with Karachi as the provincial capital.

As "Indian" Muslims who had led the movement for Muslim separation in colonial India, the refugees took a leading role in state building in Pakistan. Though they been distrustful of a centralized state in India, the Mohajirs supported a strong central government in Pakistan. They were naturally in a dominant position and were ardent supporters of Pakistani nationalism, as opposed to the regional identities professed by the Sindhis, Pathans and Punjabis. From the 1940s to the 1970s the Punjabis, the largest of the many national groups in Pakistan, and the Mohajirs cooperated in ruling the new country. The Mohajirs moved from staunch supporters of Muslim autonomy in India to advocating official Pakistani nationalism, to pursuing political identity based on ethnicity. Mohajir dominance in Pakistan's politics was gradually eroded by the Punjabi bureaucratic-military clique, and federal power gradually shifted to Punjab. As other national groups in Pakistan moved into positions of power, Mohajir nationalism was driven by relative economic and political deprivation.

The large immigrant populations in Karachi, initially Pushtuns and Mohajirs, fought for supremacy. Later, confrontations broke out between Mohajirs and the Punjabis who moved south when Karachi was designated the federal capital. The urbanization of the mostly rural Sindhis added yet another group to the mixture. When in 1972 the Sindhi provincial government declared Sindhi the sole official language of the province, the announcement set off severe rioting by the Urdu-speaking Mohajirs. The rural Sindhi population rapidly urbanized in the 1970s, causing a violent rivalry with the highly urbanized Mohajirs. Sindhi nationalism was mainly directed at the Mohajirs, who were seen as usurpers and foreigners. Mohajir nationalism is considered a product of the Karachi violence of the 1970s. The Mohajirs demanded recognition as the "fifth nationality" of Pakistan.

By the mid-1970s most of the violence was communal, pitting Mohajirs against the Pushtuns, Sindhis, and Baluch populations of the vast city. In December 1986, the worst rioting since independence in 1947 swept Karachi. Initially the riots involved Mohajirs and Pushtuns, but it quickly drew in other national groups. The rioting left over 150 dead and hundreds more injured. In late 1988, ethnic rioting occurred between Mohajirs and Sindhis in Hyderabad, then spread to Karachi, leaving over 225 dead.

In 1987, the Mohajirs published a manifesto demanding national rights within Pakistan equal to those of the Punjabis, Pushtuns, Baluch, and Sindhis. The rapid growth of ethnic communalism was reflected in the massive support for the largest Mohajir national organization, the Mohajir Qaumi Movement (MQM). In 1988, the MQM achieved widespread success in the general elections and cooperated with the governing Pakistan People's Party, but within days of the elections there were widespread arrests of MQM activists. Several MQM leaders disappeared or were killed.

Violent antigovernment demonstrations in Karachi left over 60 dead and many injured in February 1990. A curfew was imposed, and government troops were called in to restore order. The violence broke out between supporters of Mohajir demands for autonomy and the formation of a separate province, and Sindhis demonstrating for their own autonomy and against the division of their homeland to allow the Mohajirs a separate province. Gun battles between the two groups were particularly severe in Hyderabad following the arrest of Qadir Magsi, the Sindhi nationalist leader.

In 1990, the MQM again won many urban constituencies and made an alliance with the ruling Islamic party. In spite of the agreement, an army operation was launched against the Mohajirs on 19 June 1992. In subsequent elections, the Mohajir MQM carried Karachi, Hyderabad, and other large cities in southern Sind. The growing Mohajir and Sindhi national movements increasingly divided Sind province along ethnic lines. By 1992, the Mohajir national movement had split, with one faction favoring reconciliation while the more militant group advocated the immediate creation of a separate Mohajir homeland. Violence between the two groups further complicated the search for peace in the region.

The repatriation of the Biharis, an Urdu-speaking ethnic group stranded in Bangladesh since the secessionist war of 1971, further strained relations between the Mohajirs and Sindhis in 1993. The Sindhis, already a minority in their homeland, claimed that the Biharis were being settled in the urban areas to augment the Urdu-speaking population, mainly the Mohajirs. In early 1998, thousands of Biharis, who retained their Pakistani nationality, demonstrated in Bangladesh for repatriation. Their return to Pakistan was delayed until recently by fear among successive Pakistani governments of upsetting the delicate ethnic balance in Sind province.

In 1994, the entire leadership of the MQM was sentenced to prison for the kidnapping and torture of a military intelligence officer. They were later acquitted. Continued violence in Karachi in 1994–96 left hundreds dead and injured. The government in 1995 accused the Mohajirs of fomenting the violence as part of a plan to carve out a separate province for the millions of Mohajirs living in the Karachi and Hyderabad regions of Sind. The violence in 1995, the worst in Pakistan since the 1971 secession of Bangladesh, left 2,500 dead and thousands injured.

The Pakistani government accused India of supporting and training Mohajir separatists in 1995. It claimed that a training camp near Lucknow was training armed Mohajirs for a secessionist war in Pakistan. The government ordered the closure of the Indian consulate-general in Karachi. Several Urdu-language newspapers were also suspended for alleged sensational reporting.

The MQM took part in the 1997 general elections and once again carried the urban areas of southern Sind. The Mohajir leaders formed an alliance with Nawaz Sharif, the leader of the Islamic Democratic Alliance (IDA) and later the president of Pakistan, who promised to support the Mohajir position in Sind. The government eventually abrogated the agreement, and attacks on Mohajirs and their political leaders resumed in 1998. The MQM was labeled a separatist and terrorist organization. The Pakistani government in October 1998 suspended the provincial assembly and placed the Sind under direct federal rule, in an effort to curb the ethnic violence. Between 1990 and 1998 nearly 7,000 people were killed in Karachi and other areas of southern Sind.

In 1999 the Sharif government was overthrown in a military coup. The new government, although led by an ethnic Mohajir, General Pervez Musharraf, clamped down on nationalist activities. Factionalism within the Mohajirs further limited their political power and made it impossible to secure a better position in local and federal governments. The resentment of the native Sindhis against the perceived domination of the Mohajirs made accommodation extremely difficult.

The Mohajirs' demands for their rights have been branded treasonous by the Pakistani government. They are treated as criminals and are subjected to propaganda and threats in an effort to force them to discontinue their struggle for rights. The government policy, which might work against a small nation, has not deterred the millions of Mohajirs.

In the 1990s, the Mohajirs, who made up more than half the population of Sind, felt that they were discriminated against socially, politically, economically, and in education. In spite of their numbers, their representation in the Pakistani government was usually around 1% of government positions. At a provincial level, they were allocated just 28 of the 100 seats in the Sind assembly. They claimed to contribute some 70% of all tax revenue collected by the federal government, for which they received only suppression and terror in return.

The growth rate of Karachi is about 7%, compared with about 3% for the whole country. As a result city services have seriously deteriorated, and job opportunities are shrinking fast. Karachi has become a city wracked with instability, crime, and daily violence between rival national groups. Southern Sind, an explosive mixture of poverty, rampant population growth, and ethnic antagonism, is the prime evidence that Pakistan has failed to forge a unifying sense of nationhood. Ethnic rivalries are so acute that no national census has been conducted since 1981. The Mohajirs claim to constitute two-thirds of Karachi's population and a majority in southern Sind, while the native Sindhis are now reportedly a minority in their homeland.

In January 2000, Altaf Hussain, the founder of MQM, accused the dominant Punjabi establishment of destroying the concept of Pakistan and of creating the many nationalist movements tugging at the fabric of the country. He claimed that the Mohajirs were being forced to embrace separatism because the Punjabis continued to loot the national wealth, in the name of patriotism. He held that the government had a "three pronged strategy" of isolation, criminalization, and demoralization in order to crush the MQM and the Mohajirs.

For many Mohajirs, the history of the division of Pakistan into two new states in 1971 is being repeated in Sind, with the government dominated by the Punjabis to blame. Autonomy or self-determination for the Mohajirs is no longer a shocking idea in Pakistan. The talk of separation, and even independence, of Sind south of the 26th parallel began with the introduction of quota systems for government jobs in Karachi. The quota system guaranteed a percentage of jobs for Sindhis. Admissions to medical, engineering, and other professional colleges are dependent on the quota system, not on merit. Mohajir youth, adversely affected by the denial of their basic rights to education and employment, have become more nationalistic and separatist than the older generation, which helped to build the state of Pakistan.

The subcontinent was first partitioned in 1947, and Pakistan was partitioned in 1971. To the Mohajir activists, these are precedents for the partition of Sind into two political entities. In February 2000, Altaf Hussain restated the Mohajir claims to political and economic rights in the region but stopped short of openly declaring support for the secession of Mohajiristan from unstable Pakistan. He argued that Pakistan's official policy of branding the Bangladeshi peoples as traitors for their secession in 1971 was wrong and that the Punjabi establishment had made their lives unbearable and precipitated the secession. He also accused the Punjabi-dominated military government of once again risking partition by denying the Mohajirs and Sindhis their fundamental rights.

In early September 2001, Mohajir leader Altaf Hussain delivered his strongest warning yet that he will launch a struggle for self-determination in Pakistan's Sindh province. Hussain said 54 years "under the colonial yoke of the Punjabi establishment" was enough. It was time to consider the sovereignty of the Mohajir nation. The military operation launched against Mohajirs in 1992 is still continuing, he said. More than 15,000 Mohajirs had been killed in this operation, he claimed. Those killed included Hussain's brother and nephew.

The leaders of the MQM, in late September 2001, announced their support of the Pakistani government and the international coalition against terrorism and denounced the radical groups mostly based among the Pushtun groups in northwestern Pakistan and in Karachi and other areas with large Pushtun immigrant groups.

SELECTED BIBLIOGRAPHY:

Baillie, Yasmeen Lari. *Kurachee: Past, Present, and Future.* 1997.
Chitkara, M.G. *Mohajir's Pakistan.* 1996.
Ikram, S.M. *Indian Muslims and the Partition of India.* 1995.
Verkaaik, Oskar. *A People of Migrants: Ethnicity, State, and Religion in Karachi.* 2000.

Mons

Mon; Mun; Hamsavati; Talaings; Taleng; Aleng; Peguans; Takanoon; Raman

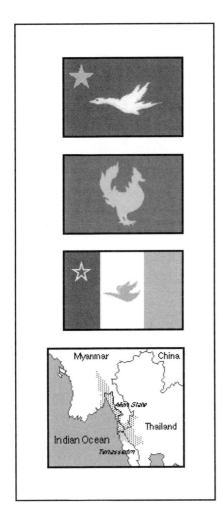

POPULATION: Approximately (2002e) 5,350,000 Mons in southeastern Asia, concentrated in southern Myanmar and Thailand. Other sizable communities live in Malaysia, Singapore, Europe, Canada, and the United States. Nationalists claim a Mon diaspora of around eight million.

THE MON HOMELAND: The Mon homeland occupies a large area of southern Myanmar and west-central Thailand stretching from the Irrawaddy Delta to the Chao Praya River. Much of the region is flat lowlands along the Gulf of Thailand and the Andaman Sea, divided by the highlands of the Bilauktaung Range along the international border. The Mon homeland has no official status in Thailand. Mon nationalists claim most of southern Myanmar as traditional Mon territory. In Myanmar the official Mon State covers a part of the traditional Mon homeland. *Mon State*: 4,478 sq. mi.—12,297 sq. km, (2002e) 2,420,000—Mons 68%, Burmans 12%, Karens* 10%, Tavoyans* 8%, other Burmese (Myanmarese) 2%. The Mon capital and major cultural center is Thaton, (2002e) 106,000. Other important cultural centers are Moulmein, called Mawlamyiang by the Mons, (2002e) 363,000, metropolitan area 522,000, and Samut Prakan in Thailand, called Paknam by the Mons, (2002e) 384,000, in the Bangkok metropolitan area.

FLAG: The Mon national flag, the flag of the national movement, is a red field bearing a centered golden sheldrake in flight and is charged with a pale blue five-pointed star on the upper hoist. The flag of the Thai Mons is a green field bearing a centered golden *hinthar*. The flag of the New Mon State Party (NMSP) is a vertical tricolor of blue, white, and red, bearing a blue five-pointed star outlined in white on the upper hoist and a golden sheldrake centered on the white.

PEOPLE AND CULTURE: The Mons are a Mon-Khmer people related to the Khmers of Cambodia. Called Taliang by the Burmans, the Mons speak a Mon-Khmer language that is related to Cambodian Khmer and the languages of some of the smaller national groups in northeastern Myanmar, but not to the languages spoken by the Burmans or neighboring peoples. The language, with its own script, an alphabet of 35 letters, has an extensive literature revered in Asia much as ancient Greek or Roman literature is in the West. The majority of the Mons live outside the designated Mon state, mostly in neighboring Pegu Division. Officially about 1.2 million Mons live in Myanmar, but unofficial sources claim that over four million people in Myanmar consider themselves Mons. Until the 1980s, assimilation of the Mons in both Myanmar and Thailand was quite advanced, but since then a reculturation has begun to reverse the process.

LANGUAGE AND RELIGION: The Mon language belongs to the Monic branch of the Mon-Khmer group of Austroasiatic languages. About half the Mons are unable to read or write Burmese, although many ethnic Mons speak Burmese as their first language. Teaching or publishing in the Mon language is forbidden in Myanmar. The language is spoken in three major regional dialects, Mataban-Moulmein, also called Central Mon, Pegu or Northern Mon, and Ye or Southern Mon. The dialects spoken in Thailand have incorporated many Thai words, and in Myanmar many Burman and Karen words and forms have influenced the Mon dialects. The oldest inscriptions in the language, dating from the sixth century A.D., are found in central Thailand.

The Mons are Buddhists, practicing Theravada Buddhism, a sect introduced to the region from India. The practices and traditions of their religion incorporate many of their pre-Buddhist beliefs, which remain an important part of their belief system. In Thailand the Mons have incorporated many Thai religious practices.

NATIONAL HISTORY: The Mons originated in the upper Mekong River region of present-day China. Along with the related Khmers, they migrated south along the upper Mekong River. While the Khmers followed the river into present-day Cambodia, the Mons veered southward to occupy the basin of the Chao Praya River in southern Thailand. In the ensuing centuries, the Mons moved westward to the Irrawaddy River delta of southern Myanmar. According to Mon legend, a sacred sheldrake carried the Buddha across the Gulf of Martaban. The ancient Mons adopted the sheldrake as their national symbol.

Several Mon kingdoms were founded in present Thailand and Myanmar. The Mons developed a highly sophisticated civilization with a strong literary tradition and an extensive classical literature. Influenced by maritime contacts with ancient India between the first and fourth centuries A.D., the

Mon kingdom evolved the most advanced and wealthy society in Southeast Asia, a brilliant civilization known as the Golden Land.

By the sixth century the Mon kingdom extended to the basin of the Chao Phraya River in present Thailand. A new capital was established at Pegu in 825; the city grew into one of the largest and wealthiest cities in ancient Asia. Mon culture and Theravada Buddhism spread across a vast region of southeast Asia. The next two centuries witnessed incessant warfare between the Mons and the Burmans.

Burman and Thai migrants from the north increased pressure on Mon territory. Burmans, a warrior people from eastern Tibet, began to penetrate the kingdom in the tenth century. They eventually moved south in large enough numbers to overwhelm the Mon kingdom in 1044. The victorious Burmans adopted much of the advanced Mon culture as their own. The Mons reestablished their kingdom following the Burman defeat by invading Mongols in 1287. The eastern Mons were absorbed by the Thai kingdom. Called Hamsavati, meaning "Sheldrake Country," the Mon kingdom in Burma entered a second golden age in the fourteenth and fifteenth centuries.

Resurgent Burmans overran the kingdom in the 1551 and established their new capital at Pegu, the capital of the defeated Mons. In 1740 the Mons' great national hero, Binnya Dala, led a 12-year rebellion against harsh Burman rule. In 1752 the victorious Dala recreated the Mon kingdom and formed an alliance with the French forces in the region. In spite of European assistance, the kingdom fell to the returning Burmans in 1757. Pegu and the other Mon cities were sacked and burned. Massacres of the populations ended the Mon threat to Burman domination for the next two centuries. Thousands of refugees fled east to the protection of the Thai kingdom.

In Thailand, the Mons were given territory and protection by the Thai king, himself a descendent of the Mons. Many settled around the Gulf of Thailand and along the Chao Praya River, where there was already an established Mon community. In both Thailand and Burma the Mons began to assimilate, mostly through intermarriage.

The Mon heartland came under British rule after the first Anglo-Burmese War in 1826, the remainder in 1852. Preferring British authority to that of the hated Burmans, the Mon became one of the most loyal of the region's peoples. Many Mons entered the local colonial administration and the colonial military forces. Western-style education, introduced in the urban areas, was embraced by the Mons as a way to improve their situation in the multi-ethnic colony.

By 1900, in spite of continuing conflict between the two peoples, most Mons had been integrated into Burman culture and no longer spoke their original language. The dominant Burmans, who had absorbed the ancient Mon culture, asserted that there had never been a separate Mon people, only an early division of the Burmans. The outraged Mons, claiming that they had created what is now called the Golden Age of Burma, began to reassert their separate culture and identity. The first cultural associations were formed in the early years of the twentieth century. Violent ethnic conflicts broke out in the 1920s as the Mons resolutely pressed their national and cultural revival.

Younger Mon leaders, educated under the British system, began to replace traditional leaders in the 1920s and 1930s. Having grown up during the Mon reculturation, the new generation was much more nationalistic and assertive. The Mon National Association was formed in 1935 among the Mon minority living in Rangoon, the Burmese capital. By the outbreak of World War II, national sentiment had spread to most Mon areas in Burma and Thailand.

In 1947, in anticipation of independence the Mons celebrated the first Mon National Day. Having been loyal to the British during World War II, the Mon petitioned for a separate state as Burma moved to independence after the war. Ignored by the British in their haste to leave Burma, the Mons unsuccessfully sought negotiations with the Burman authorities. Disappointed Mon leaders demanded the establishment of a Mon Affairs Council, their own army battalion under federal control, and parliamentary representation in proportion to the size of the Mon population in Burma. The demands were rejected. In 1948 Mon nationalists formed the Mon National Defense Organization and allied themselves to insurgent Karens despite overlapping territorial claims. Historically the Mons had maintained good relations with the neighboring Karens. Mon troops occupied Moulmein and Thaton as Burma collapsed in civil war.

Fighting during the 1950s sent a wave of Mon refugees into Thailand to join the Mons who had fled fighting with the Burmans in the sixteenth, eighteenth, and nineteenth centuries. Defeated by the Burmese military in 1958, the largest of the Mon insurgent groups, the Mon People's Front, surrendered to government forces, and 1,100 fighters gave up their arms. Despite the 10-year Mon insurgency, the Burmese government again denied the existence of the Mons as a separate ethnic group. Other Mons rejected the surrender and continued to fight. The Mons continued to suffer renewed oppression, particularly after the military took control of Burma in 1962. The Mon rebellion resumed in the late 1960s, often in alliance with other ethnic insurgent groups in Burma.

In 1974, the Burmese military government created a nominally autonomous Mon State covering Thaton and Moulmein districts, in an effort to divide and appease the Mons. The new Mon State covered only a small portion of the territory claimed by Mon nationalists. The Mon insurgents rejected the truncated state and stated that their aim was no longer autonomy but an independent Mon state. The nationalists claimed five districts—in addition to Thaton and Moulmein, the districts of Pegu, Tavoy, and Mergui. More moderate Mons limited their territorial claims to the Mon heartland in Mon State and southern Pegu Division. The nationalists called their proposed state Honsawatoi, "Sheldrake Country," a modern version of the name of their ancient kingdom. In pursuit of their aim, the Mons joined with several other national groups fighting to replace the hated Burmese state with a federation of independent states.

The Mons continued to fight the Burmese military government during the 1970s and 1980s. Although they were not involved in the opium trade to finance their insurgency, as were other rebellious ethnic groups, the Burmese government used against Mon positions military equipment provided by the United States to Burma to fight the drug trade. By the late 1980s, a renewed sense of historical separation and past glory led to widespread support among the Mons for political separation.

In 1983 several Mon organizations joined the National Democratic Front, an umbrella organization for all non-Burman national groups fighting the oppressive government. The organizations, representing about half of Burma's population, supported the creation of a democratic federation to replace the centralized military government that had controlled the country since soon after independence in 1948. Each national group in Burma would have its own autonomous state, full self-determination, linguistic and religious freedom, and representation in a federal government responsible for foreign affairs, monetary policy, and defense.

Widespread Mon support for the democracy movement in Burma in 1988–90, with its promise of independence within a democratic federation, turned to despair as the government loosed its soldiers on peaceful demonstrators and refused to relinquish power to a freely elected civilian government. The Mon insurgency, allied to the neighboring Karens, resumed in 1989 and escalated rapidly in response to the excesses of the brutal military regime. Thousands fled to Thailand to escape indiscriminate attacks on civilians in 1992–95.

The Myanmar military government declared a unilateral cease-fire in 1992 in an effort to draw the Mons into negotiations. The Mon leadership, skeptical of government intentions, refused to accept the terms. In late 1994 the government broke its own cease-fire and began a new offensive against the Mon nationalist forces. In 1995, under pressure from the Thai government, the forces of the New Mon State Party (NMSP) signed a cease-fire agreement with regime. Some factions broke away from the NMSP to form the Beik Mon Army and several small organizations that continued the armed struggle for independence. The renewed violence was due to the military's efforts to force the Mons to abandon their strongholds in an area where a natural gas pipeline was being built to Thailand. An estimated 20,000 Mons were forced to work on the Ye-Tavoy railroad and the gas pipeline being built from the Gulf of Martaban to Thailand. Massive human-rights abuses, forced labor, rape, and other atrocities against the civilian population continued in spite of the cease-fire with several Mon groups. With the exception of Moulmein, foreigners were not allowed to visit Mon areas.

The military regime, which had called itself the State Law and Order Restoration Council, changed its name in November 1997 to the State Peace and Development Council (SPDC) in an effort to reduce the negative image of the military junta. Several officials alleged to be involved in large-scale corruption were sidelined, but otherwise policies, particularly those involving antigovernment ethnic groups, remained unchanged. In October 1999, the SPDC authorities ordered the last school under government control teaching in Mon to close. In areas held by the Mon insurgents the administration and education is in the Mon language.

The Thai government, eager for economic agreements on logging, mining, and energy with the military government of Myanmar, was often accused of harassing the Mon refugees on its territory. Rising Thai nationalist sentiment against ethnic minorities, particularly refugees from neighboring Myanmar, reinvigorated Mon nationalism in Thailand in the late 1990s. In western Thailand 5,000 Mon families have been living in Thailand for more than 50 years. Although their second and third generations were born in Thailand, they have not been granted Thai citizenship. They are not allowed to leave the areas unless seriously sick and in need of hospital care. Their education is also limited to only Mathayom 3 or junior high school. Some Mons in western Thailand are the descendants of refugees who settled in the region in the early nineteenth century.

In March 2000, the Mons celebrated the 53d Mon National Day. Mon leaders reaffirmed their dedication to tripartite talks among the Burmese military government, the democratic opposition, and the leaders of the non-Burman ethnic groups as the only solution to the civil war in Myanmar.

Opposition to the Burmese state is still motivated by attitudes of superior cultural heritage coupled with the demonstrated inability or unwillingness of the majority Burmans to live in peace with, and share development and social benefits with, the non-Burman peoples of Myanmar.

SELECTED BIBLIOGRAPHY:

Guillon, Emmanuel. *The Mon: A Civilization of Southeast Asia.* 1988.
Halliday, Robert, and Christian Bauer, eds. *The Mons of Burma and Thailand.* 1999.
Lintner, Bertil. *Land of Jade: A Journey through Insurgent Burma.* 1990.
Wijeyewardene, Gehan, ed. *Ethnic Groups across National Boundaries in Mainland Southeast Asia.* 1990.

Montagnards

Dega; Degans; Moi; Austriens

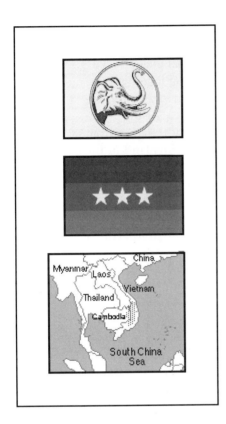

POPULATION: Approximately (2002e) 1,310,000 Montagnards in southeast Asia, concentrated in the Central Highlands of Vietnam and adjacent areas of Cambodia and Laos. There are about 3,000 Montagnards in the United States.

THE MONTAGNARD HOMELAND: The Montagnard homeland lies in the Central Highlands, the southern portion of the Annam Cordillera in southern Vietnam. Much of the region is high, forested plateaus interspersed with fertile valleys and high mountain peaks. The Montagnard homeland, called the Dega Republic by the Montagnards, has no official status in Vietnam, having been abolished in the early 1950s. It now forms the provinces of Gia Lai, Dac Lac, Kon Tum, and Lam Dong. *Dega Republic*: 21,654 sq. mi.—56,083 sq. km, (2002e) 3,772,000—Montagnards 32%, Khmer Krom* 31%, Vietnamese 28%, Chams* 6%, others 3%. The Montagnard capital and major cultural center is Lac Giao, called Buon Ama Thuot by the Montagnards, (2002e) 133,000. The other major cultural centers are Kontum, called Kon Tum, (2002e) 43,000, and Pleiku, called Play Cu, (2002e) 104,000.

FLAG: The Montagnard national flag is a white field bearing an elephant head centered. The flag of the Unified Front for the Struggle of Oppressed Races (Front Unifié de Lutte des Races Opremmées) is a horizontal tricolor of blue, green, and red, bearing three white five-pointed stars centered.

PEOPLE AND CULTURE: The hill peoples of the Central Highlands are collectively known by the French word *Montagnard* which means "mountaineer." They are the indigenous people of the region and resemble Polynesians but not the lowland Vietnamese. They call themselves Dega or the Dega People, the "Sons of the Mountains." The Montagnards are economically dependent upon shifting cultivation and upon supplementary trade in forest products and local crafts. Most live in scattered, impermanent settlements, often located on steep slopes at high altitudes. The major groups are the Jarai, Rhade, Bru, Koho, Bahnar, and Sedang, the largest of the more than 40 distinct and recognizable indigenous groups of the Central Highlands. The Americans during the Vietnam War affectionately called them "Little People" or "Yards."

LANGUAGE AND RELIGION: Many Montagnards speak a group of related Chamic dialects classified as West Indonesian languages of the Hesperonesian group of the Austronesian language family. Others speak dialects related to the Mon-Khmer language group. The most widely spoken of the dialects is that of the Jarai, with about 250,000 speakers. The other dialects are Rade, Bih, Cac Gia Roglai, Curu, Haroy, Northern Roglai, and Southern Roglai. The Chamic languages have heavy Vietnamese admixtures and resemble both the Mon-Khmer and Austronesian languages. Orthographies have been developed for most of the Montagnard languages, a work begun by the French in the early 1920s. Each of the major dialects is further divided into numerous subdialects.

The traditional Montagnard religion was an animistic belief system. Community leaders are usually attributed some shamanistic ability as curers, diviners, or trance mediums. Although their religious practices varied all of the Montagnards tried to keep in harmony with their deities. Many Montagnards are Roman Catholic, the result of early French missionary activity in the region. Later Protestant sects were active in the region, and a sizable Protestant community developed. Protestants, due to their close association with the Americans, suffered more than Catholics after 1975. The Evangelical Protestantism followed by many of the indigenous highlanders is suppressed by the government, which forbids minority Christians from gathering in churches and pressures them to renounce their faith.

NATIONAL HISTORY: The origins of the Montagnards lie in their mountains, where early tribal peoples lived in the dense forests as hunters and along the rivers and coasts as fishermen. Two thousand years ago, the Montagnards settled along the coast and in the fertile valleys of southeast Indochina. In Montagnard folklore, the mythical figures De and Ga were the first settlers of Indochina, equivalent to Adam and Eve.

Over the centuries, other cultures gradually intruded into their homeland. First, the Chams extended their kingdom throughout the coastal lowlands. Early inscriptions found among the ruins of Cham cities refer to a people who lived in the remote hinterland west of Champa, a people less advanced and viewed with disdain. These inscriptions, dating from the first century A.D., constitute the first written record of the highlanders.

The Chinese ancestors of the present Vietnamese migrated southward along the coast of the South China Sea, driving the last of the Montagnard peoples deeper and deeper into the highlands. In the isolation of their highland valleys, the Montagnards developed a unique society embedded in nature and dependent upon cosmic forces. Each of the many small groups settled a small territory, which resulted in some social-structural differences, but at the same time, adaptation to the mountains created physical and spiritual bonds that gave rise to a common highland culture.

The hill tribes were traditionally despised by the surrounding Vietnamese, Cambodians, and Thais as savages, *moi* in the Vietnamese language. The lowland peoples regarded the mountains as remote and forbidding, populated by uncultured, backward tribes. The Vietnamese mostly left the highlanders in peace while overrunning the Cham kingdom and populating the paddy fields of the Mekong Delta.

In the nineteenth century, France established colonial authority over Laos, Cambodia, and Vietnam, collectively called Indochina. The arrival of the first French missionaries in the highlands in the mid-nineteenth century began an era of ever-increasing contact between the Montagnard tribes and the outside world. As the French colonization progressed, administration of the Central Highlands became increasingly formal. As early as 1899 parts of the highlands were divided into exclusively Montagnard provinces.

Often the new contacts proved disruptive, giving rise to conflict between the Montagnard communities and the newcomers, who were looked on as unwelcome intruders. Vietnamese merchants often cheated them, and colonial officials sometimes abused them. Speculators, intent on usurping their traditional landholdings, were often supported by the colonial administration as modernizers. Several armed uprisings shook the French hold on the highlands in the early years of the twentieth century. The French military expanded its pacification of the tribes by force. Even though the number of French colonists and planters in the highlands increased, the presence of ethnic Vietnamese remained minimal throughout the 1920s.

After World War II, Vietnamese nationalists, led by the Russian-trained communist Ho Chi Minh, fought the returning French. Communist cadres moved into the Central Highlands in an effort to enlist the Montagnards in the anticolonial cause. They promised to evict foreigners and to grant autonomy to the tribal areas. To ease relations with the Montagnards, the French authorities granted them a high degree of autonomy. A federal ordinance issued on 27 May 1946 created five provinces—Koho, M'Nong, Rhade, Jarai, and Bahnar—collectively called the Montagnard Provinces of South Indochina or the Dega Republic. They were separated from the rest of Vietnam and placed under direct French rule.

The Montagnards viewed the autonomous provinces as a first step toward a separate Montagnard state in Indochina, but their hopes were short-lived. In 1951, the French administration, under increasing pressure from the Vietnamese communists and nationalists, began to transfer the responsibility for government to the Vietnamese. Bao Dai, installed as the emperor of Vietnam, annulled the French ordinance and brought the Montagnard province back under Vietnamese authority. However, he also specifically guaranteed the preservation and free evolution of Montagnard customs and protected their land rights.

The era of cooperation between the Montagnards and the government ended in 1954, when the Viet Minh communists defeated the French forces at Dien Bien Phu. Under the Geneva Accords, Vietnam was divided into two countries at the 17th parallel, American-supported South Vietnam and communist North Vietnam. More than a million refugees fled communist rule in North Vietnam, many to settle in the Central Highlands. The Montagnard homeland, never previously under direct Vietnamese rule, was incorporated into the new South Vietnamese state.

In South Vietnam, Ngo Dinh Diem became president in 1955. On 11 March 1955, the Central Highlands, the Pays Montagnard du Sud, was annexed to the Saigon government. Diem promptly declared the Montagnards as ethnic minorities and that minorities would be assimilated into the Vietnamese culture. A program was instituted in 1957 to develop the highlands economically and to bring modernization by settling massive numbers of ethnic Vietnamese in the Central Highlands. Montagnard military and civil servants were forced to take Vietnamese names, and hamlets, provinces, mountains, rivers, and other features of the highlands were given Vietnamese names as well. Teaching in Montagnard languages was prohibited, and documents and books in the languages were burned.

In 1960, the Montagnards numbered about three million, spread across a large area of South Vietnam. The resettlement program begun by the government met early resistance from the Montagnards. Many were forced to leave their villages for "regroupment" centers. The influx of Vietnamese settlers threatened their ancestral lands and their way of life. The program was harshly implemented, creating fear and antagonism among the Montagnards. By claiming that those who resisted were procommunist, the dictatorial Diem government justified the massacre of hundreds of opponents of the government.

Political activism grew as the Montagnards mobilized. In 1958, Montagnard leaders formed a nationalist organization, Bajaraka, a name derived from the initials of the four largest Montagnard tribes. United for the first time, the Montagnards called for the return of the autonomy granted by the French in 1946. The South Vietnamese government responded by jailing the nationalist leaders and cracking down on all political activity in the region. The communists of North Vietnam promised the Montagnards political autonomy once they reunited the country under their rule. By 1961, the South Vietnam government had virtually lost control of the highlands.

To offset their loss of control and communist entreaties, the government allowed American CIA and Special Forces advisers into the Central Highlands to train village defense units, border patrols, and reconnaissance groups. This represented the first direct contact between the Montagnards and the growing number of Americans in South Vietnam. Although close ties developed between the Americans and the Montagnards, relations with the South Vietnamese government did not improve. By 1964, the nationalist movement had become a movement for Montagnard independence.

The United Front for the Liberation of Oppressed Races became the leading separatist organization. After a series of armed revolts, the South Vietnamese government promised to restore a number of autonomous institutions to win back their loyalty as the Vietnam War widened. The independence movement spread awareness that the various Montagnard peoples shared a common culture, which the nationalist leaders sought to preserve.

Beginning in 1965, pressured by the U.S. forces, the South Vietnamese sought negotiations and accommodation with the Montagnards. Forced assimilation was replaced with programs to preserve their culture and identity. Montagnard law courts were reinstated, Montagnard languages and cultures were given places in regional education, and programs for granting land titles were initiated.

The Vietnam War spread and intensified, drawing more and more Montagnards into the fighting. Thousands became refugees as the war entered the highlands. Villages were emptied by communists, who needed labor, and by the American and South Vietnamese military to create free-fire zones. Many of the Montagnard refugees survived only on rice supplied by the South Vietnamese government and American aid programs.

The creation of a Ministry of Ethnic Minorities in 1969 gave the Montagnards and others a voice in government. However, the gradual withdrawal of the U.S. military in the early 1970s left them exposed. Montagnard leaders set out to establish social programs and to devise relief programs for the highland victims of the war, but the struggle for ethnic identity was soon replaced by the struggle to survive.

When the Americans pulled out in 1973, the North Vietnamese army, in spite of the cease-fire agreement signed in Paris by representatives of North Vietnam, South Vietnam, and the United States, began probing the South Vietnamese defenses. In March 1975, the communists launched an invasion through the highlands. The panicky decision by a group of South Vietnamese generals to abandon the highland towns of Kontum and Pleiku began the final downfall of South Vietnam. Their retreat precipitated the worst bloodbath of the war and the total collapse of the southern military forces. On 1 May 1975 communist troops entered the South Vietnamese capital and the Vietnam War ended; however, about 10,000 Montagnards, called the Forgotten Army, continued to fight in the Central Highlands.

The communist government offered a reward of about $400 in gold for each captured guerrilla. The Montagnard fighters became known as "Gold Heads," and the reward remains to the present.

One of the little-known consequences of the Vietnam War was the decimation and destruction of the Montagnard homeland. By 1975 some 85% of their villages were either in ruins or had been abandoned. Between 200,000 and 220,000 Montagnards had died as a result of the war. Although the two Vietnams were united in July 1976, the often-promised autonomy had only been a communist ploy. The government immediately began resettling large numbers of lowland Vietnamese in the Central Highlands in new "economic zones." At the same time, Montagnard leaders were jailed or sent to "reeducation camps." Some eluded capture and fled into the dense forests, where they joined the remaining guerrilla bands along the Cambodian border.

The Montagnards fought the communist forces, but by 1982 their forces were decimated and isolated. Without outside aid and abandoned by their former American allies, some escaped to neighboring countries and eventually resettled in the United States.

Since 1975 the Vietnamese government has institutionalized the abolition of the Montagnard way of life. They have been forced to adapt to Vietnamese culture, which is alien to the Central Highlands. Traditional ways, including religious practices and rites of passage, are forbidden. One result of the government modernization program is the deforestation of the highlands, which is proceeding at an alarming rate. The Montagnards are now fighting cultural extinction. They face forced relocation, government discouragement of ethnic languages and cultures, mandated changes in their ancient agricultural practices, and deforestation of their homeland.

A communist program called "cultural leveling," long-term ethnic cleansing, was designed to eradicate all ethnic minority cultures in Vietnam. In the 1980s and 1990s, the Montagnards suffered malnutrition, disease, and the encroachment of the ethnic Vietnamese population. In 1989, the Vietnam government began allowing political prisoners and reeducation camp survivors to apply for the Orderly Departure Program (ODP) negotiated 10 years before. In 1992, the last few hundred fighters of the Forgotten Army and their dependents were found by United Nations personnel in Cambodia and were subsequently allowed to emigrate to the United States.

Foreign organizations, mostly former American soldiers who fought with the Montagnards during the Vietnam War, began to provide medical aid, prenatal care, funding for schools and teachers, and agricultural programs. Other groups aid Montagnard refugees, convinced that the Americans owe a debt of honor to their most loyal allies. In 1994, the United States ended its trade embargo against Vietnam.

The Montagnards of Vietnam continue to suffer for their past opposition to Vietnamese domination and their association with the French and Americans. They are denied land rights, courts, and equal education. Health care is provided only for Montagnards in the labor force; all others are denied. Church services are allowed only in government-approved parishes by government-approved pastors. In rural areas gatherings of any nature are forbidden. In 2001 there was increasing official persecution of the large Christian population among the Montagnards, particularly the Protestants. The Viet government has accused Americans of stirring up the Montagnards, who retain close emotional ties to the America, where many Montagnard exiles live.

Large numbers of lowland Vietnamese are moving into the region, threatening traditional Montagnard culture. The Vietnamese see the Montagnards as backward, and want their lands to clear for coffee plantations, which grows well in the cooler highlands. Deforestation now causes severe flooding every year. Clashes over land are increasingly violent. Propaganda units from the Vietnamese army have been sent to the highlands to "educate" the Montagnards.

In February and April 2001 there were serious anti-government demonstrations by Montagnards demanding land rights and religious freedom. Renewed repression led to the flight of over 500 refugees from the Central Highlands into Cambodia between February and October 2001. Violent confrontations with security forces turned into the worst violence in Vietnam since the end of the Vietnam War.

International human rights groups and many governments, in September 2001, criticized the Vietnamese government's use of closed trials to impose harsh prison terms on fourteen Montagnards accused of anti-government activities. People's Courts imposed six- to twelve-year sentences on fourteen ethnic Jarai and Ede men for their alleged role in mass protests in February 2001, when thousands of Montagnards held protest marches in provincial towns. The demonstrators called for religious freedom, an end to encroachment on their traditional lands, and the establishment of an autonomous zone.

SELECTED BIBLIOGRAPHY:

Blondell, Anthony J. *Honor and Sacrifice: The Montagnards of Ba Cat Vietnam.* 2000.
Hickey, Gerald C. *Shattered World: Adaptation and Survival among Vietnam's Highland Peoples during the Vietnam War.* 1993.
———. *Sons of the Mountains: Ethnohistory of the Vietnamese Central Highlands.* 1982.
Mole, Robert L. *The Montagnards of South Vietnam: A Study of Nine Tribes.* 1970.

Montenegrins
Crnogorci; Chernogortsy

POPULATION: Approximately (2002e) 643,000 Montenegrins in southeastern Europe, 445,000 in Montenegro, and with communities in Serbia, Bosnia and Herzegovina, and Albania. Outside Europe there are Montenegrins living in the United States, Canada, Australia, Brazil, and Argentina.

THE MONTENEGRIN HOMELAND: The Montenegrin homeland, called Crna Gora or Black Mountain, occupies a rugged mountainous region of the western Balkan Peninsula. The forested region is traversed by high, fertile valleys and has a short coastline on the Adriatic Sea. The tiny state was recognized as an independent principality in 1878. Following World War I, the Montenegrins voted for the union of the South Slav lands, later called Yugoslavia, which broke up in 1991, leaving the Serbs and Montenegrins to form a new federal republic of two constituent republics. *Republic of Montenegro (Republika Crna Gora)*: 5,333 sq. mi.—13,812 sq. km, (2002e) 644,000—Montenegrins 69%, Sanjakis* (Sanjak Muslims) 13%, Albanians 10%, Serbs 6%, others 2%. The Montenegrin capital and major cultural center is Podgorica, (2002e) 139,000. The other important Montenegrin cultural center is Cetinje, (2002e) 18,000, the former royal capital.

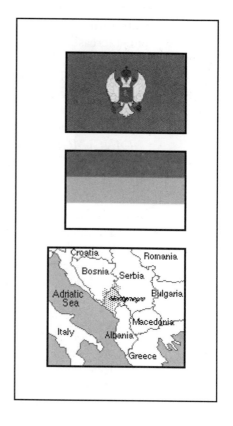

FLAG: The flag of the nationalist movement, the former royal flag, is a red field charged with a centered white eagle. The Montenegrin national flag, the official flag of the republic, is a horizontal tricolor of red, pale blue, and white.

PEOPLE AND CULTURE: The Montenegrins are a South Slav people, a robust mountain nation with a long warrior tradition. The smallest of the South Slav nations, the Montenegrins are ethnically Serbs, and although they share with the Serbs strong cultural ties, including their Orthodox faith, their history is distinct, and a majority consider themselves a separate nation. The Montenegrin culture, developed in the isolation of their mountain homeland, diverged from the Serbian culture in the fourteenth century. For centuries Montenegrin society was composed of patrilineally related extended families organized into clans. The clan system lasted well into the twentieth century, and personal tenacity and combat skills are still the most valued male virtues. Women have traditionally tended the fields, maintained the home, and raised the next generations of Montenegrin warriors. Practices such as bride theft and blood brotherhood were formerly widespread, and blood vengeance has survived to the present. Increasing urbanization has begun to break down the old clan system and vendettas, but much of the highland culture remains. Ethnically and linguistically the Montenegrins have traditionally identified with the Serbs, which complicates the growing ethnic identity in the region. Many older Montenegrins still view themselves as Serbs, while the younger, urban population have developed a distinct Montenegrin identity.

LANGUAGE AND RELIGION: The language of the Montenegrins is a dialect of the Serbian branch of the Serbo-Croatian language, which, like Serbian, is written in the Cyrillic alphabet. The Montenegrin dialect, which evolved from the upland variations of Serbian, is closer to old Serbian and lacks the Turkish admixture of the dialect spoken in Serbia. The dialect is divided into a number of subdialects based on regional geography. Each of the high valleys evolved somewhat in isolation, with its own cultural traits and speech.

The Montenegrins are mostly Orthodox Christians. The Montenegrin Orthodox Church, closely tied to their culture and history, officially separated from the larger Serbian Orthodox Church in 1993. There are Roman Catholic (mostly along the coast) and Muslim minorities, although religious friction has been kept to a minimum, and the three groups have lived together in relative harmony.

NATIONAL HISTORY: An early home of the Illyrian peoples, the highland region east of the Adriatic Sea formed part of the Roman, then Byzantine Empires before the migrating Slavic tribes settled the region in the seventh and eighth centuries. The Slavs adopted Orthodox Christianity and accepted nominal Byzantine authority.

In the twelfth century, the highlands formed part of a small Serbian kingdom, which was centered in the less accessible and more easily defensible mountains. The Venetians, in control of the coastal plain, called the highland region Black Mountain, Crna Gora in the Slavic dialect. The mountain tribes of the region were united in the early fourteenth century in the Zeta principality, which formed part of the medieval Serbian empire.

The Montenegrins' history as a separate nation began in the midfourteenth century. The Serbian Empire collapsed in 1355, leaving the highland principality of Zeta effectively independent. The Ottoman Turks, taking advantage of the regional turmoil, advanced northward from their territories in the southern Balkans. The Turkish forces defeated a combined Christian force at the Battle of Kosovo in 1389, beginning five centuries of Turkish domination of the southern Balkans.

The tiny principality of Zeta, also called Montenegro or Black Mountain, fielded a small but determined band of warriors, who defeated Turkish attempts to add their homeland to the Ottoman Empire. For centuries the Montenegrins maintained a precarious independence in their high mountain strongholds. The region became a refuge for Serbian nobles fleeing Turkish rule. Isolated from their Slavic kin, the Montenegrins evolved a warrior society, with a culture quite distinct from that of Turkish-dominated Serbia.

In 1515 the prince-bishop of Cetinje became the ruler of the small state, his office combining both the secular and religious leadership of the Montenegrins. The hereditary title traditionally passed from uncle to nephew within the Petrovich dynasty, established in the sixteenth century. The dynasty combined both secular and religious power, making Orthodox Christianity the state religion. In 1702–1703, under Prince-Bishop Danilo I, in the "Montenegrin Vespers," the Orthodox Montenegrins massacred their countrymen who had adopted the Islamic religion.

Danilo in 1715 requested and received Russian assistance against the Turks, beginning an alliance that would last until World War I. In 1796 the Montenegrins, with Russian help, defeated an invading Turkish army, and in 1799 the Ottoman authorities recognized the independence of the tiny mountain state. The reigning prince-bishop made an annual pilgrimage to St. Petersburg to reaffirm the alliance of his small state with the mighty Russian Empire.

In the early 1800s, the Montenegrin rulers began to consolidate power among the unruly Montenegrin clans. Feuding tribal chiefs surrendered power to Prince-Bishop Peter II in 1830, beginning the national revival of the decaying state. The Montenegrin state remained in practice a theocracy until 1852, when Prince-Bishop Danilo II secularized the state, giving the religious duties to the bishop of Cetinje, retaining for himself secular power as prince of Montenegro. The tiny state, allied to resurgent Serbia, again fought the Turks. At the Congress of Berlin in 1878 it was recognized as an independent state with increased territory, including a narrow outlet to the Adriatic Sea. In 1910 Prince Nicholas Petrovich proclaimed himself king of the Montenegrins.

The complicated system of alliances in the Balkans drew the Montenegrins into a number of wars in the early twentieth century. As Russia's ally, the kingdom declared war on Japan in 1905, but the declaration was never acknowledged; the Montenegrins still consider themselves technically at war with Japan. Allied to Serbia, the Montenegrins fought the

Turks in the Balkan Wars of 1912–13, and for their assistance shared the conquered territory of Sanjak with Serbia in 1913.

In 1914 the Montenegrins joined the Serbs in their conflict with Austria, the conflict became World War I. The Austrian occupation of Montenegro in 1915 strengthened the faction that favored the creation of a united South Slav state in the Balkan Peninsula. In 1917 Montenegrin delegates signed the Pact of Corfu, agreeing to merge the small kingdom into a South Slav federation at the end of the war.

The opposing political forces were deeply divided between the Greens, including the king and several powerful clans, who supported an independent Montenegrin state, and the Whites, who advocated unification with Serbia. The Whites triumphed following the surrender of the Central Powers in November 1918, and on 2 December 1918 the pan-Slav nationalists deposed the Petrovich dynasty and joined Montenegro to form the new Kingdom of the Serbs, Croats, and Slovenes. The surrender of Montenegrin sovereignty divided the clans, the crisis worsened by the takeover of their cherished autonomous church by the Serbian Orthodox hierarchy in 1920. A rebellion of the Green clans dissatisfied with the status of the former kingdom, little better than that of a Serb province, kept the area in turmoil until their defeat in 1921. The same year King Nicholas, who had done so much to modernize Montenegro, died in exile. Between 1922 and 1926 sporadic revolts erupted among the anti-Serbian Green clans.

In censuses taken during the interwar period the Montenegrins were not counted separately but classified as ethnic Serbs. Up to World War II, the Serbs claimed that the Montenegrins were only a branch of the Serbian nation. A number of clans remained unreconciled to Serb domination and again rose when Yugoslavia collapsed under German and Italian attack in 1941. The clan leaders, on 13 July 1941, declared Montenegro an independent, neutral kingdom under the deposed Petrovich dynasty. Before the clan leaders could mobilize the kingdom, Italian troops occupied it. The majority of the former Greens joined the royalist partisans fighting the Fascists. The royalists partisans also fought against the rival communist partisan groups, led by Josep Broz Tito, which drew many Montenegrin recruits from the so-called White clans.

Montenegro, with the addition of territory on the Dalmatian coast, became in 1946 the smallest and poorest of the six republics in Tito's communist Yugoslav federation. Montenegrins were disproportionately represented in the Communist Party of Yugoslavia (CPY) and in the federal government after the war. Although a large number of Montenegrins were expelled from the party for pro-Soviet sympathies after Yugoslavia broke with the Soviet Union in 1948, Montenegrins remained overrepresented in the Yugoslav bureaucracy and military hierarchy, which translated into increased development funds for their small republic.

The rapid development of mines, ports, and industries urbanized the traditionally rural Montenegrins. The urban population of the republic grew by 40% between 1948 and 1953. Several Montenegrin industries developed dramatically, although often without rational distribution of resources. Much investment was wasted, and the republic suffered from low prices for the raw materials it sold to the other Yugoslav republics. During the 1950s, Montenegro received over 50% of its revenue from the federal government, while its economy remained largely underdeveloped and neglected.

Montenegrin nationalism, dormant since 1945, reemerged in 1966–67 as part of a campaign to resurrect the separate Montenegrin Orthodox church. The relative prosperity of the 1970s, based on mining and tourism, gave the Montenegrins a new confidence. In 1981, at Tito's death, nationalism again gained support as the republics of the Yugoslav federation began to take on greater autonomy, but a government crackdown in Montenegro stifled the dissident movement in 1982–84. Fueled by economic and ethnic tension, street demonstrations broke out in the republic in October 1988, with students and workers united in calling for the ouster of the Montenegrin communist leaders.

The collapse of communism in Yugoslavia in 1989 again divided the Montenegrin clans. In free elections in December 1990 the ex-communists won, ending dissident clan efforts to move Montenegro away from Serbian domination. In June 1991, the Yugoslav federation collapsed, and the ex-communists in control of Serbia and Montenegro joined in opposing the breakaway republics and in creating a new Yugoslav federation of the two states. Montenegrin soldiers joined in the Serbian attack on Croatia; they were particularly effective in the assault on the medieval Croatian city of Dubrovnik, just north of the Montenegrin coast.

Montenegrin dissatisfaction with Serb domination grew into a strong nationalist movement; however, in a March 1992 referendum 66% voted to remain in the truncated Yugoslav state. Since 1992 Montenegrin nationalists have regained support against the misguided Serb nationalism that dragged Montenegro into war and made it an international pariah. Increasingly strident Serb nationalists deny that the Montenegrins are a separate nation and call them Mountain Serbs, which is greatly resented. Calls for Serbian annexation of the state by ultranationalist Serbian groups have strengthened Montenegrin nationalists, who work for secession from the rump Yugoslav state. Demands for equality within the Yugoslav federation have been ignored by Serbia's ruler in Belgrade, raising tension among even some pro-Serbian Montenegrin clans.

On 15 January 1998 the inauguration of a new Montenegrin president, Milo Djukanovic, was marked by violent confrontations between his supporters and supporters of the former president, an ally of President Slobodan Milosevich of Serbia. The Montenegrin nationalists also clashed with ethnic Serbians in Podgorica. The clashes, which continued sporadically, raised the specter of the post–World War I civil war between the Greens and Whites in the tiny republic. In November 1999 talks between the Montenegrin and Serbian governments on a looser federation collapsed over Serbian objections to more Montenegrin autonomy.

The Montenegrins paid a high economic and political price for their decision to remain in the Yugoslav federation in 1991. By 1997, the majority supported looser ties to Serbia and closer relations with the European Union (EU). Montenegro is Yugoslavia's sole outlet to the sea, with potential to earn foreign currency through tourism and maritime trade. Should Montenegro leave the federation, as many nationalists advocate, Serbia would be landlocked and further reduced. Serbian officials warned in 1998–99 that the Montenegrins would not be allowed to leave Yugoslavia peacefully. The EU and the United States opposed the immediate separation of Montenegro from Serbia, partly in fear of another war in the region.

The Montenegrins increasingly distanced themselves from neighboring Serbia from 1999, particularly following the oppression and subsequent North Atlantic Treaty Organization (NATO) air attacks on Serbia. In March 1999, following an ultimatum to stop ethnic cleansing of the Kosovars* of the southern province of Kosovo, NATO launched hundreds of air raids on Yugoslav territory. Although some military targets in Montenegro were hit, NATO was careful to differentiate between the two Yugoslav states. Montenegro's government tried to remain neutral in the conflict.

The pro-Western government of Milo Djukanovic supports independence but fears that a declaration of independence would trigger an armed response by Serbia. In spite of the specter of another Balkan war and the presence of up to 45,000 federal troops in the republic, the Montenegrins have created a democratic legislature, new reform laws, and their own Western-oriented foreign policy. Some Montenegrin politicians and Western leaders supported the deployment of international observers in Montenegro to monitor the delicate situation in 2000. The last two links holding the Yugoslav federation together were a shaky currency and the army, loyal to Milosevich. The Montenegrins, in response to Serbian threats and economic pressure, threatened to call a referendum on independence should their situation in Yugoslavia worsen.

In local elections in June 2000 the pro-Western forces won a majority of the vote, but the pro-Serb forces gained control of a few areas, including the important coastal town of Herceg Novi. The apparent split between the two forces in Montenegro increased the possibility of violence should the Montenegrins continue along the path to independence. In opinion polls, a large majority of Montenegrins favor looser ties with Serbia, but up to a third state that they want to preserve the Yugoslav federation. The Montenegrins, already halfway toward independence, are losing patience while waiting for the democratic change in Belgrade that the West expects, but should secession come, it will not be easy.

The election defeat of Slobodan Milosevich and the inauguration of a more moderate Serbian government under Vojislav Kostunica in mid-2000 eased tension between Serbs and Montenegrins. Although militants continue to call for secession and independence, many Montenegrins are waiting to evaluate the new government in Serbia and its response to Montenegrin demands for equal status with Serbia in the Yugoslav federation. The Montenegrin parliament continued to prepare for a referendum on independence, but although polls show that the nationalists have a slight majority, the Montenegrins are bitterly split over the issue.

In April 2001 the new Serbian government of Vojislav Kostunica, following a series of meetings with the Montenegrin leadership, seemed to accept the idea of Montenegrin independence. In late October the Montenegrin president traveled to Belgrade to discuss with Kostunica his plan to hold a referendum on independence in the spring of 2002. Despite earlier statements that seemed to favor separation, talks between the Montenegrin government and Serbian Yugoslav leaders again collapsed over the question of the Montenegrins' demands for full independence and a loose federation of two sovereign states.

SELECTED BIBLIOGRAPHY:

Denton, William. *Montenegro: Its People and Their History*. 1977.
Glenny, Misha. *The Fall of Yugoslavia: The Third Balkan War*. 1992.
Kelly, Robert C. *Serbia and Montenegro Country Review 1999/2000*. 1999.
Stevenson, Francis S. *History of Montenegro*. 1971.

Moravians

Moravans; Czecho-Moravians; Moravians and Silesians

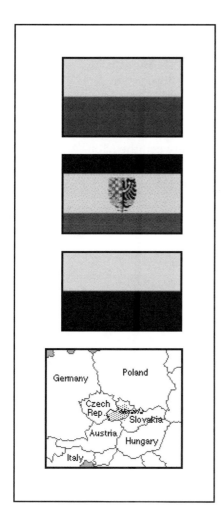

POPULATION: Approximately (2002e) 1,528,000 Moravians in the Czech Republic, concentrated in the Moravia and Silesian region of the Czech Republic. There are large communities in Prague and other parts of the republic and in Slovakia. Outside Europe there are Moravian communities in the United States, Canada, Australia, New Zealand, and Argentina.

THE MORAVIAN HOMELAND: The Moravian homeland, which includes the small Silesia region, is mostly a high plain characterized by rolling hills crossed by several mountain ranges, particularly the Bohemian-Moravian Highlands and in the north the Sudetic Mountains, which extend into Moravia from Bohemia to the west. Moravia is a historic region of central Europe that formed a separate crownland under the rule of the Austrians, and was later made a region of Czechoslovakia and the Czech Republic. The historic region is divided into four administrative regions, Brnensky, Olomoucky, Ostransky, and Zlinsky. *Region of Moravia and Silesia (Kraje Morava a Slezsko)*: 10,066 sq. mi.—26,070 sq. km, (2002e) 3,682,000—Czechs 44%, Moravians (including Silesians) 37%, Slovaks 5%, Poles 1%, Germans and Austrians 1%, Roms* (Gypsies), Ukrainians, and others 12%. The Moravian capital and major cultural center is Brno, (2002e) 382,000. The other important culltural center is Ostrava, (2002e) 620,000, metropolitan area 694,000. The cultural center of the Silesians is the city of Opava, (2002e) 61,000.

FLAG: The Moravian national flag, the unofficial flag of the Moravian regions of the Czech Republic, is a horizontal bicolor of red over yellow. The flag of the Moravian-Silesian national movement is a horizontal tricolor of black, yellow, and red, the yellow twice the width of the other stripes and charged with a composite eagle, half the red and white checked eagle of Moravia and half the black eagle of Silesia. The unofficial national flag of the Silesians is yellow over black.

PEOPLE AND CULTURE: The Moravians are a Western Slav people closely related to the neighboring Czechs. Culturally the Moravians have incorporated more Austrian influences than the Czechs and have maintained their distinct traditions and dialect. In recent government censuses and official figures the Moravians are usually counted as ethnic Czechs. The Silesians, numbering about 45,000, in northern Moravia are closely identified with their Moravian neighbors, but see themselves as a separate people traditionally more religious than the Moravians or Czechs. The focus of the national movement is the re-establishment of the Moravian and Silesian identity.

LANGUAGE AND RELIGION: The Moravians and Silesians speak dialects of Czech called Czecho-Moravian, which has been influenced by German and Polish. The Moravians claim to speak a much purer and more archaic Slavic language, while the speech of modern Bohemia is considered a type of slang. The dialects form part of the Czech group of Czecho-Slovak languages of the West Slavic branch of Slavic languages. The Silesian dialect is comprehensible to both Poles and Moravians and some Silesian dialects are transitional to both. Standard Czech, based on the dialect spoken in Prague, is quite distinct, but is spoken by all but a few in the region as a first or second language. All Czech and Moravian dialects are inherently intelligible.

The majority of the Moravians are Roman Catholic, with a small Protestant minority, mostly in the western districts. Their Catholic faith, reinforced by hundreds of years of Austrian rule, is central to the Moravian-Silesian culture. The religious festivals and commemorations marked the annual cultural year in the region. The Moravians were the first Slavic nation converted to Christianity and they were the first Slavic nation to have a literary language.

NATIONAL HISTORY: The earliest known inhabitants of the region, the Celtic Boii and Cotini tribes, were displaced by Germanic tribes in the first century B.C. Forming part of the area called Germania by the Romans, Moravia formed a frontier district lying north of Rome's Germanic provinces. Following the decline of Roman power, the region was overrun by peoples moving into the former Roman lands, the Huns and the Vandals.

In the fifth century, Slavic tribes, part of a mass migration moving from the east, settled the region. By the end of the sixth century the Slavs had taken control of Moravia, but were soon subjugated by the Avars.* The Slavs broke free under the leadership of Samo in the seventh century and established the first Western Slav state, which disintegrated with his death around the year A.D. 660.

The Moravians, taking their name from the Morava River, were first mentioned as a separate nation in historical annals written in 822. They gradually united and by the ninth century controlled Bohemia, Moravia, Silesia, southern Poland, and northern Hungary. The Moravian empire, called Great Moravia, meaning distant Moravia, was centered on Staré Mesto, which lies east of present Brno. The Moravian ruler, Duke Rotislav, appealed to the Pope for teachers, and German missionaries, Cyril and Methodius, were sent to the region in 863. The Moravians adopted Christianity and placed themselves under the authority of the Roman Catholic Church.

Germans and Jews, merchants and adventurers, settled in the cities, forming a powerful commercial class. Great Moravia reached its peak in the late ninth century, but later declined under attacks from Hungarians and Poles. In 902, the Moravians defeated the Hungarians, but by 908 the empire had been vanquished and disappeared from history. In 955, Emperor Otto I defeated the Hungarians and Moravia became a march of the Holy Roman Empire.

The Bohemians, later called Czechs, expanded their territories to include Moravia in 1029. Bohemia became a hereditary kingdom within the Holy Roman Empire in the thirteenth century, while Moravia, although under Czech rule, retained its separate diet, its parliament, and administration. At the height of its power, the Bohemian kingdom included traditionally Austrian and Hungarian territories, but defeat by Rudolph of Habsburg, in 1278, brought Moravia under Habsburg rule.

The Bohemian kingdom revived in the fourteenth century and under the rule of Charles I entered a golden age of culture, art, and power. The flowering of Czech literature and art paralleled increasing national consciousness. The golden age ended when the religious wars erupted in central Europe. With the election of the Austrian Ferdinand as king of Bohemia in 1526, Bohemia and Moravia became integral parts of the Habsburg empire.

The Moravian towns and cities, from the thirteenth century, underwent thorough Germanization. By the sixteenth century nearly the entire upper and middle classes in Moravia were German by culture and language. The German-speaking cities were surrounded by rural countryside that remained Slavic in language and culture. The Reformation and Renaissance saw a revival of religious writing and the development of liberal ideals and thinking. The Moravian Church is one of the very few Protestant churches that antedate the Reformation. It had been in existence for sixty years when Martin Luther posted his famous theses in 1517. Publishing in the Czech language, begun with the Bible, was followed by works on history, science, and medicine. Religious strife between Protestant and Catholic nobles foreshadowed the later wars of religion. During the Hussite Wars, in the fifteenth century, Moravia was separated from the Czech lands.

The disposition of the Habsburg ruler by Czech and Moravian nobles, in 1618, inaugurated the Thirty Years' War, which devastated the region. The Czechs and Moravians lost their remaining independence with the defeat of the Protestant forces at the battle of White Mountain in 1620. The war, fought from 1618 to 1648, bought the wholesale destruction of literary and artistic works followed by the repression of Moravian national life. Many Moravians fled abroad to escape oppressive taxes, religious persecution, and absentee landlords. By the eighteenth century the Czech lands were completely incorporated in the Austrian Empire. Under Empress Maria Theresa and Emperor Joseph II, the Czechs and Moravians were subjected to a program of intense Germanization. The majority of the Czech and Moravian cultural leaders worked abroad and their native language was gradually reduced to little more than a peasant dialect.

The oppression of the Czech culture and language in Bohemia and Moravia continued into the nineteenth century, but at the same time a national revival took hold, with new interest in their Slavic traditions, language, and history. Brno became the center of the Moravian cultural revival, which developed as an anti-Austrian mass movement in the region and as a rejection of the Germanization that was the official policy of the Habsburg authorities. The Czechs and Moravians led the movement for the equal rights of the Slavs of the Austrian Empire. During the Revolution of 1848, the Czechs convened a congress of Slavic leaders in Prague, but by early 1849 absolute Austrian domination had been restored. In 1849, Moravia was separated from Bohemia and was raised to the status of a separate Austrian crownland.

The establishment of the Dual Monarchy of Austria and Hungary in 1867, which gave the Hungarians rights within the empire equal to the Austrians, gravely disappointed the Slavs of Bohemia and Moravia. In spite of some concessions to the Slavs in 1879, when Czech and Moravian delegates entered the parliament at Vienna, the Czechs and other Slavs of the empire remained unsatisfied that a third Slav kingdom had not been created within the dual empire. Supported by activist immigrants in the United States, support for the autonomy of the Slav provinces within the Austro-Hungarian Empire grew in the first years of the twentieth century. A Czech National Council, including Moravian groups, was formed by exiles in the United States and began coordinate with exile Slovaks. The Czech leader, Thomas Masaryk, pressed for the independence of Bohemia and Moravia from the empire after World War I began in 1914.

The defeat of Austro-Hungary, in October 1918, opened the way for independence. On 28 October 1918, nationalist leaders declared Bohemia and Moravia independent of Austria. Two days later, on 30 October, the Slovaks declared their independence from Hungary. The union of the Czech lands and Slovakia was officially proclaimed on 14 November 1918.

The September 1919 Treaty of St. Germain between the Allies and Austria paved the way for official recognition of the new state.

The Czechs, the dominant national group in the newly independent Czechoslovakia, quickly took control of most ministries and set the tone of government. The constitution of 1920, although liberal and democratic, set up a highly centralized state and failed to address the increasingly serious question of the non-Czech groups. The German upper and middle classes continued to dominate Moravia. Moravian resentment of Czech hegemony and the anti-religious stance of the Prague government grew as Europe lurched from crisis to crisis during the 1920s and 1930s. In 1927, Moravia, along with the small section of Silesia that belonged to Czechoslovakia, was constituted as the separate province of Moravia and Silesia. The idea that Czechs and Moravians form one nation dates only to the time of the Czech "National Awakening" and the rise of nationalism in the nineteenth century.

Demands for union with Germany by the Sudeten Germans led to a serious crisis between Prague and Berlin in 1938. In September 1938, Czechoslovakia, as part of the Munich Agreement between the European powers, was forced to cede the Sudetenland, the German majority areas, to Nazi Germany. The agreement, meant to resolve the German-Czech crisis and ensure peace in Europe, prolonged the crisis. On 14 March 1939, the autonomous Slovak state declared its independence and the following day the Nazi's annexed Bohemia and Moravia as a German protectorate.

The Czech government set up a government-in-exile in London and Czech units fought with the Allies. Except for the brutalities of the German occupation, including the extermination of nearly all of the formerly large Jewish population, the Czech lands suffered little physical damage and emerged from the war with its industrial base and economy mostly intact.

The Red Army overran the region in April 1944 from the east while American and Allied troops moved into the Czech lands in the west. In March 1945, Edward Benes, who was elected president of Czechoslovakia in 1935, agreed to form a National Front government with Klement Gottwald, leader of the Communist Party of Czechoslovakia (CPCz). On 5 May 1945, the Czechs rebelled against the German occupiers. Accompanied by members of the National Front coalition government, the Allies finally took control of Prague on 12 May 1945. The fall of Prague marked the end of Allied military operations in Europe. At the Potsdam Conference of 1945 the expulsion of some three million ethnic Germans from Bohemia and Moravia was approved.

The Communist Party emerged as the strongest political party in the country in the elections of 1946. In February 1948, the Communists seized the Czechoslovak government. The new Communist administration began a campaign of repression of non-Communists. The powers held by the provinces were centralized in Prague and most levels of government were staffed with loyalists. In 1949, the province of Moravia and Silesia were replaced by four administrative regions. In 1960, a new constitution was adopted, modeled on that of the Soviet Union, which established a unitary state including Moravia, which was split into two new regions. During the 1960s, Slovak demands of communal rights triggered a parallel movement in Moravia.

In January 1968, the Slovak Alexander Dubcek became First Secretary of the Czechoslovak Communist party and introduced a program of liberal reforms, the so-called Prague Spring. The reforms included freedom of the press as well as increased contact with non-Communist countries. While the Czechs tended to emphasize democratic reform, the Slovaks and the Moravians emphasized national advances. Leaders of the Soviet Union and other East European nations feared Dubcek's program would weaken communist control in Czechoslovakia.

Under the terms of the Warsaw Pact, troops from Soviet Union, Bulgaria, East Germany, Hungary, as well as Poland, invaded Czechoslovakia on 20 August 1968. A third of the membership of the Communist party were expelled. Over 40,000 people fled the invasion and the repression that followed. The Red Army remained when the other national armies withdrew later the same year. On 1 January 1969, a federal system of autonomous Czech and Slovak governments was introduced, but power remained firmly in the hands of the Communist party. In April 1969, Dubcek was replaced, which resulted in further anti-Soviet protests. In May 1970, a new 20-year Treaty of Friendship was signed with the Soviet Union.

The Communist government of Czechoslovakia offered an amnesty to those who had fled in 1968 and many Moravian intellectuals returned to their homeland, but the government's repressive policies remained unchanged. During the 1980s, economic stagnation fed popular unrest, but the unrest was countered by increasingly repressive measures adopted as government policy.

The new spirit of openness emanating from the Soviet Union's new leader, Mikhail Gorbychev, was met in Czechoslovakia by a wave of arrests in 1988 and 1989. Pro-democratic groups organized in Brno, Ostrava, and other Moravian cities were forcibly closed. The Czechoslovak government initially aligned itself with the hard-line Communist governments in opposition to political and economic reform. In November 1989, large demonstrations broke out across the country, which culminated in the resignation of the government in December. The so-called Velvet Revolution overthrew the Communist government virtually without bloodshed.

In 1989 and 1990, mass demonstrations were held in Brno and other Moravian cities with crowds, waving the red and yellow Moravian flag, demanding autonomy for their ancient homeland. The pro-autonomy movement subsided in the mid-1990s, but a small offshoot, the Moravia-Silesia independence movement, became increasingly vocal. Claiming that the region was tightly controlled by the Czechs, they demanded the restoration of the autonomy that was canceled by the communists in 1948–49 as a first step toward greater sovereignty. Czech refusal to grant even limited autonomy or to recognize the Moravians and Silesians as distinct nations is the stimulus for the national movement. Nationalists have tapped into a vein of discontent at the growing assimilation of the Moravians into Czech culture even though over 1.4 million (1991 census) continue to declare themselves as Moravians and Silesians, not as Czechs.

In the early 1990s, the Czech government recognized Moravia and Silesia as folklore areas, but that too has been rescinded. Many local leaders who have openly discussed the situation in the region are often publicly connected with separatism. The Czechs remain very sensitive over the issue of separatism following the Slovak secession in 1993.

Multiparty elections for a new national assembly in June 1990 were won by pro-democratic parties. In Moravia, following the first taste of freedom, nationalism became an important issue. Mass demonstrations in favor of Moravian autonomy swept Brno and other cities, but waned as the country moved toward the division of its Czech and Slovak halves. On 1 January 1993, Czechoslovakia split into the Czech Republic and Slovakia, with Moravia making up one of the two parts of the new Czech Republic, Bohemia and Moravia. The Czech lands, more advanced economically than Slovakia, looked to the West for expertise and aid. The Czech economy, freed of the less prosperous Slovak economy, became one of the strongest in the former Communist block and was dubbed the Czech Miracle. Only in mid-1997 did the economy begin to show signs of weakening, leading to renewed Moravian demands for economic and political autonomy.

The Czech government, dominated by reformers and former dissidents, moved the Czech Republic into line to join NATO and the European Union. After decades of Communist repression, the Czechs and Moravians see their future security linked to a network of alliances with the most powerful states in the West. The Czech Republic has been invited to join NATO, and the continental federation, the European Union (EU).

To the Moravians, membership of the Czech Republic in the European Union would give them a greater voice in their own affairs, as European regions have increasingly demanded greater powers. Although the Moravians have rejected separatism, nationalism, the idea that their unique culture and dialect should be preserved and nurtured, has won widespread support.

SELECTED BIBLIOGRAPHY:

Dekan, Jan. *Moravia Magna: The Great Moravian Empire.* 1989.
Hochman, Jiri. *Historical Dictionary of the Czech Republic.* 1997.
Krejci, Oskar. *History of Elections in Bohemia and Moravia.* 1995.
Rees, H. Louis. *The Czechs During World War I: The Path to Independence.* 1992.

Mordvins

Mordvinians; Mordovians; Mordva; Erzya; Moksha; Mordensians; Merdensians

POPULATION: Approximately (2002e) 1,845,000 Mordvins in Europe, concentrated in the Mordvinia Republic in the Volga Basin of Russia. Other large Mordvin communities live in the Penza, Orenburg, Nizhni Novgorod, Kuybyshev, Ulyanovsk, and Saratov Oblasts, and the republics of Bashkortostan, Tatarstan, and Chuvashia. An estimated 120,000 Mordvins live in Russian Siberia and the Central Asian republics.

THE MORDVIN HOMELAND: The Mordvin homeland occupies the Volga uplands, the Oka-Don lowlands, and the wooded Mordvin Steppe in the Volga River basin of European Russia. Mordvinia, the Mordvin homeland, traditionally stretches across a broad territory from Nizhni Novgorod and Ryazan in the west to the Ural Mountains in the east. The largest concentration of Mordvin population is included in the Republic of Mordvinia, which is a member state of the Russian Federation. The republic has less than a third of the total Mordvin national population in Russia. *Republic of Mordvinia (Respublika Mordva)*: 10,116 sq. mi.—26,207 sq. km, (2002e) 915,000—Russians 52%, Mordvins 43%, Tatars* 3%, Chavash* 1%, others 1%. The Mordvin capital and major cultural center is Saransk, called Saran Os by the Mordvins, (2002e) 313,000. The other important cultural center is Arzamas, (2002e) 110,000, the center of the Nizhni Novgorod Mordvins.

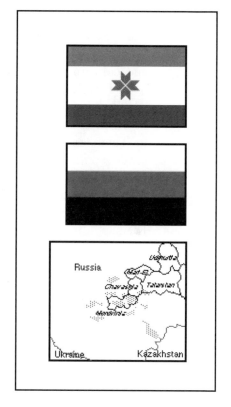

FLAG: The Mordvin national flag, the official flag of the republic, is a horizontal tricolor of red, white, and blue, the white twice the width and bearing a centered Mordvin sun symbol. The flag of the Erzya, the largest of the Mordvin groups, is a horizontal tricolor of white, red, and black.

PEOPLE AND CULTURE: The name Mordvin, which is not used by the people themselves, is used to describe five closely related peoples, of which the largest are the Erzyas and Mokshas. The Mordvins are a Finno-Ugric people, the descendents of the pre-Slav population of the Volga River Basin. They are scattered in clusters among the Russian-speaking population of the southern Volga region. Often tall and Nordic, the Mordvins, until the disintegration of the Soviet Union, had been assimilating into Russian culture. Nationalists claim a Mordvin national population of over two million in Russia. The Moksha, numbering about 500,000, live particularly in the western districts of the Mordvinian Republic, in the Penza and Orenburg Oblasts, and in Tatarstan. The Erzyas, numbering over 1.2 million, live in the northern districts of Mordvinia, in Tatarstan and Bashkortostan, and in several neighboring regions, particularly in Nizhni Novgorod. The Tengushev Mordvins live in southern Mordvinia and constitute a transitional group between the Erzya and the Moksha. The Teryukhan are Mordvins living near the city of Nizhni Novgorod who have adopted Russian as their first language, although they remain Mordvin in culture. The fifth group of Mordvins are the Karatai, who live in Tatarstan and have adopted Tatar as their first language. There are other groups that have been discovering their Mordvin identity since 1991: the Tengushen, who are ethnically Erzya but speak Moksha; Meshcheryaks, who speak Russian and live in Russian-majority regions; and Mishars, ethnic Mordvins who adopted the Tatar language and converted to Sunni Islam.

LANGUAGE AND RELIGION: The Mordvin language is actually two distinct languages, Erzya (Erzjan Kelj) and Moksha (Moksenj Kälj). Together they make up the Mordvinic branch of the West Finnic branch of the Finno-Ugric languages of the Uralian language group. The languages, although similar, are mutually unintelligible, and Russian is often used as a means of intergroup communications. Only about 70% of the Mordvins consider one of the Mordvin languages as their first language, with about 25% speaking Russian as their mother tongue. Both languages have literary status, with literary Erzya based on the dialect of the town of Kozlovka, in Atyashevo district of Mordvinia. Both Erzya and Moksha are literary languages, using the same modified Cyrillic alphabet. Some Mordvin scholars have suggested creating a single Mordvin language, but there is little interest in doing so among the speakers of the two Mordvin languages.

The majority of Mordvin believers belong to the Russian Orthodox Church. The religion, suppressed for decades under communist rule, became an underground movement and a part of the suppressed Mordvin culture. The Mordvin revival of the 1990s stressed the church's role in the preservation of the culture and its integral role in the Mordvin reculturation. Many of the Mordvins' pre-Christian traditions have been retained, and they continue to venerate native spirits, shrines, and their ancestors, often without a Christian veneer. Their beliefs include communal prayers and animal sacrifices for various spirits of nature.

NATIONAL HISTORY: The Mordvins settled the area between the Volga, Oka, and Sura Rivers more than 2,000 years ago. The Gothic historian Jordanes in the sixth century mentioned the Mordvins as tillers and herdsmen living in villages between the Oka and Volga. Many Mordvin groups had economic and political ties to the early Slavs. An early Mordvin state between the Volga, Don, and Sura Rivers became a dependency of the Bulgar Chavash state in the Volga basin in the late eighth century.

The Mordvins remained a tribal people, separated into clans and territorial groups. Ethnologists believe that between the seventh and twelfth centuries, as agriculture took hold among the Mordvins, their patriarchal and clan-based social system gave way to a more village-oriented political and social system. The city of Nizhni Novgorod was the Mordvin capital prior to its conquest by troops from three Russian principalities, Suzdal, Ryazan, and Murom, in 1172. The Russian princes of Ryazan and Nizhni Novgorod subjugated the remaining Mordvin tribes in the early thirteenth century.

The division of the Erzya and Moksha, which had begun hundreds of years earlier, was completed in the seventh century. The two closely related peoples developed distinct national identities and cooperated only when threatened by a common enemy. Geographic location dictated group affiliation, and influences from neighboring peoples colored the dialects and cultures of the regional groups.

In 1236 the Mordvin lands fell to the invading Mongols and Tatars of the Golden Horde; between 1392 and 1521 the expanding Muscovite state conquered the western Mordvin territories. Many Mordvins joined their Russian neighbors in resistance to Mongol and Tatar rule. The eastern Mordvin tribes came under the rule of the Tatar successor state, the Khanate of Kazan, which fell to Russian rule in 1552. The Mordvins, whose traditional religion revolved around ancestor worship, were forcibly converted to Orthodox Christianity between the sixteenth and eighteenth centuries.

The Russians built a strong line of military fortifications and settlements in the southeastern districts of Mordvinia in the sixteenth and seventeenth centuries to provide a defensive line against nomadic tribes. At the same time, thousands of ethnic Russians colonized the region, reducing the Mordvins to a conquered people. In the early seventeenth century, the Mordvins joined the neighboring Chavash and Maris* in a widespread revolt against Russian rule. The Russians finally crushed the rebellion in 1613; thousands of Mordvins fled across the Urals to Siberia to escape reprisals and forced conversion to Christianity. Others moved east of the Sura and Volga Rivers, where Russian authority was weaker.

The Mordvins, occupying a large area of fertile lands west of the Volga

River, were gradually reduced to serfdom on large Russian estates. The harsh Slav rule provoked sporadic Mordvin rebellions. In 1641, to better control the tribes, the Russians constructed Saransk as a fort in the center of Mordvin territory. The Mordvins again rebelled in 1670, 1743–45, and 1773–75, but Russian rule only grew harsher with each uprising.

The Mordvin economy remained overwhelmingly agricultural well into the twentieth century. Russian colonization, which advanced rapidly with the freeing of the serfs in 1861, pushed the Mordvins into scattered ethnic pockets surrounded by Slavs. Mordvin assimilation into Russian culture accelerated even as nationalism began to influence the small, educated elite, particularly with the improvement of communications brought about by the completion of the Moscow-Kazan Railroad across their homeland in the 1890s. During the revolutionary disturbances in 1905 the Mordvins rose, attacking Russian estates and settlements and skirmishing with Russian police and troops. The rebels retreated into the thick forests and continued to harass the authorities until 1907.

Mordvin nationalism grew rapidly after the outbreak of war in 1914, mainly among disgruntled soldiers. A coalition of nationalists and moderate Russian political parties took power in the region as civil government collapsed following the overthrow of the tsarist government in February 1917. A Mordvin congress sent delegates to a meeting of the region's non-Russian nations in Kazan to decide on the region's future. The majority of the Mordvins favored inclusion in a federation of states in the Volga-Ural region, or in a smaller federation with the Christian nations—the Mordvins, Maris, and Chuvash. The Mordvin debate on the future of their homeland within a democratic Russia ended with the Bolshevik coup in October 1917. In November, before the Mordvins could organize effectively, Bolshevik forces took control. Mordvin resistance ended after several weeks of fighting, and by December 1917 the Soviets had firmly established their control.

The Soviet authorities, in an effort to win Mordvin support, distributed the lands of the great Russian estates to individual farmers in 1918, just before the Russian Civil War spilled into the region. War, famine, and disease destroyed over a third of the Mordvin population of 1914 by 1921. The Soviets, emerging victorious from the civil war, created a theoretically autonomous territory for the Mordvins in 1921, but the forced collectivization of the lands distributed to the Mordvins in 1918 sparked renewed disturbances and violence in the region.

The Mordvins, despite the oppressive Soviet rule, made rapid advances in education and culture. The Soviets created a Cyrillic alphabet for the Erzya dialect in 1922 and for the Moksha dialect in 1926. There was some resistance to collectivization on the part of the Mordvin *kulaks*, free farmers, in the late 1920s, but they were mostly liquidated or deported, as were the intellectual and political leadership of the region.

The arbitrary borders of a Mordvin autonomous republic created in 1934 left a majority of the Mordvin population in neighboring Russian provinces. The majority, denied even the cultural autonomy allowed those within the autonomous republic, became the target of Soviet assimilation efforts. During World War II, when the Soviet government relocated most Russian industry away from the front, the Mordvin lands underwent dramatic demographic changes. By 1970 only 78% of the total Mordvin population considered Mordvin their first language, and the number claiming Mordvin nationality continued to decline in the 1970s and 1980s.

The liberalization of Soviet society in the late 1980s started a slow reversal of decades of Mordvin assimilation. The collapse of communism, followed by the disintegration of the Soviet Union in 1991, stimulated a Mordvin national and cultural revival. Nationalist organizations, organized among the scattered Mordvin population, began to press for the redrawing of the republic's borders to incorporate the Mordvin-populated districts of the neighboring provinces of Nizhni Novgorod, Simbirsk, and Penza.

In April 1993 the pro-reform president of the republic, in office since 1991, was toppled by the conservative, communist-dominated republican parliament in what amounted to a coup. The reformers, including the growing national movement, became the major challenge to the neocommunist republican government. Until the coup, supporters of full independence, within a Volga federation of states, made up only a small minority in the national movement. After 1993 the nationalist majority's support for economic and political autonomy in Russia was increasingly under pressure from the small but growing militant wing of the movement, which demanded reunification of the Mordvin lands in a sovereign state.

Although the numbers claiming Mordvin nationality and the numbers speaking Mordvin languages continue to fall, the decline is beginning to level off. Mordvin cultural and national associations have established language schools and cultural events, and they sponsor folklore fairs and educational events. The younger Mordvins have begun to speak the languages as a matter of pride.

The focus of Mordvin nationalism remains the unification of their nation in one political entity. The scattered Mordvin population in the Volga basin is being assimilated. Activists claim that only autonomy in a unified Mordvin republic can save their nation from extinction. Other groups advocate the creation of a separate Volga republic or a federation of the Christian peoples of the Volga. The majority of the Mordvins would probably be satisfied with cultural autonomy and protection of their language and traditions.

SELECTED BIBLIOGRAPHY:

Colton, Timothy J. *Growing Pains: Russian Democracy and the Election of 1993.* 1998.
Kirkow, Peter. *Russia's Provinces: Authoritarian Transformation versus Local Autonomy.* 1998.
Milner-Gulland, R.R., ed. *Cultural Atlas of Russia and the Former Soviet Union.* 1998.
Taagepera, Rein. *The Finno-Ugric Republics and the Russian State.* 1999.

Mormons

Latter-Day Saints

POPULATION: Approximately (2002e) 4,930,000 Mormons in the United States and Canada. The Mormons are concentrated in the state of Utah in the western United States. The world Mormon population is estimated at over 10 million, with about half in the United States, and the rest in Latin America, Europe, and parts of Oceania.

THE MORMON HOMELAND: The Mormon homeland, the state of Utah, lies in the western United States. Utah has two dissimilar regions separated by the Wasatch Range, which runs north and south through the state. To the east are high mountains and rugged plateaus; to the west of the mountains are the lowlands of the Great Basin, including the Great Salt Lake. The major population centers lie along the foothills on the western side of the Wasatch Range. *State of Utah*: 84,899 sq. mi.—219,888 sq. km, (2002e) 2,321,000— Mormons 68%, other Utahns and other Americans 32%. The Mormon capital and major cultural center is Salt Lake City (2002e) 185,000, metropolitan area 1,664,000.

FLAG: The Mormon flag of 1846 has twelve blue and white horizontal stripes bearing a blue canton on the upper hoist charged with twelve white stars surrounding a single white five-pointed star. The Deseret flag has twelve red and white horizontal stripes bearing a blue canton on the upper hoist with the Mormon symbols, a cannon, a beehive, and an eagle surmounted by twelve small white stars. The official flag of Utah is a blue field with the Great Seal of Utah centered.

PEOPLE AND CULTURE: The Mormons are considered the only indigenous American national group other than the Native Americans. They

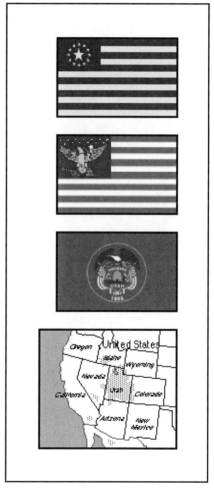

developed as a national group through the suffering and persecution of their early adherents. The story of their trek out of the United States has on them the influence of the Exodus on the Jews. Their culture evolved during the nineteenth-century migration and in the isolation of their new homeland on the Great Salt Lake. The majority of the Mormons are of Caucasian ancestry, with minorities of Native Americans, Pacific Islanders, Hispanics, and blacks. Until 1978 blacks were excluded from church office. The Mormons remain clannish and continue to adhere to a very strict social order. The Mormon tradition of isolation and self-sufficiency remains; very few Mormons receive public assistance, as the self-help tradition remains strong. The Mormon way of life is distinguished by order and respect for authority, church activism, strong group conformity, and vigorous proselytizing and missionary activity. A continuing stream of immigrants from all over the world is rapidly assimilated into Mormon society. Large families are still common; the Mormons have the highest birthrate in the United States, twice the national average.

LANGUAGE AND RELIGION: The Mormons are an American national group and speak the western American dialect of English. In the nineteenth century a phonetic alphabet for the writing of English was promulgated by the Church of Jesus Christ of Latter-Day Saints, but it never came into general use. The script consists of 38 letters, with upper and lower-case pairs that differ only in size, not in shape.

A Mormon is a member of any of several denominations and sects, the largest of which is the Church of Jesus Christ of Latter-Day Saints, that trace their origins to a religion founded by Joseph Smith in the 1830s. The religion these churches practice is often referred to as Mormonism. The church had more than 10 million members in 2000, about 50% living in the United States. The next largest Mormon church is the Reorganized Church of Jesus Christ of Latter-Day Saints, headquartered in Missouri and with a membership exceeding 200,000. The Mormon Temple in Salt Lake City, built between 1853 and 1893, is the center of the Mormon religion and culture. All Mormon males over the age of 12 are expected to join the priesthood.

NATIONAL HISTORY: The Mormon origins began with the establishment of the Mormon church by Joseph Smith at Fayette, Seneca County, New York, on 6 April 1830. According to Mormon belief, at age 14 Smith was visited by celestial personages in human form who told him to prepare himself for important tasks. About 30 years later, in 1827, they appeared again and directed him to a nearby hill where golden plates had been hidden fourteen centuries earlier by Moroni, identified as the son of Mormon, their compiler, a member of an ancient civilization. The engraved plates, which became the Book of Mormon, contained a history of the American Indians as descendents of Hebrews who sailed to the Western Hemisphere and lived in the Americas from 600 B.C. to A.D. 421. Smith translated the plates from "reformed Egyptian" with the aid of special stones. Published in 1830, the book was offered by Smith as scientific evidence of his divine calling.

Many scholars, to the present, consider the book a collection of local legends of Indian origin, fragments of autobiography, and contemporary religious and political controversies, particularly the anti-Masonic movement of the early nineteenth century, all transformed with remarkable ingenuity into a religious document. Religious leaders of the time rejected Smith's claim that his church, organized in 1830, restored the ancient, primitive Christian religion.

Smith's "revelation" on polygamy, revealed in 1852, proved to be one of the most controversial aspects of the new community. The young prophet governed the Mormons by announcing periodic revelations from God on widely divergent matters. He combined Jewish and Christian mysticism with the goal of perpetual prosperity and sought to establish Mormonism as a complete way of life.

Converts to Smith's beliefs soon experienced persecution. Joseph Smith, his brother Hyrum, and their followers moved west to Ohio, but wherever they settled they were persecuted and mistreated for their beliefs, especially the practice of polygamy. From Ohio they moved to several sites in western Missouri, where their clannishness and antislavery stance led to conflict in 1833. On 27 October 1838, the governor of Missouri proclaimed that the Mormons "must be exterminated or driven from the state if necessary to the public peace." Three days later the Missouri militia killed 17 Mormon men and boys. Despite this persecution, the Mormons continued to make converts, and their numbers increased.

The Mormons retreated east, many to Nauvoo, Illinois. At Nauvoo the Mormons built a new city, which soon had a population of over 20,000; it was the largest city in Illinois and among the most modern in nineteenth-century America. Tension and violence with neighbors continued in Illinois. Their commercial success and growing political power provoked renewed hostility from the "gentiles." Joseph Smith and his brother were killed by a mob at Carthage, Illinois, on 27 June 1844. At Nauvoo, the Mormons, to protect themselves, formed a defensive army called the Nauvoo Legion. After Smith's death, the majority of the Mormons abandoned the city of Nauvoo and determined to leave the United States.

They undertook a mass 1,100-mile (1,800 km) migration. Led by Brigham Young, long wagon trains of Mormons moved westward out of U.S. territory into the uninhabited Mexican territory west of the Rocky Mountains. They hoped to establish a commonwealth where they could practice their religion without persecution. The first Mormon wagon trains arrived in the valley of the Great Salt Lake in 1847. The Mormons again came under American authority when the region, called Deseret by the

Mormons, was ceded to the United States by the Treaty of Hidalgo, which ended the Mexican-American War in February 1848.

In 1849 a Mormon convention in Salt Lake City organized the Mormon settled region of the west into the State of Deseret; it claimed all of the present southwestern United States south of the 42d parallel and west of the Rocky Mountains. The Mormons, already under American territorial authority, applied for admission to the United States as a state. Deseret was refused recognition by the U.S. government. The Territory of Utah, named for the Ute Indians, was created with a much-reduced area in 1850, leaving large Mormon settlements in Nevada, Idaho, California, and northern Mexico outside the Mormon territory. Subsequent migrations brought to Utah the majority of the Mormons from Ohio and Missouri in 1852. Along the way many migrants stopped and settled in Iowa and in the Omaha region of Nebraska.

Congress and the administration refused to consider Utah statehood until the church (whose political arm was the People's Party) ended its economic policy by which Mormons dealt primarily with each other, and discontinued the practice of polygamy. The primary issue was polygamy, which was denounced by secular and religious authorities outside the Mormon community.

The Mormon migrations became part of the lore and culture of the developing Mormon nation. Beginning in the 1850s, a stream of Europeans converted by Mormon missionaries began to arrive in the eastern American ports and to continue directly to the Great Salt Lake valley. The Mormons became a cohesive nation through persecutions across the United States and the tales of the exodus and migration. The Mormons were the only American national group whose principal migration was an effort to leave the United States. The Mormon readiness to accept very strict social discipline arose from the harsh environment of their new homeland.

In 1857 U.S. authorities attempted to stamp out the practice of polygamy, an integral part of the Mormon culture, and to settle a controversy over control of Nevada between the Mormons and the U.S. government. Tension increased until the government dispatched troops against the Mormons in a brief war called the Winter War, or the Mormon Rebellion of 1857. Utah Territory lost territory to the east and west in the 1860s, leaving even more Mormons outside the heartland. Those living outside Utah came to be called Deseret Mormons.

The completion of the railroad from the east to Salt Lake City in 1869 facilitated Mormon emigrant movement to Utah, and the population grew rapidly. For the next three decades the U.S. government passed increasingly severe anti-Mormon laws. Many Mormon men were imprisoned for possessing more than one wife. Mormon families were known for numerous children, the largest recorded being 65.

Mormon leaders finally banned polygamy in 1890, and six years later, on 4 January 1896, Utah, reduced to its present size, was admitted to the United States, having previously tried six times. The political structure changed from theocracy to a conventional democracy, and non-Mormons were allowed to run for office, including the governorship. The Mormon church has been officially neutral in politics since the early 1900s.

Some Mormon splinter groups adopted communistic practices, particularly in Missouri. After the Church of Jesus Christ of Latter-Day Saints renounced plural marriage in 1890, some Mormon groups in Utah and in northern Arizona continued to practice it in secret.

Mormon isolation continued well into the twentieth century. Trials of Mormon polygamists continued despite the official ban on polygamy by the church authorities. In 1900 there were about 250,000 Mormons, mostly living in Utah. They took a negative view of the non-Mormons, whom they called gentiles, who settled in the state.

After 1900 many Mormons returned to Utah from scattered communities throughout the western United States, adding to the already rapid growth of the Mormon population of the state. In 1920 Utah was 56% Mormon, but by 1972 the percentage had climbed to 72%. Since the 1960s, the Mormons have taken a more closed-ranks attitude due to the chaotic state of the outside world. The Mormon Church added one million people to its rolls worldwide between 1979 and 1982 alone. With the highest birthrate in the United States, the population of Utah younger than 21 rose 50% between 1966 and 1986, as compared to a 6% decline nationwide. The Utah population grew by almost 60,000 people between July 1993 and July 1994, making it the fastest-growing state in the Union. Of the immigrants moving to the state, 61% are Mormons, mostly from the Mormon diaspora in other western states.

Rapid economic growth and a population influx into the state of Utah alarmed Mormon leaders in the 1990s. Salt Lake City became the center of one of the fastest-growing metropolitan areas in the country. The Wasatch Front metropolitan area, which snakes along the base of the Wasatch Mountains from Ogden to Provo, has a population of nearly 1.7 million and continues to grow. More than half the population of the metropolitan area are non-Mormons, including the mayor of Salt Lake City. The region will continue to grow precisely for the reason it was settled in the first place: the Church of Jesus Christ of Latter-Day Saints.

In February 1999 a scandal was revealed over payments and gifts to members of the International Olympic Committee to win the bid for the 2004 winter games for Salt Lake City. Although members of the local committee protested that they only had fulfilled demands of the international delegates, the scandal outraged the Mormon leadership.

The Church of Jesus Christ of Latter-Day Saints, headquartered in Salt Lake City, has the highest per-member income in the United States and receives revenues of more than one billion dollars per year. The Mormon church continues to exert profound influences on many facets of Mormon life, and in the local economy. The business-minded religion has assets worth a minimum of $30 billion. Its world headquarters, a vast complex that includes a huge tabernacle, temple, genealogical library, museum, administrative complex, and an apartment for the Prophet, the Mormon spiritual leader, has protected downtown Salt Lake City from the urban blight that is commonplace elsewhere.

The separation of church and state is not clearly defined in Utah, and Mormon devotion to their church supersedes all other loyalties. The Mormons remain prosperous, stable, and obsessively secret. They literally constitute a state within a state, living behind what is sometimes called the Zion Curtain.

SELECTED BIBLIOGRAPHY:

Johnson, Frank J., and William J. Leffler. *Jews and Mormons: Two Houses of Israel.* 2000.

Mauss, Armand L. *The Angel and the Beehive: The Mormon Struggle with Assimilation.* 1994.

Ostling, Richard N., and Joan K. Ostling. *Mormon America: The Power and the Promise.* 1999.

Shipps, Jan. *Sojourner in the Promised Land: Forty Years among the Mormons.* 2000.

Moros

Muslim Filipinos; Bangsamoros

POPULATION: Approximately (2002e) 6,356,000 Moros in the Philippines, concentrated in the southern islands of the archipelago. Other large communities include the mostly illegal community numbering between 300,000 and 500,000 in the neighboring Malaysian state of Sabah and in other areas of Malaysia and Indonesia.

THE MORO HOMELAND: The Moro homeland lies in the southern Philippine Islands, comprising the western part of the large island of Mindanao and the smaller islands lying to the west and south, including Basilan, Tawitawi, Palawan, and the Sulu Archipelago. The region claimed by nationalists as the Moro homeland, Bangsa Moro, comprises the provinces of Central Mindanao, Northern Mindanao, Western Mindanao, Muslim Mindanao, and the Palawan Islands of the Southern Tagalog Province. *Bangsa Moro*: 27,240 sq. mi.—70,551 sq. km, (2002e) 10,793,000—Christian Filipinos 57%, Moros 41%, interior tribal peoples 1%, others 1%. The Moro capital and major cultural center is Cotabato (2002e) 167,000, the capital of Muslim Mindanao. Other important cultural centers are Zamboanga (2002e) 152,000, Cagayan, (2002e) 421,000, Jolo, (2002e) 89,000, the center of the Sulu Archipelago, and Puerto Princessa, called Panagtaran by the Moros, (2002e) 86,000, the center of the Palawan Islands.

FLAG: The Moro national flag, the flag of the Moro National Liberation Front (MNLF), is a red field bearing a centered white Moro sword with a yellow grip, and a five-pointed yellow star and crescent moon on the upper hoist. The flag of the Mindanao Independence Movement is a horizontal tricolor of red, white, and yellow, the white twice the width,

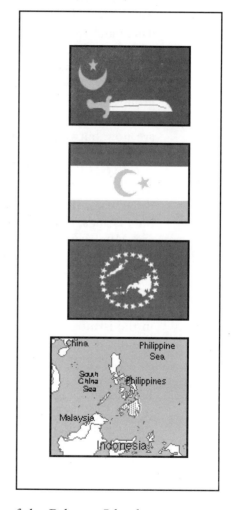

bearing a centered yellow crescent moon and five-pointed star. The flag of the Federal Republic of Mindanao is a blue field with a map of the islands within a circle of small white stars.

PEOPLE AND CULTURE: The Moros are a Malay people ethnically, religiously, and linguistically more closely related to the peoples of nearby Kalimantan (Borneo) and Sabah than to the other Filipino peoples. Although racially related to the other Filipinos, their Muslim faith and local cultures have made them the object of popular prejudice and national neglect. The Moros are not a unitary ethnic group but a conglomeration of tribes divided into 10 regional cultural-linguistic groups: the Manguindanao and the Maranao of Central and Northern Mindanao; the Tausug of Sulu and Zamboanga; the Bajaus and Sambal, concentrated on in the Sulu Archipelago; the Yakan of Western Mindanao; the Melabugnan of southern Palawan; and the Jama Mapun of the Cagayan Islands. The Moro groups are fiercely proud of their separate identities, and conflict between them was endemic for centuries. Internal differences among the groups are now outweighed, however, by commonalties of historical experience and by shared religious, cultural, social, and political traditions.

LANGUAGE AND RELIGION: The Moros speak dialects of Moro-Magindanao, a Malayo-Polynesian or Austronesian language. There are three major dialects—Tausug in the Zamboanga Peninsula region and the Sulu Islands, Magindanao in the Cotabato and Zamboanga regions of western Mindanao, and Maranao around Lake Lanao in northwestern Mindanao. There are numerous subdialects and regional differences, but since the 1970s there has been an effort to develop a standardized dialect for intergroup communication. Many of the Moros are bilingual, also speaking Tagalog, the Filipino national language, or other regional language spoken in the islands to the north.

The Moros are overwhelmingly Sunni Muslims. Because of the traditional geographic differences, religious differences remain important. The Tausugs, the first group to adopt Islam, often criticize the more recently Islamicized peoples for being less zealous in observing Islamic tenets and practices. The Islamic beliefs have been integrated into the regional cultures and differ from island to island. Many pre-Islamic beliefs and traditions continue to be important parts of Moro religious customs.

NATIONAL HISTORY: The islands, inhabited by Malay peoples who originally migrated from the Asian mainland, often formed part of the early Indo-Malay empires centered in the Malay Archipelago to the south. Islam arrived in the islands during the great Muslim missionary era, spreading from Borneo through the Sulu Islands to Mindanao between the fourteenth and sixteenth centuries. By the end of the fifteenth century several Moro sultanates had extended Muslim rule to the central islands of the archipelago. The various sultanates warred among themselves but just as often united to face common enemies.

Traders and explorers from Europe began to visit the region in the early sixteenth century. The Spanish established the first permanent European settlement in the northern Philippines in 1565. The Spanish easily conquered the mostly pagan northern islands, but when they moved into the central islands they came across the warlike tribes intent on extending Muslim rule to the north. The Spaniards called the people Moros, from a Greek word meaning "very dark." The Moros were driven back to the southern islands by the better-armed Europeans but were never conquered. For the next two centuries Moro pirates harassed Spanish shipping and terrorized coastal settlements. Internecine warfare among the several sultanates continued, the Moros uniting only when the Spanish threatened their territories.

From the sixteenth to the nineteenth centuries the Moros resisted the Spanish attempts to extirpate their "heresy." The southern islands remained outside effective Spanish control and were a meeting ground for sea traders, shell and coral producers, fishermen, pirates, and slave traders. The Moros had extensive regional contacts with Muslim countries to the south and west, and Moro raids continued to threaten areas of present-day Malaysia and northern Luzon. The Spanish colonial administration, in control of the entire archipelago except for the southern islands, launched a concerted military campaign against the Moros in 1850 but were beaten back with many casualties. Sporadic clashes continued up to the Spanish-American War of 1897–98, after which the United States was the administrator of the Philippines.

American attempts to occupy the southern islands generated a widespread armed conflict, the Moro War of 1899–1905. The Moros hoped to establish a separate sovereignty, but American troops, led by Gen. John Pershing, finally brought the islands under effective military control, ending over three centuries of Moro resistance to foreign domination. The Americans outlawed slavery and polygamy, established civil administration, and occasionally put down uprisings but generally left the Moros to their traditional way of life. The Moro islands were treated as a separate political unit under U.S. administration. A civil administration was established in 1914, and in 1915 the reigning sultan abdicated his civil powers, retaining only his rights as head of the Islamic faith in the islands.

The autonomous Commonwealth of the Philippines was established under U.S. authority in 1935. Muslim leaders petitioned the U.S. president asking that the Moro regions of Mindanao and Sulu remain under direct American administration. The petition was rejected, and in 1940 the sultan reluctantly ceded the Sulu Islands to the Philippines. The Philippine government, with a Roman Catholic minority, showed little sympathy for the problems or sensibilities of the Moros of the southern islands.

In 1941 Japanese troops invaded, driving the American troops from the islands. The Japanese attempted to extend their control over the southern islands, but like the Spanish and Americans before them found the Moros an elusive and deadly enemy. Many Moros collaborated with the Filipino resistance to fight the invaders, but many more felt that the war had nothing to do with them and that both sides were enemies of the Moros.

The Philippine government, following the independence of the country in 1946, settled on a policy of Christian colonization to dilute the Muslim majority in the south. Christian settlers, offered homesteads and generous government assistance, streamed into the area. The massive resettlement caused deep resentment among the Muslims and raised bitter conflicts over land distribution and ownership. Disputes periodically escalated into armed conflicts as both Muslims and Christians organized self-defense militias. As tension and religious violence mounted during the 1960s, the Moros organized to resist the onslaught.

In 1961 the representative of Sulu in the federal government filed a bill seeking political separation of the Sulu Archipelago from the Philippines. The bill was quickly defeated, but the idea of Moro separation began to spread. Moro nationalists formed the Moro National Liberation Front (MNLF), its stated objective an independent Moro state in the traditionally Muslim part of the southern Philippines. The Philippine army formed Christian vigilante death squads to wage a "secret" war against Moro separatists and their supporters. The central government's bias toward the Christian settlers in the competition for land and resources quickly eroded the Moro presence in their ancestral lands. By 1971 an estimated 800,000 Moros had been driven from their lands by Christians.

The Moros, threatened by the continuing Christian immigration and the widening conflict, rebelled following a local uprising in 1972. With aid from many Muslim countries, including Libya, Iran, and Saudi Arabia, the Moros attempted to drive the Philippine military and the Christian colonists from their land. Heavy fighting over the next five years devastated the region and left over 60,000 dead and 250,000 refugees. In 1977 the government negotiated an agreement that provided for an autonomous region covering 13 provinces, but the region's now majority Christian population rejected the plan, and the Moros renewed their demands for full independence. A renewed Moro rebellion followed the rejection of the autonomy plan and continued sporadically until the Philippines' new democratic government began talks in 1986.

A split emerged between those Muslims who were prepared to accept autonomy within the Philippine state and those who favored secession. The Muslims demanded an autonomous region comprising 23 provinces, to be granted without a referendum. In November 1989, a referendum was held in just 13 provinces and nine cities in the southern Philippines on proposed autonomy for these areas, with direct elections to a unicameral legislature in each province. The autonomy plan was defeated in all but four noncontiguous provinces. The four provinces were formed into a nominally autonomous region of Muslim Mindanao.

In late 1993 the government opened talks with the nationalist groups representing the Moros, but in spite of the efforts of the Indonesian government to mediate, the talks again collapsed. With negotiations stalled in 1993–94, several organizations again turned to violence—a campaign of kidnappings, bombings, and confrontations with Philippine troops. The application of Muslim Shari'a law, which would be observed only by the Moros of the region, was strongly opposed by the large Christian community.

The leader of the MNLF, Nur Misuari, signed a treaty with the Philippine government and on 30 September 1996 became the governor of the Autonomous Region of Muslim Mindanao. After years of sporadic negotiations, the agreement provided for limited autonomy and economic control. The autonomous region comprised 14 provinces with about a quarter of the Philippines' territory; it was inhabited by 3.5 million Muslims and five million Christians. Christian groups argued that the agreement did not fully reflect their interests and concerns. Several Muslim factions also rejected the treaty and continued to fight for an independent homeland. The institution of a hostile minority-Muslim government failed to alleviate the economic and communal problems of the region.

One of the major obstacles to peace is a lack of development. Government efforts to integrate Muslims into the political and economic mainstream have met with only limited success. The 1998 Asian economic collapse adversely affected the struggling economy of the region, particularly the Muslim-majority regions. The Moros did not benefit from the increasing prosperity of the Christian-dominated cities in 1999–2000.

Rebel threats to disrupt federal elections in May 1998 were countered by the deployment of half the country's armed forces in the southern regions. The various groups did not disrupt the polls, but many Moros refused to participate in a process they saw as part of the Christian domination of their homeland. The leaders of a number of Muslim organizations urged the Philippine government to appoint Muslim members of the cabinet.

The major threat to the peace agreement since 1996–97 has come from offshoots of the MNLF, principally the Moro Islamic Liberation Front (MILF), and armed gangs like Abu Sayyaf whose only purpose is robbery, extortion, and kidnapping. The more radical groups continued to resist efforts to draw them into the peace talks in the late 1990s. Attacks on Christian towns and fighting with Filipino troops continued. The slow implementation of the autonomy agreement and the lack of development raised tension in 1999–2000.

The MILF began talks with the government in May and June 1998, but the talks faltered over demands for Philippine recognition of an independent Islamic state. The talks resumed in 1999 but again collapsed, and violence was renewed.

Nur Misuari, the leader of the MNLF and the governor of the Autonomous Region of Muslim Mindanao (ARMM), threatened to return to war if a plebiscite scheduled for late 1998 was not postponed until 2003. The plebiscite on autonomy, opposed by the region's Christian majority, was finally postponed to give the Muslim leaders more time to convince the region's population of the benefits of an autonomous region and the accommodation of the Muslim population. Currently the ARMM consists of 4 provinces. The plebiscite is meant to determine if the residents of the Special Zone of Peace and Development, which covers 14 provinces and nine cities, wish to join the autonomous region.

New violence broke out in the region in early 1999. Thousands fled the renewed fighting as the army sought to contain rebel groups attacking villages. In April 2000, members of Abu Sayyaf and renegades from MNLF kidnapped 21 people from a resort in nearby Malaysia, including nationals of Finland, France, Germany, South Africa, and Lebanon along with several Malaysians. The hostages were finally released in late August 2000 following a Libyan promise to underwrite a development plan for the Moro homeland.

In June 2000, negotiators representing the MNLF and the Philippine government agreed to expand the autonomous Muslim region in Mindanao. The Moros, without forgoing their aim of an independent state, also demanded greater autonomy, protection of traditional fishing grounds from large trawlers, and the formation of a commission to examine the problems of the Moros living in neighboring Sabah. The MNLF called off the 1996 cease-fire in August 2000, and the violence escalated.

The Philippine government in September 2000 sent a force of over 4,000 troops to the strongholds of the Abu Sayyaf group, which held a number of hostages, mostly foreigners. After months of negotiations and the release of several hostages, the government finally decided to attack. Fighting on the island of Jolo was confined to the mountainous region where the separatist bases were located. The government accused the group of kidnapping foreigners to finance their separatist war.

The Philippine government, seeking to negotiate peace in the region, signed a ceasefire with the Moro Islamic Liberation Front in early August 2001. Soon after, a plebiscite on 14 August offered autonomy to parts of Mindanao and some neighboring islands. Based on a 1996 agreement between the government and the MNLF, the plebiscite promised a vote in exchange for the Moros abandoning their campaign for full independence.

Following the terrorist attacks on the United States in September 2001, ties between some Moro groups and Islamic radicals were published. Abu Sayyaf was listed as a terrorist organization and American troops were dispatched to help the Philippine military against the group.

In November 2001, about 200 followers of Nur Misuari, the deposed leader of the MNLF, broke a five-year-old peace agreement and mounted a surprise attack on army positions. Misuari, as part of the 1996 peace deal, was made governor of an autonomous Muslim region. His performance in this job was a disappointment to both the MNLF and the government. The region and people are just as poor as in 1996. Ousted by the MNLF, new elections were set for November 26, but Misuari refused to accept his dismissal. His followers took around 100 hostages, who were marched at gun-point through Zamboanga before negotiations led to their release in return for safe passage for rebels. Misuari, long the acknowledged leader of Moro nationalism, was captured after fleeing to the nearby Malaysian state of Sabah.

SELECTED BIBLIOGRAPHY:

Bauzon, Kenneth Espana. *Liberalism and the Quest for Islamic Identity in the Philippines.* 1990.
Kessler, Richard J. *Rebellion and Repression in the Philippines.* 1989.
Majul, Cesar Abid. *Muslims in the Philippines.* 1999.
McKenna, Thomas M. *Muslim Rulers and Rebels: Everyday Politics and Armed Separatism in the Southern Philippines.* 1998.

Nagas
Nagalimas

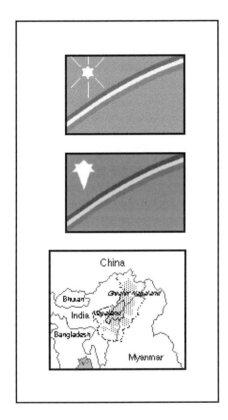

POPULATION: Approximately (2002e) 3,150,000 Nagas in India and Myanmar, concentrated in Nagaland, Manipur, Assam, and Arunchal States of India, and the Naga Hills of the Sagaing Division of Myanmar, with a population of about 1,250,000.

THE NAGA HOMELAND: Nagaland is situated at the junction of India, Myanmar, and China, occupying the Patakai Range, which runs roughly parallel to the Brahmaputra Valley. Greater Nagaland, called Naga Lim by the Nagas, as outlined by nationalists, includes Nagaland State, Manipur State, the eastern districts of Assam, the northeastern districts of Arunchal Pradesh in India, and the Naga Hills District of Sagaing Division of Myanmar, covering an area of 46,332 sq. mi.—120,000 sq. km, with a population of over three million. State of Nagaland (Naga Lim): 6,366 sq. mi.—16,488 sq. km, (2002e) 2,073,000—Nagas 91%, other Indians 9%. The Naga capital and major cultural center is Kohima, (2002e) 76,000. The other important cultural center is Dimapur, (2002e) 89,000. The cultural center of the Myanmar Nagas is Nathkaw, (2002e) 13,000.

FLAG: The Naga national flag, the flag of the national movement, is a light blue field with a curving rainbow of narrow red, yellow, and dark blue stripes from the lower hoist to the upper fly, and bearing a white six-pointed star with six white rays on the upper hoist. The flag of the National Socialist Council of Nagaland (NSCN) is a pale blue field bearing a curving rainbow of narrow red, yellow, and green stripes from the lower hoist to the upper fly, and bearing an elongated six-pointed white star on the upper hoist.

PEOPLE AND CULTURE: The Nagas are an Indo-Chinese people thought to be distantly related to the Malay peoples of Southeast Asia.

They are divided into 16 major and 20 minor tribes, the largest being the Angami, Ao, Sema, Konyak, and Chakesang. There are considerable differences in origin, culture, physique, and appearance among the tribal groups. Tribal structures also vary among groups. Traditionally some tribes had powerful hereditary chiefs, while others selected councils of elders. The Naga culture, lacking the rigid caste and class divisions of neighboring peoples, is unique in that men and women enjoy equal status. In the 1990s, drug and alcohol abuse spread through the Naga homeland, where there are few job opportunities for young people.

LANGUAGE AND RELIGION: The Nagas speak several different dialects of a Tibeto-Burman language of the Sino-Tibetan language group. The language is written in the Latin alphabet, a legacy of missionary education. There are 29 Naga languages and dozens of dialects. The major languages are Angami, Ao, Chang, Konyak, Lotha, Sangtam, and Sema, although almost every village has its own dialect. As not all the dialects are mutually intelligible, different groups communicate in broken Assamese, called Nagamese, or sometimes in English. The literary language is based on the Angami dialect, spoken around the Naga capital, Kohima.

The majority of the Nagas are Christians, primarily Baptist, with a large minority adhering to traditional beliefs, and smaller minorities that have adopted the Hindu or Buddhist religions, which dominate in India and Myanmar. Some sources claim that up to 90% of the population are nominally Christian. Since the 1930s, many Nagas were converted to Christianity, and the practice of the old tribal religion is on the wane. The Nagaland Baptist Church Council has over 300,000 members in 1,253 congregations in Nagaland and neighboring regions of India and Myanmar. The traditional supreme being is Gawang, which was easily transferred to the Christian God. Headhunting was once a traditional practice and an important part of the Naga religious ceremonies.

NATIONAL HISTORY: Little is known about the early history of the Nagas or of the origin of several large sandstone pillars at Dimapur. The ancestors of the Nagas are thought to have moved south to their present homeland from Mongolia or Tibet in the tenth century B.C., but they may have originated in Southeast Asia. The Nagas once occupied a much wider area than at present but gradually lost the lowlands to successive waves of invaders. The tribes, concentrated in the high mountain valleys, developed a culture markedly distinct from those of the neighboring peoples, including the important religious and cultural ritual of headhunting.

The Naga tribes, often warring among themselves, never developed a state system. The autonomous tribes at times came under the nominal rule of the powerful Assam or Manipur states. The earliest mention of the Nagas was recorded by the Tai Ahom invaders from present Myanmar, in grudging praise of the fierce Naga resistance. Medieval chronicles of the

Ahom kingdom of Assam tell of the Naga tribes, their customs, and their territory.

The British, after taking control of Assam in 1826, moved into the jungle-covered mountains and made their first contact with the Naga tribes in 1832. The violent encounter prompted the British to withdraw and to ignore the tribes for nearly two decades. The decision to construct a road from Manipur to Burma required the subjugation of the fierce tribes blocking the route. In 1851 a British force burned Kohima and killed some 300 Nagas. "Slaughter and withdraw," became the British policy for dealing with the Naga tribes. Finally subdued in 1881, the various Naga chiefs signed with the British authorities treaties that allowed the British to add their tribal lands to the colonial governments of Assam and Burma.

In the late nineteenth century, European and American missionaries converted a majority of the Nagas to Christianity and introduced modern education through a network of mission schools. A written form of the Naga language devised by missionaries began the process of molding the diverse tribes into a distinct nation. A Christian elite, educated in missionary schools, began to take positions of power in the tribes in the early 1920s. The Naga tribes forged a common group identity under Christian and British colonial influence.

Christian Naga leaders in 1929 demanded the unification of the several Naga districts of India and Burma under a separate administration and asked for a British promise of Naga independence should the British ever quit India. Outraged at the British failure to reply, several of the Naga tribes rebelled; the resulting disturbances continued until World War II. In 1942 the Japanese invaded northeast India and sought to win dissident Nagas with promises of independence. The collaboration of some tribal leaders seriously divided the nascent national movement.

The Naga National Council (NNC), formed during the war by Zapu Phizo to promote Naga interests, in 1945 opened negotiations on separate independence. The Nagas were the first tribal group in India to demand independence. Naga aspirations were respected by the father of independent India, Mohandas Gandhi. Although hoping that the Nagas would eventually join India, he declared, "I do not believe in forced unions. If you [Nagas] do not wish to join the Union of India, nobody will force you to do that."

Pressed by the British authorities to join India, the Nagas refused. On 14 August 1947 the Naga leaders of the NNC declared Nagaland independent of India and Burma, one day before the date set for Indian independence. Immediately after independence Ghandi was assassinated, and the Indian government, instead of fulfilling his promise, refused to recognize Naga independence and sent in the army to crush the separatist movement. Unlike other territories, Nagaland was not specifically included in the Indian Independence Act of 1947, so the Indian military occupation was technically illegal. Phizo and several other NNC leaders were arrested and imprisoned while returning from a meeting with the leaders of the Indian Union. The Nagas, despite mass killings, torture, rape, and daily harassment, resisted until the hard-pressed Naga leaders finally submitted in 1950 to inclusion in India as a district of Assam State.

Dissatisfied with the Indian administration, the Nagas organized a democratic plebiscite on 16 May 1951. The vote overwhelmingly reaffirmed their earlier declaration of independence, but the Indian government refused to accept the plebiscite's result. In 1955 the Nagas again rebelled. The rebels fought the heavily armed Indian troops at first with only bows and arrows, but later, with arms from China and Pakistan, they organized a national army of 40,000 soldiers. In 1956 the 16 tribes set aside their historical differences to form a united provisional government, the Naga Federal Government (NFG). The Indian government responded with the Armed Forces Act, which allowed the security forces broad powers, which were widely abused. The region was virtually cut off from the rest of the world, which received little news of the conflict that reportedly cost over 150,000 lives.

The Indian authorities, unable to subdue the Nagas in their highland jungles, granted them autonomy within Assam in 1960. Following renewed disturbances, the government upgraded the region's status to full statehood in the Indian union in 1962. The new arrangement failed to satisfy Naga demands for unification of all the Naga lands, and the rebellion continued. When Chinese troops invaded northeastern India in 1962, the Naga leaders offered to end their rebellion in return for Indian recognition of a democratic referendum on independence. Rebuffed, the Nagas resumed the rebellion in 1963.

A number of Naga leaders signed in 1975 the Shillong Accord by which India demanded unconditional acceptance of the Indian constitution and a surrender of arms. The accord divided the Naga leadership, leading to the creation of a number of factions. In 1980 militants formed the National Socialist Council of Nagaland (NSCN). Heavy fighting resumed, both between Naga groups and the Indian security forces and between Naga factions.

In 1990 the first nationalist leader, Zapu Phizo, died in exile in the United Kingdom. The loss of the legendary Naga leader set off tribal clashes. There were reports that some Nagas had reverted to traditional headhunting. Intertribal and intergroup conflicts made agreements on independence, autonomy, and negotiations with the Indian government exceedingly difficult.

A Naga campaign to win control of territory, beginning in 1992, focused on driving rival tribes, particularly the Kukis, from disputed territory in Manipur and other areas claimed as Naga national lands, in anticipation of a proposed referendum on reunification and thereafter independence.

The conflict was largely over control of the lucrative heroin trade route. In 1994 violence escalated as Naga nationalists attacked Kuki villages in the northern districts of Manipur. In 1995 the Indian government declared the state of Nagaland a "disturbed area," empowering the armed forces to take drastic measures to regain control.

A crackdown in 1992 by Burmese troops on militant activities of the NSCN sent an influx of refugees into Indian Nagaland. Three years later, activists moved the border posts 10 kilometers inside Myanmar, which would allow the Nagas of the area to claim Indian citizenship. The Myanmar Nagas depended on their kin in India for all of their needs, as Myanmar, under its military dictatorship, was and is the poorest country in the region.

A cease-fire agreement was announced between the NSCN and the government in August 1997, but other groups continued to fight the Indian security forces. The Indian government has claimed that the agreement covered only Nagaland, not all areas where Nagas live in northeastern India. The Naga revolt, overshadowed by the separatist violence in other parts of India and Myanmar, continues to claim lives, mostly unarmed villagers and separatists killed by Indian or Burmese troops. Younger, educated Nagas, keen to preserve their culture and eliminate the tribal and clan divisions that have seriously hampered the independence movement, are now moving into leadership positions. A 1997 referendum in Naga areas reportedly resulted in a 99% vote in favor of independence.

The Nagas and the Indian government agreed to extend the cease-fire in August 1998, but the other issues remained, and the Naga conflict continued. Talks were held between rebel leaders and representatives of the Indian government in New York in October 1998. By the end of 1998, over 20,000 people had been killed in the Naga insurgency, including many in fighting between Naga nationalist factions.

In October 1999 regional elections, several Naga organizations attempted to disrupt voting by intimidation. Federal troops were deployed in five Naga-dominated districts of northern Manipur. The NSCN called for a boycott of the elections in the Manipuri districts of Tamenglong, Senapati, Chandel, Ukhrul, and Churachandpur. The chief minister of Nagaland, S.C. Jamir, narrowly escaped an attempt on his life when suspected terrorists blew up three vehicles of his convoy. The attack on Jamir illustrated the fragile nature of the peace deals negotiated with the various Naga factions.

Naga leaders called a congress of 100 representatives of different sections of the nation in June 1999. Delegates included representatives of Naga nongovernmental organizations, political parties, the churches, and the Naga Hoho, the tribal councils. The congress reiterated the Naga demand for independence, but the government rejected any compromise on India's sovereignty, unity, or integrity in any solution to the Naga problem. The government also rejected demands for the creation of a "greater Nagaland"—to comprise the Naga-inhabited areas of Assam, Arunchal Pradesh, and Manipur. The legislatures of the three neighboring states passed resolutions opposing the integration of their Naga-inhabited areas with Nagaland. Many Burmese Nagas fled into India in September 1999, asserting that the Burmese military government and Buddhist monks were pressuring them to convert to Buddhism.

The Naga nationalists want a solution to the five-decades-old Naga conflict before any new elections are held in Naga populated regions. Negotiations between Naga groups and the Indian government were derailed in February 2000, when a key Naga leader, Thuengaling Muivah, was sentenced to a year in jail in Thailand for violating immigration laws and attempting to flee while on bail. The Naga leaders reiterated that a "sovereign Nagaland is not negotiable" and that Nagaland included all of the Naga-inhabited areas of the neighboring states of Assam, Manipur, Arunchal Pradesh, and Myanmar. Activists in June 2000 threatened to resume the 50-year-old insurgency unless the Indian government formalized a cease-fire agreement in all Naga-inhabited areas of the northeast and lifted the 1998 ban on the NSCN. In the first six months of 2000, over 100 incidents of terrorism were reported. The government extended the Nagaland cease-fire for another year in July 2000 but rejected the Naga demand for an extension of the cease-fire to Naga areas outside the state of Nagaland.

All the Nagaland nationalist groups met in Atlanta on 28 July 2001, following the extention of the cease-fire for yet another year. They met to find a solution to the insurgency which has been plaguing the state for nearly five decades. The Atlanta meeting, sponsored by the Baptist Group of America, was significant in light of the recent truce between the Naga groups to stop fratricidal killings as a step toward the unification of all underground factions for a negotiated settlement of the Naga issue.

SELECTED BIBLIOGRAPHY:

Jacobs, Julian. *The Nagas: Hill Peoples of Northeast India*. 1999.
Mao, Ashikho Daili. *Nagas: Problems and Politics*. 1992.
Singh, K.S., ed. *Nagaland*. 1994.
Steyn, Pieter. *Zapu Phizo: Voice of the Nagas*. 1999.

Navajo

Dine; Dineh; Diné; Navaho

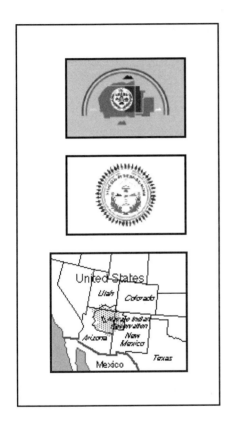

POPULATION: Approximately (2002e) 305,000 Navajo in the United States, concentrated in the southwestern states of Arizona and New Mexico.

THE NAVAJO HOMELAND: The Navajo homeland, called Diné Bikeyah or Dinetah, occupies a vast area of the southwest spreading across parts of Arizona, New Mexico, Colorado, and Utah. The lands of the Navajo encompass an area larger than the states of Massachusetts, Rhode Island, New Jersey, and Connecticut combined. They are mostly arid and generally will not support enough agriculture and livestock to provide a livelihood for everyone. Thousands earn their living away from Navajoland. The lands reserved for the Navajo were originally set aside in 1868 but were subsequently enlarged. *Navajo Reservation (Navajoland/Diné Bikeyah)*: 26,862 sq. mi.—69,572 sq. km, (2002e) 210,000—Navajo 97%, other Americans 3%. The Navajo capital and major cultural center is Window Rock, in Arizona, (2002e) 5,000. The other important cultural center is Shiprock, (2002e) 3,000. Outside the reservation there are important Navajo communities in Flagstaff, Arizona, called Kinlaní by the Navajo, (2002e) 55,000, and Gallup, New Mexico, called Na'nízhoozhí, (2002e) 20,000.

FLAG: The Navajo flag, the official flag of the Navajo Reservation, is a sand-colored field bearing an outline map of the Navajo homeland with the tribal seal centered and surrounded by four mountains of black, white, blue, and yellow at each compass point, surmounted by a rainbow of blue, red, and yellow. The tribal flag is the tribal seal on a white field.

PEOPLE AND CULTURE: The Navajo, who call themselves Diné, which means "the people," are an indigenous people of North America, belonging to the Athapaskan peoples, which also includes the closely related Apache.* The name Navajo was given them by neighboring peoples. Divided into about 60 clans, the Navajo are traditionally a matriarchal people, with descent counted through the female line. Marriage within one's clan was considered incestuous. About a quarter of the Navajo population live outside the boundaries of the reservation, mostly in neighboring areas of Arizona and New Mexico, but increasingly in the large urban areas of the southwestern states. Alcoholism is a chronic problem, and suicide rates are 30% above the national average. More than half the Navajo live below the official poverty line; unemployment is around 35% in urban areas and as high as 50% in the hot, bleak interior of the reservation.

LANGUAGE AND RELIGION: The Navajo language is a Navajo-Apache language of the Na-Dené or Athapaskan language group. The language, called Diné Bizaad, remains closely related to the language of the Apache, in spite of borrowings from Pueblo and Hopi. The language is a tonal language, meaning that pitch helps distinguish words. Nouns in the language are differentiated between "speakers," meaning humans, and "callers," or plants and animals. Because Navajo names are thought to have power, in polite address one avoids speaking another's name. The language has been tenaciously preserved, and most Navajo speak their own language along with English as a second language.

The majority of the Navajo belong to various Christian denominations, with about 20,000 belonging to the Native American Church, which combines Christian and traditional beliefs—including the use of the hallucinogen peyote. The Navajo religious beliefs are embodied in the elders and medicine people, whose mission is spiritual and moral rather than political. The traditional religious system was very intricate. Numerous rites were performed, marking the passing of each year. Most rites were primarily for curing bodily and psychiatric illnesses. In other ceremonies there were prayers or songs, and dry paintings made of pollen, seeds, flower petals, and different colored sands. Peyotism as a religious rite took hold around the 1930s and was approved by the Tribal Council in 1955.

NATIONAL HISTORY: Athapaskan nomads, moving south from their origins in western Canada, moved into the high plateau region of the American southwest around A.D. 1000. They gradually split into several distinct groups, of which the most important became the Navajo and the Apache. The Navajo settled near the agricultural Pueblo peoples, adopting their agriculture, weaving, and sand painting. By about 1500 the Navajo had evolved a distinct culture, a mixture of their Athapaskan heritage and the indigenous traditions of their new homeland in the southwest.

The Navajo, probably numbering no more than 9,000, controlled a vast territory when the Spanish, searching for the legendary cities of gold, reached the area in 1539. Unable to subdue fully the Navajo warriors, the Spanish colonial authorities generally left them to their traditional way of life. Christian missions established across the region had a greater impact than the Spanish administration, especially the introduction of European farming methods and animals. Sheep, unknown to the Navajo, profoundly changed their traditions; they adopted a seminomadic life based on large sheep herds.

By the beginning of the seventeenth century, the Navajo of the Colorado Plateau had achieved a relatively settled way of life. Pueblo* refugees from the Spanish suppression of the Pueblo Revolt settled among the Navajo, reinforcing the settled, agricultural culture. During the eighteenth century, some Hopi left their mesas because of drought and famine and came to live with the Navajo, particularly in Canyon de Chelly in northeastern Arizona.

Toward the end of the seventeenth century, Spanish colonists and Pueblo Indians attempted to establish themselves in territory claimed by the Navajo. The Navajo developed a strategy of spreading into and preying on settled communities to acquire food, sheep, horses, and cattle. The movement of Navajo bands westward into and around Hopi lands seriously threatened the precarious economy of that tribe.

The Navajo lands, under nominal Mexican rule from 1821, were among the territories ceded to the United States in 1848. The historical Navajo resistance to outside rule led to clashes and quickly escalated to war. In 1864, U.S. cavalry led by Kit Carson invaded the Navajo homeland and destroyed everything in its path, including the vast herds of sheep. Captured Navajo families—8,500 men, women, and children—were forced to march from Fort Defiance, in Arizona, to Fort Sumner, in New Mexico, a distance of 350 miles. Those that survived the hardships of the "Long Walk" were imprisoned in a squalid camp for four years before the authorities finally allowed about 8,000 Navajo to return to Arizona in 1868. The destruction of their homeland and the four-year captivity left a legacy of bitterness and distrust that has still not entirely disappeared.

A formal treaty signed in 1868 recognized the Navajo nation in exchange for the cession of huge tracts of land. The Navajo retained a reserve territory of 3.5 million acres. The treaty, its terms soon abrogated, began a century of degradation, humiliation, and neglect. Poor and uneducated, the Navajo could only protest the actions of the Indian Agency, part of the U.S. Department of the Interior, which mostly ignored their grievances. Diseases, crop failures, and attacks by neighboring tribes further reduced their numbers.

Finally provided with sheep and cattle, the Navajo began to prosper moderately. In 1884, the reservation was extended to accommodate their increasing herds. During the late nineteenth century the population doubled, and additional lands were added to the reservation. Since the Navajo lands were generally poor for farming, few attempts were made by outsiders to encroach on them. Greatly increased livestock herds presented serious problems of soil erosion and overgrazing. Eventually a livestock-reduction plan was forced on the Navajo by the U.S. government.

In 1921 the Indian Agency began to give out leases to oil and power companies without consulting the Navajo. The leases, contravening existing laws, began the development of the enormous natural resources of the Navajo reservation lands; the Navajo received nothing. The tribal government was formally organized in 1923, and in 1934 the boundaries of the reservation were established; several areas of primarily Navajo population were added.

Granted U.S. citizenship in 1924, few of the Navajo, uneducated and unable to read or speak English, were equipped to exercise their new rights. In the early 1930s concerted efforts began to end their long isolation. Between 1935 and 1940 an alphabet, devised for the Navajo language, made the spoken dialect a literary language and greatly aided the spread of education in the 1940s and 1950s.

During World War II, 3,600 Navajo served with the U.S. military; their language was used as a battlefield code, one of the few never deciphered by Axis experts. Many others left the reservation to work in nearby cities in war-related jobs. After the war many veterans found work in the uranium mines operating on reservation lands. They were not warned of the dangers or provided protection; the effects of uranium poisoning adversely effected an entire generation.

In spite of continuing poverty, the Navajo birthrate grew spectacularly. By 1950 their numbers had risen to 50,000. Eleven years later, in 1961, they numbered 85,000. In 1980 their numbers had surpassed 150,000, severely straining the limited resources of the reservation lands.

The Navajo began to make progress in education in the 1960s. A young, educated, and more militant tribal leadership introduced Navajo history and language to reservation schools, inaugurated radio in the Navajo language, and founded the first college on a reservation run by a Native American people. Granted self-government on 25 July 1972, the Navajo, for the first time in over a century, were free of outside political control. On the basis of the mineral wealth of the autonomous reservation, the Navajo became one of the world's wealthiest nations, but the wealth was only on paper. The reality of Navajo poverty, unemployment, and neglect remained unchanged.

The Navajo-Hopi Land Settlement Act, passed in 1974, clearly delineated reservation borders in the region but ignored the fact that the two peoples had shared the land since the sixteenth century. The land dispute, which envisioned the relocation of over 12,000 people, the largest forced relocation of an ethnic group since the years immediately after World War II, galvanized the Navajo. Militants formed the Diné Bii Coalition (the Coalition for Navajo Liberation), and in 1977 they joined activists from other tribes to petition the United Nations for recognition as sovereign nations. They petitioned further for the admission of delegates to represent the red race, the only one of the five world races not represented in the world body.

Militants, often comparing their small nation to the republics of the former Soviet Union, threatened in 1991 to declare independence and to take the issue before the United Nations. The majority of the Navajo would be satisfied if the U.S. government would simply honor the terms of the 1868 treaty and address unresolved Navajo land claims. In November 1992 the government unveiled a plan to award lands just outside Navajoland to the Hopi, thus avoiding a confrontation with the growing Navajo national movement.

A former Navajo tribal chairman, Peter Macdonald, was convicted of 16 federal charges of taking bribes and kickbacks to aid businessmen in gaining control of a computer company based on the reservation. He was already serving an almost six-year sentence in a tribal prison for similar offenses. Macdonald's convictions led to demands by many Navajos for a more representative and transparent tribal government.

The U.S. Interior Department, in 1994, announced tentative approval of an agreement that would cede more than 500,000 acres of federal, state, and private land in Arizona to the Hopi tribe. This agreement was meant to settle a bitter and long-standing land dispute between the Hopi and Navajo; the issue dates back to the 1880s, when increasing numbers of Navajo had begun moving into traditional Hopi lands.

In early 1995, the flag of the Navajo nation became the first indigenous American flag to fly into space. It was carried aboard the space shuttle *Discovery* by astronaut Bernard Harris. Dr. Harris, who had lived with the Navajo as a child, had asked for some token to take into space. President Albert Hale of the Navajo nation decided on the flag, upon which medicine men had sprinkled corn pollen.

The Navajo have achieved a political sophistication beyond the reach of smaller indigenous nations, including an official lobby in Washington and their own supreme court. A new generation of university-trained Navajo leaders has resolved to improve the circumstances of their nation, but this time on Navajo terms. They want to reduce the Navajo colonial dependence on the Bureau of Indian Affairs (BIA) and stimulate sustainable economic development.

In November 1999, the National Park Service ruled that the Navajo were descended from the Anasazi, who disappeared 1,300 years ago. The decision was highly controversial, because it laid the groundwork for future claims to Anasazi artifacts under the Native American Graves Protection and Repatriation Act. The Hopi and Pueblo peoples, who also believe themselves descended from the Anasazi and have a historical rivalry with the Navajo, contested the decision as prejudiced, claiming that the Navajo only borrowed from Anasazi culture after it had already died out.

The Navajo Reservation, approximately the size of Ireland, although arid and infertile, sits on 20 billion tons of coal, natural gas, oil, and uranium, while the Navajo experience mass unemployment, alcoholism, disease, and poverty. The differing policies of successive Democratic and Republican administrations have aided or harmed the situation of the Navajo, in either case mostly without consulting them.

Younger militants, tired of the red tape of state, federal, and tribal bureaucracies, are pressing for greater autonomy, particularly economic. They point out that the last time the business-licensing process was "simplified," even more steps were added. Greater autonomy, including the right to conclude economic agreements with foreign governments, would allow the Navajo to compete in the world economy. Others claim that real political and cultural autonomy will only be possible when the Navajo have been weaned from federal and state subsidies and the burden of dual taxation.

In July 2001, having lost their legal appeals, many Navajo at Big Mountain, Arizona were facing removal because they had refused to sign and accept the 1974 Relocation Act and the 1996 Navajo-Hopi Land Dispute Settlement Act. The Hopi Tribal Government began to impound livestock in the disputed areas. Militants charged that the forced removals constituted a form of genocide under the second article of the United Nations 1948 Geneva Convention on Genocide.

SELECTED BIBLIOGRAPHY:

Bonvillain, Nancy. *The Navajo: People of the Southwest*. 1995.
Garrick, Alan Bailey. *A History of the Navajo: The Reservation Years*. 1999.
Goodman, James M. *The Navajo Atlas: Environments, Resources, People, and History of the Navajo Bikeyah*. 1987.
Iverson, Peter J. *Navajo*. 1990.

Ndebele

Zambezis; Matabele; Tabele; Tebele; Northern Ndebele

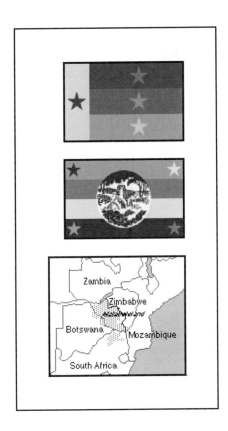

POPULATION: Approximately (2002e) 2,610,000 Ndebele in Zimbabwe, concentrated in the Matabeleland region in southern and western Zimbabwe. There are around 800,000 Ndebele, called Transvaal Ndebeles or ama-Ndebeles, in Northern and Mpumalanga provinces of South Africa, and some 300,000 in Botswana.

THE NDEBELE HOMELAND: The Ndebele homeland, Matabeleland, occupies the southern African plains between the Zambezi and Limpopo Rivers in southwestern Zimbabwe. Most of the region is rolling farm and grazing lands, rising to the Matapos Hills near Buyawayo. The homeland includes the southwestern portion of Zimbabwe's High and Middle Velds, plateau country contains the majority of the population. Matabele forms the Zimbabwean provinces of Matabeleland North, Matabeleland South, and Gweru district of Midlands province. *Region of Matabeleland*: 58,214 sq. mi.—150,813 sq. km, (2002e) 3,106,000—Ndebele 83%, Kalanga 6%, Shona 5%, other Zimbabweans 6%. The Ndebele capital and major cultural center is Bulawayo, (2002e) 813,000, metropolitan area 1,116,000. Other important cultural centers are Gweru, (2002e) 169,000, and Francistown, (2002e) 104,000, the center of the Botswana Ndebele. The center of the South African Ndebele is the town of Ekangala, (2002e) 8,000.

FLAG: The Ndebele national flag is a horizontal tricolor of black, red, and green, each stripe charged with a centered five-pointed star respectively red, green, and yellow, and with a broad yellow vertical stripe at the hoist charged with a black five-pointed star. The flag of the former Zimbabwe African People's Union (ZAPU) has four horizontal stripes of red, green, yellow, and black, the red charged with a black five-pointed star on the upper hoist and a yellow star on the upper fly, the black stripe charged with a red star on the lower hoist and a green star on the lower fly. The flag has a centered disc in yellow and black showing a scene of the ruins of ancient Zimbabwe.

PEOPLE AND CULTURE: The Ndebele, also called Matabele, are a Nguni people related to the Zulu* of KwaZulu-Natal in South Africa. The descendents of nineteenth-century Zulu migrants and the area's original Bantu peoples, the Ndebele have retained much of their original Nguni culture. Dispersed family homesteads called *kraals* remain the preferred way of life, although an increasing number have urbanized since the 1970s. Traditionally Ndebele men cared for the herds, while women had charge of farming. The related Kalangas, numbering about 160,000, are rapidly being assimilated into Ndebele society.

LANGUAGE AND RELIGION: The Ndebele language, isiNdebele, is classified as an Nguni language, related to the languages of the Zulus, although in some areas of South Africa Sotho influences are strong enough that isiNdebele is sometimes classified as a variant of seSotho. The language forms part of the Nguni group of Bantu languages of the Niger-Congo language family. Most urbanized Ndebeles, particularly in the Bulawayo metropolitan area, speak English as a second language. Many also speak Shona, the language of education and government. The Kalanga language, related to Shona, is being replaced by Ndebele in many areas of Kalanga territory southwest of the Ndebele.

Most Ndebele adhere to the various Christian sects, with traditional beliefs still followed in the more remote rural regions. Nineteenth-century missionary activities did little to change religious beliefs, but by the 1920s the majority of the Ndebele were at least nominally Christian. An important element of traditional religious customs was the institution of priestesses, older women thought to be prophets. These priestesses, called *igoso*, channel information between the Ndebele and their spirit ancestors, who in turn would pass on the prayers and wishes to the high god known as Nkulunkulu.

NATIONAL HISTORY: The Ndebeles originated as a group of related tribes in the Natal region of South Africa. Some of the tribes began migrating northward in the eighteenth century, although the formation of the Ndebele as a nation began with Mzilikazi, a Zulu military leader under the Zulu king Chaka or Shaka. In 1823 Mzilikazi gathered a large following as disputes erupted among Zulu factions. In 1827 he and his followers fled over the Drakensburg Mountains into the upland plains of Transvaal. Reinforced by Zulu deserters, the tribe coalesced into a formidable power, raiding as far south as the Orange River, destroying or absorbing conquered tribes.

Moving west, the Ndebele clashed repeatedly with Boer militiamen escorting wagon trains of settlers moving north from the Cape of Good

Hope. Threatened by the Boers, later called Afrikaners,* and by resurgent Zulus, many of the Ndebele moved north of the Limpopo River in 1837. Those that stayed in South Africa were called the Transvaal Ndebeles. In South Africa the Afrikaner leader Paul Kruger jailed or executed many Ndebele leaders, seized their lands, and dispersed others to work for Afrikaner farmers as indentured servants.

The highly sophisticated Ndebele military formations that moved north easily conquered the more numerous, pastoral Shona people. The conquerors established a large, highly centralized kingdom and controlled approximately 30,000 square miles (77,700 sq. km) of territory. The Ndebele ruled as the kingdom's pastoral aristocracy; the more numerous Shona were reduced to a serflike condition, forced to pay an annual tribute in cattle. The conquest of the Shona created an ethnic enmity that continues to the present.

Courted by both the British and the Boers of the Transvaal, Lobengula, a descendant of Mzilikazi, finally signed a treaty with the British in 1880. The treaty gave Cecil Rhodes and the British South Africa Company exclusive rights over all minerals in Matabeleland in return for £100 a month, a thousand modern rifles, and a steamboat on the Zambezi River. Assured that no more than 10 European miners would enter Ndebele territory, Lobengula was dismayed to learn that a column of 600 Europeans had crossed the frontier. The British column constructed Fort Salisbury, present Harare, in the center of the lands of the subject Shona. The British presence effectively ended the Ndebele domination of the Shona in 1889.

In 1891 the British declared protectorates over Matabeleland, Mashonaland, and Bechunaland, later called Botswana. Rhode's British South Africa Company offered 3,000-acre farms to lure European colonists, who boldly seized lands and cattle from both the Ndebele and their former Shona subjects.

Lobengula vainly attempted to avoid armed conflict, but unscrupulous Europeans, believing that the kingdom contained massive gold deposits, provoked war in July 1893. The Ndebele warriors, joined by the Shona, attacked fortified British positions, only to be mowed down by the first machine gun ever used in battle. By November 1893, the famous and previously undefeated Ndebele *impis*, or regiments, had mostly surrendered to the Europeans. In January 1894 British troops occupied the Ndebele capital at Bulawayo.

Lobengula, a victim of naked European aggression, died in late January 1894, a hunted exile in the mountains. Following Lobengula's death the kingdom collapsed, and the British took complete control of the region, offering parcels of confiscated land to European settlers. The imposition of colonial rule through military conquest completely destroyed the traditional Ndebele political structure. Ndebele nobles, artists, and warriors were reduced to selling their ostrich feather headgear to Europeans on the streets of Bulawayo.

In 1914, the Matabele National Home Society was created to work for an autonomous Ndebele homeland, the first of its kind in southern Africa. In 1923 the British authorities dissolved Matabeleland's separate colonial government and joined the province to Shonaland to form the colony of Southern Rhodesia. Although the British favored the Shona of the colony, the two nations were often united in opposition to the colonial authorities. Increasingly restrictive race laws and resentment of European privilege erupted in a general strike and violence in 1948, the first violence in Bulawayo since 1896.

In 1961 a Council of Chiefs and Assemblies Act was passed in Rhodesia giving local chiefs a policy-making role in the white-dominated government. The council was made up of equal numbers of Shona and Ndebele, with each group having five members. Many Shona resented the move, which gave the less numerous Ndebele an equal say in the council. The council and other initiatives to allow indigenous participation in the country was soon overcome by the growing anticolonial movement.

Joshua Nkomo, a young Ndebele trade unionist, formed the first nationalist organization in Matabeleland in 1957. In the name of African unity, Nkomo's nationalists joined the Shona-dominated Zimbabwe African National Union (ZANU). Differences among the Ndebele and Shona leaders led to the Ndebele withdrawal in 1963 from ZANU and the formation of the rival Zimbabwe African People's Union (ZAPU) as the focus of Ndebele nationalism. Both nationalist groups established bases in neighboring states and launched attacks on Rhodesia, which was unilaterally declared an independent white-ruled republic in 1965. The Ndebele and Shona groups, backed by Russia and China respectively, often fought among themselves. The anticolonial war cost over 35,000 lives before it finally began to wind down in 1979. The long and vicious guerrilla war came to a negotiated end in 1980, and white Rhodesia became the new African state of Zimbabwe.

The new Zimbabwe government, dominated by the larger Shona tribe, rapidly alienated the Ndebele minority. The Ndebele claimed that they had sacrificed too much for Zimbabwe's independence to fall under the rule of their former Shona serfs. Overriding Ndebele nationalist protests, Joshua Nkomo opted for peaceful unification and merged ZAPU into the Shona-dominated ZANU.

In South Africa, under the apartheid system, the Ndebeles were assigned to a bantustan called KwaNdebele, carved out of land that had been given to the son of Nyabela, a renowned warrior of Kruger's time. KwaNdebele was declared a self-governing territory in 1981, although only about a third of the Ndebele population in South Africa lived in the region. Most Ndebeles lived and worked in the Pretoria and Johannesburg urban areas.

In 1981, amid rising tension between the two peoples, Ndebele national leaders demanded autonomy for Matabeleland. The Zimbabwe government rejected autonomy as fighting broke out between Ndebele nationalists and Shona military units. Deserting Ndebele soldiers formed guerrilla groups as the fighting spread. In 1982 the Zimbabwean leader, Robert Mugabe, accused the Ndebele of separatism and dismissed Joshua Nkomo and other Ndebele government officials. Nkomo fled to exile in London but remained the leader of the Ndebele. As the Ndebele moved toward secession, an elite Shona battalion, known as the Fifth Brigade, trained in North Korea, unleashed a terror campaign across Matabeleland. Many Shonas saw the suppression of the Ndebele as revenge for nineteenth-century Ndebele raids. Between 10,000 and 20,000 Ndebele died in the "killing fields" between 1982 and 1985, yet the Mugabe government pardoned those responsible.

Serious negotiations began in an effort to avert all-out civil war. In 1985 Nkomo returned from exile and resumed his leadership of ZAPU. Talks between tribal leaders to end the violence stalled over the Shona leadership's insistence on a one-party state, at a time when many African states were beginning to move toward multiparty democracy. Nkomo signed a unity accord in 1987 under which ZAPU was absorbed by the ruling ZANU-PF party, and he became one of two vice presidents of the country. Matabaleland was at peace but remained Zimbabwe's least developed region.

In 1991 the Zimbabwe government, beset by growing unrest and economic problems, finally introduced a multiparty system and renounced its former socialist economics. The moves temporarily eased tension, but in December 1993 many Ndebele leaders, including the governor of North Matabeleland, charged the increasingly authoritarian Zimbabwean government, amid an upsurge of Ndebele national sentiment, with ethnic discrimination and unfair division of development funds.

In 1994 the homelands in South Africa were abolished, and KwaNdebele became part of a unified South Africa under a majority government. The estimated 800,000 Ndebele in the region after the end of apartheid reestablished cultural and linguistic ties to the Ndebeles of Zimbabwe and Botswana.

Zimbabwe has been run by one party, ZANU-PF, under one leader, Robert Mugabe, since independence in 1980. His rule in the late 1990s grew ever more incompetent and autocratic. In 1998, while urban poor were rioting over food prices, a fleet of new Mercedes was being ordered for the 50 top cabinet ministers. In late 1999, with chronic fuel shortages, inflation running at over 70%, a huge foreign debt, rampant cronyism, suspended foreign aid programs, and an extremely expensive military involvement in the civil war in the Democratic Republic of Congo, Mugabe increasingly baited the country's minorities—the Ndebeles, whites, and other groups, such as homosexuals. He finally hit on a strategy to end the unrest and reunite the increasingly antagonistic Shonas and Ndebeles: the confiscation of the white-owned commercial farms without compensation, and redistribution of the land to the veterans of the anticolonial war of the 1970s.

Ndebele nationalism, dormant since the late 1980s, was invigorated by the growing power vacuum in Zimbabwe. On 10 July 1999, Joshua Nkomo, the unofficial "father of Zimbabwe," died, and with him the long-term compromise between the Ndebele and Shona. A new round of assertive demands was put forward by Nkomo's successors, including compensation for the victims of the massacres carried out by the Fifth Brigade in the 1980s. Dumiso Dabengwa, a government minister and the new leader of the Ndebele, was increasingly at odds with President Mugabe.

A group of young Ndebele professionals revived the old ZAPU party, rechristened ZAPU 2000, and called for a federal system that would allow for Ndebele autonomy. The new ZAPU proposed to divide the country into a federation of five provinces, with greater autonomy and equality. They accused the Mugabe government of marginalizing the Ndebeles while government corruption and cronyism enriched the Shona political elite. Ndebele militants claimed that they were three times more prosperous in 1980 than in 2000. Militants, mostly in exile in South Africa, proposed secession from Zimbabwe and the unification of the traditional Ndebele lands of South African and Zimbabwe into an new state.

The Ndebele continue to charge the Shona-dominated government of discrimination. The civil service in Matabeleland is between 80 and 90% non-Ndebele, and the majority do not speak the Ndebele language. Educational services are very poor. Discrimination increased during the crisis of 1999–2000, with the Ndebeles and the whites vilified as foreigners and anti-Zimbabwean.

A Shona veterans' organization began to occupy white farms, often evicting or beating the owners and their families. The violence, internationally condemned, spread across the country and soon extended to the political opposition, including many Ndebele politicians. By mid-2000, Zimbabwe was near economic collapse, and political turmoil was increasing daily.

In general elections in June 2000, Mugabe's ZANU-PF carried the dominant rural Shona population, which allowed him to remain as president, but his party lost heavily in the urban areas and in Matabeleland. The election, marked by intimidation and violence, instead of reaffirming Mugabe's wobbling regime, further divided the country. The country's economic depression, worsened by Mugabe's illegal takeover of white-owned farms, continued to aggravate the region's growing poverty and to underscore the Ndebele grievance that Matabeleland has been neglected and remains underdeveloped.

The heir to the ancient kingdom of the Ndebeles in Matabeleland, in mid-2001 asserted his right to rebuild the Ndebele monarchy. Peter Komalu, Lobengula's great-grandson, is rebuilding the old royal compound near Bulawayo and hopes to revive the Ndebele monarchy and nation.

In September 2001, in spite of vote-buying and rigging on the part of the Mugabe government, the Ndebele voters supported opposition candidates for local government, particularly in the city of Bulawayo. Increasing instability in Zimbabwe fuels the resurgence of Ndebele nationalism as the country totters. Repression and violence continued to impede the growth of Ndebele separatism, but nationalism is increasingly seen as an alternative to the oppressive Zimbabwean state.

Activists of the ZANU-PF political party in Bulawayo attacked opposition political party headquarters and Ndebele cultural and political sites in November 2001. The violence spread throughout the city, with fighting between Ndebeles and the mainly Shona ZANU-PF militants. In early December, several members of the American government called for sanctions to force the Mugabe government to end the growing violence before the country disintegrates further.

SELECTED BIBLIOGRAPHY:

Beach, David. *The Shona and Their Neighbors.* 1994.
Rasmussen, Kent. *Historical Dictionary of Zimbabwe.* 1990.
Schneider, E.A. *Ndebele.* 1997.
Williams, R.H. *Matabeleland Problem: Confrontation in Zimbabwe.* 1983.

Neapolitans
Southern Italians

POPULATION: Approximately (2002e) 11,800,000 Neapolitans in Italy, concentrated in the southern regions of the Italian Peninsula. Outside the region there are Neapolitan communities in France, Switzerland, Germany, Belgium, and the United Kingdom. There are sizable Neapolitan populations in Argentina, Uruguay, Brazil, and other parts of Latin America, in the United States, and in Australia.

THE NEAPOLITAN HOMELAND: The Neapolitan homeland, popularly called the Mezzogiorno but referred to as Ausonia by nationalists, lies in the southern half of the Italian Peninsula, comprising the provinces that were formerly part of the kingdom of Naples—Abruzzi, Basilicata, Calabria, Campania, Molise, and Puglia. The region is traversed by the southern Apennines, which rise in northern Italy. Much of the land is still held by large absentee landowners. The region, called Southern Italy, or Naples (after the old kingdom), has no official status in Italy. *Southern Italy/Naples (Ausonia)*: 28,280 sq. mi.—73,224 sq. km, (2002e) 14,414,000—Neapolitans 77%, Sicilians* 10%, other Italians 13%. The Neapolitan capital and major cultural center is Naples, called Napoli locally, (2002e) 992,000, metropolitan area 3,624,000. Other important cultural centers are Bari, in Puglia, (2002e) 331,000, and Reggio di Calabria, (2002e) 179,000.

FLAG: The Neapolitan national flag, the flag of the national movement, has nine yellow and red horizontal stripes bearing a blue canton on the upper hoist bearing a mythical head and three legs. The flag of the Ausonia Movement is a white field bearing a centered orange disc bearing blue waves and crossed black and green spears. The traditional flag of the Neapolitan region is a horizontal bicolor of red over yellow.

PEOPLE AND CULTURE: The Neapolitans are the descendents of the peoples of the former Kingdom of Naples in southern Italy. Although collectively they are known by the name "Neapolitan," there are great regional differences between the peoples, particularly between those of Abruzzi and Molise in central Italy and the inhabitants of regions in the far south of the peninsula. Across the region living standards differ, as do people's capacities for thinking in the categories of responsibility and political maturity. The national character of the Neapolitans has been shaped by their distinct history, the tradition of large landholdings, and more recently by collective opposition to the policies of Rome and the northern Italians. Organized crime, which grew from poverty and past injustices, remains a serious problem and continues to deter investment in the region. The major groups include the Camorra in Naples and Campania, the 'Ndrangheta in Calabria, and the United Sacred Crown in Puglia.

LANGUAGE AND RELIGION: The Neapolitans speak a Romance language called Neapolitan-Calabreze, which is spoken in three major dialects and many regional varieties. The language is not intelligible to speakers of standard Italian; many of its speakers do not speak the Italian national language, particularly in rural areas. The use of the language remains vigorous, and attempts are under way to standardize its usage and teaching. There is a large amount of literature, written mostly in the Neapolitan dialect. The dialects associated with Neapolitan in the northern regions differ considerably from the Calabreze dialects spoken in Calabria, Basilicata, and Puglia. The other regional dialects are Aquilano, Abruzzese, Pugliese, and Milisano, spoken in the eastern parts of the peninsula. An estimated half the population of the region uses the one of local dialects as their first language.

The Neapolitans are overwhelmingly Roman Catholic; the religion forms an integral part of the regional culture. Although the influence of the church has declined, church holidays remain an integral part of daily life. In recent decades evangelical sects have been making inroads.

NATIONAL HISTORY: The southern part of the Italian Peninsula was early conquered and colonized by Greeks, who founded cities and established Greek culture throughout the region. The city of Naples was founded by refugees from a fallen Greek city on the site of ancient Parthenope. The settlement, called the new city, Neapolis, grew into one of the most important of the Greek cities.

Romans, expanding from central Italy, conquered the Greek city-states in the fourth century B.C. The Romans established a tradition of large landholdings, often owned by absentee landowners, that survives to the present.

In the sixth century A.D., southern Italy passed to Byzantine rule, but the region soon broke up into several small duchies, including the duchy of Naples. Conquered by the Normans* in the eleventh century, the area was incorporated into their kingdom of Sicily. The region passed to the Hohenstaufens in the twelfth century. In 1268, the region was taken by Duke Charles of Anjou. When Sicily passed to the Aragonese* in 1282, the separate kingdom of Naples was created by the Angevins. Naples and Sicily were reunited under Alfonso V of Aragon, the self-styled king of the Two Sicilies, between 1443 and 1458, but the two territories were again separated again upon his death.

Rival French and Spanish claims to the kingdom of Naples in the late fifteenth century led to armed conflict. The French occupied the kingdom, leading to the temporary partition of Neapolitan territories and finally to the Spanish conquest of the kingdom in 1503. The Spanish reunited Naples and Sicily. Under the terms of the Treaty of Utrecht in 1713 the region was ceded to the Austrian Hapsburgs, but it was reconquered by the Spanish Bourbons in 1734. The Bourbons reestablished the Kingdom of the Two Sicilies.

The French invasion of Italy by Napoleon in 1798 forced the Bourbon monarch to flee. Napoleon again partitioned the region, including Naples in the French-dominated Parthenopean Republic in 1799. The Bourbons, with the aid of an English squadron under Lord Horatio Nelson, returned to Naples, where they carried out severe reprisals against those who had supported the revolution. In 1806 King Ferdinand and Queen Marie Caroline were again driven from Naples by a French invasion. Joseph Napoleon, made king by his brother, was replaced in 1808 by Joachim Murat, the husband of Napoleon's sister Carolina. Murat's beneficent reforms were revoked after his fall and execution in 1815 by Ferdinand, who was restored to the throne of Naples.

The two crowns of Naples and Sicily were officially merged by King Ferdinand in 1816. A revolt in Naples in 1820–21 forced King Ferdinand to grant a constitution, but the uprising was suppressed with the aid of Austrian military forces; his absolute powers were restored in March 1821. The reactionary regimes that followed were increasingly unpopular with the Neapolitans. Most Neapolitans supported Giuseppe Garibaldi's expedition, which, beginning with his landing in Sicily, finally swept the Bourbons from power in Naples in 1860. The Neapolitan territories were incorporated into the new Italian kingdom.

The diversity of the new Italian kingdom's component regions as well as the resentment against the growing influence of the north-Italian Piedmont convinced the kingdom's leaders that some measure of devolution ought to be granted. The Farini-Minghetti Bill was prepared in 1861 and was approved by the cabinet, but it was withdrawn when it became clear that centrifugal forces, particularly in the Neapolitan southern provinces, could jeopardize the newly unified kingdom. The danger of Italy splitting into its constituent parts forced even the most liberal of government ministers to impose a uniform administrative system.

The most pressing issue for the ruling class after unification was how to "harmonize" regional differences. The centralized system had shown the weakness of the agrarian and industrial bourgeoisie that had been the driving force behind unification. In place of the decentralizing Farini-Minghetti Bill, the government passed a law in 1865 that introduced a rigid prefectorial system along Napoleonic lines. The prefecture became the representative of executive power at both local and provincial level.

The adoption of a Tuscan dialect as the national language was widely rejected in southern Italy, where regional dialects were virtually unintelligible to Tuscan speakers. In 1870, only about 10% of Italy's population spoke the new standard Italian; over 90% of the Neapolitans continued to use the Neapolitan-Calabreze dialect.

In the late nineteenth century poverty, regional conflicts, and corruption (particularly associated with the Camorra, the Neapolitan Mafia) remained widespread. Malaria, malnutrition, and illiteracy forced hundreds of thousands of Neapolitans to emigrate. Many sailed to North America, where Neapolitan communities grew up in New York, Montreal, and other eastern cities. Others, unable to meet the requirements for immigration for the United States or Canada, left for Argentina, Uruguay, and southern Brazil. The Neapolitan diaspora maintained close ties to the homeland, and remittances from overseas Neapolitans became a mainstay of the regional economy.

Italy's entry into World War II in 1915, following Allied promises of territory from the Austro-Hungarian Empire, led to conscription riots in southern Italy, where many people felt that the war was for territory in northern Italy and had little to do with them. The resentment of conscription and the confiscation of crops and goods led to serious demonstrations and violence in 1918–19.

Fascism's rise to power in Italy was partly due to the overly centralized character of the Italian state. Neapolitans widely supported Benito Mussolini, the Fascist leader, with his calls for the return of ancient glory. It was not until the end of the Second World War that administrative decentralization was once again seriously considered, partly due to rising regionalism in both northern and southern Italy. Many felt that a more balanced division of power would prevent the recurrence of authoritarianism, such as the former Fascist government. Despite these aspirations, there was no clear answer to the demands for regional autonomy. The powerful socialist and communist parties were particularly suspicious of any form of federalism. The result was the 1948 Italian constitution, which established regions with very limited legislative powers. In spite of demands for a united Naples, to include all the territory south of Rome, the historic region was split into six administrative regions.

The economic and social changes of the 1960s reopened the question of Neapolitan autonomy. The emergence of new social and interest groups alongside the traditional Neapolitan elite and the still-powerful Camorra was accompanied by the success of leftist political parties that favored regional autonomy and an end to the Christian Democrats' monopoly of political power in Italy. The grant of regional autonomy in 1972 coincided with the beginning of European integration and demands across northern Italy for an end to the government subsidies that had sustained southern Italy but had also enriched the Camorra and other illegal organizations and supported widespread corruption. Vast amounts of money earmarked for Neapolitan development had gone instead to strengthen the political bases of leading politicians.

In the 1970s and 1980s, unlike the northern and central Italian peoples, who were dissatisfied with the central government but favored their regional governments, the Neapolitans were dissatisfied with all levels of government. Alongside their traditions, the low level of economic development, uneven distribution of resources, and corruption were the major reasons for the growth of Neapolitan regionalism. The differences between the Neapolitans and the rest of Italy—differences referred to as the "Southern Question"—had widened since the 1950s, when the industrialization of the north had further divided the country. Between 1945 and 1970, an estimated 4 million left the region for northern Italy, other parts of Europe, or the Americas.

In the late 1980s the Northern League, popular in Lombardy and other northern regions, campaigned for a federal state in Italy or, failing that, secession of the northern regions as part of the growing European Economic Community (EEC). The nationalists in northern Italy believe that northern and southern Italy represent two distinct and nonconverging societies that ought to go it alone; this view resonated among the Neapolitans.

Paradoxically, the revival of national sentiment based on traditional regions took place at a time when Italy had reached a high degree of cultural homogeneity, particularly from a linguistic point of view. Although the Neapolitan-Calabreze dialect had not disappeared, census results in the early 1990s indicated that standard Italian had become dominant, that the majority was able to speak both standard Italian and a local dialect. Its was not linguistic "nostalgia" that provoked demands for Neapolitan autonomy. Rather, it was the deterioration of political institutions, the growth of organized crime, and endemic corruption in business transactions involving party, regional, and state officials. Resentment of northern nationalists, who blamed the "Neapolization" or "Southernization" of the Italian state—that is, the emergence of a widespread corrupt and clientelistic system of government—fueled the growth of Neapolitan nationalism and regional movements in the Mezzogiorno.

Regional policy and regional development schemes since the early 1950s have failed to solve the basic north–south divide, but there were also other differences between the regions. The collapse of the socialist and Christian Democratic parties following a series of scandals created new divisions in the country in terms of political behavior, with the possible consequence of a more drastic political split. The growing regionalist response to nationalism in northern Italy and south of Rome were partly a political backlash to Rome's inefficient government, but their basis remains the underdevelopment of the entire territory. The absence of an indigenous entrepreneurial culture and the lack of resources, as well as pervasive corruption, doomed all efforts to raise the Neapolitan homeland to the industrial and social levels of the regions north of Rome. The Cassa per il Mezzogiorno, a state within a state that dispensed huge handouts to the south, was finally closed down in 1993.

In the 1990s, the regional split in Italy led to electoral victories by the Northern League and associated groups in the North, the Democratic Party of the Left (PDS) in the center, and several heterogeneous coalitions in the south, generally made up of regional parties and anti-Mafia and anti-Camorra alliances. In some areas of the south, however, the vote-controlling traditional political machinery survived almost unscathed.

More than 40 years of government subsidies and regional policy have left southern Italy at best modernized, but not developed. There is now a growing consensus across the region that there must be an end to indiscriminate subsidies and centrally controlled handouts. Much of the land is still held by large absentee landowners. By 2000 the differences between northern and southern Italy were no less than they had been in the 1960s, and the gap was again widening. Productivity of Neapolitan labor has been stuck at around 80% of that of the north since 1970. In the 1990s, the southern growth rate was only half that of the north. Activists claim that the south still suffers from its traditional inertia, obedience to authority, and a lack of enterprise, the results of 140 years of paternalistic government.

National fiscal austerity required to qualify for monetary union in Europe led to cuts in public spending in the Mezzogiorno equivalent to roughly 5% of local output. The phasing out of special tax breaks for Neapolitan manufacturers, which broke European Union (EU) rules on state aid, was another blow to the region. Combined with cuts in state-owned industries, these measures eliminated thousands of jobs in the region leading to tension and greater support for self-government and control of the local economy.

Since 1992, Italian governments have not been as dependent on local potentates in the Mezzogiorno as formerly. The election reform of 1994 further limited the previously chronic cronyism and nepotism. The loss of the funds formerly dispensed by local political bosses allowed a break with the traditional system and the growth of movements that would have been unthinkable a decade before, such as the Ausonia Movement, which seeks autonomy for the Neapolitan regions.

The worst effect of the dependence on regional aid had been to debilitate Neapolitan enterprise. Local businessmen looked to public contracts, not export markets. Workers sought the lifetime security of jobs in the public sector. Most Neapolitans accept that aid has failed and that organized crime has been toxic; they are starting to believe that private enterprise and the EU will finally end the backwardness and underdevelopment of their homeland. Where once emigration was the answer, Neapolitans, except the most highly qualified, are now staying where they can depend on extended families, and where housing is less expensive than where the jobs are, in the north.

Nationalists formed the Lega Sud (the Southern League), and the Movement for the Autonomy of the Two Sicilies in the mid-1990s. Claiming that the south had suffocated by the state, nationalists wanted widespread autonomy and eventually independence within the EU. The movements' aim is to form a single political block representing the entire southern part of the Italian Peninsula, realizing the interests of those peoples who originally belonged to the Kingdom of the Two Sicilies—a European state that flourished in southern Italy for eight hundred years. Although the Sicilians have shown little interest, the movement has won support across the southern peninsula. Militants call for secession and the creation of a Federal Republic of Ausonia, the name given to the Neapolitan regions by nationalists. The more moderate leaders of the national movement want the Neapolitans to become an autonomous nation within the EU and to end the politics the region has suffered from since Italian unification.

SELECTED BIBLIOGRAPHY:

Carello, Adrian N. *The Northern Question: Italy's Participation in the European Economic Community and the Mezzogiorno's Underdevelopment.* 1989.

Chubb, J. *Patronage, Power and Poverty in Southern Italy.* 1990.

Hine, David. *Governing Italy: The Politics of Bargained Pluralism.* 1992.

Levy, Carl, ed. *Italian Regionalism: History, Identity and Politics.* 1996.

Nenets

N'enet's'aî; N'enyts; Nentsy; Hasavans; Hasaba; Hasawa; Yuraks; Yurak Samoyeds; Khasova; Nenec; Nenetz

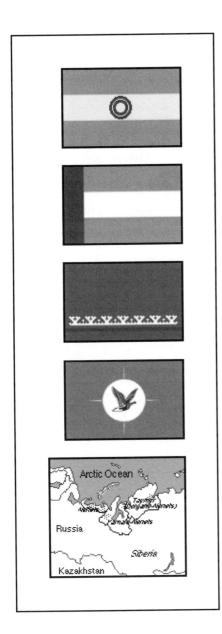

POPULATION: Approximately (2002e) 42,000 Nenets in Russia, mainly in the Nenets, Yamalo-Nenets, and Taimyr (Dolgano-Nenets) Autonomous Districts in northern Russia. If the small, related groups—the Enets, Selkups, and Nganasans—are counted, the national population numbers over 50,000.

THE NENETS HOMELAND: The Nenets homeland occupies an enormous region of tundra, taiga, and permafrost just north of the tree line. The region lies almost entirely within the Arctic Circle, stretching from the Kola Peninsula in northwestern European Russia to the Taimyr Peninsula in north-central Siberia. The region, which includes a number of large islands in the Kara and Laptev Seas of the Arctic Ocean, is covered by snow for up to 260 days a year. The Nenets homeland comprises three autonomous districts of the Russian Federation—Nenets, Yamalo-Nenets, and Taimyr. *Nenets Autonomous Okrug (Nenëtsie Avtonomnyj Ñokruk)*: 68,224 sq. mi.—176,600 sq. km, (2002e) 46,000—Russians 68%, Nenets 17%, Komis 10%, Enets, Nganasan, and others 5%. *Yamalo-Nenets Autonomous Okrug (Jamaly'-Nenëtsie Avtonomnyj Ñokruk)*: 289,691 sq. mi.—750,300 sq. km, (2002e) 493,000—Russians 77%, Ukrainians 8%, Nenets 4%, others 11%. "Yamal" means the "end of nowhere" in the Nenets language. *Taimyr (Dolgano-Nenets) Autonomous Okrug (Dolgany-Nenëtsie Avtonomnyj Ñokruk)*: 332,857 sq. mi.—862,100 sq. km, (2002e) 41,000—Russians 81%, Dolgans 11%, Nenets 8%. The Nenet capital and major cultural center is Nar'yan Mar, called Njar'jana

Mar' in the Nenets language, (2002e) 19,000. The other important cultural centers are Salehard, called Sal- ja'xarad, (2002e) 33,000, and Dudinka, called Dudinkê or Kojkë, (2002e) 26,000.

FLAG: The Nenets national flag has three horizontal stripes of pale blue, white, and pale blue charged with two concentric red rings centered. The flag of the Nenets Autonomous Region has three stripes of pale blue, white, and pale blue with a vertical red stripe at the hoist. The flag of Yamalo-Nenets is a pale blue field with a red stripe and a traditional white design on the lower half. The flag of Taimyr is a pale blue field bearing a black, white, and red goose in flight.

PEOPLE AND CULTURE: The Nenets, formerly called Yurak Samoyeds, are the largest of several related peoples living in Arctic Russia. Their name means "real people" in their language. Traditionally the Nenets were nomadic reindeer herders, but most now live in settled communities. The two major divisions of the Nenets are the Tundra Nenets in the north, and the Forest Nenets, also known as Khandeyar, in the southern districts. A third group, the Komi Nenets, has emerged as a result of intermarriages between Nenets and the Izhmi subgroup of the Komis.* A strong and enduring people, the Nenets resisted suppression and assimilation under dictatorship and communist rule, but that resistance cost many lives. The pollution of heavy metals has been transferred to humans through mosses and reindeer meat and has become a severe health risk. The average life expectancy of the Nenets is only 45 to 50 years, and the suicide rate is unusually high. Nearly 60% of the Nenet adults are unemployed, while most others work in jobs with low qualifications. In 2000 the first feature film in the Nenets language, *Seven Songs from the Tundra*, was made by a Nenets filmmaker living in Finland.

LANGUAGE AND RELIGION: The Nenets speak a Samoyed language called N'enytsia vada, in the Finno-Ugrian (Uralic) language group. There are two major dialects, Tundra Nenets and Forest Nenets, and numerous subdialects, due to the vast national territory. The language was formerly called Yurak, but the name is now considered derogatory. Tundra Nenets is spoken in the northern regions, while Forest Nenets is spoken in the southern Yamal Nenets region and in the Khanty-Mansi region. Although the Soviet system almost eliminated illiteracy, very few Nenets receive an adequate formal education. The Nenets written language was created in 1932 on the basis of the Latin alphabet, which was replaced in 1937 with the Russian Cyrillic alphabet. The literary language is based on the Tundra dialect. In 1989 about 77% of the Nenets listed their own language as their first language, but since then the Nenets reculturation has revitalized the language.

The majority of the Nenets adhere to traditional beliefs; only about 4% belong to various Christian denominations, mainly Russian Orthodox. Their shamanistic beliefs involve an unseen world of gods, demons, and ancestral spirits, as well as many elements of Christianity. They believe that a shaman is the only mediator between humans and the spirit world. Witch doctors are sought to cast magic spells, heal the sick, predict the future, and contact the dead. Although shamanistic traditions were suppressed under communism, there was a marked revival of the Nenets traditional religion during the 1990s. The Nenets continue to recognize many gods, while nature is the Nenets church.

NATIONAL HISTORY: The Nenets are believed to be descended from early groups that split from the Finno-Ugrian migrations around 3,000 B.C. They moved east, where they mixed with Turkic-Altaic peoples around 200 B.C. For centuries the Nenets and the related tribes herded reindeers across the vast reaches of the Arctic, moving their herds to the seasonal grazing lands in the tundra and taiga lands north of the tree line. Their society was carefully organized into well-defined clans, each with its own grazing, hunting, and fishing territories, as well as its nomadic routes.

European chronicles first mentioned the northern reindeer herders in the eleventh century, and some groups came under Slavic influence around A.D. 1200. In the thirteenth century the western tribes came under the sway of the mercantile republic of Novgorod, which demanded taxes and tribute. In the fourteenth century, taxation by the Tatars* was added to that of the Slavs.

At the end of the fifteenth century some of the western tribes became tributary to the duchy of Moscovy. Between 1552 and 1596 the majority of the Nenets and Enets, called Nentsy and Entsy by the Russians, came under direct Russian rule. A series of Russian forts was constructed across the region; Russians collected the despised fur tax but left the actual administration to the traditional local rulers. The western tribes trapped the valuable fur animals in order to pay the ever-increasing annual taxes and tributes demanded by Moscow.

Any Nenet who converted to Christianity was offered full Russian citizenship. Along with Christianity, the Russians brought tools, firearms, and various trade goods, including alcohol, which has plagued the Nenets since. They also inadvertently introduced European diseases, to which the Nenets had never been exposed. Smallpox and cholera devastated the tribal peoples.

Protected by the Ural Mountains, the tribes of the Yamal Peninsula remained free of Russian domination until 1628. The tribes of the Taimyr Peninsula and the Yenisei Valley came under Russian rule in the late seventeenth century. Small in numbers and spread across vast territories, the Nenet tribes found themselves nearly powerless to resist the determined capitalists of prerevolutionary Russia, but the Russians were dismayed at the number and ferocity of the frequent Nenets uprisings, which continued until 1746. In 1824 the government organized a large-scale conversion to Orthodox Christianity.

The Russians called the tribes Samoyeds, a word denoting "cannibal." The tribes traditionally ate raw reindeer meat, particularly at ceremonies, though never slaughtered more of their reindeer than immediate needs required. The reindeer herds, closely tied to the Nenets' traditional way of life and even their ancient religious beliefs, provided the nomadic tribes with food, shelter, and clothing.

In the 1870s, the tsarist government confiscated large parcels of Nenets lands in the west. Many tribal peoples were resettled to northwestern border areas of Russia. Russian became the language of local administration and education. By 1900, a few Nenet families had amassed thousands of reindeer, but most herds were much smaller, ranging from several dozen to several hundred.

The arrival of the communists after the Russian Civil War of 1918–20 saw the implementation of the Soviet plan to create a modern socialist society in the region. In 1924, a Committee of Assistance of Peoples of the North was established. They first proposed large reservations where the indigenous peoples could continue their traditional way of life. Instead, the Soviet authorities decided to integrate the Nenets into Soviet society. The plan involved the confiscation of all "surplus wealth" from the Nenets. Their reindeer herds taken away; the authorities allowed each herder to retain just four animals. Each band's hunters were relieved of any furs they had stored. As an average band needed at least 250 reindeer just to survive, thousands of Nenets perished of hunger.

The consolidation of Soviet power included theoretical autonomy for non-Russian national groups. When the Soviet authorities began to exploit the Nenet lands, they organized nominally autonomous regions—for the Nenets in 1929, and for the Yamalo-Nenets and Dolgano-Nenets in 1930. Stalin's collectivization of the late 1920s forced the surviving nomads to work for the state and to move to permanent settlements chosen by local Soviet bureaucrats. The reindeer herders rebelled against collectivization and attacked the mining town of Vorkuta. The Red Army used aircraft to subdue the Nenets, attacking herds, villages, and even the new collective farms.

In the early 1950s, the Nenets religion was suppressed, prompting several Nenet rebellions in the Arkhangelsk region. The uprisings were suppressed, and the rebel leaders either executed or sent to remote slave-labor camps. The Nenets were broken morally and as a nation; the traditionally nomadic groups were forced to adopt a Soviet life on collective farms.

The Nenets' only source of income became the huge Soviet enterprises that invaded the region from the 1950s onward. Even Nenets who found employment received wages a quarter or a third of those of the "incomers." The discovery of huge oil and natural gas reserves, in the 1960s, brought a renewed influx.

Communist development plans devastated the fragile Nenets homeland, which was treated as a classic colony to be exploited. Some 20 million hectares of land were destroyed by careless mining and drilling between 1979 and 1989 alone. The region was the site of Russia's richest gas and oil fields, and the indigenous Nenets were carelessly pushed aside in the rush to exploit it. The Yamal-Nenets region had a population of 80,000 in 1970, which grew to 486,000 by 1989.

The era of liberalization of the late 1980s allowed the first Nenet attempts to organize resistance to the despoliation of their lands. A nascent national movement organized the first protests against the suffering caused by decades of communism and collectivization, which had resulted even in the dumping of radioactive waste in the Kara Sea and along the shore of the island of Novaya Zemlya. Military officials determined which settlement areas, positions, rights, and privileges were available. Nuclear experiments have been carried out unobstructed on Novaya Zemlya. The Norilsk nickel refinery alone polluted over five million hectares of Nenets grazing lands and almost a million hectares of virgin forest.

The Nenets, although they value education, increasingly resent the need to allow their children to attend large boarding schools in towns far away from their families. After 10 years of Russian education, children become alienated from their traditional way of life and language, but they are not accepted into the Russian community either. The vast influx of Russian-speaking newcomers already threatens their culture as assimilation continues in many areas.

The governments of the three autonomous regions, dominated by ethnic Russians, declared the regions autonomous states in the autumn of 1990. The taste of autonomy only whetted the Nenet appetite for more. Following the collapse of the Soviet Union in 1991, the Nenets refused to recognize the authority of the regional governments and began to organize in the Nenet majority regions in the far north.

In March 1993 the leaders of the Yamalo-Nenets struggled to take control of their national wealth from the bureaucrats, setting off a well-organized effort to regain control of their homelands across the Nenets regions. In the east the Nenets and Dolgans fought for the Great Arctic Reserve, finally designated a safe environment area in the Taimyr Peninsula in July 1993. The northern peoples shared a sense of outrage at the abuses they had suffered and felt that only by regaining their right to self-determination could they reestablish their identity and begin to rebuild their Arctic homeland.

In 1996, the legislature of Yamalo-Nenets, an autonomous region within the province of Tyumen, voted not to participate in the Tyumen Oblast gubernatorial elections in December. The Nenets Autonomous Okrug legislature voted in October 1996 not to participate in the Arkangelsk Oblast gubernatorial and legislative elections. The increasingly separatist attitudes of the regional governments has spurred a growing movement for the

Nenets-populated region to secede and to form a new nation separate from the areas dominated by the Slavic newcomers.

Nenets activists, in early 2001, presented a plan for a new autonomous region to include the northern districts of the three administrative regions from the Taimyr Peninsula in the east to the Kanin Peninsula to the west. The plan, which would include areas of vital economic interest to the Russian government, was accepted for study, but the Nenets and the other small national groups of the vast region have little hope that their desires will be respected.

SELECTED BIBLIOGRAPHY:

Abramovich-Gomon, Alla. *The Nenets' Song: A Microcosm of a Vanishing Culture.* 1999.

Bartels, Dennis A. *When the North Was Red: Aboriginal Education in Soviet Siberia.* 1995.

Osherenko, Gail. *Siberian Survival: The Nenets and Their Story.* 1999.

Pika, Alexander, ed. *Neotraditionalism in the Russian North: Indigenous Peoples and the Legacy of Perestroika.* 1999.

Nevisians

Nevis Islanders

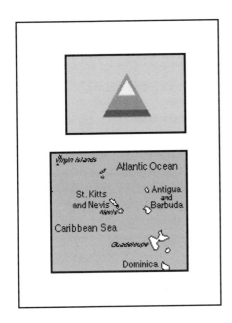

POPULATION: Approximately (2002e) 30,000 Nevisians in the Caribbean, concentrated on the island of Nevis, part of the Federation of St. Kitts and Nevis. There are sizable Nevisian communities living in other areas of the Caribbean and in the United States and Canada.

THE NEVISIAN HOMELAND: The Nevisian homeland, the island of Nevis, lies in the Caribbean Sea in the northern Leeward Islands. The island is of volcanic origin and is rugged and mountainous. The island is nearly circular, being eight miles (12 km) long by six miles (10 km) wide, and rises symmetrically to the central volcanic cone of Nevis Peak. A fertile coastal strip surrounds the central mountain. Officially Nevis forms a constituent part of the Federation of St. Kitts and Nevis. *Nevis*: 50 sq. mi.—130 sq. km, (2002e) 9,000—Nevisians 95%, other Caribbean islanders, some British, Portuguese, and Lebanese 5%. The Nevisian capital and major cultural center is Charlestown, (2002e) 1,500.

FLAG: The Nevisian national flag, the flag of the national movement, is a yellow field bearing a centered green triangle representing Nevis Peak with a smaller white triangle at the top over a base of dark blue.

PEOPLE AND CULTURE: The majority of the Nevisians are descendents of black slaves imported from Africa to work the early plantations. There is a considerable European admixture, the result of alliances between slaves and masters in centuries past. There are also small East Indian and white Nevisian groups. While sea-island cotton for the Japanese market has replaced sugar as the staple crop, most Nevisians remain subsistence farmers. The high level of emigration offsets natural increase and enables the island to maintain a fairly stable population although the population continues to decline. The emigrant population elsewhere in the Caribbean, in the United States, and in the United Kingdom, maintains close family and political ties to the island, and remittances from emigrants form an important source of foreign exchange.

LANGUAGE AND RELIGION: The Nevisians speak the Caribbean dialect of English, a melodious dialect with a sing-song accent, along with an English patois that is the language of daily life on the island. The Nevisians have one of the highest literacy rates in the Caribbean. The official language of the island is English.

Most Nevisians belong to Protestant churches, the main denominations being Anglican and Methodist. Evangelical Protestant sects, active in the islands since the 1960s, have gained considerable followings. There are small groups of Moravians and Roman Catholics.

NATIONAL HISTORY: The fertile coastal strip that surrounds the central peak of the island was sparsely settled by Carib Indians, who had driven the more peaceful Arawaks from the island, when Columbus encountered the islands in 1493. Columbus named the island Nuestra Senora de las Nieves, chosen because of the mountain in the center in a circle of white mist that reminded him of snow. Columbus claimed the island for Spain, but the Spanish authorities—interested not in agriculture but in the gold and riches of other American cultures—ignored the island, which remained almost uninhabited for over a century.

The first English colony in the Caribbean was established on nearby St. Kitts in 1623. Settlers from St. Kitts crossed the narrow strait to colonize the neighboring island in 1628. The Spanish name of the island, Nieves, was retained as "Nevis," for Ben Nevis mountain in Scotland, which the early settlers thought resembled Nevis Peak. Nevis became the second English colony in the region but remained subservient to neighboring St. Kitts. The capital of the island, Jamestown, was destroyed by a devastating tidal wave in 1680. A new capital, Charlestown, named for the English king, was founded. The settlers established sugar plantations but, in need of labor, began importing black African slaves as workers.

The island, also claimed by Spain and France, was often threatened or attacked. In 1782, the French took control of Nevis but a year later, under British pressure, abandoned its claim.

In the eighteenth century, Nevis became an aristocratic resort for the plantation aristocracy of the British islands in the Caribbean. Planter families from Jamaica and other islands annually traveled to Nevis to enjoy the elegant society of the island, often called the Bath (after the English resort city) of the Caribbean. The Bath House Hotel became one of the most famous establishments outside Europe. In 1757 Alexander Hamilton, one of the framers of the U.S. Constitution, was born on the island. In 1787, Adm. Horatio Nelson married Frances Nisbet in Charlestown. The opulent way of life of the European planter society gained Nevis the reputation and name of "Queen of the Caribees."

The abolition of slavery in 1833 ended the sugar boom. Many of the wealthy planters left the island, while others turned to small farming, hiring former slaves. Many of the former slaves also took up subsistence farming and fishing. The island became a neglected outpost, its uneducated, backward former slaves living mostly on what they could grow or gather for themselves or working on the former great sugar plantations as wage laborers.

In 1871 Nevis became part of the British colony of the Leeward Islands. St. Kitts, with its larger population, came once again to dominate neighboring Nevis in the late nineteenth century and early twentieth century. Government officials and bureaucrats from the larger island generally filled the few official posts on the island. The islands of St. Kitts, Nevis, and Anguilla were united in a federation by an act of Parliament in 1882.

Nevis remained part of the Leeward Islands, in a political association with St. Kitts and Anguilla, until 1956. In 1958, the British authorities formed the Caribbean territories into an autonomous West Indies Federation. The Nevisians, along with the Anguillans,* indicated a preference for a status within the new federation separate from St. Kitts, but they were ignored. From 1958 to 1962, Nevis formed part of the St. Kitts-Nevis-Anguilla presidency of the federation.

The larger islands of the federation, Jamaica and Trinidad, withdrew to declare separate independence, and the federation collapsed in 1962. In 1967, over Nevisian protests, the island was included in the new British Associated State of St. Kitts-Nevis-Anguilla. The Nevisians formed the Nevis Reform Party (NRP), which opposed rule from St. Kitts. When the Anguillans unilaterally seceded from the state, many Nevisians favored the same route for their island, but they were opposed by a majority that feared violent upheavals. The Nevis Reform Party, when finally given a place in the state government, came out against secession.

In the 1970s the Nevisians increasingly resented heavy-handed rule from St. Kitts. In 1977, the British-associated states in the Caribbean moved toward separate independence. The residents of Nevis voted 4,193 to just 14 to sever their ties to the larger island and to petition the British government to restore Nevis's status as a separate colony. The government of St. Kitts ignored the Nevisian vote, but continuing Nevisian opposition delayed the independence of the joint state, while the other associated states gained independence from 1978 onward.

The Nevis Reform Party continued to support demands for autonomy for Nevis but remained in the state government until the 1980 elections. In 1982, an agreement was finally reached on independence from the United Kingdom, with the Nevisians entitled to one-third of the seats in the National Assembly. Nevis was also granted its own assembly and a certain amount of autonomy within the federal structure. The Nevisians, still opposed to inclusion in the joint state, were to vote, 18 months after independence, on separation from the new state should they feel that continued association with St. Kitts harmed their interests. Their options, should they wish to separate, were full independence or a return to British administration.

On 19 September 1983, St. Kitts–Nevis was granted independence, and the new state joined the United Nations. In March 1985, the Nevisians voted to remain an autonomous part of the St. Kitts–Nevis. In the 1987 elections, the Nevis Reform Party took all the Nevisian seats, on a platform of greater autonomy for the island but not separation.

A lack of economic opportunities drove many younger Nevisians to emigrate in search of work. One of the main sources of income became money sent by Nevisians working overseas. Tourism, supported by the government, brought the construction of resort hotels, but this increased Nevisian resentment; they rejected the idea of becoming an island of anonymous hotel workers.

The Nevis International Exempt Trust Ordinance of 1994, amended in 1995, established the government of Nevis, under a premier, the head of the majority party in the House of Assembly. The law, increasingly used to separate Nevis politically from St. Kitts, became the basis of a renewed nationalist movement. The law was used by the Nevisians to turn down a dozen applications for Internet "virtual casinos," on the ground that they would damage its reputation as an emerging independent state.

In June 1996, Premier Vance Amory of Nevis declared that he had instructed the island's legal department to prepare a bill for secession from the two-island federal state. His decision stemmed from the rising nationalism among the Nevisians, a reaction to the central government's assertion of control over Nevis's affairs, including the thriving financial industry. The declaration set off a serious political crisis, as secession fever swept Nevis.

The Concerned Citizens Movement (CCM), headed by Vance Amory, was returned to power in the Nevis Assembly election in February 1997. The now pro-independence Nevis Reformation Party held on to the other seats in the assembly. In October 1997, nationalists presented a motion in the assembly calling for separation from St. Kitts. The motion was widely supported by both Nevisian political parties.

A referendum to confirm the resolution was scheduled for the August 1998. The the Caribbean Community, Caricom, and the United States, had urged the Nevisians not to secede. In the referendum 62% of the voters in Nevis backed independence and separation from St. Kitts, just short of the two-thirds needed under the constitution.

Elections were held in St. Kitts and Nevis on 6 March 2000, with the majority on St. Kitts voting for the Labour Party, out of loyalty to Robert Bradshaw, a sugar workers' leader prominent in St. Kitts politics since the late 1970s. Mr. Bradshaw's contempt for Nevis, which lacked cane cutters for him to organize, continued to cause separatist feelings on the island.

Another referendum on independence is being organized. According to militants on the island, Nevis will form one of the world's smallest independent states following the next plebiscite.

Activists on the island are organizing another referendum, probably in 2003 or 2004, but they must first convince all Nevisians that separation would not harm the already fragile economy or the Nevisians'access to St. Kitts, just a 2-mile ferry ride across a narrow strait. Secessionists believe Nevis could survive and prosper on its own.

SELECTED BIBLIOGRAPHY:

Ewing, Debra, ed. *Saint Kitts and Nevis Country Review 1999/2000*. 1999.

Hubbard, Vincent K. *Swords, Ships and Sugar: A History of Nevis to 1900*. 1997.

Olwig, Karen Fog. *Global Culture, Island Identity: Continuity and Change in the Afro-Caribbean Community of Nevis*. 1993.

Richardson, Bonham C. *Caribbean Migrants: Environment and Human Survival on St. Kitts and Nevis*. 1983.

New Englanders

Yankees

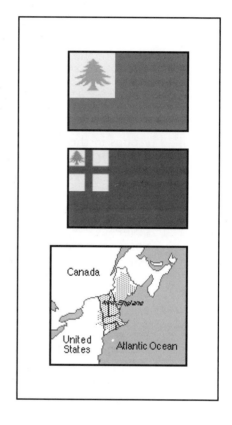

POPULATION: Approximately (2002e) 15,200,000 New Englanders in the United States, concentrated in the northeastern states of Connecticut, Maine, Massachusetts, New Hampshire, Rhode Island, and Vermont. Other large New Englander communities live in New York and other eastern states, and on the west coast of the United States.

THE NEW ENGLANDER HOMELAND: The New Englander homeland occupies the northeastern corner of the United States. In the north and west the land rises to the New England system of the Appalachian Mountains. From the Green Mountains, the White Mountains, and the Berkshire Hills, the region slopes gradually to the Atlantic Ocean. Because of the generally poor soil, agriculture has never, except for the early colonial period, been a major part of the regional economy. Much of the region is forested, particularly in Maine. The southern region in Connecticut, close to New York City, is heavily urbanized. *Region of New England*: 66,667 sq. mi.—172,668 sq. km, (2002e) 14,098,000—New Englanders 88%, other Americans 12%. The New Englander capital and major cultural center is Boston, (2002e) 595,000, metropolitan area 5,532,000.

FLAG: The New Englander flag, the traditional flag of the region, is a red field bearing a white canton on the upper hoist bearing a green pine tree. The flag of the autonomy movement is a red field bearing a white canton on the upper hoist bearing a red cross and a green pine tree.

PEOPLE AND CULTURE: The New Englanders are an American group shaped by the long and particular history of their region. Although most American regions have lost their local cultures to the homogenization of American society, the New Englanders have retained much of theirs, including their reputation for forthrightness and honesty. A long commercial tradition of the legendary Yankee trader remains to the present, making Boston and other regional centers important banking and financial markets. The architecture, cuisine, and art of New England remain important parts of the regional culture. The majority of the people of the region feel American, but they also nurture a strong regional identity.

LANGUAGE AND RELIGION: The New Englanders speak the New England dialect of American English, although in the twentieth century the distinctive features of the dialect were lost to urbanization. Curious and antiquated words and sayings, legacies of the region's early English settlers and of the region's colonial isolation, remain as colorful reminders of the region's past. New England has long been a literary and educational center of the United States.

The New England region was originally settled by Puritans and other religious dissenters, but modern New Englanders mirror the religious diversity of the United States. Although Protestant denominations still predominate, there are large Roman Catholic, Jewish, and other religious groups in the region.

NATIONAL HISTORY: Capt. John Smith, sailing under the sponsorship of a group of London merchants, explored the shores of the region in 1614. He called the region New England, because of its resemblance to the English coast. The region was inhabited by several indigenous tribal groups when it became the site of the earliest European settlement in northern North America. Religious intolerance had driven the first settlers, Puritans who called themselves Pilgrims, to abandon England for life in the new world. Their ship, the *Mayflower*, landed at Plymouth Rock in 1620, where they founded the colony of New Plymouth, which was governed under the Mayflower Covenant. Other religious dissenters established a colony at Providence in 1636. French colonists founded several settlements in the northern region they called Maine.

The Penacook people living in the region have been credited with teaching the settlers the skills they needed to avert starvation during the winter of 1621–22. The forests surrounding the settlement were teeming with game and wild food unfamiliar to the Pilgrims. The Penacook showed them how to use and prepare them. According to New England traditions, the Penacook also taught the Pilgrims elementary democracy, which the Penacook in turn had learned from the Iroquois.*

The Pilgrims believed in simplicity and had an aversion to idleness and luxury that well served the fledgling communities, where the work to be done was so prodigious and the hands so few. Contingents of colonists from Massachusetts settled the neighboring regions of Connecticut and Rhode Island in the 1630s. The New Haven colony was established in 1638.

The New England Confederation was formed in 1643, for "mutual safety and welfare," by the representatives of the colonies of Massachusetts Bay, Plymouth, Connecticut, and New Haven. The delegates met in Boston and adopted a written constitution binding the colonies in a league known as the United Colonies of New England. The chief purpose of the confederation was defense and the settlement of boundary disputes. The internal affairs of the individual colonies were to be left to local leaders. Maine and Narragansett Bay (Rhode Island) sought admission to the confederation but were refused on political and religious grounds. In 1652, Massachusetts Bay acquired the northern province of Maine, and in 1691 it absorbed Plymouth. Connecticut and New Haven colonies were united in 1664 and were granted a strip of land extending to the Pacific Ocean.

During the seventeenth century, enlightened leadership and the high esteem in which an educated clergy was held encouraged the development of public schools as well as such institutes of higher learning as Harvard, founded in 1636, and Yale, 1701. The region became the intellectual and commercial center of the American colonies.

Isolated from the mother country, the New Englanders evolved representative government, including the institution of the town meeting, an expanded franchise, and broad civil liberties. The area was initially a region of self-sufficient farms, but its rich forests, streams, and harbors soon promoted the growth of industry and commerce. The New England confederation endured until 1684. The Dominion of New England formed a single province in 1668. Under the rule of Sir Edmund Andros, the colonies of New Hampshire, Rhode Island, and later New Jersey and New York were added to the dominion. Andros was overthrown by dissidents in the region in 1689, and the colonies resumed their separate existences.

The New England colonies carried on extensive trade with the other British colonies, particularly the so-called Molasses Triangle. New Englander shipping companies were involved in a triangular trade with Africa and the Caribbean, exchanging manufactured goods for Caribbean sugar and African slaves.

In the eighteenth century, New England became a center of revolutionary agitation for independence from the United Kingdom. Many of the major events of America's colonial period, including the start of the American Revolution, took place in New England. British troops withdrew to Boston after colonial uprisings at Lexington and Concord, Massachusetts, in 1775, the first skirmishes of the Revolutionary War. New England patriots played leading roles in establishing the new United States of America. In the early decades of independence, the New Englanders supported a policy of federalism, with broad autonomy for the individual states.

Before the American Revolution, Vermont formed a part of the colony of New York. However, Vermonters never felt great attachment to the government in Albany but thought of themselves as New Englanders. They took advantage of the revolution to declare their independence as the Republic of New Connecticut on 15 January 1777. The name of the republic was changed to the Republic of Vermont on 4 June 1777. The newly established

Committee of Public Safety guided Vermont through the revolution, mostly remaining neutral. Under pressure from New York, Congress refused to acknowledge the new state. Ethan Allen and his brothers quickly assumed a major role in Vermont's government. In 1791, the Vermonters decided to join the United States and duly ratified the Constitution.

The war of 1812 had an adverse effect on the New Englanders' trade, and hostility to the war between the new American federation and the United Kingdom was widespread. Opposition became so hardened that the New Englanders threatened secession. After the war, the growth of manufacturing was rapid, and the region became highly industrialized.

In 1785–86 the New England states of Massachusetts and Connecticut gave up claims to western territories originally included in their colonial charters. Scattered rebellions against government economic policies were common between 1786 and 1800. Maine separated from Massachusetts and was admitted to the Union as a separate state under the Missouri Compromise of 1820. The northern boundary of New England was settled by treaty with the British government in 1842.

In the nineteenth century, New England experienced a cultural flowering characterized by its literature and a deep evangelical sense that frequently manifested itself in support for reform movements. Temperance, abolition of slavery, improvement in prisons and insane asylums, and an end to child labor all had widespread support in the region. The antislavery movement was the most prominent; New Englanders stoutly supported the Union cause in the American Civil War from 1861 to 1865.

The westward expansion of the American frontier drew many New Englander emigrants, who carried with them their culture and governmental traditions. The Industrial Revolution also began during this period, and manufacturing, along with fishing and whaling, came to dominate the regional economy. Itinerant Yankee peddlers carried such New England products as clocks, shoes, textiles, and hardware as far west as the Mississippi River. Both before and after the Civil War a new labor force, mostly from Ireland and Eastern Europe flooded into the region, causing a cultural revolution and forcing the traditional Protestant culture and religion to make space for the growing number of Roman Catholics.

In the early years of the twentieth century many changes were evident, but the traditional New England culture and customs continued to characterize the people. In the years after World War II, New England's once-flourishing textile and leather-goods industries virtually deserted the region for the South, where labor and land costs were more attractive.

The loss of manufacturing in the 1960s and 1970s was somewhat offset by the growth of new transport and electronic industries, and in the 1980s and 1990s by the proliferation of high-technology and service-based economic enterprises. The formerly heavily regulated manufacturing era gave way to a technology revolution that required much less government supervision and fewer regulations. The high-technology culture, paralleled by the traditionally independent New Englander character, spawned a regionwide movement for greater autonomy in the 1990s.

The autonomy movement, led by the New England Confederation (NEC), with chapters in all six states, stated its aims in the Lowell Declaration in 1997 and the Portland Resolution of 1999. The activists believed that the United States had grown too large, was out of touch with the nation's peoples, and was too expensive to maintain. They believed that the U.S. government had often usurped the constitutional limits set by the Tenth Amendment to the Constitution and that the federal government should return many of its powers to the states and regions. The purpose of the movement was to work for greater cooperation among the six New England states, with the goal of greater autonomy in economic, political, and social policy.

Nationalists point out that New England is a historically, geographically, culturally, and politically recognized region and that the New Englanders have crucial factors in common that they do not wholly share with other nations, states, or regions. They want New England to recover its regional authority and reassert its voice within the communal life of the United States. Home rule, as outlined by the nationalists, would divest the federal government of all rights and powers not specifically granted to it by the Constitution and would create a New England regional legislative body that would exercise New Englander self-government in matters of regional economic and commercial interests, environmental affairs, education, urban planning, migration, and foreign trade. A united New England political front in Washington would push for the devolution of government and tax revenues to the individual states.

The autonomy movement is founded on the belief that democracy cannot be practiced on a large scale. In order to preserve New England's unique democratic traditions, it holds, power must be returned to the region from the bloated bureaucracy of the United States. The devolution must occur at all levels: political, economic, social, cultural, and emotional. Traditional New England democracy, based on the town meeting, was a participatory democracy where local citizens had the right to voice their opinions in public forum. Activists claim that that traditions is being brushed aside by the increasingly bureaucratic federal and state governments.

SELECTED BIBLIOGRAPHY:

Hale, Judson. *Inside New England.* 1982.
Milburn, Josephine. *New England Politics.* 1981.
Pierce, Neal R. *The New England States: People, Politics, and Power in Six New England States.* 1976.
Zimmerman, Joseph F. *The New England Town Meeting: Democracy in Action.* 1999.

Newfies

Newfoundlanders

POPULATION: Approximately (2002e) 720,000 Newfies in North America, concentrated in the Canadian province of Newfoundland. Other important Newfie communities are in Ontario and Quebec in Canada, and in the New England region of the United States.

THE NEWFIE HOMELAND: The Newfie homeland is one of the four Atlantic provinces of Canada, constituting the easternmost portion of the North American continent. The province comprises the island of Newfoundland in the Gulf of St. Lawrence and the huge mainland territory of Labrador, which makes up about three-quarters of the total territory but has a population of only about 35,000. The island is separated from the mainland by the Strait of Belle Isle. Newfoundland has a coastline highly indented by small bays. The province, formerly a distinct dominion, joined Canada in 1949. *Province of Newfoundland*: 143,488 sq. mi.—371,634 sq. km, (2002e) 534,000—Newfies 96%, Innu,* Inuits,* other Canadians 4%. The Newfie capital and major cultural center is St. Johns, (2002e) 98,000, metropolitan area 211,000. Another important cultural center is Corner Brook, (2002e) 21,000, urban area 53,000. The major cultural center of Labrador is Labrador City, (2002e) 12,000.

FLAG: The Newfie national flag, the flag of the national movement, is a vertical tricolor of pink, white, and pale green. The official flag of the province is a white field with a stylized Union Jack. The flag of Labrador is a horizontal tricolor of white, green, and blue, in the proportions two to one to two, bearing a green spruce bough on the upper hoist.

PEOPLE AND CULTURE: The Newfoundlanders, popularly called

Newfies, are a distinct North American people. The greater part of the Newfie population are extraordinarily homogenous: about 95% trace their origins to the southwestern counties of England or the southwestern region of Ireland. The origins of the Newfies are 76% English and Scots, 18% Irish, and 2% French. A small number trace their ancestry to other English and Irish counties, Scotland, Wales, the Channel Islands, or the coasts of Normandy and Brittany in France. Although the Newfies became Canadian citizens in 1949, they retain closer ties to the British Isles in accent, appearance, and family connections. The major occupation of the region, fishing, is not just a livelihood but the basis of the distinct Newfie culture, one of the unique regional cultures in North America. Newfoundland has been characterized as a living archive of folklore, folktales, and folk songs. About half the population still live in small fishing villages along the coasts.

LANGUAGE AND RELIGION: The Newfie language, a mixture of archaic West Country English and Erse (Gaelic), with borrowings from French and the Indian and Inuit languages, has developed over centuries, producing many words and constructions not found in other English dialects. The comparative isolation of the region has preserved much of the seventeenth-century West Country speech and other British dialects that have disappeared elsewhere. The dialect has been modified only by the influence of the Irish, who constituted half the total population in the mid-nineteenth century. Although there is a standardized dialect, Newfies claim that there are as many dialects as there are bays. The differences between the Newfie dialect and standard English are in not only accent but vocabulary, sounds, and syntax. An immense body of folk tales and music has been preserved and forms an important part of the Newfie culture.

Historically, social groups in Newfoundland have been defined along lines of denominational rather than by linguistic or ethnic origin. The three principal denominations are Roman Catholic, Anglican, and United Church of Canada. Historically the churches controlled much of the region's social life and educational system.

NATIONAL HISTORY: Newfoundland island was originally settled by Algonquins, while Inuits inhabited the northern reaches of Labrador. Traditionally Vikings visited Labrador in A.D. 985 or 986, although researchers have found no definite proof of such an early expedition. Vikings certainly reached the Newfoundland island in 1285, but a Viking settlement, under Landa-Rolf, ultimately failed. Giovanni Caboto, known in history as John Cabot, sighted the island in 1497 and called his discovery "New-founde-land."

The Grand Banks, one of the world's great fishing grounds, were discovered soon after Cabot's voyage and attracted competing fishing fleets. Traditionally, the English government regarded the Grand Banks as a preserve of the mother country and discouraged colonial settlement of the island. Small settlements established by the fishermen of several European countries sprang up in the isolated coves in the 1500s despite English territorial claims. To consolidate English domination, the Crown formally annexed the island in 1583 as England's first overseas possession. The French founded a rival colony on the island in 1662, but English sovereignty was confirmed in 1713. French claims to the region ended with the cession of Labrador in 1763, although they retained the two small islands of Saint Pierre and Miquelon, just south of Newfoundland.

The region developed separately from the British Canadian territories. It was not until 1824 that a settled colony, with a resident governor and council, was finally acknowledged by the British government. In 1832 Newfie agitation led to the creation of a popularly elected assembly.

The population grew slowly, the majority of the inhabitants living in small, isolated coastal settlements, where they retained customs and speech patterns that disappeared elsewhere. An influx of Irish immigrants, fleeing famine in Ireland, settled in Newfoundland in the 1840s, giving the emerging Newfie culture a definite Irish flavor, particularly noticeable in music and folklore. By the end of the nineteenth century a working class of Irish Roman Catholics and a middle class of Protestant tradesmen and fishermen had developed.

In 1855 Newfoundland won dominion status, autonomy under a regional government. Four of Britain's other North American provinces united to form the Dominion of Canada in 1867. The Newfies rejected British moves to add their island to Canada in 1869, preferring to retain dominion status, equal to but separate from Canada. In the 1880s, ignoring vehement Newfie protests, the British government granted fishing rights in the Grand Banks, the dominion's major asset, to other fishing nations. In the 1890s, when the question of joining Canada again came up, the precarious state of the Newfie economy precluded any serious discussion of union with Canada. Fishing in the Grand Banks, mainly for cod, was virtually the only industry in Newfoundland until the beginning of the twentieth century.

Foreign access to the Grand Banks, without benefit to Newfoundland, awakened a latent nationalism. In 1904 the Newfies managed to eliminate France's special fishing rights, and in 1906 they signed a fishing agreement with the United States, the dominion's major trading partner. New radical social policies appeared with the formation of the People's Party in 1907 and the Fishermen's Protective Union in 1908.

When war began in 1914 the Newfies put aside their grievances and joined the other British dominions in sending troops to Europe. During the war the nationalists gained support, and in 1917 the Newfies elected a nationalist government under William Lloyd, who attended the 1919 Paris Peace Conference as the head of a victorious nation.

The huge territory of Labrador, after lengthy negotiations with the Canadian government, became part of Newfoundland in 1927. The exploitation of Labrador's vast iron reserves replaced fishing as the major source of revenue. The forestry industry also aided the declining Newfie economy, based mainly on fishing and mining. Newfoundland suffered severe reverses during the depression of the 1930s. Unable to meet interest payments on government loans, the dominion government requested aid from the imperial treasury. The aid request, incompatible with dominion status, forced the Newfies to comply when London suspended the constitution and withdrew dominion status in 1933. The state, over widespread domestic opposition, thus gave up its independence and became the first member country to withdraw from the British Commonwealth.

Newfoundland's return to colonial status roused Newfie nationalism, many of the islanders blaming British policies for the state's economic problems. Nationalists called for independence and proposed an economic union with the United States, but nationalism waned with the outbreak of World War II in Europe. The site of major Allied bases during the war, Newfoundland prospered from money spent by thousands of American soldiers.

Dominion status, restored in 1946, failed to satisfy the two major political factions, respectively pro–independence and pro–Canada. A plebiscite held in June 1948 gave the Newfies three choices—eventual independence, confederation with Canada, or continued dominion status. None of the choices received a majority, but a second plebiscite in July produced a slight edge for confederation. On 1 April 1949 Newfoundland joined Canada as the 10th province. Nationalists protested by chopping down hundreds of maple trees, the symbol of Canada.

Nationalist protests and demonstrations gradually declined as confederation brought development funds and the benefits of Canada's welfare state. Modernization in the 1950s coaxed the Newfies out of hundreds of small ports and into a more urban life, but without the loss of their distinctive culture. Family-run operations were replaced by large fisheries and canneries.

Newfie nationalism, dormant for nearly three decades, reemerged following the discovery of oil and natural gas in nearby waters in 1979, opening a passionate dispute between the provincial and federal governments over the control of natural resources. The resurgent nationalism sparked parallel cultural and linguistic revivals. Television and radio had been eroding the culture, as had the large influx of non-Newfie professional people. The care and preservation of their distinct culture became the focus of Newfie cultural nationalism, which became a vital force in provincial life. The first dictionary of the Newfie language appeared in 1982. The younger generation began using the dialect as a matter of pride. The reculturation fostered a revival of the arts, theater, and literature in the dialect.

In 1983 nationalists formed the Party for an Independent Newfoundland, with the aim of secession from Canada and the recuperation of Newfie independence. In 1989, the Newfies noted but did not celebrate the fortieth anniversary of union with Canada. Fervent opponents of union admitted that it brought limited prosperity, including welfare and money to pave roads, but they feared that union with Canada was submerging their unique culture in the English-speaking culture of North America. Nationalists were outraged to learn that on the anniversary the Canadian government had agreed to allow French ships to take an extra 11,000 tons of fish from Newfie coastal waters.

The enormous hydroelectric-power resources of mainland Labrador have become of great importance to the industrial development of the province. A 1969 agreement to sell power to neighboring Quebec later became a focus of Newfie grievances; Quebec pays very low prices for Newfoundland's hydroelectric power and sells the same power to New England at world prices.

From its inception, Newfoundland has been a staging point for further emigration, and in the twentieth century there was a high level of emigration to the United States and other parts of Canada, although without loss of contact with the dialect and culture. The trend toward urbanization was accelerated by government policies aimed at reducing the cost of services by centralizing the Newfie population. In 2000 more than half the population was urban, nearly half living in the metropolitan areas of St. John's and Corner Brook.

The province's isolation helped perpetuate sectarianism in the school system. In 1997, the Newfies voted resoundingly to take control of the province's educational system away from the churches. In a referendum, 73% supported the establishment of a single, secular school system, rather than have six Christian churches operating their own schools, resulting in 230 separate school boards in the province. The decision was opposed by the Roman Catholic Church, the largest denomination in the province, and the Pentecostals. Other churches supported the reform movement.

Depletion of the fish stocks in the Grand Banks resulted in a two-year moratorium on fishing in May 1992. The moratorium, blamed on Canadian government policies, was extended until the year 2000; it affected 35,000 Newfie fishermen and raised the unemployment rate to around 20%. The economic problems of the 1990s spurred nationalist sentiment to levels not seen in the province since 1948–49.

In 1997 a 600,000-ton oil rig in the Hibernia field in the Grand Banks began pumping oil from Newfoundland's extensive offshore oil fields. By 2002 two more offshore oil projects should be operating. The oil, and a newly discovered cache of nickel at Voisey Bay in Labrador, promise a brighter future after several decades of a declining fishing economy. The newfound riches could stimulate a new round of Newfie regionalism and nationalism.

The controversy over the provincial riches, particularly oil and natural gas, continues to be the focus of nationalists. In early 2001 demonstrations against the Canadian government's policies on petroleum products were accompanied by many waving the Newfie nationalist flag as a sign of their defiance.

SELECTED BIBLIOGRAPHY:

Hiller, James, ed. *Twentieth-Century Newfoundland.* 1994.
Johnson, Wayne. *The Colony of Unrequited Dreams.* 1999.
LeGrow Chris. *Bound Down for Newfoundland.* 1998.
Long, Gene. *Suspended State: Newfoundland before Canada.* 1999.

Nogais

Nogays; Noghays; Noghais; Nogalars; Nogai Tatars; Nogay Tatars; Mangkyt; Volga Muslims

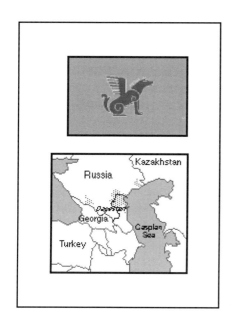

POPULATION: Approximately (2002e) 105,000 Nogais in the Russian Federation, concentrated in the Nogai, Babaurt, Tarum, and Kizlar districts of the Dagestan Republic, the adjoining Neftekumsky and Achikulak districts of Stavropol Krai, the Shelovsk district of the Chechen Republic, and the Sholkovsky district of the Karachai-Cherkessia Republic in the North Caucasus region of southern European Russia. There are other communities outside the region, notably in Rostov, Astrakhan, and farther north in Russia. Outside Russia there are about 50,000 Nogais in Bulgaria, Romania, Ukraine, and Turkey.

THE NOGAI HOMELAND: The Nogai homeland lies in the vast Nogai Steppe west of the Caspian Sea between the Terek and Kuma Rivers in the Republic of Dagestan, Stavropol Krai, and northeastern Chechen Republic. Most of the region is high, flat pastureland rising from the coastal plain on the Caspian Sea. The Nogais are traditionally cattle and sheep herders, although farming has become more widespread in recent decades. The region inhabited by the Nogais has no official status but remains divided between several administrative regions, with only about 20% of the Nogai Steppe still in use by the Nogais. Nogai nationalists seek a separate, sovereign homeland in the region, but their aspirations have not been recognized by the government of the Russian Federation. The Nogai capital and major cultural center is Kizlyar, (2002e) 47,000, the center of the Kara Nogais. The other important Nogai centers are Babayurt, (2002e) 23,000, and the town of Terekin-Mekteb, (2002e) 16,000.

FLAG: The Nogai national flag, the flag of the Nogai National Movement, is a pale blue field bearing a centered, green winged dog or wolf, outlined in yellow.

PEOPLE AND CULTURE: The Nogais are a Turkic people related to the Kumyks.* They are of Central Asian origin, being descended from the different Turkic and Mongolian tribes of the Golden Horde. Their name derives from Nogai, the grandson of Genghis Khan, who led the Nogai Horde until he was killed in the late thirteenth century. Traditionally tribal identities remain strong, although the Nogais are divided into three hordes that cross tribal and clan lines—the Ak (Aq) or White Nogais in the west, the Archikulak or Central Nogais in the center, and the Kara (Qara) or Black Nogais in the east. They are further divided into four major tribes (Bujak, Edisan, Jambulak, and Edishkul) and five minor tribes (Mansur, Kipchak, Karamurza, Tokhtam, and Novruz). Another group of 35,000 Nogais live in the Astrakhan region, and are divided into four clan groups—Yurt, Kundrovets, Karagash, and Utar-Alabugaty. Nogai identification with their tribe is often more powerful than identity as Nogais, although the recent growth of nationalism is changing attitudes. The Nogai culture and language have been greatly influenced by contacts with neighboring peoples, including Russians. Traditionally nomadic herders living in mobile houses called *cutan*, all Nogai groups are now settled, and besides cattle and horse breeding they have taken up farming. Since the 1980s there has been a migration to the cities.

LANGUAGE AND RELIGION: The Nogai language belongs to the Kipchak or Northwestern group of the Turkic languages and is one of the least studied of the Turkic languages. The language is divided into three major dialects—Kara or Black Nogai, Achikuluk or Central Nogai, and the Ak or White Nogai dialect, spoken in the Kuban region. The literary language is based on the White Nogai dialect. The dialectical differences are the result of long geographical separation. About 90% of the Nogais speak the language as their first language, although about 75% are bilingual in Russian. Many also speak one or more Caucasian languages. Until 1957, the teaching of Nogai was widespread in the Nogai homeland, but now it is largely restricted to the northern region of Dagestan. Secondary education in the Nogai language is available only in the Nogai District of Dagestan, which has a Nogai majority.

The Nogais mostly adhere to the Hanafi school of Sunni Islam. Many pre-Islamic beliefs, including reverence for their traditional god, Tengri, associated with their Turkic origins. Many still believe that inanimate objects have spirits. The Nogais practice a liberal, less rigid form of Islam and with increased assimilation into Russian religious practices have become even more relaxed.

NATIONAL HISTORY: The Nogais are thought to have originated in the steppe lands of Central Asia and later to have mixed with the peoples of the Kipchak tribal confederacies, particularly the Turkic-speaking Polovtsy. They were conquered by the expanding Mongol-Tatar empire, the Golden Horde, probably in the early thirteenth century, and moved west with the other subject peoples. Traditionally the Nogais claim descent from one man, Nogai or Nogay, grandson of Genghis Khan. Nogai, who controlled the Nogai Horde in the late thirteenth century, was killed either in 1294 or 1300, and the horde disintegrated. The sense of Nogai ethnic identity remained and his name remained, denoting the nomadic peoples of the steppe lands by the Sea of Azov. In early Russian manuscripts the Nogais were referred to as the North Caucasian Tatars.

The nomadic Nogai tribes roamed the vast plains between the Danube River and the Caspian Sea until the sixteenth century, when Tsar Ivan IV of Russia conquered Astrakhan and Kazan, bringing most of the Nogai territories under Russian rule. The Nogai Horde split into two groups. One, known as the Great Horde in the lower Volga region, came under nominal Russian domination in 1557; the other, the Little Horde, occupied the right bank of the Kuban River, the area east of the Sea of Azov, and southern Ukraine. The hordes were known as fierce opponents to Russian expansion.

The two Nogai hordes reunited in the seventeenth century after the Little Horde was driven south by an invasion of warlike Kalmyks* in 1634. Other clans of the Great Horde, to escape the Kalmyks, moved north into the lower Volga region, around Astrakhan. The united Nogais then came under the political control of the Crimean Tatars.* In the seventeenth century, some of the Nogai chiefs entered into an alliance with Moscow, sometimes fighting as Russian allies against the Kabards,* Kalmyks, and the Caucasian nations of Dagestan.

In 1723 the Russians took formal control of the Nogai homeland in the North Caucasus. Russian rule was formally recognized by the Ottoman Turks in 1724. The Nogais managed to exercise a degree of autonomy over the next century, but in 1859, when the Russians finally pacified the mountainous areas to the south, all the peoples of the region were brought under closer Russian authority. During the 1860s, when significant Russian expansion into their territory began, there was a large-scale emigration of Nogais to Turkey, the Crimea, and Romania. Most Nogai tribes remained nomadic and dispersed, but they were united by shared political and economic interests. In the early nineteenth century the majority of the tribes settled the Nogai Steppe region of North Caucasia. There they began to lose their former tribal structures and to mix across tribal and clan lines. The Kara Nogais in the east continued as nomads, but the Kuban or White Nogais to the west left their nomadic life to settle along the Greater and Smaller Zelenchuk Rivers and the Lower Uruk and Laba Rivers, beginning in the late eighteenth century. There they took up farming, although horse breeding also remained important.

Throughout their history, horse breeding remained the primary activity. Horses were used for transport; battles were fought by mounted cavalry; horse milk was the main drink, and horse meat the main staple. From the seventeenth century horses were sold annually to agents of the Russian government. Until the early 1900s most Nogais remained pastoral, semi-nomadic herders. They traveled in large groups known as *auls*, made up of different families and tribes, and smaller groups called *otars*, members of one extended family. The two groups often traveled together during the winter then spread across the steppe lands during the summer.

The Muslim Nogais openly supported the Turks when war began in 1914 and became effectively independent when civil administration collapsed during the Russian Revolution in 1917. A Muslim conference elected Mullah Gotinsky as its political and religious leader in May 1917. The Bolshevik takeover of the Russian government in October 1917 created chaos in the region as local Bolsheviks attempted to take power. The Muslim peoples joined with the Terek Cossacks to declare an independent Terek-Dagestan republic on 20 October 1917, but the new state, undermined by ethnic, religious, and territorial disputes, collapsed in December 1917.

The Muslim peoples of Dagestan formed a separate republic in March 1918 and attempted a cooperative defense as the Russian Civil War spread south. The anti-Bolshevik forces, the Whites, took control of the region in January 1919, but forced conscription of Muslims incited strong resistance. Promised autonomy, the Nogais mostly went over to the Reds. The last of the Whites withdrew in January 1920. The regional leaders, disappointed at their treatment by the Soviet authorities, demanded the promised regional autonomy. Rebuffed by the Soviets, the Muslim peoples rebelled and held out until finally subdued in May 1921, having inflicted over 5,000 Soviet casualties. In 1922 the Nogai territory in Kizlar, Tarumovsky, and Nogaisky Districts was added to the expanded Dagestan autonomous republic, while other Nogai-populated regions were added to other North Caucasus territories.

Soviet linguists created a standardized Nogai language based on the Kara dialect, on the grounds that it was the language of the working masses. The Nogai written language, based on the Arabic alphabet, was changed in 1928 to the Latin alphabet; the first spelling book was published in 1929. Schoolbooks, several dictionaries, and an orthographic manual followed. In 1936, in an effort to standardize further the language, a new literary language was developed, but in 1938 the Cyrillic alphabet was introduced, as a means of introducing the Russian language.

In spite of being administratively divided, the Nogai clan and tribal system ignored administrative boundaries, and many government policies, such as education, were extended to all the Nogai districts. In 1938, all the land north of the Terek River was transferred to Astrakhan Oblast, which included a large Nogai community. In 1931 the Narimanovsk District comprised the Tatar-Nogai National Territory, but all administrative autonomy was ended with the dissolution of the territory 10 years later.

Between 1944 and 1957 the Nogais were forcibly deported to various rural areas in Dagestan, Chechnya, and Stavropol. Others were arrested and shipped east to Central Asia. Until 1957, the Nogai language was taught everywhere in the Nogai Steppe region for the first five years of schooling, but the administrative changes that year divided the Nogais into three administrative regions, with different educational policies. The Nogai territory west of the Kizlar District was transferred to Chechnya. In Stavropol Krai and Chechnya, Nogai language teaching was ended; Nogai language schools continued only in the northern districts of Dagestan.

The Nogai way of life changed rapidly during the 1950s and 1960s. State enterprises and collective farms became the norm, reducing the semi-nomadism that had characterized traditional Nogai life. Most Nogais became employees of the state. The economic integration of the Nogai was accompanied by their increasing social integration into Russian culture.

After World War II, several waves of immigration swept over the Nogai territories. The first, in the 1960s, were Avars* moved to the lowlands steppes from their mountain regions by the Soviet authorities. Massive resettlement of Dagestanis* occurred in the 1970s and 1980s. Ethnic tension resulted. The migrations led to the domination of both urban society and much of the rural steppe by the former mountain peoples. The migrants introduced intensive cultivation to areas traditionally inhabited by the pastoral Nogais. Other migrants took up horse and cattle herding in direct rivalry with the Nogai.

The Soviet authorities mostly ignored the Nogai districts. Roads were primitive, and communications almost nonexistent. In many villages water supplies were deficient. The result of underdevelopment and an influx of non-Nogai migrants was that many Nogai began to leave their historical districts to move to cities, where they joined Nogai cultural organizations in an effort to preserve their formerly rural culture. By 1970 only 20% of their historical territory was occupied by Nogais. The Astrakhan and Crimean Nogais were rapidly being assimilated.

In the 1970s the threat to their remaining pasture lands prompted the formation of a movement for a separate autonomous state within Soviet Russia. The movement strengthened in the late 1980s, particularly following the relaxation of Soviet rule after 1987. In the 1989 census, thousands of ethnic Nogais, formerly counted as other ethnic groups for political or economic reasons, registered as members of the Nogai nationality. Two newspapers in the Nogai language were begun, but due to poor road conditions and poorly managed communications, their distribution was not wide. The first fledgling Nogai political groups were dismissed as extremists. Nonetheless, the movement toward autonomy, particularly calling for the autonomy they enjoyed before 1957, sent petitions to the authorities in Moscow.

The Nogai national movement, Birlik (Unity), in existence since 1957 as a cultural organization, was transformed into a political movement in

December 1989, when it came out in favor of an autonomous Nogai republic to include parts of Dagestan, Stavropol, and Chechnya. The goal of Birlik was to undo the division of the historical Nogai homeland among three present administrative entities, in which the Nogai form small minorities. In May 1991, the Nogais opposed a Dagestan sovereignty resolution because it failed to address the demand for a separate Nogai republic within the Russian Federation. They demanded that the large Kislyar district, abolished in 1957, be restored on the left bank of the Terek River and separated from Dagestan.

In the 1990s, the Nogais mobilized to save their small nation from extinction. Administratively divided and with education in their language limited, they were nearly assimilated in the 1970s, but a reversal of that trend and the reculturation of the Nogais in the years since the disintegration of the Soviet Union revived the language and culture and brought the Nogais back from the edge of extinction.

The Nogais living in the Chechen Republic were caught up in the Russian war against the independence movement of the Chechens.* Most fled the region in 1994–95 and took refuge among the Nogais of Dagestan. The remainder, living in southern Chechnya, left the region during the renewed fighting in 1999–2000. Around 10,000 Nogais are now in refugee camps in northern Dagestan.

The national movement now focuses on the creation within the Russian Federation of a separate Nogai republic that would facilitate the gathering of the Nogai from other regions. The Nogais want to reoccupy their traditional territory in the Nogai Steppe in northern Dagestan, although at present they are dispersed across several Dagestani districts and in other areas of the North Caucasus. In 1999, in an informal poll of ethnic Nogais in the North Caucasus, over 35% expressing their willingness to return to their historical homeland in the Nogai Steppe if a sovereign homeland were to be created.

SELECTED BIBLIOGRAPHY:

Matveeva, Anna. *The North Caucasus: Russia's Fragile Borderland.* 2000.
Olson, James S. *An Ethnographic Dictionary of the Russian and Soviet Empires.* 1994.
Tutuncu, Mehmet, ed. *The Turkic Peoples of the Caucasus.* 2001.
Warhola, James W. *Politicized Ethnicity in the Russian Federation.* 1996.

Normans

Normands

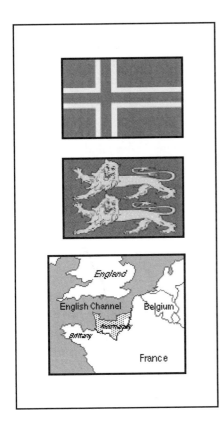

POPULATION: Approximately (2002e) 4,030,000 Normans in France, most concentrated in the Normandy region of France, but with large communities in Paris and other large French cities.

THE NORMAN HOMELAND: The Norman homeland lies in northwestern France, a region of flat grasslands and farmlands rising to the Hills of Normandy in the southeast, and including the Cotentin Peninsula and the Norman coast on the English Channel, locally called the Norman Channel. Most of Normandy is flat farmland, forests, and gentle hills, including the western spur of the Massif Armoricain. The coast has a number of excellent harbors, particularly Le Havre and Cherbourg. The historical region of Normandy has no official status but forms two administrative planning regions of the French republic, Basse-Normandie and Haute-Normandie, comprising the departments of Manche, Calvados, Orne, Eure, and Seine-Maritime. *Region of Normandy (Normandie)*: 11,521 sq. mi.—29,840 sq. km, (2002e) 3,223,000—Normans 91%, other French 8%, English 1%. The Norman capital and major cultural center is Rouen, (2002e) 104,000, metropolitan area 461,000. The other important cultural center is Caen, (2002e) 115,000.

FLAG: The Norman national flag, the flag of the national movement, is a red field bearing a red Scandinavian cross, outlined in yellow. The flag of the region of Normandy is a red field bearing two yellow lions, called Norman Lions—the same lions featured on many of the personal flags of the British royal family and on flags used in the Channel Islands.

PEOPLE AND CULTURE: The Normans are a French-speaking nation, the descendents of Germanic Franks and later Norse Vikings. The original Normans, from "Nortmanni," or Northmen, were pagan barbarians from

Denmark, Norway, and Iceland known for plundering the coasts of Europe in the eighth century. The early Normans were characterized by their courage, love of fighting, and a precocious sense of the use and value of money. The modern-day Normans, true to their Scandinavian heritage, are generally taller, fairer, and more often light-eyed than the other French peoples. The Normans, particularly since the beginning of urbanization of the 1960s and 1970s, have been plagued by rural depopulation since World War II. The names of places and families reflect Nordic, Anglo-Saxon, and Frankish backgrounds. An important part of the Norman culture is cuisine, which differs considerably from the French cuisine of Paris and makes extensive use of dairy and apple products, and fish.

LANGUAGE AND RELIGION: The Normans have retained a distinctive culture and dialect, which predates modern French and displays many Norse and English words and forms. The Normans are bilingual in the standard French of Paris, but the language of daily life remains the Norman dialect, which is spoken in several subdialects that correspond to the historical districts of Normandy. The use of the Norman patois, which incorporates numerous English expressions and words of Scandinavian derivation, is declining, although part of the Norman reculturation of the late twentieth century was a strong movement to save what was increasingly called the Norman national language. In recent years dictionaries and grammars have been published in the Norman dialect.

Although the majority of the Normans are believers, with a large Roman Catholic majority and a Protestant minority, they tend to be less intensely religious and more skeptical than is usual in France. The Catholic Church is still highly influential in the daily life of the Normans, particularly in charities and other organizations sponsored by local parishes. There were many converts to Protestantism after 1528, and sizable communities remain in Rouen, Caen, and the village of Luneray in Seine-Maritime.

NATIONAL HISTORY: The coastal region facing Britannia across the narrow channel formed part of Roman Gaul for centuries but suffered economically and politically following the Roman withdrawal from Britannia in A.D. 410. Invading Germanic Franks, moving into the crumbling Roman Empire, settled the region in 486. In the sixth century the region was brought under the authority of the Frankish kingdom of Neustria. The area's only large population center evolved around the coastal ports and in the valley of the Seine River, while rural lords held most of the land in small feudal holdings.

Vikings, called Norsemen, began to raid the coastal regions in the early ninth century and by 841 controlled most of the coastal districts. The Norsemen established large colonies on the English Channel and pushed inland against French resistance. Unable to defeat the fierce Vikings, the French king Charles the Simple finally accepted Norse control of the region. The duchy of Normandy was created in 911, when the Viking chief

Rollo, or Hrolf, received lands around Rouen and Evreux from the king by the Treaty of St. Clair-sur-Epte. With its pastures, fisheries, and forests, this land was a rich prize. Rollo's successors extended their authority aggressively. Large number of Scandinavians immigrated to settle the new Norse land. The Norsemen, later called Normans, eventually accepted Christianity and the French language as the price of French acceptance. Early Norman history, lacking the records that only Christian clerics could write at the time, is not well documented.

The second duke of Normandy, William I, called William Longsword, was murdered by the Flemish* in 942, and Norman possessions were threatened. Only under his son Richard I was administrative continuity established, based on a peaceful succession as the new duke and control of the church, which was increasingly involved in the politics of the duchy. The Norman dukes allied themselves with the French duke Hugh Capet and were rewarded when he became king of France in 987. At this time a new Norman aristocracy took shape.

The Normans gradually lost contact with Scandinavia, but not the Norse craving for adventure and conquest. On the pretext of expelling the Byzantine Greeks and Arabs from Roman Catholic lands, Normans, led by Tankard de Hauteville, conquered southern Italy and Sicily between 1057 and 1091. Another Norman army, under Duke William II of Normandy, crossed the Channel to conquer Saxon England in 1066. Duke William had to put down a dangerous rising of Norman barons in 1047 to establish central control of castles, which was without precedent in France, before crossing the English Channel.

Many of the Norman leaders of Normandy, England, and Sicily were among the most powerful and successful rulers of their age in Western Europe. Their ability to create political institutions that were both stable and enduring stemmed from a capacity to imitate and adapt existing systems. The Normans had begun as pagan raiders bent on plunder and slaughter, but they quickly became missionaries and proselytizers of the societies that they had attacked and that ultimately absorbed them.

Norman rule in England changed the history of the island. In the conquered areas Norman architecture, noted for frequent use of round arches, lack of adornment, and massive proportions added a new element to the English landscape. The French-speaking Norman conquerors established a landed nobility over the majority Saxons and remained a separate people for centuries.

The dukes of Normandy ruled both England and Normandy until the French conquest of the mainland Norman territories in 1204. The Norman king of England renounced his title to Normandy in 1259, but his descendents returned to the mainland to reconquer Normandy in 1346. England returned Normandy to the French by treaty in 1360, although the region again came under English rule in 1417–18, during the Hundred

Years' War, which arose from Norman claims on both sides of the English Channel. A young Frenchwoman, Joan of Arc, burned at the stake in Rouen by the English in 1431 during the long war, became the patron saint of Normandy. In 1450 the defeated English abandoned mainland Normandy, retaining only the Norman Islands, later renamed the Channel Islands.

King Louis XI of France gave the duchy of Normandy to his brother Charles in 1465 but soon brought it back under his rule. In 1468 he persuaded the French estates-general to declare Normandy an inalienable part of the French crown. Thereafter the province of Normandy was governed directly by the monarch. Succeeding French kings worked to assimilate the Normans and Norman institutions into the French system. A Norman legislature, the *parlement*, was established at Rouen in 1499 as a focus for Norman loyalty; the Normans retained many such local liberties and privileges. The legislature exercised considerable regional power for nearly 300 years, until the French Revolution in 1789 and the dissolution of all provincial autonomy. The revocation of the Edict of Nantes in 1685 led to a mass emigration of Huguenots, who had contributed greatly to the prosperity of the region, but the Normans soon recovered.

Divested of all traditional privileges, the Normans turned against the French Revolution they had enthusiastically welcomed in 1789–90. Rebellion broke out in Normandy in 1793; the rebels took the name "Chouans," meaning "owls" in the Norman dialect. The rebel bands used owl hoots as signals. The Chouans fought a bitter guerrilla war against the revolutionary forces but were ultimately defeated with great loss of life. The crushing of the Chouan revolt is still referred to by Normans as the first modern genocide. Boats filled with rebels and their families were sunk in the Seine, while whole villages were burned and their inhabitants massacred or scattered.

Napoleon Bonaparte, coming to power in the aftermath of revolution and war, in 1791 split France's historical regions into small departments to undermine local loyalties. Under Napoleon all power was centralized in Paris, where it remained until the late twentieth century. The Norman Chouans again rebelled against the loss of their rights in 1815, forcing Napoleon to divert troops from the decisive and final battle at Waterloo.

In the nineteenth and early twentieth centuries, Normandy remained pastoral and underdeveloped, with most industry, government, and culture centralized in Paris. Normans had to leave their homeland in order to excel in the arts, literature, government, or education. Resentment of the need to emigrate and the threat to their culture it represented incited the beginning of a modest Norman national movement, one of the few in Western Europe in the late nineteenth century not based on language. The nationalist movement spurred a revival of the Norman culture. The early nationalists claimed to be French but also Norman, a revolutionary idea in highly centralized France. Following the canonization of Joan of Arc in 1920, the Normans adopted her as their unofficial patron saint, even though she had not been born a Norman.

In the years prior to World War II, nationalist and radical political parties proliferated in Normandy, stimulated by the region's economic backwardness. In 1939 workers in Paris earned an average 40% more than their Norman counterparts. Although the region remained economically backward and underdeveloped, the Norman ports remained important in France's trade with the British Isles.

Normandy was occupied by Nazi German troops in 1940 and became part of the front line, facing Britain across the Channel. A concerted German campaign during the war to win Norman support by stressing common Nordic origins of the German and Norman peoples met with little success; the vast majority remained loyal to the French state. The first region of continental Europe to be liberated from Nazi occupation, Normandy sustained massive damage during the Allied invasion in June 1944, which began on the Norman beaches. Normandy recovered from the damage done by the war by the early 1950s and experienced a modest prosperity based on cross-Channel trade.

A regionalist movement, claiming that Paris appropriated Normandy's finest resources and most talented people, gained support after France's entry in the European Economic Community (EEC) in 1960 shifted French trade to the east and away from Normandy and the Channel. In 1969 the regionalists created the Mouvement de la Jeunesse de Normandie, which demanded the creation of autonomous universities specializing in the occupations of the region. The debate over the reunification of historical Normandy soon became the focus of local nationalism, led by the Union for the Normandy Region. In 1971 the Normandy Movement was formed by several regionalist and nationalist organizations. A regional assembly was created at Rouen in 1972 but had little power.

The Normans, but not the French government, supported Britain and Ireland's bid to join the EEC, finally realized in 1973. The increasing integration of Europe gave new impetus to the growing Norman national movement. Few Normans saw the sense of applying to Paris, to the east, for trade agreements with Normandy's natural trading partners, Britain and Ireland, to the west.

A socialist government elected in France in 1981 promised certain powers to planned new regions based roughly on France's historical regions, but the limited powers only brought demands for greater home rule. The government, over the protests of the Norman regionalists, divided historic Normandy into two distinct regions. The national movement, modeled on that of the neighboring Bretons,* with whom the Normans have close historical ties, focused on the unification of the historical Norman territories and demands for greater economic autonomy. The survival of the declining Norman dialect became a major nationalist issue in the 1990s.

In early 1989, as the French prepared to celebrate the 200th anniversary of the French Revolution, many Normans demanded that their martyrs and the horrors of the revolution in Normandy should be remembered. They especially wanted an official apology to the Chouans, considered the first Norman nationalists, who had been hanged from lampposts, guillotined, and shot before the revolution could be forced on the reluctant Normans.

The nationalists at the beginning of the twenty-first century published their demands, which included: cultural and economic autonomy, by returning to the sovereignty of the years 911–1204; the reunification of historical Normandy, according to the slogan "one plus one equals one"; the extension of regional development projects; the promotion of Norman identity and dialect; the teaching of particular Norman history in regional schools; and an end to the "Jacobite" centralization that stifled regional development. Except for a small, militant minority, the major organizations rejected separatism and violence.

In a poll of the region's inhabitants in 1998, over 65% favored the reunification of the two Norman regions to reconstitute the historical united Normandy. For the small but growing number of pro-European Norman nationalists, the survival of the Norman culture, economy, and dialect depends on achieving Norman reunification and sovereignty in a united Europe formed from regions.

SELECTED BIBLIOGRAPHY:

Chrisp, Peter. *The Normans*. 1995.
Christiansen, Eric. *History of the Normans*. 1998.
Jewett, S. *The Story of the Normans*. 1990.
Palgrave, Francis. *History of Normandy and England*. 1995.

North Chadians

Muslim Chadians

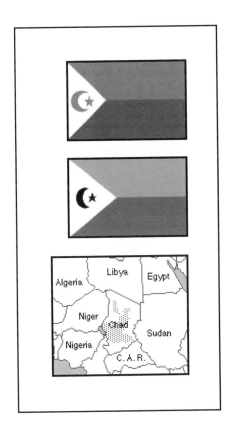

POPULATION: Approximately (2002e) 3,320,000 North Chadians in Chad, concentrated in the prefectures north of the Chari River. Other North Chadian communities live in southern Libya and around N'Djamena, the Chadian capital.

THE NORTH CHADIAN HOMELAND: The North Chadian homeland lies in the Sahara Desert in north-central Africa, occupying the arid Tibesti Mountains in the north, the bush lands and savanna in the south, and the Ennedi Plateau. Much of the region is arid and unproductive; its population is concentrated in the region's grazing lands and limited agricultural lands. North Chad has no official status. The territory claimed by North Chadian nationalists includes the Chadian prefectures of Borkou-Ennedi-Tibesti, Kanem, Lac, Batha, Biltine, Ouaddaï, Chari-Baguirmi, Guéra, and Salamat. *Region of North Chad*: 403,196 sq. mi.—1,044,055 sq. km, (2002e) 3,813,000—North Chadian 80%, Mabas* (Ouaddaians) 14%, Kanuris* (Kanembu), 5%, other Chadians 1%. The North Chadian capital and major cultural center is N'Djamena, (2002e) 607,000.

FLAG: The North Chadian national flag, the flag of the national movement and of the proposed Islamic Republic of North Chad, is a horizontal bicolor of red over green bearing a white triangle at the hoist charged with a green crescent moon and five-pointed star. The flag of the largest national organization, the Chad National Liberation Front, is the same as the national flag, except that the bottom stripe is blue.

PEOPLE AND CULTURE: The North Chadians are a Muslim people comprising dozens of distinct peoples representing several cultural and linguistic groups united by religion and history. Most of the North Chadian peoples are of mixed Arabic, Berber, and black African descent. The

North Chadians formed as a nation during the colonial era due to their shared rejection of French colonial authority and of domination by the Logonese* peoples of the south. Most of the groups in north Chad are affiliated with the Arab and Saharan/Sahelian Muslim culture that dominates the northern, central, and eastern parts of Chad. A contentious claim that the North Chadians are ethnic Libyans has complicated political and ethnic relationships in the region since the colonial period. The largest of the North Chadian groups are the Sudanic Arabs, about 41% of the total, comprising the Zagawa, Baggara, Shuwa, and Oueler Shiner tribes; the Tedas, with about 27% of the population; the Mabas, Masalits, and Mimi, collectively called Ouaddaians or Wadaians, making up about 17%; and the Kanembu or Kanuris, about 8%. Other sizable groups are the Hausas,* Fulanis, Bertis, Tamas, Dagus, Dazas, Toubou, Tauregs,* Hadjeraï, and Baguirmis.

LANGUAGE AND RELIGION: The largest segment of the North Chadian nation is represented by Sudanic Arabs speaking Sudanic dialects of Arabic, the lingua franca of the region. Other languages widely used are the Nilo-Saharan languages and Maba. The majority of the North Chadian peoples are nomadic or seminomadic herders.

The North Chadians are overwhelmingly of the Sunni Muslim faith, which spread through the region from the tenth century. Islam is well established in most major towns and wherever Arab or Arabized populations are found; in the isolated mountainous regions of Guéra and among some ethnic groups, religious practices are mixed with pre-Islamic customs and traditions. Islam has attracted a wide variety of ethnic and linguistic groups and has forged a certain degree of unity. The Chadian government, currently controlled by the North Chadians, has proposed the institution of Shari'a, Islamic laws, and the Arabic language, the language of their Muslim religion, as the justice system and official language of the Chadian state even though Chad is only about 50% Muslim; the remainder of the population is about 30% Christian and the rest animist.

NATIONAL HISTORY: Known to the ancient Egyptians, the peoples of the region absorbed cultural influences from the civilizations of North Africa and the Christian kingdoms that later grew up just to the east. The area south of the Sahara, mentioned in the early seventh century A.D. by Arab historians as settled by nomadic pagan Arabs, received an influx of Berber refugees fleeing the Arab invasion of North Africa in the seventh and eighth centuries. The Arab and Berber peoples conquered or weakened the tribal states in the region, and an Arab-Berber culture spread across the region.

In the eighth century, newcomers from the upper Nile Valley moved into the area and established walled city-states in the fertile lands in the south. Zagawa Arab nomads, possibly of Berber origin, conquered much of the region in the ninth century, laying the foundations for the states that developed as regional powers in the eleventh and twelfth centuries. The degree of ethnic variety in the region increased as the southern Sahara became a linguistic, social, and cultural crossroad.

Invading Muslim Arabs conquered the area and introduced Islam, traditionally in the year 1090. Controlled by a sophisticated Muslim Berber-Arab pastoral elite, the states of the region, including Wadai, Bagirmi, and Fitri, grew wealthy on the trans-Saharan caravan trade. The Muslims raided the black African tribes to the south for captives to send to the slave markets of North Africa. Even before European colonization there was a history of confrontation between the Muslims and the animist black Africans.

The empire of Kanem-Bornu of the Kanembu Kanuris, centered on Lake Chad, conquered the numerous small warring states in the thirteenth century. Its mounted and armored warriors swept across the region and to the east, eventually destroying the Christian kingdoms west of the upper Nile Valley. At the height of its power in the sixteenth and early seventeenth centuries, Kanem-Bornu controlled a vast empire in central Africa.

The Fulani, a powerful warrior people, conquered most of the Muslim states south of the Sahara in the early nineteenth century, except for Kanem-Bornu. The Kanembu defeated the Fulani in 1812, but the effort so weakened the state that it began to disintegrate. The ancient empire was wracked by civil wars and clan and tribal conflicts when the first Europeans visited the region in 1822.

In the 1890s the Madhists, Islamic fundamentalists from present-day Sudan, conquered the districts in the east. In the west, Rabah Zobeir, also called Rabah Amoney, a Sudanese ex-slave turned slave trader and military chieftain, rose to power. Called the "Napoleon of Africa," Rabah led a vast Muslim army west, defeating and absorbing tribes and states. Alarmed by his advance, the rulers of Kanem-Bornu requested French military aid in 1893. In 1900 a combined European military force defeated Rabah's army, and in 1902 the Europeans divided his empire between their various colonial empires.

The new French territories officially became part of Chad, a French colony south of Lake Chad since 1897. From the beginning, the Muslim peoples rejected inclusion in a territory occupied by tribes they had formerly raided for slaves and booty. The French military finally subdued the Muslim tribes in 1912. Although officially in civilian-ruled French West Africa, the Muslim northern districts of Chad remained under virtual French occupation, due to the frequent uprisings.

Almost as soon as they took control, the French began leaving, except for the military, preferring to rule the Muslim areas through payments to local leaders. Educational opportunities, existing mostly in the southern black areas, were not extended to the north. The Logone peoples of the south progressed much more rapidly into the civil service and the colonial military. Antagonism increased during the 1950s, when the Logonese virtually ran the region, under the supervision of the French colonial authorities. When independence approached, the southern tribes controlled the state; the Muslims were mostly excluded from power. To the Muslims, who viewed the black Africans as either subjects or slaves, the idea of being ruled by a black-dominated government was unthinkable.

Chad became an independent republic in 1960. The first postcolonial government of François Tombalbaye, dominated by the black African tribes of the south, was rejected in the Muslim north. The French maintained a strong military presence, which maintained a precarious calm, but in 1965 the Chadian government requested their withdrawal. In 1966, no longer constrained by the French troops, several Muslim leaders demanded the secession of the northern provinces and the establishment of an independent Islamic Republic of North Chad. The Front de Libération Nationale du Tchad (FROLINAT) assumed the leadership of the diverse groups. The nationalists' demands for autonomy, a larger share of power, and a fairer distribution of development funds were rejected by the French-backed Chadian government in N'Djamena.

In spite of several French-brokered truces and cease-fires and, in 1968, military intervention, rebellion spread across the region in 1970, setting off a vicious civil war. Libyan troops entered the country in 1971, supplying arms to the rebels. President Tombalbaye finally agreed to negotiations, but then he apparently went insane. In a frenzy of voodoo and nationalistic fervor, he forced the entire population of Chad to take traditional African names and made the whole civil service undergo the initiation rites of his own Sara tribe. Anyone who refused was summarily executed. In 1975 he was overthrown by southern rivals, and a new government was installed.

In 1978 the FROLINAT forces gained control of most of North Chad, but again the French intervened and forced negotiations. A government of national reconciliation, including Muslim leaders, fell apart, and the rebellion resumed in 1979. Chad's postindependence history became a monotonous litany of military coups, rebellions, and violence. Ethnic, religious, economic, and political factors continued to divide the over 200 ethnic groups of the country.

The cause of Muslim unity and separation from the infidel south spread through the region in the 1970s, spurred by the growth of Muslim fundamentalism across the Muslim world. In March 1979 the FROLINAT forces took control of N'Djamena and drove the southern tribes from power.

The dozens of ethnic and language groups making up the Muslim population of Chad, frequently split into several subgroups, remained united against the Christian government, but as always in the bellicose north, the coalition began to fragment. The factionalism of the civil war underscored a tendency to find allies among neighboring subgroups rather than with a larger inclusive religious, ethnic, or linguistic group. Splinter groups proliferated based on groups, subgroups, and regions.

After 1980 the confused shifting of alliances and fighting between various Muslim factions splintered the North Chad national movement. The repeated military intervention by the French and Libyan incursions exacerbated the chaos in the region. Idriss Déby led a coup in 1990 and was later installed as president. In October 1992 the French dispatched troops to protect a Chadian government that commanded little loyalty in either Muslim northern Chad or in Christian and animist Logone Chad in the south. In August 1994 a rebellion against the minority Muslim government spread across the south, and isolated outbreaks of unrest occurred in the north.

Déby was reelected in 1996 in an election marked by fraud, vote rigging, and local irregularities. The former unity of the Muslim peoples of North Chad splintered again, and regional and ethnic conflicts proliferated in the 1990s. The government was unable to exert effective control over many parts of the country, but it continued to attempt to reach agreements with the many rebel groups. By 1997 most of the rebel groups, cut off from rear bases and supplies in neighboring countries, had been forced to sign peace agreements.

In late 1997, a former leader of FROLINAT was accused of supporting nationalist groups in a conspiracy to create a Toubou-Taureg state in the northern districts of Chad and Niger. Other northern leaders accused the government of fomenting the rebellion to encourage support in Niger for a consolidated push against the increasingly troublesome North Chadian rebels.

Atrocities carried out by the Republican Guard, the government's mostly Zagawa elite guard, reignited ethnic and regional unrest in 1997–98. A northern rebel group led by members of the Toubou ethnic group, which includes a former defense minister, Youssouf Togoimi, staged a widespread rebellion in the northwest in October 1998. In the late 1990s, Chad was a highly centralized republic dominated by Idriss Déby. Déby and his Zagawa ethnic group, supported by the Hadjeraï, dominated the government and the economy. Ethnic and regional discrimination remained widespread, fueling the continuing regional conflicts within the country. Societal discrimination continued to be practiced routinely by members of all ethnic groups in the region, with de facto segregation in urban neighborhoods. There were few interethnic marriages, even though the groups shared the Muslim religion and culture.

Political parties and groups are readily identifiable on regional or ethnic bases. Muslim nationalists, who support the expulsion of French troops and foreign oil companies, want to separate from Logone Chad, which forms part of black Africa, and to create a separate Islamic Republic of North

Chad based on Islamic culture and Shari'a law. Ethnicity continues to influence government appointments and political alliances. The Zagawas are dominant in the public sector; they largely control the economy and are overrepresented in key institutions of state power, including the military.

The government, in recent years, has attempted to defuse the many ethnic and regional conflicts in order to facilitate the extraction of large oil reserves in the south of the country. A pipeline, planned to carry oil from the fields to ports on the Atlantic, is being constructed through francophone Cameroon, though a route through Nigeria would be more direct. The pipeline, financed by France and the World Bank, is denounced by many opposition groups as making military intervention in support of the government much more likely in the event of a serious threat to the Déby regime. The present fragile truce is being put at risk by the prospect of huge oil wealth in the south that would be controlled by the Muslim north.

SELECTED BIBLIOGRAPHY:

Azevedo, Mario J., ed. *Chad: A Nation in Search of Its Future.* 1998.

Berberoglu, Berch. *The National Question: Nationalism, Ethnic Conflict, and Self-Determination in the 20th Century.* 1995.

Manning, Patrick. *Francofone Sub-Sahara Africa 1880–1985.* 1988.

Safran, William, and Ramon Maiz, eds. *Identity and Territorial Autonomy in Plural Societies.* 2000.

Northern Cypriots

Kibris; Turkish Cypriots

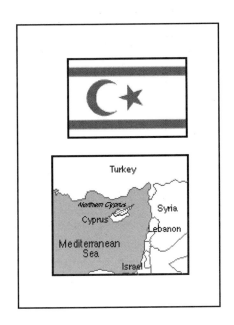

POPULATION: Approximately (2002e) 145,000 Northern Cypriots in Cyprus, concentrated in the northern third of the island of Cyprus, the Turkish Republic of Northern Cyprus. Other Northern Cypriot communities live in the United Kingdom and in cities on the Turkish mainland, where an estimated 40,000 Northern Cypriots now reside.

THE NORTHERN CYPRIOT HOMELAND: The Northern Cypriot homeland occupies the northern part of the island of Cyprus in the eastern Mediterranean Sea, 40 miles south of the Turkish mainland and 60 miles west of Syria. The region includes highlands north of Nicosia and coastal lowlands in the east. Northern Cyprus forms a self-proclaimed republic under Turkish occupation and protection. The official status of the region remains in dispute. *Turkish Republic of Northern Cyprus (TRNC/Kuzey Kibris Türk Cumhuriyeti)*: 1,295 sq. mi.—3,354 sq. km, (2002e) 188,000—Northern Cypriots 80%, Turkish 18%, Greek Cypriots 1%, others 1%. The Northern Cypriot capital and major cultural center is the divided city of Nicosia, called Lefkosa in Turkish, (2002e—Turkish sector) 41,000. The other major cultural center is Famagusta, called Gazi Magusa by the Northern Cypriots, (2002e) 24,000.

FLAG: The Turkish Cypriot national flag, the official flag of the republic, is a white field, with narrow, horizontal red stripes near the top and bottom, bearing a red crescent moon and a red five-pointed star near the hoist.

PEOPLE AND CULTURE: The Turkish Cypriots are a Turkish people, descendents of medieval settlers from the Turkish mainland. Centuries of mixing with the Greeks and other Mediterranean peoples evolved a unique Turkish-speaking group on the island with their own culture, dialect, and history. Better educated and more prosperous than the mainland Turks, the Cypriot Turks are separated from the Turks by centuries of history.

Since 1974 over 60,000 mainland Turks, called Anatolian Turks, have settled in the region, not counting the 29,000 Turkish soldiers and their families. The massive influx of mainland Turks has raised tension between the islanders and the newcomers.

LANGUAGE AND RELIGION: The Northern Cypriots speak the Kibris dialect of Osmanli Turkish, which incorporates many English, Greek, and Armenian words and forms. Most Turkish Cypriots speak standard Turkish and often English as a second language, but few speak Greek.

The Turkish Cypriots are Sunni Muslims, although religious practices tend to be more moderate than on the Turkish mainland. Turkish Cypriot women have higher status and are allowed more freedom than most Turkish women, the result of decades of British rule.

NATIONAL HISTORY: The largest island in the eastern Mediterranean, Cyprus received colonists from most of the ancient empires that rose in the Middle East, North Africa, and southern Europe, although the Greeks formed a majority from about 295 B.C. Conquered by the Romans in 58 B.C., the island remained a part of the eastern Roman Empire when the state divided in A.D. 395. Captured by the European Crusaders in 1191, the island became a territory of the French Lusignan family from 1192 to 1474. In 1489 the maritime empire of the Venetians* added Cyprus to their growing Mediterranean empire.

Ottoman Turks invaded the island in 1562 and overwhelmed the last Venetian stronghold in 1571. The Turks imposed a harsh rule, suppressing the majority Greek Christians and settling thousands of Muslim Turks on confiscated lands. Frequent Greek rebellions, crushed with great severity, exacerbated the ethnic enmity between the island's two largest national groups.

Mainland Greece, independent of Turkish rule in 1829, supported majority Greek Cypriot demands for *enosis*, union with Greece. Greek volunteers aided a sporadic rebellion against Turkish rule. The Ottoman government, unable to crush the uprising, leased the island to Great Britain in 1878. Modern education and health care, introduced by the British administration, greatly benefited both ethnic groups and raised living standards on the island far beyond those of mainland Turkey or Greece.

Great Britain formally annexed the island when the Ottoman Empire joined the Central Powers as war began in 1914. In 1915, the British government offered Cyprus to Greece as an inducement to enter the war on the Allied side, but King Constantine of Greece declined the politically charged offer. Turkey, defeated along with the other Central Powers, recognized British annexation of the island through the 1923 Treaty of Lausanne.

Relations between the Turkish and Greek Cypriots deteriorated in the early twentieth century. In spite of the material benefits of British rule, Greek Cypriot agitation for *enosis* continued to sour relations between the island's two peoples. The Turkish Cypriots vehemently opposed inclusion in the Greek state. The dispute exploded in violent ethnic clashes in 1931, and with periodic disturbances up to World War II. In 1941 the British authorities allowed formerly forbidden political meetings.

A new round of violence erupted in 1954, provoked by renewed Greek Cypriot demands for union with Greece. The Turkish Cypriot minority, rejecting both Greek Cypriot domination and union with Greece, demanded *taksim*, the partition of the island between the two national groups. Negotiations between the two groups and the British authorities broke down in 1955, when the Greek Cypriot Organization launched a violent campaign to drive the British from the island and achieve union with Greece by force. An agreement reached in 1959 precluded either union with Greece or ethnic partition. The compromise paved the way for Cypriot independence in 1960. The United Kingdom, Greece, and Turkey signed the independence agreement as guarantors of Cypriot peace and territorial integrity. The constitution provided for a Greek Cypriot president, a Turkish Cypriot vice president, a council of ministers with seven Greeks and three Turks, and a House of Representatives of 50 members.

For hundreds of years, the island of Cyprus had been home to a mixed population of ethnic Greeks and Turks. Their cultures, influenced by the other, differed considerably from the cultures of mainland Greece and Turkey, and the two peoples had much in common. However, even after Cyprus became independent, the members of the Greek Cypriot community continued to agitate for formal union with Greece, increasingly alarming and alienating the Turkish-speaking Cypriot community.

Greek Cypriot domination, often brutal and heavy-handed, culminated in the death of two Turkish Cypriots at the hands of Greek Cypriot police in December 1963. The Turkish Cypriots rebelled. The uprising set off a vicious civil war and brought Greece and Turkey close to war. Isolated Turkish Cypriots moved into the relative safety of Turkish enclaves. By the early 1970s, Cyprus was effectively partitioned, with fortified Turkish Cypriot enclaves scattered across the northern part of the island. With funding from the military junta controlling Greece, Greek Cypriot militants formed armed guerrilla groups.

Amid the violence, Greek Cypriot military officers of the Cyprus National Guard led a coup that overthrew the island's government on 16 July 1974. The coup leaders demanded immediate *enosis*. Diplomatic efforts failed, and four days later the Turkish government, citing its obligations as a signatory to the 1959 independence agreement, launched an invasion of the island. Forty thousand Turkish troops landed on the northern coast and quickly took control of half the island, provoking a crisis in Greece that led to the collapse of the military junta. Two hundred thousand Greek Cypriots fled south, while 45,000 Turkish Cypriots fled north to the occupation zone. After a month of fighting, a cease-fire line was established.

The Turkish invasion led to the complete partition of the island, as well as to thousands of deaths.

International efforts to mediate the dispute foundered as the Turkish Cypriots demanded legal partition and declared an autonomous state in the 37% of the island under Turkish occupation. The Turkish government began to settle colonists from its underdeveloped eastern provinces on lands abandoned by Greek refugees. Repeated attempts at negotiations failed over Turkish insistence on a bizonal federation in the face of Greek Cypriot demands for a unitary state.

Frustrated by the lack of progress after several rounds of negotiations, the Turkish Cypriot leader Rauf Denktash declared the independence of the Turkish Republic of Northern Cyprus on 15 November 1983, but left open the option of later federation. The new state, recognized only by Turkey, insisted that its independence was not negotiable during talks that dragged on throughout the 1980s. In May 1985 a constitution of the Turkish Republic of Northern Cyprus was approved by referendum. International sanctions damaged the northern economy; the average difference between annual incomes between the Turkish and Greek Cypriots widened from $425 in 1976 to over $4,500 by 1989.

The large number of Anatolian Turks settled in the state became a point of contention with the Turkish Cypriots. Although they shared language and religion, they had little else in common. The Cypriots world outlook and economic development had diverged from those of the mainland centuries before. Cypriot incomes, averaging 70% higher than the mainland, became an issue between the two Turkish peoples. The Turkish Cypriot community feared that their unique island culture would be swamped by immigration from the mainland, but an even greater fear was the loss of Turkey's military protection.

In early 1992 the United Nations put forward new proposals for a single Cypriot state made up of two zones, but again the negotiations failed. The Turkish Cypriots reiterated that independence was not negotiable, though a federation of independent states on the island would meet the requirements of both national groups. The Greeks rejected the proposal. Incidents along the dividing line between the Turkish and Greek sectors continued.

In August 1994, following a new round of failed talks, the European Union complicated the situation by suggesting that Greek Cyprus join the EU on its own. The EU also imposed import restrictions on goods from Northern Cyprus; the European Union had taken 74% of Northern Cyprus's exports in 1993. The European Union's intervention exacerbated the Turkish Cypriots' sense of isolation and strengthened their determination to maintain their independence. Rauf Denktash in 1998 reiterated Turkish Cypriot demands for a confederation of two independent and equal Cypriot states. The United Nations, European Union, and the Greek Cypriot government rejected the demand.

The Greek Cypriot government is acknowledged internationally as the government of the whole island, a point disputed by the Northern Cypriots. The Northern Cypriot state, although recognized as independent only by Turkey, functions as de facto independent state. Residents of each sector are allowed to cross the border to visit sites of religious and historical importance. Formal accession talks with the European Union (EU) were begun by the Greek Cypriot government, representing the entire island, in 1998.

Severe earthquakes in both Turkey and Greece in 1999 began a process called by some "earthquake diplomacy." A thaw in relations between Turkey and Greece as a result of their shared disasters and the mutual help offered by both governments to victims made a solution to the seemingly intractable Cyprus problem appear closer.

In December 1999, the leaders of the Turkish and Greek Cypriot states, Rauf Denktash and Glafcos Clerides, met in New York for the first time in two years. They received pressure from many sides: American president Bill Clinton, European leaders, and from inside Cyprus, where the Greek Cypriots were enjoying unprecedented prosperity, denied the Northern Cypriots due to trade embargoes and sanctions.

The Turkish government, facing the cost of rebuilding following the massive earthquake, is anxious to reduce the military cost of its presence in Northern Cyprus. Relations between the Turkish government and the Northern Cypriots, tense throughout the 1990s, deteriorated with increasing Turkish pressure to reach an accord with the Greek Cypriots. In July 2000, five Northern Cypriots, including three journalists, were arrested by Turkish troops on suspicion of espionage. They were among a growing number of Northern Cypriots calling for the police to be placed under the control of the civilian Northern Cypriot authorities.

The Greek Cypriot government, after years of negotiations, has accepted the idea of a loose federal state in Cyprus. But the Turkish Cypriots maintain that only independence will protect them and their unique culture. The two sides continue to talk, but a solution remains elusive. The hope is that the prospect of EU membership will lure the two governments into agreement; however, the two peoples, whatever the attractions of EU membership, deeply mistrust the motives of each other. The Greek Cypriots have to give up the idea that Cyprus is essentially a Greek island, while the Turkish Cypriots have to be convinced that they can avoid being dominated by the Greeks.

The current plan, based on a proposal put together by the United Nations in 1992, would divide the island into two self-governing zones with separate parliaments. A weak central government would be confined to such matters as foreign policy, customs, currency, and postal services. Turkey and Greece, along with the former colonial power, the United Kingdom, would guarantee the settlement. The agreement would give the

Turkish Cypriots 28% of the island, compared with the 37% they have controlled since 1974.

Rauf Denktash stated in 2000 that the Turkish Cypriots must have more than 28%, while most Greek Cypriot politicians claim that 25% is the maximum the Turkish Cypriots should be allowed to control. Other problems remain; Denktash is firmly against Greek Cypriots' returning to live in Northern Cyprus, as the agreement would allow. The Greek Cypriots and the EU are pressing for agreement on the right to live and own property in all parts of the island for both Cypriot peoples. The Northern or Turkish Cypriots, though determined to resist anything that amounts to subjugation by the Greek Cypriots, increasingly realize that without an internationally recognized settlement, their small republic will get steadily poorer than its southern neighbor.

Negotiations resumed in mid-2000, but with little progress. The Northern Cypriots continue to insist on sovereign status in a bizonal federation, which the Greek Cypriot leadership has long rejected. Efforts to find a middle ground in the talks continue, but the chances of persuading the Northern Cypriots to accept anything less than full self-government are not good. In December 2000, Rauf Denktash pulled out of talks until the TRNC is recognized as an independent political entity, with a status equal to Greek-Cypriot part of the island.

A poll, taken in early 2001, found that only 8% of Northern Cypriots want integration with Turkey, 32% want a loose confederation of two Cypriot states, 23% want full recognized independence, 5% return to old undivided island. However, 90% agree on the European Union (EU), they want to join along with Greek-Cypriots.

The issue of Turkish Cyprus has become a major stumbling block to Turkey's own desire to enter the EU, which increased pressure on the Northern Cypriots. In November 2001, following a proposal to begin negotiations with the Greek Cypriots' entry into the EU, but not to begin negotiations with Turkey, the Turkish government threatened to annex Northern Cyprus.

SELECTED BIBLIOGRAPHY:

Dodd, Clement H. *The Cyprus Imbroglio.* 1998.

Joseph, Joseph S. *Cyprus, Ethnic Conflict and International Politics: From Independence to the Threshold of the European Union.* 1999.

Stefanidis, Ioannis D. *Isle of Discord: Nationalism, Imperialism and the Making of the Cyprus Problem.* 1999.

Streissguth, Thomas. *Cyprus: Divided Island.* 1998.

Northern Irish

Ulster Irish; Scotch-Irish; Ulstermen; Ulsterfolk; Orangemen

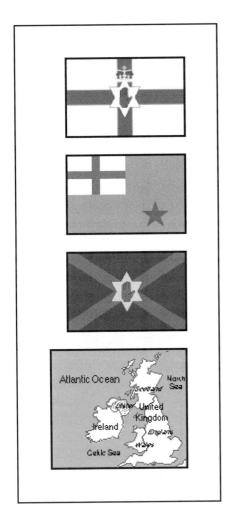

POPULATION: Approximately (2002e) 1,100,000 Northern Irish in the United Kingdom, concentrated in the province of Northern Ireland. Other large Northern Irish communities live in England, particularly the London region, in northern England, and in Scotland. Outside the region there are large Northern Irish communities in the United States, Canada, Australia, New Zealand, and South Africa.

THE NORTHERN IRISH HOMELAND: The Northern Irish homeland lies in the northeastern corner of the island of Ireland, comprising 6 of the 9 counties of the old Irish province of Ulster. Most of the region is rolling hills climbing to the highland areas in Tyrone and Londonderry in the west. The province lies on the North and Irish Seas on the north and west, and borders the Irish Republic on the south. Northern Ireland forms an integral part of the United Kingdom of Great Britain and Northern Ireland. *Province of Northern Ireland (Ulster)*: 5,452 sq. mi.—14,121 sq. km, (2002e) 1,744,000—Northern Irish (Protestants) 53%, Irish (Roman Catholics) 46%, other British 1%. The Northern Irish capital and major cultural center is Belfast, called Bilfawst in the local dialect, (2002e) 257,000, metropolitan area 815,000. The other important cultural center is Londonderry, called Lunnonderrie in the Ulster Scots dialect, (2002e) 83,000.

FLAG: The flag of the Northern Irish, the unofficial flag of the province, is a white field divided by a centered red Cross of St. George, bearing a centered six-pointed star charged with a red hand below a gold crown. The flag of the largest Northern Irish organization, the Orange Order, has an orange flag bearing the Cross of St. George as a canton on the upper hoist and a purple five-pointed star on the lower hoist. The flag of the pro-independence movement is a blue field bearing a centered six-pointed yellow star charged with a red hand centered on a red St. Patrick's Cross.

PEOPLE AND CULTURE: The Northern Irish, increasingly calling themselves Ulstermen or Ulsterfolk, are the Protestant descendants of Scots* and English colonists of the seventeenth and eighteenth centuries. The Northern Irish, even after centuries of living in Ireland, consider themselves British, not Irish. The Northern Irish birthrate, lower than that of the Catholic Irish minority, threatens their hold on the province as the Catholics may soon be in a majority. The distinct culture includes an emerging musical tradition known as Orange music. As is the case with most aspects of life in Northern Ireland, it is difficult to distinguish between indigenous and imported cultural traits, but apart from some traditional Irish musical groups, few traces of Irish culture predating the Protestant Ascendancy remain. Folk participation and recreation are generally focused on religious ceremonies and procession, often tragically violent. Generally, the Northern Irish share the culture of the British Isles and have few distinctive regional characteristics. Nationalists claim that the Northern Irish are the seventh Celtic nation.

LANGUAGE AND RELIGION: The Northern Irish speak English along with a Scotch-Irish dialect of English that includes remnants of their original Scots and northern English dialects brought to the island by early Protestant colonists. The dialect, called Ulster Scots, persists as education in the province is segregated, with Protestants attending state schools, while Catholics attend schools run by the Roman Catholic Church. The language evolved from the dialects brought to the region by the Scottish immigrants and is considered a variety of Lallans, the English dialect spoken in lowland Scotland. About 100,000 people are able to speak Ulster Scots although the dialect is declining rapidly in spite of efforts to revive its use as a regional language.

The Northern Irish are a Protestant people, their national identity closely tied to their religion. Protestantism has shaped the character of the people and to an extent unknown in the rest of the European Union (EU), religion determines a person's way of life.

NATIONAL HISTORY: The northern part of the island of Ireland was included in the ancient Celtic kingdom of Ulster. In the fifth century the island was converted to Christianity by St. Patrick. In the sixth century Vikings began raiding the coastal regions, bringing chaos to the kingdom. Threatened by the Vikings until the ninth century, the regional culture declined and fortified settlements replaced the formerly flourishing ports and farms. By the eighth century, the island's clans had grouped themselves into five kingdoms, of which Ulster under the Uí Néill dynasty was the leading state until the eleventh century. During one of the many sea attacks on the province, the leader of the attackers promised a valuable prize to the first man to touch land with his right hand. One of the raiders, a left-handed man, cut off his right hand and threw it onto the shore. The hand became the national symbol of the region.

Normans* crossing from England conquered Ireland in 1169–71, bringing all of Ireland under the rule of the English crown. Ulster shared the history of Ireland until the reign of Elizabeth the First of England in the late sixteenth century. After crushing a third Irish Catholic rebellion against harsh English Protestant rule, the colonial authorities confiscated much Irish land in Ulster and colonized the region with Protestant Scots. Another Irish rebellion in 1641–51 was brutally suppressed by the English under Oliver Cromwell, who dispossessed many thousands of Irish in Ulster and settled loyal English Protestants on their lands. Over the next century many more Protestants were settled in the region by the English government and Ulster became separate from the rest of Ireland, taking on a distinct culture and character by the eighteenth century.

Protestant Prince William of Orange led the Protestant forces against the Catholics under King James II at the Battle of the Boyne in 1690. The victorious Protestants established their domination throughout Ireland, beginning centuries of discrimination and repression. To ensure continued Protestant domination, regional leaders formed the Orange Order in 1795. The Protestant population increased still further in when the region became a refuge for Protestant Huguenots fleeing religious persecution in France after the revocation of the Edict of Nantes in 1685. The immigrants' skills contributed to the development of the textile industry that became the foundation of the nineteenth-century industrialization.

Subsequent British government policies favored the Protestants and discriminated against the Roman Catholic Irish. Bitter rebellions and savage repression continued through the eighteenth and nineteenth centuries. In the eighteenth century the rise of Irish nationalism made the Protestant minority in Ulster even more pro-British. Many Northern Irish, usually called Scotch-Irish, immigrated to the United States, Canada, Australia, and New Zealand. The 1801 Act of Union created the legislative union of Great Britain and Ireland under the name of United Kingdom.

In the 1800s, Irish Catholics agitated for home rule for all of Ireland, particularly following the thousands of deaths attributed to the great famine of the 1840s, which was blamed on British government policies. The Northern Irish, who saw themselves as a separate national group, neither British nor Irish, remained strongly pro-British and anti-Catholic. The "Irish Question" continued to plague Britain through the end of the end of the nineteenth century, with sporadic violence, rebellions, demonstrations countered by repression, often brutal, and virtual military occupation of the island.

The industrialization of the northern province of Ulster in the nineteenth century further differentiated the region from the mainly agrarian southern provinces. The utilitarian approach to life in the industrial Victorian era set the tone for life in the province. The rise of an urbanized industrial class stimulated the first stirrings of a particular Protestant Northern Irish nationalism.

As World War I approached, the British government moved to grant home rule to Ireland in an effort to quell the sporadic uprisings and violence. Home rule sparked serious rioting by the Northern Irish opposed to Irish home rule in 1914–16. Despite a ban by the British authorities, the Protestants succeeded in landing arms and ammunition in July 1914. On 10 July 1914, the Northern Irish leaders declared a provisional government in Ulster with the power to call up volunteers, called the "Ulster Volunteers," to fight for Britain during the world war.

The Roman Catholic Irish rebelled in 1916, setting off the "Easter Rebellion." The Irish rebellion was brutally crushed by British troops aided by the Ulster Volunteers. The leaders of the rebellion were executed but guerrilla warfare continued as the Irish rejected home rule and fought for independence from Britain. The Northern Irish, fearing domination by the hated Catholics, violently opposed the Irish aim of independence from the United Kingdom and settled for home rule, even though they preferred union with Great Britain.

Irish nationalists declared Ireland independent of Britain on 21 January 1919, but the movement was quickly suppressed by British troops. In 1920 British reinforcements, called the Black and Tans, were dispatched to Ireland, setting off months of ferocious warfare. In December 1920, the British government passed the Government of Ireland Act, giving Northern and Southern Ireland separate parliaments. Northern Ireland comprised 6 of the 9 counties of Ulster. Southern Ireland was made up of 23 counties, including 3 counties of Ulster with Roman Catholic majorities. A Council of Ireland representing the two parts of the island in an attempt to effect common action in affairs affecting both parts of the island. Ireland was granted dominion status as the Irish Free State, while the six counties with large Protestant populations were separated and placed under direct British rule as a temporary measure. In June 1921, the first Northern Irish parliament was created at Stormont in Belfast. From 1921 to 1940 Northern Ireland was an openly sectarian state, controlled by the Northern Irish majority and ruled in their interest.

The Irish minority in Ulster rejected separation from Ireland, but in 1925 the boundary between the Irish Free State and Ulster was fixed after long negotiations. Under the Protestant Northern Irish government in Ulster, the Roman Catholic Irish minority in the region was discriminated against in education, employment, and religion. Religion became an integral part of both Irish and Northern Irish nationalism.

The Irish Republican Army (IRA) was formed by Catholics in both

Southern and Northern Ireland to fight for the secession of Ireland from the United Kingdom and the creation of a united Irish republic. Attempts at unification continued until 1938, when elections in Northern Ireland resulted in an overwhelming victory for the Unionists, the pro-British Protestants Northern Irish. The Unionist victory ended any hope of the merger of the two territories.

Southern Ireland, the Irish Free State, remained neutral during World War II, while Ulster, as an integral part of the United Kingdom suffered heavy bombing. After the war, in 1949, Southern Ireland was declared the Republic of Ireland and withdrew from the British Commonwealth. The Northern Irish of Ulster declared their loyalty to Britain and their virulent opposition to any ties to Catholic Ireland.

Discrimination against the Irish minority in Northern Ireland became even more severe as tensions mounted in the 1950s. Ulster had one of the lowest crime rates in Europe, partly due to the presence of British troops in the province. The Catholic minority, watching American civil rights demonstrations on television, began to organize demonstrations for Catholic Civil Rights in 1966. Three years later violence broke out between Catholics and Protestants with street fighting and communal fighting. The British government intervened militarily to quell the violence. The two communities became armed camps. The IRA and other Catholic groups turned to terrorism in an attempt to force the unification of the island in a socialist republic. The Provisional IRA, the military wing of the Irish Republican Army, fought pitched battles with British forces and Northern Irish paramilitary groups, the Ulster Defense Association (UDA) and the Ulster Volunteer Force (UVF).

The continuing violence was countered by the stationing of over 21,000 British troops in the province by 1972. Peace proposals, supported by the British and Irish governments, were opposed by both the IRA and the Northern Irish extremists led by hard-line Protestants such as the Reverend Ian Paisley. The ongoing violence led to the suspension of autonomous government, the closing of the Stormont parliament, and the imposition of direct rule from London.

A coalition government was formed in 1973 when moderates won elections to a new assembly, but a Protestant general strike brought down the new government in 1974 and the province again reverted to direct British rule. Pro-independence groups, including the Ulster Independence Party (UIP), called for an independent Ulster and population exchanges with the Irish Republic. Attempts at home rule in the province continued to be undermined by the hatred and violence between the Northern Irish Protestant majority and the Irish Catholic minority.

Terrorism and violence continued to undermine efforts to reach a peace agreement. The assassination of Earl Montbatten of Burma, the senior statesman of the British royal family in 1979, was one of the more infamous acts of the IRA. The violence brought increased poverty. By 1984, Northern Ireland had the highest unemployment rate in Western Europe, over 50% in some Roman Catholic districts. The conflict, Europe's longest, left over 2,400 dead and 21,000 wounded by the mid-1980s and continued to cost the British government over $2.8 billion a year. In a June 1986 Gallup Poll in England, Scotland, and Wales, only 26% wanted Ulster to remain in the United Kingdom, while 48% felt that the province's future should be left to its residents.

In the 1990s, after three decades of violence and terror, various proposals have been presented by the British and Irish governments, but with little impact. Northern Irish nationalists, although a minority among the pro-British Protestant population, propose an independent Protestant Ulster republic within the British Commonwealth, including detaching the predominately Roman Catholic districts west of the Bann River. This would move about 300,000 Roman Catholics into the Irish Republic. Protestants in the region opposed to inclusion in the Irish Republic would move across the river. According to the nationalist propaganda, after the Belfast slums were cleared, Ulster would have a Catholic minority of about 10%.

The repressive tactics of the Northern Irish police and the British military presence, viewed by many Catholics as a foreign occupation force, added to the volatility of the situation. Paramilitaries on both sides carried out bomb and sniper attacks Northern Ireland, Great Britain, and the Republic of Ireland during the 1990s. The latest hope for a peaceful resolution is the Good Friday Accord, signed in April 1998. The accord provides a framework for ending the violence, although the implementation of the accord stalled over the issue of "decommissioning." Northern Irish Unionist politicians have demanded that the IRA surrender its weapons before its political wing, Sinn Féin, be allowed to join the new autonomous Northern Ireland assembly. In August 1998, twenty-eight people were killed by a car bomb in Omagh, the worst atrocity in nearly 30 years of violence.

Northern Irish nationalists argue that independence, the so-called third way, would finally bring peace to the troubled province. A sovereign Ulster state would end the bogey of British imperialism on the island and allow the two Irish states to peacefully coexist within the European Union (EU). The strife that has continued for over 30 years has killed over 3,600 people, but numerous attempts at peace have failed. Independence, encompassing both the Protestants and Catholics, could be the solution to one of Europe's longest and bloodiest conflicts.

Renewed tensions in mid-2001 included efforts to save the power-sharing agreement set up in 1998. Also harassment of Irish Catholic school children passing a Northern Irish neighborhood in Belfast focused on the ongoing conflict. The Protestant Northern Irish are losing ground, politically and economically, to the Irish-oriented Catholics, which continues to add to the attraction of nationalist sentiment.

The decision of the largest of the Catholic groups, the Irish Republican Army, the IRA, to begin disarming in October 2001 allowed the peace process to restart. Relative peace could end the trend to violence by the Northern Irish. In previous years, many of the deaths in the province were blamed on Catholic groups, but between January 2001 and December 2001 fourteen people died violently in Northern Ireland, two killed by the IRA, but the other 12 were killed by Northern Irish paramilitaries.

SELECTED BIBLIOGRAPHY:

Brewer, John D. *Anti-Catholicism in Northern Ireland.* 1998.
Hewitt, Brian George. *The Times Guide to the Peoples of the World.* 1994.
Miller, David, ed. *Rethinking Northern Ireland.* 1998.
Ruane, Joseph, and Jennifer Todd. *The Dynamics of Conflict in Northern Ireland.* 1999.

Northern Tai

Tai; Northern Thai; Chwan; Chuang; Zhuang

POPULATION: Approximately (2002e) 24,500,000 Northern Tai in China, concentrated in the western half of the Kwangsi Chuang Autonomous Region, and in Kweichow, Yunnan, and Hunan provinces.

THE NORTHERN TAI HOMELAND: The Northern Tai homeland lies in southern China south of the Nan Mountains. Most of the region is composed of hilly country of upland grazing lands and fertile valleys devoted to rice cultivation on the terraced, narrow mountains. The traditional homeland forms part of the provinces of Yunnan and Kweichow (Guizhou) and the autonomous region of Kwangsi-Chuang (Guangxi-Zhuangzu). The Northern Tai heartland forms an autonomous region of the People's Republic of China, however the Northern Tai are concentrated in the western

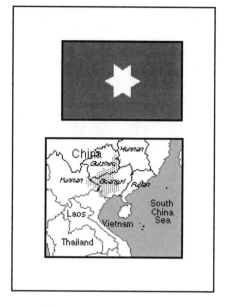

two-thirds of the region, while the eastern third is mostly Han Chinese. *Kwangsi Chuang Autonomous Region (Guangxi Zhuangzu Zizhiqu)*: 85,096 sq. mi.—220,399 sq. km, (2002e) 45,600,000—Han Chinese, 46%, Northern Tai 39%, Miao 11%, Yao 1.5%, others 2.5%. The Northern Tai capital and major cultural center is Bose, called Paise by the Northern Tai, (2002e) 145,000.

FLAG: The Northern Tai flag, the traditional flag of the national movement, is a red field bearing a centered yellow six-pointed star representing the six major Northern Tai groups of southern China.

PEOPLE AND CULTURE: The Northern Tai are a Thai people related to the Thai of Thailand comprising a number of closely related Tai groups in southern China including the Chuang (Zhuang), numbering 17 million, Puyi (Buyi/Bouyei), 3.1 million, Tung (Dong), 3 million, and the smaller Sui (Shui) (370,000), Mulam (180,000), Maonan (85,000), and Primni (50,000). The largest subgroup of the Northern Tai are the Chuang, called Zhuang in the Chinese Pinyin system. The Chuang are often referred to as "water dwellers" as they traditionally built their settlements close to water and their dwellings are often constructed on piles or stilts. The second largest of the subgroups, the Puyi or Buyi (Bouyei), live to the north of the Chuangs in Kweichow province. The official division between the Chuang and Puyi is determined by provincial borders. At times all the Northern Tai groups, including the Chuang, are called Puyi. The origins of the widely scattered Tung or Dong, the third largest group, live in Kwangsi and Kweichow, are not clear, but they are generally considered to be a branch of the Chuang, whom they closely resemble in culture and language. The Chuang maintain many social customs that differ from the Chinese, including premarital sexual freedom and free marriage without middlemen, the bride staying at home with her parents until the birth of the first child. Centuries of Han Chinese domination has resulted in the widespread cultural assimilation of the Northern Tai peoples although the largely rural population has maintained its separate identity.

LANGUAGE AND RELIGION: The Northern Tai speak two closely related languages classified as Northern Tai and Central Tai, the linguistic dividing line being the Xiang River of southern Guangxi province. The Wu-ming dialect of the Central Tai or Chuang language, now accepted as the standard language of the region, uses the Latin alphabet with six additional letters. The Northern Tai dialects are tonal languages, using pitch differences to distinguish words. The dialects include many borrowings from the Chinese languages, both archaic and modern. The language, the lingua franca of the mountainous region, is the second language of the non-Tai peoples who speak Tibeto-Burman languages, the Miao or Hmongs,* the Yao, and the She. The Chungkia (Zhungkia) or Ikia, counted as ethnic Chinese, are the descendants of early Chinese settlers who now speak the Northern Tai language. The language is used in instruction in primary and secondary schools where the size of the Tai population warrants it. Cantonese is widely spoken as a second language by the Northern Tai, a result of over two millennia of coexistence with the neighboring Han Chinese. In the northern districts many speak Mandarin. A Romanized Northern Tai alphabet has been created and is one of four writing systems to be printed on Chinese bank notes. Scholars are currently working on a dictionary of Zhuang-Chinese-English.

The majority of the Northern Tai are Buddhist or Taoist, although their traditional religion, polytheism, remains strong, particularly in rural areas. Magical rites, sorcery with human figurines, and the ancestral cult remain important to the religious beliefs. Spirits, often malicious, believed to control daily events must be appeased. In recent years Christian missionaries have converted a large number to evangelical Protestant sects. In 2000, the Christian population is estimated at about 1% of the total Northern Tai population.

NATIONAL HISTORY: The ancestors of the Tai peoples first came into contact with the Chinese about 2,500 years ago. Tai peoples inhabited much of southern China before the establishment of the Chinese Empire in 221 B.C. The advance of the Han Chinese culture and the boundaries of their empire pushed the Tai peoples southward. Their homeland, later called Kwangsi, was known as the land of Pai-Yüeh, meaning the Hundred Yüeh, which referred to the indigenous, non-Han peoples of the region.

A subgroup of the Northern Tai, the Chuang, with an advanced economy based on irrigated rice cultivation was the only ancient nation known to the Han Chinese who were not considered barbarians as they possessed a sophisticated state system and a developed culture. Eastern Kwangsi was conquered by the Han Chinese in 214 B.C. under the Ch'in dynasty.

An independent state known as Nan Yüeh was created, with Chuang support, at the end of the Ch'in dynasty and existed until it was annexed in 112–111 B.C. under the Han dynasty. The Northern Tai's written history began in 45 B.C., during the late Chou dynasty. A powerful Tai state, Nan Chao, erected in the third century A.D., controlled a large territory in present southern China. The highly evolved Tai culture, including a refined system of writing and an illustrious literature, culturally influenced areas far beyond the state's borders. The influx of Yao tribes increased racial tensions in the region between the seventh and tenth centuries.

The Chinese advance slowly pushed the Tai peoples into the more mountainous south and west and eventually into the lowland valleys of present Thailand, Myanmar, Laos, and Vietnam. China's Sung dynasty prepared the way for Chinese domination by defeating the Tai in the twelfth century, winning for China the rice lands of Kwangtung (Guangdong). The name Kwangsi is derived from time when the region was known as Kuang-nan Hsi-lu, meaning Wide South, Western Route, or western half of the territory south of the Nan Mountains. Chinese migration to the conquered lands began the long process of assimilation of the lowland Tai. The Chuang trace their descent from this period of Chinese expansion, when their ancestors developed as a distinct nation from a mixture of refugees fleeing the Chinese onslaught and the Tai mountain tribes who took them in.

Their traditional homeland, divided by a line from Kuelin (Guilin) to Nanning, remained Tai in the west, but was increasingly colonized by Han Chinese in the east. In 1052 a Northern Tai leader, Nung Chih-kao, led a revolt against Chinese domination and set up an independent kingdom in the south. The revolt was crushed a year later, but the region remained unsettled. The Chinese Sung dynasty governed the region from 971 to 1279 by the alternate use of force and appeasement, a policy that neither satisfied the aspirations of the Chuang nor ended the unrest among the non-Chinese population.

The Northern Tai state survived in the mountains until its conquest by the Mongols of Kublai Khan in 1253. Marco Polo visited the fallen state soon after the Mongol conquest. Under successive Chinese dynasties the authorities encouraged Chinese migration to the region, leaving only the less productive lands and the mountain areas to the Northern Tai and other minority peoples. Mostly ignored by the Chinese Imperial Government, the minority peoples developed their own systems under local rulers. The Manchu, after their conquest of China in 1644, finally imposed direct imperial administration on the minority regions of south China in 1650.

The Northern Tai territory area came under French colonial influence in the nineteenth century. The French established a sphere of influence in the Chuang region following the Franco-Chinese war of 1884–85. French domination of neighboring Vietnam exposed the Chuang homeland to foreign encroachment and in 1898 France obtained a sphere of influence that included the Tai homeland. Unhindered by the weak Manchu government, French missionaries introduced modern education and the Latin alphabet. The turbulence of the last years of the Manchu dynasty and the Chinese Revolution in 1911, gave the Northern Tai, led by the Chuang, effective independent control of their homeland, under French political influence, between 1910 and 1916.

The mountainous regions of the Northern Tai homeland became the base of the Nationalist revolution led by Sun Yat-sen. The feeble Chinese republican government, installed following the Chinese Revolution in 1911, exerted some influence in the southern border regions in 1916, but again lost effective control during the chaos that swept China after 1917. Badly treated by the Chinese republican troops during the government's brief control of the region in 1916–17, the Northern Tai resisted Han Chinese incursions.

Northen Tai peasants began organizing forces controlled by local Han Chinese landlords and established an independent base at Tunglan in 1926. On 12 January 1927, the rebel leaders declared the region independent of China and appealed to the French in neighboring Tonkin for support. The Northern Tai and other minorities resisted the return of the Nationalist Chinese following the rise of Chiang Kai-shek in 1927. Leaders formed the Kwangsi Clique in opposition to Chiang. This group did much to modernize the region, but their revolt was crushed by Nationalist troops in 1929.

Communist organizers infiltrated the area and declared it the Right River Soviet in 1929, followed by the establishment of the Left River Soviet further to the south. The Northern Tai, distrustful of both communist and capitalist Chinese, continued to fight until they were defeated by forces loyal to a local warlord allied to the Nationalists in 1930. The region, controlled by local warlords, remained virtually independent during the Chinese Civil War of the 1930s. An agreement, reached in 1936, allowed the Nationalist Government to reassert its authority in the region.

During World War II, Nationalist forces and American military units garrisoned the strategic region. With the Allies present, the Nationalist

Chinese were careful to suppress all signs of minority dissent. The cities and bases in the region were major targets of Japanese attacks.

The Chinese Communists, victorious in the civil war that resumed in 1945, drove the last Nationalist forces from the area in November 1949. Greeted as liberators, the Communists soon proved as harsh as the Nationalists although they applied the communist theory of limited autonomy. In 1950 the Northern Tai revolted with the covert aid of the French in neighboring Vietnam. Dubbed bandits, the Communist authorities executed thousands of minority rebels and civilians. In 1952, as part of its nationalities system, the Communists erected an autonomous region, only to dissolve it six years later amid charges of separatism. To prevent the minority peoples from consolidating in a viable nation, the Communist authorities split the large minority region among several provinces. The Chuang Autonomous Region of Kwangsi, created in 1958, was announced as a step designed to help foster the cultural autonomy of the Northern Tai, but the new region remained dominated by the Han Chinese majority in the province and demands for real autonomy and the unification of the Northern Tai in one region were ignored.

China's cultural revolution, beginning in 1966, led by the fanatical Red Guards, destroyed non-Han shrines, institutions, and monuments to force assimilation. The government, between 1958 and 1977, outlawed many traditions and cultural traits judged detrimental to development. A period of relative leniency in the 1980s ended with the crushing of the pro-democracy movement in 1989. The Chinese leaders, fearing that the disintegration of the Soviet Union would spread nationalist ideas to the minorities, imposed new restrictions on the Northern Tai and reinforced government control at local levels.

The Northern Tai and other non-Han peoples of the region, despite over seven centuries of Chinese domination, retain a strong urge to unite in an independent state. Nationalists claim that they are a nation by all modern criteria: a long and separate history, separate language and culture, and a compact ethnic national area. Whether or not China splinters like the Soviet Union when communism is finally overthrown, many in the region have already begun to view their homeland as a natural part of Southeast Asia.

Assimilation into Chinese culture, considered more advanced than in China's other autonomous regions, began to reverse in the 1990s under the influence of the rapid political and economic changes in Asia. At the turn of the new century, ethnic tensions in the region are economic and geographic factors that have exerted a powerful influence on Chuang cultural trends. The Northern Tai have been largely left out of the modernization and industrialization of southern China since 1990 resulting in a return to their ethnic roots and the beginnings of reculturation that could reverse their assimilation into Chinese culture.

The political openness between Thailand and China in the 1990s enabled academic cooperation between Thai and Northern Tai scholars. Thai academics and archeologists visiting the region confirmed the ancient ties between the two peoples that goes back over 3000 years, making the Northern Tai homeland the oldest known center of the Tai peoples. Many Thai linguists are studying the related Northern Tai languages, which are intelligible to Thai speakers.

SELECTED BIBLIOGRAPHY:

Collier, Mac. *China in Disintegration, 1912–1949.* 1977.
Harrell, Steven, ed. *Cultural Encounters on China's Ethnic Frontiers.* 1996.
Heberer, Thomas. *China and Its National Minorities: Autonomy or Assimilation?* 1989.
Kaup, Katherine Palmer. *Creating the Zhuang: Ethnic Politics in China.* 2000.

Northumbrians

Geordies; Northern English

POPULATION: Approximately (2002e) 3,495,000 Northumbrians in the United Kingdom, mostly in the northern counties of England, but with sizable concentrations in London and other large British cities.

THE NORTHUMBRIAN HOMELAND: The Northumbrian homeland, commonly called the North, occupies a region of rolling hills and lakes between the Irish and North Seas in northern England, just south of the Scottish border. The region is level along the North Sea but is hilly in the interior, with the Cheviot Hills on the northern border and the Pennine Chain in the south. Inland are highland moors, which alternate with fertile valleys. The most important rivers are the Tyne and its tributaries, which flow into the North Sea. Northumbria has been designated a European region, but in England the region remains divided between the metropolitan counties of Tyne and Wear, and the nonmetropolitan counties of Cleveland, Northumberland, and Durham of the North-East planning region, and the nonmetropolitan county of Cumbria of the North-West. *Region of Northumbria*: 5,944 sq. mi.—15,401 sq. km, (2002e) 3,041,000—Northumbrians 90%, Scots* 5%, other English 5%. The Northumbrian capital and major cultural center is Newcastle upon Tyne, (2002e) 187,000, metropolitan area 1,281,000. The other important cultural center is Middlesbrough, (2002e) 144,000, metropolitan area 688,000.

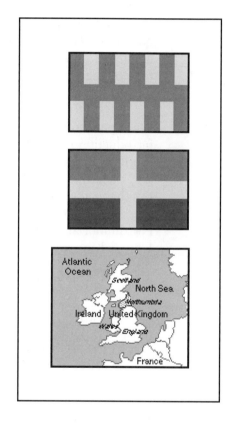

FLAG: The Northumbrian flag, the ancient flag of Bernicia, is widely used; it has eight red and gold vertical stripes and a centered horizontal red stripe. The flag of the national movement is a horizontal bicolor of blue over red charged with a centered, broad yellow cross, the cross of St. Cuthbert.

PEOPLE AND CULTURE: The Northumbrians, popularly called Geordies, particularly in the Tyneside region, are also sometimes called Northern English. The Northumbrian character and culture, incorporating both English and Scottish influences, retain many traits and traditions that disappeared in other parts of England. The Northumbrians are divided into several regional groups. The real "Geordies" live on either side of the River Tyne. The culture of the North developed around the ancient coal mines, and mining dictated the way and rhythm of life for centuries. The Northumbrians increasingly consider themselves a distinct British people and a separate European nation. One of the crucial components of Northumbrian nationalism is a dislike of the outside groups that seem to dominate, especially London and Londoners. There is a deep-seated hatred of the metropolitan elite that dominates the region politically and socially.

LANGUAGE AND RELIGION: The Northumbrians speak a dialect that developed from medieval Northumbrian, a language not influenced by the introduction of Norman French in the south of England in the eleventh century. The dialect, rooted in the ancient Celtic and Viking languages, is spoken in seven subdialects that roughly respond to the historical counties that make up the region—Geordie, Cumberland, Central Cumberland, Durham, Northumberland, Newcastle Northumbrian, and Tyneside Northumbrian. Education in the region is among the poorest in the United Kingdom, a fact that has perpetuated the use of the dialect. The thick local dialect is not quite a language according to linguists, but to many English speakers it is unintelligible. There remain similarities between local expressions that have their origins in the Viking occupation and in nearly identical expressions in the Danish language. There are significant variations, including the softer Tees Valley dialect in the south.

NATIONAL HISTORY: The Celtic Ottadeni of the narrow region of Britain between the North and Irish Seas came under Roman rule in the first century A.D. Their Latinized homeland formed the northern frontier of Roman Britannia. In an effort to protect the northern districts from attacks by Picts and Celts, the Romans constructed the long defensive structure known as Hadrian's Wall between A.D. 120 and 123. The modern city of Newcastle began as a station, called Pons Aelii, on the wall. The region, prosperous under Roman rule, declined rapidly with the collapse of Roman power and the withdrawal of the Roman garrisons from Britannia in 410.

Angles and Jutes, Germanic tribes from the European mainland, invaded the region in the early sixth century. The Germanic tribes created a separate kingdom, Bernicia. The kingdom later united with neighboring Deira to form the Kingdom of Northumbria, one of the seven Anglo-Saxon kingdoms of England. From the mid-sixth to the mid-eighth centuries, Northumbria experienced a golden age, a great flowering of the arts, literature, and scholarship. Its military strength was greatest in the seventh century, when the supremacy of its rulers was recognized by the southern English kingdoms. The inhabitants of the region accepted Christianity in 627 and thereafter incorporated Christian themes in their culture. Concurrent with the cultural golden age, however, was almost constant political discord and upheaval.

The cultural life and political unity of Northumbria were destroyed by the arrival of the Danes. The coastal districts of Northumbria came under Viking attack in the ninth century, and the southern part of the kingdom was conquered by the invaders in 867. The Viking invasion ended North-umbria's preeminent position in England. Early in the tenth century other Vikings entered and settled western Northumbria from the Irish Sea. In the north, the newly formed kingdom of Scotland pushed the Northum-brian boundary back to the River Tweed. The Angles, maintaining a small kingdom north of the Tees River, accepted the authority of the king of Wessex in 920 and became part of the united English kingdom. Successive English kings gave the bishop of Durham princely status and considerable political autonomy, allowing him to raise taxes and armies to fight off periodic invasions by the Scots. After the last Viking ruler was expelled in 944, there ceased to be independent kings in Northumbria, which then became an earldom within the kingdom of England.

The conquest of England in 1066 by the Normans* from mainland Europe introduced a more centralized form of government. The North was divided into counties administered by Norman nobles, and the traditional liberties of the Anglo-Saxon inhabitants were greatly curtailed. Reaction to authoritarian Norman rule, especially among the Anglo-Saxon majority, led to the reestablishment of political and personal freedom with the signing of the Magna Carta, in 1215, and the creation of an English parliament in 1295.

Henry VIII's conflicts with the Roman Catholic church ended the semi-autonomous status of the region under the bishop of Durham in 1537. Troops smashed open the tomb of the region's patron saint, St. Cuthbert, and carried off the famed Lindisfarne Gospels, a beautifully lettered and illustrated Latin text of four Christian gospels produced in the seventh century to commemorate St. Cuthbert. The saint had been the prior of Lindisfarne, also known as Holy Island, at a time when it was famed throughout Europe for Christian scholarship. By the mid-sixteenth century the political power of northeastern England had waned.

Northumbria, forming the English frontier on the Kingdom of Scotland, suffered during centuries of border wars until the two kingdoms united under the Stuarts in 1603. Scotland joined the United Kingdom of Great Britain in 1707, ensuring the security of Northumbria. Peace on the border allowed the industrial revolution to spread to the North; there followed a rapid development of large industrial enterprises, ports, and mines, largely based on the region's important coal deposits—the world's oldest coal field and the center of Northumbrian life. Rapid industrial expansion converted the region into a powerhouse of English industry, spurred by the expansion of the overseas British Empire. The profits from the industrialization of Northumbria, however, mostly went to the industrialists and the government based in London. Far from the center of government, the North experienced serious unrest in the early nineteenth century; Geordie industrial workers demanded the same rights as those enjoyed by the more prosperous South.

The industrially important region was vital to the British war effort during World War I, but the long conflict seriously drained its wealth and manpower. Severe economic problems in the 1920s made the declining northern counties a bastion of unionism and antigovernmental sentiment, and also a center of support for the new Labour Party. Economically devastated by the depression of the 1930s, the region revived during World War II as its industries turned out war goods. A Labour government, elected in 1945, nationalized the mining industry and introduced the British welfare system in 1948, which helped to eliminate regional economic and social differences. In 1950 Northumbrian incomes drew equal to those of the South.

The Northumbrian region began a long decline following the election of a Conservative government in 1951, exacerbated by the increasing centralization of political power in London and the southeastern counties. Chronic unemployment, decaying cities, and aging industries raised social tension and sparked a renewal of a regionalist movement and a resurgence of separate Geordie identity. The growing regional movement demanded a fairer distribution of development and investment to the perennially depressed northern counties.

The United Kingdom's entry into the European Economic Community in 1973 further concentrated investment and development in the prosperous counties around London, a center of continental trade. By 1985, incomes in the North had fallen to 3% below the national average, while incomes in the southeast climbed to 5% above the average. The gap continued to widen thereafter.

Demands for autonomy and devolution of political power by the Scots, Welsh,* and Cornish* in the United Kingdom resonated in the Geordie North. Proposals for regional government, more responsive to local needs, met with repeated rejection in London. Geordie regionalism grew rapidly during the 1980s amid increasing unrest and growing unemployment, up to 30% in some areas. The so-called North-South divide became very real to the Northumbrians. In 1991 severe rioting swept the region, highlighting its massive political and economic problems. Many claimed that Northumbria continued to have a semicolonial relationship with England and that the Northumbrians, like the Scots and Irish, had been conquered by the English.

The economic decline, the longest since the depression of the 1930s, blamed on the Conservative government, raised demands for economic independence. The region, strongly supporting the devolution of power, increasingly looked to Europe, with a nationalist minority advocating independence within a federal United Kingdom or even within a united, federal Europe. Following the overthrow of communism in Eastern Europe, Northumbria was often called the only remaining one-party state in Europe—a state ruled by a political party, the Conservatives, that have never won an election in the region.

The election of a Labour government in the United Kingdom in 1997 somewhat eased regionalist tension in the northern counties, but expectations were high. The Geordies became determined to bring their region into the European mainstream. The region, a Labour stronghold, helped the party to power and expected to gain by doing so, but the economic decline continued. In 1999, Prime Minister Tony Blair admitted that the Labour government had failed to make significant inroads in bridging the regional divide. The northeast remains blighted by higher crime, worse housing, higher unemployment, and poorer health than in the South.

The evolution of a particular national identity in the region, based on dialect, history, and culture, accelerated in the 1990s. In 1995, a group of historians were awarded a million pounds to investigate what exactly makes up the national identity of the natives of the northern English counties. Northumbrians argue that their national character has survived the demise of the steel, shipbuilding, and coal industries, and that they have never looked for sympathy. A fierce brand of patriotism, not found in other parts of England, has always carried them through the region's many economic downturns.

The British government's decision to repatriate the Stone of Scone from Westminster Abbey to the Scots was a sign of the growing power of Scottish nationalism. In 1998 the Northumbrians demanded the return of one of their own national symbols, the Lindisfarne Gospels. They are currently kept in the British Library in London, but a campaign, with decidedly nationalist overtones, has mobilized Northumbrian pride and is seeking to have the book brought back permanently to the region. The campaign has become linked with efforts to persuade the British government to set up an elected northern regional assembly. In March 1998, nationalists surrounded the British Library with a celebration of Northumbrian culture, featuring folk musicians and choral groups. The campaigners then invaded Downing Street with a petition to Prime Minister Blair pleading for the return of the book to the Northumbrian homeland.

Northumbrian nationalists have modeled their campaign for autonomy on the highly successful crossparty Scottish Constitutional Convention, which led to the creation of a separate Scottish legislature. Mirroring the political role played by his medieval predecessors, the present bishop of

Durham, Michael Turnbull, is chairing the new convention, but the British government, once a proponent of regional devolution, in 1999–2000 became noticeably more cautious. Undeterred, Bishop Turnbull has used his contacts to involve the region's universities and their research skills in advancing the cause of regional autonomy.

The redrawing of boundaries by the new Regional Development Agency left Cumbria out of the official region. Northumbrian irredentists resent this and sense a conspiracy to downsize their region and sideline its growing national movement. Local businessmen, however, are quietly antagonistic to the idea of devolution, on the grounds that it would cost more in taxes than it would bring in and that it would bring more red tape, bureaucracy, and government regulations. The level of cynicism is considered a result of the low esteem in which local government is held in much of the region. Allegations of incompetence and political infighting are common.

Confusion about the government's aims is causing irritation in the region. While promising devolution, the Labour government has imposed so many restrictions that little is accomplished. Local councils are agitating over spending curbs, and regional budgets are a collection of subsidies from 10 different ministries. Government policies are decentralizing and centralizing at the same time.

In August 2000, a report stated that the North–South economic divide is widening, along with the political divide. Though spurred by the 1999 creation of a Scottish parliament, many Northumbrians, who formerly opposed Scottish nationalism, see Scotland as not only an inspiration but a rival for government funds and investment. Many politicians and nationalists argue that until the region gets its own assembly and prime minister, its voice will continue to be drowned out in both London and the European Union.

The Northumbrians' peculiar fanaticism for local football and their avid interest in local historical symbols, nationalists claim, are part of the same deep-rooted desire to regain their cultural identity. which reaches back to a time when the region was great and powerful. This desire, coupled with a resentment of London and the south of England, is the basis of the growing national movement.

SELECTED BIBLIOGRAPHY:

Bainbridge, Beryl. *Forever England: North and South.* 1999.
Bogdanor, Vernon. *Devolution in the United Kingdom.* 1999.
Fraser, C.M., and K. Emsley. *Northumbria.* 1989.
Jewell, Helen M. *The North-South Divide: The Origins of Northern Consciousness in England.* 1994.

Nuba

Nubans

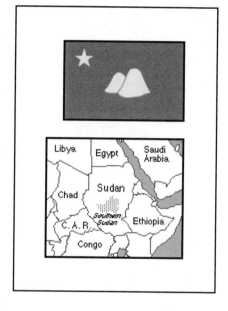

POPULATION: Approximately (2002e) 2,800,000 Nuba in Sudan, concentrated in the Nuba Mountains in the central Sudanese province of South Kordofan. Outside the region there are sizable Nuba communities living in cities and other regions of Sudan, often in refugee camps or shanty towns around the large cities.

THE NUBA HOMELAND: The Nuba homeland lies in the Nuba Mountains in the central Sudan. Most of the region is studded with rugged, fertile, granite hills that rise sharply from a wide clay plain. The Nuba peoples live in or near the hills, while the lowlands are inhabited by Muslim Baggara Arabs. The Khartoum government insists that the Nuba homeland is part of the north, which is exclusively Arab in culture and Islamic in religion. The Nuba Mountains cover about 30,000 sq. mi. (78,000 sq. km), mostly in the Sudanese province of South Kordofan, although the Nuba homeland has no official status in the country. The Nuba capital and major cultural center is Tabanyaat, called Tabanya by the Nuba, (1998e, prior to its capture by government troops) 25,000. The official capital of the region is Kaduqli, called Kadugli by the Nuba, (2002e) 79,000.

FLAG: The Nuba national flag, the flag of the Nuba Mountains United Front, is a horizontal bicolor of pale green with two yellow hills centered and a yellow five-pointed star on the upper hoist.

PEOPLE AND CULTURE: The Nuba are resilient and self-reliant people comprising twelve closely related tribal groups collectively called Nuba, after their mountains. In place of previous reluctance to use the term "Nuba" for all non-Arabic groups of the mountains, successive calamities have imposed a common identity. The groups differ in physical type and culture but share a long history, as well as opposition to Muslim domination. Kinship is normally matrilineal in the south and patrilineal in the north. Most of the Nuba are agriculturists; many crops are grown on terraced hills and in larger cultivations on the plains. Traditionally Nuba men went naked, and women wore beads and lip plugs, but this has disappeared except in the most remote areas. Wrestling and stick fighting remain the most important pastimes of Nuba men; Nuba culture emphasizes power and strength. The African identity of the Nuba culture is slowly being eroded by forced Arabization and Islamization. Many Nuba claim descent from the ancient Kush kingdom of the eighth century B.C. and believe that theirs is one of the oldest cultural heritages in Africa.

LANGUAGE AND RELIGION: The Nuba language is a group of related dialects belonging to the Eastern Sudanic or Kordofanian group of the Chari-Nile branch of Nilo-Saharan languages. The Nuba dialects are roughly grouped by region—the Niger-Kordofanian languages in the east, the Nilo-Saharans in the northwest and center, and the Kadugli-Krongo group in the southwest. The dialects, further divided into about 50 sub-dialects, are for the most part mutually intelligible. The largest of the dialects are Keiga, Jirru, Dabri, Nyimang, Dilling, Dair (Ghulfan), Masakin, Tagale (Taqalawin), Moreb (Tgaoi), Tira, Koalib, Moro, Otoro, Laro, and Krongo. Many Nuba are bilingual in Arabic, which serves as a lingua franca; a smaller number speak English as a second language, as the result of missionary education.

The Nuba mostly adhere to traditional religious beliefs linked with agricultural rituals and ancestral spirits. Priests and rainmakers have important positions in Nuba society. Various degrees of Islamization can be observed, depending on the geographic situation. A growing number are accepting Christian beliefs, although most missionary activity has been banned by the Sudanese government. It is quite common to find Muslims, Christians, and animists who follow the traditional religious beliefs, in the same family.

NATIONAL HISTORY: Little is known of the history of the Nuba, but they are thought to be the earliest inhabitants of the Kordofan region. They probably inhabited a much wider region but were gradually driven from the plains by other groups that ruled the banks of the Nile River, and by interior tribes. In the seventh century they fled the invasion of nomadic Muslim tribes who were zealously converting all conquered peoples. They retreated to the mountains, where there was fertile land, adequate water, and a number of easily defensible positions.

The more recent history of the Nuba begins in the early sixteenth century, when pastoral tribes began moving south, confining the agricultural Nuba to the region known as the Nuba Mountains. This movement coincided with the establishment of the kingdom of Sennar in A.D. 1504. According to Tegali tradition, a holy man known as Muhammad al-Jaali came to Tegali from Sennar to teach Islam around 1530 and stayed to marry the daughter of the chief of Tegali. His son, al-Jaili abu Garida, became the legendary first king of the Tegali dynasty in 1560. Although

Islam was introduced to a large number of Nuba tribes, it apparently did not weaken the people's identity as Nuba. Despite strong relations between Tegali and the other Nuba peoples, the hill tribes were not brought under the effective rule of a central authority.

Around 1800 the Baggara tribes, which had previously roamed the plains of northern Kordofan and Darfur, began to move into the valleys of the Nuba Mountains in search of water and pasture for their livestock. The Baggaras divided the plains into territorial zones and drove the Nuba tribes into the higher valleys and hills. The Baggara invasion coincided with the beginning of slave raiding in the region.

The Nuba, driven into the hilly country, turned to terrace farming to survive. Gradually they established a barter relationship with the Baggaras. Each subtribe of the Baggaras protected the Nuba hill tribes in its own territory in return for supplies of grain and slaves. The extent and limits of these relationships between Nuba and Baggara varied greatly from one area to another; the most prominent feature of relations between the two peoples was slave raiding by Baggara warriors.

In 1821, the Egyptians conquered the Sudan as agents of the Ottoman Empire. The Turkish governors of Kordofan sent expeditions into the Nuba Mountains in search of gold and slaves but never attempted to extend their authority to the region. Baggara slavers were particularly active under Turkish rule.

The rise of the Islamic Mahdist movement in the 1880s brought a new crisis to the mountains. Some Muslim Nuba supported the Mahdi, thought to be the new prophet, while the majority resisted. The brutal harassment of the Nuba continued after the defeat of the Mahdist state by the allied forces of Egypt and Britain and the establishment of a new administration in Anglo-Egyptian Sudan in 1898. In spite of their devastating experience during the Mahdi period, the Nuba resisted the extension of government administration to their homeland. It took almost 30 years to subdue the different Nuba tribes completely.

In the nineteenth century, Western Christian organizations, dedicated to evangelizing the non-Muslim peoples of the region, began a campaign against the slave trade practiced by the Arabized Muslims. Missionary schools and stations began the modernization of the region, and many Nuba accepted the new religion.

In the early twentieth century, many Nuba began to come down from the protection of the hills to farm and live on the plains. The movement was encouraged by the colonial government as a means to end resistance in the mountains and more effectively administer the region. Modern agricultural practices were introduced, and cotton became a valuable cash crop for Nuba farmers.

The government finally introduced large-scale schooling to the area in 1940. The emergence of an educated elite became a significant unifying factor for the scattered Nuba tribes. Cultural and linguistic differences became less pronounced as education highlighted the similarities and common factors.

Sudan was granted independence in 1956. Immediately after independence, the teaching of the Koran was required in all schools, and missionary schools were nationalized. In 1962, the Missionary Societies Act imposed discriminatory licensing requirements on Christian missions. Independence also accelerated the opening of the mountains to resource development and intrusions by national and international agents of trade and politics. The racist and discriminatory attitude of the Muslim-dominated government in Khartoum gradually hardened Nuba attitudes to that and all subsequent regimes. Much of the Nuba land, particularly in the plains, was taken by the government for distribution to absentee Muslim landlords.

A Sudanese civil war began in 1983, when President Jaafar Muhammad Nimeiri tried to impose Muslim Shari'a law on the non-Muslim regions of the country. In 1984 the civil war spilled into the Nuba Mountains; heavy fighting spread across the fertile region, driving the people toward either garrison towns or the refuge of rebel-held areas. By 1987 the Nuba had mobilized, and insurgent groups allied to the Sudan People's Liberation Army (SPLA) of the Southern Sudanese* were fighting government troops and armed Muslim militias.

Since an Islamic, fundamentalist general of the National Islamic Front came to power in Sudan in 1989, an attempt to defeat the Nuba rebellion has grown into a scorched-earth war of annihilation against a people whose tradition of political and religious tolerance threatens the Sudanese government's vision of Islamic extremism. The government began a program of forced Islamization and Arabization. Northern elites seized much of the fertile land for huge mechanized farms. Nuba migrant workers in northern towns experienced blatant racial discrimination. Christianity, seen by the regime as a rival to Islam, became the government's particular target; a *jihad*, a holy war, was declared against the non-Muslim peoples of the Nuba Mountains by the governor of South Kordofan in January 1992.

Sudanese leaders believe that to be Sudanese is to be Muslim. Some of the most discriminatory legislation was amended following the visit of Pope John Paul II in 1993, but persecution continued. A *fatwa*, a religious decree, was issued in December 1993 by Muslim clerics in Khartoum declaring it the holy duty of all Muslims to kill people in the Nuba Mountains that refuse to convert to Islam.

Armed militias, called *murahleen*, formed under the Popular Defense Act of 1990, have taken thousands of Nuba as slaves. In many cases the militias accompany military units, raiding along the way and returning to their bases with captured slaves. Although the Sudanese government continues to deny that slavery is practiced in Sudan, there is overwhelming evidence that slavery, in its classic sense, has in fact reemerged in the country. Attacks on the Nuba make no distinction between Muslims, Christians, or animists. Churches, mosques, Christian missions, and Quranic schools have all been indiscriminately shelled. Educated Nuba of whatever faith have been singled out and often summarily executed.

Nuba leaders mostly support the idea of a secular, democratic state in Sudan in which non-Muslim peoples would be equal to those of the Arabized north. Other demands include the expulsion of Baggaras who came to the mountains to escape drought in the lowlands, and the end of official discrimination. Smaller, more militant groups work for an independent Nuba homeland in federation with the Southern Sudan proposed by the insurgent peoples to the south.

The first documentation of government depredations against the Nuba became available through international sources in 1995, finally exposing the little-known war in the Nuba Mountains. Since that time human-rights organizations, Christian churches, and other groups have attempted to bring the situation to the world's attention, but with only limited success. The Sudanese government continues to deny the existence of warfare in the region and to accuse rights groups of fabrication and selective reporting.

None of Sudan's insurgent national groups can overthrow the ruling National Islamic Forces alone. Sudan's opposition groups have a common enemy in the Khartoum government, but establishing a workable alliance proved difficult in the late 1990s. The National Democratic Alliance was formed in 1995 when seven northern opposition groups forged an alliance with the SPLA. A separate peace agreement was signed by the Sudan government and a faction of the Nuba Mountains United Front of the SPLA in 1997, but continuing raids by government-armed Baggaras and the refusal to allow outside observers ended the agreement within months. Wholesale forced population movements and massacres by the Baggara Arab militias followed.

Famine struck the devastated region in 1998. The Sudan government in June 1999, for the first time in 10 years, allowed international aid agencies to deliver food aid to rebel-held areas of the Nuba Mountains. Attacks by government militias on relief centers, however, hampered the effort to stave off mass starvation. Food stores were looted, and thousands of head of cattle were stolen. Many women and children were taken to be sold in the Muslim north. Many Nuba were forced to convert to Islam in order to receive food.

The government, in spite of international pressure to allow the delivery of food aid, realized that assistance from the United Nations could alter the balance of power by stopping the flow of hungry Nuba to government-held areas and thereby strengthening the rebel position. From 1989 to

1999, Sudan's Islamic government lured people out of the mountains by permitting UN aid and other assistance only to government towns and camps. The government cut off all access to the mountains in an effort to force starving civilians out of areas controlled by the rebels of the SPLA and its Nuba allies. In mid-1999, international pressure forced Sudan's Islamic government to allow UN relief into the Nuba mountains for the first time in more than a decade.

Hundreds of thousands of Nuba starved out of the mountains are held in so-called peace villages, where men are armed and compelled to fight against fellow Nuba. Children are separated from their parents and conscripted into Islamic militias. Reportedly many women are raped, to dilute Nuba ethnicity. In May 2000 the major Nuba center, Tabanyaat, was overrun by government troops, forcing over 15,000 Nuba to flee to the mountains.

The Nuba, brutally dragged into the modern world, have been fighting to preserve their homeland and culture, but with little outside help. Aid agencies were expelled from the region in 1991, and little international aid has been allowed into rebel-held areas since. Journalists and other foreigners have also been barred. In government-held areas the situation is nearly as bad; there the Islamic government is forcing assimilation. Hunger, the product of the government's scorched-earth policy, threatens thousands of lives. The survival of the Nuba as a distinct African nation is at serious risk; an estimated 300,000 have been killed between 1989 and 2001, and many more have been driven from their homelands in nearly half a century of war and repression.

The government's program is dedicated to the eradication of all that is essential to Nuba society, whose very existence challenges the foundation of the government's claim that it can create an Islamic state in northern Sudan because all the citizens are Muslims who support that goal. The war in the Nuba Mountains is a war for the identity of Sudan.

In November 2001, the UN brokered a 4-week cease-fire to allow food aid to be distributed. Thousands are starving in the area, which in normal times, produced a surplus. The Nuba were happy to see the food sacks, which showed that they had not been completely forgotten by the outside world.

Successive Sudanese governments have discriminated against the Nuba: in education, in development, in social services, and in political office. The military government of President Omer al Bashir and Hassan al Turabi, that seized power in 1989, have escalated this into a war of annihilation.

SELECTED BIBLIOGRAPHY:

Baumann, Gerd. *National Integration and Local Integrity: The Miri of the Nuba Mountains in the Sudan.* 1988.

Davidson, Andrew P. *In the Shadow of History: The Passing of Lineage Society*. 1996.
Manger, Leif O. *From the Mountains to the Plains: The Integration of the Lafofa Nuba into Sudanese Society*. 1994.
Riefenstahl, Leni. *Last of the Nuba*. 1995.

Nyoros

Banyoros; Runyoros; Bunyoros; Kitara

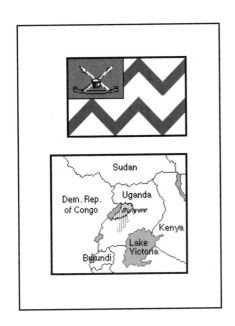

POPULATION: Approximately (2002e) 1,412,000 Nyoros in East Africa, concentrated in west-central Uganda south and southeast of Lake Albert. Nyoro nationalists claim that the national group makes up 14% of the Uganda population, making a national population of nearly three million.

THE NYORO HOMELAND: The Nyoro homeland occupies a well-watered, fertile plateau region in western Uganda east of Lake Albert and west of the Victoria Nile River. The population mostly live in scattered settlements in savanna lands. The homeland, traditionally a kingdom, was partially restored in 1993. The region comprises the present districts of Hoima, Masindi, Luwero, Kibaale, and Kiboga. The Mubende District, forming part of Buganda, is claimed as the heartland of the kingdom. *Kingdom of Bunyoro*: 9,831 sq. mi.—25,461 sq. km, (2002e) 1,424,000— Nyoros 88%, Toros* 8%, Gandas* 3%, other Ugandans 1%. The Nyoro capital and major cultural center is Hoima, (2002e) 15,000, the capital of the kingdom. The other major cultural center is Mubende, (2002e) 31,000, the traditional capital now included in the kingdom of Buganda.

FLAG: The Nyoro national flag, the flag of the former kingdom, is a white field crossed by two serrated blue lines, bearing a red canton on the upper hoist charged with a white drum surmounted by crossed spears.

PEOPLE AND CULTURE: The Nyoros, popularly called Banyoro, have a complex heritage that embraces three historical divisions—the tall, slender, light-skinned Bito, descendents of sixteenth century Nilotic invaders; the Huma, related to the Hima and Tutsi farther south, light-skinned Hamitic herdsmen who settled in the region in the Middle Ages; and the Bairu (Iru), dark-skinned Bantu agriculturists. Nyoro acculturation and sense of nationhood and shared destiny have been forged only since Ugandan independence in 1962. Until the 1960s the three groups remained separate, and intergroup marriage was forbidden. Population density is considerably less than that of neighboring peoples, in part because the Kabarega National Park, created in the northern part of Bunyoro. The Nyoro observe patrilineal descent and are divided into a number of exogamous clans. The once-large herds have been decimated by disease and warfare, although cattle raising is still a prestigious occupation, generally reserved for Nyoro of Huma descent. The average life span, just 42 years, is 10 years less than in 1980.

LANGUAGE AND RELIGION: The Nyoro language, Lunyoro, is a Western Lacustrine Bantu language, part of the Southern Bantu group of languages. The language is a dialect of the Nyoro-Toro branch of the Bantu languages, with narrow dialectical differences between the Nyoros and the Toros to the south. Although Bantu in structure, Lunyoro shows considerable Nilotic influence. Spoken in two major dialects, Rutagwenda and Orunyoro or Nyoro, the language is one of the most important in Uganda. Lunyoro is used in primary schools, an advanced literacy campaign, and in a growing Nyoro literature. Education for children of over 10 years is mostly in English. All three Nyoro peoples speak Lunyoro, which was the language of the original Bantu inhabitants.

The majority of the Nyoros are Christian, with a small Roman Catholic majority and an important Muslim minority concentrated in the north. The Nyoros were not heavily influenced by the introduction of either Christianity or Islam, and most see Christian, Islamic, and traditional rituals as equally valuable. They observe all these rituals scrupulously.

NATIONAL HISTORY: Bantu peoples settled the fertile lands around Lake Albert between A.D. 1000 and 1100 and gradually united as a tribe under a paramount king. The Bairu (Iru), also called the Bachwezi, who were skilled farmers, developed a structured, pacific society under a feudal hierarchy. The legendary kingdom of Bunyoro-Kitara controlled present-day western Uganda, eastern Congo, western Kenya, and parts of northern Tanzania.

In the open grasslands of Bunyoro there are impressive earthworks whose makers and functions are not yet completely understood. Also, many hills are important historically, particularly Masaka Hill and Mubende Hill, with its sacred Nakaima tree. All of the historical sites are associated with the Kitara or Bachwezi culture that flourished in the region between the fourteenth and sixteenth centuries.

Hamitic migrants, the Huma (Hima), thought to have originated in present-day Ethiopia, conquered the kingdom and established themselves as a pastoral aristocracy. In the early sixteenth century a tall Nilotic people, the Bito Luo, replaced the Huma as the kingdom's dominant people. The conquerors reestablished the kingdom under the Bito dynasty. The Luo adopted the culture and language of the more advanced Bairu. The Bairu were relegated by the Nilotic aristocrats to a serflike condition and forbidden to own cattle, the new measure of wealth in the kingdom. The Bito mostly dominated the northern districts, while the Huma continued to control the southern districts as vassals of the Bitos.

The *omukama*, or king, was believed to be descended from the first ruler, Kintu, whose three sons were tested to determine the relationship that would endure among their descendents. The eldest son became a servant and farmer, the second became a herdsman, and the third son became the ruler of all. This tale served to legitimize the social stratification of Nyoro society, which viewed the pastoral way of life as more prestigious than of peasant agriculture. It also served to emphasize the belief that the socioeconomic roles of the three castes were divinely ordained. Even now, when many Nyoros have departed from their traditional occupations, these putative lines of descent, to some extent, justify social behavior.

The kingdom, Bunyoro-Kitara, dominated a large area of the lakes region in the sixteenth and seventeenth centuries, by controlling the salt trade. Invasions and civil wars eventually divided the territory into a number of rival kingdoms, including Rwanda, Burundi, Karagwe, and Buganda. Buganda gradually assumed the position of the premier kingdom and expanded at Bunyoro's expense. In the 1840s the southern region of the kingdom seceded to become the separate kingdom, called Toro. The succession of an adroit king, Kabarega, to the throne in 1869 restored Bunyoro power; the kingdom engaged rival Buganda in a long series of wars in the second half of the century.

British influence, established in rival Buganda in 1888, made Bunyoro a center of resistance to the Europeans and their Ganda allies. In 1894 a suspected Belgian advance from the west provided the British and Gandas with a pretext for war. Defeated by the combined force, the *omukama* could not resist the incorporation of his kingdom into British Uganda in 1896. The Kyanyangire Abaganda Rebellion in 1899 erupted over Nyoro grievances and grew into an attempt to reestablish the sovereign kingdom. The rebellion ended with the exile of Omukama Kabarega to the Seychelles, a British island group in the Indian Ocean.

The British authorities allowed Kabarega to return to Bunyoro in 1900 but forced him to sign the Buganda Agreement, giving all Nyoro lands south of the Kafo River, the provinces of Buyaga and Bugangaizi, to Britain's ally and Bunyoro's ancient enemy, Buganda. The "Lost Counties" territorial dispute continues to the present, since the two counties include Bunyoro's ancient center, Mubende, and the traditional burial site of Bunyoro kings. Ganda chiefs were employed in Bunyoro as agents of the British government and Luganda, the Ganda language, was employed as the language of administration. By 1907, the Nyoro succeeded in having Ganda agents withdrawn in exchange for guaranteeing the peace in the region.

Stripped of their salt monopoly and of outlying territories, the Nyoros remained less developed throughout the colonial period. They accused the British of trying to punish them for their unwillingness to accept protectorate status as did the neighboring kingdoms. They were the outcasts of the colonial administration, victimized by the British and the other tribes.

Ganda domination and the Lost Counties controversy initiated the growth of modern Nyoro nationalism. The movement began as an anti-Ganda popular movement. The Nyoro also saw the British as their enemies, powerful protectors of their ancient rivals in Buganda. In 1921 Nyoro nationalists formed a political group called Mubende-Banyoro, which quickly became the kingdom's most popular political party; its demands included the return of the Lost Counties and secession from British Uganda. The British treated the kingdom as conquered territory until 1933, when the king finally signed a protectorate agreement.

The territorial dispute between Bunyoro and Buganda acquired renewed importance when Britain prepared Uganda for independence. In 1961 the *omukama* refused to attend a constitutional conference until the British authorities resolved the conflict. The Ganda refused to negotiate, setting off a serious crisis as Bunyoro moved toward secession and prepared for war. British mediation produced an agreement to hold a plebiscite in the disputed area, finally allowing Uganda to achieve independence in 1962. The Kingdom of Bunyoro reluctantly agreed to accept autonomy and a semifederal status within Uganda.

In 1964 the inhabitants of the Lost Counties voted to return to Bunyoro. The conflict again became a crisis when the Ganda government refused to accept the results of the plebiscite. Nyoro soldiers gathered in Hoima and prepared for war, but the dispute quickly lost importance as even more serious threats menaced the kingdoms. The Ugandan government, dominated by non-Bantu northern tribes, instituted laws to curtail the kingdoms' autonomy. In 1966 the government abrogated the autonomy statutes and in 1967 abolished the kingdoms as administrative units.

Nyoro nationalists enthusiastically supported the overthrow of the hated government in 1971 by a young army colonel, Idi Amin Dada. Amin's new government, a brutal dictatorship dominated by Amin's small northern Muslim tribe, soon lost all support in Bunyoro. In 1972 Nyoro leaders, sickened by the excesses of the Amin regime, called for Bunyoro secession, but the movement lost momentum as Amin's henchmen systematically eliminated its leaders.

The infamous Amin regime, finally overthrown in 1979, gave way to a series of weak, unstable Ugandan governments. A large resistance movement arose among the southern Bantu peoples of the former kingdoms of the southwest, led by Yoweri Museveni, an ethnic Ankole.* After years of bush warfare, Museveni took control of Uganda in 1986 and created the country's first Bantu-dominated government.

Relative peace and democracy permitted the rebirth of Nyoro nationalism, based on demands for the restoration of the kingdom. A more radical minority advocated the secession of Bunyoro from Uganda, arguing that the kingdom's inclusion in the multi-ethnic state had brought it only terror, death, and destruction. In July 1993 the government allowed the partial restoration of the kingdom and the enthronement of a new Nyoro king, Solomon Iguru, a descendent of Kabarega and the 27th monarch of the Bito dynasty. In September 1993 nationalists demanded the restoration of the kingdom's traditional boundaries, including the Mubende area of Buganda, the Lost Counties.

The first national elections in 16 years were held in Uganda in April 1996. The majority of the Nyoros supported President Museveni, fearing the chaos and violence of the north of the country. The vote generally split along regional lines in Uganda, with the Bantu south supporting Museveni, while the Nilotic north supported opposition leaders.

For decades the Nyoros had been among the poorest of the peoples of Uganda, but in the 1990s they experienced a resurgence due to a new emphasis on cash-crop production by small-scale farmers. New prosperity and the partial restoration of the kingdom fueled demands for greater autonomy and for real political power for the new *omukama*. Presently the king is a cultural leader, with no political or administrative power, but under his patronage the Nyoros are striving to salvage and maintain their age-old culture and kingdom.

In May 1998, a land-reform bill raised fears that the Nyoros would lose land to other ethnic groups. Nyoro leaders claimed that the bill favored the Ankole, President Museveni's ethnic group, further souring relations between the government and Nyoros, who also accused Museveni of favoring of the people of his homeland in the far southwest in his government.

Uganda's support of rebel groups in neighboring regions of the Democratic Republic of Congo in 1999–2000 raised tension in the region as resources were drawn off to support the military campaign. The growing disillusionment with the Museveni government is based on the relatively disadvantaged economic situation of the Nyoros and the perceived decline in government development funds since the war in the neighboring Congo drew in the Ugandan government in 1999. The dispatch of 15,000 troops into neighboring areas of Congo in support of antigovernment rebels in 1999 further alienated the Nyoros, who claim that the military intervention is draining away funds badly needed for regional development in Uganda.

In May 2001, the kingdom government took control of two palaces, royal burial grounds, and other cultural sites in the region from the Ugandan government. The monarchy has begun to reunite the Nyoros, who have had no unifying symbol since 1967. Demands are now being voiced for all-weather roads—there are none in the kingdom—to allow the

Nyoros to engage in trade and to allow for better communication throughout the ancient territory.

SELECTED BIBLIOGRAPHY:

Apuuli, Clarence. *A Thousand Years of the Bunyoro-Kitara Kingdom*. 1981.
Mutibwa, Phares. *Uganda since Independence*. 1992.
Nyakatura, V.W. *Anatomy of an African Kingdom: A History of Bunyoro-Kitara*. 1973.
Sathyamurthy, T.V. *The Political Development of Uganda 1900–1986*. 1986.

Ob-Ugrians

Khanty-Mansis; Hanty-Mansis; Ostyaks-Voguls; Obdors; Berezovs; Yugras; Jugras

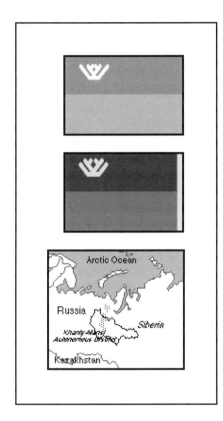

POPULATION: Approximately (2002e) 50,000 Ob-Ugrians in Siberia, concentrated in the Khanty-Mansi Autonomous Region, with smaller communities in Yamalo-Nenets Autonomous Region, Tobolsk, Tyumen, and Sverdlovsk Oblasts. The actual population of the Ob-Ugrians is difficult to calculate, as the present population figures are based on language use.

THE OB-UGRIAN HOMELAND: The Ob-Ugrian homeland, called Yugra, lies in northwestern Siberia along the lower reaches of the Ob River. The Ob-Ugrians mostly live in the basin of the Ob River, in the Western Siberian Plain. Much of the region is Arctic tundra and taiga, with deep northern forests and swamplands that remain frozen for much of the year. The region forms an autonomous district of Tyumen Oblast in the Russian Federation. *Autonomous District of Khanty-Mansi (Yugra)*: 201,969 sq. mi.—523,100 sq. km, (2002e) 1,341,000—Russians 79%, Ukrainians 10%, Ob-Ugrians 3%, others 8%. The Ob-Ugrian capital and major cultural center is Khanty-Mansiysk, called Samarovo by the Ob-Ugrians, (2002e) 37,000. The other important cultural center is Salehard, at the head of the Ob River, (2002e) 38,000.

FLAG: The Ob-Ugrian national flag, the flag of the national movement, is a horizontal bicolor of pale blue over pale green bearing the national symbol in white on the upper hoist. The official flag of the Khanty-Mansi Autonomous Okrug is a horizontal bicolor of blue over green bearing the Ob-Ugrian national symbol on the upper hoist and a narrow white vertical stripe on the fly.

PEOPLE AND CULTURE: The Ob-Ugrians comprise two closely related peoples, the Khants, numbering about 35,000, and the Mansis, numbering some 15,000. In response to the harsh environment, the

Ob-Ugrians developed a set of distinct social and economic practices and traditions. Traditionally the tribal peoples were grouped into a system of patrilineal clans organized into tribes, divided in turn into three ethnographic groups—northern, southern, and eastern—with distinct cultural features and dialects. The ancient social system severely restricted women's rights and movements. The presence of women was thought to defile religious idols and lead to temptation for clan and family members; therefore, women were veiled. Modern Ob-Ugrian culture is a blend of indigenous and Russian ways. Traditional beliefs and cultural traits survived most clearly among the rural clans, but the majority of the small nation's members cling to their traditions. In the 1960s, the government sponsored "open face" ceremonies to encourage Ob-Ugrian women to abandon their traditional veils.

LANGUAGE AND RELIGION: The Ob-Ugrians speak Ob-Ugrian dialects of the Ugrian branch of the Finno-Ugrian group of languages. The closely related Khant and Mansi languages are related to the language of the Magyars, the Hungarians of Central Europe. The Khant language is spoken in 10 distinct dialects grouped into three dialectal groups, the northern, southern, and eastern. Mansi is spoken in three dialects, also northern, southern, and eastern, with several subdialects that blend into Khant. The number of dialects reflects the vast area and sparse population of their homeland. The dialects have gained abundant loanwords from the neighboring Komis,* Tatars,* Nenets,* and Russians. The first publication in the language, part of the Bible, appeared in 1868. School primers, written by clerics, appeared in 1897. The modern literary language is based on the Kazym dialect, but at present education is in Russian.

The Ob-Ugrians are nominally Orthodox Christians, but they have continued to follow traditional beliefs. Their religion has many gods, great and small, the most important being called Numi-Torem. Their religious beliefs, developing in their northern environment, stresses reincarnation. Each newborn baby is seen as the reincarnation of a deceased member of the tribe. Traditional practices included the worship of wooden idols that represented clan ancestors and sacred animals. Funeral rites, formerly involving piling the deceased's possessions on the grave, have been modified; symbolic sleds and other miniatures are now used in place of the actual possessions. Government pressure, based on economic need, has curtailed the sacrifice of animals. An estimated 5–10% are practicing Christians.

NATIONAL HISTORY: Theories differ as to the origins of the Ob-Ugrians. Archeological finds indicate that the ancestors of the Khants, Mansis, and Hungarians inhabited the western Siberian taiga and wooded tundra three to four thousand years ago. One theory suggests that they originated in the valley of the Pechora River in northern European Russia and crossed the Urals to the Ob River region in the first century B.C. Others believe they evolved east of the Urals from a mixture of Uralian and other groups. Around 500 A.D., the Ugrian tribes were forced to leave their homeland to move northeast, crossing the Ural Mountains to settle the basin of the Ob River, while their kinsmen moved west, eventually settling in Hungary.

The first European reference to the Ob-Ugrians, then called the Jugras, is found in a Novgorodian chronicle from 1096. In the thirteenth century, the Ob-Ugrian tribes became tributaries to the mercantile republic of Novgorod. About the same time, the Khant and Mansi languages began to diverge. Slavic expeditions explored the region 1483 and 1499.

The Ob-Ugrians came under Russian control during the late sixteenth and early seventeenth centuries. The first mention in Muscovite archives of the tribal groups appeared in 1572. Following the penetration of Siberia by the Cossacks and the defeat of the Tatars in 1581–82, Russian fur traders established themselves in the Ob Valley. They were soon followed by government officials. In 1595, a Russian fort was established at the mouth of the Ob River, on the site of a Khant town. A fur tax was imposed on the tribal peoples, but the rugged terrain made it possible for the Khants largely to escape Russian rule by moving away from the Russian settlements. The Mansis, who had earlier fought the Tatars, stayed to fight the new invaders and were decimated.

The tribal peoples, enticed by iron and steel goods, and later by firearms, were slowly brought under the authority of the colonial administration. Large numbers also adopted the harmful use of alcohol. The Russians also brought European diseases, especially venereal ones. The Ob-Ugrians entered a long period of decline that continued until the mid-eighteenth century.

Orthodox Christian missionaries, most notably the monk Fyodor, officially converted the Ob-Ugrians between 1715 and 1722, but the conversions were only nominal. Tsar Peter I had directed that those who resisted be killed. Traditional religious beliefs and customs remained more important than the new Christian religion. The Russian government authorized the granting of citizenship to any indigenous person who converted to Christianity, a process that led to forced conversions. Citizenship brought the tribes under the authority of civil servants and the military, leading to the virtual enslavement of the tribal groups to increase fur trapping.

Russian traders and colonists began encroaching on traditional tribal lands and fishing grounds. The remoteness of the region and the lack of a government presence in many areas prevented effective enforcement of laws passed to shield the native Siberian peoples from exploitation. The tribal peoples were economically subjugated with the help of a combination of debt and liquor provided by Russian merchants and officials.

The Ob-Ugrians, until well into the twentieth century, remained largely a nomadic hunting and fishing people, with others engaged in herding reindeer. Virtually untouched by World War I, the Ob-Ugrians began to feel strong Russian influence only in the wake of the Bolshevik revolution of 1917. A special government body, the Committee of the North, was created in 1924 to deal with the small northern nations. It introduced basic elements of administration, medical care, and primary schools. It also launched a campaign to end the subjugation of women.

The tribal peoples of the northern regions were organized on a territorial basis at the close of the 1920s. As part of this process, the Ostyak-Vogul National Area was formed in 1930–31. Although in theory the Ob-Ugrians were to be self-governing, government policies were actually designed to assimilate the tribal peoples into the larger Russian culture. A literary language was developed, using the Latin alphabet, but in 1939 it was changed to the Russian Cyrillic alphabet. Compulsory attendance at Russian-language schools introduced the children to Russian culture.

The Slavic impact on the Ob-Ugrians intensified after 1929, a time when all of the Soviet Union was being reshaped under Stalin's dictatorship. The tribal lands and herds were collectivized, while Russian officials and settlers conducted a campaign against the native religious practices. Such social practices as the abduction of brides and the treating of diseases by shamans were condemned and outlawed. The more prosperous tribal leaders and the shamans were liquidated, and sacred groves and burial grounds were desecrated. Ob-Ugrian children were forcibly removed to Russian-speaking boarding schools.

In 1933 the tribal peoples, threatened by Stalinist excesses, forced Russification, and separation from their children, rebelled across a wide region. The Kazym Revolt pitted the poorly armed Khants and Mansis, led by the tribal elders, against the well-armed Russian colonists. The Soviet authorities called in troops, and the rebellion was brutally crushed. Many villages were burned and their inhabitants forced to settle in sites controlled by the military. More distant villages were bombed by the Soviet air force. In 1940, however, in an unusual concession, the name of the region was changed from Ostyak-Vogul to Khanty-Mansi, replacing the Russian names for local names.

The life of the Ob-Ugrians remained mostly traditional until the 1960s. Although the region was known to contain resources, there were severe impediments to their exploitation. The area was densely forested and traversed by hundreds of low-watershed rivers. There was also a huge marshland extending from the Baraba Steppe in the south to the Arctic Circle. The relative isolation began to change quickly, however, when huge deposits of oil and natural gas were discovered. Pipelines were laid across the region, and a railway was constructed. In 1960 alone, six million hectares of grazing land was destroyed, and 200,000 hectares of waterways, rich in fish, were heavily polluted. As a consequence the herds of reindeer decreased, and the yearly catch of fish declined rapidly.

The Ob-Ugrians have probably never been numerous, but during the twentieth century they decreased, particularly in 1926 and 1970–79. The first decrease was a result of the Stalinist repression, when large numbers of Ob-Ugrian men were massacred. Since 1970, the number of Ob-Ugrians speaking their native languages has decreased due to the Russification of the population.

Soviet economic policies had virtually destroyed much of the region by the late 1980s. Extensive oil-extraction projects, accompanied by massive pollution, all but ruined the fishing grounds, and a variety of large-scale development projects did similar damage to traditional reindeer pasturage. The recent discovery of new oil and natural gas deposits in the region promises even more damage to the land and identity of the Ob-Ugrians.

The liberalization of Soviet life under Mikhail Gorbachev in the late 1980s fueled the growth of a local Ob-Ugrian nationalism and allowed the airing of decades' worth of grievances. Many who had been assimilating into Russian culture began to take a new interest in their traditional culture and language. Increased contact with Hungarians and Estonians brought much-needed financial aid and published materials. In 1997 the Hungarian president visited the region during an extended visit to Russia.

In May 1991, delegates protested to the Council of Ministers of the Soviet Union against a decision to start oil exploitation at Tyanovsk in the Khanty-Mansi Autonomous District. In response to their protest, 35 Khant families were forcibly deported from their homes. In the wake of the disintegration of the Soviet Union, in late 1991, local Khant and Mansi leaders proclaimed the sovereignty and independence of the region, but local Russian *soviets* (councils) refused to recognize the change, primarily due to its implications, including Ob-Ugrian control over natural resources. In April 1993 there were disturbances following the death of a Khant activist.

The Ob-Ugrians live in 72 national settlements, many still without electricity, or with light provided only for a certain number of hours a day. In many settlements there are no hospitals, schools, clubs, or even shops. There are also a number of settlements that are considered "liquidated," nonexistent, but people continue to live in them. They completely lack amenities, and the inhabitants have only themselves or their neighbors when help is needed.

Many educated Ob-Ugrians have joined cultural and national groups protesting the environmental disaster overtaking their homeland and the assault on their national identity. The groups have joined environmental and interest groups representing indigenous peoples, and they support demands for more controlled development policies that will permit the survival of the Ob-Ugrians and their culture. The region's population, around 150,000 in 1970, swelled to nearly 1.5 million by 2000. Oil spills and pollution blacken the wetlands, raised roads cause flooding and ruin the forests, fires caused by carelessness and petroleum-soaked debris send columns of smoke into the air, while acid rain blights huge areas.

In March 1997, the Khants in North Priobskoye on the Ob River rejected a proposal by the regional government to auction off their traditional lands for oil development. The Khant leaders of the area refused consent because of the potential impact on their subsistence livelihoods. The region represents the last, large, contiguous and virtually undeveloped tract of middle Siberian taiga. Indigenous activists also point out that the area is home to over 200 types of birds, seven of which are endangered species.

In the late 1990s, the exploitation and derision of the "blacks," as they are called by the Russian colonists, went unpunished. Thus a part of the Ob-Ugrians embraced a nationalist sentiment. Another part responded to the derision of the Russians with self-denigration. They left their homeland and tried to live as Russians. Although assimilation slowly began to reverse in the 1990s, the suicide rate among the two small peoples remained extremely high.

Ob-Ugrian activists, realizing that Russian control of their vast former homeland is irreversible, in 1998 proposed the creation of new autonomous region around the area at the confluence of the Kazym and Sosva Rivers. The much-reduced homeland would give the Ob–Ugrians control over their lives and allow them to sustain their traditional culture. One of the major points of the proposal, which had not been officially addressed in late 2001, would be a ban on the exploitation of the new region's oil and natural gas deposits.

SELECTED BIBLIOGRAPHY:

Forsyth, James. *A History of the Peoples of Siberia.* 1992.
Mandelstam, Majorie. *The Tenacity of Ethnicity: A Siberian Saga in Global Perspective.* 1999.
Miller, Marc, ed. *State of the Peoples: A Global Human Rights Report on Societies in Danger.* 1993.
Olson, James S. *An Ethnohistorical Dictionary of the Russian and Soviet Empires.* 1994.

Occitans

Occitanians; Provençals; Languedociens

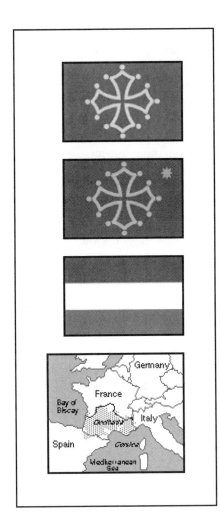

POPULATION: Approximately (2002e) 12,200,000 Occitans in southwestern Europe, with 10,840,000 in the Occitania region of France and other large concentrations in Paris and northern France. A small group, numbering around 5,000, called Aranese, live in the Aran Valley of northern Spain, and some 300,000, called Transalpin Occitans, live in adjacent areas of northwestern Italy.

THE OCCITAN HOMELAND: The Occitan homeland lies in southern France, comprising the historical regions of Auvergne, Bourbonnais, Béarn, Dauphiné, Foix, Gascony, Guyenne, Languedoc, Limousin, Marche, Provence, and Venaissin. The region is largely mountainous: the large plateau region, the Massif Central, in the center; the Alps in the east and in Italian Occitania; and the Pyrenees in the south. The valley of the Garonne, the coastal lowlands in the west, and the coastal plains of the Mediterranean and the valley of the Rhone in the southeast are the most densely populated. Occitania has no official status in France. Historical Occitania embraces the French regions of Aquitaine, Auvergne, Languedoc, Limousin, Provence-Alps-Côte d'Azur, Midi-Pyrénées, and the southern departments of Rhone Alps Region. *Region of Occitania (Occitanie):* 83,371 sq. mi.—215,987 sq. km, (2002e) 14,902,000—Occitans 71%, other French 14%, North Africans 10%, Spanish 1%, others 4%. The Occitan capital and major cultural center is Toulouse, called Tolosa in the Occitan dialects, (2002e) 404,000, metropolitan area 982,000. Other important centers are Bordeaux, called Bordèu, (2002e) 217,000, metropolitan area 942,000, and Marseilles, called Marselha, (2002e) 811,000, metropolitan area 1,533,000, and Nice, known as Niça, (2002e) 336,000, metropolitan area 945,000. The capital and major cultural center of the Aranese, the Spanish Occitans, is Viella, called Vielha locally, (2002e) 3,000.

FLAG: The Occitan flag, the unofficial flag of the nation, is a red field charged with a red Cross of Toulouse outlined in yellow. The flag of the national movement is the national flag with the addition of a seven-pointed yellow star on the upper fly. The unofficial flag of the Aranese, the Occitans in northern Spain, is a horizontal tricolor of blue, white, and green.

PEOPLE AND CULTURE: The Occitans are the descendents of the Latin peoples of Roman Gaul, more closely related to the Catalans* of northeastern Spain and the Piedmontese* and Ligurians* of northwestern Italy than to the Germanic descendents of the Franks in northern France. The Occitans, unlike the northern French, are a Mediterranean people, having mixed very little with the Franks, and they tend to be shorter and darker than the inhabitants of Paris and northern France. The Occitans, who mostly identify with regional identities, have only recently begun to view themselves as a united national group. The inhabitants of southern France often refer to the northern French as "Franks," referring to their Germanic origin. The Occitans of the Aran Valley of northern Spain are the only Occitans whose language is officially recognized.

LANGUAGE AND RELIGION: The Occitan language, often called Langue d'Oc, is considered the closest to the original Latin of the modern Romance languages and is the oldest of the Romance languages still in use. The language, forming the Occitano-Romance group of languages, has never been standardized and is characterized by a group of six related Oc dialects—Auvergnat, Alpin, Gascon, Languedocien, Limousin, and Provençal. Auvergnat or Auvernhas is spoken in the central Augergne region in two subdialects, Haut-Auvergnat and Bas-Auvergnat. Alpin, often considered a dialect of Provençal, is spoken in the Alpes from Valence to Grenoble. Gascon is spoken in the southwest and includes four subdialects—Landais in the west, Béarnais in Béarn, Ariégeois in Foix, and Aranese in the Aran Valley in the Spanish Pyrenees. Languedocien or Lengadoucian is spoken in the southern region of Languedoc and the central and western region of Guyenne; it includes four subdialects—Bas-Languedocien, Languedocien Moyen, Haut-Languedocien, and Guyennais. Limousin or Lemosin is spoken in Limousin and Marche and comprises two subdialects, Haut-Limousin and Bas-Limousin. The most widely spoken of the dialects is Provençal, with over 250,000 fluent speakers; over a million have some knowledge of the language. Provençal is spoken in the southeast, in Provence, eastern Languedoc, and Venaissin in five subdialects; Niçard or Niçois in the Nice region; Maritime Provençal around Marseilles, Toulon, and in the department of Var; Gavot in Dauphine, Rhodanien or Nimois west of the Rhone River around Nîmes; Dauphinois or Dromois in southern Dauphine; and Tranalpin in the adjacent districts of Piedmont in northwestern Italy. The dialects are structurally separate languages; none of the dialects are universally accepted as the standard literary language, although all are mutually intelligible. Since the 1970s a voluntary and deliberate return to the regional dialects has reversed centuries of assimilation and acculturation and has prompted the cultural and nationalist revolution of the 1980s and 1990s. A modern literary language is being developed based on the Languedocien dialect, which is linguistically conservative and still close to the troubadour language of the thirteenth century.

The Occitans are mostly Roman Catholic, with small Protestant minorities, mostly in the mountainous and rural areas. The Cathar heresy was wiped out during the Middle Ages, but remnants of the belief system remain, particularly in religious ceremonies and celebrations.

NATIONAL HISTORY: Greeks visited the coastal areas on the Mediterranean as early as the sixth century B.C. Greek colonies were founded, and Greek culture spread along the coast and influenced the Celtic tribes living in the area. The flourishing Greek port cities fell to Roman rule in the second century B.C., forming part of the first Roman possession outside Italy. Julius Caesar conquered the interior districts in the Gallic Wars, from 58 to 51 B.C. The Romans called the region Gaul, the Latin name for the area's Celtic inhabitants. Roman Gaul developed as a prosperous center of Roman commerce, art, and culture.

Roman power collapsed in the fifth century A.D., leaving the region open to invasion and Germanic tribes—Visigoths, Vandals, Burgundians,* and Franks. The most powerful of the Germanic tribes, the Franks, settled in northern Gaul in the sixth century. The region, retaining many Roman institutions and traditions, remained more culturally and politically advanced than the Frankish north. The countship of Toulouse, founded in 788, and the kingdom of Provence, established in 879, evolved as the major states in the politically divided area. The Occitan states carried on an extensive trade with North Africa, enjoying luxuries and inventions unheard of in most of Europe.

The Oc dialects flourished as the court languages of the states of southern France from the ninth to the thirteenth centuries. Occitania experienced a great cultural flowering in the eleventh and twelfth centuries, when the whole area south of a line running from Bordeaux to Grenoble spoke Oc dialects. From its inception in Limousin, the budding "troubadour culture" spread across the region, carried by wandering troubadours, who turned the Oc dialects into a standardized Romance language. The cultural awakening, a forerunner of the Renaissance, developed an extensive Occitan literature, marked by new forms and a striking lyric poetry. Official documentation used Occitan, while northern France still used Latin. A standardized literary language spread across the region, although many different dialects continued to be spoken.

The cultural flowering coincided with the spread of an eastern religious sect, the Cathars or Cathari. The troubadour culture and the Cathar beliefs became closely intertwined in the brilliant medieval Occitan civilization, which combined Roman heritage, sophisticated Arab imports, and Christian concepts. The Cathar sect, originating in the Balkans, gained converts in the region from the eleventh century. The converts, called Albigenses (after Albi, one of the major Cathar cities), were branded heretics by the Catholic Church. The Cathars were not heretics or even Christians, but adherents of a dualistic system believing in good and evil, body and soul, etc. The Albigenses, very aesthetic in comparison to the local Roman Catholic clergy, gained many converts. Supported by many powerful nobles, the Cathar sect became a virtual state religion in many of the Occitan states.

The Cathars earned the wrath of the Catholic Church by criticizing its wealth and vast land holdings. In spiritual questions the Cathars attacked the very foundations of Christianity, denying the value of the sacraments. The pope sent missionaries to Occitania to stop the rapid spread of the Cathar heresy and issued increasingly stringent instructions for dealing with heretics and nonbelievers. Efforts to bring the heretics back to the church having failed, the pope, encouraged by the French, proclaimed a crusade against the Cathars in 1208. The French kingdom, to the north of the Oc states, answered the pope's call, seeing in the wealthy south a chance for conquest, expansion, and plunder. Cathar nobles, backed by the Catholic Aragonese,* united to resist the French invasion. The Albigensian Crusade of 1209–29 quickly became a political war, with the Occitan states as the battleground.

Rampaging French knights, under the guise of stamping out heresy, plundered and devastated Occitania driving thousands of refugees, both Catholic and Cathar, across the borders into Spain and Italy. Massacres of Occitan populations marked the French acquisition of the Oc lands. Pope Gregory IX in 1233 established a system of legal investigation in the conquered Albigensian centers, the beginning of the infamous Inquisition.

In 1229, Languedoc was partly annexed by France, and in 1271 the county of Toulouse was incorporated into the French kingdom, while other areas retained some independence until after the Hundred Years' War in the fifteenth century, which again devastated much of the region. Under the Inquisition and the revitalized Catholic Church, the Albigensian sect disappeared within a century. The Occitan dialects, suppressed in favor of the Oïl French spoken in Paris, were downgraded to folk languages spoken in rural areas and were finally banned in 1539. The Wars of Religion, from 1562 to 1598, further devastated the region, and massacres of Protestants echoed the earlier Cathar massacres.

Occitania was divided into provinces, which retained some local autonomy until the French Revolution swept away the local *parlements* in Toulouse, Aix-en-Provence, Grenoble, and other provincial capitals. Until the revolution, the Occitan provinces remained outside the French Tariff Union as "provinces considered foreign." For centuries after the Albigensian Crusade, Occitania remained the poorest region of France, although the vitality of the Occitan culture and language was evidenced by their refusal to die under massive French government pressure.

With the French Revolution in 1789 began a period of severe repression of regional identities. In 1794, during Robespierre's reign of terror, the regime's policy was to erase dialects and make the French language universal. After the revolution, Napoleon divided France into numerous departments in an effort to blunt regional loyalties. The emergence of a French press in the early nineteenth century further eroded the use of regional dialects in southern France. In the 1850s, however, one in five Frenchmen still could not speak standard French.

The Occitans, during the revolutionary upheaval in 1851, began to revive their culture and language, and to demand a federal system in France. An Occitan cultural organization, Felibrige, formed by the famed Provençal poet Frédéric Mistral in 1854, stimulated a resurgence and a new interest in the Occitan history, language, and culture. The cultural movement stimulated demands for cultural and political autonomy in highly centralized France. Mistral, in attempting to standardize the Occitan language, produced a monumental two-volume dictionary plus a collection of Occitan poetry that won him the Nobel Prize in 1904.

Following the introduction of universal education in France in 1872, the use of regional languages was rigorously repressed in the interest of national unity. Pupils using languages other than standard French were punished, particularly after the introduction of compulsory schooling in 1882. The Occitan dialects remained the language of daily life until the early twentieth century; many writers, as part of the Occitan revival, used the language despite French cultural pressure.

The Occitan movement lost support during World War I, but the Escola Occitana was established in 1919 to promote the revival of the language and culture. Official suppression hampered the effort to revive the language, and by the 1930s standard French had replaced the Occitan dialects as the language of daily life across the region.

During World War II, Occitania formed part of unoccupied France, under the authority of the regime at Vichy, in northern Occitania. The Germans sought to garner support by emphasizing the Latin heritage of the region, but with little success. Liberated by American troops, the Occitans remained pro-American in the postwar era, while the attitude of the northern French and the French government became increasingly anti–American as France lost it place as a major world power.

In 1951 the French government removed the ban on regional languages, stimulating the rebirth of the Occitan movement. In the 1960s, local politicians, aware that the Occitans had a weak sense of national identity, at first turned to ecological and other regional issues, but a regionalist movement soon emerged. Regionalist political groups, Lutte Occitane and VVAP (Volem Viure al Pais), grew from local action committees formed to resist pressure from the central government. The generations born in the 1960s and 1970s learned to speak Occitan as a matter of pride and were able to communicate with their grandparents in their own language. By the 1970s autonomist and nationalist sentiment in the region had begun to politicize the Occitan population.

The political integration of Europe, in the 1970s and 1980s, gave the movement focus. Occitan nationalists claimed that the region, like the Mezzogiorno in Italy, was at once colonized, neglected, and underdeveloped. With the socialist victory in France, in 1981, some powers were returned to the regions, but a regional Occitan assembly demanded by Occitan nationalists was rejected by the French government. Massive Muslim immigration from the former French colonies in North Africa became a major issue, generating support for racist, reactionary political groups.

In the 1980s militants and academics successfully forced the government to introduce Occitan into regional schools, and by 1991 an estimated six million people spoke or had some understanding of the Occitan dialects. The Occitan dialects have been introduced in a number of regional schools and universities, primarily in areas where nationalist feeling is present. Nationalists note that the French government struggles to maintain a multilingual Europe while English is becoming dominant, but at the same time refuses to countenance a multilingual France.

The Occitans still recall that they were forcibly joined to France through the devastation of their troubadour culture in the Albigensian Crusade and the Hundred Years' War. The national movement, in the 1990s, looks back on the massacres and horrors visited on their nation by "foreign invaders" from northern France in the thirteenth century. Modern Occitan nationalists seek independence within a united Europe and see the Albigenses as the first Occitan nationalists. The setting-up of an Assembly of the Autonomous Occitan Community in 2001, with an appointed executive and regrouping the elected members for Auvergne, Dauphiné, Gascony, Guyenne, Languedoc, Limousin and Provence in the French Senate was arranged as a demonstration in favor of regional autonomy but was denounced by the government as separatist and illegal.

SELECTED BIBLIOGRAPHY:

Brustein, William. *The Social Origins of Political Regionalism: France, 1849–1981.* 1982.

Costen, Michael. *The Cathars and the Albigensian Crusade.* 1997.

Lambert, Malcomb. *The Cathars.* 1998.

Roche, Alfonse. *Provençal Regionalism.* 1954.

Ogonis

Koana-Gokana; Kanas; Khanas

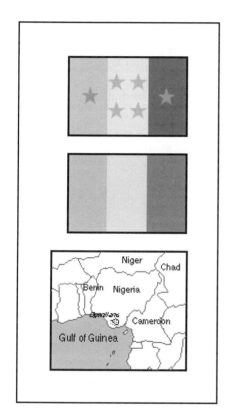

POPULATION: Approximately (2002e) 560,000 Ogonis in Nigeria, concentrated in the Ogoniland region of Rivers State in the Niger River delta in southern Nigeria. Outside Nigeria there are sizable Ogoni communities in the United Kingdom, Canada, and other African states.

THE OGONI HOMELAND: The Ogoni homeland, Ogoniland, lies in the Niger Delta region of southern Nigeria. Ogoniland has the dubious distinction of being the area where oil was first extracted in Nigeria in 1958. Historically densely populated, Ogoniland is divided into six kingdoms. The region, in Nigeria's Rivers State, is currently divided between the Bori Local Government region, which includes the Khana and Gokana Ogonis, and the region of Otelga, including the Tai and Eleme Ogonis, along with Ijaw* and Ibo* groups. Region of Ogoniland: 704 sq. mi.—1,823 sq. km, (2002e) 625,000—Ogonis 89%, other Nigerians 11%. The Ogoni capital and major cultural center is Bori, (2002e) 35,000. The other important cultural center is Port Harcourt, where a large Ogoni community lives, just outside Ogoniland.

FLAG: The Ogoni national flag is a vertical tricolor of pale green, yellow, and pale blue bearing six red stars. The flag of the Movement for the Survival of the Ogoni People (MOSOP), is a vertical tricolor of green, yellow, and blue.

PEOPLE AND CULTURE: The Ogonis are a Bantu people, part of the large Bantu population of west and central Africa. The Ogonis are relatively short and stocky, and are known for their strength and endurance. The Ogonis are divided into four major groups—the Gokana, Tai, Eleme, and Khana—which correspond to the major geographical regions of the homeland. The Ogonis are mainly subsistence farmers and fishermen. Until 1993, the Ogoni were politically inactive. The Ogonis only recently came to consider themselves a nation, as formerly they identified with their region, kingdom, or linguistic group. Archaeological and oral historical evidence suggests that the Ogonis have lived in the Niger Delta for about five centuries. Marriage with neighboring proples, except the Ibibios*, is forbidden by Ogoni custom and traditions.

LANGUAGE AND RELIGION: The Ogonis belong to the Ibibio or Semi-Bantu linguistic group of the Benue-Congo group of Niger-Congo languages. The language is spoken in four major dialects that correspond to the four major divisions of the small nation—Gokana, Tai, Eleme, and Khana. The dialects correspond to two primary divisions, East Ogoni and West Ogoni. Tai is often considered a dialect of Khana. Some Ogonis speak English or Ibo as a second language.

The majority of the Ogonis are Christians, most belonging to Protestant evangelical sects. Much of their pre-Christian belief system have been retained and mixed with Christianity to create a unique religion. Until recently the superstitious Ogonis normally killed twins, as they believed that a woman could only have one baby at a time, so one of the twins had to be a devil. Despite the introduction of Christianity, many aspects of indigenous beliefs remained. The land on which they live and the rivers that surround them are very important to the Ogonis. They not only provided enough food but are believed to be gods and are worshiped as such, which explains why the Ogonis view the degradation of their homeland as more than just an enviornmental disaster.

NATIONAL HISTORY: The history of the Ogonis, except for fragments contained in their oral traditions, is mostly a mystery. For centuries the Ogonis lived in six autonomous tribal groups under paramount chiefs or kings. Their fertile homeland in the Niger Delta supported a dense agricultural population. The region was often the target of slave raiders, because the mainly Muslim peoples from the north were forbidden to enslave fellow Muslims.

In the late fifteenth century Europeans appeared along the coast to the south. Under European impetus, the coastal tribes, the Ibibios and Ijaws,* raided the interior for slaves to sell to the insatiable Europeans. Thousands of Ogonis were captured and sold in the slave ports to be shipped to the labor-short territories of various European empires.

Europeans moving north from the coast explored Ogoniland in the 1700s. They were followed by European missionaries in the early 1800s. The Ogonis were receptive, and by the 1830s Christianity had begun to gain a foothold among the peoples of the six kingdoms. Although they benefited from the beginning of European education and the growing anti-slavery movement, Ogoni leaders resented the increasing loss of their traditional powers. In 1884 Ogoniland was included in the territories organized as the British Oil Rivers Protectorate.

European authority was finally extended to all of Ogoniland at the end of World War I. Population pressure forced many Ogonis to seek jobs in administration and trade in the coastal ports or the administrative towns beyond Ogoniland. The Ogoni peoples, formerly identifying with their tribe or kingdom, began to see themselves as one nation; the designation "Ogoni," used by the British administration since 1947, began to be used for all the smaller related groups collectively. The first grammar school was established in Ogoniland in 1958, exactly 100 years after the establishment of the first grammar school in Nigeria.

The Anglo-Dutch company Shell Oil began exploration in the region in 1937, but only after World War II was oil found in commercial quantities. Shell drillers discovered oil in Ogoniland in 1958, and drilling began across the region. The Ogoni had no say in the oil exploitation or in forced population movements to make way for oil drilling. Millions of dollars' worth of oil was extracted in the 1960s and 1970s, but almost nothing was returned to the region, one of the poorest in Nigeria.

Nigeria gained independence in 1960, amid growing regional and ethnic rivalries involving the country's largest and most powerful national groups. Being a small national group in a country of hundreds of tribes, the Ogoni had no effective say in national politics. Along with other groups in the Niger Delta, the Ogoni resented the domination of the Ibos, who controlled the Eastern Region of Nigeria.

In the early 1960s rivalries between Nigeria's three largest tribes, the Ibos, Hausas,* and Yorubas,* led to violence, particularly against people from the Eastern Region living outside their home areas, particularly in the Muslim Hausa Northern Region. Thousands of Ogonis, living and working in Muslim northern Nigeria, fled the violence and returned to their homeland, where agitation was growing for separation of the Niger Delta from the Ibo-dominated Eastern Region.

In May 1967, the Ibo leadership of the region declared the Eastern Region independent as the Republic of Biafra, including the reluctant non-Ibo peoples of the Niger Delta. The ensuing civil war devastated Biafra as federal troops fought their way across it. The Ogonis, in spite of supporting the federal cause, were treated as enemies by Nigerian troops and suffered along with the Ibos and other peoples. Tens of thousands died in the war and in the famine that accompanied the fighting, including an estimated 30,000 Ogonis. In 1970 the Ibos surrendered, and the reconstruction of the region was undertaken.

Oil production began almost immediately after the Biafra surrender, often carelessly, with massive oil spills and pollution. By the early 1980s, the oil boom had turned nearby Port Harcourt and Owerri into major oil ports, drawing many Ogonis from their overcrowded homeland to live and work in the urban areas. Pollution from the oil industry ruined the extraordinary fertility of the Niger Delta, devastating the subsistence farming and fishing that traditionally occupied the majority of the Ogonis.

The continuing rivalry between Nigeria's largest tribal groups systematically excluded the Ogonis and other smaller groups from positions of power. Laws were passed that favored the larger tribes; for instance, the 1989 constitution allows the federal government, a body never responsive to Ogoni grievances even under the occasional "democratic" regimes, to hold all mineral rights in the country.

When the Ogonis began their protests, Nigeria was under the military dictatorship of a Muslim from northern Nigeria, Gen. Ibrahim Babangida. He held out the promise of democracy in Nigeria by calling presidential elections in June 1993; they were won by a southern Christian. The victory was unacceptable to the military regime, and power was handed over to a military-appointed interim national government, which was in turn ousted by yet another military coup, led by Gen. Sani Abacha, in November 1993. As the situation in Nigeria deteriorated, the government became more repressive.

The environmental effects of more than 100 oil wells, mostly owned by Shell, have been devastating. Between 1976 and 1991 almost 3,000 separate oil spills, averaging 700 barrels each, occurred in the Niger delta. Oil leaked into the water supply and made formerly fertile farmland unusable. Gas flares, burning 24 hours a day, are often situated near Ogoni villages. The villagers have to live with the constant noise of the flares, which cover their homes and fields in thick soot, which further contaminates water supplies when the rains come. Air pollution from the flares results in acid rain and respiratory problems. Oil pipelines pass through villages and over what was once agricultural land.

The Nigerian government echoed Shell's lack of concern for the effects of oil production on the Ogonis. In response to protests and petitions, the government announced that since Ogoniland was one of the first places in Nigeria in which oil production was undertaken, it is reasonable that the environmental impact should be more pronounced there.

Kenule Beeson Saro-Wiwa, an noted Nigerian playwright, led a campaign against the Western oil companies in the late 1980s and early 1990s. By sensitizing the Ogonis and other ethnic groups in the Niger delta to their exploitation, he came to be viewed as a threat to the status quo—as the oil industry in Nigeria is the only part of the economy that continues to function. He founded the Movement for the Survival of the Ogoni People (MOSOP) in 1992. Until then the international community had ignored the Ogoni struggle to expel Shell Oil Company from their lands, and no one wanted to hear about the pollution and destitution brought about by uncontrolled oil drilling. Saro-Wiwa found an ally in a British firm, the Body Shop, known for its natural ingredients and environmental concerns. Executives of the Body Shop poured resources into a campaign to draw the world's attention to the destruction of the Ogoni nation.

The Ogoni region, which produced about 5% of the oil from the Niger Delta, was left with a badly polluted landscape, dead rivers, and desolation. To the Ogonis, Shell and the Nigerian government were waging environmental war against their small nation. They responded by mobilizing. The conflict resulted in the evolution of a strong national identity that had historically been lacking. The Ogonis believe they either win this war or be exterminated.

On 4 January 1993, over 300,000 Ogonis staged a peaceful protest against Shell Oil, the Nigerian government, and the environmental destruction of their homeland. This action was timed to coincide with the beginning of the Year of Indigenous People of the United Nations (UN). The situation in Ogoniland soon deteriorated. In response to an attack on a Shell employee, the company withdrew its staff from Ogoniland, bringing a strong response from Nigeria's military regime. Activists were harassed, and Ken Saro-Wiwa and others were arrested and held for periods without charges. In April the military fired on 10,000 Ogonis protesting against the construction of a new pipeline, wounding a number of the protesters. Ogoniland was sealed off by the military, and indiscriminate beatings and arrests followed during months of violent confrontations.

Twenty-nine leaders of MOSOP were arrested during the violence that spread across Ogoniland. The leaders of MOSOP were charged with sedition and inciting nationalism. In 1995, after a show trial condemned internationally as a sham, Ken Saro-Wiwa and eight others were publicly hanged for the deaths of four chiefs during disturbances in the region. The nine men were buried in anonymous graves in a military cemetery in Port Harcourt. The campaign then shifted from MOSOP to the Ogoni people themselves. A series of brutal attacks on Ogoni villages left over 750 dead and 30,000 homeless. The attacks were reported by the government as ethnic clashes between Ogonis and neighboring peoples.

The campaign to expose the devastation finally resulted in Nigeria's expulsion from the Commonwealth, promises by Shell to reform its operations, and government promises to share more of the proceeds of the oil wealth with the regions where it is produced. During the campaign the Ogonis organized a grassroots liberation movement, with their own flag, anthem, heroes, martyrs, and politics.

The Ogonis, devastated by generations of neglect and denial, remain suspicious of the Nigerian government. In spite of promises from both the Nigerian government and Shell, there has been almost no compensation, reparation, development, or cleanup. A hospital at Gokona, part of Shell's 1996 "Ogoni Reconciliation" plan, was agreed to in an effort to combat international concern over the company's poor environmental and human-rights record. The hospital reportedly has no mattresses, few medicines, and no electricity, but it is still the best and only hospital in a region with a population of over 200,000 people. Twenty-five miles away the Shell hospital for its own employees is newly refurbished, well staffed, and supplied with all modern amenities.

Living in an area where schools and health services have collapsed and poverty is endemic, many Ogonis focus on Shell and its gleaming employee compound in Port Harcourt as both the problem and the solution. Shell has stepped up its contributions to communities in the region, but how the money is spent has only increased the agitation. Ogoni leaders accuse the company of incompetence in development work, neglecting consultation, and being paternalistic at best. Most of the health, environmental, educational, and agricultural projects supported by Shell are dismissed as ineffective, unnecessary, or simply as aimed at the company's press relations. At a special congress in 1998, MOSOP leaders demanded a role in assessing the development projects that Shell backs; the demand was rejected by the company.

On 8 September 1998, the twenty Ogoni leaders arrested with Ken Saro-Wiwa and the other eight martyrs were finally released from prison. The release of the prisoners is considered the first positive step in the Ogoni struggle since it began in 1990. The men had been held without trial, which has now been deemed unconstitutional, illegal, and unlawful. The men were suffering serious injuries and untreated illnesses, having been consistently denied medical care in prison. In January 1999, the acting president of MOSOP and many other nationalists were arrested in Bori to prevent them from celebrating Ogoni Day.

Shell employees, after years of conflict in the region, fear going into Ogoniland and often work through local chiefs, so development funds rarely reach grassroots level. Other projects use corrupt local contractors; millions of dollars have been wasted, while Shell turns a blind eye. Shell's official policy is to repair relationships and rebuild communities, but most believe that the company hopes eventually to restart oil pumping in the region.

In February 2000, the new democratic Nigerian government gave permission for the bodies of the nine executed Ogoni leaders to be returned to their families. The family of Ken Saro-Wiwa confronted MOSOP over plans to exhume his body and rebury him and the other eight executed Ogoni leaders in Ogoniland. MOSOP leaders wished to rebury the Ogoni martyrs and had the backing of some of the families of the executed men, but the Wiwa family objected, setting off a heated controversy. Ken Saro-Wiwa left a will with specific instructions about his funeral, and the family had its own plans to rebury him. Others criticize MOSOP for using the reburial of the martyred men for political ends.

The World Wildlife Fund (WWF) nominated Shell Oil to receive the British Columbia Minister's Environmental Award for 1997 following the company's agreement to give up exploration rights in the homeland of the Haidas* and Tlingits* in western Canada. At the same time, the repression in Ogoniland continued. The state-orchestrated violence in Ogoniland, by late 1999 had claimed more than 2,000 lives, and left over 30,000 Ogonis internally displaced within the region. Several thousand escaped to neighboring regions or have been forced into exile as refugees. Shell Oil is heavily implicated in the repression and violence in Ogoniland.

Royal Dutch Shell, in July 2001, announced that it wished peace with the Ogonis and suggested negotiations and reparations, but the negotiations never began. In September, following an attack on a Shell installation, Shell Oil sued the local Ogoni community for millions in damages.

Most Ogonis now agree that they would have been better had oil not been discovered in their homeland. They have not benefited economically, and their lands have been polluted. They have been repressed, killed, tortured, and driven from their homes. Anger continues to feed the development of the nationalist movement. Militants and pacifists, though they support opposing ideas of how to move ahead, agree that their nightmare will come to an end only when the Ogoni nation regains control of its destiny, its land, and its resources. Even politically moderate Ogonis declare that the minimum needed for the salvation of their nation is the unification of all Ogoniland in a single administrative region, cultural and political autonomy, and control of their own resources.

SELECTED BIBLIOGRAPHY:

Na'Allah, Abdul-Rasheed, ed. *Ogoni's Agonies: Ken Saro-Wiwa and the Crisis in Nigeria.* 1998.

Osaghae, E. *The Ogoni Uprising: Oil Politics, Minority Agitation and the Future of the Nigerian State.* 1995.

Saro-Wiwa, Ken. *Genocide in Nigeria: The Ogoni Tragedy.* 1992.

Wente-Lukas, Renate. *Handbook of Ethnic Units in Nigeria.* 1997.

Ojibwe

Anishinabe; Anishnabeg; Ojibway; Ojibwa; Chippewa; Chippeway; Otchipwa

POPULATION: Approximately (2002e) 225,000 Ojibwe in North America, 147,000 in the United States and 78,000 in Canada. The Ojibwe are concentrated around the Great Lakes, mostly in the states of Wisconsin, Minnesota, and Michigan in the United States and the Canadian province of Ontario. The closely related Ottawa or Odawa number about 17,000, and the Potawatomi about 28,000. In 2000, less than half lived on reservations, including those forcibly moved to Kansas and Oklahoma during the nineteenth century.

THE OJIBWE HOMELAND: The Ojibwe homeland, called Anishinaabenaang, lies in the region around Lake Superior and Lake Huron in the Great Lakes region of the United States and Canada. Although there remain many unresolved land claims, there are a number of small reservations, including 83 Ojibwe reservations, 3 Potawatomi reservations, and 1 Ottawa reservation. Ojibwe bands inhabit a large territory between the lower peninsula of Michigan and adjacent parts of Ontario to the east, through Minnesota and Wisconsin, to the plains of eastern Saskatchewan to the west. Their nothern extension runs north to Lake Winnipeg. The major Ojibwe cultural centers are Bemidji (Bemijigamaag), Minnepolis (Gakaabikaang), Duluth (Onigamiinsing), and St. Cloud (Ozaagiiziibiing) in Minnesota, Green Bay (Boojwiikwedong), Ashland (Gichi-wiikwedong), and Rhinelander (Zhede-zhiibiing) in Wisconsin, and Ironwood (Maananoonsing) in Michigan, and Owen Sound (Namewiikwedong), Fort Frances (Nicickousemenecaning), Stony Point (Aazhoodena), and Sault Ste. Marie in Ontario, and Gypsumville in Manitoba.

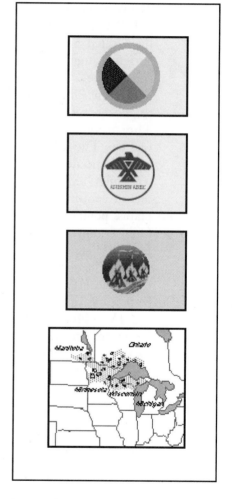

FLAG: The unofficial flag of the Ojibwe in the United States is the Four Winds flag, a white field bearing a central disk divided into four quarters of white, black, yellow, and red. The unofficial flag of the Canadian Ojibwe is the Thunderbird flag, a stylized black bird and the name of the nation, Anishinabek, within a black circle on a white field; the circle is often shown with four quarters of white, black, yellow, and red. The flag of the Council of Three Fires, also called the Three Fires Confederacy, is a tan field bearing a central disk bearing three fires. Each band or reservation has its own distinctive flag, but they generally recognize the two regional flags.

PEOPLE AND CULTURE: The Ojibwe, popularly called Chippewa in the United States, call themselves Anishinabe, meaning "true people" or "original men." The related Ottawa and Potawatomi also call themselves Anishinabe. At sometime in the past the three tribes were a single tribe. The name Ojibwe comes from the Algonquin word *otchipwa* which means to pucker, referring to the distinctive puckered seam of Ojibwe moccasins. The major cultural distinction is between the Woodlands and Plains Ojibwe. The Plains Ojibwe are distinct in language, social organization, art, ceremonies, and traditional dress. They are derived from small groups who migrated west into the plains, beginning near the end of the eighteenth century. There they adopted many of the traits of the northern plains peoples, including a bison-hunting economy. The Woodlands Ojibwe represent the classic Ojibwe culture, which was imortalized by Henry Wadsworth Longfellow in his 1855 epic poem, *The Song of Hiawatha*. The stories related in the poem are nearly all Ojibwe even though the name Hiawatha is drawn from the Iroquois.* Since the 1950s, urbanization has drawn many young Ojibwe to the nearby cities and towns.

LANGUAGE AND RELIGION: The Ojibwe speak a Central Algonkian language, Anishinaabemowin, that is also spoken by the Ottawa and Potawatomi. Due to their dispersal and their relatively large population, there are some regional dialectical differences. The major dialects are the Woodlands or Ojibwe proper, which includes Northern Ojibwe, also called Salteaux, and Southern Ojibwe or Chippewa. There are a number of regional dialects and subdialects. The major dialect spoken by the western bands is Plains Ojibwe or Bungi. The language is dying out in many areas, but is still spoken by many adults and some younger people. Concerted efforts to revive the language include teaching it in public schools and its use by tribal councils and governments. All are thought to be bilingual in English, the major language in the United States and Canada. Historically the Ojibwe had a unique form of picture writing that was intimately connected to the Midewiwin society. Many Ojibwe words have entered the English language, including Mississippi (Miziziibi), moccasin (makizin), moose (mooz), toboggan (zhooshkodaabaan), and Milwaukee (mino-aki).

The Ojibwe, while nominally Christian, often combine traditional beliefs and Christian traditions in a unique belief system. Many converted to Christianity during the nineteenth and twentieth centuries. Some never gave up their traditional beliefs, and still others are returning to those beliefs as they strive to reclaim their identity. Ojibwe mythology is elaborate; the chief religious and ceremonial rites centered around the Medewiwin, the Grand Medicine Society.

NATIONAL HISTORY: The Ojibwe were among numerous tribal groups that lived on the Atlantic coast of North America, called Great Turtle Island. Many ancient Ojibwe sites were continuiously inhabited since the Middle Woodland period, about 200 B.C. Oral traditions of the Ojibwe, Ottawa, and Potawatomi claim that at one time all three tribes were one people who lived in the region around the Straits of Mackinac. From there they split off into three different groups, although their cultures and languages are nearly identical. Each year they united in the annual celebration of the Grand Medicine Society, a secret organization open to both men and women.

At the end of the seventeenth century the Ojibwe had settled a small region adjacent to northern Lake Huron and eastern Lake Superior. Then, in a series of migrations and conquests, they expanded to the west and north, driving the Sioux* from present Wisconsin and Michigan. By the mid-1700s, the Ojibwe had settled in the region around Mille Lacs in what is today central Minnesota. They lived by hunting, fishing, and gathering, particularly the cereal later known as wild rice. Their population was estimated at 25,000 to 30,000 in the 1770s. The Ojibwe were not prominent in colonial history because of their remoteness from the frontier during the colonial wars.

The Ojibwe are believed to have made contact with Europeans in 1615 when the French explorer Samuel de Champlain arrived at Lake Huron, where some Ojibwe bands lived. In 1622, one of Champlains associates, Etienne Brule, explored the Lake Superior territory and made contact with Ojibwe groups farther to the west. The French called the Ojibwe by the name Saulteaux, referring to the rapids of the St. Mary's River where an important Ojibwe town was located. In 1667, the French established a Christian mission at the rapids, called Sault Ste. Marie in the French language

The Ojibwe were forced westward beginning in the 1640s when the Iroquois Confederation began to attack other tribes in the Great Lakes region in an effort to monopolize the fur trade with the Europeans. The Ojibwe resisted and by the 1690s had won some impressive victories against the Iroquois. The Iroquois sued for peace with the French and their Ojibwe allies in 1701.

Allied economically and militarily to the French, who dominated trade in the Great Lakes region, the Ojibwe expanded west to find richer fur-trapping regions in order to trade furs for European trade goods. Moving west they encountered the Santee Sioux. During the 1730s, the Ojibwe and Sioux went to war over the region around the western point of Lake Superior and the headwaters of the Mississippi River in Minnesota. The war lasted sporadically until the 1850s. The generally victorious Ojibwe pushed the Sioux farther west into Minnesota and present North and South Dakota.

In 1745, the Ojibwe of Lake Superior began to move inland into Wisconsin, with their first permanent settlement at the headwaters of the Chippewa River. Later they expanded into other parts of northern Wisconsin, particularly the lands around Lac du Flambeau.

The Ojibwe sided with the French during the colonial wars between the French and British in North America between 1689 and 1763. They were particularly active during the final conflict, the Seven Years' War, popularly called the French and Indian War in North America, from 1754 to 1763.

When the French lost Canada and the upper Midwest to the British in 1761–63, the Ojibwe did not trust the British colonial authorities. Unlike the French, the British generally treated the indigenous tribes with contempt and distain. Many Ojibwe joined the Ottawa chief called Pontiac in a widespread rebellion against British rule in 1763. They were defeated by British troops in 1765. Afterward, the British authorities took a more conciliatory approach to the Ojibwe bands and they became staunch British allies. The Ojibwe fur trade prospered under British rule.

The new United States gained control of all lands south of the Great Lakes after the American Revolution that ended in 1783 with the signing of the Treaty of Paris. British fur trading companies in Canada, particularly the extensive North West Company, continued to operate trading posts in the Ojibwe lands of northern Wisconsin and Minnesota until 1815. The United States government, concerned by British influence in the region, sent an expedition led by Lieutenant Zebulon Pike in 1805–6. Pike attempted to undermine British influence and to end the Ojibwe-Sioux wars, but with little success. Like many tribes, the Ojibwe generally favored the British as they feared that the United States government would take their lands. Many became adherents of Tecumseh and the Shawnee brothers in Ohio who preached a doctrine of resisting American expansion.

White settlers moving west in the early nineteenth century increasingly threatened Ojibwe lands and resources. The United States government, recognizing the Ojibwe tribal government, negotiated several treaties. The first was in 1837, when the Ojibwe sold most of their territory in north-central Wisconsin and eastern Minnesota. The next was signed in 1842 and ceded the remaining Ojibwe lands in Wisconsin and upper Michigan. Miners and lumbermen moved into the ceded lands, driving many Ojibwe from reserved lands.

In 1855, an Ojibwe chief named Shawbashkung signed what was called a "treaty of peace and friendship" on behalf of his people. In 1862, some Ojibwe joined the Sioux in fighting the encroaching Americans, but others, including those in the Mille Lacs region, remained neutral and often protected their white neighbors. For this they were classified as "non-removable" and when other bands were forced to leave their traditional lands, they remained. Ojibwe chiefs traveled to Washington in 1849 and again in 1852 to plead with the government officials, including the president, for the right to stay on their lands. A further treaty, signed in 1854, ceded the last important territories in Minnesota to the United States in return for reserved lands in their traditonal territories.

The Ojibwe, once the reservations were established, were unable to support themselves by hunting and gathering. Many worked as lumberjacks or miners for white-owned companies. While lumbering brought some economic benefits to the Wisconsin Ojibwe, it also brought continued land loss. In 1887, the Dawes Act was passed. Called the General Allotment it was designed to help the native peoples live more like whites by dividing up reservation lands so they could all own individual plots. All surplus reservation land was confiscated by the state authorities and sold off to lumber companies or white farmers. The land in northern Wisconsin and Minnesota was not good for farming, and many Ojibwe, unaware of the value of the land, sold theirs to lumber companies to supplement their wages. On some reservations, over 90% of the land passed into white hands. By 1930 over half the Ojibwe population lived off the reservations and many were forced into poverty. Alcohol abuse became a serious problem and did petty crime.

The Ojibwe, because of their relative isolation, escaped the great epidemics that decimated the tribes to the east, but they still lost population to diseases brought to the area by settlers. By 1910 their numbers had fallen to about 30,000 in the United States and about 20,000 in Canada. The 1930 census showed just 21,500 Ojibwe in the United States.

In the 1930s, during the administration of President Franklin D. Roosevelt, several Ojibwe communities in Wisconsin, which had not received reservations in the 1854 treaty, finally received reservation lands in 1937–38. The new reservation lands are compact as most other reservations lands were a patchwork of Ojibwe and white-owned parcels.

Well into the twentieth century the Ojibwe were not allowed to practice their religion, teach their language and culture to their children, or to govern themselves. Traditionally the Ojibwe were divided into numerous bands united in permanent clans. One of the clans claimed the hereditary chieftainship of the entire tribe while another claimed precedence in the councils of war.

When the Ojibwe signed the 1837 and 1842 treaties, they reserved the right to hunt and fish on lands ceded to the United States. For many years, the state authorities in Wisconsin and Minnesota arrested and convicted

Ojibwes who fished or hunted off their reservations without licenses. In January 1983, the federal district court in Chicago affirmed their rights under the terms of the treaties.

Many Ojibwe bands took their land claims to court in the 1980s and 1990s. But having exhausted all legal recourse, many gave up the fight. The implication was that they had no legal right to traditional lands stolen or given up to the United States and Canada. The only legal recourse in the United States is the Indian Claims Commission, which pays for land claims, but does not return land to tribal control.

The opening of casinos, in the 1990s, banned in the surrounding areas, but allowed on the territory of the sovereign reservations, have been an economic boon, creating jobs, opportunities, and hope. While some bands are engaged in the traditional occupations of hunting, fishing, and harvesting wild rice, others now run manufacturing and casino businesses.

In 2000, the Ojibwe constitute the third largest indigenous nation in the United States and one of the largest in Canada. They remain divided into numerous bands and reservations, but have begun to organize into larger units that allow them to use their numbers and votes to better the overall situation of tribal members. Some bands are still seeking redress for the loss of hunting and fishing rights stemming back to the treaties made in the 1840s and 1850s. The traditional Three Fire Confederacy of the Ojibwe, Ottawa, and Potawatomi has been renewed and revitalized as the Nation of the Three Fires.

SELECTED BIBLIOGRAPHY:

Benton-Banai, Eddy. *The Mishomis Book: The Voice of the Ojibway.* 1988.
Hickerson, Harold. *The Chippewa and their Neighbors: A Study in Ethnohistory.* 1970.
Jones, Dennis. *Ojibwe Culture and History.* 1998.
Legay, Gilbert. *Atlas of Indians of North America.* 1995.

Okinawans

Ryukyuans; Riukiuans; Nansei; Riukiu Islanders; Ryuku Islanders; Luchu

POPULATION: Approximately (2002e) 1,420,000 Okinawans in Japan, concentrated in the Ryuku Islands, which stretch from the major southern Japanese island of Kyushu to Taiwan. Other large Okinawan communities live in central Japanese islands and in the western part of the United States.

THE OKINAWAN HOMELAND: The Okinawan homeland lies in the East China Sea; it is a string of 143 subtropical islands strategically located between the Japanese archipelago and Taiwan. The islands, known as the Ryukus, include three major groups—the Sakishima Islands in the south near Taiwan, the Okinawa Islands in the center (both groups returned to Japanese sovereignty in 1972); and the Amami Islands, which returned to Japan in 1953 and now form part of Kagoshima Prefecture of Kyushu, the most southerly of the major Japanese islands. The Okinawa and Sakishima Islands form a separate prefecture. *Prefecture of Ryuku Islands (Okinawa)*: 848 sq. mi.—2,196 sq. km, (2002e) 1,354,000—Okinawans 96%, other Japanese 4%. The Okinawan capital and major cultural center is Naha, (2002e) 319,000, metropolitan area 524,000. The center of the Anami Okinawans is Nishinoomote, (2002e) 19,000.

FLAG: The Okinawan national flag, the flag of the national movement, is a white field with a centered disc made up of the traditional symbols of Okinawa's Sho kings, three tear-shaped devices of red, yellow, and blue. The flag of the largest national organization, the Okinawa Independence Party (OIP), is a diagonal bicolor of green over blue, upper hoist to lower fly, separated by a narrow white stripe, and bearing in a centered white disc the three devices

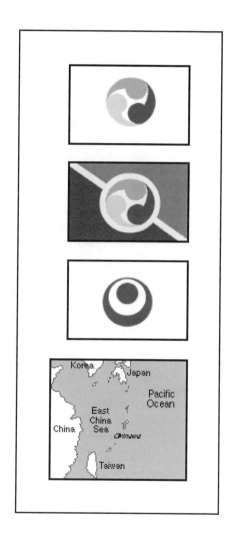

of the Sho kings. The official flag of the Prefecture of Okinawa is a white field bearing a red sun within a red ring.

PEOPLE AND CULTURE: The Okinawans, though an Oriental people, are thought to include in their ancestry the original Caucasian inhabitants of the islands. They are related to the Ainu* of northern Japan, with later admixtures of Chinese and Japanese. Generally taller and darker than the Japanese, the Okinawans are geographically divided into seven major groups. Through centuries of close relations with China, the Philippines, and Southeast Asia, the Okinawans developed a unique culture with a distinct language, traditions, and social customs. The Okinawan culture has revived since World War II. The Okinawans, unlike the reserved Japanese, are known for courtesy, warmth, generosity, and directness. The family remains the center of Okinawan life; extended families often live together.

LANGUAGE AND RELIGION: The Okinawan language, called Nantö, is divided into six major dialects—Northern Amami, Southern Amami, Toku, Oki, Ryukyan, and Yayeyama. The language is related to Ainu, the language of the Japan's ancient Caucasian inhabitants. There are numerous subdialects, which each island representing a dialectical region, and subdialects often vary from village to village. Assimilation has decreased the use of the Okinawan dialects; Japanese has been the medium of administration and education.

The majority religions are Buddhism and Shintoism, with an important Christian minority, about 3%, the result of American missionary activity after World War II. Traditional shamanistic practices are still prevalent, with belief in unseen gods, demons, and ancestral spirits. The spirits of ancestors are believed to live in the tombs where they were buried and must be invited back into the lives of their descendents so that they may continue to exist. They also believe that unseen powers known as *kami* control the ancestral spirits and other parts of nature, including the sea and land.

NATIONAL HISTORY: Inhabited in ancient times by a Caucasian people, over thousands of years the islanders absorbed immigrants from neighboring areas while retaining their original language and much of their ancient culture. The islands were early divided into three kingdoms corresponding to the three island groups, but they were later unified under the Sho kings of the central island of Okinawa. Following the unification, weapons were banned, and the unified kingdom, called Liuchiu or Luchu, was pursued a policy of peace and trade with neighboring nations.

From the seventh century A.D., when the Okinawans repelled an invasion from the mainland, the Chinese constantly threatened the island kingdom. In the fourteenth century the Chinese forced the Sho kings to swear allegiance to the Chinese emperor and to pay annual tribute as a vassal. Influenced by Chinese culture, the kingdom entered a golden age, a great flowering of Okinawan culture, literature, and eventually political power.

Throwing off Chinese hegemony, the kingdom expanded to control the large island of Taiwan just off the coast of the Chinese mainland.

In 1609, the Tokugawa military government of Japan gave the Satsuma Samuri clan permission to invade the Ryuku Islands. Forced to pay tribute to both China and Japan, the kingdom declined, losing Taiwan to Chinese colonization. For the next two centuries the kingdom maintained a precarious independence amid increasing poverty as the Japanese and Chinese fought for control.

Commodore Matthew Perry of the U.S. Navy landed at Naha in 1853. The Americans established friendly relations with the Okinawans and used the kingdom as a base for the eventual penetration of the "hermit kingdom," Japan. During one of his visits to the islands Commodore Perry acquired an ancient Okinawan temple bell, the Gokokuji Bell, which was used to ring out the score at Army-Navy football games until its return to Okinawa in 1988.

Increased rivalry with nearby China prompted the Japanese government to send troops to occupy Okinawa in 1872. Two years later Japan annexed the kingdom, over dogged Okinawan resistance. The occupation authorities deposed the last Sho king in 1879 and instituted a policy of assimilation into Japanese culture. The Okinawan language and culture were banned. China, defeated by the Japanese in a brief 1895 war, finally recognized Japan's claim to the Ryuku Islands.

Prior to World War I, the Japanese were taught that the Japanese empire included many *gaichijin*, nationals of colonial origin, such as Taiwanese and Koreans, and *naichijin*, non-Japanese nationals of the home islands, the Okinawans. It was accepted that Japan was a multi-ethnic country. Assimilating and incorporating the minorities into the Japanese people was considered an important national task.

Resistance to assimilation pressure stimulated Okinawan nationalism after World War I. The national movement, in demanding autonomy and linguistic rights, was modeled on those of the ethnic minorities in Europe. Discrimination against and intolerance of the Okinawan nation, however, increased as the military hierarchy gradually took control of Japan in the 1920s and 1930s. Nationalists in the islands formed the Okinawa Independence Party in the 1930s and openly advocated secession and independence until its suppression in the late 1930s. By 1938, with Japan under a military dictatorship, most of the Okinawan nationalist leaders were dead or in prison.

Japan's military government, preparing for war, suspected the loyalty of the Okinawan population. The islands, particularly the largest, Okinawa, were heavily fortified as the tide of war turned against Japan. The Okinawans, never enthusiastic about the war, came under increasing pressure as the Americans neared the home islands.

In early 1945 American troops invaded the islands, beginning a three-month battle to oust the Japanese. The Okinawans, forced to continue to resist the Americans long after the outcome was decided, lost over a third of their population. Fierce fighting devastated the islands, including many cultural treasures. The Battle of Okinawa is still commonly referred to as the "Typhoon of Steel." Over 75,000 Okinawan civilians were killed, and in the capital, Naha, 94% of all buildings were destroyed. The scale of the slaughter was one of the main factors in the U.S. decision to drop atomic bombs on Nagasaki and Hiroshima rather than risk an invasion of the Japanese home islands.

Placed under American military occupation in August 1945, the islands rapidly recovered with the aid of the U.S. forces. Huge American military bases became major sources of income. The governor of the islands, Oshiro Shikiya, presented a plan for an independent Okinawa in January 1950. Initially the Americans supported the proposal, but continuing Japanese opposition led to a change of policy, and the independence proposal was rejected in March 1950. In 1953, despite Okinawan protests at the division of the islands, the Americans returned the northern Amami Islands to Japan. The disposition of the other islands became a major source of friction between the United States and Japan.

In postwar Japan, the Japanese ideology of racial superiority was transformed to stress simply the uniqueness of the Japanese people. Part of this ideology was the now-unquestioned description of Japan as a mono-ethnic state. Scholars, intellectuals, and political leaders commonly based their discussions of Japanese culture, society, and national character on the assumption of social homogeneity. The Okinawans, not fitting the national stereotype, were considered foreign and were expected to assimilate. The fact that minorities have existed and have been subjected to discrimination has been conveniently denied at all levels of Japanese society.

Okinawan nationalism reemerged under the American administration. The nationalists sought American support for independence and vehemently opposed Japanese demands for sovereignty over the islands. In 1968 the islands elected their first chief executive, and their government was granted considerable autonomy. Because of the near-total destruction of the material culture on the main island during the war, a growing nationalist sentiment and cultural revival of the 1960s drew on the undamaged, traditionally Okinawan, smaller islands. In the early 1970s, the restoration and recuperation of Okinawan historical treasures became a national obsession.

The United States and Japan, over strong nationalist opposition but with much popular support in the islands, reached an agreement on the islands' return to Japan in 1971. On 15 May 1972 the United States formally ceded the islands to Japan. Nationalists drew up a proposal for an independent Republic of the Ryukus, to include all the Ryuku Islands, including the northern group returned to Japan in 1953, but they were ignored by both governments.

The Okinawans, whose incomes had been higher than the Japanese average until 1972, now began to lose their economic base. Japanese businessmen descended on the islands to open polluting factories away from the environmental restrictions of the main Japanese islands. Although industrial output expanded, the Okinawans were mostly left out of the Japanese economic miracle. In the 1990s the Okinawan living standards were only 70% of those of the Japanese home islands, adding economic grievances to the growing list of nationalist issues. The Okinawans suffered unemployment rates twice the national average, and their economic and industrial structures were weakened by dependence on the central government.

The twentieth anniversary of the reversion of Okinawa to Japan in 1992 increased interest, particularly among young Okinawans, in their unique culture. Okinawan music, crafts, and traditions were revived, and the use of the language increased. Many Okinawans used the anniversary to expose the Japanese nation to their cultural heritage, although having been under pressure to assimilate for over a century, it is questionable how much distinctive Okinawan culture remains. Perhaps in its present diluted form it is less threatening: it has become an object of interest to the wider Japanese population.

Many Okinawans would like to be seen as fellow Japanese by their compatriots on the islands to the north, but because of continuing discrimination there is a growing movement to reverse the process of assimilation and revive the Okinawan culture and language. The nationalists believe that the Okinawan culture has deep roots and has not died, that in fact it can be fully revived. But reviving the culture means confronting the powerful mono-ethnic Japanese myth.

Tension between the Okinawans and the American military bases, growing since the 1970s, erupted into angry protests in 1995, when three U.S. marines were convicted of raping a twelve-year-old schoolgirl. The American ambassador to Japan was forced to apologize formally, but that did little to assuage Okinawan sensibilities. Okinawa remains the home of 50,000 U.S. service personnel living on bases that cover some 20% of the land of Ryuku Islands prefecture.

Mass demonstrations against the military bases swept the island in 1996–97, partly in response to the refusal of the prefecture's governor, Masahide Ota, to sign renewed leases for the bases. The Japanese prime minister, Ryutaro Hashimoto, signed the leases himself in order to meet the deadline, creating a serious rift between the Okinawan and central governments. Although an estimated 35,000 Okinawans are economically dependent on the bases, the ordinary Okinawans want a greater part of the subsidies paid the prefectural government by both the American and Japanese governments to maintain the military forces in the islands.

Many Okinawans see their islands as a center of regional peace, coexistence, and self-reliance in an increasingly unstable region. But to establish themselves as a bridge between the regional powers, they want to pursue an independent and internally driven development program, through political and cultural autonomy. The first step, the creation of a regional assembly, was proposed as part of an autonomy plan for the islands but was rejected by the Japanese government.

Since 1995 many Okinawans have concluded that closing the military bases would clearly threaten the regional economy. Local polls in 1997 found that only between 14 and 23% of the Okinawans want the bases closed. The American military, however, contributes only about 7% of the Okinawan economy, down from 41% in 1972, when most of the islands returned to Japanese sovereignty. Okinawan unemployment is nearly twice the Japanese average. Were the bases to go, the Japanese government would end many of the subsidies to the islands, which would leave Okinawa a backward farming sector, mostly dependent on sugarcane, with little local manufacturing, and its tourism shackled by very high air fares from the main Japanese islands and Japanese government restrictions on direct international flights to Okinawa.

A plan put forward in 1997 would turn Okinawa into a free trade zone under a "one country, two systems" formula. The plan would offer the islands a more flexible tax and regulatory regime than mainland Japan. Prime Minister Hashimoto made several trips to Naha in a bid to mend relations with the restive islands, officially apologizing for past neglect and renewing the government's pledge to bring the Okinawans' standard of living up to the Japanese average.

Okinawan nationalism and national sentiment remain a potent force in the islands, continually stimulated by the dismal Japanese attitude to minorities. The Japanese approach, called by Okinawan nationalists a form of quiet apartheid, is summed up by the often-repeated Japanese assertion that there are no ethnic or linguistic minorities in Japan.

SELECTED BIBLIOGRAPHY:

Boan, Jim. *Rising Sun Sinking: Okinawa*. 2000.
Johnson, Chalmers. *Okinawa: Cold War Island*. 1999.
Kerr, George H. *Okinawa: The History of an Island People*. 2000.
Sakihara, Mitsugu. *A Brief History of Okinawa*. 1987.

Orcadians

Orkney Islanders

POPULATION: Approximately (2002e) 40,000 Orcadians in the United Kingdom, concentrated in the Orkney Islands of northern Scotland. Outside Scotland there are Orcadian communities in other parts of Britain, and in the United States, Canada, Australia, and New Zealand.

THE ORCADIAN HOMELAND: The Orcadian homeland forms a group of about 70 islands in the Atlantic Ocean and the North Sea, north of the Scottish mainland. The islands, generally low-lying and treeless, have a mild, wet climate and comprise one of Scotland's richest farming counties. The largest of the islands are Mainland, the central island, Hoy, South Ronaldsay, Stronsay, Sanday, Westray, and Rousay. The closest of the islands is only ten miles north of the Scottish mainland,

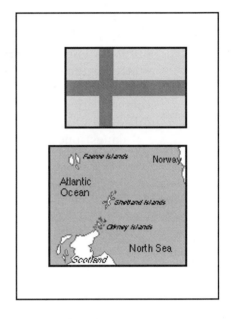

from which they are separated by Pentland Firth. County of Orkney: 376 sq. mi.—974 sq. km, (2002e) 20,500—Orcadians 94%, other British 6%. The Orcadian capital and major cultural center is Kirkwall, (2002e) 8,000.

FLAG: The Orcadian national flag, the flag of the autonomy movement, is a yellow field bearing a red Scandinavian cross called the St. Magnus cross.

PEOPLE AND CULTURE: The Orcadians are of mixed background, being the descendants of early Scandinavian settlers and later Scottish colonists. Ethnically and historically the islanders are more closely related to the peoples of Iceland and the Faeroe Islands than to the other national groups of the British Isles. Orcadian culture, long isolated from the majority Scottish culture of the northern part of Britain, retains many customs and traditions brought to the islands by the early Vikings.

LANGUAGE AND RELIGION: The Orcadians speak standard English, but have retained their own distinct dialect that is virtually unintelligible to mainlanders. The Orcadian dialect combines Old Norse, Celtic, and English influences. Radio transmissions, since the 1970s, have used the local dialect for island programming. Island children, until the 1970s, were rebuked for speaking the dialect in school, but it has now taken on a new authenticity and interest in reviving and protecting the unique dialect is growing.

The majority of the Orcadians are devout Christians, mostly Roman Catholic, but with an influential Protestant minority. Many of the pre-Christian traditions and holidays are still observed as they form an integral part of the Orcadian culture.

NATIONAL HISTORY: The original inhabitants, Bronze Age Picts, settled the islands between 3,800 and 3,200 B.C. The Standing Stones of Stenness and the Ring of Brodgar were constructed for religious and political purposes. The islanders lived in small farming villages, with an elaborate religious and social culture when the Romans conquered most of Britain. In A.D. 78, the Roman general Agricola visited Orkney while circumnavigating the island of Britain. In classical literature the islands were called the Orcades.

Vikings appeared off the islands in 787, their first attacks on the British Isles. By the early ninth century Scandinavian colonists had settled many of the islands, the earlier inhabitants absorbed into Viking culture. Annexed by Harold Fairhair, the first king of Norway, the Orkney and Shetland islands were organized as a separate earldom in 875. Details of the Norse conquest and settlement are recounted by the Orkneyinga Saga, a Norse epic.

Earl Sigurd was forced to convert to Christianity in 995 by the Norwegian king Olaf Tryggvason. He soon extended the new religion across the islands, supporting the founding of churches and monasteries. Magnus, the earl of Orkney from about 1080 until 1115, when he was murdered by his co-ruler Hakon Palsson, was declared a saint in 1135, and was adopted as the patron saint of the Orcadians. In 1180, St. Magnus Cathedral was founded in Kirkwall to honor their national hero.

In 1196, Shetland was separated from the Orkney earldom. The Norse line of rulers died out in 1231, and their successors, the Scottish Angus line, ended in 1325. Shetland was reunited with Orkney in 1379, the same year that Norway, Sweden, and Denmark were joined in the Union of Calmar.

The island remained a Norwegian dependency until the Norwegian kingdom, along with its possessions and dependencies, passed to Denmark in 1397. The Danish king, Christian I, in 1468, pledged the islands to James III of Scotland as security for the dowry of Margaret of Norway on her marriage to the Scottish king. King James, not in receipt of the dowry, annexed the islands to his kingdom in 1472. Scottish King James V visited Orkney in 1540 and granted the islands separate status as a county.

Scotland's union with England in 1707 began a long campaign in Orkney for separation from Scotland and for a distinct legal status within the

United Kingdom. The Orcadians demanded the political and economic autonomy that would recognize their distinct culture and history, a status similar to that granted the Manx,* the Guernseians,* and the Jerseians* of the United Kingdom. Relative isolation and a small population facilitated the efforts to preserve the unique island culture and dialect, even though the English language spread to the isolated islands in the eighteenth and nineteenth centuries. A lack of industry and high unemployment caused the islands' population to decline from about 1871.

The sea north of Scotland developed as the United Kingdom's major fishing region while excess population left the islands for the mainland, keeping the population nearly constant during the early decades of the twentieth century. The relative prosperity of the region gave the Orcadians a new confidence and renewed the campaign to win separate legal status within the United Kingdom.

Orkney, particularly the important anchorage at Scapa Flow in the Orkneys, became important to the British fleet during both world wars. In November 1939 the islands were the target of the first German air raids on the United Kingdom following the outbreak of war in Europe. Many of the island children were evacuated to safer areas, but the majority of the Orcadians refused to leave their islands in spite of the danger.

The population of the islands began to drop after World War II and the post-war decline of the fishing industry. The Orcadians, forced to leave in search of work, denounced the lack of opportunities as the result of their colonial political status. The discovery of oil in the North Sea off the islands in 1970 stabilized the population and reversed the long decline. The islands became a center of the North Sea oil industry with oil workers from many parts of the world brought in by the British and international oil companies. Exploitation of North Sea oil resulted in the construction and operation of a major oil terminal in Scapa Flow. The oil industry offers employment, where previously emigration was the only choice.

The idea of home rule for the islands north of the Scottish mainland emerged in 1962 after a local delegation visited the Faeroese* homeland. The vigor of the autonomous government of the Faeroe Islands stimulated the growth of local nationalism in Shetland. Their culture and way of life threatened by the massive influx of oil workers and companies, the islanders began to mobilize during the 1970s. Nationalist organizations demanded autonomy and separate legal status to protect their unique culture and to give them local control over the ecological damage done by the oil companies. In 1979, the islanders threatened secession as their pristine islands were practically overrun by the oil companies going after the rich oil deposits in the North Sea. Local groups, the Shetland Movement and the Orkney Movement, led the campaign for greater autonomy.

The region's oil wealth, which stimulated Scottish nationalists to demand that the British government leave the control of the booming industry to the Scots, also roused island demands that the Scots keep their hands off the islands' North Sea oil. The nationalist upsurge, with growing support for island control of development and the offshore oil fields, and demands for a fairer share of the oil revenue, added another element to the dispute between Scotland and the government of the United Kingdom over control of natural resources.

Scottish nationalism, advocating independence within a united Europe, stimulated Orcadian sentiment for separation from Scotland in the 1980s and 1990s. The Orcadians, culturally and historically distinct, in numerous polls expressed their preference for separate legal status within the United Kingdom rather than remain part of an autonomous Scottish state. In the 1990s, pro-European sentiment gained support with the realization that future European regulations and funding will be more important to the islands than decisions made in either Edinburgh or London.

The Orcadians, part of Scotland through a quirk of history, mostly oppose Scottish nationalism and prefer loose ties to the London government rather than rule from Edinburgh. On 21 February 1994, along with the Shetlanders,* the Orcadians called for a referendum on independence from the rest of Scotland and the establishment of sovereignty and ties directly to the central government in London. Many Orcadians advocate a status similar to that of the Manx or the Channel Islands.

The Orcadians voted overwhelmingly against the proposal for a Scottish parliament in the 1979 referendum. In the 1997 referendum, the Orcadians emerged as the most reluctant of Scotland's voters to support Scottish tax-paying powers. The suspicion of urban domination continues to fuel the national movement and led to a successful demand for an Orcadian member of the Scottish parliament rather than to share the member with the Shetlanders as it does in the British government.

In 1999, the establishment of a separate Scottish parliament raised new fears in Orkney that politics and their destiny will be dominated by "central belt" politics. The islanders fear that they will be at the mercy of a parliament run by an urban elite from Glasgow and Edinburgh and the rest of the urbanized central belt, where the bulk of the Scottish population lives.

The Orkney Movement, which wants more autonomy for the islands, has become an umbrella group for nationalists, ecologists, and pro-British–anti-Scottish separatists. The nationalists use the Scottish slogan "small is beautiful," but claim that smaller is still more beautiful. The movement works to ensure that devolution does not stop with Edinburgh. Once devolution is well established in Scotland, the Orcadians feel that the Scots would be hypocritical if they opposed demands for autonomy for the Orkney Islands. Many Orcadians seek the same political status that the Channel Islands, the Isle of Man, and the Faroese Islands enjoy. In 1999, proposals were published for the inclusion of Orkney and Shetland in the Scandinavian cultural and political group, the Nordic Council.

In 2000–2001, a revitalized oil industry built on the Flotta oil terminal reactivated the national movement as competition between the Orcadians and Shetlanders. Demands for greater local control of the vital oil industry is the main focus of the nationalists, but questions of language, culture, and education are also being raised

SELECTED BIBLIOGRAPHY:

Barry, George. *The History of the Orkney Islands.* 1988.
Buxton, Anne. *The Orkney Chronicles, 1900 & 1989.* 1990.
Ritchie, Anna, ed. *Orkney.* 1997.
Thomas, William P. L. *History of Orkney.* 1991.

Oromos

Oromoos; Gallas

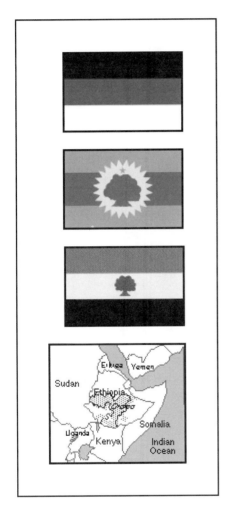

POPULATION: Approximately (2002e) 23,500,000 Oromos in Ethiopia, concentrated in Oromo state in the central and southern parts of the country. Outside the region there are Oromo communities in neighboring Somalia and Kenya. Oromo nationalists claim an Oromo national population of up to 30 million in Ethiopia.

THE OROMO HOMELAND: The Oromo homeland, called Oromia or Oromiyaa, sprawls across central and southern Ethiopia. Oromia is a region of great physiographic diversity, lying partly in the Great Rift Valley, including high, rugged mountains, high plateaus, deep river valleys, and rolling plains. The region is characterized by different climate types, ways of living, and resources. The traditional Oromo territory was never delimited; the present states of Oromo, Dire Dawa, and Harar, with Oromo majorities, are claimed by Oromo nationalists. *Oromo Regional State (Oromia/Oromiyaa)*: 136,560 sq. mi.—353,690 sq. km, (2002e) 23,644,000—Oromos 85%, Amhara* 10%, Gurage 2%, other Ethiopians 3%. *Dire Dawa State*: 497 sq. mi.—1,288 sq. km, (2002e) 318,000—Oromos 49%, Amhara 27%, Western Somalis* 4%, Gurage 3%, other Ethiopians 17%. *Harer State*: 117 sq. mi.—304 sq. km, (2002e) 165,000—Oromos 53%, Amhara 32%, Harari 7%, Gurage 3%, other Ethiopians 5%. The Oromo capital and major cultural center is Addis Ababa, called Finfinnee by the Oromos, (2002e) 2,630,000. Other important cultural centers are Nazret, (2002e) 162,000, and Debre Zeyit, (2002e) 93,000. Dire Dawa is the capital of Dire Dawa state, (2002e) 208,000. Harer, capital of Harar state is also an Oromo cultural center, (2002e) 95,000.

FLAG: The Oromo national flag, the flag of the proposed independent state of Oromia, is a horizontal tricolor of black, red, and white. The flag of the largest national organization, the Oromo Liberation Front, has green, red, and green horizontal stripes with a centered yellow star of 26 points charged with a centered green tree surmounted by a small, five-pointed red star. The official flag of Oromo state in Ethiopia is a horizontal tricolor of red, white, and black bearing a centered green tree.

PEOPLE AND CULTURE: The Oromos, formerly called Gallas, are a tall, Hamitic, pastoral people related to the neighboring Somalis, but without the Arabic admixture that characterizes the Somali. They are the largest single national group in Ethiopia, constituting about a third of the total population. Oromo activists claim they are the single largest national group in Africa. The peoples collectively known as Oromo comprise 16 major tribes and numerous subtribes and clans representing diverse cultural, linguistic, and political backgrounds. The Oromos are an ancient people, often considered the indigenous people of the Horn of Africa. They are broadly divided into four main groups—the Western Oromos, the source of the early nationalist leaders; the Northern Oromos, including the urban population around Addis Ababa, the most assimilated into Amhara culture; the Arsi and Borana of the south, still living a seminomadic lifestyle; the Eastern Oromos, including the urban populations of Harar and Dire Dawa and large rural populations farther west. The Eastern Oromos show the most Arabic influence on their culture and language. About 85% of the Oromo population live in rural areas.

LANGUAGE AND RELIGION: The majority of the Oromos speak an East Cushitic language of the Afro-Asiatic language group. The Oromo language, called Afaan Oromo, is spoken in numerous dialects reflecting the wide geographical dispersal of the Oromos. Some Oromo subgroups have adopted Amhariya or other regional languages. Until the 1970s, the language remained essentially a well-developed oral tradition. When the Oromo National Liberation Front began to use the language as the official language of the liberated area under its control, its use became widespread. The Latin alphabet was adopted, which had been banned until the revolution of 1974.

The primary Oromo religion is Sunni Islam, mostly in the south and east, with large animist and Christian populations in the southwest and the central highlands. The Western Oromos are largely Christian, belonging to the Protestant Mekane Yesus Church. Many of the Northern Oromos belong to the Ethiopian Orthodox Church. The southern Arsi and Borana, with a Muslim minority, mostly remain animist, believing in a sky god. In some areas Protestant missionaries have had a degree of success.

NATIONAL HISTORY: The Hamitic Oromos are thought to have displaced the original black tribes of the region in the early Middle Ages.

The Oromo nation earlier developed its own social, political, and legal system, called *gadaa*. This system, still present among the southern Arsi and Borana groups, guided the religious, social, political, and economic systems. The system grouped society according to their age and responsibilities. The Oromo religion, based on worship of Waaqa, the supreme god, played both a religious and political role; ceremonies were organized by the priesthood.

The Oromos are thought to have migrated from present Somalia and southeastern Ethiopia to the region around Lake Rudolph in the late fifteenth and early sixteenth centuries, in search of grazing lands, with no political or warlike intent. The Oromo migrants traveled in individual clans, united only by culture and religion, not by a central authority. Further migrations between 1550 and 1670 brought the Oromos into the Ethiopian highlands and into conflict with the Christian Amhara kingdom. They occupied all of southern Ethiopia, some settling along the Tana River in present Kenya.

Oromo legends tell of five "fathers" who established the five historical divisions of the Oromo nation. Wherever the Oromos settled in their widely dispersed areas, they assimilated local customs and intermarried to such an extent that their original cultural cohesiveness and racial homogeneity were largely lost. In the east the Wallo Oromo adopted Islam. The Mecha and Tulema moved into the highlands, adopted Christianity, and mixed with the Semitic Amhara. In the south the Borana and Bartumma settled less populated lands and retained their traditional Oromo culture. A number of small Oromo states grew up south of the highlands in the seventeenth century, their expansion checked by the powerful Christian Amhara states.

The political divisions of the scattered Oromo groups facilitated their eventual subjugation by the Amharas, the major national group in Ethiopia. The Amhara-dominated, Christian Ethiopian empire conquered most of the Oromo clans in the seventeenth and eighteenth centuries. Many Oromo groups accepted the authority of the emperor and often provided mercenary troops to the imperial army. Several Oromos held high positions in the imperial government in the eighteenth and nineteenth centuries.

A series of weak rulers effectively decentralized the Ethiopian state between 1769 and 1855, with many Oromo regions becoming autonomous. In 1855, Emperor Theodoros II consolidated his authority and reunified the empire. The imperial capital, Addis Ababa, was founded in traditional Oromo territory in 1883, partly to ensure Oromo loyalty to the Ethiopian emperor.

Garrison towns, called *ketemas*, were established throughout the Oromo lands as military centers and to disseminate the Christian Amhara culture to the Oromo regions. Thousands of Oromo tribesmen were recruited from the poor rural populations. Oromo soldiers served in the armies that fought invading Egyptians in the 1870s and Italians attempting to extend their empire in the 1890s.

The Amhara-dominated Ethiopian empire, in the late nineteenth and early twentieth centuries, conquered Jimma, Kaffa, and the other remaining Oromo states. Oromo resistance to Christian Ethiopian rule provoked frequent uprisings. A number of clans united, for the first time, in a widespread revolt in 1928–30, a forerunner of the later Oromo national movement. In 1930, Haile Selassie I became emperor. Because the state's financial well-being was heavily dependent on coffee produced in peripheral Oromo areas, Haile Selassie tried to win Oromo loyalty through alliances with key Oromo leaders. Relations between the Amhara and Tigrean landlords and their Oromo tenants were often tense, but they became set in a feudal manner, with many Oromos tied to the land by law.

In 1936 Oromo nationalists led a revolt in the southwestern provinces. The Oromo rebels attempted to lead several provinces into secession before their defeat by imperial troops, who included a large number of ethnic Oromo soldiers. Italian troops from Eritrea conquered Ethiopia later in 1936. The invasion by the Italians ended the Oromo revolt. Many Oromo leaders viewed the Italians as liberators from Amhara rule; the clans that collaborated with the invaders faced punishment and reprisals following the Allied liberation of Ethiopia in 1941. After the end of World War II the Ethiopian government cracked down on growing ethnic unrest, particularly in the Oromo provinces, where an active national movement had widespread support.

In the 1960s the Ethiopian administration outlawed all languages other than the official language, Amhariya. The language issue fueled an Oromo cultural and linguistic revival, and resistance to the government edicts spread. In 1963–64 a rebellion erupted among the Borana Oromos in the south. By 1965 the rebels controlled much of Bale Province and had been joined by insurgent Somali groups in the region. The Mecha-Tulema Movement, formed among the Arsi Oromos, was involved in the first terrorist act by Oromo nationalists, the bombing of a cinema in Addis Ababa in 1966. The rebellion was not fully suppressed until 1970, when the rebels lost the support of the neighboring government of Somalia.

The relative success of the rebel southern clans inspired nationalist sentiment in other Oromo regions. In 1973 several clan organizations united to form the Oromo Liberation Front (OLF), which supported the popular revolution that finally overthrew Ethiopia's feudal monarchy in 1974. The Marxist leadership of Ethiopia, called the Derg (meaning "the committee" in the Amhara language), under Haile Mariam Mengistu, nationalized all land, industry, banking, insurance, large-scale trade, and many private properties, virtually wiping out the economic base of the former ruling classes. Rejecting wholesale this land confiscation and refused autonomy, the OLF led a separatist campaign to establish an independent Democratic Republic of Oromia and to integrate various Oromo regional and religious groups into one state. Forced collectivization and strict Marxist control alienated the majority of the Oromo clans. The Oromo nationalist revolt spread even to the clans that had been assimilating into the dominant culture of the Amharas for decades.

The Marxist Derg moved against the Oromo rebels in 1980–81. There were mass arrests of suspected supporters and closures of churches and mosques, which the government claimed served as centers of sedition. Universal conscription, often at gunpoint, forced thousands of young Oromos into the huge army fighting the ethnic insurrections in Tigre and Eritrea, in northern Ethiopia.

The OLF joined a coalition of insurgent groups in 1990. Allied to the northern rebel groups, the Oromo guerrillas moved on Addis Ababa from the south. Attacked on all sides, the beleaguered Derg began to collapse in early 1991, and in late May the Ethiopian capital fell to the rebel alliance. The allied insurgent organizations formed a coalition government and began to devolve power to ethnically based regional states.

Relations between the insurgent Oromos and the leading rebel group, the Tigreans,* began to deteriorate because of Oromo fears of Tigrean domination. Oromo national leaders demanded a referendum on autonomy within two years; the demands split the national movement between supporters of independence and those favoring autonomy within a loose federal system. Territorial claims sparked violence between Oromo nationalists and rival peoples in several areas. The growing rift between the Oromos and their former allies worsened, and in June 1992 the OLF withdrew from Ethiopia's coalition government, and the Oromo insurgency resumed, amid demands for secession and independence. Thousands fled the fighting, many taking refuge in Somalia or Kenya.

In mid-1993 the government moved against the OLF and other Oromo groups suspected of harboring separatist rebels. The growing chaos in Ethiopia greatly increased the chances that the multi-ethnic state could splinter along ethnic lines. The Ethiopian government in 1994 attempted to establish autonomous ethnic states and confirmed the right to secession by the state's various national groups. For Oromo nationalists this meant that for the first time in their modern history an independent Oromo state was a real possibility, but in fact the government actively opposed secession and pressed Ethiopia's many ethnic groups to remain within the increasingly Tigrean-dominated Ethiopian federation. The aspirations of the Oromos for self-determination were thus not met, and fighting resumed in 1993.

In 1995 the government arrested 280 members of the OLF in the town of Zeway, 120 miles south of Addis Ababa. They were accused of waging war against the interim Ethiopian government, but in 2002 most continue to be held without trial. Hundreds more were arrested in 1996 on suspicion of supporting Oromo opposition groups. In 1997, after a number of government troops of Oromo origin defected to an Islamic group, the government accused the Oromo nationalists of planning to establish an Islamic state. Actually, the Oromos include large numbers of Christians and animists who would oppose an Islamic government.

The migration of ethnic Amhara farmers toward the Wollega region of Oromia sparked renewed tension in July 1997. The migration was provoked by land shortages and legislation introduced in Amhara State that dispossessed farmers suspected of supporting opposition groups. The land issue became particularly acute when famine spread across central Ethiopia in the summer of 1997. The drought, which drove many farmers from northern Ethiopia into the Oromo areas in the south and west, was seen as a Tigrean plot to dilute the Oromo population centers.

Fighting between Oromo nationalists and government troops intensified in early 1999. In August, a battle close to Addis Ababa left over 140 dead. A number of Oromo leaders were arrested. The government has lost the support of the majority of the Oromos. Only one government-supported Oromo political party still participates in the federal government in 2002.

SELECTED BIBLIOGRAPHY:

Aguilar, Mario I. *Being Oromo in Kenya*. 1998.
Jalata, Asafa, ed. *Oromo Nationalism and the Ethiopian Discourse: The Search for Freedom and Democracy*. 1998.
Legesse, Asmarom. *Oromo Democracy: An Indigenous African Political System*. 2001.
Melbaa, Gadaa. *Oromia: An Introduction to the History of the Oromo People*. 1999.

Ossetians

Ossets; Osetes; Ossetins; Osetiny; Alans; Digor; Ir; Iristi; Ironi

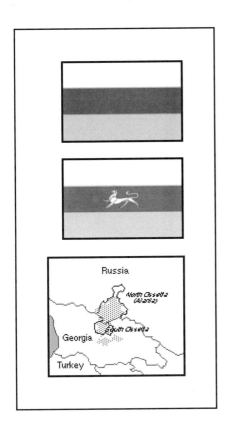

POPULATION: Approximately (2002e) 725,000 Ossetians in the former Soviet Union, with 400,000 concentrated in the North Ossetia (Alania) Republic of southern Russia and 170,000 in South Ossetia and neighboring regions of north-central Georgia. Other Ossetian communities live in the Kabardino-Balkar Republic, Stavropol Krai, Moscow, Chechenia, Rostov Oblast, Krasnodar Krai, and Dagestan Republic of the Russian Federation, and in the Central Asian republics, Azerbaijan, and Turkey.

THE OSSETIAN HOMELAND: The Ossetian homeland lies in southern European Russia and north-central Georgia, occupying the northern and southern slopes of the central Caucasus Mountains and the Mozdok and Ossetian lowlands, drained by the Terek River and its tributaries to the north. The Ossetian homeland straddles one of the world's most forbidding mountain ranges, so there is tremendous environmental diversity according to the altitude. The Ossetian republic in Russia, called North Ossetia or Alania, is connected with South Ossetia in Georgia by the Ossetian Military Road, which leads over the Caucasus through the Mamison Pass near Mount Kazbek, one of the highest of the Caucasian peaks. The homeland forms two distinct political entities, the Republic of North Ossetia, often called Alania or Iryston in the Ossetian language, a member state of the Russian Federation; and South Ossetia, a nominally autonomous province within the Republic of Georgia. *Republic of North Ossetia-Alania (Iryston/Caegat-Irystony Alanijy Republika)*: 3,089 sq. mi.—8,001 sq. km, (2002e) 679,000—Ossetians 56%, Russians 26%, Ingush* 15%, Ukrainians 2%, Kabards* 1%. *Autonomous Region of South Ossetia (Xussar Iryston)*: 1,506 sq. mi.—3,901 sq. km, (2002e) 97,000—Ossetians 63%, Georgians 34%, Russians 2%, others 1%. The

Ossetian capital and major cultural center is Vladikavkaz, called Dzaujikau by the Ossetians, (2002e) 313,000. The city of Tskinvali, called Tchereba by the Ossetians, (2002e) 41,000, is the major Ossetian cultural center of the South Ossetians.

FLAG: The Ossetian national flag, the official flag of North Ossetia, is a horizontal tricolor of white, scarlet, and yellow. The flag of the South Ossetians is a horizontal tricolor of white, red, and yellow bearing a centered white, crouching snow leopard.

PEOPLE AND CULTURE: The Ossetians, calling themselves Iristi and their homeland Iryston, are the most northerly of the Iranian peoples. Intermarriage and centuries of contact with neighboring peoples have greatly influenced the Ossetian culture and language. Despite their Iranian language and their origins in the steppe lands, the Ossetians have a culture similar to that of neighboring Caucasian peoples. The Ossetians are divided into five principal groups and many subgroups or clans, dwelling in villages under the authority of elders. The Kurtats and Alagirs never developed a class system, but the Tagaurs and the Digors, under Georgian influence, retain a four-class society. Formerly Ossetian traditions included such practices as clan warfare, bride stealing, and vendettas. Marriage was forbidden between blood relatives, or anyone with the same surname. Until the Russian Revolution, divorce was permitted only among the Muslim Ossetians.

LANGUAGE AND RELIGION: The language of the Ossetians, called Iron Avsag, is an Iranian language somewhat modified by borrowings from their Caucasian and Turkic neighbors. Dialectical differences originally followed tribal divisions, but one dialect, called Iron, has been recognized as the basis of standard Ossetian. Ossetian is spoken in six dialects—Iron, Digor, Tual or Tuallag, Tagaur, Kurtat, and Allagir. Iron is spoken in the eastern districts of North Ossetia, Digor is spoken in the Digor Valley of western North Ossetia, and Tual is mostly spoken south of the mountains in Georgia. Most Ossetians speak Russian as a second language. The first written example of the language—known as the "Zelenchuk inscription"—is dated A.D. 341. From 1923 until 1938 the language was written in an adapted Latin alphabet, but a new system, based on the Russian Cyrillic alphabet, was made official in 1938. The literary language is based on the Tagaur dialect.

There is profound religious division in the Ossetian nation, which affects the culture and relations with other nations. The Irons and Tuals are mostly Orthodox Christians, while the Digors are mostly Sunni Muslims. Between 15 and 20% of the Ossetians are Sunni Muslims and have been affected by the spread of radical Islamic doctrines. Both the Christianity and Islam practiced by the Ossetians incorporate many ancient pagan traditions and practices. The groups share similar, uniquely Ossetian celebrations surrounding deaths and marriage.

NATIONAL HISTORY: The Ossetians trace their ancestry back to the ancient Scythians, but this theory is disputed by historians who believe they descended from a division of the Sarmatians, the Alans, who inhabited the grasslands between the Volga and Don Rivers, north of the Caucasus Mountains. Between 72 and 135 A.D., the Alans raided south into Armenia and the Caucasus region. They, in turn, were pushed out of the Terek River lowlands and into the Caucasus foothills by invading Huns in the fourth century A.D., while other Alan groups joined the Huns and moved west into the territory of the Roman Empire. Waves of invaders pushed the Alans of the Caucasus farther back into the mountain gorges; some moved to the southern slopes of the Greater Caucasus.

The high passes of the Caucasus Mountains that united the scattered Alan tribes, also called Ossetes, served as major invasion routes between Europe and Asia. The Ossetians organized a state structure between the ninth and thirteenth centuries but maintained only a precarious independence against the region's numerous invaders—the Huns, Khazars, Arabs, Seljuk Turks, and Georgians. The Ossetians north of the mountains were constantly at war with the neighboring Kabards and often raided into the southern Caucasus. The Darial Gorge, which cuts through the high Caucasus, was formerly called Dar-i-Alan, or Gate of the Alans.

In the twelfth century, Georgia's Queen Tamara persuaded the Ossetian population to adopt Christianity, the religion of the Georgian state. The Mongols overran Georgia and the Caucasus in the thirteenth century, and the Christian Ossetian homeland was devastated by the merciless destruction of the conquerors. In the fourteenth century the recovering Ossetians won religious freedom under the rule of the Mongols' successor, the Golden Horde. The Kabards imposed their rule on most of the Ossetians in the early eighteenth century. The Digors, whose territory lay closest to Kabardia, were more culturally influenced, and they converted to Islam.

The entire Caucasus was the center of a fierce struggle for dominance by the Turkish Ottoman Empire and the Persians in the fifteenth century. The expanding Russian state to the north, taking advantage of the chaos created by the Muslim rivals, began to penetrate the region in the sixteenth century. Christian Russian influence, particularly in the Ossetian region north of the mountains, brought the Christian Ossetians a degree protection against the depredations of the warlike Muslim tribes of the Caucasus Mountains.

The Ossetians came under nominal Russian influence in 1792. The Ossetians welcomed the Russians, since they offered protection against the Kabards and permitted the Ossetians to repopulate the plains to the north. The key fortress of Vladikavkaz, founded in 1784, became a center of Russian expansion in the Caucasus. Resistance to Russian rule replaced the earlier good relations when tsarist bureaucrats attempted to take control of all aspects of Ossetian life. In 1794 the Ossetians rebelled; following their defeat, their territory was annexed to the Russian Empire between 1801 and 1806. Sporadic rebellions continued in Ossetia until 1850, with a serious, widespread insurgency in 1842. In 1865 over 3,000 Muslim Ossetian families left to settle in the Ottoman Empire.

The Ossetians, through their early good relations with the Slavs, became the most advanced people in the Caucasus, favored by the tsarist authorities over their Muslim neighbors. Many Ossetians left the mountains to settled in the northern plains, where they developed agricultural communities. In 1844, a Russian linguist created a literary language based on the Cyrillic alphabet. Serfdom, abolished in the Russian Empire in 1861, was finally ended in Ossetia in 1867. In 1889 the Ossetian Military Road was hacked through the 9,000-foot Mamison Pass, facilitating contact between the northern and southern Ossetian clans.

The Caucasian Muslim peoples, generally sympathetic to Muslim Turkey when war began in 1914, viewed the Orthodox Ossetians as Russian agents; violence and tension increased as the war dragged on. The Ossetians, to protect themselves in the spreading chaos, formed an alliance with the Terek Cossacks* to the north, the dominant military power in the region. The Russian Revolution in February 1917 escalated the confusion in the Caucasus. In April 1917 the Ossetians called a national congress to establish organs of self-rule within a new democratic Russian state.

Frightened by the Bolshevik coup in October 1917, the Ossetian national congress supported the creation of a joint Christian-Muslim government in the region. The alliance collapsed in December 1917, when fighting broke out between the Muslim tribes and the Cossacks in the Terek River valley. In January 1918 a new council brought together the anti-Bolshevik groups in the region—the Ossetians, the Terek Cossacks, some Muslim groups, and delegates from the major Russian political organizations.

Bolshevik officials declared Ossetia an autonomous Soviet republic in March 1918, but their effective authority to do so was limited. The spreading Russian civil war spilled into the region in mid-1918. Bolshevik troops allied to the Muslim Chechens* and Ingush overran Russian Ossetia in November 1918. The Ingush captured and looted Vladikavkaz. Under the direction of the Bolshevik leader G. K. Ordzhonikidze, the Bolsheviks and Muslims unleashed a reign of terror, arresting and executing Ossetian, Terek Cossack, and anti-Bolshevik Russians. The Ossetians viewed the terror as perpetrated by the pro-Bolshevik Ingush.

The South Ossetians, under Georgian rule, revolted against the declaration of a independent Georgian state in May 1918. The rebellion was put down with brutal efficiency by Georgian forces, opening a serious rift in relations between the two peoples. In February 1921, when Bolshevik forces invaded Georgia, the Ossetians aided the invaders. In 1922 the southern part of Ossetia was made part of Soviet Georgia, and the Soviet government established an autonomous South Ossetian region on 20 April 1922.

The Bolsheviks in January 1920 created the Mountain Autonomous Republic, which included most of the territory of the Caucasus region. Regional and ethnic disputes caused the breakup of the Mountain Republic; North Ossetia was created a separate autonomous region in 1924, but the majority of government posts were held by ethnic Russians. Local Ossetian leaders appealed for the creation of a united Ossetian republic, to include the South Ossetians, within the Soviet state in 1925. Their request was denied by nationalities minister, Joseph Stalin.

The autonomous region was raised to the status of an autonomous republic within the Russian Federation in 1936. The Sovietization of Ossetia, including collectivization and the elimination of the landowning classes, was carried out with great brutality. Some aspects of Ossetian culture, particularly clan loyalties and polygamy, proved especially difficult for the Bolsheviks to eradicate.

During World War II, German columns invaded the Caucasus region and occupied North Ossetia in 1942. The Ossetians remained unmoved by the overtures of the Nazi authorities, but once the Germans were driven back in early 1943, the Muslim Digors received the same treatment from the Soviets as the other Muslims in the region: they were deported to Central Asia on Stalin's orders. In 1944, Stalin, after deporting the Digors, arbitrarily enlarged the North Ossetian republic with the addition of districts separated from Stavropol Krai and the western district of Ingushetia, the Prigorodny region. Prigorodny had been inhabited by Ingush, but following their deportation, it was repopulated by ethnic Ossetians. An estimated 50% of the deported Digors died during the brutal dispersal throughout Central Asia.

In the postwar period, particularly following Stalin's death in 1953, literary and artistic expressions of Ossetian culture were encouraged by the Soviet government. After 1954, the writing system of the South Ossetians, which had been based on Georgian, was changed to the Cyrillic alphabet used in North Ossetia. The Digors, rehabilitated in 1956, began to return to their homeland in 1957, although Ossetian communities remain scattered throughout Central Asia.

In the 1970s, evidence emerged that some elements of the Communist Party of Georgia was pursuing a long-term strategy of assimilation of the Ossetian minority. In spite of the nominally autonomous government of South Ossetia, most political posts were held by Georgians and Russians, Georgian and Russian were the official languages, and discrimination on the basis of ethnic origin was widespread.

The Soviet liberalization of the late 1980s sparked a rapid and dramatic rise of nationalism among the divided Ossetian peoples. In 1988 the South Ossetians in Georgia demanded secession and unification with North Ossetia. The secessionist demands set off violent clashes between Ossetians and Georgians, often with the encouragement of the ethnocentric Georgian government of Zviad Gamsakhurdia. Over 1,500 died in the fighting, and 40,000 Ossetian refugees fled across the mountains to North Ossetia, their plight fanning nascent nationalism in Russian Ossetia. On 11 December 1990 the nationalist Georgian government rescinded South Ossetia's autonomy and renamed the region Shida Khartli, Inner Georgia. The following day, the region's nationalist leaders declared the independence of the South Ossetian Democratic Republic, which was not recognized by the governments of Georgia or Russia.

The disintegration of the Soviet Union allowed long-suppressed grievances to be aired. The Ingush renewed their old claim to territory transferred to North Ossetia in 1944 laying claim to the northern Prigorodny region and also the city of Vladikavkaz. In May 1992, after separating from Chechnya, the Ingush demanded the return of their traditional territory, but Ossetian nationalists reacted by driving the Ingush inhabitants of Vladikavkaz from the city and attacking Ingush villages in the disputed districts. Over 60,000 Ingush refugees fled across the border into Ingushetia, but the dispute remained unsettled. Sporadic fighting in the region left hundreds of dead and injured.

North Ossetia became an important outpost after the declared secession of Chechnya; Vladikavkaz and Mozdok became the primary Russian military bases during the Russian assaults on the Chechens in 1994–95 and 1999–2000. In the conflict between the Ossetians and Ingush, the Russian government favored the "always loyal Ossetians" over the discontented Muslim Ingush.

The conflicts with the Georgians in the south and the Ingush in the west have fueled the growth of Ossetian nationalism, but the majority hope for autonomy, not full independence, fearing the loss of Russian protection in the volatile region they have inhabited since ancient times. The Ossetians, although needing Russian protection in the mostly Muslim region, continue to work for the unification of their small nation in a single political entity. In 1996, the governments of North and South Ossetia signed a treaty of friendship and cooperation.

Relations between the South Ossetians and the Georgian government improved in the late 1990s. The Georgian government of Eduard Shevardnadze proposed in June 1998 a loose federation of Georgia, Abkhazia, Ajaria, and South Ossetia. The two sides signed agreements on economic reconstruction and the return of refugees, but the political situation remains unsettled and Russian peacekeepers remain in the region.

An estimated 13,000 of the 60,000 Ingush refugees who fled the violence in North Ossetia had returned to their homes in the Prigorodny region by March 1999, but meetings between Russian, Ingush, and Ossetian officials were unable to resolve the conflict. A deterioration of the situation in the Prigorodny led to extremism on both sides.

In September 1999, Merab Chigoev, the head of the breakaway Republic of South Ossetia, accused the Georgian government of reneging on a previous agreement to provide economic aid to South Ossetia. The Georgian authorities cut off power supplies to the region on 1 September, because the South Ossetian government had failed to pay previous energy debts. The conflict jeopardized the negotiations on defining relations between South Ossetia and the Georgian government.

The Ossetians in both Russia and Georgia remain one people, with a strong sense of identity. Demands for unification continue to color the political situation in both countries, although relations between the Ossetians and their neighbors have improved since the early 1990s. Currently most Ossetians favor a special relationship between North and South Ossetia, with cultural, political, and economic autonomy for both Ossetian states.

SELECTED BIBLIOGRAPHY:

Matveeva, Anna. *The North Caucasus: Russia's Fragile Borderland.* 2000.
Olson, James S. *An Ethnohistorical Dictionary of the Russian and Soviet Empires.* 1994.
Trepavlov, V.V., and A.N. Sakharov, eds. *Russia and North Caucasus: 400 Years of War?* 1999.
Wesselink, Egbert. *Minorities in the Republic of Georgia.* 1992.

Pa-O

Pao; Paoh; Pa'O; Pa'U; Taungthu; Black Karens; Kula

POPULATION: Approximately (2002e) 1,430,000 Pa-O in southeast Asia, concentrated the Mong Pan district of Shan State in Myanmar and adjacent areas of Thailand.

THE PA-O HOMELAND: The Pa-O homeland, called Paoh, occupies the mountainous region around the valley of the upper Salween River just south of the Shan Plateau in the Tanen Taungyi Range in east-central Myanmar. Paoh has no official status, the region forms the districts of Hsuphang, Mong Pan, Mong Kang, and Mauk Mai of southeastern Shan state of Myanmar. *Region of Paoh*: 6,690 sq. mi.— 17,336 sq. km, (2002 e) 1,780,000—Pa-O 75%, Shans* 11%, Karennis* 7%, Lahus* 4%, Palaung 2%, Lisu and other Burmese 1%. The Pa-O capital and major cultural center is Hsuphang, (2002e) 10,000.

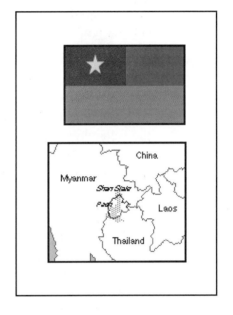

FLAG: The Pa-O national flag, the flag of the national movement, is divided horizontally, the lower half green, the upper half divided vertically into two equal rectangles, red on the fly and blue at the hoist, the blue charged with a white, five-pointed star.

PEOPLE AND CULTURE: The Pa-O are a tribal people who have retained their traditional tribal and caste structures and their ancient culture in the isolation of the heavily forested mountains around the upper Salween River. The tribes collectively called Pa-O have only united in recent decades and still display great differences in culture, dialect, and political organization. They are also known as Taungthu, which can be translated as "southerner" or "mountaineer." In Thailand they are often called Kula, derived from a derogatory term meaning dark or black used for Indians. The Thais often call Myanmar the country of the Kula. The Pa-O, although linguistically related to the Karennis* and Karens,* they claim they are more akin to the Shans* from whom they have borrowed many cultural traits, including the Buddhist religion.

LANGUAGE AND RELIGION: The Pa-O speak a Karen language of

the Sino-Thai branch of the Sino-Tibetan languages. The language, forming part of the Pho group of Karen dialects, is related to the other Karen dialects, but shows considerable borrowings from the neighboring Shan language. The language is spoken in many dialects, each area and often each village speaking a related dialect.

The majority of the Pa-O are Buddhists, which was introduced to the Paoh uplands from the neighboring Shans. There is considerable interplay between traditional animist rituals and Buddhist practices. A small Christian minority, mainly Roman Catholic, is the result of missionary activity in the region in the late nineteenth and early twentieth centuries. Pa-O villages tend to be predominately one or the other of the three religions, while there are more mixing of faiths and places of worship in the urban areas.

NATIONAL HISTORY: The Pa-O are believed to have originated in eastern Tibet,* their ancestors having migrated south along the rivers in ancient times. Following the course of the Salween River the tribes settled the valley lowlands before the sixth century A.D. Forced into the less accessible mountains by stronger peoples, the Pa-O settled in small, autonomous villages based on tribes, clans, and family groups. United only when faced with a common threat the various groups often warred among themselves. The tribal culture, based on small units, evolved a tradition of fierce independence.

Conquered by the Shans, a Thai people, in the seventh century, the Pa-O paid annual tribute to the feudal Shan princes but mostly continued to live a traditional way of life. In the ninth century the Burmans, a people linguistically related to the Pa-O, began to penetrate the Shan states. The long rivalry for control of the region forced the majority of the Pa-O to retreat into the forests and high mountain valleys. In the seventeenth century, the Pa-O came under the nominal rule of the Burman kings of the Irrawaddy delta.

The British took control of Upper Burma from the Burmese kingdom in 1886. The European authorities established a tradition of indirect rule, signing treaties with various Pa-O tribes living in the regions nominally ruled by the Shan principalities. British and American missionaries, in the 1890s, introduced the Pa-O tribes to Christianity and Western education. In the first decade of the twentieth century a small educated group of chief's sons took the first tentative steps to try to end the endemic tribal conflicts.

During World War II, the Pa-O formed guerrilla bands behind the Japanese lines. Trained and armed by Allied officers parachuted into the region, the fierce Pa-O guerrilla bands terrorized the Japanese patrols and served as guides for Allied forces crossing their rugged terrain. The guerrillas, after the end of the war, formed the nucleus of a Pa-O national army and the growing nationalist movement.

Promised local autonomy, the Pa-O districts remained part of Shan State when Burma gained independence in 1948. Soon after independence the Burmese government abrogated the autonomy statute. In 1949, Buddhist monks led the Pa-O in revolt against taxation by local landlords. The revolt spread across Paoh and the uprising took on a definite nationalist flavor. Led by the former guerrillas of World War II, the Pa-O, with arms from China, and often allied to the Burmese Communist rebels operating in the jungle region, pursued a war against the Burmese government during the 1950s. The common goal of self-rule united the diverse tribes and for the first time the Pa-O began to see themselves as a nation rather than as a group of unrelated tribes and clans.

The Pa-O insurgents, nearly defeated by government forces in 1958, retreated into the inaccessible jungles. Many rebels, unable to find arms, surrendered during a general amnesty. In 1961, the government's military commander in the region announced that the Pa-O rebellion had finally been eradicated. The next year, following the 1962 coup that brought a military government to power in Rangoon, the indiscriminate attacks by government troops on Pa-O villages reignited the nationalist movement and renewed the Pa-O insurgency.

Allied to other ethnic insurgent groups, the Pa-O leaders, in 1972, put aside demands for autonomy and proclaimed the ultimate goal of independence within a federation of states what would replace Burma's brutal military government. To finance the separatist war the Pa-O depended on modest teak logging and smuggling across the Thai border. In the 1980s, when Thai companies, granted logging concessions by the Burmese government, devastated the teak forests, many of the Pa-O tribes turned to the lucrative opium trade to finance the ongoing war with the government forces in the region.

The Pa-O's increasing involvement in drug trafficking opened rifts between the Pa-O bands and other ethnic groups. In the late eighties, fighting erupted for control of the drug trails along the Thai border. In early 1994 the Thai government sealed the border to stop the flow of drugs crossing into Thai territory.

The Pa-O, threatened by increasing violence, deforestation, and the denial of land rights, agreed to open negotiations with the government in 1994. The nationalists, after decades of fighting, continue to claim that to surrender will mean the extinction of their small nation, but armed resistance has become more difficult as arms and funds from outside their territory have begun to dry up as Thai economic interests replaces cooperation.

In December 1994, attacks by government troops, the first in over two years, renewed fighting in the region. The rebels, falling back on jungle strongholds, began to coordinate their armed struggle with the other insurgent groups under renewed attack by the government. Nationalist leaders reiterated their aim of Pa-O independence within a federation of states when the brutal military junta is finally driven from power.

In an effort to cut off support for the rebels, the government began to forcibly relocate many villagers to the outskirts of government-controlled towns. The relocations were accompanied by killings, rape, and other abuses. Many Pa-O are believed to have died from malnutrition and disease due to the poor conditions in the government camps. In some areas relocated villagers were forced to work on road building projects. Other Pa-O were killed on the Thai border when they could not afford to bribe the border guards. Government efforts to block rice supplies to areas where insurgents were active led to severe malnutrition in 1996–97.

The Pa-O insurgents finally made a cease-fire deal with the ruling military government, the State Law and Order Restoration Council (SLORC), renamed the State Peace and Development council (SPDC) in 1997 in an effort to reduce the negative image of the brutal military government. The insurgent Pa-O capitulated after government troops began holding entire populations hostage and conducting systematic executions. Although the leaders surrendered, splinter groups held out and continue to operate in the region, particularly in sabotage raids. Thousands of Pa-O remain in refugee camps in Thailand or in camps along the Thai-Myanmar border.

Myanmar was formally admitted to the Association of Southeast Asian Nations (ASEAN) in 1997, a grouping of the capitalist, mostly democratic states in the region. Although promises were made, there has been no appreciable improvement in the treatment of non-Burman national groups despite the policy of "constructive engagement" by its regional partners. The Myanmar government continues to commit human rights abuses against the country's ethnic minorities with complete impunity.

Pa-O women, traditionally subservient, became more assertive as war and repression ravaged their homeland. The women set up their own nationalist organization on 5 November 1999. The Pa-O Women Union aims to promote Pa-O culture and literature, and to ultimately protect the culture until the hated military government is finally overthrown and the peoples of Myanmar win their self-determination within a federal system or separately as sovereign nations. One of their most pressing needs is to promote unity among various Pa-O movements. The other important work is the care of Pa-O refugees on the Thai-Myanmar border.

The government's frontier battalions, lacking major confrontations, turned to profit-making enterprises by mercilessly exploiting indigenous Pa-O groups. Money, goods, and crops are demanded of helpless villagers. Lucrative resource extraction, particularly mines and timber, use forced labor recruited at gun-point from the local population. Well-intentioned international organizations, including the United Nations (UN), have funded development projects in the region, but turn a blind eye to the slave labor used to implement the projects. Slavery, forced labor, forced relocation, and arbitrary executions continue throughout the Paoh region. Refugees crossing into Thailand in 1999–2002 report increased attacks on unarmed villages, the looting of food and other supplies, and extrajudicial killings by government soldiers. The military reportedly targeted Christian and animist villages particularly.

SELECTED BIBLIOGRAPHY:

Diran, Richard K. *The Vanishing Tribes of Burma*. 1997.
Lintner, Bertil. *Land of Jade: A Journey through Insurgent Burma*. 1990.
Mirante, Edith. *Burmese Looking Glass: A Human Rights Adventure*. 1993.
Smith, Martin. *Ethnic Groups in Burma: Development, Democracy and Human Rights*. 1994.

Palaungs

Padaungs; Palongs; Ta-ang; De'ang; Pale; Palay

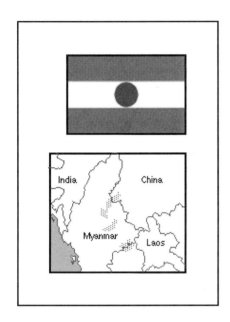

POPULATION: Approximately (2002e) 1,300,000 Palaungs in southeast Asia, including about a million living in the Shan State of Myanmar, 240,000 in adjacent areas of China, and about 60,000 in Thailand. Outside the region there are Palaung communities in Rangoon and other areas of southern Myanmar, and in Bangkok.

THE PALAUNG HOMELAND: The Palaung homeland lies in northeastern Myanmar and adjacent areas of China and Thailand. The region occupies the mountainous area between the upper Salween River and Irrawaddy rivers. The homeland, which stretches from Tawngpeng in nothern Shan to Kengteng in southern Shan, is the center of highland tea production in Myanmar and China. The Palaung homeland has no official status in any of the three countries. In Myanmar, the region forms several districts of Shan State. The Palaung capital and major cultural center is Hsenwi in Myanmar, (2002e) 20,000.

FLAG: The Palaung national flag, the flag of the national movement, has three equal stripes of green, white, and green bearing a centered red disk.

PEOPLE AND CULTURE: The Palaungs are a tribal peoples related to the Mons* of Myanmar and Thailand, and the Khmers of Cambodia. Divided into a five distinct groups, the Golden or Shwe Palaung in Myanmar and China, the Bonglong of China, the Rumai, and Riang-Lang, and the Silver or Ngwe Palaung. In China the Palaungs are normally called De'ang and in Thailand they are the Palongs. They are further divided into classes, clans, and family groups. Palaung society is based on age, gender, and wealth. Some Palaung groups are patrilineal, while others are matrilineal or recognize inheritance from both parents. The Palaungs are known for the elaborate brass rings worn on the neck, arms, legs, and necks of women, the famous giraffe women. Some groups, such as the Rumai, live in the higher altitudes, while the lower elevations are populated by the Silver Palaungs, who grow rice rather than tea. Since there are no Palaung traditions forbidding inter-group marriage, mixing with other groups and inter-marriage are common, which is why their culture shows definite Shan influences.

LANGUAGE AND RELIGION: The Palaungs speak Palaungic, a language belonging to the Palaung-Wa branch of the Mon-Khmer language group. There are many dialects and subdialects, with fifteen dialects spoken in Myanmar alone. The Silver Palaung speak their own language, which is not mutually intelligible to speakers of other Palaung dialects. In China the language is called Benglong. Because they generally share villages with other ethnic groups, many of the Palaungs are bilingual, speaking their own language within the group, but using Burmese or Shan in public. Shan is generally used as a lingua franca between different Palaung groups and between the Palaungs and the neighboring peoples. The Palaung language closely resembles that spoken by the Wa* farther east, but there is no close cultural connection between the two peoples.

The majority of the Palaungs are Buddhists, belonging to the Theravada branch of Buddhism. Buddhism coexists with various local cults associated with the Palaungs' pre-Buddhist religious beliefs, including belief in evil spirits called nats. The Palaungs believe that while all nats are inherently evil, some are more evil than others and a person must appease them. If the nats are pleased the people will prosper and enjoy good health. Ancestor worship also remains a part of the local belief system and shamans remain powerful figures in Palaung society. About 2% of the total Palaung population is Christian, the result of missionary activity in the region in the 1920s and 1930s.

NATIONAL HISTORY: The Palaungs are thought to migrated to the region known as the Shan Plateau from the upper Salween and Mekong rivers in eastern Tibet. They followed the rivers south in the seventh and eighth centuries and spread across the highlands. Some of the Palaung groups came under Chinese authority in the eighth century. In the twelfth century the Shans, a Tai people, migrated to the region from China, driving the Palaungs from the lowlands into the less accessible mountains. Burman invaders from the Tibetan plateau began infiltrating the region in the ninth century.

Many invaders crossed the Palaung homeland, but the tribes stubbornly resisted all invaders and maintained their independence in the mountains. The ornamentation of Palaung women, with rows of brass rings on their arms, legs, and elongated necks is thought to have begun in an attempt to make the women unattractive to enemies.

The Shans established a number of small territorial states that nominally included the Palaung territories, but Shan control was generally limited to the lowland Palaung regions. In the mid-eighteenth century, the Palaungs repulsed an invading Chinese army, but lost the eastern districts to Chinese rule. Burman pressure from the lowlands increased in the eighteenth and nineteenth centuries, following the Burman defeat of the dominate Shans. By the mid-nineteenth century, the Shan states paid tribute to the Burman king. Tribute was also extracted from the Palaungs in the form of gems, tea, rice, or other forest products.

In the late 1870s, the Shan principalities renounced their allegiance to the Burman kingdom, plunging northern Burma into war. The turbulence gave the British a pretext for intervention. Following the Third Anglo-Burmese War in 1885–86, the British occupied the Shan Plateau region, although the Shan princes were allowed to continue their rule under the supervision of British advisors, who were also responsible for the Palaung tribes. Palaungs in the more remote areas continued to fight British rule until the 1930s.

British and American missionaries arrived in the region in the late nineteenth century. Some Palaung leaders converted to Christianity, mostly sensing material benefits. During the colonial period, most missionary education was in English, the official language of the colony. Both English and Burmese were later made compulsory subjects in area schools. Since the knowledge of English became a valued asset, many Palaungs learned to speak it.

A small English-speaking elite emerged, missionary educated and determined to bring their small nation into the modern world. In 1923, the first Palaung cultural organization was formed among the mission-educated minority. The educated elite gradually molded a Palaung nation out of the dispersed tribes and clans formerly united only by language and cultural affinities.

In the late nineteenth century, other peoples, the Dai and Han Chinese in China, and the Shan and Burmans in Myanmar, gradually infiltrated the Palaung homeland. By the early 1950s, the Palaungs had lost or sold about 85% of their rice lands. Many Palaungs were reduced to tenant farming on lands owned by other groups.

During World War II, the Shans at first favored the Japanese, who promised independence. The Palaungs remained loyal to the British and formed guerrilla groups that fought Japanese incursions into the high mountain valleys. The Japanese and their Burman and Shan allies often attacked unarmed villages in reprisals. When Allied troops began to infiltrate the region late in the war, they found the Palaungs to be willing guides and ferocious troops.

At the end of the war the British announced their intention to grant independence to Burma. The Shan leaders demanded separate independence, which stimulated Palaung demands for autonomy and control of their traditional territories. The Palaung demands were ignored in the rush to independence. The Palaungs neither agreed to join Burma nor have they accepted their inclusion in the state. The Burmese government promised autonomy to the country's many ethnic groups, but within months of independence in 1948 the new government abrogated the constitution and attempted to impose direct rule. Clashes between Palaung groups and government troops rapidly politicized the Palaungs in the early 1950s. The Palaung leadership formed the Palaung State Liberation Party (PSLP), and its military wing, the Palaung State Liberation Army (PSLA), to fight for separate statehood within a democratic Burmese federation.

In the 1950s, the Palaung population of China had the highest infant mortality rate in the country. China's medical care has greatly improved since then, and their population growth has been steadily since the 1960s. Traditionally, all land was held in common by the village, with each family having the right to use the land, but not to own it. The imposition of communism and the collectivization of all lands severely strained the traditional culture.

Allied to the Shans, the Palaungs fought the Burmese government troops that entered their hills from the late 1940s. By the early 1960s, several Palaung nationalist groups had formed, evidence of their growing independence of the Shan leadership. The expansion of opium production in the so-called Golden Triangle in the 1960s provided the Palaungs with a means of bettering their dismal economic situation and to earn the funds needed to continue their fight for self-determination. Many Palaung farmers greatly increased their incomes by growing and selling opium. Some groups set up their own processing plants in the jungle to increase their incomes by producing the finished drugs.

The military coup in Burma in 1962 ended the use of English in Palaung education, with Burmese, the only official language in the country, becoming the language used in teaching and education. The Palaung dialects, disparaged as folk tongues, were forbidden in any official function.

Heavy fighting periodically swept the region in the 1970s and 1980s, often between rival groups involved in the growing drug trade. Many Palaungs withdrew further into the rugged mountains, but the war seemed to follow them. Civilian casualties, particularly from hunger and disease, devastated the region.

In 1975, the PSLP joined eight other insurgent groups in the National Democratic Front (NDF) dedicated to replacing the hated military government of Burma with a loose federation of independent national states. The Palaung groups, often allied to the neighboring Shans and Burmese Communists, came under attack by government troops utilizing military equipment supplied by the U.S. government to fight the drug trade.

In May 1991, the Palaungs were ordered to sign a cease-fire with government forces. Soldiers held entire villages hostage and indiscriminate executions continued until the Palaung elders finally agreed to sign the peace accord. Splinter groups continued to fight the government. At the slightest hint of rebellion, the government attacks violently. Government troops, at checkpoints along the main trade routes, prevent the Palaungs from maintaining their traditional trade with the lowland Shans.

Government troops, moving into the region to oversee the exploitation of natural resources, regularly force villagers to work as porters or unpaid labor on development projects. Thousands of Palaungs fled across the border into Thailand in the mid-1990s to escape relocations to so-called "peace villages" under the close control of the military. Many remained in refugee camps across the border or in inaccessible jungle areas in 1999–2000. A shortage of weapons and a crackdown on rebel activity by the Thai authorities have curtailed Palaung insurgent activities to low-level guerrilla activities and sabotage against government positions and Thai logging operations that are devastating their homeland.

The Thai government is cooperating with the military government in a grandiose "development" scheme to build a string of huge dams on the Salween River, where it forms the border between Myanmar and Thailand. Intended to provide energy-hungry Thailand with electricity generating power, the dams will eventually flood the lowland parts of the Palaung homeland.

The Palaungs have survived centuries of invaders, and intend to survive the current military government and its brutal methods. They continue to hold out hope for the eventual overthrow of the hated government and the democratization of the region, but until then they will continue to resist government efforts to suppress their traditional independence. To the Palaungs, the Burmese government has been one of their five traditional enemies, along with fire, famine, flood, and plague.

SELECTED BIBLIOGRAPHY:

Horowitz, Donald L. *Ethnic Groups in Conflict.* 1987.
Schaefer, Richard T. *Racial and Ethnic Groups.* 1999.
Silverstein, J. *Burmese Politics: The Dilemma of National Unity.* 1980.
Smith, M. *Burma: Insurgency and the Politics of Insurgency.* 1991.

Palestinians

Falastins; Palestinian Arabs

POPULATION: Approximately (2002e) 6,240,000 Palestinians in the Middle East, 2,910,000 in Gaza, the West Bank, and East Jerusalem, 750,000 in Israel, and large communities in Jordan, Lebanon, Syria, Egypt, the Gulf States, and other Arab states in the Middle East. Outside the region, the largest populations are in Europe, the United States, and North Africa.

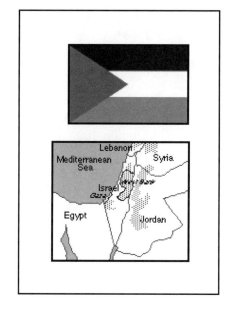

THE PALESTINIAN HOMELAND: The Palestinian homeland, as defined by the Palestine Liberation Organization, comprises the so-called Occupied Territories (which include the West Bank), the former Jordanian territory west of the Jordan River, the Gaza Strip (just north of the Egyptian border), and Al-Quds ash Sherif (East Jerusalem). The West Bank and Gaza are divided by 20 miles of Israeli territory, and the status of Jerusalem remains unsettled. The Palestinian Authority rules the autonomous Palestinian state, made up of the West Bank and Gaza, that was created in 1994. *Palestine (Falastin)*: 4,998 sq. mi.—12,948 sq. km, (2002e) 3,248,000—Palestinians 97%, Israelis 3%. The Palestinian capital and major cultural center is East Jerusalem, called Al-Quds ash Sherif in Arabic, (2002e) 155,000, urban area 361,000. The temporary capital of the autonomous Palestinian state is Ramallah, called Ram Allah, (2002e) 23,000, urban area 81,000. The major cultural centers are Gaza, called Gazzah by the Palestinians, (2002e) 397,000, metropolitan area 1,278,000, and Nabulus, the major city of the West Bank, (2002e) 113,000.

FLAG: The Palestinian national flag, the flag of the national movement and the official flag of the autonomous region, is a horizontal tricolor of black, white, and green bearing a red triangle at the hoist.

PEOPLE AND CULTURE: The Palestinians are an Arab people, the Arab inhabitants of the area called Palestine (including present-day Jordan and Israel) created after World War I. The majority of the Palestinians live in other Arab countries, many in long-established refugee camps in the states bordering Israel. The Palestinian diaspora since 1948 has evolved a large intellectual and professional class. The Palestinian population of the Occupied Territories does not include the nearly 800,000 Palestinians who live in Israel and are Israeli citizens.

LANGUAGE AND RELIGION: The Palestinians speak the Palestinian dialect of Arabic, although many different dialects are spoken in the diaspora. The local dialects, based on the peasant dialect of nineteenth-century Palestine, contains many Turkic borrowings and later English admixtures. The standard dialect, based on the Jerusalem dialect, is the basis of the Palestinian literary language. The language is the official language of the autonomous Palestinian state and is taught in schools and used in administration. Hebrew and English are widely spoken as second languages.

The majority of the Palestinians are Sunni Muslims, belonging to the orthodox branch of Islam. A large but declining minority are Christians, both Roman Catholic and Protestant. Some of the Christians trace their religion back to ancient times, others to nineteenth-century missionary activity. Radical Islamic organizations have gained support since the early 1990s, partly as a reaction to the frustration felt by the Palestinians over the lack of results after years of negotiations between the Palestinian leader, Yasser Arafat, and various Israeli governments.

NATIONAL HISTORY: The Israelites, led out of slavery in Egypt in the twelfth century B.C., eventually occupied the lands of the Canaanites. The ancient Hebrew kingdom, established in 1025 B.C., was nearly constantly at war with the Philistines of Gaza and the coastal cities. The Philistines are claimed as the ancestors of the Palestinians by some groups. Successively part of the Assyrian, Chaldean, and Persian empires, the region came under Roman rule in 63 B.C. Roman Judea was the scene of Christ's life and the inception of Christianity.

The Jews, refusing to accept Roman gods and culture, revolted in A.D. 70 and again in A.D. 135. The Romans finally dispersed the defeated Jews from the region; only a small Jewish minority remained by the end of the second century. Following the dispersal, the Roman authorities renamed the province Palestine, after the earlier Philistines. By the fourth century the majority of Palestine's inhabitants had become Christians.

Poor and backward after the Roman decline, the region fell to Muslim Arab invaders in 636–40. The invaders converted most of the population to the new Islamic religion, but Jews and Christians that refused Islam were tolerated as "peoples of the book" (the Bible). The Muslim conquerors erected a great mosque, the Dome of the Rock, on the site of the ancient Jewish Temple of Solomon in Jerusalem, in the belief that Mohammed halted there on his flight to heaven. Angered by the stubborn refusal of Christians and Jews to accept Islam as the logical successor to their religions, the Muslims replaced their tolerance with suppression.

Persecution of the Christians between 996 and 1021, particularly the destruction of churches, was partly responsible for the Christian Crusades from Europe. In 1099 the Crusaders captured Palestine and created the Latin Kingdom of Jerusalem, one of a string of Crusader states erected along the Mediterranean coast. The resurgent Muslims regained most of Palestine in 1187, and the last of the Crusader states fell in 1291.

Conquered by the Ottoman Turks in 1516, Palestine declined through three centuries of neglect, corruption, and isolation. The population of the region fell to a historical low of 350,000 in 1785. Egyptian authorities, under nominal Turkish rule, took control of the province in 1831, opening the region to European influences. In 1882 Russian Jews, fleeing pogroms, joined the small Jewish minority in the area and became the forerunners of the Zionist movement, the campaign to return the Jewish diaspora to the ancient Jewish homeland in Palestine.

In the late nineteenth century, Arab nationalists became active in the region. The movement, organized as an anti-Turkish campaign, became active in opposing further Jewish settlements. In the years before World War I, Arab nationalists focused on the creation of a separate Arab state within the multi-ethnic Ottoman Empire.

The history of the Arab-Israeli conflict began with the wave of Jewish immigration to Turkish Palestine in 1882. In late-nineteenth-century Europe, the reaction of a growing number of Jews to anti-Semitism and continuing discrimination and persecution was nationalism. The Jews, they believed, were a distinct nation, different from others only because they lacked a national homeland. Political Zionism advocated the return of the Jews to their ancient homeland in Palestine. An Arab nationalism grew in the region in reaction, and opposition, to Zionism.

A new wave of immigration from Europe, beginning in 1904, brought a new type of Jewish immigrant. Primarily socialist and interested in the national revival of the Jewish nation, the immigrants built communal organizations, such as the *kibbutzim*, intended only for Jews. Although this was not meant specifically to exclude Arabs, it led to the creation of a separate Jewish society in Palestine.

On the eve of World War I, the Zionists, having failed to gain the approval of the Ottoman sultan, turned to the British. The British vaguely promised support, but to win Arab support when war began in 1914 they promised them a proposed united, independent Arab state to be carved out of the defeated Ottoman Empire. The British also negotiated the Sykes-Picot Agreement with France, in which the allies agreed to carve up the Middle East once Turkey had been defeated.

Pressed by their allies and influential members of the Jewish diaspora, the British government issued the Balfour Declaration in November 1917, just before British troops and their Arab allies captured Palestine. The declaration supported the establishment of a Jewish national home in Palestine. It was understood that nothing would be done that would prejudice the civil and religious rights of the non-Jewish population in Palestine. The wording was vague, promising a "national home" for the Jews but not a state, and leaving discussion of borders for a later date.

At the end of the war, contrary to earlier promises to the Arabs, Great Britain and France carved up the former Turkish provinces into League of Nations mandates. The Palestine Mandate included the present states of Israel and Jordan, and the modern Palestinian Authority areas of Gaza and the West Bank. In 1921 the British authorities divided Palestine to create the Kingdom of Trans-Jordan, as partial compensation for the unkept promises to their Arab allies. Tension between Arabs and Jews—both groups having been promised the remainder of Palestine—erupted in violence in 1920–21. Bowing to Arab pressure, the British placed restrictions on further Jewish immigration to Palestine, but anti-Jewish rioting again erupted in 1929 and in 1936, when more Jews, frantic to leave Europe (where the Nazis had taken control of Germany) began to arrive illegally.

The Jews worked with the British authorities, viewing them as sympathetic to their interests. The Arabs, on the other hand, saw British rule as facilitating Jewish immigration and land purchases that were slowly pushing them off their best lands. Because most land in Palestine had been registered in the name of wealthy absentee landlords, often residents of Beirut or Damascus, rather than the Palestinian *fedayeen*, the peasants who worked it, Jewish agents were able to buy it with little opposition. There were some evictions from land Arabs had lived on and worked for centuries.

The British Peel Commission, sent to Palestine in 1937, recommended the partition of the mandate into Arab, Jewish, and British regions, the latter to include Jerusalem and the shrines sacred to the three major religions. The Jews reluctantly agreed, but the Palestinian Arabs rejected the plan entirely. With another European war looming, the British government feared that the Arabs might form alliances with the Fascist powers.

Knowing that the Jews would never turn to Nazi Germany, the British government in 1939 issued a white paper declaring that Palestine would become an independent state within the British Empire within ten years. Although the point was not spelled out, the state would be under Arab rule, since Jewish immigration was to be limited to just 75,000 over the next five years. The white paper repudiated the Balfour Declaration and reversed 20 years of British policy in Palestine. The white paper did not sway Arab opinion, but it both enraged and frightened the Jews, who were becoming desperate in the face of growing anti-Semitism in Europe.

The Jews and many Arabs supported the British during World War II; the Muslim religious leader of Palestine, the mufti of Jerusalem, spent most of the war as Hitler's guest in Berlin. The Holocaust brought the Jews widespread international sympathy. British efforts to keep the Jewish survivors from reaching Palestine deepened international sentiment in favor of a Jewish state in Palestine as the only solution to "the Jewish problem."

In 1945, caught between international opinion and the growing power of the oil-rich Muslim states, the British failed to satisfy either side. Growing violence and attacks on British targets made the mandate increasingly ungovernable. Unable to find a solution, the British government finally turned the problem over to the new United Nations in 1947.

The UN Special Committee on Palestine suggested partition into Arab and Jewish states, with Jerusalem under UN administration. The Jews accepted the compromise, but the Palestinian Arabs, supported by the surrounding Arab states, rejected the plan. The Arab leaders proposed that the entire region be turned over to Arab rule, with guaranteed rights for the Jewish minority.

The Palestinian Jews, supported by United Nations resolutions, declared the independence of the State of Israel on 14 May 1948. The armies of the neighboring Arab states immediately invaded. Thousands of Palestinian Arabs fled the fighting, were driven from their homes by the victorious Jews, or left the region, assured by Arab leaders that overwhelming military power would allow them to return very soon. The armies cf the five neighboring Arab states, intending to destroy the Jewish state, were defeated as much by a lack of coordination as by the hastily organized Israeli army. The defeat, called by the Palestinians *Il Nakhbah*, the Catastrophe, began the Palestinian diaspora.

One of the primary causes of the collapse of Arab society in the region was the prior flight of the Palestinian Arab elite. Fearing for their lives and obviously not caring for the peasant majority, the local mayors, judges, and community and religious leaders fled to neighboring Arab countries. As Palestinian society had been semifeudal in nature, the townspeople, villagers, and peasants were left virtually helpless. Thousands fled the war zone, intending to return when the Arab armies had driven the Jews into the sea. By the end of the war, between 600,000 and 800,000 refugees had left the areas that fell to Israeli control.

A United Nations–brokered cease-fire left the Israelis in control of 30% more territory than had been envisioned in the UN compromise. Of the remaining Palestinian territories, Egypt took control of the Gaza Strip, and Jordan annexed the West Bank. In the camps, Palestinian nationalists mobilized and formed a number of organizations. No peace settlement was possible; neither side would compromise. The Israeli government refused to allow the Palestinian refugees to return except as part of a comprehensive peace agreement.

The 120,000 Palestinians that remained in Israel, still in control of their lands, chose to express their nationalism through *sumud*, steadfastness. They stayed in the Jewish state, denying the Zionists a homogenous Jewish state. They carefully obeyed the laws, so that the authorities would have no excuse to deport them. Many diaspora Palestinians despised the Israeli Palestinians for submitting to their status as second-class citizens in the Jewish state, but they were also envious of the benefits the Israeli Palestinians received and their increasing prosperity in the Israeli state. The Palestinians were placed under military rule, which was not lifted until 1963, refuting Israeli claims that the Arabs were equal citizens.

The Arab states, each hoping to become the leader of pan-Arabic nationalism, took up the Palestinian cause. The official policy of the neighboring Arab states left thousands of Palestinian refugees in squalid camps, a ready pool of zealous anti-Israeli fighters. Only Jordan granted citizenship rights to the Palestinians who had fled there. At a summit of Arab states in Cairo in 1963, the Palestine Liberation Organization (PLO) was formed to control the Palestinian national movement. Originally the PLO was under the control of the Arab governments, but other groups, particularly Fatah, led by Yasser Arafat, became more active. By organizing raids into Israel, Fatah created the image of guerrilla fighters popular throughout the Palestinian diaspora. Fatah hoped to provoke a military confrontation in which Arab numbers would finish the Jewish state.

A series of inconclusive wars and skirmishes polarized attitudes on both sides. Once again Arab disunity and incompetence betrayed the Palestinians. During the 1967 war, Israeli forces overran the West Bank and the Gaza Strip, and despite international pressure, they refused to relinquish the territories until the Palestinians and other Arabs recognized Israel's right to exist. The Israeli state came into control of 1.3 million Palestinians in the Occupied Territories. The Palestinian Arabs of the Occupied Territories, not granted the same rights as the Palestinian population in Israel, remained under military rule.

Demanding independence from the meddling of various Arab governments, Fatah took control of the PLO when the various Palestinian groups were admitted to the Palestinian National Council (PNC). Yasser Arafat became the chairman of the PLO and presided over the PNC and its dozens of splinter groups. Throughout the 1970s and 1980s, groups associated with the PLO carried out numerous acts of terrorism, including airline hijackings, the massacre of Israeli athletes at the 1976 Munich Olympics, and attacks on civilian targets.

The Palestinians' relations with Arab governments varied over time. The most significant conflict, known as Black September, occurred in Jordan. Guerrilla organizations ran the refugee camps in Jordan as fiefdoms and often defied the Jordanian authorities. When the Popular Front for the Liberation of Palestine (PFLP), which called for the overthrow of the Jordanian kingdom as a first step to the recovery of Palestine, hijacked four Western airliners to the desert near Amman, King Hussein decided to act. On 16 September 1970, when the hostages had been released and the planes blown up, the king sent in his army. Pitched battles were fought, but the Jordanians finally triumphed on 25 September. Thousands of Palestinians fled from Jordan to overcrowded refugee camps in Lebanon and Syria.

In October 1973, during the Jewish new year celebrations, the armies of Egypt and Syria launched a coordinated surprise attack on Israel. After initial successes, the Israelis, supported by the United States, turned the Arab armies before the Americans managed to impose a cease-fire. In the wake of the October War, the PLO was recognized by the Arab world as the sole legitimate representative of the Palestinian nation.

In 1987 the frustrated Palestinians began the *intifada*, a Palestinian uprising against Israeli military rule and the growing number of Jewish settlements constructed in the territories. The Palestinian leadership, realizing that decades of terrorist attacks on Israeli and Western targets had achieved little and had brought international condemnation, in 1988 renounced violence and the long-held goal of the destruction of Israel. The Palestinian National Council, meeting in Algiers, proclaimed the independence of the State of Palestine on 15 November 1988. Dozens of states established diplomatic relations with the Palestinian government, even though its national territory remained under Israeli military occupation.

In 1991, in the wake of the Gulf War, the first face-to-face talks were held between the Palestinians and the Israelis. A series of negotiations finally reached agreement in August 1993 on autonomy for the Gaza Strip and the Jericho District of the West Bank; the Palestinian autonomous authority was intended eventually to extend to the rest of the West Bank. The contentious issue of Jerusalem, claimed as the national capital by both peoples, remained unresolved. In May 1994 Israeli troops withdrew from the new Palestinian Autonomous Area.

Continued talks between the Palestinian Authority, the government of the autonomous area, and the Israeli government resulted in the transfer of additional lands on the West Bank to the Palestinian Authority. Negotiations sponsored by the United States in 1998–99 were unable to overcome the intractable problem of the final status of Jerusalem. Hard-line elements on both sides opposed the concessions needed to reach a final peace agreement.

Yasser Arafat, following inconclusive talks in 1999–2000, planned to declare the independence of the Palestinian state on 13 September 2000 but was persuaded by Arab and Western governments to postpone the proclamation and to continue to negotiate. The disposition of Jerusalem, sacred to Jews, Muslims, and Christians, was the major point blocking a comprehensive peace agreement. The Clinton administration brought the two sides together for a last try at accommodation before the new American president was inaugurated in January 2001, but once again the talks collapsed.

Violence continued as both military and diplomatic efforts to end the conflict continued to fail. Israeli attacks aimed at eliminating the more radical Palestinian leadership led to the assassination of a number of Palestinians. In elections in February 2001, Palestianian Israelis boycotted the vote, with barely 18% of the 500,000 elegible to vote participating, against almost 75% in earlier elections, which aided the election of Ariel Sharon, the hard-line politician whose visit to the Dome of the Rock has ignited the so-called second intifada in early 2000.

On 11 September 2001, terrorists attacked New York and Washington leading to some televised celebrations in Palestine when the news reached the region. The majority of Palestinians abhorred the massacre in the United States and leaders, led by Yasser Arafat, quickly aligned themselves with the growing number of world leaders that condemned the acts. Arafat denounced statements by Osama bin-Laden and other radical Islamists who claimed that the attacks were carried out in the name of the Palestinians.

The response to the terrorist acts included growing pressure by Israel for Arafat to condemn terrorist acts carried out in Israel by groups such as Hamas and Islamic Jihad. Several suicide attacks led to the virtual occupation of a number of Palestinian cities. International efforts to restart the peace process were put aside following a series of deadly suicide attacks in Israel in December 2001. Israeli retaliation, the bombing of police stations, and Palestinian Authority buildings in the Occupied Territories provoked threats of even more attacks by radicals and threatened the authority of Yasser Arafat.

SELECTED BIBLIOGRAPHY:

Aburish, Said K. *Arafat: From Defender to Dictator*. 1998.
McDowall, David. *The Palestinians*. 1998.
Said, Edward W. *The Politics of Dispossession*. 1994.
Smith, Charles D. *Palestine and the Arab-Israeli Conflict*. 1995.

Pattanis

Patanis; Pattani Malays; Patanians

POPULATION: Approximately (2002e) 3,165,000 Pattanis in Southeast Asia, concentrated in the Phatthalung Division of southern Thailand and the adjacent areas of Malaysia. Outside the region there are sizable Pattani populations in other parts of Thailand, in southern Malaysia, and Sumatra. Over 100,000 Pattanis work in Saudi Arabia and the Gulf States, and many students attend universities in the countries of the Arabian Peninsula.

THE PATTANI HOMELAND: The Pattani homeland, called Pattani Raya, occupies a heavily forested region of the central Malay Peninsula stretching from the Thale Luang Lake to the Malaysian border, between the South China Sea and the Andaman Sea. Unlike other areas of Thailand, Pattani is jointly administered by the Department of Interior Affairs and the Department of Defense and Security. Pattani has no official status but is co-terminous with the Phatthalung Division of Thailand, comprising the seven provinces of Patani (called Pattani in the Malay languages), Yala (Jala), Narathiwat (Bangnara), Satun (Setul), Trang, Phatthalung (Patalung), and Songkha (Singora). *Division of Phatthalung (Pattani Raya)*: 11,008 sq. mi.—28,518 sq. km, (2002e) 4,371,000—Pattanis 68%, Thais 26%, Chinese 4%, Sakai, Semang, and others 2%. The Pattani capital and major cultural center is Patani, called Pattani in Malay, (2002e) 44,000. The other important cultural centers are Songkha, Singora in Malay, (2002e) 86,000, and Hat Yai, (2002e) 184,000.

FLAG: The Pattani national flag, the flag of the national movement, is a horizontal bicolor of red over white with a wide vertical green stripe at the hoist bearing a white crescent moon and five-pointed star. The unofficial flag of the Pattani region, Negara Pattani Raya or Greater Pattani State, is a horizontal bicolor of red, white, and green, with a broad black vertical stripe at the hoist bearing the ancient symbol of the Pattani kingdom. The flag of the major nationalist organization, the Pattani United Liberation Organization (PULO), has four horizontal stripes of red and white, with a black canton on the upper hoist charged with a yellow crescent moon and five-pointed star.

PEOPLE AND CULTURE: The Pattanis are a Malay people closely related to those of the lower Malay Peninsula. The Pattani culture has been influenced by long association with the Thais to the north and by early contact with the Chinese. The Pattanis are divided into two groups, the Pattanis and the Melajus (who number about 500,000). Most Pattanis are independent farmers and fishermen, although urbanization is accelerating. Pattani society is organized much like the neighboring Malays of Malaysia, who have a culture based on Islam. Local society remains divided between a ruling class and commoners, beginning with the hereditary Pattani sultan. One of the most contentious issues between the Pattanis and the Thai government is the ban on Muslim women attending schools veiled or wearing the *hijab*, traditional Muslim clothing. There are pockets of Muslims as far north as the Isthmus of Kra.

LANGUAGE AND RELIGION: The Pattani speak a Malay dialect (with a Thai admixture) belonging to the Austronesian language group. In the northern and western districts a minority has adopted the Thai language. The language is written in its own script called Jawi, which is based on archaic Arabic. Although similar to the dialects spoken in the neighboring Malaysian states of Kelantan and Trenganu, the dialect is quite different from standard Malay.

The majority religion is Sunni Islam, which is closely identified with the Pattani culture. Except for a small elite of theologically trained believers, the Islamic faith in Pattani has incorporated many beliefs and practices not integral to Islam. Animistic practices indigenous to traditional Malay culture, including practices used to drive off evil spirits, are part of local Islamic ceremonies. The Pattanis closely adhere to Shari'a, or Islamic law, which is taught in the traditional Muslim schools, called *pondoks*, that flourish throughout the region. There is a small Shi'a minority, the result of early trading and cultural ties to the Middle East.

NATIONAL HISTORY: The ancestors of the Malays probably originated in southern China. Small migrations began to filter down the long Malay Peninsula about 2000 B.C. The migrants settled in the coastal zones, regions of wooded lowlands and swamps. Their colonization gradually pushed the native Negrito peoples into the dense jungles in the center of the peninsula. Around the beginning of the Christian Era, Buddhist and Brahman missionaries spread new religions among the pagan population.

Small Hindu-influenced states developed in the region. One of the small states, Langkasuka, based in the present Kedah region of Malaysia, eventually expanded to control most of the central section of the peninsula. The state grew wealthy on trade; ships arrived in its port towns from as far away as China and the western Indian Ocean. The Hinduized kings of Langkasuka are mentioned in Arab and Chinese records of the sixth through the eighth centuries.

In the second half of the eighth century, the Sailendra rulers of the Sri Vijaya kingdom of Sumatra extended their influence up the peninsula to absorb Langkasuka. Pattani developed as one of the centers of the Sailendra's empire, even rivaling Palembang, the Sailendra capital, in splendor and wealth. Sailendra rule, eclipsed in Java and Sumatra, continued in Pattani, where the Sailendras moved their power base.

Pattani remained a center of Sailendra influence until the Cholas, from southern India, overran the peninsula in the eleventh century. After a half-century of Chola domination, the Sailendras reasserted their power in the region. Pattani regained its importance as a center of Sailendra naval power. Sailendra hegemony continued into the thirteenth century, but eventually it fell to the expanding Sukothai kingdom of the Thais. The Thai king, Rama Kamheng, who began his 40-year rule in 1275, conquered the northern part of the peninsula and brought the various states under nominal Thai domination.

Islam, introduced to the peninsula through the port of Malacca, the Thai's rival power to the south, spread to Pattani in the fifteenth century. The Muslim empire centered on Malacca disputed Thai influence in the northern Malay states, but Malacca's power ended in 1511 with the Portuguese conquest of the capital city. In the north the Thais reasserted their authority over the various small Muslim states. The Islamicized Malay states maintained considerable autonomy, while acknowledging the Thai kings as suzerains.

The first European ships appeared in the port cities in the sixteenth century. The first expeditions, mainly Portuguese traders, spread stories in Europe of the region's wealth and brought back the exotic spices so prized in Europe. English and Dutch expeditions explored the coasts, and from 1612 to 1623 the English maintained a trading "factory" at Pattani. Concentrating their activities to the south, however, the Europeans then abandoned the region for over a century.

The Thais, expanding to the south, invaded the Pattani kingdom in 1786 but were driven back. The Thais returned in 1789, 1791, and 1808, finally conquering the southern districts of the kingdom in 1832. In 1826 the Thais signed a treaty with the British that opened the port cities of the Siamese-controlled Malay states to British trade. Thousands of Pattanis fled to the neighboring Malay states or Sumatra. The Thais divided the kingdom into seven divisions, each under a local sultan. The sultans paid tribute to Bangkok in the form of the flowers of gold every three years.

In 1902, the Thai government proclaimed Pattani legally part of the Thai kingdom. The seven sultanates were reorganized into four provinces governed directly by appointed governors. The Malay language was prohibited, and the Pattanis were forced to adopt Thai customs and dress.

The Siamese Malay states shared in the growing commercial prosperity of the British protected Malay states to the south, but did not attain the commercial importance of the southern states. Growing British influence in Pattani and the other northern states resulted in Siam's 1909 transfer of suzerainty of Kelantan, Perlis, Kedah, and Trengganu to Great Britain. In spite of increasing European pressure the Thais managed to retain control of Pattani, Yala, Satun, and the other northern states.

The anticolonial movement, spreading from the British Malay states, stimulated a parallel movement in the Thai states. In the late nineteenth century the Pattani formed the first nationalist organization of Muslims under Thai rule. The resurgence of the Malay's Muslim religion spurred the movement, the Muslim nationalists being vehemently opposed to rule by Buddhists.

The Thais, nominal allies of the Japanese during World War II, gradually lost control of the region. The Pattanis, led by the prince of Pattani, Tun Mahmud Mahyuddin, took advantage of the chaos to reassert their independence. The prince cooperated with the British authorities in neighboring Malaya, but on 8 December 1941 Japanese troops took control of the Pattani region. The return of the Thai authorities in 1946 marked the beginning of the modern Pattani national movement. The Pattanis were officially renamed Thai Muslims, and a program of assimilation within 25 years was launched.

The Pattani nationalists demanded the self-government extended to the British Malay states in 1948; some Pattanis called for union with the British-sponsored federation. In the fifties, spurred by the independence of Malaya in 1957, the Pattani demanded independence from Thailand, and skirmishes with the Thai military broke out. Communist insurgents operating along the Thai-Malayan border supplied arms and logistical support.

In the 1960s separatist violence and fighting spread, in what was described by radicals as a Muslim holy war. The separatists received support from the several Muslim states, particularly Libya. The United States military provided extensive military aid and technical assistance to the counterinsurgency program of the Thai government. When the Americans withdrew their support of the effort in the mid-1970s, a military stalemate set in. In December 1975, following the murder by Thai soldiers of five Pattanis who had refused to worship an image of the Buddha, thousands of people demonstrated for 44 days demanding punishment of guilty soldiers. The government promised to prosecute, but the matter was later dropped.

The Pattani provinces remained economically neglected well into the 1970s, increasing the resentment of the largely Muslim population. Government efforts to establish firm control of the region stimulated a strong, although unorganized, local resistance. In the late 1970s the Pattani national movement evolved a coordinated resistance. By 1981, the nationalists fielded a formidable force of several thousand fighters. A change in Thai government policy in the mid-1980s brought greater regional autonomy, increased social and economic development, and religious toleration. The insurgency lost popular support; by 1988 only a few hundred rebels were operating in the region.

A new Thai constitution adopted in 1990 for the first time recognized the right of minorities to practice and propagate their languages. It also provided support for the administration of Islamic affairs and the teaching of minority languages. However, new mosques, built with government funds in the major Pattani cities, incorporated the Buddhist lotus symbol into their designs, which outraged the Muslim population.

In the mid-1990s the Pattani nationalist movement, dormant for nearly a decade, again become active, partly in response to renewed Muslim militance and economic grievances. In August 1993 the separatists launched a new campaign to win independence, burning Thai-language schools, ambushing trains, and attacking Thai military targets. A government crackdown led to the arrests of political leaders and teachers accused of supporting the separatists. In August 1995 the Thai government resumed peace talks that had been suspended since 1992.

Violent confrontations increased along the Thai-Malayan border in 1997; many rebels were allowed refuge in the Malaysian state of Kelantan, which is ruled by an Islamic government. In an effort to promote better relations, leading Muslims elected a former parliamentarian, Sawasdi Sumalayasak, to be the advisor to the Thai king on Islamic religious affairs, but the event was overshadowed by a series of bomb attacks across the region.

The majority of the Pattanis resisted the more radical forms of Islamic thought in the 1990s, but a small minority embraced Islamic fundamentalism, demanding the introduction of Shari'a law and the creation of an Islamic state, possibly in conjunction with the neighboring states of Malaysia. Religious tension exacerbated the ethnic and linguistic conflict in the southern Thai provinces. The Thai army launched a large-scale security operation in the Muslim-dominated south, incorporating both the military and police in late 1999. The Thai and Malaysian governments cooperated in a new crackdown, primarily to quell demands for greater local control of recently discovered offshore oil and natural gas fields.

Thai government concessions, including autonomy for the Pattani provinces, and a lack of discrimination in daily life has led to little support for separatism and independence, but a growing radical Islamic influence could change attitudes in the region. A series of bombings across the region in May 2001 were the most serious outbreaks of violence since the 1960s.

The Pattanis, in spite of the rich natural resources of their homeland, are increasingly being marginalized as the region is industrialized; control of industries and resources is being centralized in Bangkok. Moderate nationalist Pattanis continue to demand religious, cultural, and political autonomy in a loose federation with the Thai state. More militant nationalists call for independence, claiming that integration into Thai society is impossible due to the preeminent status of Buddhism there.

SELECTED BIBLIOGRAPHY:

Che Man, Wan Kadir. *Muslim Separatism: The Moros of Southern Philippines and the Malays of Southern Thailand.* 1994.

Fraser, Thomas M. *Fishermen of South Thailand: The Malay Villagers.* 1984.

Smalley, William A. *Linguistic Diversity and National Unity: Language Ecology in Thailand.* 1994.

Syukri, Ibrahim. *History of the Malay Kingdom of Patani.* 1985.

Permyaks

Komi Permyaks; Komi Otir; Komi-Voityr; Permyakis; Kama Permyaks

POPULATION: Approximately (2002e) 158,000 Permyaks in Russia, concentrated in the Komi–Permyak Autonomous Region in northeastern European Russia. Other Permyak populations live outside the autonomous region in Perm Oblast; in other areas of Russia, including Siberia; and in Ukraine and Kazakhstan.

THE PERMYAK HOMELAND: The Permyak homeland occupies part of the forest zone in northeastern European Russia in the oblasts of Perm and Kirov west of the central Ural Mountains. The southern districts of the region are flat steppe lands rising to wooded highlands in the north. Most of the traditional Permyak homeland forms an autonomous district in Perm Oblast. *Komi-Permyak Autonomous Okrug (Komi-Permjacköj Avtononöj Okrug)*: 12,703 sq. mi.—32,901 sq. km, (2002e) 151.000— Komi-Permyaks 74%, Russians 19%, Ukrainians 3%, Komis* 2%, Belarussians 1%, others 1%. The capital and major cultural center of the Permyaks is Kudymkar, (2002e) 34,000.

FLAG: The Permyak national flag, the flag of the national movement, is a horizontal tricolor of white, pale green, and blue, bearing the Permyak national symbol, in red, on the upper hoist. The official flag of the Komi Permyak Autonomous Okrug is a horizontal tricolor of red, white, and blue, bearing the red national symbol centered.

PEOPLE AND CULTURE: The Permyaks, also known as Komi-Permyaks, are part of the Finno-Ugrian Permian peoples, being closely related to the Komis* and Udmurts.* Separated from the Komis about A.D. 500, the Permyaks retained more of the ancient Permian culture than the Komis, who moved north and mixed with other national groups. The Permyaks are divided into two major groups—the Yazvinians or Yazva, living in the Yazva River area of northwestern Perm Oblast; and the Zyuz-

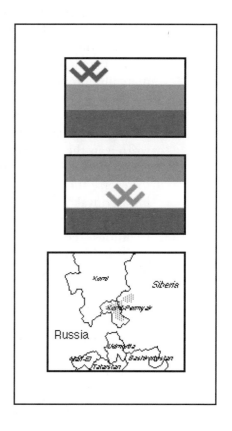

dinians or Kirov Permyaks, living along the Zyuzda River in the Komi Permyak Autonomous Okrug. The alphabet reforms and mass education of the Soviet era generated a literary renaissance, which continues as part of the recent Permyak cultural revival.

LANGUAGE AND RELIGION: The language of the Permyaks, closely related to those of the Komis and Udmurts, forms part of the Permian group of Finno-Ugrian languages. The language is spoken in three major dialects—North Permyak or Kosinsko-Kama, South Permyak or Inyven, and Zyudin. Another dialect, Yazva, intelligible to Permyak speakers, often included as a dialect of Komi, is more accurately a transition dialect between Permyak and Komi. The Permyak language has ancient literary and cultural traditions separate from Komi, but the two languages remained mutually intelligible. In 1923 the language was definitely separated from the closely related Komi by the Soviet authorities, with separate writing systems created for the two languages. The language is now about 80% intelligible to speakers of Komi or Udmurt. The first modern literature written in the language were portions of the Bible in the late nineteenth century. The Permyak reculturation that began in the late 1980s has begun to reverse the process of assimilation, and the number of Permyaks claiming Permyak as their mother language is rising.

The Permyaks are mostly Russian Orthodox, but their religious traditions remain laced with the shamanistic traditions of their pre-Christian heritage. A substantial number of the Permyak Orthodox population are Old Believers, who adopted their religious beliefs from Russian Old Believers who settled in the region to escape persecution by the Orthodox authorities.

NATIONAL HISTORY: The Permian peoples are descended from ancestors who originally inhabited the middle and upper Kama River area. During the first millennium before the Christian era, they split into two major groups, Komis and Udmurts. Around 500 A.D., the Komi group split, with some of the clans migrating from the upper Kama River region to the Vychegda Basin. The clans that remained behind in the Kama River basin became known as Komi Permyaks, or simply Permyaks.

The Permyaks were first mentioned by traders from Novgorod who entered the Ural Mountains to collect furs and taxes in 1187. The Russians of the rival Muscovite duchy began to penetrate the Vychegda River area in 1450. Expanding their influence into the Kama region, the Muscovites introduced their Orthodox religion. In 1463 the first Permyaks were baptized. The Permyak homeland became an outpost for trade with Siberia, and later of the conquest of Siberia. Although more blond and Nordic than the Russians, the Permyaks were subjected to prejudice and a harsh colonial regime.

Russians colonists settled the region from the sixteenth century, establishing a flourishing trade in salt and minerals. Many Permyaks were reduced to serfdom on Russian estates or were forced to labor in the mines, suffering extreme poverty and the loss of their traditional way of life. Conversion to Christiantiy and assimiliation into Russian culture were the official government policies. The northern districts became places of exile for criminals and tsarist political exiles.

The abolition of serfdom in Russia in 1861 led to a massive influx of freed serfs into the region. Land shortages and growing discrimination forced many Permyaks to migrate east into the vast reaches of Siberia. Permyak resentment of the Slav colonists, who appropriated the best lands, led to violent confrontations in the 1870s and 1880s.

Their treatment by the growing Russian population in their territory triggered a national revival. A Permyak cultural movement in the late nineteenth century emphasized their language, particularly the distinguished tradition of oral epics and folk literature. The revival began to reverse centuries of forced assimilation and prompted demands for equality and cultural rights. A parallel movement, heavily influenced by the attitudes and ideals of the large population of political exiles in the region, evolved a Permyak national sentiment, antigovernment and anti-Russian.

The outbreak of World War I reinforced the growing antitsarist movement. Many young Permyaks took refuge in the forests to escape conscription. The overthrow of the tsar in February 1917 raised Komi expectations that the abuses and wrongs of the past would finally be addressed. The Permyaks sent delegates to a Komi congress in the summer on 1917 that voted for autonomy for the Permian peoples in a new democratic Russia and sent a formal petition to the Provisional Government.

The Bolshevik coup in October 1917 swept away the remaining Russian authority in the region. Left virtually independent, the Komi leaders, aided by the numerous freed political prisoners, began to organize the institutions of self-rule, but troops of the new Soviet government overran the region in 1918–19, ending the attempt to set up an autonomous government. The Komi autonomous province was organized in 1921. After several years of discussion on whether to try to include the Permyaks in this administrative unit, the authorities in 1923 finally decided to create a separate Permyak homeland. The autonomous district of the Komi-Permyaks was established in 1925 within Perm Oblast. In 1929 its status was upgraded to that of an autonomous region.

To disseminate information over the large territory populated by the Permian nations, a new alphabet was devised to fit the Permian languages by the Soviet authorities. The alphabet, using mixed Latin and Cyrillic characters, was used in printing after 1920, but in 1938 the authorities eliminated the distinctive alphabet, and the Russian Cyrillic script was substituted. The Russian language became the only language of administration and education.

The Permyaks experienced cultural progress, with schools and books in their own language, but the economy stagnated, and poverty remained widespread. In the 1930s, collectivization and repression led to famine and a sharp decline in the Permyak population. The Permyak homeland gained new importance during World War II as threatened industries and populations shifted east and north from the provinces overrun by the Germans. Many of the factories and elements of the Soviet's wartime infrastructure were constructed by slave labor drawn from the "Gulag," the vast system of labor camps established during the purges of the 1930s.

At the end of World War II many Slavs returned to western Russia, leading to an upsurge in national sentiment. Purges ordered by Joseph Stalin during the late 1940s and early 1950s mostly eliminated the cultural and political leadership of the Permyaks. Ethnic Slavs filled nearly all the positions in the local government and Communist Party hierarchies. In the 1960s, the region became more important economically as the extensive minerals began to be exploited. Assimilation into Russian society accelerated with increasing urbanization and industrialization.

The reforms introduced by Mikhail Gorbachev in the late 1980s had an immediate impact on the region. Decades of Permyak grievances were suddenly talked about, particularly poverty and discrimination. Economic demands gave way to political demands, including calls by some national leaders for the reunification of the Komi and Permyak lands divided between 1925 and 1929. Organized movements to revive the Komi languages, traditions, and religious practices developed in the late Soviet period. The disintegration of the Soviet state in 1991 fueled a dramatic increase in the Permyak national awareness and demands for closer ties to the related Komis and Udmurts.

Several Permyak national organizations, formed mostly since 1991, have increasingly demanded local control of the region's mineral resources and dedication of a larger share of the revenues to local development projects, particularly the lucrative logging operations. Economic demands have grown since the economic collapse of the Russian economy in 1998.

The Permyak rebirth accelerated in the post-Soviet period, into a mass cultural movement. Many Permyaks continued to press for unification with the neighboring Komis, but others demanded the upgrading of the autonomous region to the status of a full republic, which would give the Permyaks greater cultural autonomy and wider official use of the Permyak language.

The Permyaks mostly reject Komi claims that they form a branch of the Komi nation. Permyak leaders have proposed close cultural and political ties to the Komis, but have rejected incorporation into the Komi nation. National sentiment, based on their distinct history, dialects, and geographic location, originally developed only after division by Soviets and began to take on a life of its own in the 1950s. By 2000, the Permyaks had developed a national sentiment as strong as that of the neighboring Komis.

Environmental concerns became the focus of Permyak nationalism in 2001–2, particularly the dangerous conditions of the important mining operations. Pollution from the mines has also drained into drinking water and has ruined pasture and agricultural lands. The Russian government's slow response to demands for compensation and clean-up fueled a drive to win more control over development projects and funds set aside for the rehabilitation of heavily polluted zones.

SELECTED BIBLIOGRAPHY:

Kozlov, Viktor. *The Peoples of the Soviet Union*. 1988.

Olson, James S. *An Ethnohistorical Dictionary of the Russian and Soviet Empires*. 1994.

Warhola, James W. *Politicized Ethnicity in the Russian Federation: Dilemmas of State Formation*. 1996.

Wixman, Ronald. *The Peoples of the USSR: An Ethnographic Handbook*. 1984.

Piedmontese

Piemontesi; Piemonti; Piemontese

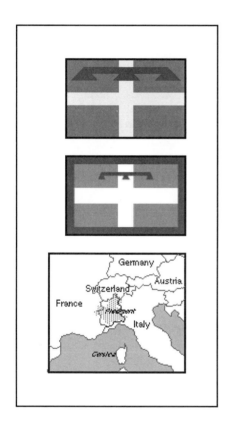

POPULATION: Approximately (2002e) 3,750,000 Piedmontese in Italy, concentrated in the northwestern Piedmont region. Outside the region there are Piedmontese communities in other parts of Italy, particularly in Rome and Milan, and in France, Switzerland, North America, and South America.

THE PIEDMONTESE HOMELAND: The Piedmontese homeland occupies part of the Po Valley, historically called Val Padana, a fertile upland plain drained by the Po River and its tributaries. The region is nearly surrounded by mountains—the Cotian and Maritime Alps on the west, the Graian and Pennine Alps on the north, and the Apennines in the south. In the west, high valleys lead into the Alps along the French border. In the south, Piedmont is separated from the Mediterranean Sea by the homeland of the Ligurians.* Piedmont forms a semi-autonomous region of the Italian Republic; it was established in 1948 and received limited autonomy in 1970. *Region of Piedmont (Regione Piemonte)*: 9,807 sq. mi.—25,399 sq. km, (2002e) 4,274,000—Piedmontese 77%, Occitans* 7%, other Italians and non-Italians 16%. The Piedmontese capital and major cultural center is Turin, called Torino in Piedmontese and Italian, (2002e) 901,000 (metropolitan area 1,724,000), the former capital of the Kingdom of Sardinia and the first capital of united Italy. Other important cultural centers are Alessandria, (2002e) 90,000, urban area 142,000, and Novara, (2002e) 102,000, urban area 151,000.

FLAG: The Piedmontese national flag, the flag of the national movement, is a red field divided by a centered white cross and bearing an inverted blue crown on the top half. The official flag of the region is similar, a white cross on a red field with an inverted blue crown, with a narrow blue stripe all around.

PEOPLE AND CULTURE: The Piedmontese are a Latin nation of mixed Italian, French, and Occitan ancestry. The culture of the Piedmontese is quite different from the standard Italian culture of central and southern Italy, being a basically alpine culture, with considerable French influence. The long, separate history of the Piedmontese sets them apart from other Italians, as do their culture and dialect. The Piedmontese define their distinct identity by their traditional culture, language, and historical values. Nationalists like to quote Marie-Henri Beyle, the nineteenth-century French novelist better known as Stendal, that the distance between the Piedmontese and the Italians is greater than that between the French and English. A revival of the Piedmontese culture, begun as Europe began to integrate, has emphasized the declining alpine culture and the language.

LANGUAGE AND RELIGION: The language spoken in Piedmont, along with standard Italian, is Piedmontese, which is distinct enough from standard Italian to be considered a separate Romance language. Piedmontese belongs to the Western branch of the Gallo-Romance languages. The language, with considerable French and Occitan borrowings, is spoken in two dialects, High Piedmontese and Low Piedmontese, and remains the language of daily life for most of the Piedmontese population. The language, called a Gallo-Italic language, displays a close affinity to French in the pronunciation and truncated word endings. Publishing in the language began between the 1830s and 1860 but declined following Italian unification in 1861. Recent efforts to revive the literary language has prompted new publications, including grammars and dictionaries. In 1990 the majority of the Piedmontese described themselves as bilingual. Only 36% spoke Italian only, but just 17% continued to use Piedmontese as the only language of daily life. The revival of the 1970s and 1980s reinforced the Piedmontese literary tradition and the vibrant middle-class culture of the region.

The majority are Roman Catholics, with a small but influential Protestant minority. Since the 1920s, the Piedmontese have become more secular and less attached to the teachings of the Roman Catholic Church. Dissatisfaction with traditional belief systems has led to the rapid growth of evangelical Protestant sects, particularly among the urban young.

NATIONAL HISTORY: Originally settled by early Celtic peoples, the Piedmont region came under Roman rule between 177 and 121 B.C. Called Pedemontium by the Romans, meaning "at the foot of the mountains," the province formed part of Cisalpine Gaul. The Celtic town of Taurini, later called Turin, became the center of Roman culture in the area. The mountainous regions remained outside Roman control until 25 to 15 B.C., when the Celtic tribes were defeated and the Roman provinces in Italy and Gaul were united. The region formed a prosperous part of the Roman Empire for over five centuries.

In the fifth century, Roman power collapsed, leaving the wealthy region open to invasions by tribes from outside the empire. Huns overran and ravaged the region in A.D. 452, and in the sixth century Germanic Longobards or Lombards* conquered the fertile Po River basin. The Lombards incorporated Piedmont into their kingdom in 568, and modern Piedmont developed from the western districts of Turin and Ivera of the Lombard kingdom in the early Middle Ages.

The Franks absorbed Piedmont into the their growing empire in 774. The Frankish empire of Charlemagne, later the Holy Roman Empire, united much of west-central Europe. In the eleventh century parts of the region passed by marriage to the House of Savoy. Free communes emerged as alternate power centers in the twelfth century, while other districts remained under the rule of feudal lords, the most powerful being the counts (later dukes) of Savoy, and the marquises of Saluzzo and Montferrat.

In the fifteenth century the Savoyards* emerged as the most powerful regional force, their territories straddling the mountains that traditionally divided the Italian and French territories of southern Europe. The multiethnic Savoy duchy, dominated by the French-speaking Savoyards, was occupied by French troops in 1536. Later restored, the duchy moved its capital from Chambéry to Turin, although the language and tone of the court remained French until the eighteenth century, when the Piedmontese identity emerged. The early 1700s were a period of consolidation of the nation and of linguistic and cultural reforms. Piedmontese national awareness was accompanied by the territorial and economic consolidation of the state.

The Po Valley was often a battlefield; the Savoyard state was variously at war or allied to the powerful neighboring French state or the Austrian Hapsburgs. Savoy, under the terms of the Treaty of Utrecht that ended the War of the Spanish Succession in 1713, extended its territory in Italy and won possession of Sicily; the duke was awarded the title of king. In 1720 the Piedmontese acquired the island of Sardinia in exchange for Sicily and renamed the state; the monarch took the title of King of Sardinia.

During the French Revolutionary Wars, the kingdom fell to Napoleon in 1797 and was annexed to France. At the Congress of Vienna, at the end of the Napoleonic Wars in 1815, the Sardinian kingdom was reestablished and the kingdom acquired additional territories in 1848, including the remaining Piedmontese territories and Liguria on the Mediterranean, the former Genoese maritime republic.

The Sardinian kingdom became a center of the Risorgimento in the 1850s, the movement to unite the numerous Italian states under the rule of the House of Savoy. The Piedmontese led attempts at Italian unity in 1848 and 1859. Napoleon III, for his help in uniting Italy, demanded the cession of the culturally French western regions of the kingdom—Savoy, Nice, and Menton; they were ceded to France in 1860. Turin was named the capital of the newly united Italian kingdom in 1861, when Victor Emmanuel II, formerly king of Piedmont and Sardinia, became the first ruler of united Italy.

A Tuscan dialect spoken around Florence was finally adopted as the new national language, over unwavering Piedmontese opposition. The Tuscan dialect, spoken by less than 10% and written by only 1% of Italy's population, was considered more representative of the majority of the spoken dialects in both northern and southern Italy than the distinct Piedmontese language.

The new Italian kingdom finally wrested Rome and the central provinces from papal rule in 1870, and the authorities transferred the capital of the kingdom to that more central city. The Italian government's move to Rome dealt a severe blow to Piedmontese pride that is still an issue in the region. The loss of prestige and power undermined Piedmontese enthusiasm for Italian unification. A movement formed in the 1870s to protect the Piedmontese dialect from Italianization incited a literary revival and over the next decades spurred a cultural revival. The Piedmontese revival coincided with the development of a large industrial middle class that further divided the region from agrarian central and southern Italy.

The Piedmontese were influential in drawing Italy into the First World War in 1915, partly to aid their traditional ally, France. Fascism gained strength in Italy after World War I, but its base lay in Rome and the poor, backward south. Nationalists and communists gained support in industrial Piedmont; the rival ideologies led to frequent violent clashes, particularly in industrial Turin.

The Fascist Italian government, allied to the Axis powers in the late 1930s, won enthusiastic Piedmontese backing with promises to recover the territories lost to France in 1860. The enthusiasm declined rapidly after fighting broke out on the nearby French border in June 1940. The Italian government surrendered to the Allies in 1943, and the Germans quickly occupied the northern Italian regions, treating their former allies as a conquered people. Liberated from German rule in 1945, the Piedmontese began agitation for autonomy; the movement gain support following a 1946 Italian referendum that eliminated the beloved monarchy, the House of Savoy, that had ruled Piedmont for over 900 years. In 1948 a separate Piedmont region was created, but with limited powers; all important decisions remained with the bureaucrats in Rome.

Piedmont's industries boomed in the 1950s and 1960s, attracting hundreds of thousands of workers from Italy's underdeveloped southern regions. Forced to communicate, the workers and their Piedmontese supervisors replaced their mutually incomprehensible dialects with standard Italian in the workplace. In 1950 approximately 60% of the Piedmontese spoke only the Piedmontese dialect; the percentage dropped rapidly with the influx of southerners and the spread of mass media over the next two decades. Fearing unrest in the northern regions that were leading Italy's postwar economic recovery, the government promised self-rule, but after numerous delays finally granted only semi-autonomous status in 1970.

The so-called Italian economic miracle, confined to the northern regions, raised the Piedmontese levels of industrial production and incomes to the level of neighboring European regions but greatly increased Piedmontese frustration with the cumbersome and inefficient Italian state. Resentment that their taxes were being squandered on the corrupt and backward south became more acute with the increasing integration of the northern regions into mainstream Europe in the 1970s. The Europeanization of Piedmont fueled a strong desire to participate in the continental federation, the European Union, without the encumbrance of the Italian bureaucracy or the poor, crime-ridden southern regions of the republic. A Piedmontese nationalist movement emerged in the 1980s, closely allied to other such movements evolving across the prosperous northern regions, particularly in neighboring Lombardy. By 1992 an alliance of northern Italian nationalist, autonomist, and separatist groups, the Northern League, had become a major political force.

The construction of an all-weather road between Piedmont and France, which passes through a 7.3-mile (11.7 km) tunnel under Mont Blanc, has facilitated the growing relationship between the Piedmontese and the neighboring Occitans of southern France. Proposals for the creation of a Euro-region, which would include Piedmont and the French departments to the west, is based on the regions' long historical, and growing economic, unity.

The northern Italian regions in the 1990s increasingly demanded greater economic and cultural autonomy. The frustration with the creaking Italian state manifested itself in growing support for a separate federation of independent states in northern Italy, which nationalists call Padania.

The pro-European sentiment stimulated the growing national movement, which led the Piedmontese reculturation. In 1995–96, Piedmontese cultural associations began organizing free language courses in an effort to stem the decline of the language. After decades of forced conformity to an Italian stereotype that began under the Fascist government in the 1920s and 1930s and continued into the 1980s, the Piedmontese now see themselves as the nation that had the strength to unite Italy in the nineteenth century and now has the strength to participate in the unification of Europe as a distinct European nation. In the late 1990s, environmentalists influenced the national movement with growing demands for the Italian government to address the serious and growing rate of genital cancer and tumors caused by chemical pollutants in the water supply. Rome's slow response to such concerns is one of the causes of the widespread support that the nationalists enjoy.

SELECTED BIBLIOGRAPHY:

Cardoza, Anthony L. *Aristocrats in Bourgeois Italy: The Piedmontese Nobility, 1861–1930*. 1997.

Carello, Adrian N. *The Northern Question: Italy's Participation in the European Economic Community and the Mezzogiorno's Underdevelopment*. 1989.

Hine, David. *Governing Italy: The Politics of Bargained Pluralism*. 1992.

Levy, Carl, ed. *Italian Regionalism: History, Identity and Politics*. 1996.

Pomaks

Pomatsi; Bulgarian Muslims (Bulgaromohamedani); Rhodopes (Rhodopa); Achrjanis

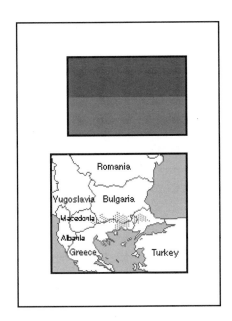

POPULATION: Approximately (2002e) 385,000 Pomaks in southeastern Europe, concentrated in the Rhodope Mountains in southern Bulgaria, with 285,000, and northern Greece, with about 50,000. There are smaller communities in eastern Macedonia, Romania, Turkey, and Albania. The Pomak population is not usually included in census and estimates of the total population vary from 150,000 to over a million in the Balkans, including about 300,000 in European Turkey.

THE POMAK HOMELAND: The Pomak homeland lies in the southern Balkan Peninsula, in the region traditionally called Western Thrace. The area, lying mostly in the Rhodope Mountains, slopes down to a narrow coastal plain on the Thracian Sea west of the Turkish border with Greece. In Bulgaria the Rila-Rhodope Massif rises from the Thracian Plain to the north. The homeland has no official status in Bulgaria or Greece. The Pomak capital and major cultural center is Razlog in southwestern Bulgaria, (2002e) 22,000. Other important cultural centers are Smolyan, called Smiljan by the Pomaks, in Bulgaria, (2002e) 32,000, and Ekhinos, in Greece, (2002e) 11,000.

FLAG: The Pomak national flag, the traditional flag of the region, is a horizontal bicolor of dark blue over red.

PEOPLE AND CULTURE: Some argue that the name "Pomak" comes from the Turkish word *pomagach*, "helper," recalling the fact that the Pomaks once guarded caravans passing through the Rhodope Mountains. Others claim the name loosely translates as "collaborators" or comes from *pomachen*, meaning "forced," referring to their forced conversion to Islam. Traditionally the Pomaks are farmers or mountain herders. The Pomak culture evolved in the isolation of the rugged mountains, retaining customs and a dialect that disappeared elsewhere. They are often treated as second-class citizens, and in both Greece and Bulgaria the "Pomak" is used as an insult. The Pomaks never emigrated in large numbers and do not consider emigration a viable option now. They are officially called Bulgarian Muslims in Bulgaria and Muslim Greeks in Greece. In both Bulgaria and Greece the denial of the Pomak identity has made it difficult to express their identity freely and to maintain their culture. Prejudice and coarse jokes about the Pomaks and prejudices are common in Bulgarian society, and many Pomaks feeling forced to hide their origin. The Pomaks of Greece have never been seen by Bulgarians as kinsmen living outside the fatherland. Ethnic marginality is the essence of Pomak national identity.

LANGUAGE AND RELIGION: The Pomaks speak an archaic dialect of Bulgarian, a language of the Bulgaro-Macedonian group of South Slav language. The language, called Rhodope, Pomakika, or Pomakci, is spoken in several dialects corresponding to the isolated geography of the Rhodope Mountains. The dialect contains many words that have disappeared from standard Bulgarian; it is a mixture of Slavic, Kuman Turkish, and Orguz Turkish. Some of the words still in use derived from the dead Thraco-Illyrian language. The dialect is close to both Bulgarian and Macedonian, with geographical shadings toward each. Some Pomaks speak Turkish as a second language and as the language of Muslim religious life. The first Greek-Pomak dictionary was published in Athens in 1996, causing protests by the Bulgarian government to the Greek government.

The Pomaks are mostly Sunni Muslims of the Hanafite rite, although after decades of official atheism in Bulgaria and oppression in Greece, a number have become atheists or have converted back to Orthodox Christianity. Those that did were still not accepted by the Bulgarians and remained culturally Pomak. Many of the Pomak leaders are atheistic or secular intellectuals who emphasize their Muslim religion as merely part of their culture. The Muslim saints are practically unknown, while the feast days of various Christian saints are observed. Weddings and other ceremonial occasions often combine Muslim and Christian traditions.

NATIONAL HISTORY: The Pomaks are thought to be descended from ancient Thracians who were Hellenized during the expansion of Greek culture in the eastern Mediterranean. Theories abound as to their origins, but most scholars believe their ancestors were the indigenous peoples of the region who settled Thrace during the second millennium B.C. The coast was colonized by Greeks in the seventh century B.C. The Thracian tribes were gradually absorbed or driven into the less accessible mountains by invaders in the lowlands. In isolation they developed a distinct alpine culture and in the early Middle Ages adopted the Bulgarian language.

The Ottoman Turks first came to the Balkans as mercenaries of the Byzantines in the 1340s. A decade later they returned as conquerors. Between 1359 and 1362 the Turks conquered much of Thrace from the Byzantines and captured Adrianople, the major Byzantine city of the region. Most of the Christian population of the Balkans remained Christian, but the inhabitants of the Rhodope Mountains were converted to Islam, mostly between the sixteenth and eighteenth centuries. One explanation as to why the Bulgarians of the Rhodope region were singled out for forced conversion concerns the Turkish sultan, who used the area as a huge hunting reserve: he, his family, and his retainers needed to be served during their stays, but they could be served only by Muslims. Most Pomaks were forcibly converted, but others accepted Islam to escape poverty, taxes, and discrimination. The Muslim Pomaks enjoyed privileged status, since non-Muslims were officially denied Ottoman citizenship.

The Pomaks in the Rhodope Mountains, isolated from the plains below, did not mix with the Turks during the long Turkish occupation of Thrace. They retained much of their former culture, in addition to their Slavic physical features. Because the Turks showed little interest in the Pomak lands, and because the Pomaks were converted relatively late, their customs and alpine culture remained intact and they continued to speak their Bulgarian dialect.

The Pomaks helped Turkish troops to crush a Christian Bulgarian uprising in 1876, and they opposed the subsequent Treaty of San Stefano, which led to the creation of Great Bulgaria. They revolted and set up an autonomous administration that survived for many years in over 20 localities in the Rhodope Mountains. The Ottoman Turks created the autonomous province of Eastern Rumelia in northern Thrace in 1878. The region was annexed to the Bulgarian kingdom in 1885. Southern Thrace remained under Turkish rule until the First Balkan War in 1912–13 and the region's cession to Bulgaria. On 8 July 1913, Pomak leaders proclaimed the short-lived Republic of Gumuldjina in Thrace following the withdrawal of Bulgarian and Turkish troops.

The large number of Muslims incorporated into Bulgaria presented a problem for the Bulgarian government. The Turks and other Muslims were ignored, but the Pomaks, speaking a dialect of Bulgarian, were subjected to a campaign of conversion to Orthodox Christianity, because of the close relation between religion, language, and ethnicity in the Bulgarian kingdom. The formation of the Pomaks as a separate national group corresponded to the acute incompatibility to their faith with the Bulgarian nationality of their new masters, and of their language with Turkish of their former masters.

Boundaries in the region were again rearranged after the Second Balkan War in 1913 and World War I. Greece received Western Thrace in 1919, while Eastern Thrace was returned to Turkish rule in 1923. Massacres, forced and voluntary migrations, and forced conversions accompanied the boundary and population changes. Under the terms of the 1923 Treaty of Lausanne, the Greek government recognized only a Muslim minority, not ethnic minorities. Under the terms of the treaty, Muslims were allowed to stay in Greek Thrace, and Greeks remained in Istanbul.

Bulgarian Pomaks forced to convert to Christianity continued to suffer discrimination on the basis of their culture and origin. The government of independent Bulgaria in the early twentieth century sought to weaken the Pomaks' distinctive identity, a campaign that intensified during the nationalistic fascism of the 1930s. The imposition of a communist government in Bulgaria in 1946 brought new tension to the border region and its many Pomak inhabitants. Whole villages near the border with Greece, over 15,000 people, were forcibly displaced from their homes between 1948 and 1951. Others were displaced because they were considered hostile to the "people's authorities." Most were jailed or imprisoned in camps. By 1955 the policy was deemed a failure, and many returned to their border villages.

The Greeks instituted a system of restrictions on the border region. In 1951, the Greek government introduced Turkish-language education for Pomaks in an effort to distance them from Bulgarians. Under the Greek military dictatorship of 1967–74, the situation of the Pomaks worsened. Financial inducements were offered to Christian groups to move into Western Thrace to dilute the Muslim population of the region.

The Bulgarian communist government had by the mid-1960s failed to deliver on promises of prosperity. It had to find an alternative way to legitimize continued communist rule, and it chose nationalism. A campaign to assimilate the minorities was pushed to extremes. In 1972–73 the authorities forced all Pomaks to "Bulgarianize" their family and given names. Over 500 Pomaks were arrested and imprisoned in order to break Pomak resistance to these measures. Muslim traditions were also banned, including circumcision, funeral and wedding rituals, and Muslim holidays. The Pomak dilemma was whether to attempt to assimilate into Bulgarian society or lose their identity in a greater Muslim but Turkish-dominated minority.

The growth of nationalism was hindered by the divisions within the Pomak nation. Some favored Bulgarian identity and others identified with the Muslim Rumelian Turks,* though a majority increasingly demanding recognition of their own ethnic identity. To the Bulgarians the Pomaks are Bulgarians, particularly when their votes are needed in elections, but they are generally ignored. The Turks also claim the Pomaks, again especially before elections. The majority now support their own national identity, as neither Bulgarians nor Turks.

In the waning years of the Bulgarian communist government, the dictator Todor Zhivkov played his "Turkish card." The Bulgarian government embraced Bulgarian nationalism and again launched a campaign to assimilate the Muslim minorities, including the Pomaks, in 1984–89. The brutal campaign of forced name changes, religious restrictions, and repression drove over 300,000 people, Pomaks, Turks, and Roms,* across the border into Turkish territory by mid-1989. Some Pomaks were subjected to a second name change if the names they received in the early

1970s were not considered definitely Bulgarian. Unrest flared when Pomaks from the Gotse Delchev region were refused passports that would have enabled them to emigrate. Local officials banned public gatherings of more than three Pomaks and forbade residents to leave their villages.

The exodus provoked the political changes that began in the country in November 1989. Zhivkov resigned and was replaced by younger, reform leaders. The collapse of communism allowed the Pomaks to regain their national identity in Bulgaria. As it became evident to the new Bulgarian government that the Pomaks were far from eradicated, they were again viewed as a problem. Pomak nationalism spread with the democratization of Bulgaria, and demands for cultural, religious, and economic autonomy arose. The movement split the Pomaks into pro-assimilation groups and elements seeking self-rule and recognition as a separate national group in both Bulgaria and Greece.

The Greek government pursued an active policy of "ethnic homogenization" that weakened the national identity of the Pomaks in the 1970s and early 1980s. As part of this program, Pomaks were forced to adopt Christian names, and their Bulgarian dialect was banned. Greece's entry into the European Economic Community (EEC) in 1981 required Greek adoption of minority-protection policies; despite the EEC rulings, little changed for the Pomaks in Greece. In 1995, restrictions on entry into zones along the Bulgarian border, areas populated by Pomaks, were abolished for all Greek citizens.

The rate of employment of Pomaks in the public sector and in state-owned industries and corporations is much lower than the claimed percentage of the total regional population. They did not urbanize but stayed in their mountain villages during the communist era, which crippled their ability to compete for government positions. Small factories in the Rhodope villages and the introduction of tobacco increased the prosperity of the Pomaks but also drew in a sizable non-Pomak population.

The Bulgarian census of 1992 gave no specific Pomak identity; the Pomaks had to identity themselves as Bulgarians or Turks. The Pomak national group in Bulgaria was then officially split between Bulgarian and Turkish, but at the same time a Pomak political movement was gaining support with demands for recognition of the Pomaks as a national group in Bulgaria.

In June 1994, Pomak children aged eight through 14 were forced by local Bulgarian authorities to give blood samples, which were tested for DNA clues to the Pomak ethnic origins. Fingerprints were also studied and heads measured in an experiment carried out in the middle Rhodopes. The results confirmed, according to the Bulgarian government, the Pomaks' Indo-European origins and Slavic physical background. In elections that year, the Pomak political party, the Democratic Party of Labor, in spite of Bulgarian government claims that they were ethnic Bulgarians, won over 100,000 Pomak votes with its demand for recognition as a separate ethnic group.

The Bulgarian prime minister, Kvan Kostov, declared in December 1998 that there was no Pomak nation. His statement was published just before Pomak nationalists demonstrated for the removal of a long fence along the Bulgarian-Greek border and for permission to meet with relatives and pasture cattle on traditional pasture lands on both sides of the boundary.

The Greek government did not keep up with the changes that swept through the Balkans in the wake of the democratic revolution in the early 1990s. The demise of the totalitarian regime in Bulgaria led to the radical improvement in the treatment of the northern Pomaks, but those in Greece continued to suffer discrimination and neglect. In the late 1990s, Greece's treatment of its national minorities was severely criticized by various human-rights organizations and the European Union (EU). In 1999 the Greek and Bulgarian governments agreed to open mountain passes, improve roads, and cooperate on economic themes in the region. The project included free-entry zones on both sides of the international border.

In July 1997 President Petur Stoyanov of Bulgaria apologized to the Pomaks and other Muslim groups for the communist-era "Regeneration Process" under which Pomak names were forcibly changed to traditional Slavic names. Even though restrictions have been lifted and tolerance is the official government policy, Orthodox Christianity constitutes one of the cornerstones of Bulgarian nationality. Separation of the religious-cultural groups, a legacy of the millet system of the Ottoman Empire, continues to be the norm in the Balkans.

The Bulgarian government ratified a General Convention of Minority Rights in March 1999. The convention recognizes the existence of national minorities. The document is the first accepted by Bulgaria to use the word "minority," and it states that the country is engaged in implementation of a policy of protection of human rights and tolerance toward members of national minorities. The convention was drafted with consultations with the Turkish, Pomak, and Rom minorities and was welcomed by the leaders of the three groups.

The Bulgarians, Greeks, and Turks all claim the Pomaks as a component of their respective nations or simply want to assimilate them. Each provides a different "national history" that highlights the Pomaks' ties to their nation. Over many decades the Pomaks have been divided in their loyalties, and they remained divided in the late twentieth century, but since the early 1990s a separate ethnic identity has spread through the Rhodope region that may finally end the long controversy.

At the conference on "Borders and Minorities in Balkans," held on 6 October 2001 in Thessaloniki, under the auspices of the Greek newspaper "Makedonia," several important recommendations were adopted, which were presented to the governments of the Balkan region. Participants attending the conference agreed to appeal to the governments in the region to take the necessary measures to facilitate the free flow of information, ideas and people across national borders within the Balkan region. The recommendations, enthusiastically endorsed by the Pomaks, led to new demands that the Greek government recognize the Pomaks as a distinct Balkan national group.

SELECTED BIBLIOGRAPHY:

Asenov, Boncho. *Nation, Religion, Nationalism.* 1994.
Ilieva, Irena. *Balkan Minorities.* 1994.
Kalionski, A. *The Pomak Dilemma.* 1993.
Poulton, Hugh, and Suha Taji-Forouki, eds. *Muslim Identity and the Balkan State.* 1997.

Pueblo

Tema; Toma; Tima; Zuni; Hopi

POPULATION: Approximately (2002e) 102,000 Pueblo in the United States, concentrated in the states of New Mexico and Arizona in the southwestern United States. Smaller Pueblo communities live in Colorado, Utah, and Texas. The closely related Hopi number about 17,000 and the Zuni about 15,000. The Pueblo, Hopi, and Zuni are historically, culturally, and linguistically one nation. Some activists claim a national population of up to 200,000 including those that are not officially registered with local tribal governments.

THE PUEBLO HOMELAND: The Pueblo homeland lies in the southwestern United States, in the states of New Mexico and Arizona. Most of the region is arid or semi-arid, except in the foothills and in the basin of the Rio Grande River, which flows through the homeland. The territory remaining to the Pueblo is made up of 21 separate entities, mostly along the Rio Grande, but with the Zuni on the New Mexico-Arizona border and the Hopi in northeastern Arizona. The important cultural centers are the cities and towns

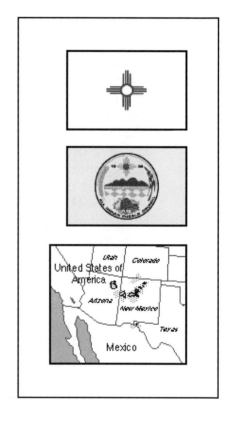

adjacent to or surrounded by Pueblo lands, Albuquerque, Santa Fe, Taos, Bernadillo, and Española in New Mexico. The Hopi capital and major cultural center is Kykotsmove, the seat of the Hopi Tribal Government.

FLAG: The sun flag of the Zia Pueblo, a red stylized sun with 16 rays on a white field, is widely recognized due to the use of the Zia symbol on the official flag of the state of New Mexico. The flag of the All Pueblo Indian Council has the same symbol at the top over a scene of mountains, desert, and agriculture in various colors on a white field.

PEOPLE AND CULTURE: Pueblo is the name given a number of related tribal groups that used similar architecture to build their towns, pueblos in Spanish. The Pueblo include the Keres nation, with its subdivisions

1523

Acoma, Cochiti, Laguna, Santo Domingo, San Felipe, Santa Ana, and Zia. The Tewa include the Nambe, Pojoaque, San Ildefonso, San Juan, Santa Clara, Tesuque, and the Hopi Tewa. The Tiwa include the Isleta, Picuris, Sandia, Taos, and the Tiguas of Texas. The Towa have just one division, the Jemez. The Zuni also no subdivisions. Traditionally Pueblo society was constructed around the cultivation of corn. The Pueblo are a matrilineal society, with descent and inheritance through the female line. Women have traditionally played an important role in Pueblo society. The Pueblo are divided into two major divisions, eastern and western, also called summer and winter or the corn and turquoise division. The eastern division is in New Mexico, made up of the various Pueblo groups, the western division is comprised of the Hopi, Zuni, Acoma, and Laguna and two dozen smaller bands. High unemployment and a lack of opportunities continue to plague the Pueblo. The average annual income is considerably less than the national average.

LANGUAGE AND RELIGION: The Pueblo speak six different languages of two language families. Languages of the Tanoan branch of the Aztec-Tanoan languages are spoken at 11 pueblos. Languages of the Keresan branch of the Hokan-Siouan group are spoken by all the Hopi groups except the Hano, who speak a Tanoan language. The Zuni language may be related to Tanoan, falling within the Aztec-Tanoan group. Only a small minority are not bilingual in English, which is language of education, administration, and inter-group communications.

The Pueblo build large underground chambers called kiva for secret ceremonies. The kiva is rectangular or circular with a fire pit in the center and usually a timbered roof. An opening in the floor represents the entrance to the lower world and the place through which life emerged into this world. The indigenous religion, called the Kachina religion, remains strong in the pueblos of the Hopi and Zuni, but fades eastward in the Pueblo heartland in New Mexico. The Pueblo remain deeply religious with ceremonies that coincide with the agricultural seasons. Even though they have been officially Christianized for several centuries, they have retained many of their ancient beliefs. Prayers and thanks are offered for crops, rain, and other blessings. Spirits, known as kachinas, are revered as the bringers of good fortune.

NATIONAL HISTORY: The Pueblo homeland has been inhabited for thousands of years. The first petroglyphs were carved into the faces of cliffs over 3,000 years ago. Over a thousand years ago the Four Corners, the meeting point on the Colorado Plateau of the states of New Mexico, Arizona, Utah, and Colorado, was inhabited by the Hisatsinom "The Ones who Came Before," the ancestors of the modern Pueblo, Zuni, and Hopi. The Hisatsinom are more popularly known by their Navajo name, Anasazi. The Hisatsinom culture was the oldest and most advanced north of Mexico. The transition from hunting and gathering to a settled agricultural culture is thought to have taken place around the first century A.D.

The Hisatsinom were sedentary farmers, while traditionally the men were weavers and the women were potters. Pottery manufacture began around the year 400. The area is littered with the ruins left behind by this advanced society, including the impressive Chaco Canyon. Oraibi, established around 1100 A.D. and though to be of Hisatsinom origin, is the oldest continuous settlement in North America. Originally the Hisatsinom are thought to have lived in small, scattered villages. By the early 1100s, they had left these small villages to live in larger, more compact towns.

The cause of the collapse of the Hisatsinom empire has long been one of the most perplexing mysteries of Southwestern archeology. Careful study of tree-ring records established that in the late 1200s a prolonged drought interrupted agriculture in the area. Many scholars believe that it was not severe enough to drive the Hisatsinom to abandon their magnificent stone villages on the Colorado Plateau and move to the Hopi Mesa in present northeastern Arizona, then to the Zuni lands on the present New Mexico-Arizona border, and to build dozens of new adobe villages in the basin of the Rio Grande River. Recent studies show that the evacuation began before the long dry spell set in. Some researchers believe that internecine warfare, drought, and a religious crisis all conspired to end the Hisatsinom civilization.

In their new territories, the Pueblo groups built small towns known for the stone or adobe apartment-like structures of homes built on terraced roofs. The roof of one home is reached from the level below by a movable ladder. Traditionally the dwellings did not have windows or doors on the lower floors, with access through trapdoors in the roof. This was a protection against enemies. Each town was self-governing. Several of the surviving pueblos have retained pre-European social systems and community organizations to a degree.

Pueblo life was build upon a foundation of work, together with religious observances and practices. Based on their Hisatsinom tradition, the Pueblo tribes further developed farming, pottery, textiles, and a complex mythology and religion. The highly developed agricultural economy was the labor of all inhabitants of the towns as the Pueblo did not practice slavery or anything like the feudal labor practices of Europe. Each Pueblo family had its own land, to be cultivated with the aid of clan and tribal groups. Whole towns banded together in hunting, food gathering, farming, irrigation, and the care of children and the land.

The Spanish of Mexico, dazzled by tales of the fabled Seven Cities of Cibola, sent a large expedition to the north led by Francisco Vásquez de Coronado. When the Spanish entered the region from the south in the 1539 there were well over 80 independent Pueblo nations living along the Rio Grande River. The seven cities of Cibola, believed to be rich in gold, were at first mistaken for the high-rise Pueblo towns. Finding neither splendor nor riches in the towns, in the 1540s Coronado, believing that the indigenous peoples were hiding their riches, attacked the Zuni pueblos, upsetting what were initially friendly relations between Spanish and the inhabitants of the seven Zuni pueblos.

Each of the tribes had a well-organized system of administration with an efficient system of law and order that protected Pueblo society as well as the rights of the individual. The towns were called pueblos by the Spanish were because they resembled Spanish towns. Gradually the name Pueblo was applied to all the related tribes who inhabited the multi-story dwellings in the stone and adobe towns.

The Spanish, called Castillas by the Pueblo, began to impose European-style administrative systems and attempted to outlaw the traditional religious practices. A Pueblo governor was put in place to be democratically elected and to serve for the period of a year. In 1620 the Spanish governor presented the Pueblo with the Cane of Authority, which acknowledged Pueblo sovereignty. The Spanish also began to centralize the Pueblo groups, so that in the years following the Spanish invasion the number of pueblos fell from eighty to about twenty-five. Pueblo men were forced to work for the Spanish and to give them some of their crops. Many Pueblo were taken for sale as slaves in Mexico. The Spanish introduced the horse, goat, cow, and sheep. From then on wool replaced cotton as the main textile. By about 1630 the Spanish had established missions in nearly every pueblo and officially 60,000 Pueblo had been converted to Christianity.

Spanish colonization increased pressure on the existing food supplies. Demands for food from the Pueblo supplies strained relations. Tensions between the Spanish and the initially friendly Pueblo groups grew as colonists moved north. From 1667 to 1671, epidemics, Apache raids, and a five-year drought ravaged the region. In 1675, Spanish soldiers confiscated Pueblo religious items, burned kivas, and hanged three Pueblo religious leaders. Another 43 leaders were publicly flogged in the plaza of Santa Fe for practicing witchcraft. Pueblo warriors surrounded the plaza and demanded the release of their leaders. The Pueblo prevailed, but relations with the Spanish worsened.

In 1680, the Pueblo, led by Po'pay, one of those whipped in Santa Fe, rose and drove the Spanish from their territory, killing 380 settlers, including 31 priests. The remaining Spanish fled south to El Paso. The Pueblo religious practices, outlawed by the Spanish, were resumed. Traditional culture, although now incorporating many Spanish traits, flourished. The Pueblo, never unified before the 1680 revolt, found they had in common their hatred of the Spanish system and the suppression of their religious practices. United by Po'pay the Pueblo groups found strength and purpose that remains to the present.

Twelve years later the Spanish returned, and after much bloodshed, reconquered the Pueblo homeland although some in the west, including the Hopi, remained independent. Tanoan-speaking Pueblo moved southward into present Texas between 1670 and 1675 as a result of devastating attacks by Apache. A second movement to the south took place after the Pueblo revolt of 1680 and again during the reconquest in 1692. The expansion of Spanish controlled-territory eventually brought all the Pueblo groups under Spanish administration. In negotiations for surrender, the Pueblo leaders demanded an end to forced labor and to interference in their internal affairs, particularly their religion. The Pueblo again rebelled in 1696, killing the priests who had returned to work for their conversion to Christianity. They were again defeated and settled into a tranquil existence, mostly ignored by the Spanish authorities and populations in the cities of Santa Fe and Albuquerque that had been built on Pueblo lands.

The Europeans who settled the region adopted the adobe structures and compact village plans of the Pueblo. The Pueblo, for their part, adopted many domestic animals and assorted European crafts such as blacksmithing and woodworking.

Mexico declared its independence from Spain in 1821. The new Mexican government reiterated its claim to all Spanish territory in North America. Like the Spanish, the new Mexican government presented the Pueblo with the Cane of Authority, acknowledging their historical sovereignty. The Mexicans, like the Spanish, generally left the Pueblo groups to govern themselves in return for taxes, paid in crops, labor, or crafts.

The United States gained the territory from Mexico as a result of the Mexican War of 1846–48. During the war the Pueblo mostly supported the Americans. By signing the Treaty of Guadalupe Hidalgo of 1848, the United States agreed to uphold the Pueblo land titles, which had been recognized by both the Spanish and Mexican governments. In 1863, like the Spanish and Mexican authorities, representatives of the United States government officially presented the Pueblo with the Cane of Authority.

The Pueblo population remained practically stationary from the mid-nineteenth century. The population of 8,400 in 1887, had grown very little by 1900. Improvements in health care and education, begun in the first years of the twentieth century, gradually led to an increase in population.

The native peoples of New Mexico and Arizona were granted United States citizenship in 1924, but were denied the vote. Miguel Trujillo, an Isleta Pueblo, sued the government with the argument that he was a tax-paying citizen. He finally won the vote for those in New Mexico in 1948.

During World War II, members of the New Mexico National Guard, federalized in January 1941, were sent to the Philippines just three months before the attack on Pearl Harbor. They courageously held out for four months against the Japanese invasion of the Philippines, using the language of the Pueblo soldiers for communication. The Pueblo soldiers were the first Code Talkers of World War II. Only a few of the Pueblo soldiers, most from Taos, survived. Some were subjected to Japanese medical experiments to prove they were of Mongolian ancestry. Although the soldiers bravely served their country, they were not able to vote until three years after the war ended.

In 1965, the All Indian Pueblo Council (AIPC), representing the 19 pueblos in New Mexico, adopted a constitution. The AIPC sought to promote justice, encourage a common welfare, foster social and economic of all the Pueblo, to preserve and protect their common interest. The AIPC provides essential services that would otherwise be inaccessible to the Pueblo, including health services, education, job training, economic development, environmental protection, and child welfare.

The Red Power movement of the 1960s translated into a more militant stance in the 1970s and 1980s. In 1970, the Taos Pueblo won title to Blue Lake, a lake sacred to the people of the region. The government had made it part of a national forest, excluding Pueblo rights. Militancy increased among the Pueblo, although the movement never developed a radical fringe as did parallel movements of other native American peoples.

Sovereignty, although some link it with the sovereignty of the United States, actually predates that of the United States. Organized tribes existed in the area before the European incursions. The significance of Pueblo self-government was acknowledged from the onset of European contact. The evidence of their sovereign powers, the Canes of Authority, were presented to the Pueblo by the governments of Spain in 1620, Mexico in 1821, and the United States in 1863. The state of New Mexico, where the majority of the Pueblo live, presented the state Cane of Authority in 1980. The Lincoln Cane, presented in 1863, symbolizes the perpetual acknowledgment and commitment of the United States to honor Pueblo sovereignty.

The modern Pueblo continue to live a life of economic struggle, characterized by unemployment, low incomes, poor health, and inadequate education. A resurgence of cultural identity since the 1980s had led to a backlash against American-European culture. A resurgence of Pueblo culture, particularly religion, in the 1980s and 1990s strengthened their demands for greater autonomy and the recognition of their historical sovereignty.

During 1998, celebrations were held throughout the region to mark the 400th anniversary of the first Spanish settlement. The celebrations, including contributions by several Pueblo groups, sparked a lively debate over the future of the Pueblo nation. Activists want closer ties between the various autonomous groups in order to strengthen their political clout. Some activists denounced the celebrations as glorifying the beginning of the colonial era and discounting the impact on the Pueblo and other indigenous peoples.

In 2001–2 the Pueblo were in a struggle to hang on to their sovereignty.

Legislation being proposed in the U.S. Congress would weaken the sovereignty of the tribal groups. Pueblo activists rejected any move to infringe on their nation's sovereignty as symbolized by the canes presented by Spain, Mexico, and the United States. The Pueblo, who control less than 9% of their original homeland, are the national group that has lived in the same location longer than any other in the United States. Claiming that their sovereignty predates that of the United States, activists have demanded the return of vast territories to Pueblo control. A minority advocates a sovereign Pueblo nation in all aspects, including international relations.

A statue of Po'pay, the leader of the 1680 revolt, called by the Pueblo the first American revolution, is scheduled to be placed in the National Statuary Hall in Washington D.C. in 2002. The placement of the statue is the culmination of a long and arduous campaign by the Pueblo.

SELECTED BIBLIOGRAPHY:

Folsom, Franklin. *Indian Uprising on the Rio Grande: The Pueblo Revolt of 1680.* 1996.
Pike, Donald G. *Anasazi: Ancient People of the Rock.* 1986.
Sando, Joe S. *Pueblo Profiles: Cultural Identity Through Centuries of Change.* 1998.
Yue, Charlotte. *The Pueblo.* 1986.

Puerto Ricans

Borinquenos

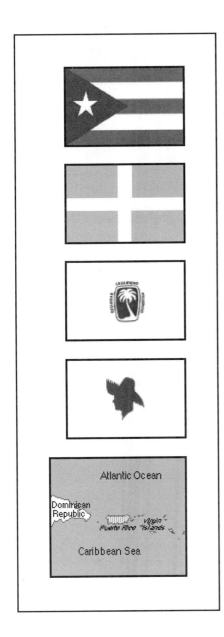

POPULATION: Approximately (2002e) 5,750,000 Puerto Ricans in North America, concentrated in the island of Puerto Rico in the Caribbean and on the U.S. mainland, particularly the large cities of the northeastern states and Florida.

THE PUERTO RICAN HOMELAND: The Puerto Rican homeland lies in the northern Caribbean Sea, forming the smallest and most easterly of the Greater Antilles, between the Dominican Republic and the Virgin Islands. The island is mountainous with a fertile coastal plain, which is quite narrow in the south. Puerto Rico forms a self-governing commonwealth in free association with the United States. *Commonwealth of Puerto Rico (Estado Libre Asociado de Puerto Rico)*: 3,515 sq. mi.—9,106 sq. mi. (2002e) 3,916,000—Puerto Ricans 88%, Crucians* 5%, other Caribbean Islanders 4%, other Americans 3%. The Puerto Rican capital and major cultural center is San Juan, (2002e) 425,000, metropolitan area 1,974,000. The other important centers are Ponce, (2002e) 156,000, metropolitan area 278,000, the major city in the southern part of the island.

FLAG: The Puerto Rican national flag, the official flag of the commonwealth, has five horizontal stripes of red and white bearing a blue triangle at the hoist charged with a single five-pointed white star. The flag of the independence party is a green field with a centered white cross. The flag of the Popular Democratic Party, the commonwealth party, is a white field bearing the profile of a *jibaro*, an island peasant, wearing a *pava*, a wide-brimmed woven-straw hat. The flag of the Progressive Party, the pro-statehood party, is a white field with a centered white palm tree on a blue background surrounded by the words "statehood, security, and progress" in Spanish.

PEOPLE AND CULTURE: The Puerto Ricans are a homogenous Caribbean people, a mixture of diverse strains, mainly Spanish-colonist and African-slave. Estimates of the makeup of the Puerto Rican people are 20% of European descent, 20% of African descent, and 60% of mixed background. The primary language of the island is Spanish, with English widely spoken. The bilingual majority reflect the island's culture, an ebullient mixture of Caribbean, African, Spanish, and North American cultural influences. Over two million Puerto Ricans live on the American mainland, mostly concentrated in the northeastern states and Florida. An estimated half of all Puerto Ricans spend some part of their lives away from the island, usually to live for some years in the mainland United States. Family-planning programs and birth-control measures have contributed to the sharp decline in the birthrate since the 1960s. Emigration to the mainland continues to alleviate the island's chronic overcrowding. The Puerto Rican culture is vigorous and not endangered. The Puerto Ricans have the highest standard of living in Latin America.

LANGUAGE AND RELIGION: The Puerto Ricans speak a Caribbean dialect of Spanish that incorporates many borrowings from various African languages and English. Although both Spanish and English are official languages, most Puerto Ricans are Spanish-speaking, yet many, including those who have lived on the U.S. mainland, speak English as a second language. Numerous attempts at bilingual education were made throughout the twentieth century, but Puerto Ricans remain predominantly Spanish-speaking.

The majority of the Puerto Ricans are Roman Catholic, the legacy of centuries of Spanish rule. The liturgical year, marked by saints' days and celebrations, continues to set the rhythm of daily life. In the nineteenth century, the church's loyalty to the Spanish kingdom eroded much of its popular support. About 15% of the Puerto Ricans are not Catholics but adhere to various Protestant sects (many of them evangelical groups from the mainland United States), or belong to Caribbean religions that combine Christianity with beliefs brought from Africa by black slaves.

NATIONAL HISTORY: The first inhabitants of the island were probably from the Florida Peninsula, reaching the island more than 1,000 years before the Spanish. By the year A.D. 1000 Arawaks migrating north from the South American mainland had taken control of the island, then called Borinquen. The island was sparsely populated by agricultural groups numbering between 20,000 and 50,000 when it was sighted by Columbus on his second voyage to the New World in 1493. The Spanish called the island the "rich port," Puerto Rico.

The Spanish founded a colony at Caparra in 1509 but were forced to abandon the settlement two years later by Arawak attacks. In the first four years of Spanish rule, forced labor, mistreatment, and disease decimated the Arawak population, leaving only about 2,000 survivors in 1500. In need of laborers to replace the disappearing indigenous peoples, the Spanish authorities began to import African slaves in 1513.

The island grew rich on tropical agriculture and the treasure-laden galleons from South America that anchored at San Juan on the long voyage to Spain. The Spanish sea routes and the port cities attracted the attention of English and Dutch buccaneers. In the late sixteenth century the Spanish built strong fortifications on the island, but otherwise Puerto Rico remained largely undeveloped until the late eighteenth century.

In the eighteenth century, as Spain's vast colonial empire declined, Puerto Rico settled into a quiet plantation existence. The colonial calm of the island ended in the 1820s with calls by a nascent nationalist movement for Puerto Rican independence as the other Spanish American colonies threw off Spanish rule. The abolition of slavery in 1873 exacerbated island discontent with Spanish rule, particularly among the influential planter class. The Spanish government hastily granted the Puerto Ricans autonomy in early 1898, when the Spanish-American War began, to ensure their loyalty. Seven months later, in October 1898, U.S. troops occupied the island. By the terms of the peace treaty Puerto Rico was ceded to the United States on 18 October 1898. In December 1898, the U.S. Senate set up mechanisms for policing the island, establishing sanitation, constructing highways and other public works, and operating a system of public education.

The island remained under military occupation until a civil administration took control in 1900. The U.S. administration of the island, distasteful to many Puerto Ricans, was amended to allow wider native participation in the island's government. The Olmstead Act, approved by Congress on 15 July 1909, placed the supervision of Puerto Rican affairs in the jurisdiction of an executive department designated by the president. The Puerto Ricans demanded greater autonomy, and the majority asked for American citizenship. An Organic Act that came into effect on 2 March 1917 made Puerto Rico an organized but incorporated territory and granted collective citizenship. Citizenship allowed military conscription during World War I. Thousands of Puerto Rican conscripts, classified as nonwhites, were drafted into Negro regiments. The Puerto Ricans, particularly the majority of European descent, greatly resented their arbitrary classification as second-class citizens.

The Puerto Ricans, in spite of the legal limitations on political autonomy, slowly came to accept the climate of freedom that resulted from the change of sovereignty. At first mistrusted, resented, or misunderstood, gradually the American administration was recognized as beneficial, and the democratic system was accepted by the islanders. The separation of church and state greatly changed the educational system and social values. Government programs that dealt with the needs of the population for education, health and sanitation, and labor regulation all reflected efforts to remedy centuries of Spanish neglect.

However, there was no clear government policy on Puerto Rico's eventual political status. This approach created strong resistance to groups advocating stronger ties to the United States from many local leaders, especially Luis Muñoz Rivera, who had fought for Puerto Rican autonomy under Spanish rule. Political parties formed, mostly advocating full independence or statehood.

Sugar and other products experienced a sevenfold expansion between 1899 and 1939, but a rapidly growing population remained mostly rural and poor. The application of modern sanitation spurred a population explosion; the population grew from 950,000 in 1899 to over 1.5 million in 1930. Between 1930 and 1940 the population explosion resulted in a 21% increase, and overpopulation became a critical problem. Glaring inequalities of wealth distribution remained, sharpening social and political tension. Fleeing poverty and underdevelopment, thousands of islanders moved to the mainland between the 1930s and 1950s, most settling in separate districts of the northeastern industrial cities. Mainland discrimination against the dark, Spanish-speaking Puerto Ricans provoked the first stirrings of nationalist sentiment.

During World War II the administration again assigned Puerto Rican draftees to black regiments. The indignation of the Puerto Rican soldiers fed the growing nationalism taking hold on the island. In 1946, President Harry S Truman named Jésus T. Piñero as the first Puerto Rican governor. Congress amended the Organic Act of Puerto Rico to permit election of governors by popular vote. In 1950 Puerto Rican nationalists nonetheless attempted to assassinate Truman. Puerto Rico became a commonwealth in 1952, electing its own government and representatives in the House of Representatives and Senate, but despite some concessions the U.S. authorities remained firmly in control. In 1954 radical nationalists attacked the House of Representatives, wounding five congressmen. Armed separatist groups, formed after World War II mostly by returning soldiers, began to operate on the U.S. mainland.

In the 1960s the island government launched Operation Bootstrap, luring manufacturing to the island with tax incentives and low wages. By the late 1960s Puerto Rico had become the most prosperous and industrialized island in the Caribbean, although average incomes remained well below those of the U.S. mainland.

Advocates of statehood gained support in the 1960s and 1970s, while the small independence movement splintered. More militant nationalists conducted a campaign of sabotage and terrorism in the late seventies, but they failed to win widespread support for independence. Leftist groups, aided by communist Cuba, advocated the creation of a socialist Puerto Rican republic. In September 1982 the United Nations General Assembly voted 70 to 30 to defeat a Cuban motion to label Puerto Rico an American colonial possession.

The leading political parties—pro-commonwealth, pro-statehood, and a smaller independence party—reflected the debate on the island's future. Support for independence declined in the 1970s, when the island achieved the highest standard of living in Latin America. (In the early 1990s improved conditions prompted a small movement from the mainland back to the island.) In 1989 the island's governor called for a plebiscite giving the voters three choices—enhanced commonwealth, full statehood, or independence. The plebiscite, originally scheduled for 1992, was postponed when the enabling legislation stalled in Congress.

In November 1992 elections the pro-statehood political party won, vowing to hold a referendum on statehood in 1993. In January 1993 the legislature overturned a law making Spanish the only official language, effectively reinstating English as the island's second language. Puerto Rican voters participated in the long-postponed plebiscite on 14 November 1993, voting by 48% to 46% to retain the island's commonwealth status rather than apply for statehood. The option of seeking full independence received less than 5% of the vote.

The small pro-independence movement claimed that Puerto Rico possesses all the elements necessary for independence: a homogeneous population, a common language, distinct borders, and a distinct culture. The majority of the Puerto Ricans fear the uncertainties of independence, most preferring to retain their ties to the United States in some form.

A Bill forcing Puerto Ricans to decide their future relationship with the United States passed the U.S. House of Representatives in March 1998. The Bill, HR 356, calls for a series of plebiscites, beginning in late 1998, to determine if Puerto Ricans prefer statehood, independence or sovereignty with "free association" ties to the United States. If Congress agrees, the U.S. commonwealth could become a state or a sovereign country within 10 years depending on the outcome of the plebiscites. The Bill, which faced stiff resistance in the Senate, requires plebiscites to be held every 10 years until they choose the statehood or independence option.

In the 1990s, the forces pushing for U.S. statehood grew steadily stronger. Though advocates of full independence constituted only a tiny minority, the desire to maintain the Puerto Rican cultural identity has not disappeared but has remained strong among all segments of the population, including the pro-statehood group. The Puerto Rican culture has stood up to the invasion of mainland culture, although the inroads made by popular American culture complicate the political situation and the controversy over the future status of the island. Pro-statehood, pro-commonwealth, and pro-independence parties all profess to protect the culture and claim that the statuses they respectively advocate are the best ways to ensure the future of the island. A plebiscite in December 1998 failed to yield a clear majority for statehood or commonwealth status. Once again the pro-independence groups received less than 5% of the vote.

In 1999, the small island of Vieques, used since 1941 as a target range by the U.S. Navy, became a highly charged nationalist issue. On 4 July 1999 tens of thousands of Puerto Ricans marched through San Juan demanding that the U.S. Navy leave the small island. Vieques became an issue after an errant bomb killed a security guard on 19 April 1999. Other issues were also aired, including demands for the release of Puerto Rican nationalists called terrorists by the U.S. government. In a recent poll most of the Puerto Ricans stated that they are not anti-American and truly value their U.S. citizenship, yet 72% want the Navy out of Vieques. The Vieques issue has polarized Puerto Rican opinion, with the statehood groups viewing the controversy as a matter of civil rights and social justice for American citizens. The pro-independence minority see the issue as a step toward demilitarization and freedom.

In July 2001, Puerto Ricans voted in an unofficial referendum that demanded an immediate end to U.S. Navy bombing in Vieques. The Navy stopped the bombing during the referendum, but resumed four days later. A proposed referendum among the 9,500 residents of Vieques, scheduled for 6 November 2001 was postponed until January 2002. The residents will be asked to decide if they wish the bombing to stop by 1 May 2003 or to continue indefinitely in return for a $50 million economic aid package. The issue, which has rallied nationalist groups, continues to divide Puerto Ricans.

The passionate campaign for Puerto Rican statehood, opposed by about half the Puerto Ricans, is also opposed by many mainland politicians. Legislative initiatives on the issue have been raised many times, but all remain stalled. The Puerto Ricans continue to vote on the issue periodically; the vote remains split between the two most powerful blocs, pro-statehood and pro-commonwealth. Most Puerto Ricans shun outright independence on the grounds that they have lived with the United States for over a century but have not become Americans.

SELECTED BIBLIOGRAPHY:

Cripps, L.L., and Louise Cripps Samoiloff. *Puerto Rico: The Case for Independence.* 1993.

Davila, Arlene M. *Sponsored Identities: Cultural Politics in Puerto Rico.* 1997.

Monge, Jose Trias. *Puerto Rico: The Trials of the Oldest Colony in the World.* 1999.

Negron-Muntaner, Frances, and Ramon Grosfoguel, eds. *Puerto Rican Jam: Rethinking Colonialism and Nationalism.* 1997.

Pushtuns

Patans; Pakhtuns; Pakhtoons; Pashtuns; Pushtoons; Pukhtuns; Pashtos; Pukhtos; Pashtus

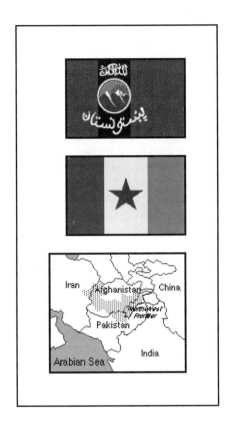

POPULATION: Approximately (2002e) 28,850,000 Pushtuns in South Asia, concentrated in the northwestern Pakistan, with about 11 million, and southern Afghanistan, with 16 million. Outside the region there are large Pushtun communities in other parts of Pakistan, particularly Karachi, in northern Afghanistan, in Western Europe, and in the countries around the Persian Gulf.

THE PUSHTUN HOMELAND: The Pushtun homeland occupies a mountainous region in South Asia lying partly in the Himalayas and the Hindu Kush west of the Indus River and as far west as the Seistan Plateau in Iran. Much of the region is in a chain of barren, rugged mountains in which lie the Khyber Pass, the major invasion route into India for centuries, and many fertile plains and valleys. The Pushtun region in southern and eastern Afghanistan has no official status. The Pushtun homeland in Pakistan forms the North-West Frontier Province (NWFP) and the federally administered Tribal Areas of the Islamic Republic of Pakistan. *North-West Frontier Province and Tribal Areas (Pukhtoonkhwa/Pushtunistan)*: 39,242 sq. mi.—101,740 sq. km, (2002e) 22,895,000—Pushtuns 82%, Afghan Pushtuns 11%, Punjabis 3%, other Pakistanis 4%. The Pushtun capital and major cultural center is Peshawar, (2002e) 1,093,000, metropolitan area 1,605,000. The capital and major cultural center of the Durrani Pushtuns of Afghanistan is Kandahar, (2001e) 335,000, prior to the outbreak of hostilities in the region in October 2001.

FLAG: The Pushtun flag, the flag of the 1947 republic, is a red field divided by a broad vertical black stripe offset toward the hoist and charged with an overlapping white disc bearing three snow-capped green mountains set against a pale blue sky and backed by a yellow rising sun. The flag of the national movement in Pakistan is a vertical tricolor of red, white, and green with a centered red star.

PEOPLE AND CULTURE: The Pushtuns, formerly known as Patans or Pathans, are an Indo-Iranian people comprising four major divisions. One is the Durrani of Afghanistan. The other three are Pakistani—the Ghilzai or Gilzai, the highland nomads called Tribals including a number of distinct groups living along the Afghan border, and the Lowland Pushtuns (the most integrated into Pakistani society). The divisions are further fragmented into some 60 tribal groups. The tribal and subtribal divisions remain the focus of Pushtun loyalty even though the nation now includes a diverse population, from highly educated urban dwellers to tent-dwelling nomads. The Pushtuns have a strong sociocultural identity that transcends the tribal divisions and the international border that divides Pakistan and Afghanistan. All Pushtuns honor the *pushtunwali*, the "way of the Pushtuns," a strict unwritten code of honor that imposes three obligations—*nanawatai*, giving asylum to any refugee, even a mortal enemy; *melmastia*, extending hospitality to all strangers; and *badal*, exacting revenge for wrongs.

LANGUAGE AND RELIGION: The Pushtun language, called Pashto, is an Indo-Iranian language belonging to the southeastern group. The language is divided into Pakhto, the northern variety, and the softer Pashto, spoken in the south. It is further divided into four major dialects—Pakhto or Eastern Pashto, the major dialect in northeastern Pakistan; Southern Pashto in central Pakistan and Afghanistan; Durani or Western Pashto in western Afghanistan and Iran; and Mahsudi or Central Pashto, spoken in the tribal areas. The dialects are each divided into several subdialects and regional variations. Pashto is written in a modified Perso–Arabic script. The Yusufzai dialect of Eastern Pashto is the basis of the literary language in Pakistan. The Kandahari dialect is the standard in Afghanistan. The Pashto language is one of two official languages in Afghanistan. It has no literary tradition, although it has a rich oral tradition.

The Pushtuns are overwhelmingly Muslim, but are divided into often conflicting sects, primarily Sunni and Shi'a, with smaller numbers of Ishmailis, Christians, and Ahmadis.* Although passionately devoted to their religion, the Pushtuns are known for their pursuit of pleasure and their fierce vendettas. Islam came to the Pushtuns as a great liberating and unifying force, and it remains the cornerstone of Pushtun identity, although the majority of the Pushtuns consider themselves more Pushtun than Muslim. In recent years radical Islamic groups have introduced a more restrictive form of Islam, which became the basis of the Taliban movement in Afghanistan.

NATIONAL HISTORY: The origins of the Pushtuns are unclear. Their legends claim that they are descended from Afghana, the grandson of the Hebrew King Saul. Most scholars believe they probably developed from ancient Aryan tribes intermingling with subsequent invaders. The mountainous region, containing the main passes leading into the Indian Plain, was a corridor for invaders for thousands of years.

A center of the ancient Buddhist kingdom of Gandhara, the region was reached by the Macedonian soldiers of Alexander the Great. In the first century A.D. the Kushans overran the region. Fair Aryan tribes driven from the Iranian Plain occupied the mountains in the seventh century and created small tribal states in the high mountain valleys.

Conquered by the Muslim warriors of the Afghan Empire in the tenth century, the Pushtun tribes adopted Islam. Centuries of invasions by Afghans, Persians, Indians, and Mongols, converted the Pushtun tribes into a warrior people, possibly the best guerrilla fighters in Asia. The tribes united only when threatened, more often warring among themselves. Historically, the Pushtun homeland formed part of the territories of the ruling dynasty of Kabul.

The Afridi Pushtuns rallied the tribes to defeat a Mogul army of 40,000 in the seventeenth century. Only partially subduing the Pushtuns after repeated attacks, the Indian Moguls initiated the practice of paying local rulers to keep the peace on the volatile frontiers. The Mogul Empire declined rapidly after 1707, leaving the Pushtuns to unite under the Durrani Sultanate of Afghanistan in 1747. As the Pushtuns gained control over the country, many settled in other areas, particularly around Kabul.

The Sikhs, expanding from the Punjab lowlands, drove the Durrani Pushtuns from the territory east of the Khyber Pass in 1823. The Afghan ruler initially sought the help of the British to recover the territory taken by the Sikhs. The eastern Pushtun territories, along with the rest of the Sikh empire, passed to British rule following the defeat of the Sikhs in 1849. The Afghans, unable to convince the British to return the territories, turned to the Russian Empire for support, thus bringing about a clash of the two colonial powers. The British eventually excluded the Russians from Afghanistan, and the kingdom's foreign policy came under British influence.

During the Sepoy Mutiny of 1857, the Pushtun ruler of Afghanistan, Dost Mohammad Khan, exchanged his neutrality for British recognition of his suzerainty over Peshawar and the frontier zones. During the next decades, the boundaries of Afghanistan were settled through arbitration or agreement between the British and Russians. The weak rulers of Afghanistan unwillingly accepted the division of the Pushtun nation between Afghani and British territory. The frontier that crossed historical Pushtunistan was fixed by British arbitration in 1872 and 1875. Following the Second Anglo-Afghan War, the Durrani state of Afghanistan became a virtual British protectorate.

The British garrisoned the main towns but, unable to pacify the tribal areas, continued their predecessors' practice of paying local rulers to keep the peace. The stipends became the region's major source of legal income, aside from smuggling and other prohibited activities. Military expeditions attempted to subdue the tribes in the 1880s and 1890s, but with little success.

In 1901, having failed militarily, the British authorities created a semi-autonomous region, the North-West Frontier District, comprising the four districts of Peshawar, Kohat, Bannu, and Dera Ismail Khan. British garrisons in the district effectively controlled only a third of the Pushtun territory.

The Montagu-Chelmsford Reforms of 1919 introduced provincial democracy in India, but the North-West Frontier Province was excluded from the democratic experiment. Rule through the local Pushtun *jirgas*, local tribal leaders, remained the policy in British Pushtunistan. A Pushtun majority in Afghanistan ethnically distinguished the population of the province from the rest of British India.

In 1919–20 the tribal groups of Waziristan, in the mountainous west of the NWFP, rebelled against British rule. The rebellion spread, forcing the British to mobilize 30,000 troops before the rebels were finally subdued. In the 1930 the Afridi Pushtuns, led by a local religious leader, the *fakir* of Ipi, rose against the British; over 10,000 Pushtuns died before the British finally triumphed. The *fakir* of Ipi became a national martyr, and the British are still despised today.

Afghanistan was recognized as an independent multiethnic state in 1921, under a royal government dominated by the Durrani Pushtuns. The Afghan amir laid claim, on historical and ethnic grounds, to the Pushtun territories under British rule. The Pushtuns of the region acknowledged neither Kabul nor Calcutta. The Afghans, like the British, paid local Pushtun leaders to keep the mountain passes open and to control local smuggling and tribal uprisings.

Pushtun resistance to British rule continued through the 1940s and World War II, forcing the diversion of units of the hard-pressed British army in India to fight tribal uprisings. The Afghan government in 1944 emphasized its interest in the Pushtun area in a letter to the governor of British India. The British dismissed the Afghan interest as Pushtun irredentism, but the movement for an independent Pushtunistan received overt and persistent support from the Afghan government.

After the war, as British India moved toward independence, the major political party, the Frontier Congress (Khudai Khidmatgar), won widespread support with demands for separate status. The Afghan government proposed that the Pushtuns of the NWFP be allowed to vote on joining Afghanistan, Pakistan, India, or for separate independence. The Frontier Congress in the 1946 elections defeated the Muslim League, the organization dedicated to the formation of a Muslim state. The only choices finally offered by the British authorities were attachment to Muslim Pakistan or Hindu-dominated India.

Pushtun nationalists of the Frontier Congress formed Khuda-i-Khidmatgar (Servants of God), popularly called the "Red Shirts," which called for a nationalist boycott of the accession referendum and refused to be bound by the result of the vote, which was accession to Muslim Pakistan. The Red Shirts launched a terrorist campaign against the new Pakistani state and on 2 September 1947 declared the province independent as Pushtunistan, the Land of the Pushtuns. Pakistani troops invaded the breakaway state, provoking rioting in the Pushtun cities. The Pushtun uprising became the first serious threat to Pakistan's fragile unity. The Pushtuns were finally incorporated into Pakistan, and their demands for provincial autonomy thereafter played a vital role in their relationship with the central government.

The Afghan government opposed the incorporation of Pushtunistan into Pakistan and voted against Pakistani membership in the United Nations in 1949. The negative vote was cast on the grounds that the Pakistanis illegally occupied historically Afghan territory in the NWFP. The Afghan government also declared all agreements on boundaries with the British illegal and reiterated its support of Pushtun self-determination. Many Pushtuns slipped across the Afghan border to collect arms and ammunition, which resulted in the widespread militarization of Pushtun society in the NWFP. Most tribal leaders accepted arms and money from both governments; in the process, the area prospered.

In 1950 Pakistan adopted a unitary framework that frustrated any aspirations for provincial autonomy. The elite of the new state, mostly ethnic Punjabis and Mohajirs,* having used religious zealotry to mobilize Muslims for a separate homeland, were now faced with demands for federalism and autonomy from several groups, particularly the Pushtuns of West Pakistan and the Bengalis of East Pakistan. The numerical dominance of the Bengalis was the major reason that the new Pakistani government rejected any form of power sharing and suppressed national and linguistic identities in broader framework of Islamic unity and identity. Provincial autonomy became anathema.

The Pakistani government, unable to subdue fully the rebellious tribes, finally adopted the earlier practice of paying local chiefs to keep the peace. Pushtun separatism, supported by Afghanistan and the Soviet Union, continued to destabilize the region in the 1950s and 1960s. In 1952 some 5,000 Pushtun nationalists, trained in Afghan camps, invaded the Peshawar Valley to plant the flag of Free Pushtunistan. Eight years later, the Pushtun frontier tribes mobilized to defeat an incursion of Afghan troops disguised as Pushtun tribesmen and drove them back. Pakistani troops controlled the major highways and garrisons, but most of the Pashtun territory in northwestern Pakistan remained outside government control. Crises in relations between Afghanistan and Pakistan over the Pushtunistan issue were particularly serious in 1955–57 and 1961–63.

Beset by nationalist movements in several provinces in the 1960s and 1970s, the government outlawed political parties, banned regional assemblies, and suppressed nationalist groups. In 1971 the secession of East Pakistan, renamed Bangladesh, provoked a crisis as Pushtun nationalists pressed for their homeland to follow the Bengalis into secession. A government crackdown on nationalist activity forced many Pushtun leaders to leave the country, mostly to the Pushtun regions of neighboring Afghanistan. The Afghan government reaffirmed its support for a separate Pushtun state in Pakistan in 1972 and was blamed for increased separatist violence in the early 1970s. Moderate political leaders requested that the name North-West Frontier Province, a colonial legacy, be officially changed to Pushtunistan, but the request was rejected as nationalist by the Pakistani government.

The Soviet invasion of Afghanistan in 1979 sent over six million refugees into the NWFP, about 85% of them ethnic Pushtuns. The Afghan civil war after the Soviet withdrawal in 1989 pitted Pushtun groups against the non-Pushtuns of northern Afghanistan. A militant Islamic organization, the Taliban, founded by Afghan Pushtun students studying in Pakistan in the mid-1990s, took control of all but a small portion of the country by 1998.

The Taliban, mostly students from radical religious schools in the North-West Frontier Province of Pakistan, were initially welcomed in Afghanistan as peace-makers following years of civil war, imposed a harsh form of Islamic law. Women were especially targeted; they were prohibited from working outside the home, receiving education after the age of eight years, or receiving medical attention. Afghan men were required to grow untrimmed beards, and all music, television, sports, and other amusements were banned.

The radicalization of the Muslim religion in the 1990s reverberated in the North-West Frontier Province. In November 1994 Pushtun fundamentalists took control of the tribal Malakand District and demanded the creation of an Islamic state in the region. The Pakistani government, aware of the unrest and nationalist stirrings, conceded an Islamic government in Malakand District but rejected the rebels' political demands.

The Pakistani government has always attempted to suppress Pushtun demands for the creation of a federal state, viewing federalism as a prelude to separatism. The leadership of the Pakistan, mostly drawn from the predominantly Punjabi heartland, recall the separatist movement of the 1940s and 1950s and remain suspicious of the strength of Pushtun loyalty to the unitary Pakistani state.

The legislature of Pakistan's Northwest Frontier Province passed a resolution, sponsored by the Awami National Party (ANP), calling upon the government of Pakistan to rename the province after the majority Pushtun population—Pukhtoonkhwa or Pushtoonkhwa. In March 1998, ANP ministers in the province resigned as a protest against the government's refusal to rename the province. The ANP stated in June 1998 that it favored the maximum provincial autonomy within the federal structure.

Violence, particularly between the Pushtuns and Mohajirs in Karachi, left many dead and injured in confrontations in early 1998. The violence in Karachi, which reflected the unrest across the country, led to a nationalist conference in mid-1998 of Sindhis,* Pushtuns, Baluch,* and Seraikis. The meeting resolved to stand united against the domination of the Punjabis and warned that the Pakistani state could collapse if the non-Punjabis were not given equal rights. The conference also launched the Pakistan Oppressed Nations Movement. Pushtun leaders reiterated their demand for renaming the Pushtun homeland in Pakistan.

The Pakistani state, after more than 50 years of independence, has yet to build a strong national identity and remains a collection of distinct Muslim nations loosely bound by the military threat perceived from India. Its objective of attaining parity with India has been effectively used to divert public opinion from domestic issues and to provide legitimacy to autocratic and military rule.

The terrorist attacks in the United States in September 2001 were quickly traced to Osama bin-Laden, the honored guest of the Taliban government of Afghanistan. United States military strikes against Taliban positions led to widespread demonstrations among the Pashtuns of Pakistan. Thousands of Pashtuns crossed the border to fight for the Taliban and their allies, called terrorists by the U.S. president. The U. S. bombing raids aided the non-Pushtun groups fighting the Taliban in the north of the country. In November the Taliban began to collapse as their opponents advanced, aided by continued American bombing. Thousands fled back to the Pushtun heartland areound Kandahar. In early December the city, the last Taliban stronghold in Afghanistan, fell to the opposition forces. An interim Afghan government, led by an anti-Taliban Pushtun leader, Hamed Karzai, promised to reintegrate the Pushtuns into Afghan national life, including many Taliban fighters who surrendered.

The ongoing ethnic conflicts in both Pakistan and Afghanistan reignited calls by nationalists for the reordering of regional borders to reflect the historical and ethnic geography. Militant Pushtuns in Pakistan put forward a plan for an Islamic Republic of Pushtunistan to incorporate Pakistan's North-West Frontier Province, the tribal areas, and the southern and eastern provinces of Afghanistan.

SELECTED BIBLIOGRAPHY:

Caroe, Olaf. *The Patans, 550* B.C.–A.D. *1957.* 1958.
Jansson, Erland. *Nationalist Movements in the North-West Frontier Province, 1937–47: India, Pakistan, or Pakhtunistan.* 1981.

Malik, Iftikhar H. *State and Civil Society in Pakistan: Politics of Authority, Ideology and Ethnicity*. 1997.

Nichols, Robert. *Settling the Frontier: Land, Law and Society in the Peshawar Valley, 1500–1900*. 2000.

Québecois

Québecers; Quebeckers, French Canadians;
Franco-Canadians; Fransaskois

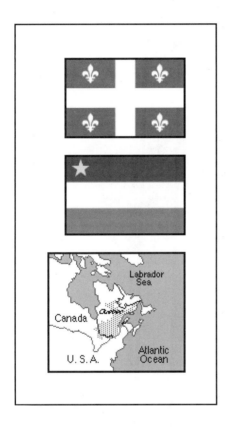

POPULATION: Approximately (2002e) 5,750,000 Québecois in North America, concentrated in the Canadian province of Quebec in eastern Canada. Outside the province there are Québecois communities in other parts of Canada and in the United States and Europe.

THE QUÉBECOIS HOMELAND: The Québecois homeland occupies a large part of eastern Canada, a heavily wooded region between the Hudson and Ungava Bays on the north and the Gulf of St. Lawrence on the south. The huge area includes a sparsely populated north and a heavily populated and urbanized south. The region is rich in minerals and with 7% of the earth's fresh water, hydroelectric power; the southern counties are highly industrialized. Quebec is a province of Canada. *Province of Quebec (Province de Québec)*: 524,861 sq. mi.—1,359,743 sq. km, (2002e) 7,492,000—Québecois 78%, English Canadians 10%, Indigenous groups 10%, other Canadians 2%. The Québecois capital and major cultural center is Quebec City, called Québec locally, (2002e) 171,000, metropolitan area 706,000. The other major cultural center is Montreal, (2002e) 1,037,000, metropolitan area 3,492,000.

FLAG: The Québecois national flag, the official flag of the province, is a blue field divided by a centered white cross, each blue rectangle charged with a white fleur-de-lys. The flag of the major nationalist political party, the Parti Québecois (PQ), is a horizontal tricolor of green, white, and red, bearing a five-pointed yellow star on the upper hoist.

PEOPLE AND CULTURE: The Québecois, descendents of early French colonists, are a French-speaking North American people with a New-World French culture unique on the North American continent. The low birthrate is offset by a constant stream of immigrants; however, the newcomers tend to vote against secession. The Québecois culture and law set them apart from other North Americans. Culturally the Québecois retain much of their colonial culture of the eighteenth century, with a modern evolution into a French-speaking, advanced industrial society with a high standard of living. The Québecois do not want to end up as a colorful ethnic subculture known for their music, cooking, or their quaint linguistic history; they have embraced nationalism as a means to survive in an English-speaking continent of 300 million.

LANGUAGE AND RELIGION: The devoutly Catholic Québecois speak a French dialect called Québécois that retains many words and forms of the French spoken in the eighteenth century. Québecois forms part of the French dialects of the Gallo-Romance group of Romance languages. The dialect is considered a national language by the Québecois. Although inherently intelligible to other speakers of French, the dialect uses a simplified syntax and borrowings from indigenous languages and English.

The majority of the Québecois are Roman Catholic. Prior to the 1960s the Catholic Church was influential in all aspects of provincial life, including education, social services, and government. The modernization of the postwar era, including separation of church and state, ended the Catholic monopoly. There is a small Protestant minority, and a growing number of evangelical sects are active in the region.

NATIONAL HISTORY: The coastal areas, sparsely populated by diverse tribal peoples, were claimed for France by Jacques Cartier, who visited the Gaspé Peninsula in 1534. He later sailed up the St. Lawrence River to claim the vast interior for France. Samuel de Champlain built a trading post on the site of modern Québec City on the upper reaches of the St. Lawrence in 1608. In that year French colonization officially began. The town that grew up around the post became the center of missionary and exploration activities for all the enormous colony of New France. The royal government of New France was created in 1663. By 1700 over 12,500 French colonists, mostly farmers, had settled in the fertile southern districts. In the early eighteenth century the colony grew rapidly with increased European settlement and government-sponsored immigration.

French and British rivalry in North America led to a series of wars, culminating in the French defeat on the Plains of Abraham outside Québec's city walls in 1759. New France, with its 70,000 French citizens, was ceded to British authority in the 1763 Treaty of Paris. After a failed attempt to assimilate the Québecois into an English-speaking colony, and with rebellion growing in the 13 colonies farther south, the Parliament passed the Quebec Act of 1774, which divided Canada into French-speaking Lower Canada and English-speaking Upper Canada. The division guaranteed the Québecois land tenure and cultural, linguistic, and religious rights. The Québec culture and legal system were thereafter protected under colonial law. The Québecois, satisfied with these guarantees, refused to join the American colonies in revolt against British rule in 1776.

Québecois dissatisfaction with British rule, however, heightened in the early nineteenth century. In 1837 the Québecois rebelled, under the influence of Louis Papineau, the leader of the French Canadian Reform Party. The rebels, known as Patriotes, attempted to create an independent republic, Laurentia, before their final defeat in 1838. Lower Canada, dissolved in 1840, became part of a united province called East Canada, which also included Ontario. In 1867 the province was separated once again and, renamed Québec, joined with three English-speaking provinces to form the new Canadian confederation under the British North America Act.

The Québecois, mostly rural, poor, and staunchly Roman Catholic, looked to Québec City as the bastion of French culture and language. Their largest city, Montreal, became one of North America's greatest immigration melting pots; French, English, Italian, Portuguese, Irish, Jewish, and Eastern European immigrants crowded into the city. English gradually replaced French as the language of business and culture in the city.

In the late nineteenth century, responding to the growing threat to their language and culture, Québecois began to organize in nationalist groups, such as the Sons of Liberty and the Association of St. Jean Baptiste, to press for Québecois political and linguistic autonomy. Political unrest led to short-lived rebellions in 1870 and 1884. As discontent surged in the 1890s, the Québecois pressed for greater provincial powers.

A massive Québecois shift to the burgeoning cities between 1901 and 1921 reinforced the language and culture, particularly the all-important influence of the extremely conservative Catholic church. The severe hardships of the Great Depression particularly affected the Québecois areas, where families of a dozen children were common. The dominance of the church extended to all aspects of Québecois life: books from France were censored, and women had no voting rights until 1940. The only careers open to Québecois women were motherhood or the convent until the liberalization of the 1960s.

During World War II, mirroring attitudes during the First World War, the Québecois generally supported the Allied cause. While 80% of English-speaking Canadians approved of conscription, 72% of French-speaking Canadians were opposed, partly on the ground that Québecois soldiers could not be sure of serving under French-speaking officers.

After World War II, church power declined as education and greater opportunities began to spread. Québecois traditions were put aside to the extent of allowing women to enter the workforce. Québec society liberalized as urbanization accelerated; a burgeoning French-speaking middle class entered business and the professions. In the 1960s the "quiet revolution" swept the province, a period of modernization and renewed social structures. The Québecois finally attained a standard of living equal to that of the English-speaking North Americans. The modernization transformed Québec from an underdeveloped backwater—Catholic, agrarian, and conservative—into an advanced, French-speaking industrial state. It was at this time that some Québecois began to believe that their future should lie in a separate French-speaking republic.

President Charles de Gaulle of France, on an official visit to Canada in 1967, ignited modern Québecois nationalism when he proclaimed during a speech, *"Vive le Québec Libre!"* ("Long live free Québec"). De Gaulle's proclamation became the rallying cry of the nationalists. The rise of nationalist sentiment split the movement into a moderate element seeking independence by democratic means, and militants, demanding immediate independence and willing to use any means. A moderate separatist party, the Parti Québécois, led by René Levesque, appealing to the deep nationalist sentiment of generations of Québecois, was organized in 1968. In 1970 the largest of the militant groups, the openly Marxist Front for the Liberation of Québec (FLQ), turned to terrorism to publicize its commands, but it found little popular support.

Members of the FLQ kidnapped a British trade commissioner, James Cross, and Québec's labor minister, Pierre Laporte, whom they later murdered. The Québec government requested federal help, and the War Measures Act was proclaimed. Civil liberties were suspended, some 500 activists were arrested, and federal troops moved into the province. At the height of the separatist campaign over 200 bomb attacks occurred across the province.

The Canadian government made French the second official language across the federation offered numerous concessions to francophone sensitivities. A renovated constitution spelled out in detail the equality of French with English; yet the Québecois, alone among the peoples of the ten provinces, withheld their approval of the new constitutional amendments. In 1974 French was made the official language of Québec, sparking violent opposition by anglophones and immigrant groups who supported bilingualism.

The Parti Québécois won the 1976 provincial elections with vows to hold a referendum on independence. A French-only language law passed in 1978 drove out much of the province's powerful English-speaking business community, raising fears that independence would aggravate Québec's economic problems. A 1980 referendum on independence failed 58.2% to 41.8%, demonstrating the widespread fear for the future of the Canadian federation. Following the plebiscite, the economy replaced nationalism as the province's primary concern. Young Québecois quickly moved into leadership positions in commerce and industry in the 1980s. The increasingly alienated English-speaking minority began leaving the province, many companies moving to Ontario or other provinces. Between 1976 and 1996 at least 400,000 non-Québecois left the province.

Attitudes to separation from wealthy, secular Canada were regularly gauged by polling the Québecois and other Canadians. In 1984, polls showed only 4% favored complete independence, 15% "sovereignty association," 23% special status within Canada, and 52% continued provincial status with safeguards for the Québecois language and culture.

The nationalist debate resurfaced in 1986, provoked by a conflict over a controversial language law and Québecois demands for recognition as a distinct society within Canada. Proposed changes to the federal constitution were blocked by groups in other provinces, which in turn prompted a nationalist resurgence in Québec. The Canadian federal system afforded the Québecois wide-ranging autonomy as well as the advantages of an economic union with the other nine provinces, but for the nationalists this was not enough. Believing that Québec possesses the confidence, resources, and economic infrastructure to sustain independence, the nationalists vowed to settle for nothing less than the creation of an independent Québecois state in North America.

The Québecois nationalist movement in the early 1990s took in many of Québec's successful entrepreneurs and businessmen, the sector most opposed to separation in 1980. Supported by the belief that Québec had become an economically viable industrial state, the nationalists gained support in local elections. In late 1993 the nationalists took 54 of the 75 Québec seats in the Canadian Parliament, making the Québec nationalists the official opposition on a Canadian national level.

In 1994 the Parti Québecois won provincial elections on a platform committed to independence. A meeting of the 10 provincial leaders of Canada hammered out the Meech Lake Accord, which would have recognized the Québecois as a "distinct society" and generally satisfied the Québecois, but it failed to win full national ratification and was scrapped. In a second referendum on secession on 30 October 1995, the Québecois voted 49.44% for separation against 50.56% against, falling just 53,498 votes, or one percentage point, short of authorizing the Québec government to begin negotiations on separation. Nationalists pointed out that the vote showed a majority of about 60% of Québecois favored secession but that various small non-Québecois groups opposed Québecois independence. Negotiations would also have to address the problem of northern Québec, where the Cree* have consistently voted against separation.

In the late 1990s the Québecois economy was stable, and the Québecois shared the North American way of life. High technology had revitalized the economy of Montreal, the world's second-largest French-speaking city, and had increased trade with the nearby northeastern states of the United States. Should Québec separate from Canada, it would become the sixth largest trading partner of the United States.

The Canadian Supreme Court began hearings to decide the constitutionality of Québec's referenda on unilateral separation from Canada and independence. The Québecois boycotted the proceedings, claiming that only they should have the right to decide on their independence. The court ruled that Québec could not unilaterally secede but that should a clear majority vote in favor of sovereignty, negotiations should begin. The court did not make any clear declaration with respect to the indigenous peoples of Québec. Most Québecois leaders rejected the court's rulings, claiming that independence was a political question, not a legal one. In December 1998, the Québecois returned an openly separatist provincial government in local elections.

The French, often blamed for the rise of Québecois nationalism in the late 1960s, were again part of the conflict in March 1999. The French government extended an invitation to representatives of the Québec government to a reception exclusively for representatives of national governments. The Canadian government refused to attend, protesting that the French were promoting Québecois nationalism.

Lucien Bouchard, the premier of Québec, who had led the campaign for independence during the 1990s, was readying the Québecois for a third referendum on separation when he suddenly resigned in January 2001. His absence from the secessionist movement reduced demands for an immediate referendum.

The nationalists, edging closer to a majority vote with each referendum, are determined to fulfill what they consider Québec's destiny as an independent, French-speaking nation-state in North America. However, although between 40 and 60% of the population remain fervently nationalist, the time for separatism may be passing. For over 30 years the issue of Québec's separation has dominated Canadian politics, and both the Québecois and other Canadians are tiring of the tension it has produced. Younger Québecois, their flourishing culture and language safeguarded by some of the world's most stringent cultural-protection laws, are less inclined than their predecessors to support separatism or to give up the many benefits of Canadian citizenship. A report sponsored by the Québec government published in June 2001 indicates that French is not under serious threat in the province, contradicting the perception of the more militant nationalists and language activists.

In mid-2001 an outspoken new premier in Québec, Bernard Landry, considered a strident separatist by other parts of Canada, angered Québecois and other Canadians by calling the Maple Leaf flag a red flag. Landry is the leader of the PQ took power in the winter of 2000–2001. In a July 2001 poll, only about half the Québecois supported Landry's plan for sovereignty, and only 15% said that they would favor outright independence of Quebec. Following the September 2001 attacks on the neighboring United States, the economy floundered and secession became a lesser issue.

SELECTED BIBLIOGRAPHY:

Kizilos, Peter. *Québec: Province Divided*. 1999.

Scowen, Reed. *Time to Say Good-Bye: The Case for Getting Québec Out of Canada*. 1999.

Tanguay, Brian. *Contemporary Québec Politics and Society*. 1999.

Young, Robert A. *The Struggle for Québec: From Referendum to Referendum?* 1999.

Quechua-Aymara

Quechuaymara; Runa Kuna; Quechwa-Aimara; Aymara-Qhichwa; Kollas; Kechua-Aimara; Incas; Inkas

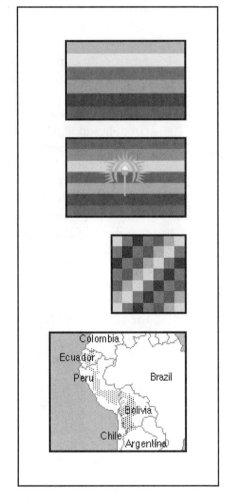

POPULATION: Approximately (2002e) 17,500,000 Quechua-Aymara concentrated in the highland regions of Peru, Bolivia, and Ecuador. Other important communities live in Colombia, Chile, and Argentina. Outside the Andean region there are growing communities in the large cities, especially Lima in Peru. The Aymara, numbering about 2.5 million, are concentrated in Bolivia, with about 500,000 in Peru and 100,000 in Chile.

THE QUECHUA-AYMARA HOMELAND: The Quechua-Aymara homeland, called Tawaninsuyo, meaning the Four Quarters, lies in the Andean regions of Peru, Bolivia, Ecuador, Chile, and Argentina. The heartland is in the highlands around Cuzco in Peru and Lake Titicaca in Bolivia. Most of the region forms part of the Andes Mountains and is often called the Tripartito, as it lies on the borders of Peru, Bolivia, and Chile. The most important Quechua-Aymara cultural centers are Cuzco, called Qosqo locally, meaning "navel of the world," (2002e) 282,000, Cajamarca, Caxamarca, (2002e) 104,000, Ayacucho, Ayakuchu, (200e2) 114,000, and Juliaca, called Juleaqa, (2002e) 156,000, in Peru; Cochabamba, called Kuchawampa, (2002e) 563,000, Sucre, Sukri, (2002e) 183,000, and Oruro, called Ururu, (2002e) 217,000 in Bolivia; Riobamba, (2002e) 128,000, and Ibarra, (2002e) 124,000 in Ecuador. Other important cultural centers are Lima, the capital of Peru, La Paz in Bolivia, and Quito in Ecuador.

FLAG: The flag of the Quechua-Aymara national movement, the Tawantinsuyo flag, has six horizontal stripes of red, yellow, green, pale blue, dark blue, and purple. The same flag with the addition of a golden torch centered is the flag of the Quechua in Ecuador. The flag of the Aymara is a square flag of 49 squares of the same colors as the Tawantinsuyo flag.

PEOPLE AND CULTURE: The Quechua-Aymara are the indigenous nation in the Andean region of western South America, the descendants of the peoples of the Inca Empire. The nation, unified by over four centuries of abuse, is made up of the majority Quechuas and the Aymaras, who inhabit the Altiplano, mostly in Bolivia. The Quechua-Aymara are remarkably well adapted to the climate and altitudes of the high Andes Mountains. Most still live in rural areas, often on lands belonging to absentee landowners. Urbanization has accelerated since the 1960s partly due to land scarcity and increasing population. Much of the original culture of the Quechua-Aymara has been retained even though they have been systematically oppressed since the Spanish conquest of the sixteenth century.

LANGUAGE AND RELIGION: The Quechuas and Aymaras speak languages of the Andean branch of the Andean-Equatorial languge family. The languages are highly expressive, including bipersonal conjugation and conjugation dependent on mental state or veracity of knowledge. Quechua, which is spoken from southern Colombia to northern Chile and Argentina, includes a number of distinct dialects and numerous subdialects. Quechua and Aymara are official languages in Bolivia and Quechua is an official language in Peru. Aymara, which belongs to the Aru or Jaqi language family, is spoken around Lake Titicaca in Bolivia, Peru, and Chile. Other members of the language family, Jaqaru and Kawki, spoken around Lima, in Peru, are nearly extinct.

Officially, the Quechua-Aymara are Roman Catholics, with 95% listing the faith as their principal belief system. In recent years Protestant sects, particularly Evangelical Methodists, have won converts. The great gods of the Incas were the powers of nature especially the sun, called Inti, and the moon, Quilla. Other important deities were the thunder and rainbow gods and the bright planets. Over all reigned Viracocha, the creator. He was both father and mother of the sun and moon. He was often thought as an old man with white hair and beard. He was supposed to be the ruler of destiny and was invisible. His place in the heavens was the dark area in the Milky Way known as the Coal Sack.

NATIONAL HISTORY: The Andean highlands were settled at least 21,000 years ago. Records are fragmentary but suggest that agriculture was developed about 3000 B.C. and that the smelting of metals, especially copper, began about 1,500 years later. By 600 B.C., the first great Andean empire had emerged among the Aymaras on the high plateau later known as the Altiplano. The empire, Tiahuanacan, was centered on Lake Titicaca and included urban centers around the lake, as well as enclaves in different zones from the eastern valleys to the Pacific Coast.

The center of the empire, Tiahuanaco, was a great center of trade and religion, and the impact of its advanced culture spread far beyond the highland plateau. The empire's rapid expansion after 1000 and its sudden collapse around 1200 are still poorly understood. Seven small Aymara successor states developed, but by the fifteenth century the Aymaras had been brought under the rule of the Incas of the Quechua.

After the collapse of Tiahuanacan, a small Quechua-speaking state emerged in the Cuzco Basin. The people whose rulers were called Incas were originally a highland Quechua tribe ruled by a god-king known as the Sapan Inca. According to a mythological account, they migrated from the south to settle the Cuzco basin, where they established a small state. They began to expand by absorbing neighboring tribes about 1100 A.D. The economy was based on an intensive terracing of mountain slopes and irrigation. The Inca civilization, which developed urban centers, an extensive road network, and a well organized and efficient administration, began as a Quechua empire, but with the incorporation of the highlands to the south included a large Aymara population. The Incas, taking their name from that of their ruler, ruled the largest and most advanced state in the Americas before the arrival of the Europeans. At its height in the fifteenth century, the empire, called Tawantinsuyu, extended from northern Ecuador to central Chile and from the Andes Mountains to the coastal lowlands and had a population of between 9 and 16 million.

The Quechua-dominated empire was remarkable as it was achieved without benefit of either the wheel or a formal system of writing. Instead of a script, the Incas used a highly accurate *khipu* (knot-tying) system of record keeping. Their achievements were even more remarkable considering the brevity of the period during which the empire was built and the formidable geographic obstacles. The Inca society was very organized. Everyone knew his or her position in the social pyramid. At the top of the pyramid was the *Sapan Inca* and his wife, who was traditionally his sister. Next were the high priest and the military chief followed by the four *apus*, the chief officers of the four quarters of the empire.

In 1470, several Aymara kingdoms rebelled against Inca rule. The Incas completely defeated two states and pacified the region by sending Quechua colonists, especially the southern valleys and the Aymara valleys east of the Andes. The present Quechua population of Bolivia are the descendants of the Inca colonists. Quechua and Aymara traditions were very similar and were finally unified under the rule of the Incas.

Spanish explorers, sailing south along the Pacific Coast from Panama to confirm the legendary existence of a land of gold called Biru, first made contact with the Inca Empire in 1524. Because the rapidly expanding empire was internally weak, the Spanish were able to conquer it with remarkable ease. After the Inca Huayna Capac died in 1527, his sons Huascar and Atahualpa fought over the succession. Although Atahualpa defeated Huascar, he had not yet consolidated his power when the Spaniards returned in 1532.

Atahualpa did not attempt to defeat the Spaniards led by Francisco Pizarro and Diego de Almagro on the coast because he was convinced that those who commanded the mountains also controlled the coast. When Pizarro formed alliances with rebellious subject tribes and supporters of his dead brother, Atalhualpa moved to meet him. Atahualpa was captured during the first encounter. He was later executed, even though the Incas had paid a ransom equvalent to half a centure of European gold and silver production. One year later Cuzco, the center of the Inca Empire, fell to the victorious Spanish.

Despite Pizarro's rapid victory, rebellions by Quechuas soon began and continued periodically throughout the colonial period. In 1537, Manco Inca, established as a puppet emperor by the Spanish, rebelled against the conquerors and restored the Inca state. This state continued to challenge Spanish authority even after they had suppressed the revolt and beheaded the Inca heir, Túpac Amaru, in the public square of Cuzco in 1572.

Pizarro and Almagro divided the Inca territory, with the north under the control of Pizarro and the south, in present southern Peru and Bolivia, under that of Almagro. Fighting between the two broke out in 1537 when Almagro seized Cuzco after suppressing the Manco Inca rebellion. Pizarro defeated and executed Almagro in 1538 but was himself assassinated three years later by former supporters of Almagro. The fighting between the Spanish factions continued until 1548, delaying the Spanish settlement of the Altiplano.

According to Spanish archives, the Quechua-Aymara declined by 75% between 1561 and 1796, mostly due to the diseases introduced by the Europeans. The rapid loss of population further disrupted the economic and social systems. In some provinces two-thirds of the surviving population was conscripted to work in the silver mines, where thousands died. Another estimate, for 1800, counted the Quechua-Aymara at just 10% of their pre-conquest population.

The conquistadors, the Spanish conquerors, came to the New World in search of riches. Leaving their families behind in Europe, many took Quechua-Aymara women as wives. Their offspring, called Mestizos or Mixed, formed a population of uncertain social position. Mestizo children of marriages recognized by the Catholic Church were frequently assimilated by the ruling group. They formed a distinct social group that was Spanish speaking and closer to the colonial rulers than the mass of rural natives, yet they were clearly separate from the Spanish elite.

Spanish rule created a highly stratified society in which whites and Mestizos controlled the Quechuas and Aymaras living in the form of indentured servitude on large haciendas. The Spanish justified the harsh treatment of the former Inca peoples as a means of converting them to Christianity, a goal that was most often subordinated to the quest for wealth. Slavery, forced labor, and diseases decimated the Quechua-Aymara tribes and ruptured many indigenous communities and kin-groups.

The Spanish Catholic missionaries, needing an instrument for the extention of Catholic dogma, used Quechua as their means of communication. Quechua was extended to areas where other dialects were traditionally spoken. The use of the language became widespread, both in religion and as a lingua franca for the entire Andean region.

Discontent with Spanish domination led to numerous uprisings. The pace of the insurrections increased dramatically in the eighteenth century, with five in the 1740s, eleven in the 1750s, twenty in the 1760s, and twenty in the 1770s. The underlying causes of the uprising were largely economic. Land was becoming increasingly scarce because of illegal purchases by colonists at the same time that the Quechua-Aymara population was once again growing after the long decline following the conquest. Most of the revolts in the highlands were usually local in nature, the exception being the great rebellion led by Túpac Amaru II. In 1780 José Gabriel Condorcanqui, a wealthy mestizo descendant of the Incas who sympathized with the oppressed majority, seized and executed a notoriously brutal landowner. He then raised a poorly-equipped army of tens of thousands of natives, assuming the name Túpac Amaru II after the last Inca, to whom he was related. Drawing on a rising discontent and nativism, he advocated a return to a mythic Inca past at a time of increased economic hardship. Captured by royalist forces in 1781, Condorcanqui was tried and like his namesake, cruelly executed, along with several relatives, in the main square in Cuzco. In response to the revolt the colonial authorities finally undertook to carry out some of the reforms that the leaders of the revolt had advocated.

The system of peonage, tying the Quechua-Aymara to the Spanish plantations, mines, and haciendas, continued through the independence of Peru and Bolivia in the early nineteenth century. Political independence transferred power into the hands of the Creole descendants of European colonists and the larger Mestizo populations, changing little for the majority Quechua-Aymara.

In the late nineteenth century, various Quechua-Aymara regional movements were organized to address the four centuries of abuse. Between 1879 and 1965 there were thirty-two peasant revolts and movements, denying the traditional view that the Quechua-Aymara passively accepted serfdom. Few of the uprisings threatened the white hold on the region, but all testified to the burgeoning feelings of frustration, anger, and alienation that had built up over centuries. Demands for redress of the situation led to the reestablishment of the official Indian Community in Peru in 1920. Subsequently, communities that could prove that they had held colonial title to lands were permitted to repossess it, a long and arduous bureaucratic process.

Most Quechua-Aymara were tenants on large rural estates by the end of the sixteenth century. Their languages were discouraged and Spanish was the language used by the masters and workers. The wealth of the white elite depended on the agricultural estates, and they firmly resisted any effort to change the status or outlook of their Quechua-Aymara labor force, scornfully called peons. As a result, the economic and social culture of the hacienda, and with it the status of the Quechua-Aymara, continued into the twentieth century.

Uprising and rebellions, mostly local in nature, continued to challenge white control of the Andean region. The chronic instability of the Peruvian and Bolivian governments added to the tensions. In the 1920s, there were several uprising in the Bolivian Altiplano culminated in a widespread rebellion in 1930–33. The rebels, who proclaimed a Republic of the Original Peoples and Nations, were ultimately defeated.

Language served a major role in shaping ethnic identification and intergroup relations. Traditionally, the inability to speak Spanish contributed to the vulnerabilty of the Quechua-Aymara. Mestizos and whites controlled access to the larger society through their use of Spanish. Until the latter part of the twentieth century, only very small numbers of Quechua-Aymara were bilingual; for many of these, learning Spanish was simply a step in severing their links to their own people. Only in the 1960s and 1970s did a significant number of Quechua-Aymara learn and use Spanish, many being trilingual, also speaking the other indigenous language along with Spanish. Between 1950 and 1975, the number of monolingual Quechua dropped by nearly 40% and monolingualism among the Aymara dropped about 50% during the same period.

Education was predicated on the goal of "Hispanicizing" the Quechua-Aymara, but the majority retained a strong positive orientation to their ethnic background. This well-educated minority formed the nucleus of a native intelligentsia in the 1970s and 1980s. Renewed interest in their traditional culture and their past fostered a strong cultural movement and a general reculturation of the entire regional population.

In April 1952, the Quechuaymara in the mountains of Bolivia took up arms against the Bolivian government and the mining companies in the first widespread uprising. The Bolivian government in response to the uprising finally adopted agrarian reform that ended the traditional system of serfdom. Peru adopted similar legislation in 1969.

Activists rejected the political passivity of the past in the 1990s. Several leaders accused Spain of genocide and renamed the Spanish Conquest the Andean Holocaust. Others demanded the return of the Huarochirí manuscript, an ancient Quechua document, one of the few that survived the Spanish conquest, from the Biblioteca Nacional in Madrid. The removal of their past to European museums and collections is seen as a form of cultural genocide, while the imposition of European states in their divided homeland is called the genocide of the Quechuaymara nation.

Some Quechua-Aymara idealized the Inca past, others viewed the path of development in a return to the pre-Columbian past of communal values, autochthonous technology, and the Inca genius for production and organization. They reject the Spanish version that they conquered a continent of primitive peoples in South America, but instead claim that the Conquistadors plundered the lands of highly advanced civilizations symbolized by the Inca empire. The name of the empire, Tawantinsuyo, is proposed as the name for a reconstituted Quechua-Aymara state, with Cuzco, under its former name of Qosqo, its capital.

In April and September–October 2000, several activists were killed by security forces during serious demonstrations in Cochabamba, Bolivia. In a symbolic declaration the Quechua-Aymara of Bolivia proclaimed their self-determination in April 2001. Activists announced the establishment of an autonomous state, given the ancient name of Kollasuyu or Qullasuyu. The declaration, called the Jach'ak'achi Manifest, was dedicated to the martyrs of the nation. Colonalism stripped them of their power as a nation and their families of their properties, transforming freedom into slavery. The declaration asks how long this situation can continue. What are the physical and juridical privileges that safeguard the position of a minority that has usurped the Quechua-Aymara lands and territory?

In 2001–2, the Quechua-Aymara are the largest indigenous group in South America, and one of the largest in the world not to have broadcasting and communications in their own language. There is some radio, but only in local dialects, and no television or other means of communication in the Quechua-Aymara languages.

The Quechua-Aymara are increasingly rejecting their isolation and centuries of servitude. Growing ties to other indigenous American groups and the activities of the local organizations and federations have greatly increased their participation in the world. Representatives of the Quechua-Aymara nation now regularly attend United Nations deliberations on indigenous peoples and similar groups within the Americas. One result of the growing contacts with other non-state nations is the increase in militancy. The Quechua-Aymara, according to the Spanish-speaking rulers of their homeland, are legendary for their patience. This may be changing.

SELECTED BIBLIOGRAPHY:

Abercrombie, Thomas Alan. *Pathways of Memory and Power: Ethnography and History Among an Andean People.* 1998.
Gade, Daniel W. *Nature and Culture in the Andes.* 1999.
Klaren, Peter F. *Peru: Society and Nationhood in the Andes.* 1999.
Osborne, Harold. *Indians of the Andes: Aymaras and Quechuas.* 1988.

Rabhas

Ravas; Rabbhas

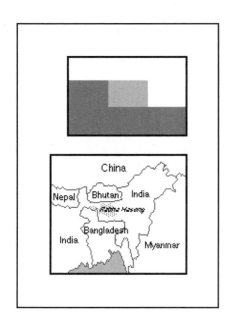

POPULATION: Approximately (2002e) 310,000 Rabhas in India, concentrated in the northeastern state of Assam, but with sizable communities in the neighboring districts of the states of West Bengal and Meghalaya.

THE RABHA HOMELAND: The Rabha homeland lies in northeastern India in western Assam, in the Darrang, Goalpara, and Kamrup districts, northwestern West Bengal, the Jalpaiguri and Cooch Behar districts, and the East Garo Hills District of Meghalaya. Some nationalists claim a wide territory in all three states that they call Rabha Hasong or Rabhaland, but most claim the Assamese districts of Goalpara, Bongaigaon, and Dhubri as the limits of their homeland. The proposed Rabha Hasong Autonomous Council covers the district of Goalpara in Assam. *Rabha Hasong Autonomous Council:* 2,117 sq. mi.—5,484 sq. km, (2002e) 822,306—Assamese 33%, Bengalis 29%, Rabhas 22%, Bodos* and Garos 14%, other Indians 2%. The Rabha capital and major cultural center is Tamulpur, called Bishnu Rabha Kshetra by the Rabhas, (2002e) 22,000. The other important center is Dudhnai (2002e) 14,000.

FLAG: The Rabha flag, the flag of the national movement, has three horizontal stripes of white, a center strip of a traditional design in red, yellow, and white, and a lower red stripe.

PEOPLE AND CULTURE: The Rabha are a Tibeto-Burman nation ethnically and historically related to the other Tibeto-Burman nations of northeastern India, the Bodos,* Masas,* and Mikirs.* Originally the Rabha occupied a larger territory, but over many centuries they were pushed into the hills by stronger nations. Known for their arts and crafts, Rabha tribal art has gained an appreciative audience around the world, particularly carvings of elephants. Elephants occupy a distinct place in Rabha mythology and are symbols of good luck. Historically the Rabhas were a matrilineal people, but in the twentieth century they underwent a transition to a patrilineal system. Rabha men marry as many women as they can afford as polygyny is recognized by Rabha custom and has the force of law. Women have begun to demand their rights, which the state does little to protect. The most important yearly festivals are Farkhanthi, which honors the dead Rabha kings, and Baikhu, also called Khaksi, which is a fertility festival.

LANGUAGE AND RELIGION: The Rabha language belongs to the Koch subgroup of the Bodo-Garo group of languages of the Tibeto-Burman language family. The language, close to the language spoken by the Kacharis and Bodos is spoken in two major dialects, Maitaria and Rangdania, which reflect the regional dispersion of the Rabha people. The language has incorporated considerable borrowings from the neighboring Indo-European languages, Assamese and Bengali. English words have often been adopted for items or activities brought to the region during colonial times.

The majority of the Rabhas adhere to a form of Hinduism called Vaishnavism. The Vaishnavite sect appeals to the tribal peoples because of its repudiation of caste privilege. Under the Brahman system of central India, tribals are relegated to the lowest rungs of the rigid caste system. One ancient belief system, the worship of a cow goddess, was incorporated into the Rabha belief system. The Rabhas firmly believe that any man or woman can clandestinely learn the secret art of witch-craft. Periodic witch hunts often lead to deaths. About 2% belong to various Christian sects, primarily Baptist.

NATIONAL HISTORY: The original inhabitants of the Brahmaputra Valley were Australoid groups who were later absorbed by the Tibeto-Burmans who entered the region from the Tibetan Plateau in the twelfth century. The Tibeto-Burman tribes settled the highlands north and south of the Aryan-dominated flood plains. Their territories were gradually divided into regions controlled by individual tribes.

Much of the jungle-clad highlands came under the nominal rule of Hindu states in the Brahmaputra lowlands. Isolated from the mainstream of Indian civilization, the area lay outside most of the great states that arose on the subcontinent. In the early Christian era the Hindus of the valley formed a state tributary to the Gupta Empire of northern India, but were unable to bring the tribal regions under their rule. At times the Rabhas formed a separate kingdom, but during most of their early history they lived in autonomous communities that were united only by culture and custom.

The Tibeto-Burmans, called Kacharis or Kiratas, created an independent kingdom with its capital at Pragjyotishpura, near present Guwahati. The kingdom, an ally of the Indian Gupta Empire, adopted Hinduism, but it is unclear to what extent the indigenous population embraced the new religion. By the early thirteenth century the centralized kingdom had collapsed into a fragmented system of tribal polities and loose confederations of principalities.

In 1229, the Brahmaputra Valley, then in turmoil, was overrun by invading Ahoms, a Thai people from present north Burma-China border region. The Ahoms arrived at a time of turmoil in the region, with only the larger Tibeto-Burman tribes able to offer some resistance. The Ahoms introduced the writing of history and kept meticulous records in handwritten tomes called *burajnis*. The first written records of the Rabhas appeared in these Ahom archives.

The Ahoms erected an independent kingdom and mixed with the conquered Aryans to form the Assamese people, but like the former kingdoms they were unable to effectively extend their rule much beyond the Brahmaputra River valley to the hill tribes. The Tibeto-Burman tribes withdrew to their jungle strongholds and maintained their control of much of present Assam around the vast river valley. The Ahom victory pushed the Rabhas and other smaller Kachari tribal groups south into the highlands. Separated from their kin north of the Brahmaputra River, the Rabhas developed a distinct culture based on shifting agriculture and influenced by the cultures of other highland groups. By the sixteenth century the majority of the Rabhas in the east had been subdued and brought under Ahom rule. The Rabhas living farther west came under the Kamata kingdom of the Rajbangsis.*

During the latter half of the sixteenth century, a revered teacher, Shankara Deva, inspired a popular religious reform movement within Hinduism called Vaishnavism. The movement sought to reform the rigid esoteric practices of Tantric Hinduism and to limit the prerogatives of the Brahmans attached to the Ahom court. Vaishnavnite monasteries played an important part in the reclamation of wastelands for wet-rice cultivation, which quickly spread to the Rabha tribal territories. The Vaishnavite creed, which repudiated caste privileges and the discrimination against tribal groups practiced by Tantric Hinduism, appealed to the broad tribal base within the Ahom kingdom.

After much fighting, the Brahmaputra Valley and its rich rice lands finally fell to the Muslim Moguls in 1661–62, but their hold was tenuous and they were quickly expelled by the Ahom, now called Assamese. However, repeated invasions by the Burmans from the east had a more lasting impact on the Tibeto-Burman tribes. The Assamese requested aid from the British in Bengal against the Burmans in the early 1700s. In 1792, the Rabhas joined a widespread rebellion against Assamese rule and the Assamese again requested British help to put down the rebellion, setting a pattern for later confrontations.

Civil strife in the Ahom kingdom, including continued rebellions by the Rabhas and other indigenous groups, weakened the Ahom and allowed the Burmans to invade from the east in 1817. The Burmans again invaded the Brahmaputra Valley in 1822, one of the reasons for the first Anglo-Burmese War in 1824–26. The Burmans were forced to cede all of Assam, including the Rabha tribal areas in the Rabha Hills, to British rule in 1826, when Assam became a British protectorate.

The Rabha territories, administered by British commissioners that accompanied military garrisons, formed part of British Bengal until 1874, when they were included in the new Assam province. The British developed the Rabha homeland, called Rabha Hasong, for agriculture and commercial plantations. The government offered incentives to Europeans to start plantations of rubber, cinchona, hemp, jute, and tea. Because the Rabha were unwilling to do plantation work, impoverished tribes from southern and central India were recruited.

The colonial administration made Bengali the official language of Assam and staffed administrative and professional positions with educated Bengalis. Conflicts between the Rabhas and the Bengali administrators often led to violence, which was put down by British troops. Early in the twentieth century, the British government of India made vast tracts of tribal lands available to predominately Muslim farmers from the provinces of East Bengal. Nepalis were also imported to work as dairy herders and similarly were encouraged to colonize tribal lands that had not been set aside as reserved territories.

Some Rabhas were converted to Christianity by British and American missionaries in the nineteenth century. Western-style education began a process of change among the tribals. New leaders, educated at mission schools, soon challenged the traditional hold on power of the chiefs and village headmen. Several Rabha leaders, educated by Christian missionaries, asked the British authorities for help in preserving their language and culture and for other small cultural concessions in 1929.

During World War II, when Assam was the object of a Japanese thrust into India, the Tibeto-Burman tribes were at first courted as Japanese allies, but their refusal to join the anti-British forces led most to join the British forces fighting the Japanese. After World War II the British prepared to grant independence to the subcontinent, but rejected numerous demands for separate statehood and finally agreed to the partition of British India into two large states, India, a secular state dominated by Hindus, and Pakistan for the Muslims.

Following Indian independence in 1947, the Assamese won control of their state assembly and launched a campaign to reassert the preeminence of Assamese culture and language and to improve the employment opportunities of the native Assamese. This led to the gradual alienation of the Rabha and other tribal groups. In 1950 a small group of Rabha students first suggested the idea of separation from Assam and the creation of a Rabha majority state within India.

The state of Assam, which included many non-Assamese tribal groups, remained a center of nationalist tensions. Regional cultures and variations were too distinct to remain within a single political administration. New tribal states were carved out of Assamese territory, Nagaland in 1963, followed by Meghalaya and Mizoram in 1971, and Arunchal Pradesh in 1972. The creation of these states spurred numerous separatist movements among the remaining tribal groups in Assam.

Following the Pakistan civil war in 1971, nearly two million Bengali Muslim refugees settled in Assam, often in lands claimed by the Rabhas and other tribal groups. Their illegal settlement and then their electoral support of Indira Gandhi's Congress Party government in New Delhi aggravated Rabha fears of domination and central government ambitions to support assimilation into Bengali or Assamese culture.

In the late 1970s and early 1980s, there were persistent conflicts between local government officials and Rabha students over the rights of the illegal Bengali settlers. A mass movement to safeguard Rabha interests, led by the All Assam Rabha Students Union, won the support of almost all the Rabhas in Assam. The movement stimulated the growth of parallel organizations among the Rabha populations in West Bengal and Meghalaya. The Rabha considered their fight a war for survival against the onslaught of millions of non-tribal migrants.

Reports of government representatives exerting pressure on tribal chiefs to send Rabha women to be sterilized in the early 1980s led to the political mobilization of the Rabhas. In the mid-1990s, a group of Rabha students, unable to see any progress by peaceful means, formed the Rabha National Security Force (RNSF) to fight for a sovereign Rabha homeland to be called Rabha Hasong.

In early 2000, the RNSF intensified its activities in the Rabha heartland in Assam. Militants collected funds from businessmen and supporters to buy arms and to finance their guerrilla war against Indian rule. Stepped up violence, often coordinated with other militant groups in the region, followed the mobilization of the Rabha nation. Militant cadres, led by Jabrang Rabha, having undergone training in camps along the Assam-Meghalaya border, often under the supervision of militant Assamese of the United Liberation Front of Assam (ULFA). Joint attacks on plantations controlled by Bengalis or other non-indigenous peoples were carried out by activists of the RNSF and ULFA in 2000–2.

Various Rabha factions, meeting in April 2000, after long deliberations, agreed to set aside their factional differences in order to find ways for the all-around development of the Rabha nation. Under the auspices of the Rabha People's Conference, the various Rabha leaders decided to work for greater self-government within the auspices of the proposed Rabha Hasong Autonomous Council.

In late 2000, the Assamese legislature passed a bill for an autonomous Rabha council, which would give the Rabha some limited self-government.

The bill, denounced by the militants, restricted autonomous control to the district of Goalpara. The Assamese government, in January 2001, circulated a list of towns and villages proposed for inclusion in the Rabha Hasong Autonomous Council. Moderate tribal leaders demanded the demarcation of a wider council area to include all the Rabha in Assam. Others rejected the limited autonomy and reiterated their aim of a separate Rabha state to include territory in Assam, Meghalaya, and West Bengal.

Thousands of Rabhas rallied in Tamulpur in February 2001 during a festival of Rabha culture that was held in spite of the threat of militant disruptions. Over 5,000 people, most in traditional dress, cheered leaders demanding Rabha self-government and demands for over 300 posts in local governments to be filled by Rabhas. Other leaders demanded respect for local languages and the development of the Rabha language and culture.

In July 2001, pro-statehood groups outlined a plan for an expanded Rabha territory and full statehood within the Indian union. The more militant groups again rejected the plan as too limited and also rejected moderate claims that "self-determination" did not imply secessionist tendencies. Openly separatist Rabha groups say that too much time and too many lost opportunities leave them just one option, full independence, possibly within a federation of independent states that would replace the Indian occupation of the northeast.

SELECTED BIBLIOGRAPHY:

Karlsson, B.G. *Contested Belongings: An Indigenous People's Struggle for Forest and Identity in Sub-Himalayan Bengal.* 2000.
Sen, Sipra. *Tribes and Castes of Assam.* 1999.
Singh, K.S., ed. *Tribal Ethnography, Customary Law and Change.* 1993.
Tripathy, S.N. *Glimpses of Tribal Development.* 2000.

Rajbangsis

Koch-Rajbangsis; Koche; Kamatapuris; Rajbongshis; Tajpuris; Koach-Bongshi; Kock-Rajvanshi; Kamatas

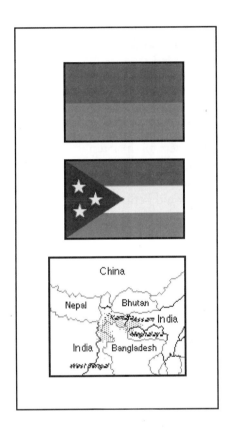

POPULATION: Approximately (2002e) 2,645,000 Rajbangsis in India, concentrated in northeastern India, in the northern districts of West Bengal State, in Assam, and Meghalaya. There are important Rajbangsi communities in Bangladesh, with about 200,000, and in Nepal, about 105,000.

THE RAJBANGSI HOMELAND: The Rajbangsi homeland, called Kamatapur, lies in the high plains of northern West Bengal and western Assam in northeastern India. The region includes the narrow neck of Indian territory, just 20 kilometers wide, that connects India proper with the isolated region of North Bengal and the seven states of northeastern India. The region includes the valleys of the Tista, Torsa, Jaldhaka, and Ranjit rivers. Variations in altitude result in great variety in the nature and climate. The region includes a number of small enclaves belonging to Bangladesh. Nationalists claim the West Bengal districts of Cooch Behar, Jalpaiguri, the plains of Darjeeling, North and South Dinapur, and Malda, the Assamese districts of Kokrajhar, Bongaigaon, Dhubri, and Goalpara, the western territories of West Garo Hills of Meghalaya, and the Dinapur and Saidpur regions of Bangladesh. The Rajbangsi heartland in West Bengal, called North Bengal or Kamata, forms the districts of Cooch Behar and Jalpaiguri. *North Bengal (Kamata):* 4,468 sq. mi.—11,572 sq. km, (2002e) 4,821,000—Rajbangsis 48%, Gorkhas* 24%, Bengalis 20%, Bhutanese and other Indians 7%. The Rajbangsi capital and major cultural center is Cooch Behar (2002e) 85,000. Other important cultural centers are Siliguri (2002e) 298,000, metropolitan area 637,000, and Jalpaiguri (2002e) 87,000. The center of the Rajbangsis in Assam is Dhubri, called Dhubguri by the Rajbangsis, (2002e) 83,000.

FLAG: The Rajbangsi national flag, the traditional flag of the nation, is a horizontal bicolor of blue over green. The flag of the Kamatapur Liberation Organization is a tricolor of blue, white, and green, with a large black triangle at the hoist charged with three white stars.

PEOPLE AND CULTURE: The Rajbangsis are a people of mixed Dravidian, Aryan, and Tibeto-Burman ancestry. Culturally they are related to the Bengalis and Assamese,* but their culture also shows influences from the pre-Aryan cultures of the plains of northeastern India. Originally one people, the Koch who adopted Hinduism were called Rajbangsi. Although not officially a scheduled tribe, they are considered a tribal people by the Bengalis. The Rajbangsis are called Koch or Koch-Rajbangsi in Assam. Most of the Rajbangsis are farmers although since the 1980s they have been urbanizing. The Rajbangsi language and culture are distinct from the dominate cultures of Bengal and Assam. The Rajbangsi tradition of illustrated books with small illuminations came to the region with the Neo-Vaishnavism in the sixteenth century.

LANGUAGE AND RELIGION: The language of the Rajbangsis is an Indo-European language belonging to the eastern group of Bengali-Assamese languages. The language has only one major dialect called Bahe. Koch, spoken by about 50,000 people, is a Tibeto-Burman language; it is not linguistically related although the majority of the ethnically and historically related Koch also speak Rajbangsi. Koch, spoken in Assam, has a number of regional dialects. Some speak Bengali as their mother tongue. English is also favored as a second language.

The majority of the Rajbangsis are Hindu, although a large minority adheres to an indigenous religion called Khavas Tharu. Vaishnavism, a form of Hinduism, spread across the region in the sixteenth century. Historically the Rajbangsis worshipped a supreme god called Ai. Once a year they held a feast, during which many animals were sacrificed along with the *bhogis*, a class of men who devoted their lives to Ai. From the time that they became *bhogis* they were pampered and given anything they wished, but after the span of one year they were killed during the yearly rituals.

NATIONAL HISTORY: Aryan tribes, originally from the Iranian Plateau, swept across northern India in ancient times. The tribes drove the earlier Tibeto-Burmans tribes from the plains which they occupied about 1200 B.C. The tribes gradually formed small kingdoms that maintained trade and cultural relations with China, other parts of India, and as far west as Greece and Rome.

The isolation of the highland plains led to the separation of the inhabitants from mainstream Bengal. In the eighth century, the region came under the rule of the Buddhist Pala kingdom. By the eleventh century, Hinduism had replaced Buddhism as the major religion. Muslims of Turkic origin conquered southern Bengal in the thirteenth century further isolating the Rajbangsi groups in the north.

The Rajbangsis, also called Koch, the inhabitants of the plains at the foothills of the Himalayas, created several small kingdoms, the most important being Kamarupa or Kamata, established in 1250, and the Koch kingdom established in sixteenth century by Biswa Simha. Naranarayana, the ruler of Kamarupa in the mid-sixteenth century united large portions of northern Bengal and western Assam and extended Koch-Rajbangsi influence to the neighboring kingdoms of Cachar, Tripura, and the small states of the Khasi and Jaintia Hills. The kingdom's political power was paralleled by a great flowering of Rajbangsi arts and literature. In 1511, the Koch dynasty, led by Khandan Narayan, gave its name to the expanded Rajbangsi state, Koch Bihar, with its capital at Kamatapur. After Naranarayana's death in 1584 the kingdom disintegrated. The Rajbangsis in the western districts fell prey to invading Muslim Moghuls while those in the east became vassals of the Ahom kingdom of Assam. The remnants of the kingdom survived in the reduced state of Cooch Behar (Koch Bihar).

British influence extended to the Rajbangsi homeland in the late eighteenth century. The defeat of the Moghuls by the British at the Battle of Plassey in 1757 ended Muslim rule in Bengal. The Rajbangsis, weakened by a serious famine in 1769–70, suffered an invasion by Bhutanese in 1770. The raja of Cooch Behar appealed to the British, which provided Bengal Governor General Warren Hastings with the opportunity to expand British influence. British military aid was provided only on the condition that the British East India Company gain sovereignty of the state. After the British defeat of the Bhutanese in 1772, Hastings extended British rule to Cooch Behar. In 1826, the British extended their authority to Assam, uniting the Rajbangsis under their colonial administration of Bengal.

In 1783, the Narayana dynasty was established in Cooch Behar under Raja Harendra Narayana. The Narayana rajas took the elevated title of maharaja in February 1880. The Narayanas supported British rule, which gave them security from stronger neighboring states and promoted trade across the vast British Indian territories. Under Nripendra Narayana, who ruled from 1884 to 1911, the Cooch Behar kingdom flourished. The kingdom, the focus of Rajbangsi loyalty, formed part of the British Eastern States Agency with a British advisor at the kingdom's court. In 1874, Assam was separated from Bengal, effectively dividing the Rajbangsi and Koch nation.

After World War II, as the British began to prepare India for independence, the Rajbangsi demanded negotiations for separate status for an expanded Cooch Behar state to include all Rajbangsi districts in Bengal and Assam. In August 1947, the British authorities granted independence to the subcontinent, divided into two states, Hindu-dominated India and Muslim Pakistan, including East Bengal, called East Pakistan. The southern districts of the traditional Rajbangsi homeland, with a slight Muslim majority was included in Pakistan. Cooch Behar was included in India as a separate state, but the Narayana dynasty was officially ended.

In 1950, the government of West Bengal, led by Bidhan Chandra Roy, convinced the Indian government to allow West Bengal to absorb the state of Cooch Behar. Rajbangsi leaders, beginning in the 1950s, deprived of their own state, demanded scheduled tribe status, which would give the Rajbangsis greater protection and opportunities. Agitation for scheduled tribe status laid the foundation of the later separatist movement. Neglect and underdevelopment allowed Rajbangsi national leaders to gather widespread support. In 1966, they were granted scheduled tribe status, but after the ordinance was renewed three times, the government allowed it to lapse. As a result, from the 1970s, the Rajbangsis were treated as a backward caste group and were denied the benefits of their former status.

Following the Pakistani civil war in 1971, hundreds of thousands of Bengali Muslim refugees poured into the region. Their illegal settlement and then their electoral support for Indira Gandhi and India's Congress Party aggravated Rajbangsi fears of Bengali cultural domination and Indian government ambitions to push for the assimilation of the Rajbangsis into the larger Bengali society. In the late 1970s and early 1980s, there were persistent disputes between the Rajbangsis and the state governments of West Bengal and Assam over the rights of illegal immigrants to citizenship.

The grass-roots political movement demanding safeguards for Rajbangsi culture and interests was initially peaceful and had the support of the majority of the Rajbangsis. As Bengali immigration grew, the Rajbangsis considered it a war for survival against the onslaught of uncontrolled migrations from Bangladesh and elsewhere. The West Bengal state government and the Indian federal government responded by the use of force to suppress the movement.

In the mid-1990s, the Rajbangsis, never part of Bengali or Assamese society, put forward demands for a separate homeland in the northern districts of West Bengal and the western districts of Assam. The neglect of the region by the state governments and the economic deprivation led to agitation for separation. The Rajbangsi nationalists major demands are separation from West Bengal and Assam, the inclusion of their language in the eighth schedule of the Indian Constitution, and broadcasting and television in the Rajbangsi language.

Rajbangsi organizations in the 1990s staged demonstrations, strikes, and cultural events to propagate Rajbangsi culture throughout their homeland. Spurred by continuing Bengali immigration to their region, including many illegals from Bangladesh, the Rajbangsis demanded a ban on all settlement in the region by non-Rajbangsis. The Indian government responded to Rajbangsi demands with the widespread use of force. The 1990s were marked by violations of human rights by the Indian Army and police. Mostly unable to apprehend militants, the police and soldiers often harassed innocent civilians.

Nationalists claimed that the region of the proposed Kamatapur state in West Bengal is 80% Rajbangsi, but the West Bengal government countered that only about 30% of the population is Rajbangsi. The more militant nationalists, who claim territory in West Bengal, Assam, and in historic Rajbangsi land in Bangladesh, claim a national population of over 4 million.

The majority of the Rajbangsis support moderate, democratic groups dedicated to the creation of a separate Kamatapur state within India, however a small militant minority formed the Kamatapur Liberation Organization (KLO) which launched a violent campaign for separation. One faction of the militants works for an independent Kamatapur. The KLO, led by Tushar Das, was trained and armed by the United Liberation Front of Assam (ULFA). Militants, from bases in neighboring Bhutan, attacked police stations and non-Rajbangsis in the six northern districts of West Bengal beginning in 1995. In 1998, the government of West Bengal demanded the deployment of special police along the state's border with Bangladesh and Bhutan to disrupt outside support for the growing Kamatapur movement. The KLO targeted tea plantation owners and rich businessmen for extortion to finance their activities.

The Rajbangsi allege that their homeland has been ignored by both the West Bengal and Indian governments. No major industries have been created and an apathetic attitude towards the region fueled dissatisfaction and separatism. The West Bengal government officials branded the Rajbangsi nationalist leaders as secessionists, extortionists, and anti-socials. Memorandums sent to New Delhi have been ignored.

The Indian government, after years of deliberation, rejected Rajbangsi demands for scheduled tribe status in August 2000. The rejection fortified the separatist movement, whose leaders claimed that only a separate state could provide the protection and security their nation lacked as part of West Bengal. In October 2000 agitation for a separate Kamatapur state spread from West Bengal to the Koch-Rajbangsi population of the adjacent areas of Assam and Meghalaya.

The KLO formed a military alliance with the Assamese militants of the United Liberation Front of Assam. The combined groups, in 2001–2, kidnapped several owners or managers of tea plantations and fought skirmishes with Indian police and soldiers. The government, in an effort to curb the growing violence, sent additional military and paramilitary troops to northern West Bengal in October 2001. The increasing incidents of violence, both by the Rajbangsi militants and the Indian security forces, has polarized the civilian population. Many have rejected violence from whatever quarter, others have embraced the militant demand for a united, independent Rajbangsi state to be carved out of Indian and Bangladeshi territory.

SELECTED BIBLIOGRAPHY:

Das, A.K. *Tribal Situation in West Bengal.* 1990.
Lieten, G.K. *Continuity and Change in Rural West Bengal.* 1992.
Prasad, Sachchidananda, and R.R. Prasad. *Encyclopaedic Profile of Indian Tribes.* 1996.
Sarup, C. *Encyclopaedia of Indian Tribes.* 2000.

Rapanui

Rapa Nui; Easter Islanders; Rapanuians

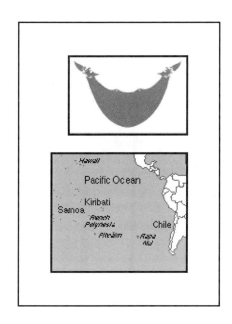

POPULATION: Approximately (2002e) 11,000 Rapanui in the South Pacific, concentrated in Easter Island, called Rapa Nui, mainland Chile, and Tahiti. Outside the region there are Rapanui communities in Hawaii and North America.

THE RAPANUI HOMELAND: The Rapanui homeland, commonly called Easter Island, is one of the most isolated places on earth. A triangular volcanic island, Easter Island is over 2,000 miles (3,218 km) from the nearest important population center and 2,300 miles (3,702 km) west of Chile. The island has volcanic craters, lava formations, and hundreds of huge stone statues. The island forms a province of the Republic of Chile. *Isla de Pascua/ Easter Island (Rapa Nui)*: 46 sq. mi.—119 sq. km, (2002e) 3,000—Rapanui 85%, other Chileans 15%. The Rapanui capital and the only settlement on the island is Hanga Roa.

FLAG: The Rapanui national flag, called the Reimiro (bird men) flag, is a white field bearing a red design representing a canoe and two figures based on the ancient ceremonial wooden pectorals worn by chiefs.

PEOPLE AND CULTURE: There is considerable controversy concerning the origins of the Rapanui. Norwegian Explorer Thor Heyerdahl proposed that the people who built the statues were of Peruvian descent, due to the similarity between Rapanui and Incan stonework. In the 1950s, Heyerdahl sailed westward from Peru in a reed raft called the Kon-Tiki, trying to prove that early South Americans may have settled on the island. But subsequent archeological studies produced convincing evidence that the island's early inhabitants were all of Polynesian origin. Archaeological evidence supports the theory that the island was populated by Polynesians. Cannibalism was formerly practiced on the island, partly as a religious sacrifice, and partly due to the lack of fresh meat. In terms of distance, the Rapanui are the most isolated nation on earth. Their nearest neighbors are the less than 100 inhabitants of Pitcairn Island, 1,200 miles (1,931 km) to the northwest. Most Rapanui now work in the tourist industry, fish, or are craftsmen.

LANGUAGE AND RELIGION: The Rapanui language, also called Rapanui or Rapa Nui, is a Polynesian language called Pascuense in Spanish. The language is an isolated dialect belonging to the Rapanui branch of the East Polynesian group of Polynesian languages. The closest relatives are the Hawaiian, Mangareva, and Rarotonga languages spoken in other parts of Polynesia. Spanish, the official language of Chile, is widely spoken as a second language. Only between a quarter and half the population is literate. Rongorongo, the hieroglyphic script, has remained a mystery since its discovery. For over a century controversy has raged over the meaning and source of the enigmatic characters. According to a 1992 study, only 5% of the Rapanui schoolchildren spoke the Rapanui language, down from 70% in 1977. Efforts to avert the extinction of the language is an integral part of the growing national movement, which claims that the loss of the language would mean the loss of one of the strongest indicators of cultural identity.

The Rapanui are now mostly Roman Catholic, the religion introduced by the mainland Chileans. Traditionally their belief system included ancestor worship, with the huge Moai representing each clan's most revered forebears, which were believed to bestow powers on living leaders. Because the powers were transmitted through the Moai, the clans or tribes competed to build bigger and bigger statues and altars. Making more Moai became a national obsession. At any given time in the island's pre-European history, the whole Rapanui society was dedicated to the production and transport of the Moai.

NATIONAL HISTORY: Most scholars believe that Polynesians discovered the island about A.D. 400, driven west probably in quest of fertile land. According to Rapanui legends, the group of migrants came from the east and was led by Hotu Matua. On the island the migrants created an impressive and enigmatic culture. They created massive statues, the Moai, and developed the Rongorongo script, the only written language in Oceania. The hundreds of Moai, statues of human figures averaging about 15 feet (4.6 m.) in height, were erected across the island. The early Polynesian settlers called the island Te Pito O Te Henua, the naval of the world.

The settlers used the typical Polynesian slash-and-burn agricultural techniques, razing more and more of the island's natural woodlands as the population grew and prospered. Recent investigations show that by about 1500, there was little or no timber left on the island. The population of the island reached its peak of about 10,000, far exceeding the capabilities of the small island's ecosystem. Resources became scarce, and the once lush palm forests were destroyed, cleared for agriculture and moving the massive stone Moai, which occupied increasingly large labor forces. The island became a metaphor for ecological disaster, with depleted soils and little wood left for canoes, limiting fishing activities. The thriving and advanced social order began to decline into bloody civil war and later cannibalism. Eventually, all of the Moai standing along the coast were torn down by the islanders themselves. All of the statues now standing are the result of recent archaeological efforts. Conflict and upheaval climaxed in the 1600s. Archeological studies and oral Rapanui traditions have yielded strong evidence of bloody battles and massacres, mass destruction and anarchy.

The overthrow of the old religion as the Moai cult faded was replaced by a "bird man" cult in which athletes competed to bring back the first egg of the nesting season from terns on a nearby islet. The tribal competitors raced out to the islet and back on reed floats. The tribe whose designated athlete brought back the first egg ruled the island for the next year. According to tradition, the "bird man" system survived into the nineteenth century.

On Easter Sunday 1722, the island's 1,400 years of isolation ended when three Dutch ships under the command of Admiral Jacob Roggenveen sighted the low, flat island, which he called Easter Island. The next morning they saw smoke rising from various locations on the island, but stood out to sea due to bad weather. They were amazed by the large statues they thought were made of clay. The equally amazed Rapanui, having believed that they were the only people in the world, brought them bananas and chickens, but following a misunderstanding 9 or 10 islanders were shot by the nervous Dutch sailors before the fleet departed.

In 1770 the Spanish, under Don Felipe Gonzalez de Haedo, arrived at the island, which they claimed for the king of Spain in a ceremony that included placing three Christian crosses at strategic point on the island. An official document was signed by some of the Rapanui using the island's unique Rongorongo script. Captain James Cook reached the island during his exploration of the South Pacific in 1774. In need of water and fresh provisions, he was disappointed at how little they found on the island. Cook, familiar with other Polynesian peoples, recognized the Rapanui as being of the same race and origin as the other Pacific islanders. A French expedition, led by J.F.G. de la Pérouse, spent 11 hours ashore in 1786. The French made an attempt to introduce plants and animals to help the starving islanders. Goats, hogs, and sheep were set ashore, and various plants, such as citrus and vegetables were given to the estimated 1,200 islanders that appeared. The first Europeans to visit Rapa Nui found a society in crisis, although they did not recognize it as such. Noting the impoverished Rapanui who could offer them little in the way of food supplies, and contrasting their condition to the huge statues, the Europeans concluded that some earlier race had constructed the monuments.

Discovery by the Europeans had a catastrophic effect on island society.

Slavery and disease reduced the population. By 1862, the population was estimated at about 6,000, but contact with the South American mainland included disastrous slave raids by Peruvians and others, which reduced the island population by one-third. An estimated 90% of the Rapanui, often sent to the guano mines, died within one or two years of capture. Eventually the Catholic Bishop of Tahiti led a public outcry that so embarrassed the Peruvian government that the few survivors were rounded up and returned to the island. Smallpox broke out on the ship carrying the survivors home, and only 15 arrived at the island. The resulting smallpox epidemic nearly wiped out the remaining island population.

French Catholic missionaries established a mission station in 1864, converting the majority to Catholicism. The missionaries attempted to protect the islanders, who were often shot by foreigners, sometimes just for the sport. The ship captain that brought the missionaries, Jean Baptiste Dutrou-Bornier, decided that the island had possibilities. He traded for some land and quickly became a power in the island. With fire and gun he intimidated the missionaries, who eventually fled, and kept the dwindling number of Rapanui in virtual slavery. He then declared himself king. The population dropped to an almost unsustainable 111 people in 1877 when the Rapanui rose and murdered Bornier. The Rapanui culture nearly disappeared along with the murdered, enslaved, or disappeared kings, priests, and learned men.

In 1888, the Chilean government took control of the island, until then unclaimed by any foreign government. The island was an unattractive target for acquisition as it lacked rivers and trees, and the rugged coastline left no room for a safe harbor. The Chilean government assumed that the island had agricultural potential and strategic possibilities for a naval station. Formal annexation brought little change to the island until 1896 when the government placed the island under the jurisdiction of the department of Valparaiso.

Through a series of forced land deals and irregular rental contracts, a private sheep ranch was created that occupied nearly all of the island's 40,000 acres in 1895. The ranch authorities, under the direction of a Chilean businessman, Enrique Merlet, confiscated buildings and all animals left to the Rapanui by the missionaries, who fled the island. The Rapanui were forced to build a stone wall around the village of Hanga Roa and, except for work, permission was needed to leave the area, even to fetch water. Those Rapanui who rebelled against the harsh treatment were exiled to the mainland and few ever returned.

A Scots-Chilean company, Williamson Balfour, in 1903 created a subsidiary, the Easter Island Exploitation Company, which took over all of the island outside Hanga Roa. The island was given over to commercial production of wool and animal byproducts. These activities further harmed the vegetation of the island and many archaeological sites were destroyed to make sheep pens and other structures. Successive Chilean governments renewed the company's contracts until 1953, even though in 1935 the island was declared a national part and historic monument. The plight of the impoverished Rapanui, who lacked even such essentials as soap and adequate clothing, was mostly ignored. At one point the desperate islanders petitioned the government to allow them to emigrate to Tahiti.

From 1953 to 1965, the Chilean Navy governed the island, an administration that proved even harsher that that of the commercial company. Between 1944 and 1958, a known 41 Rapanui attempted to escape their island "prison" in open boats. Some made it to the Tuamotus in French Polynesia, but at least half disappeared at sea. In the 1950s, a Norwegian archaeological expedition and systematic surveys awakened the government to the possibility of attracting tourists and opened new vistas for the remaining islanders. The government, in response to a revolt by the Rapanui, gave the island a civilian administration similar to the mainland provinces and began several development projects in 1965. Before 1965, there were no airline flights and supply ships visited the island only once or twice a year.

The construction of an airfield led to the construction of small hotels and inns, tourist agencies, restaurants, and curio shops in Hanga Roa. Mainland business people and television arrived, adding to the foreign influences. What was left of the Rapanui Polynesian culture began to quickly fade. Subsistence agriculture declined as food imports increased. Social problems, particularly alcoholism, became serious.

In 1994, the Rapanui demanded control of their own affairs in order to save the remnants of their culture, including their language. Increased tourism and other contacts with the mainland flood the island with foreign influences. For many Rapanui, restoring their ancestral monuments is parallel to reclaiming land rights and cultural identity. A power struggle developed between two rival groups that claimed leadership of the Council of Elders, a community organization based on traditional Rapanui social structure. The issue was how the islanders should regain control of government lands and what interests should prevail in the island's development.

Since the 1970s, the Council of Elders had been led by Alberto Hotus, the mayor of Hanga Roa in the early 1990s. He and his supporters backed a Chilean government plan to distribute surplus government land to the Rapanui. The plan would also give them greater say in the administration of the remaining government lands, which include a 16,000-acre cattle ranch and a 16,000-acre national park. The opposition, led by owners of tourist businesses, challenged Hotus' leadership and elected a new council, but Hotus refused to step down. The challengers rejected the government plan to share responsibliliy for government lands under the Indigenous Peoples Act. Instead, they want the lands to be directly ceded to the Rapanui for administration in coordination with the national government. The challengers accepted communal ownership of the cattle ranch, with leases to private users, but rejected any plan that would allow parts of their ancestral lands to remain under government control.

After decades of neglect, the Rapanui have begun to take pride in their heritage. Aided by fellow Polynesians, they began to recover much of their lost culture. Activists demanded that many artifacts be returned to the island from the Valparaiso museum on the mainland. The restoration of AhuTongariki, the greatest monument of prehistoric Polynesian culture was completed in the late 1990s. Thirteen of the massive Moai have been resurrected on the huge stone altar, the ahu. The Moai stand as tall as 27 feet (8.2 m.), with elongated heads and shortened torsos, long ears, prominent noses, and pursed lips. The restoration at Tongariki is seen by the Rapanui as a landmark in their efforts to preserve the remains of the civilization that flourished on the island in a past era of glory.

Weekly flights from Santiago, Chile and Tahiti have made tourism the major industry. By the early 1990s, more than 7,000 people a year were visiting Rapanui. On New Year's Eve 1999–2000, the Rapanui flag was raised with the Chilean flag beneath it. The Chilean government demanded that it be brought down as the only official flag allowed to be hoisted is the flag of Chile. During the Tapiti festival, which celebrates the island's Polynesian heritage, held in late January and early February in 2000, nationalists for the first time marched through Hanga Roa bearing their nationalist flag and were applauded by many of the tourists.

SELECTED BIBLIOGRAPHY:

Dos Passos, John. *Easter Island*. 1971.
Guy, Jacques B.M. *Easter Island Tablets*. 1990.
Matraux, Alfred. *Easter Island: A Stone-Age Civilization of the Pacific*. 1957.
Stanley, David. *South Pacific Handbook*. 1999.

Réunionese

Réunionais; Reunion Islanders; Reunionese; Renyons

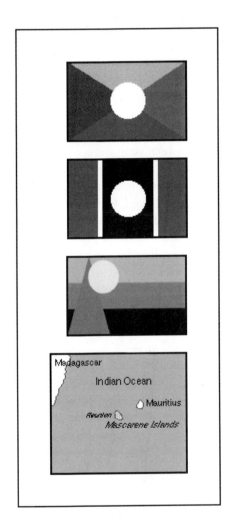

POPULATION: Approximately (2002e) 690,000 Réunionese in the Indian Ocean region, concentrated in Réunion, one of the major islands of the Mascarene Islands. Other large communities live on nearby Mauritius, with a Réunionese population of over 40,000; on Madagascar, with 20,000; and in metropolitan France, where 350,000 live.

THE RÉUNIONESE HOMELAND: The Réunionese homeland, called Renyon in the Creole language, is a large island lying in the Indian Ocean 425 miles (684 km) east of the island of Madagascar, which lies off the coast of southeastern Africa. The island is part of the Mascarene Islands, a group that also includes the independent island state of Mauritius. The island is mountainous with a flat, heavily populated plain around the central rugged core. The island's population density is high, even in areas that typically would be considered too mountainous to support a dense population. The island forms an overseas department of the French republic. *Department of Réunion (Renyon)*: 969 sq. mi.—2,511 sq. km, (2002e) 744,000—Réunionese 91%, French (Metros) 6%, others 3%. The Réunionese capital and major cultural center is St. Denis, (2002e) 138,000, metropolitan area 251,000. The other important center is St. Paul, (2002e) 93,000, metropolitan area 146,000.

FLAG: The Réunionese national flag, the flag of the national movement, has four triangles, yellow on the top, blue on the hoist, green on the bottom, and red on the fly, bearing a centered white circle. The flag of the Réunion Movement has three vertical stripes of red, black, and red, the black twice the width of the red and bearing a centered white circle.

The flag of the Understanding and Helping Hand Movement is a horizontal tricolor of pale blue, green, and black bearing a red triangle and yellow circle near the hoist.

PEOPLE AND CULTURE: The Réunionese are an island people, a mixture of the descendents of French settlers, African slaves, Malagasy immigrants, Indian and Chinese indentured laborers, and later Malay and Indochinese laborers from the former French Asian colonies. About a quarter of the Réunionese are of French descent, with many living in the mountainous interior, where they have preserved many archaic traditions and dialects; another 25% are of Indian descent, mostly Tamils,* living in the coastal lowlands; and about 45% are Creoles, of African and mixed background, inhabiting the lowlands and the growing urban areas.

LANGUAGE AND RELIGION: The most widely spoken language is a French patois called Creole. French is the official language and is the language of administration and education. Literacy is high; about 80% are able to read and write French. Creole, also called Réunion Creole French, is spoken by over 90% of the population and is gaining status as a national language. There are two dialects, informally called the urban dialect and the popular dialect. The urban dialect is closer to spoken French, while the popular dialect, also called Deep Creole, is spoken mostly in rural areas and has more borrowings from Bantu and other African languages.

The majority of the Réunionese are Roman Catholic, about 85%, with smaller numbers of Hindus, Muslims, and Buddhists. The Roman Catholic religion has become an integral part of Réunionese culture; religious festivals and ceremonies are attended by all segments of the population as cultural events.

NATIONAL HISTORY: The island was known to Arab traders sailing the Indian Ocean but was uninhabited when first visited by Portuguese explorers in 1502. The islands were again visited by the Portuguese in 1513; the archipelago was named Mascarene for the explorer Mascarenhas, who came to the islands in 1545.

The French claimed the island in 1642 and four years later designated it a penal colony. French settlers arrived in 1649, including many prisoners sent from metropolitan France. In 1665, the island, called Bourbon for the French dynasty, became an important post on the trade routes to India and the East. With no indigenous population to exploit, the French began to import slaves from the African mainland. In 1715 coffee was introduced, and vast sugar plantations were established with slave labor. From the 17th to the 19th centuries, French immigration, supplemented by influxes of Africans, Chinese, Malays, and Malabar Indians gave the island its ethnic mix.

The French Revolution, which ended the Bourbon dynasty, reached the island in 1793; many planter families were sent to guillotines set up in the main squares of the largest towns. The name of the island was changed from Bourbon to Réunion to symbolize the reunion of the government and people under the new French republic. In 1804, when Napoleon became emperor of France, the island was again renamed—Bonaparte, for the new French dynasty.

The British took control of the Mascarene Islands during the Napoleonic Wars in 1810. Réunion was returned to France in 1815, although the British retained control of Mauritius. During the Bourbon restoration in 1815 the island was again named Bourbon but reverted to the name Réunion in 1830.

Slavery was outlawed by France in 1848, leading to a labor shortage on the plantations. Indentured laborers were imported from the Malabar Coast of India and from among the Malays of nearby Madagascar and the French colonies in Asia. Authority on the island remained in the hands of the powerful French planter aristocracy, with the aid of bureaucrats and troops sent from continental France. The opening of the Suez Canal in 1869 cost the island its importance as a stopover on the East Indies trade route.

The mixed population of the island developed a French patois for intergroup communications. Most assimilated into the Creole French society, although the small Chinese and Muslim groups remained separate. By 1880 Réunion had a burgeoning population of over 200,000. The French majority continued to control the island's politics and economy, stirring up the first movements for equality and rights by the non-French groups.

The population dropped during World War I and by 1920 stood at just 173,000. The one-product economy, based on sugar and its offshoot, rum, and the lack of cultivable land forced many to emigrate to France in search of work, although plantation laborers continued to be imported from the French Indochina colonies. Neglect left the island underdeveloped and dominated by the small planter aristocracy.

The French government changed the island's status after World War II from a colony to an overseas department, with all the rights and financial subsidies of the metropolitan departments. The French welfare system was extended to the island, bringing unprecedented prosperity and a dramatic population increase in the 1950s and 1960s. All segments of the population enjoyed a considerable increase in standard of living, but power remained with the French planters and the "Metros" sent from Europe to fill government positions.

The national liberation movement that swept Africa in the 1960s led to the politicization of the Réunionese; pro-French and pro-independence groups proliferated. The Parti Communiste Réunionais advocated autonomy, socialism, and the adoption of Creole as the official language. By the early 1970s several groups were pressing for complete independence.

To counter growing unrest, the government designated Réunion a governmental region in 1974, but with little real power. In 1978 the Organization of African Unity (OAU) demanded that France decolonize the territory, the last important European territory in the Indian Ocean. The large French population opposed moves toward self-government, as did the French government, as the island was the last French military base in the region. Separatists from Réunion joined other nationalist groups of Bretons,* Guadeloupeans,* and groups from other French possessions in an attack on the Palace of Versailles outside Paris in 1978. Although there were other attacks during the 1970s and early 1980s, the assimilation of the majority of the population into French society muted calls for independence and kept separatist activity to a minimum.

Even anti-French groups were not anxious to lose the generous financial subsidies that Paris lavished on its remaining overseas possessions. In 1979 an estimated 75% of the Réunionese received welfare payments. Nonetheless, in the late 1980s most of the wealth of the island was in the hands of the French minority; discontent was growing among the agricultural workers, among whom unemployment was high. Although Réunion had the highest standard of living in the Indian Ocean, overcrowding was a major problem, and distribution of wealth was uneven. The stagnant economy and substantial emigration kept the population fairly constant throughout the 1980s, with about 5,000 Réunionese emigrating to mainland France every year.

In 1981 a number of autonomy and independence groups formed the Movement for the Liberation of Réunion with the support of several African countries and the OAU. Pro-French groups formed a loose organization called the French Réunion Association. In 1983 local elections the pro-independence grouping won over 50% of the vote. The leftist elements generally favored greater autonomy or independence, while pro-government groups feared the loss of French and European Union (EU) financial subsidies.

In the late 1990s, 66% of the island's trade was with France, and 75% with the EU as a whole; financial ties to Europe remained strong. The Réunionese, due to the financial subsidies, had incomes estimated at four times those of neighboring, independent Mauritius. Despite French efforts to diversify the economy, sugar and rum still accounted for 90% of exports. The apparent prosperity of the Réunionese was artificial, being based on aid and the salaries of civil servants.

In 1991, the French authorities attempted to close down the television station run by Dr. Camille Sudre, the moving spirit behind the separatist Fre-Dom Party. Creoles surrounded the station, and violence broke out. Within days rioting engulfed the island, with pro-independence groups demanding immediate independence. Troops flown in from France finally got control of the situation, but not before 11 people had died. Separatist sentiment is especially strong among the large Creole population, which increasingly sees itself as the only indigenous population of the island.

There remains considerable backing for greater autonomy, although pro-independence groups have lost support since the 1980s. The main political debate in 1999–2000 was over the appropriate degree of autonomy and the importance of continued French and EU financial subsidies. The island produces only a small fraction of what it consumes, and under the present situation could not survive without financial subsidies and food aid. France has created a situation that keeps the Réunionese dependent on the French government just to survive. An onofficial poll taken in early 2001 showed that support for some form of self-determination has grown to over 60%, but that those favoring full independence has fallen to less than 40%.

SELECTED BIBLIOGRAPHY:

Brehony, Kevin J., and Naz Rassool, eds. *Nationalisms Old and New*. 1999.
Gotthold, J.J., and D.W. Gotthold, eds. *Indian Ocean*. 1988.
Robert, Maurice. *Réunion*. 1976.
Safran, William, and Ramon Maiz, eds. *Identity and Territorial Autonomy in Plural Societies*. 2000.

Rhinelanders

Rheinlanders; Rheinfränkisch

POPULATION: Approximately (2002e) 13,765,000 Rhinelanders in Germany, 11,500,000 in the Rhineland region of Germany, and other large Rhinelander communities in Berlin and other parts of Germany. There are small Rhinelander populations in Belgium, France, and the Netherlands. Outside Europe there are Rhinelander populations in Canada, the United States, and in Brazil and Argentina.

THE RHINELANDER HOMELAND: The Rhinelander homeland lies northwestern Europe, mostly in the valley of the Rhine River, primarily on the west bank but with small areas also on the east. The northern districts include part of the industrialized Ruhr district; the south has some of Europe's most celebrated wine-producing districts. The area has no of-

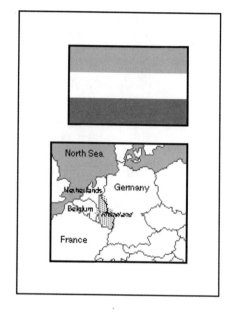

ficial status. The historical Rhineland region is split between various territories, including the *länder*, or states, of Saarland and Rhineland-Palatinate, and the northwestern districts of Baden-Württemberg, western Hesse, and southwestern North Rhine–Westphalia. *Region of Rhineland (Rheinland)*: 9,454 sq. mi.—24,485 sq. km, (2002e) 13,763,000—Rhinelanders 83%, other Germans 11%, Turks 4%, others 2%. The historical Rhinelander capital and major cultural center is Cologne, Köln in German, (2002e) 951,000, metropolitan area 1,893,000. Other important cultural centers are Dusseldorf, (2002e) 574,000, metropolitan area 1,321,000, the capital of North Rhine–Westphalia; Wiesbaden, (2002e) 260,000 (923,000), the capital of Hesse; and Bonn, (2002e) 295,000 (592,000), the post–World War II capital of the Federal Republic of Germany.

FLAG: The Rhenish national flag, the flag of the post–World War I national movement, is a horizontal tricolor of green, white, and red. The flag was subsequently adopted as the official flag of the German state of North Rhine–Westphalia.

PEOPLE AND CULTURE: The Rhinelanders are a German people of

Franconian descent, traditionally oriented to the French and the West, not to Berlin and the East. The Rhenish culture is distinct from the Prussian-influenced culture of Berlin and has been shaped by liberal ideas and historical ties to the West since the Roman conquest of the region. The Rhenish homeland contains some of the most densely populated areas of Europe. The Rhinelanders have historically formed a frontier between the East and West, between the French and the Germans, and between Protestants and Catholics.

LANGUAGE AND RELIGION: The language of the Rhinelanders is a Low German dialect, mainly the dialect called Rheinfränisch, spoken extensively in the Rhine Valley. The Rhenish dialects did not experience the "second consonantal shift" of the eighth and ninth centuries. The language, not mutually intelligible with other German dialects, is actually a group of dialects spoken in geographically distinct areas and descended from medieval Franconian. The Rhinelanders are bilingual, with standard German spoken in all areas, although Rhinelanders are readily recognizable by their characteristic pronunciation.

The Rhinelanders are divided religiously; about two-thirds are Roman Catholic and about a third Protestant, mostly in the northern districts. Religion has historically played an important part in local culture, but in the twentieth century religious influence diminished.

NATIONAL HISTORY: Celtic tribes long inhabited the fertile territory along the Rhine River, but the first organized government of the region was established by the Romans, who conquered and colonized the region from the first century A.D. Many of the present Rhenish cities are of Roman origin. Latinized in culture and language, the inhabitants developed a sophisticated, advanced culture that lasted for nearly four centuries. The Romans viewed the region as a buffer zone between Gaul and the Germanic peoples to the east.

Roman rule ended in the fifth century, and the region was overrun by Franks, Germanic tribes from outside the Roman Empire. By the sixth century the Franks controlled the Rhineland, much of western Germany, and northern France. In the eighth and ninth centuries, the Rhineland formed the heartland of the Frankish realm under Charlemagne, whose capital was at Aachen. In 843, Charlemagne's heirs divided his empire into three parts, with the Rhineland included in the middle kingdom, Lotharingia or Lorraine.

The Rhenish territories were included in the Holy Roman Empire, which reached its peak of power and influence in the mid-eleventh century. Following the breakup of the duchy of Lower Lorraine in the eleventh century, the Rhineland split into more than 100 ecclesiastic and secular fiefs and free imperial cities. In 1356, the several Rhenish rulers—the archbishops of Mainz, Trier, Cologne, and the Count Palatinate of Rhine—became electors of the empire.

The region remained a Roman Catholic stronghold during the Protestant Reformation and the religious wars in the sixteenth century. Politically divided into a number of petty states, the region was often a battleground for competing powers and religions. The devastation of the period left most Rhinelanders looking toward Paris and the West as new and liberal ideas began to be felt in Europe. In the East, Brandenburg and its successor, Prussia, came to represent to the Rhinelanders the harsh militaristic and Protestant influences in Germany.

The Prussians first gained control of the small territories of Kleve and Mark in the Rhine region in 1614, forming the nucleus of future Prussian power in the Rhineland. The feudal system, which generally disappeared from Europe by the eighteenth century, remained a force in many of the small Rhenish states. During the eighteenth and nineteenth centuries hundreds of thousands of Rhinelanders emigrated, mostly to North America, to escape the feudal backwardness and poverty of the region.

Thousands of fugitives from the terror of the French Revolution took refuge in the region, but with the rise of Napoleon it became a target of French expansion. The first Rhenish republic, the Republique Cisrenane, was created by the French in 1797. Napoleon later abolished most of the small Rhenish states and in 1801 created the Rhine Confederation. In 1803 Napoleon annexed all of the Rhineland west of the Rhine River to France, the first time all of ancient Gaul had been under one government since the fall of the Roman Empire. Napoleon's reorganization of the Rhineland eliminated the numerous petty states but prepared the way for Prussian control.

At the Peace of Vienna in 1815, Prussia received most of the Rhineland. The Westernized, mainly Roman Catholic Rhinelanders greatly resented the harsh, conservative, Protestant Prussians, especially since it was the industrialization of the Ruhr in the late nineteenth century that in large part made Prussia the strongest power in Europe. The Rhineland, despite rule by reactionary Prussia, remained one of the centers of liberal German thought, spiritually and culturally closer to Paris than to Berlin. Dissatisfaction with "foreign" Prussian rule came to a head during the revolutionary upheavals in Europe in 1848–49. Democratic and Rhenish separatist groups fought pitched battles with Prussian troops. The Rhenish revolution was finally put down, with brutal reprisals and increased oppression.

In 1866, the French supported the creation of an independent buffer state in the Rhineland, an idea that the Prussians supported in exchange for French neutrality during Prussia's war with the Austrians. The subsequent Prussian failure to live up to its promises was to be one of the causes of the Franco–Prussian War in 1870. Rhenish nationalism evolved as an anti-Prussian mass movement in the late nineteenth century. Nationalists in the region supported the idea of the separation of the Rhineland, now called the Rhine Province, from Protestant Prussia.

The Rhineland's industries were very important to the German war effort after 1914. The collapse of the German Empire in November 1918 was followed by widespread revolution in Germany. A Rhenish separatist movement formed in Koblenz and Aachen, and disturbances were instigated in the Rhenish cities by separatists and radicals opposed to the National Congress of Soldiers and Workers Councils that met in Berlin in December 1918 to form a new German government.

On 4 December 1918, a meeting in Cologne of the Catholic Center Party adopted a resolution in favor of a Rhenish-Westphalian Republic as part of a new German federation. The separatists had the support of much of the Catholic population of the region. The Catholics hoped to end the privileged position the Protestants had enjoyed under Prussian rule. The French and Belgian governments, seeking a neutral space between their borders and those of Germany, supported the erection of an independent Rhenish buffer state at the Paris Peace Conference in 1919, but they were opposed by President Woodrow Wilson of the United States and by other allied leaders.

Separatists, supported by the French, proclaimed on 1 June 1919 the independence of the Rhenish Republic, with its capital at Koblenz. A Rhenish government was formed under the leadership of Hans Dorten, but by the terms of the Treaty of Versailles Allied troops occupied the Rhineland (British and Belgian troops in the northern districts and American troops in the south), and the Dorten government collapsed.

The Saar Territory in January 1920 was given the status of a sovereign state under French military occupation and the League of Nations. By the terms of the treaty, the Saarland's future would be decided by plebiscite in 1935; the choices would be inclusion in Germany, union with France, and separate independence.

In March 1920, a communist "Red Army" of 50,000 to 80,000 took over the major industrial centers, but were driven underground by "Freikorps" troops dispatched by the German government. The French and Belgian governments used instability in the region and default by Germany on reparations as excuses to occupy the region in January 1923. Widespread passive resistance by the Rhinelanders resulted.

Unable to persuade the other allies to support its annexation of the Rhineland or the creation of a Rhenish buffer state, the French government supported a Rhenish rebellion. On 21 October 1923, separatist uprisings broke out in Dusseldorf, Bonn, Koblenz, Weisbaden, and Mainz. The separatists included Konrad Adenauer (who would be a member of the provincial diet from until 1933 and a post–World War II chancellor of West Germany). The separatists proclaimed the independence of the Rhineland Republic (Rheinische Republik) with its capital at Aachen on 22 October 1923. The new republic was created as a federation of three states, North State, South State, and Ruhr State. Rioting by communists, fighting between Rhenish separatists and the Freikorps, the opposition of the United States and the United Kingdom, and the assassination of the Rhenish president brought about the collapse of the republic on 31 January 1924. Many Rhenish nationalists fled to France, and in 1925 Germany and the allies signed the Locarno Pact, which regulated the administration of the Rhineland under allied occupation and reaffirmed the demilitarization of the region. Support for Rhenish nationalism faded with the return of constitutional government.

In 1930, the last allied troops withdrew, but under the terms of the Locarno Pact the Rhineland remained demilitarized. The rise of the National Socialists—the Nazis—in the early 1930s was accompanied by agitation for the reoccupation of the Rhineland. In January 1935 a plebiscite was held in the Saarland after a massive propaganda campaign by the Nazis. The result was 90.7% in favor of reunion with Germany. Soon after the plebiscite the German government purchased the Saar mines from France. The heavy industries of the Rhineland were crucial to the Nazis' plans for rearmament and for the later conquest of Europe. On 8 March 1936, Adolf Hitler denounced the Locarno Pact; on the same day, German troops crossed the Rhine and occupied the Rhineland. All important Catholic, socialist, nationalist, and communist leaders were removed from official posts, and the many anti-Nazi organizations and political parties were forcibly abolished. Despite the suppression of all opposition, the region, particularly Cologne, remained an anti-Nazi stronghold for several years.

The Siegfried Line, the German fortifications in the Rhineland, were penetrated by the Allies during World War II only after very heavy fighting. The region was heavily bombed, particularly the industrial cities of the Ruhr. Aachen was the first important German city to fall to the Allies, in October 1944. In 1945 French troops occupied the districts of Trier and Koblenz, while British troops occupied the Cologne, Dusseldorf, and Aachen districts. The French government again proposed and supported the separation of the Rhineland from Germany, but the plan was stopped by the British and Americans, who opposed the breakup of Germany into a number of small, hostile states.

In 1946 the region was reorganized. The state of Rhineland-Palatinate was formed from the merger of the Rhenish Palatinate, Rhenish Hesse, the southern districts of the former Prussian Rhine Province (including Koblenz and Trier), and a small district of the former Prussian province of Hesse–Nassau. North Rhine–Westphalia was formed through the union of the former Prussian province of Westphalia, the northern districts of Prussia's Rhine Province, and the state of Lippe. The Saarland, again under French occupation, was made a self-governing state under the auspices of the United Nations. The new states had little national or historical unity or political cohesion.

Konrad Adenauer, the former Rhenish nationalist leader, was elected chancellor of the Federal Republic of Germany in 1949. Adenauer, mayor of Cologne until dismissed by the Nazis in 1933, had twice been imprisoned. He was the cofounder of the Christian Democratic Union in 1945 and was the party's president from 1946 and 1966. He was reelected chancellor in 1953, 1957, and 1961.

In spite of the division into several states, the Rhinelanders retained a sense of cultural and historical unity. The Rhenish Catholic vote remained important, and in the 1960s and 1970s the Rhinelanders were among the most avid supporters of European unity. The Rhine River links the economically inseparable areas of eastern France, the Rhineland, and the Low Countries.

In the 1990s the Rhineland split between a prosperous south and an economically ailing north, a consequence of a postwar effort by leaders of the industrial Ruhr to discourage industries moving from East Germany from settling there. The industries generally went to the southern districts, where they became among the most prosperous in Germany. In the state of Lower Saxony, the Rhinelanders formed a separate regional league with responsibility for traffic, cultural affairs, and welfare.

The economic and political integration of Europe in the European Union has again stimulated interest in Rhenish autonomy. The region, closely tied economically and historically with the neighboring French, Belgians, and Dutch, remains oriented toward Paris and Brussels, not to Berlin. The transfer of the German capital from Bonn, in the Rhineland, to the historical capital of Berlin at the end of the twentieth century raised Rhenish fears that Germany would once again shift its attention to the East.

SELECTED BIBLIOGRAPHY:

Ardagh, John, and Katharina Ardagh. *Germany and the Germans: The United Germany in the Mid-1990s.* 1996.

Bunn, T. Davis. *Rhineland Inheritance.* 1993.

Craig, Gordon A. *The Germans.* 1991.

Medlicott, W.N. *The Rhineland Crisis and the Ending of Sanctions, March 2—July 30, 1936.* 1978.

Riffians

Riff; Riffs; Riffi; Rifi; Ruafas; Rifias; Riffian Berbers; Imazighen; Amazigh

POPULATION: Approximately (2002e) 2,610,000 Riffians in North Africa, concentrated in the Rif region of Morocco and the Spanish coastal enclaves. Outside the region there are substantial Riffian populations in adjacent areas of Algeria and in France.

THE RIFFIAN HOMELAND: The Riffian homeland occupies a hilly coastal lowland in northern Morocco and northwestern Algeria, extending west to the Strait of Gibraltar and south to the Rif Mountains, which divide the region from the rest of Morocco. The Rif region includes five enclaves, holdovers from the colonial period, that are claimed by both Spain and Morocco. The territories—Ceuta, Melilla, Penon de Vélex de la Gomera, Penon de Alhucémas, and the Chafarinas Islands—are administered by Spain's region of Andalusia. The

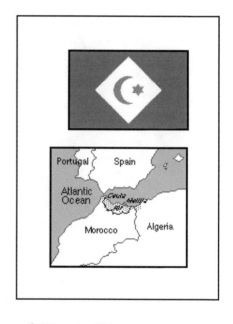

Riffian territory in Morocco forms all or part of Tangier-Tétouan, Chaouia-Ouardigha, Oriental, and Taza-al Hoceima-Taounate provinces. *Rif (Er Rif/Tamazgha)*: 6,584 sq. mi.—17,052 sq. km (2002e) 2,607,000— Riffians 74%, Arabs 21%, Spaniards 4%, others 1%. The Riffian capital and major cultural center is Tétouan, called Tittawen by the Riffians, (2002e) 342,000. The other important cultural centers are Chaouen, called Cefcawen locally, (2002e) 38,000, and al-Hoceims (al-Husaymah), (2002e) 63,000, and the Spanish enclaves of Ceuta, called Sibta by the Riffians, (2002e) 77,000, and Melilla, called Tamlit, (2002e) 69,000.

FLAG: The Riffian national flag, the flag of the former republic, is a red field charged with a centered white diamond bearing a green crescent moon and six-pointed star.

PEOPLE AND CULTURE: The Riffians are a Berber people, descendants of the region's indigenous pre-Arab population. The Riffians, calling themselves Amazigh, are divided into 19 distinct tribal groups based on geographic distribution, five in the west along the Mediterranean coast, seven in the center, five in the east, and two in the southeastern desert area. More closely related to the European peoples than to the Semitic Arabs, the Riffians' high incidence of fair hair—25% blond and 4% red—is roughly the same as Ireland and Scotland and would seem to validate theories that ancient Celts crossed to North Africa. The Riffians have as little to do with government as possible. Most local problems never reach the attention of government officials but are solved by tribal elders. National consciousness, developed in the early twentieth century, remains strong. The Riffian material culture is based on agriculture, herding, and sardine seining. Before their loss of independence in 1926, the Riffians were organized by kinship into graded age units; each unit elected or appointed a council of renowned fighters. There is today a large group of urbanized, Arabized Riffians, known as *muarabeen*, in Casablanca, Rabat, and other large Moroccan cities. The Riffian citizens of the Spanish enclaves, making up about half the population of the enclaves, are the only indigenous Berber population in the European Union (EU).

LANGUAGE AND RELIGION: The Riffian language, called Tarifit, belongs to the Tamazight group of Berber group of the Afro-Asiatic languages. Tarifit is spoken in four major dialects—Urrighel, Arzeu, Igzennaian, and Iznacen or Beni Iznassen. The language is not recognized officially in Morocco or Spain, where it is called Rifeño. Most Riffians also speak Arabic, as the language of administration and religion. One of the central Riffian tribes speaks Arabic, as do sections of the five western tribes. Many are also able to speak French and even more use Spanish, both formerly colonial languages. Due to difficulties in writing and expressing their traditions in Tarifit, many Riffian writers use other languages, primarily Spanish or Arabic. In 1999 the translation of 114 *suras* (chapters) of the Koran from Arabic into Tarifit was finished. Many predict that the translation will shake Morocco much as the translation of the Bible into vernacular translations shook medieval Europe. The Riffians, however, have a low literacy rate, primarily because children are taught in a language they do not understand.

Overwhelmingly Sunni Muslim, the Riffians have retained many pre-Islamic customs and traditions, including equal status for women. The Riffian religion, known as Maraboutic Islam, retains many practices more ancient than Islam, such as observance of the cults of saints. Belief in *marabouts*, wise men who practice healing and cast out evil spirits, is widespread.

NATIONAL HISTORY: The ancient Berbers traded with the Phoenicians as early as the seventh century B.C. The Carthaginian Empire, which was of Phoenician origin, controlled the coastal regions until its defeat in the second century B.C. by the Romans. Following the Roman destruction of Carthage, the Berbers formed a separate kingdom called Mauretania. Roman rule extended to Mauretania in 25 B.C.; the Romans subdued the last Berber tribes in A.D. 41–42.

Berber-populated Mauretania, a prosperous agricultural province, suffered invasions by barbarian tribes from Europe after the Roman collapse in the fifth century. Germanic Vandals defeated the remnants of the Roman garrisons and overran the mostly Christian province. The wanton destruction of the wealthy region gave the world a new word, "vandalism." Thousands of Berber refugees fled to sanctuaries in the mountains. There the Berbers created a loose tribal confederation that resisted later incursions.

Invading Muslim Arabs conquered the lowlands in 683, destroying the remnants of Christianity in the region, but Arab incursions into the Berber mountains met fierce resistance. Unable to defeat the tribes, the Arabs eventually formed alliances with tribal chiefs. Isolated in the Rif Mountains, the Berbers became known as "Riffians" (the name "Rif" comes from an Arab word meaning "edge of cultivated area") and the Arabs of the lowlands "Fasis," meaning "people of Fez." Slow to adopt the Arabs' Islamic religion, the tribes molded the new faith to their ancient customs; the unveiled Riffian women retained their pre-Islamic freedom and respect.

The coastal tribes and their Arab neighbors turned to piracy in the twelfth century, their swift raiders preying on European shipping. The Portuguese attacked the pirate bastions, seizing the Riffian port of Ceuta in 1415 and thereby initiating the European conquest of Africa. Spanish forces conquered Melilla in 1497 and took Ceuta from the Portuguese in 1578.

The European powers, competing for influence in Morocco in the eighteenth and nineteenth centuries, played on traditional Arab–Berber enmity. In 1904 Spain and France divided Morocco into spheres of influence; most of the Rif was assigned to the Spanish zone. Spanish military columns moved out of the port cities in 1909, intent on subduing the troublesome Riffian tribes. Badly mauled, the Spanish retreated back to the garrisons, pursued and harassed by Riffian warriors. The Spanish authorities, although their authority remained restricted to the fortified ports, claimed the Rif as part of a protectorate called Spanish Morocco, created in 1912.

Repressive Spanish rule aroused the Riffian inhabitants of the coastal towns. Muhammad Ibn 'Abd el-Krim Al'Khattabi, employed as a newspaper editor in Melilla, became disillusioned with Spanish rule. Eventually imprisoned, he escaped in 1918 and was made a *qadi* (Muslim judge) and tribal chief. Joined by his brother, 'Abd el-Krim led a widespread Riffian rebellion, the precursor of the anticolonial struggle for independence. He became the hero of the Berber peoples of North Africa by forming a modern army that annihilated a Spanish force of 60,000 at the Battle of Anual in July 1921. The Riffians pursued the fleeing Spanish to the walls of their fortified positions on the coast. At Chaouan 16,000 Spaniards were slaughtered and 40,000 driven from the city. In the east the Riffians overran Melilla, sending a flotilla of terrified refugees back to Spain.

United for the first time in centuries, the Riffians seemed invincible to the Spaniards huddled behind the walls of the few ports still in Spanish hands. 'Abd el Krim overcame tribal rivalries and created a civil administration for the tribal confederation. The new government adopted modern judicial and legislative systems. On 19 September 1921 'Abd el-Krim declared the independence of the Confederal Republic of the Tribes of the Rif. He defeated another Spanish army sent against him in 1924.

Riffian tribes in the south, living on both sides of the border between the French and Spanish zones, began to attack French outposts, finally drawing France into the war in the spring of 1925. Faced with el-Krim's successes and seeing his movement as a threat to their colonial possessions in North Africa, the French met with the Spanish in Madrid and decided on joint action. A combined Franco-Spanish force of over 250,000 men, the largest European army to operate in Africa until heavily armed and technologically advanced, moved on the Riffian state in late 1925. Defeated in May 1926, the Riffians surrendered, ending the twentieth century's first attempt at Berber independence. El-Krim was exiled to the French island of Réunion in the Indian Ocean. He died in Cairo in 1963, having refused to return to Morocco as long as French troops remained on North African soil.

The Spanish authorities began to exploit the iron mines of the Rif Mountains in the 1930s, during a period of relative peace. In 1936, Gen. Francisco Franco launched his attack on the Spanish Republic from Morocco, having recruited a large number of Arab and Riffian volunteers, who served him loyally during the Spanish Civil War. The Spanish made no attempt to set Berber against Arab as did the French authorities.

The Riffians nonetheless again rose against the Spanish authorities in 1954–55; the rebellion gradually became part of the Moroccan independence movement. Granted independence in 1956, the Spanish zone, except for five small enclaves, became part of the united Moroccan kingdom. Promised autonomy, the Riffians celebrated Moroccan independence and pledged loyalty. The change of currency, however, caused a rapid rise in the cost of living, and difficulties arose from the introduction of French-speaking Moroccan officials. Mostly excluded from government and under pressure to assimilate, the Riffians lost their enthusiasm and turned first to resentment and then violence. In 1958 the Riffians rebelled again, only to suffer defeat by mechanized Moroccan troops in 1959. The leaders were rounded up, packed into helicopters, flown out to sea, and shoved overboard, supposedly at the orders of the crown prince and army chief, later King Hassan.

A failed Riffian coup in 1971 began a period of severe cultural repression. The Riffian language was purged, and Egyptian and Syrian teachers were posted in the highlands to inculcate Arabic in the Tarifit-speaking Riffians. Demands for linguistic and cultural rights again provoked large demonstrations in 1981. As unrest spread new demands were raised—Berber studies in schools and universities, and the release of Riffian nationalists jailed by the Moroccan authorities.

Emigration to Europe and a government crackdown on cannabis production—the region's only lucrative export—became nationalist issues in the 1980s. A Berber political party was a member of the ruling coalition government of Moroccan legislature from 1984 to 1993, although the king's authority superseded that of the legislature, and advances for the Riffians remained minimal.

For several months in mid-1986, violent clashes occurred in the Spanish enclave of Melilla between the authorities and the Riffians, who made up about a half of the city's population. The Spanish government charged that Morocco was fomenting unrest in an effort to redirect Riffian anger from the repression in Morocco. The Moroccan government, bogged down in a seemingly endless war against the Sahrawis* of Western Sahara, greatly feared the spread of unrest to the Rif. In 1993 Riffian nationalists appealed to Spain, the former colonial power, to intervene in order to save the Riffian homeland from the ravages of emigration and depopulation.

A widespread protest in May 1994 by Riffian activists demanding recognition of their language and culture was countered by the arrest of 28 militants. Three of the militants were later sentenced to prison. However, later in 1994, the government commenced Berber-language television and radio news broadcasts. In August 1994, King Hassan announced that the Berber languages would be taught in primary schools in areas with Berber majorities, but the program was never fully implemented. Meetings by Riffian cultural associations continued to be banned. In February 1996 Riffian nationalists called on the Moroccan government to recognize their language as an official language and to make its teaching obligatory in schools.

The annexation of Melilla by Spain five centuries before was celebrated in October 1997, although neither the Spanish king nor the head of government attended due to security concerns. The enclaves, not listed by the United Nations as colonies, because they had been settled long before Morocco existed in its present shape, were becoming an uncomfortable issue between the European Union and Morocco, yet it was the Riffians who had the most valid historical claim.

One of the mainstays of the Riffian economy is money sent by emigrants working in France. Hundreds of thousands of Riffians live and work in Europe, often making annual trips to their homeland to visit families and bring goods purchased in Europe. Riffians who remain in the homeland mostly survive by raising cannabis, and its finished product, hashish, which has become the major export, although it remains illegal. Plans for an automobile tunnel from near Tangier across the Strait of Gibraltar to Spain were begun in 1979. Tests and plans continue, although little has actually been constructed. The possibility of driving from the Rif to France, where hundreds of thousands of Riffians live and work, would dramatically change their lives.

In July 1999, King Hassan II, the ruler of Morocco since 1961, died. With the death of the dictatorial monarch and the accession of his son, Mohamed VI, the pressure on the Riffians eased somewhat, but economic and political autonomy remain a distant dream. The Riffians hoped that the neglect and backwardness they had endured since the 1958 rebellion would finally end.

The question of the five Spanish enclaves continues to irritate Riffian sensibilities. The Spanish government claims the enclaves on historical grounds and argues that military bases in the territories are important for Spanish national security. The Moroccans argue that the UN principles of decolonization should be applied, that Spanish bases threaten the security of the kingdom and provide havens for dissident groups. The Riffians claim that the disposition of the territories, like that of the rest of the Rif, is not a bilateral issue between Spain and Morocco but concerns the future of the Rif homeland.

In July 1999, following a scandal that brought down the local autonomous government, Mustafa Aberchan became the first Riffian and Muslim to become the mayor of the autonomous city of Melilla. The Spanish enclaves have little economic value and have become centers of money laundering, drug smuggling, and illegal immigration. Tensions between the Andalusian Christians and the Riffian Muslims are becoming serious problems.

The Riffian revival of the 1990s brought nationalists into conflict with the Islamic movement in Morocco. The Islamic radicals accused Riffian activists of treachery and of adhering to the ideology of the former colonial rulers. Thirty years ago the Riffians wanted only language parity with Arabic, but after three decades without appreciable change, militant groups are demanding Riffian supremacy and increasingly are willing to fight for that ideal.

The Moroccan government accused the Berber movement of opposing standardization and thereby disturbing national unity. In 1997 the government introduced new measures outlawing Berber names and restricting Berber children to approved Arab and Muslim names.

The question of the enclaves soured Spanish-Moroccan relations in 2001. Following Riffian demands for the language rights they enjoyed in the enclaves to be extended to the neighboring Moroccan territories the Moroccan government withdrew its ambassador from Madrid. Riffian activists announced plans to make the language issue the focus of a campaign to win their rights as a distinct North African nation.

Riffian activists call the government's Arabization program the second Arab conquest of North Africa. The Arabization policy generated a movement of culturally genocidal proportions. It is actually trying to subdue local identity in order to augment the numbers of so-called Arabs.

King Mohammed of Morocco met a long-standing demand from the nation's Riffian community by setting up an institute dedicated to their cultural heritage in October 2001. Berber leaders, while applauding the new institute, published a manifesto calling on the state to license a Berber television station, teach Berber in schools, and end restrictions on registering Berber names for their children. Riffian activists said the longer the government denies them their cultural rights, the greater the tensions will grow.

SELECTED BIBLIOGRAPHY:

Brett, Michael, ed. *The Berbers.* 1997.

Gellner, Ernest, and Charles Micaud, eds. *Arabs and Berbers: From Tribe to Nation in North Africa.* 1972.

Hart, David M. *Tribe and Society in Rural Morocco.* 2000.

Zartman, William I, and William Mark Habeeb, eds. *Polity and Society in Contemporary North Africa.* 1993.

Romands

Romandes; Suisse Romands

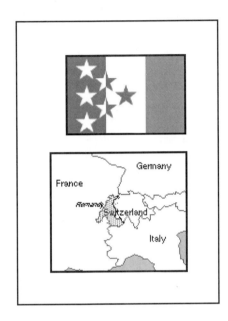

POPULATION: Approximately (2002e) 1,420,000 Romands in Switzerland, 1,290,000 in the Romande region of Switzerland, and the remainder in other regions of Switzerland and in France, particularly Paris.

THE ROMAND HOMELAND: The Romand homeland, popularly called the Swiss Romande, lies in western Switzerland, occupying the western part of the Swiss Plateau and bounded by the Jura Mountains on the west and the Pennine Alps in the south. The Romande includes the lake regions around Lake Geneva (Lac Léman), the Lake of Neuchâtel, Lake Morat, Lake la Gruyère, and Lake Bienne (Bielersee). Much of the region is composed of the fertile uplands and grassy meadows of the western Swiss Plateau, which has the majority of the population. The Romande has no official status. The region forms the majority French-speaking cantons of Fribourg, Geneva, Jura, Neuchâtel, and Vaud, and the western districts of Valais and Bern Cantons. *Romandy (Swiss Romande/Romandie)*: 3,934 sq. mi.—10,189 sq. km (2002e) 1,562,000—Romands 82%, other Swiss 14%, Portuguese, Spaniards, Turks, and others 4%. The Romand capital and major cultural center is Geneva, Genève in French, (2002e) 172,000, metropolitan area 608,000. The other important Romand center is Lausanne, (2002e) 114,000, metropolitan area 262,000.

FLAG: The Romand national flag, the flag of the Mouvement Romand, is a vertical tricolor of blue, white, and red, bearing three white stars on the blue stripe, two stars divided vertically white and blue at the juncture of the blue and white stripes, and a single blue star centered on the white strip. A white star on the upper fly, representing Switzerland, was removed in 1992 following the negative vote of the Swiss Germans in a referendum on closer economic ties to the rest of Europe.

PEOPLE AND CULTURE: The Romands are a distinct Romance people whose national identity has been shaped by Protestantism and their long separate history rather than by ethnic or linguistic considerations. Ethnically and linguistically the Romands are related to the Burgundians* and Savoyards* in the adjacent areas of France. For over a century the Romands have lived in isolation from the neighboring French and have evolved a distinct French-speaking Swiss culture. The Roman national identity is now that of a French-speaking, Protestant nation, but a part of the French nation. The descendents of ancient Latinized Celtic tribes, the Romands have only recently become politically mobilized, one of the latest groups in Europe to define its national identity as a distinct European nation.

LANGUAGE AND RELIGION: The language of the Romands is French; the majority speak both the standard French, based on the Paris dialect, and the local Romand dialects of Franco-Provençal, which differ considerably from standard French. An estimated third of the total Swiss population is able to speak French, although the Romands account for less than 20% of the total population. The dialect spoken around Geneva is the standard for the region and was the official language of the Swiss Republic for some time. Many of the isolated alpine valleys have preserved individual dialects. Since the sixteenth century there has been literature in the local dialects, notably in those of Geneva and Fribourg.

The majority of the Romands, estimated at over 75%, are Protestants, and a minority, about 23%, are Roman Catholic. The Protestant religion is central to the national identity of the Romands, and it differentiates them from the majority of the French-speaking populations in Europe. Geneva was a center of the Protestant Reformation and remains one of the great centers of Protestant culture in Europe.

NATIONAL HISTORY: Ancient Celtic tribes—Allobroges, Sequani, and Helvetii (or Helvetians)—inhabited the region around the highland lakes by the sixth century B.C. Part of the Celtic culture that extended across the European continent, the Celts remained tribal and never developed a state structure. Disunited, the tribes fought valiantly, but the region fell to Roman rule in 58–57 B.C. The Celts adopted the Roman culture and language, and the Latinized Celtic towns became centers of Roman culture. Roman culture left a lasting legacy in the language and culture of the region.

The decline of Roman power in the fifth century opened the way for invasions by barbarian tribes from outside the empire. Invading Germanic Burgundians devastated the Roman towns in the region in A.D. 442–43. The Burgundians eventually settled the region, and Geneva became the seat of a Burgundian kingdom. Another Germanic tribe, the Franks, conquered the area in 534–36 and joined it to their kingdom, the forerunner of the Holy Roman Empire.

The Romande formed an important and prosperous part of Charlemagne's empire. At the division of the Holy Roman Empire among Charlemagne's heirs in 843, the Romande was included in the middle kingdom of Lotharingia. Later, from 888 to 1032, the region was included in the successor kingdom known as Transjurane Burgundy. In 1033 the Holy Roman Empire gained control of the Romande area.

Politically divided, the region included the ecclesiastical states of Lausanne and Geneva, Habsburg territory in Fribourg and other areas, and French-speaking districts controlled by the German-speaking Bernese. In 1285 the citizens of Geneva placed themselves under the protection of the rulers of Savoy, and by 1387 they enjoyed wide powers of self-rule. Savoyard control of the bishops of Geneva nearly resulted in subjugation of the region. In 1481 Fribourg became the first of the Romande states to join the expanding Swiss Confederation.

In 1533, Geneva formed an alliance with two Swiss cantons, Fribourg and Bern, to resist Savoyard pressure. In 1536 Geneva, where the French theologian John Calvin had just settled, revolted against the duchy of Savoy and refused to acknowledge the authority of its Roman Catholic bishop. The citizens expelled the Savoyard bishop, and many turned to the new doctrine, that of the Protestant Reformation. The German-speaking Bernese conquered Lausanne and the Vaud region in 1536, facilitating the eastward expansion of the Protestant Reformation to the other Romande states.

In 1538 the Genevans expelled Calvin and many of his followers, but 1541 the majority accepted his doctrine. Calvin organized his church democratically, incorporating ideas of representative government. From 1541 to 1564 Geneva became the stronghold of the Calvinist brand of Protestantism. Calvin established at Geneva a theocratic state that became a leading political and intellectual center of Protestant Europe. Geneva's preeminence grew with the arrival of thousands of Protestant Huguenot refugees fleeing persecution and massacres in Roman Catholic France.

The French-speaking Romande states, both inside and outside the Swiss Confederation, were protected by a network of political and defensive alliances. The Romands, both Protestant and Catholic, prospered; the old ruling classes were gradually replaced by patrician elites more concerned with commerce than politics or religion. Carefully avoiding involvement in the sporadic wars that convulsed the surrounding regions, the Romands in the eighteenth century grew rich on trade and services.

Buffeted by the chaos and upheavals that followed the French Revolution in 1789, the Romande states became a refuge for people fleeing the revolutionary excesses in France. Occupied by French troops in 1798, the states were forcibly joined to Napoleon's Helvetic Republic. In 1803 the Swiss Confederation was partly restored, including the new French-speaking canton of Vaud and the important city of Lausanne. Following Napoleon's final defeat in 1815, Geneva, Neuchâtel, and Valais joined the

Swiss Confederation. In 1848, after a nearly bloodless civil war between the Protestant and Catholic cantons, the Swiss adopted a new constitution that guaranteed cantonal autonomy.

The Swiss carefully avoided involvement in the European wars of the nineteenth and twentieth centuries while developing as one of Europe's major banking centers. Strict banking and secrecy laws allowed the Swiss banks to do business without consideration of their clients' politics or crimes; they even established secret financial ties to the Nazis during World War II.

The confederation remained a prosperous, multinational, and multireligious island of tolerance in the center of turbulent Europe. Switzerland's strict neutrality precluded membership in the League of Nations, the United Nations, or any international organization; however, Geneva became the headquarters for many such organizations, including the League of Nations and many branches of the United Nations. In 1959 a referendum allowed Switzerland to join the European Free Trade Association (EFTA). In February 1971 women were for the first time allowed to vote in federal elections, and women have greatly affected subsequent elections.

Modern Romand nationalism grew from a movement of the French-speaking western districts in the Jura Mountains to separate from the predominantly German-speaking Bern Canton. In 1978 the majority French-speaking districts of northwestern Bern voted to form a new canton called Jura, but the separatists failed to win enough votes in the mixed districts around Lake Bienne (Biel). The controversy opened a bitter rift between the French and German cantons of Switzerland. Nationalist organizations called not just for the separation of Jura but for the separation of the French-speaking Romande from Switzerland.

The end of the Cold War pushed the traditionally neutral Swiss into closer cooperation with their European neighbors. In May 1992, the Swiss government formally applied for membership in the European Economic Community (EEC). A referendum in December 1992 on membership in a joint EEC-EFTA trading area failed, primarily due to opposition in the German-speaking cantons. To the chagrin of the pro-European Romands, Switzerland was left out of the continental trading system.

A growing rift separated Switzerland's two largest groups, the Romands and the Swiss-Germans, exacerbated the Romand perception that the Swiss-Germans were usurping Swiss identity and shunting the Romands to the margins of Swiss political life. The so-called "fried potato ditch," the *Rösti-Graben*, has become more than just the imaginary line dividing the two peoples. For centuries Swiss identity has been defined in negative terms—as not German, not French, not Italian, and not part of any international organization. The changing reality in Europe is also changing Romand perceptions of themselves; they have begun to redefine their identity as a separate European nation.

In February 1998 the Swiss-German canton of Zurich announced plans to start compulsory English in cantonal schools from an early age. The initiative of the cantonal government, which gained favor in other parts of German-speaking Switzerland, threatened the teaching of French in the region and infuriated Romand leaders, who denounced the move as a threat to Switzerland's unity. The perceived threat to their culture and its place in Switzerland led to some militant demands for a referendum on the Romands continued ties to the Swiss-Germans.

On 21 May 2000 voters in Switzerland approved a plan to open Switzerland up to the European Union (EU) in a number of economic and political agreements. The vote, seen as ending Switzerland's long isolation, lessened tensions between the Romands and the dominant Swiss Germans, who had repeatedly rejected closer ties to the continental system. The Romands overwhelmingly (80%) supported the initiative and backed bilateral agreements with the EU; they are the most pro-European of the Swiss groups.

The Romands gained by the referendum just the part of European integration they desired, economic and cultural benefits, without any loss of Switzerland's sovereignty to Brussels. Many Romands, particularly younger people, regret the sense of aloofness and apartness that traditional Swiss neutrality brought. Moderate Romand leaders, however, welcomed the result, which helped to calm the growing number of militants in the region. In a referendum on EU membership in March 2001, the majority of Swiss voters, 76.7% voted against, with 23.3%, mostly in the Romand region, voting for integration in united Europe.

SELECTED BIBLIOGRAPHY:

Berlin, Peter. *The Xenophobe's Guide to the Swiss*. 1993.
Bullen, Susan. *The Alps and Their People*. 1994.
Grotzer, Pierre. *1919–1939: The Swiss Romande between the Wars*. 1997.
Steinberg, Jonathan. *Why Switzerland?* 1996.

Romansh

Grischa; Rhaetians; Romansch; Romanche; Romontsch; Rumantsch

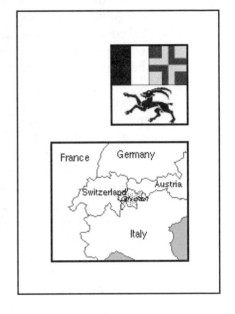

POPULATION: Approximately (2002e) 75,000 Romansh in Switzerland, concentrated in Grisons (Graubünden in German) Canton in the southeast. There are small Romansh communities in other parts of Switzerland, particularly in Zurich and other large urban areas.

THE ROMANSH HOMELAND: The Romansh homeland, called Grischun, lies in the Rhaetian and Leopontine Alps in southeastern Switzerland. The region has peaks, glaciers, forested highlands, and fertile valleys, including the famed Engadin Valley of the Inn River, the valley of the Upper Rhine, and the Rheinwald Valley on the Lower Rhine River. The homeland forms a canton of the Swiss Confederation. The canton, called Grisons in French and Graubünden in German is the largest and least populated of the Swiss cantons. The Romansh population is concentrated in the valleys of the central districts of the canton. *Canton of Grisons/Graubünden (Grischun)*: 2,745 sq. mi.—7,111 sq. km, (2002e) 174,000—Romansh 39%, Swiss-Germans 37%, Italian Swiss 22%, others 2%. The Romansh capital and major cultural center is Chur, called Cuira in the Romansh language, (2002e) 33,000. Another important cultural centers are Saint-Moritz, called San Maurezzan in Romansh, (2002e) 7,000, site of the Winter Olympic games in 1928 and 1948, and Davos, called Tavau locally, (2002e) 12,000, site of many international conferences.

FLAG: The Romansh national flag, the official flag of the canton, is a square banner divided horizontally, the lower half bearing a black mountain goat on white, the upper half, divided vertically, has blue and gold squares on the upper fly and black and white vertical stripes on the upper hoist.

PEOPLE AND CULTURE: The Romansh, calling themselves Grischa, are a Rhaeto-Romantic people, one of the group of Rhaeto-Romantic nations that inhabit the eastern Alps and includes the Ladins* and Friulis.* The descendents of Latinized alpine tribes, the Romansh are one of the four recognized nations within Switzerland. A conservative people, the Romansh have preserved their unique culture and dialects in the isolation of their high mountain valleys. There has been a flourishing local literature since the nineteenth century.

LANGUAGE AND RELIGION: The Romansh language belongs to the Rhaeto-Romance branch of the Romance language group. The language is spoken in five well established and distinct dialects: Sursilvan or Romontsch in the upper Rhine or Vorderrheintal region, Sutsilvan in the lower Rhine or Hinterrheintal and in Nidwald, Surmeiran in the Surmeir and Albulatal Valleys, Putèr (Upper Engadine) in the upper Engadin, and Vallader (Lower Engadine) in the lower Engadin and Münsteral valleys. The language is the direct descendent of the Roman language brought to the region by the Roman legions, although the dialects more closely resemble French than Italian. Romansh is the official language in 82 of the 120 communes in the canton, one of three official languages of the canton, and one of the four official languages of Switzerland. Interest in the language remains high, and there are a number of Romansh newspapers, radio stations, and television. It was not until 1982 that a consistently written form, called Rumantsch Grischun, was adopted.

The majority of the Romansh are Protestant, although the population of the canton is almost evenly divided between Protestants and Roman Catholics. The historical bishopric of Chur was for centuries both a religious and temporal power in the region, and the bishopric remains an important focus of the Romansh religion.

NATIONAL HISTORY: The high alpine valleys were originally settled by the Raeti or Rhaeti, a people thought to be Celtic in origin. According to classical authors, the Raeti spoke an Etruscan dialect when the region was conquered and annexed by the Romans in 15 B.C. The use of Vulgar Latin began to spread, gradually blending with the local pre-Roman languages. Incorporated into the Roman province of Rhaetia, named for the Celtic inhabitants, the region had practically no economic importance, but Roman control of the high mountain passes was militarily important for communications and trade between Italy and the northern Roman provinces. Christianity, brought to the region by the Romans, was solidified by the establishment of a bishopric at Chur in the early fifth century.

The Latinized Celts, later called the Romansh, fought to preserve their Latin language, laws, and culture against the Germanic tribes that invaded the crumbling Roman Empire in the latter fifth century. Overrun by Ostrogoths in A.D. 493 and by the Franks in 537, the region eventually came under the authority of the Frankish kingdom, the forerunner of the Holy Roman Empire. The migrations of Germanic peoples from the fifth to tenth centuries began the progressive erosion of the territory of the Romansh.

The region was designated a county by the emperor Charlemagne in

806. In the ninth century the bishops (after 1170 prince-bishops) of Chur, a free imperial city of the Holy Roman Empire, began to attain prominence, having allied themselves to the rising power of the Hapsburgs. Their power, however, was checked and gradually reduced by leagues of free communes and feudal lords that formed in the region between 1367 and 1436.

The League of God's House, the Gotteshausbund, formed an alliance to stem the bishop's rising power in 1367. It was followed in 1395 by the Graubünden, or Gray League, of the upper Rhine Valley. The gray, Grisch in the Romansh language, referred to homespun gray clothing and gave rise to the name of the canton, the Gray Leagues. The leagues made the Grisons a regional military power, leading to an alliance with the Swiss Confederation in 1496. In 1512 the leagues conquered the Valtellina region from Milan and ruled the area, which was richer and more populous than their alpine homeland, as a subject territory. In 1526 the last traces of the temporal jurisdiction of the bishops of Chur were abolished.

The majority of the population of the leagues, including the Romansh, accepted the Protestant Reformation in 1524–26, but the Catholic subjects in the Valtellina staunchly resisted it. The Lutheran Jacob Bifrun's translation of the New Testament into the Upper Engadine dialect of Romansh helped to disseminate Protestantism throughout the Romansh valleys. Most of the earliest records of written Romansh date from the sixteenth century, when advocates of both the Reformation and Counter-Reformation published works in the language.

The Grisons, unlike the other Swiss cantons, did not remain neutral during the Thirty Years' War, which began in 1620 when the Valtellina Catholics rose and massacred their Protestant masters. The ensuing conflict eventually drew in most of the European powers. Restored to league rule in 1639, the Valtellina remained a subject territory until its incorporation into the French-dominated Cisalpine Republic created by Napoleon in 1797. Two years later Grisons, more popularly known by its German name, Graubünden, was forced to join Napoleon's Helvetic Republic. In 1803 the territory joined the restored Swiss Confederation with German and Italian, but not Romansh, as official cantonal languages.

Mass emigration of the rural population, mainly to the Americas during the drought and depression after 1815, greatly reduced the number of German speakers in the canton, giving the native Romansh more access to local authority. A bitter controversy in the early nineteenth century over Switzerland's political system underscored religious and cultural differences and marked the beginning of a particular Romansh nationalism. The conflict, settled in a nearly bloodless civil war of 1847–48, resulted in a new Swiss constitution that guaranteed cantonal autonomy in a loose confederal political system.

The Romansh, protected by Switzerland's armed neutrality during

World War I, launched a peaceful campaign to end their domination by the German-speaking Swiss population and to win equal linguistic and cultural rights. The campaign, led by an active and persistent national movement, continued for over two decades. In 1937 the Swiss government finally accepted the Romansh language as one of the confederation's four official languages, but for use within the canton, not at the federal level. Added protection for Romansh group, linguistic, and cultural rights were included in the revised confederation constitution.

The proportion of Romansh speakers in Grisons Canton fell from two-fifths of the total population in 1880 to one-fourth in 1970, mostly due to migration from the Italian-speaking districts to the east and south. As their national identity was protected by cantonal autonomy and guaranteed by the Swiss constitution, few Romansh felt culturally or linguistically threatened in multinational and multireligious Switzerland until the 1970s. The small national movement remained on the fringes of political life until the late 1980s, when a debate arose over Switzerland's relations with a uniting Europe. Linguistic and cultural organizations mobilized to protect the language in the 1980s and early 1990s,

The growth of pro-European sentiment in the canton paralleled the emergence of a new awareness of a right to recognition as a separate European people. In May 1992, the Swiss government formally applied for membership in the European Community, a move widely supported by the Romansh. In December 1992 the Romansh, like the other non-Swiss-German national groups, voted for closer ties with the European Community, but the vote, due to the opposition in the German-speaking cantons, was narrowly defeated; Switzerland as a result remained outside the continental economic system.

The integration of the European continent animated the long-dormant Romansh national movement in the 1990s. The movement's leaders stressed that the national movement was a pro-European movement and was not directed against the Swiss Confederation, which had sheltered the Romansh nation for nearly two centuries. The growing pro-European faction of the national movement foresaw Romansh sovereignty transferred from the Swiss Confederation to a united and secure federal Europe that would protect the independence of one of Europe's smallest but most ancient nations.

A referendum in 1996 accorded the Romansh language semiofficial status and permitted its use at the federal level. Romansh nationalists continued to demand that the language become the fourth official language of Switzerland, but they were actively opposed by the large German-speaking population of the Grisons, who claimed that Romansh is not a language at all but a confection of regional dialects.

In August 1998, the bishop of Chur was replaced, partly due to his failure to relate to the Romansh population of the region. A new bishop,

Amédé Grab, became the 99th holder of a position considered as part of the historical continuity of the Romansh nation.

Rifts between Switzerland's two largest national groups, the Romands* and the Swiss-Germans and between the Protestants and Roman Catholics raised tensions in the country that were exacerbated by the growing discussion over ties to the rest of Europe. The Romansh have reiterated their desire to be a part of a united Europe, but without loosing their historic ties to the other Swiss peoples.

SELECTED BIBLIOGRAPHY:

Head, Randolph C. *Early Modern Democracy in the Grisons.* 1995.
Mayer, K.B. *The Population of Switzerland.* 1982.
Snyder, Louis L. *Global Mini-Nationalisms: Autonomy or Independence.* 1982.
Steinberg, Jonathan. *Why Switzerland?* 1996.

Roms

Gypsies; Romani; Roma; Rroms; Ciganos; Gitanos; Tsigani; Tziganes; Zigeuners

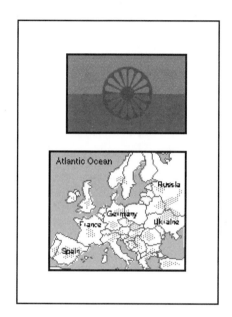

POPULATION: Approximately (2002e) eight to 12 million Roms in Europe, about four-fifths of the total in eastern Europe and the former Soviet Union. World estimates vary from 12 million to over 15 million. Statistics on Rom population are notoriously contradictory and unreliable because of difficulties in classifying them. Roms can be hard to define as there is no clear definition of what Roms are. Most definitions include dark-skinned and Romany-speaking, but not all Roms are dark-skinned and only about 4 million speak some dialect of Romany. Accurate estimates are difficult to obtain, as many governments count only nomadic Rom, others misrepresent Rom population figures, and some governments even deny the existence of Rom populations in their countries. Only about a half-million maintain the Roms' traditional nomadic way of life.

THE ROM HOMELAND: The Rom are dispersed throughout the world, with the largest concentrations in Europe, particularly the countries of Central and Eastern Europe. In the majority of European states the Rom have few or no rights or official status. In Western and Central Europe many Roms live in shantytowns or marginal neighborhoods on the outskirts of large cities such as Madrid, Prague, Budapest, and Rome. In Eastern Europe the majority live in smaller towns or in rural areas. There is no official Rom political territory. Estimated numbers: 2.5 million Romania, 800,000 Bulgaria, 800,000 Spain, 600,000 Hungary, 550,000 Slovakia, 500,000 Turkey, 430,000 Yugoslavia, 400,000 Russia, 350,000 France, 300,000 Czech, 250,000 Macedonia, 200,000 Greece, 120,000 Germany, 100,000 Great Britain, 100,000 Italy, 85,000 Albania, 50,000 Poland, 50,000 Bosnia.

FLAG: The Rom flag, recognized and used by all Rom communities, is a horizontal bicolor of pale blue over green charged with a centered red wheel, or *chakra*, with sixteen spokes. Local Rom flags, used by regional groups or political parties, use the blue-over-green flag, although the wheel is often changed to white, and the number of spokes varies.

PEOPLE AND CULTURE: The Roms, popularly called Gypsies, a medieval corruption of "Egyptian," are a transnational group with communities scattered across Europe, parts of Asia, North and South America, Australia, New Zealand, North Africa, and the Middle East. The Roms call themselves Gajo, Rom, or Romani and refer to all non-Roms as "Gadje." The European Roms comprise four major divisions—the Lowara, Machwaya, Kalderasha, and Churara—each with numerous subdivisions. The most important of the European Rom groups are the Gitanos in Spain, Portugal, and North Africa; the Manouche or Sinti in France; Sinte in Germany and Italy; Rom and Kalderash in Eastern Europe and the former Soviet Union; Romnichals in the British Isles; Boyash or Bayash in Romania; and the Xoraxaya in European Turkey. The Rom have adopted local languages and religions while retaining their separate cultures and languages. Intermarriage with Gadje has been limited, but some mingling over the centuries has given the Rom populations a wide range of physical appearances, from very dark to very fair. The Rom birthrate, estimated at an average 3% across the continent, is thought to be the highest in Europe. Policies toward the Roms, although they vary from country to country, invariably constitute a negation of the nation, their culture, and their dialects. Government policies can be roughly grouped into three categories—exclusion, containment, or assimilation—and are often a combination of all three.

LANGUAGE AND RELIGION: The Rom language, called Romany or Romani, is spoken in 17 major and minor dialects, many mutually unintelligible. The language belongs to the Indo-Iranian language family and is closely related to the languages of the northwestern Indian subcontinent. The dozens of Romany dialects and subdialects vary greatly from region to region. There are three major language groups—the Domari in the Middle East and Eastern Europe, the Lomarvren in Central Europe, and the Romani of Western Europe. Within these groups they are further divided into four main and about 10 smaller tribes or groups. Education across the continent generally ignores Rom needs and children are often automatically put into "remedial" classes or schools for retarded children, or even taken into custody and placed in Christian orphanages. Activists now demand that Rom dialects and history be taught in countries with large Rom populations; they also want adult literacy classes. In 1998–99 primary schooling in the Rom language was begun. Each of the dozen dialects in Europe has absorbed words from the numerous languages with which they have been in contact throughout the centuries. There is a movement to promote a standard and written form of the language.

In religion the Roms have adapted to local traditions, so European Roms display a wide variety of religious beliefs. The majority of the Roms are

Christian, with Orthodox, Roman Catholic, and Protestant groups, but others adhere to Islam or other belief systems. Islam is particularly prevalent in the southern Balkans and in parts of Russia. Traditionally the Roms adhere to a unique, syncretic mixture of belief and practice rooted in Hinduism, often mixed with Christian and Islamic elements.

NATIONAL HISTORY: According to Rom legends, their original homeland lay in the present province of Sind in southeastern Pakistan. Some Rom nomads are thought to have migrated westward between 500 and 600 B.C., but the main migration arrived in Iran in the first millennium A.D. The migration is thought to have begun with refugees fleeing the Muslim conquest of Sind in A.D. 711–12. During their time in Iran the nomads split into three groups—the Gitanos, Kalderash, and the Manush—the predecessors of the modern Rom tribes. Some Roms later moved into Egypt and North Africa, and in 835 they were reported in Byzantine territory. Rom groups first entered Russia in the tenth century.

Rom groups were first reported as moving into Eastern Europe from Asia Minor in the fourteenth century, and by the fifteenth century they first appeared in Western Europe. Many of the Roms settled as sedentary farmers and tradesmen, but others, less fortunate in the attitudes of local governments, were hounded from place to place. Smithing and metal-working developed as the primary occupations, valuable skills to offer settled populations. The name "Gypsy" began with the name "Egyptian," arising from the mistaken idea that the Roms originated in a mythical Little Egypt—although some Roms in fact entered southern Europe from North Africa, having passed through Egypt. The name was eventually applied to all the European Roms.

The first Roms arrived in Western Europe in the early fifteenth century, being recorded in Paris in 1427 and Barcelona in 1447. By the mid-fifteenth century, hostility to the Roms was widespread, and anti-Gypsy laws affected all Roms in Europe. Their eastern origins gave rise to many myths associated with the Roms, and a magical aura grew around them that persists to the present. Rom women were often famous and sought-after fortune-tellers. By the sixteenth century, the Roms in Europe were reduced to despised outcastes. Their darker skin, different languages, and lack of an organized religion provoked widespread prejudice and opposition from the three pillars of European society, church, state, and the trade guilds. The Roms were barred from many established churches, as legends associated the Roms with the crucifixion of Jesus, child stealing, and cannibalism.

The Ottoman conquest of southeastern Europe forced many Roms to migrate to Western Europe, while others fled west to escape enslavement by feudal lords. By the late fifteenth century most European states had passed stringent anti-Gypsy laws. The most abhorrent allowed enslavement or death, with bounties paid for Gypsies, dead or alive. Tales associating the Rom with the Crucifixion were used to justify the persecutions, expulsions, and suffering that followed the Rom throughout Europe. In the sixteenth and seventeenth centuries the first Rom prisoners were forcibly transported to the New World, often as slaves. The Rom in the Middle East and North Africa, where nomadic peoples were common, generally fared better than their kin in Europe.

In the eighteenth and nineteenth centuries, European governments often treated the Roms very much like the Jews, subjecting them to special taxes, restrictions, official discrimination, and religious persecution. Only in the late nineteenth century did some European states rescind the more odious anti-Gypsy laws. Immigration to North America became one of the few options for the persecuted Roms of Europe. A nineteenth-century French observer describes the Roms as "Europe's Negroes." They were often enslaved or lynched with impunity. Roms were still being bought and sold in Romania and the Balkans as late as the 1860s.

New restrictions and discrimination became common in Western Europe following World War I. In 1890, a conference was organized by the German military to discuss the problem of the *Zigeunergeschmeiss*, meaning "Gypsy scum." In 1899, the German government established the Central Office for Fighting the Gypsy Nuisance. A policy conference in 1909 recommended that all German Roms be branded for easy identification. As late as 1927 a group of nine Roms stood trial in Slovakia for cannibalism.

In the first years of Soviet rule, the Roms of Russia and Ukraine were recognized by the Soviet nationalities program. Their educational level was raised, professional Rom training was begun, newspapers and magazines were published, and preparation was made for Rom schools. By the late 1920s, however, the program had mostly been abandoned, and by the 1930s the Roms of the Soviet Union shared the destiny of other deported populations. Thousands were arrested and deported to Siberia and Central Asia. In 1956, the Soviet government adopted a decree forbidding the remaining Roms to move from where they were officially registered.

German law had already legalized many anti-Gypsy restrictions when the Nazis came to power in 1933. The Nazis refused to accept the Roms as an Aryan nation, even though their language is of Aryan origin. Considering the Rom, like the Jews, to be of Asiatic origin, official Nazi persecution of them escalated during the 1930s. In 1936 the first group of 400 Roms was imprisoned at the Nazi concentration camp at Dachau. Genealogical investigations, initiated in December 1938, followed a decree labeling the Rom as a menace to German society. Roms were selected for sterilization by injection, and laws were passed forbidding Germans from marrying Jews, Gypsies, and Negroes. Even persons with an eighth part of Gypsy blood became subject to the increasingly harsh strictures. Although the Germans had nothing to gain by persecuting the Roms, the treatment of Rom populations worsened radically following the outbreak of war in September 1939.

In 1940 many thousands of German Roms were transported to concentration and work camps in occupied Poland. The first mass genocide action took place in January 1940, when 250 Rom children were used to test cyanide gas crystals at Buchenwald concentration camp. By the summer of 1942 the Nazi hierarchy had decided to exterminate Europe's Roms. On 16 December 1942, Heinrich Himmler signed a decree sending the remaining German Roms to the extermination camp at Auschwitz. Germany's allies—Italy, Vichy France, Croatia, Romania, Slovakia—and neutral Spain issued similar decrees. The Gypsy Holocaust, called *Porrajmos* by the Roms, meaning "the devouring," claimed some two million lives during World War II. Most died in massacres or of hunger and disease, but 500,000 Rom perished in the Nazi death camps. At the end of the war not one Rom was called to witness at the German war crimes trials at Nuremberg in 1945–46. West Germany and other Western countries denied compensation to the surviving Roms, and throughout Europe many Roms were declared stateless. Thousands emigrated to the United States, Canada, South America, and to Australia and New Zealand.

In the postwar years the Roms began to form closer intergroup contacts within the various Western European countries and to develop ways to protect Europe's remaining Rom population. In the early 1950s Rom leaders pleaded at the United Nations for the establishment of a Rom "Israel," an independent homeland to be called Romanistan, the Land of the Rom. The Rom petition did not receive a sympathetic hearing, and discrimination in many areas continued. Governments, often well intentioned, pressed assimilation and forced nomadic groups to settle, often in urban or rural slums, where unemployment, violence, and crime added to the general poor public opinion of the Roms. Several governments placed severe curbs on religious and cultural practices. According to the 1954 Geneva Convention, the Roms were a "stateless people."

There were few contacts between the various dispersed groups until the 1960s, but Rom nationalism asserted itself in spite of official opposition in many countries. In the early 1970s Rom leaders from many areas formed the World Romani Congress (WRC). In April 1971 the WRC brought together representatives of Roms from 14 countries, representing over three million Roms. In 1976 the first International Rom Congress, held in India, brought together the representatives of the global Rom populations. In 1978 a second congress was held in Geneva, Switzerland. Each year the European Roms gather in the southern French town of Saintes-Maries-de-la-Mer.

Still surrounded by mystery, myth, and superstition, the Rom have become the targets of ethnic hatred released by the overthrow of communism in Eastern Europe and the Soviet Union. The frustrations and economic hardships of converting command economies to free markets are all too often turned on the most defenseless minority, the Rom. Attacks on Roms were particularly severe in Romania and the states of the former Soviet Union in the early 1990s. The most serious anti-Rom riots took place in Odessa, Ukraine, in 1992.

An influx of Roms into Western Europe fleeing economic hardships and discrimination created large illegal Rom populations throughout the European Union (EU). The German government sold a group of handcuffed Rom asylum seekers back to Romania for $21 million. Some of the Roms committed suicide rather than return to Romania. In France, the Roms are the only group given a different identity card, which obliges them to present themselves every three months to the police. The French government also actively opposes the recommendation of the Council of Europe to recognize the Roms as a "nonterritorial cultural minority." The French government deported over 2,000 Romanian Roms in December 1993.

Rom nationalists believe that the anticommunist revolution of 1989–91 may have opened their last opportunity to join the world community. In October 1991 a conference of European Gypsies put forward a new proposal for the recognition of the Rom as a transnational European community, a nation without a state, but with the same guaranteed cultural, economic, and political rights everywhere in a united, federal Europe. During the rapid political and economic changes that accompanied the collapse of command governments in Eastern Europe, the Roms were often forgotten or kept on the fringes.

At the turn of the twenty-first century, many of the European countries with the largest Rom populations were doing all they could to ensure that the European Union saw them as potential members; however, the Roms living in these countries continued to suffer discrimination. Rom groups across the continent pressed for equal participation in the social, economic, and political life of the European Union. Despite some improvement, hundreds of Czech and Slovak Roms sought political asylum in Canada and the United Kingdom, charging human rights abuses in their homelands. In September 1993, two Roms were lynched and another was killed by a mob in Romania after they were accused of murdering a Romanian.

Outside Europe, the Roms of the United States and Canada faced the least discrimination. In late 1998, the state of New Jersey removed a 1917 anti-Rom bill from the books. The law was the last in North America aimed at a particular ethnic group. In a region with so many vocal ethnic groups, the Roms are hardly noticed. Their numbers range from about 100,000, according to the U.S. Census Bureau, to more than a million, according to Rom sources.

During the Kosovo conflict in 1999, many Roms were accused of collaborating with the Serbs in oppressing the Kosovars.* Once NATO bombs had driven the Serbs from the region, thousands of Roms were forced to flee along with the Serb population. Many Roms had in fact collaborated with the Serbian authorities; all Roms were blamed and driven from their homes. An estimated Kosovar Rom population of between 50,000 and 80,000 remains in refugee camps or has emigrated to Western Europe.

The stereotype of the Roms across Europe is generally the same—dirty, lazy, stupid, and prone to crime. That the Roms are active in the black market, drugs, and prostitution and have a disproportionately high crime rate perpetuates this stereotype. The poor economic status of the Roms, which is partially due to these prejudices, is largely responsible for this high crime rate. Thus, the Rom stereotype in Europe is self-perpetuating.

The European Roma Rights Center claimed that the Rom population in Europe exceeds 12 million people. Some activists claim a Rom population of about 15 million. In early 2000, a Rom congress in Prague declared the Roms to be Europe's first transnational nation. The delegates put forward a demand for a Rom seat in the United Nations. The congress also addressed the question of immigration, which many Western governments fear is turning into a Rom invasion from the East. The Roms work for recognition as the first nation that is not territorially consolidated. Their struggle for self-determination does not necessarily aim for statehood but rather at greater control over their own lives. Throughout their history in Europe, the Roms for the most part remained outside the mainstream political, cultural, and social systems, whether feudal, socialist, or capitalist.

The striving of the countries of Central Europe to enter the European Union (EU) may offer an unprecedented chance to Europe's Roms to be recognized as a nation, even without a defined territory. The International Romany Union, which claims to represent 10 million Roms in more than 30 countries, has set up an office in Brussels and announced plans to create a Rom parliament while demanding representation in the European Parliament. Despite changes in Europe, the Roms remain much as they have always been: Europe's phantom nation.

SELECTED BIBLIOGRAPHY:

Crowe, David M. *A History of the Gypsies of Eastern Europe and Russia*. 1994.
Kuznetsova, Ljalja. *Gypsies*. 1998.
Ligeois, Jean-Pierre, and Nicholas Gheorge. *Roma/Gypsies: A European Minority*. 1995.
Moreau, Roger. *The Rom: Walking in the Paths of the Gypsies*. 1997.

Rumelian Turks

Bulgarian Turks; Danubian Turks; Tourkos; Tourkikos

POPULATION: Approximately (2002e) 1,320,000 Rumelian Turks in southeastern Europe, concentrated in southern Bulgaria and northeastern Greece, and smaller groups in eastern Macedonia, Yugoslavia, and Albania. Some Turks claim a Rumelian Turk population of over 2 million in the Balkans.

THE RUMELIAN TURKISH HOMELAND: The Rumelian Turkish homeland, called Rumeli by the Turks, lies in the southern Balkans, occupying the Danubian Plain and the Rhodope Mountains in Bulgaria, Greece, and Macedonia. The major concentrations of Rumelian Turks are in Kürdzhali Province and neighboring areas of the Rhodope Mountains in southern Bulgaria and northeastern Greece, along the Danube River in northern Bulgaria, and in the provinces of eastern Bulgaria. The Rumelian Turks have no official political entity in the region but remain dispersed among a number of Bulgarian provinces and the provinces of Western Thrace in Greece. The Rumelian Turkish capital and major cultural center in Bulgaria is Kürdzhali, called Kircaali by the Rumelian Turks, (2002e) 44,000. The other important cultural center in Bulgaria is Plovdiv, called Filibe by the Turks, (2002e) 346,000. The major center of the Rumelian Turks in Greece is Komotini, called Gümüljina locally, (2002e) 41,000. The major center in Macedonia is Strumica, called Ustrumca in Turkish, (2002e) 36,000.

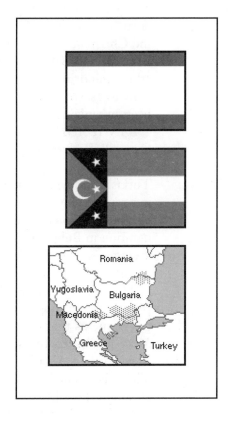

FLAG: The Rumelian Turkish national flag, the flag of the Movement for Rights and Freedoms in Bulgaria, is a white field bearing two narrow red stripes at the top and bottom. The flag of the Rumelian Turks of Western Thrace in Greece has three horizontal stripes of red, white, and red, bearing a red triangle at the hoist charged with a white crescent moon and five-pointed white star over a black stripe divided into triangles bearing white five-pointed stars.

PEOPLE AND CULTURE: The Rumelian Turks are part of the Turkish nation, although their modern history has divided them from the Turks of Turkey. Natural growth and a high birthrate have been balanced by continued emigration to Turkey. They number about 950,000 in Bulgaria, 120,000 in Greece, 80,000 to 200,000 in Macedonia, 60,000 to 100,000 in Yugoslavia, some 50,000 in the Dobruja region of Romania, and smaller numbers in other Balkan states. Typically the Rumelian Turks have been portrayed as devious, duplicitous, and rapacious, the traditional enemy of the Christian peoples of the Balkans. Estimating the number of Rumelian Turks in the Balkans is problematic, as census returns often do not count ethnic minorities, as in Greece, or because Turks have registered as Christians to escape discrimination. Since the 1970s, the Rumelian Turks have been urbanizing, particularly in Bulgaria and Greece.

LANGUAGE AND RELIGION: The Rumelian Turks speak dialects of Osmanli Turkish, the official language of Turkey. The four major dialects spoken in the Balkans are Danubian Turkish, Razgrad Turkish, Dinler Turkish, and Macedonian Turkish. The Turkish language is gradually being replaced by national languages—Bulgarian, Greek, or Macedonian—although national identity remains strong. The language has official recognition in Bulgaria and Greece. Literacy rates are lower than the national averages, as Turkish-language schools are generally overcrowded and underfunded.

The majority of the Rumelian Turks are Sunni Muslims, although a portion of the population adopted the official atheism of the communist governments that controlled Bulgaria and Yugoslavia after World War II. Most belong to the Hanefite rite, although there are small numbers of Alevis, called Alijanis locally, who adhere to the Shi'a Muslim tradition. There is a small Christian population, the result of forced assimilation, although the Christians remain Turkish in culture and language.

NATIONAL HISTORY: The Turks first began their conquest of the Balkans in the mid-fourteenth century. The land was divided into fiefs of various size that were administered by cavalry officers and local nobles who converted to Islam. The Turks called their European territories Rumeli, meaning "land of the Romans." The region became a center of Ottoman Islamic culture, with famed religious schools and mosques in the major cities. Many Turks migrated to the new territories to settle as landlords, soldiers, or local functionaries.

In the fifteenth and sixteenth centuries, Rumelia functioned as a source of the *devsirme*, the levy of Christian boys, who were taken and trained as soldiers and administrators. Turkish landlords reduced much of the Christian population to a serflike condition, with few rights and many obligations. Most of the land was owned by Turks in the form of estates held by Turkish nobles, mostly absentee.

In the early nineteenth century, Bulgarian, South Slav, and Greek nationalism became major forces in Rumelia. Bulgarian and Greek nationalism were virtually equated with anti-Turkish sentiment. The mobilization of the Christian nationalities of the region began as mass movements against Turkish rule. Rebellions and repression continued to disrupt the region.

The administrative boundaries of Turkish Rumelia changed frequently until 1864, when the unit of administrative division became defined as the province, or *vilayet*. The Danube *vilayet* was formed first, in 1864, and included the bulk of the Turkish population in the Balkans. In 1876 the Bulgarians rebelled against Ottoman rule. Ottoman troops responded with great brutality and massacres, the "Bulgarian Horrors." About 15,000 people were massacred at Plovdiv, and many villages and monasteries were destroyed. In spite of widespread indignation in Europe, the major powers did little to alleviate the situation.

The Russians, the self-proclaimed protector of the South Slav nations in the Balkans, attacked the Ottoman Empire in 1877, forcing the Turks to sue for peace. The Treaty of Berlin in 1878 disbanded the Danube *vilayet*, and the independent state of Bulgaria was formed under Ottoman suzerainty. Present southern Bulgaria formed the autonomous province of Eastern Rumelia with its capital at Plovdiv. In 1885, the Bulgarians annexed Eastern Rumelia, with its large Turkish population. Some scholars estimate that the Rumelian Turks formed a majority of the population of the new Bulgarian state, but emigration to Turkish territory, which began just after independence, led to a sharp decline.

The Turkish population of Balkan Rumelia was estimated at about seven million in 1900, including the European provinces of Eastern Thrace. The Balkan wars of 1912–13 virtually eliminated Turkish authority in most of the Balkans region, which was divided among Greece and the Slavic states. In Bulgaria the first attempt to force the remaining Turkish population to take Slavic names was instituted between 1912 and 1914.

The independence of the Balkan states forced most Rumelian Turks to emigrate to Turkey, leaving about 1.5 million by 1925. The 1923 Treaty of Lausanne, which recognized the Republic of Turkey after World War II, brought on a massive population exchange between Greece and Turkey; hundreds of thousands of Turks were repatriated to Turkey. The treaty obliged the Greek government to recognize a Muslim minority, but not minority national groups.

An estimated 220,000 Rumelian Turks migrated to Turkey from Bulgaria between 1923 and 1949. Another wave of immigrants, numbering 155,000, was either expelled or "allowed to leave" in 1949–51. The number of immigrants would have been higher had the Turkish authorities not closed the international border twice during the period. The communist authorities restricted Muslim religious practices and prohibited religious publications. Rumelian Turks in Bulgaria could easily obtain the works of Marx or Stalin written in Turkish, but not the Koran.

In 1968 an agreement reopened the Bulgarian Turkish border to close relatives of persons already living in Turkey. The agreement remained in effect from 1968 to 1978. Serious concern developed over the low birthrate of the ethnic Bulgarian population in the 1970s. Numerous programs were instituted to stimulate growth, but without success. The birthrate of the Rumelian Turks remained over 2%, while the Bulgarian rate was barely above zero. In late 1984 the government began a major campaign to "Bulgarize," or assimilate, the Rumelian Turks. The government claimed that all Muslims in Bulgaria were descended from Bulgarians forced to adopt the Islamic religion during the Ottoman era; therefore the Muslims were "voluntarily" to take new Slavic names as part of their "rebirth" process. The campaign included the forced abandonment of Turkish-language publications and radio broadcasts, and it required the Turk towns and villages to adopt Bulgarian names.

Many Rumelian Turks resisted assimilation, and serious clashes broke out with local authorities. Many were killed in the confrontations, and many others were sent to labor camps or were forcibly resettled. On 29 May 1989, the Bulgarian communist leader Todor Zhivkov demanded that Turkey open its border in order to receive all "Bulgarian Muslims" who wanted to leave Bulgaria. Over 310,000 Rumelian Turks fled or were driven across the frontier before the Turks closed the border to stem the influx, which was overwhelming resources. At the height of the assimilation crisis, in 1987–89, the Turkish government claimed that 1.5 million Turks resided in Bulgaria, while the Bulgarian communist government claimed there were none.

The Rumelian Turks in Western Thrace in Greece began to complain of their deteriorating position in the early 1980s. The protests gathered force in the late 1980s, and in 1988 there were large-scale demonstrations by Rumelian Turks. A number of bomb attacks against mosques and other Muslim properties aggravated the situation. The Rumelian Turks of Western Thrace took their grievances to the United Nations and the Council of Europe. The increasing polarization of the communities in Western Thrace was the result of the continuing assimilationist policy of the Greek government in the 1990s.

In August 1989, Zhivkov was replaced as Bulgaria's leader, and by the end of 1989 communism had collapsed in the country. Zhivkov's successors endorsed a policy of democracy and halted the repression of the Rumelian Turks. During 1990, some 150,000 Rumelian Turks who had left during the 1989 exodus returned to Bulgaria. A 1991 law gave the Rumelian Turks three years to restore their original names. Turkish-language lessons were reintroduced for four hours per week in parts of the country having substantial Turkish populations. The Rumelian Turks made significant strides in the area of cultural expression and identity. Many of the polices to suppress their religious practices and language during the communist era were rectified, although the Turks remained objects of suspicion for many Bulgarians.

The revival of Bulgarian nationalism with the overthrow of communism in Eastern Europe in the early 1990s manifested itself in opposition to Rumelian Turkish empowerment and participation in administrative structures, particularly in mixed areas. In May 1994, extremist groups, who had been keeping a low profile, stepped up their activities with small rallies and threats against Bulgaria's Turkish community. Many Bulgarians reacted negatively to government policies aimed at integrating the Rumelian Turks into the cultural and economic life of the country. Many Bulgarians, who had profited from the Rumelian Turkish exodus by purchasing houses, goods, and livestock at artificially low prices, agitated against the return of the Turkish-speaking population.

The Rumelian Turkish political party, the Movement for Rights and Freedoms (DPS), won 26 towns in municipal elections in November 1995, including the city of Kürdzhali. The leader of the DPS, Akhmed Dogan, protested to the president of Bulgaria against the deliberate delaying of the convening of municipal council of Kürdzhali by the regional governor. The "Kürdzhali problem" marked a new and more aggressive phase of the Rumelian Turks' fight for self-determination. On 5 February 1996 the results of the Kürdzhali election were annulled. Thousands demonstrated in the city against the decision until the Bulgarian supreme court confirmed the DPS election victory in Kürdzhali in 1995.

In Greece the names "Tourkos" or "Tourkikos," which connote Turks or Turkish, are prohibited. In 1996, a dozen schoolteachers from Western Thrace were sentenced to eight months in prison for using the name "Turkish Teachers of Western Thrace" in a union document.

The Rumelian Turks continue to suffer a host of human-rights violations in Greece. The Greek government denies the Turkish identity and accepts the existence of a Muslim minority only in Thrace. Protests by other governments, including the European Union (EU), to which Greece belongs, are routinely ignored. The Rumelian Turks are viewed by the state with suspicion, the strength of which largely reflects the current state of relations between the Turkish and Greek states. A citizenship law, finally abolished in 1998, allowed the state to revoke the citizenship of non-ethnic Greeks unilaterally and arbitrarily. Between 1955 and 1998 an estimated 60,000, mostly Rumelian Turks, lost their citizenship under this law.

Peter Stoyanov, with the backing of several opposition parties, including the DPS, won presidential elections in Bulgaria in November 1996. The

DPS, as part of the coalition the United Democratic Forces, formed part of the new Bulgarian government, bringing Rumelian Turks into the Bulgarian government for the first time.

Emigration to Turkey, partly due to discrimination and partly economic, continued from 1989 to 1993, when the Turkish government imposed visa restrictions. The economic discontent remains strong, and Rumelian Turks continue to leave Bulgaria to find work in more prosperous regions of European Turkey. In the late 1990s, middle-aged and elderly Rumelian Turks have had difficulty obtaining Turkish visas, although younger working-age applicants had no problems. In 1997 the Turkish government began sending back people who were in Turkey illegally or whose visas had expired.

Disputes among the leadership of the Rumelian Turks in Bulgaria flared up over a decision by the DPS to form an election coalition with monarchists, agrarian groups, and liberals. The DPS pulled out of the coalition rather than allow the organization to factionalize between those seeking minority status for the Rumelian Turks in Bulgaria and those who believe that they should integrate into Bulgarian society. The DPS split in late 1998 into the Movement for Rights and Freedoms and the National Movement for Rights and Freedoms.

In spite of advances, there is increasing unrest among the Bulgarian population who fear an Islamic resurgence in parts of Bulgaria where ethnic Bulgarians are in the minority. Other Bulgarians are concerned that neighboring Turkey might gain more influence over Bulgaria's political life. The Rumelian Turks, in Bulgaria and other areas of the Balkans, continue to face job and cultural discrimination, which fuels demands for official recognition, language rights, and political mobilization.

SELECTED BIBLIOGRAPHY:

Anson, Jon, ed. *Ethnicity and Politics in Bulgaria and Israel*. 1993.

Karpat, Kemal H. *The Turks of Bulgaria: The History, Culture, and Political Fate of a Minority*. 1991.

Poulton, Hugh. *The Balkans: Minorities and Governments in Conflict*. 1993.

———. *Minorities in Southeast Europe: Inclusion and Exclusion*. 1998.

Ruwenzoris

Konjos and Ambas; Bakonjo-Baamba; Konzo-Amba; Ruwenzurus

POPULATION: Approximately (2002e) 640,000 Ruwenzoris in Uganda and the Democratic Republic of Congo, including 420,000 Konjos and 220,000 Ambas. Outside the region there are Ruwenzori communities in the lowlands of western Uganda.

THE RUWENZORI HOMELAND: The Ruwenzori homeland occupies a rugged, mountainous region in the Ruwenzori Mountains, which straddle the international border between Uganda and the Democratic Republic of Congo north of Lake Edward. The mountains, popularly called the Mountains of the Moon, contain high peaks that are often hidden by clouds and capped by snow and glaciers. The southern districts are inhabited by the Konjos, who call their homeland Busongora, while the Ambas inhabit the high plains beyond that stretch into Congo; they call their homeland Bwamba. *Region of Ruwenzori (Busongora-Bwamba)*: 2,634 sq. mi.— 6,822 sq. km, (2002e) 737,000—Ruwenzoris 82% (Konjos 56%, Ambas 26%), Toros* 12%, other Ugandans 6%. The Ruwenzori capital and major cultural center is Bundibugyo, (2002e) 11,000. The other important cultural center is Kilembe, (2002e) 9,000.

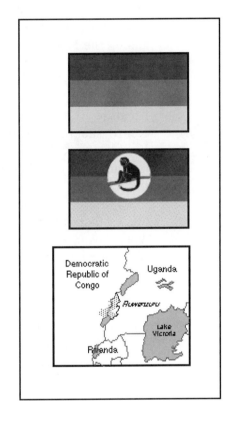

FLAG: The Ruwenzori national flag, the flag of the national movement, is a horizontal tricolor of blue, green, and yellow. The same flag, with the addition of a white disk on the upper two-thirds charged with a black monkey sitting on a brown branch is the flag of the Ruwenzuru Movement.

PEOPLE AND CULTURE: The Ruwenzoris comprise two closely related Bantu peoples of the Western Lacustrine branch of the Bantus. They are more closely related to the Gandas* of east-central Uganda than the non-Bantu Hamitic Toros who dominate the region. Traditionally the two peoples have a common origin and share a highland Bantu culture adapted to the steep slopes and climate of the Ruwenzori Mountains. The Konjos, or Bakonjo, inhabit the higher altitudes of the Ruwenzori Mountains, maintaining close relations with the Ambas, also called the Baamba or the Humu in Congo, of the high plains west of the mountains. The two Ruwenzori peoples have maintained an alliance for over 80 years, first against Toro domination, then against the British colonial state, and more recently against the Ugandan nation-state. Marriage among the Ruwenzoris is a matter of great social concern, and it is usual for children to be betrothed early in life. Dowries, or bride wealth, are important and are normally paid in goats. The Ruwenzori peoples also share the initiation ceremonies for youngsters reaching puberty. Communication by whistling developed among the Konjos as a means for hunters to convey messages and is still used by rebel groups in the mountains.

LANGUAGE AND RELIGION: The Ruwenzoris speak two closely-related Bantu languages of the Southern Bantoid group of Benue-Niger languages. The Konjo language, called Rukonjo or Konzo, belongs to the Konzo subgroup of the Bantu languages. The Amba language, called Kwamba or Ku-Amba, forms part of the Bira-Huku subgroup, more numerous in neighboring Congo. The first secondary school was opened in the region in 1976, but illiteracy remains widespread. In the 1990s there was a literacy campaign supported by the regionalist movement. The Bible was partly translated into the Konjo language in 1914. Proficiency in the Toro language, used in churches in the region, is limited.

Traditionally the Ruwenzoris believed in two supreme beings, Kalisa and Nyabarika, and constructed shrines on mountain slopes. Sacrifices were made by hunters before expeditions, and pieces of meat were often left. Ancestor worship remains widespread. Many of the Ruwenzoris are now nominally Christians, both Roman Catholic and Protestant. Evangelical Protestant sects have been active in the region despite the growing violence of the antigovernment movement.

NATIONAL HISTORY: Bantu agriculturists, the ancestors of the Ruwenzoris, settled the lowlands, probably before A.D. 1100, living in autonomous villages united only by culture and tradition. According to Ruwenzori tradition, they originated around Mount Elgon in eastern Uganda but migrated west during a period of invasions. They continued the migration until they encountered the Ruwenzori highlands, which had a climate similar to their original homeland.

Around 1500 tall Hamitic herdsmen, probably from present-day Ethiopia, conquered the region around the highland lakes, driving many of the Bantus into the Ruwenzori Mountains. The invaders created a large, centralized kingdom dominated by a Hamitic aristocracy. The warlike Hamitic nomads relegated the more advanced Bantu to a lower class of serfs, craftsmen, farmers, and herdsmen forbidden to own cattle, the measure of Hamitic wealth. Nilotic invaders from the north conquered the kingdom in the sixteenth century. The Nilotes divided the region into a string of small independent kingdoms.

Around 1830 a prince of the Nyoros broke away from the kingdom and with his followers moved south to create a separate kingdom in the southern districts south of Lake Albert. The prince, the first *omukama* (king) of Toro, controlled the lowlands but asserted only nominal control over the mountainous Ruwenzuru region to the west. The inhabitants of the region in the Ruwenzori Mountains, the Konjo and Amba tribes, considered primitive by the more cultured lowlanders, acknowledged the authority of the Toro kingdom government while maintaining only rare and often acrimonious contact. Many were taken as tribute or slaves to work the estates of Toro aristocrats.

The two groups, the Ruwenzoris and the Toros, differed on the basis of language, customs, culture, systems of justice, history, and ethnic identity. The Ruwenzoris had no interest in socially or economically interacting with the Toros, who were prejudiced and in the past had sold entire villages into slavery with the Arabs.

European explorers visited the kingdom in the 1850s and were astounded at the highly stratified and sophisticated society of the Toro kingdom. The highland Ruwenzoris were mostly ignored. Over the next decades the kingdom established trade relations with the British and allowed Protestant and Roman Catholic missions to operate, with some moving into the Ruwenzori Mountains. Christian missionaries actively opposed the slavery that had oppressed the Ruwenzoris for centuries.

The Toro kingdom signed a diplomatic treaty with the British authorities in 1890. Five years later, reacting to interest by other European powers, the British declared Toro a protected state. The king finally signed a protectorate agreement in 1900. The logic of British colonialism dictated that the Ruwenzoris be integrated first into the Toro kingdom and then later into the national structure of Uganda. British assistance to the Toros allowed them to consolidate their hold on the kingdom. In 1906 the Ruwenzoris were for the first time brought under the direct authority of the kingdom's government. The Rukurato, the Toro parliament, became a partly elected legislature under British influence, with delegates from all districts, allowing the Ruwenzoris some say in the government of the kingdom.

A boundary agreement between the British and Belgians signed in 1910 divided the Konjos, Ambas, and the related Nandes, who inhabited the western foothills. Until the 1960s, the peoples of the region mostly ignored the international boundary and crossed to trade or visit kin without hindrance. The artificial division of the Konjo-Amba-Nandi population cluster remains a focus of nationalist sentiment to the present.

The British allowed the Toros to have full political and legal jurisdiction over the Ruwenzori region. The Toro government immediately posted Toro representatives as tax collectors and placed Toros in all other administrative positions in the highlands. In 1919, the Ruwenzoris, led by the Konjo chiefs, rebelled against Toro domination. The Konjo rebels repelled the king's troops but met defeat when British forces were dispatched to the kingdom. The rebellion ended when three leaders were publicly hanged, thus becoming martyrs for the later nationalist movement.

The traditional political relationships of clientship, serfdom, and slavery gradually disappeared, although the dominant Toros continued to discriminate against the Ruwenzori peoples in education, administration, and the economy. The discrimination, only partly ethnic and cultural, was aggravated by the inaccessibility of the Ruwenzoris' mountain homelands.

In the 1920s and 1930s the colonial authorities gradually reduced the power and independence of the kingdom. The British attempted to bring the Ruwenzoris into the administration, but they remained isolated, and the Baamba homeland was connected by road only in 1938. The Ruwenzori districts were the richest in the kingdom, particularly the mines opened and operated by the British authorities.

After World War II, Toro nationalism focused on assimilating the Ruwenzoris, particularly after 1949 colonial legislation recognized the kingdom as the basis of local government. In 1953 the Toro royal government demanded federal status and the extension of the Toro language, Lutoro, to all the kingdom's schools, particularly those in the Ruwenzuru region. Ignoring Ruwenzori protests, the British, believing that Ugandan independence was still decades in the future, encouraged the development of Toro nationalism and authority. The result of British policy was increased pressure on the Ruwenzoris to assimilate into Toro society.

The issue of domination intensified as independence for Uganda neared in the late 1950s. The rapid growth of Toro nationalism paralleled the growing nationalism of the Ruwenzoris, a reaction to increasing assimilation. By the late 1950s, the Rwenzururu Movement was so strong that in 1961 its main leaders Isaya Mukirane, Yeremiya Kawamara and Petero Mupalya (both the latter being Ambas) along with 18 other Ambas and Konjos were elected to the Toro Rukurato (parliament) after prolonged resistance by the Toro kingdom.

The Ruwenzoris demanded separation from Toro and the creation of a separate Ruwenzuru district within Uganda. In 1960 the Ruwenzoris insisted that a new constitution for the kingdom be adopted that recognized the three tribes as the peoples of Toro, replacing the ethnocentric view that the Toros were the only legitimate inhabitants. In early 1962, consultations took place in the Toro parliament, but the Ruwenzori leaders broke off the talks when their demands for recognition were rejected. The leaders were arrested for insulting the Toro king. On the eve of Ugandan independence in October 1962 the Toro kingdom adopted a new constitution that ignored the Ruwenzoris' demands for official recognition of the kingdom's three peoples. The Toro kingdom accepted semifederal status within the newly independent Ugandan state. Toro nationalists, somewhat mollified by official recognition of the kingdom, blocked Ruwenzori efforts to separate themselves.

In early 1963 the Ruwenzoris rebelled against Toro domination, and violence spread across the kingdom. The Ruwenzoris initially demanded separate district status, but government refusal prompted the more militant leaders to espouse separatism. On 13 February 1963, Ruwenzori leaders declared the independence of the Kingdom of Ruwenzururu, extending their territorial claims to all of Toro. Copies of the declaration were sent to the Ugandan government, the United Nations, and the Organization of African Unity. The Ruwenzoris, led by their elected king, Isaya Mukirane, asserted that they were the rightful inhabitants of the Toro kingdom and that the Toros must return to Bunyoro where they originated. In 1964 the Ugandan army attacked the Ruwenzori rebels, but they held out in their mountain strongholds. The Ruwenzoris attempted to unite with the Konjos, Ambas, and Nandis of neighboring Congo. The Konjos and Ambas were supportive, but the Nandis, who had never been suppressed by the Toro kingdom, showed little interest.

In the 1960s coffee, mountain tourism, and the mine at Kalimbe brought relative prosperity and improved health services and infrastructure in the region. Agriculture, the main occupation of the majority of the population, remained the mainstay of the local economy, and few of the rural Ruwenzoris benefited from the improvements in the towns.

Uganda's government, dominated by northern tribes, had little sympathy for the traditional Bantu monarchies in the southern districts. In 1967 the government abolished the kingdoms, including Toro, as centers of local nationalism and separatism. Having overthrown the Toro kingdom, the Ugandan government of Milton Obote sent troops into the Ruwenzuru region, where the Ruwenzori rebels were finally defeated in 1970. The regime of Idi Amin, which took power in 1971, gained infamy as Africa's most brutal. Amin was finally overthrown in 1979, to be succeeded by a series of unstable and often repressive governments.

In 1980 the Ugandan government took a more conciliatory stance to the continuing Ruwenzori insurgency. A couple of health dispensaries were opened in the region, but the government had more pressing problems, and the region remained isolated and neglected. Charles Iremangoma, the last Ruwenzori king and the leader of the separatist movement, the Ruwenzuru Movement, surrendered to government troops in 1983.

A resistance movement among the southern Bantu peoples of Uganda finally took control of devastated country in 1986. The movement formed the country's first government controlled by the Bantus, but relative peace allowed old grievances to resurface. The Ruwenzoris quickly lost faith in the new government, which ignored their petitions for regional autonomy. The 40-year Ruwenzori rebellion resumed.

In July 1993, with government approval, the Toro kingdom was partially restored, and Patrick Olimi Kaboyo took the throne as the new omukama. The Ruwenzoris initially refused to relinquish the former royal lands they had occupied, but in March 1994 senior members of the Ruwenzuru Movement, acknowledged the new king, officially ending the conflict that had begun three decades before. The Ruwenzuru Movement continued to demand autonomy for the mountain region of the indigenous Ruwenzoris.

A group operating near the Rwenzori Mountains, the Allied Democratic Forces, mostly militant Ruwenzoris, emerged as a localized threat in 1996 and has inflicted substantial suffering on the population in the area. An ADF-affiliated group, the National Army for the Liberation of Uganda (NALU), also claimed responsibility for terrorist attacks that resulted in fatalities.

In neighboring Congo, the outbreak of civil war in 1996 sent a stream of refugees into the Ruwenzori region. Fighting between immigrant Rwandans and the indigenous Nandes and other groups escalated in the late 1990s. Many of the refugees formed armed groups to fight in both Congo and Uganda. In 1998–99, the government encouraged the Bwisis and other regional groups to arm themselves against the Ruwenzoris, who are perceived as the major group in the multi-ethnic Allied Democratic Forces (ADF), formed in 1996.

Militant Ruwenzoris of the ADF continue to fight Toro domination and the Uganda government. Having enlisted recruits from armed groups in eastern Congo, they increasingly threatened both moderate and progovernment Ruwenzoris and troops sent to extract valuable cobalt from the waste dumps from the Kilembe mines. In 1998–99, ADF forces were accused of abducting children to be trained as guerrillas.

The current relationship between the Ugandan state and the Ruwenzoris is one of mutual distrust, each side discounting the legitimacy of the other. The current Uganda administration under President Yoweri Museveni is ultra-nationalist and views the Rwenzururu Movement as an enemy of the ultimate statist third world political goal of national unity. The Ruwenzoris have fought to preserve their traditional independence for hundreds of years and vow to continue to fight until they are recognized as the indigenous people of the Ruwenzori Mountains region, achieve democratic self-government, and gain control of their natural resources.

SELECTED BIBLIOGRAPHY:

Ahmed, Sayed Z. *Ruwenzori: Mountains of the Moon.* 1996.
Kasozi, A.B.K. *The Social Origins of Violence in Uganda 1964–1985.* 1994.
Rotberg, Robert, and Ali Mazrui, eds. *Power and Protest in Black Africa.* 1970.
Yeoman, G. *Africa's Mountains of the Moon: Journeys to the Snowy Sources of the Nile.* 1989.